D0501973

THE FORCE OF DESTINY

The FORCE of DESTINY

A HISTORY OF ITALY SINCE 1796

Christopher Duggan

HOUGHTON MIFFLIN COMPANY

Boston · *New York*

2008

Copyright © 2007 by Christopher Duggan

ALL RIGHTS RESERVED

First published in Great Britain in 2007 by Allen Lane,
an imprint of Penguin Books

For information about permission to reproduce selections
from this book, write to Permissions, Houghton Mifflin Company,
215 Park Avenue South, New York, New York 10003.

www.houghtonmifflinbooks.com

Library of Congress Cataloging-in-Publication Data
Duggan, Christopher.
The force of destiny : a history of Italy since 1796
/ Christopher Duggan.
p. cm.
Includes bibliographical references and index.
ISBN-13: 978-0-618-35367-5
ISBN-10: 0-618-35367-4
1. Italy—History—1789–1870. 2. Italy—History—
1870–1914. 3. Italy—History—1914–1945.
4. Italy—History—1945– I. Title.
DG551.D84 2008
945'.08—dc22   2007041643

Printed in the United States of America

MP 10 9 8 7 6 5 4 3 2 1

For J.

'Cela est bien dit . . . mais il faut cultiver notre jardin.'

Contents

PART THREE:
Poetry, 1846–60

PART FOUR:
Prose, 1861–87

PART FIVE:
War, 1887–1918

CONTENTS

PART SIX:
Fascism, 1919–43

PART SEVEN:
Parties

List of Illustrations

Photographic acknowledgements are given in parentheses.

1. An allegory of the invasion of Italy, 1796 (Museo Centrale del Risorgimento)
2. The horses of St Mark's being shipped off to France, 1797 (University of Reading Library)
3. Antonio Canova's monument to Vittorio Alfieri (Alinari Archives, Florence)
4. *Pietro Rossi, Lord of Parma*, by Francesco Hayez (Pinacoteca di Brera, Milan)
5. *Peter the Hermit Preaching the Crusade*, by Francesco Hayez (Giulio Einaudi Editore/private collection)
6. A meeting of Carbonari, 1821 (Museo Centrale del Risorgimento)
7. An engraving celebrating Pope Pius IX's allocution, 10 February 1848 (Museo Centrale del Risorgimento)
8. *La Meditazione*, by Francesco Hayez (Civica Galleria d'Arte Moderna, Verona)
9. Giuseppe Mazzini (Alinari Archives, Florence)
10. Count Camillo Benso di Cavour (Istituto Mazziniano, Genoa)
11. King Victor Emmanuel II and Rosa Vercellana (Giulio Einaudi Editore/private collection)
12. The bandit leader Nicola Napolitano (Editori Riuniti)
13. Giuseppe Garibaldi wounded, 1862 (Museo Centrale del Risorgimento)
14. Francesco Crispi meeting Bismarck at Friedrichsruh, 1887 (Rizzoli Editore)
15. The Battle of Adua, 1896 (Fototeca Storica Nazionale Ando Gilardi)

xi

Preface

The composer Giuseppe Verdi was not a man with particularly strong or sophisticated political views, but he was almost unerringly alert to the mood of his audiences; and when, at the beginning of 1861, just a few months after the extraordinary chain of events that had led, in what many observers felt had been a providential fashion, to the unification of Italy under King Victor Emmanuel II of Piedmont–Sardinia and his prime minister, Count Camillo Cavour, he was approached by the Imperial Theatre of St Petersburg to write a new opera, he quickly alighted for his subject on a play that had been written nearly thirty years earlier by a well-known Spanish writer and politician, the Duke of Rivas, *Don Alvaro o la fuerza del sino* – *Don Alvaro, or the Force of Fate*. Verdi worked on the opera in the late summer and autumn of 1861, and in November 1862 *La forza del destino* (*The Force of Destiny*), as it was now called, received its premier in St Petersburg. It was a considerable success, and the composer was rewarded by the Tsar with the Order of St Stanislas – though the third performance was marred by a demonstration staged, it seems, by Russian musical nationalists who were unhappy at the official accolades being meted out to a foreign work.[1]

La forza del destino was not an overtly political opera – though it contained invocations to war against the Austrians ('the eternal plague of Italy and her sons') that were guaranteed to excite Italian audiences when it toured the peninsula: a large part of north-eastern Italy was still under the rule of Austria in 1862 and there was much talk at the time of the need for a fresh military offensive to finish the work of unification. But running through Verdi's opera (the only one to which he gave an abstract title) was an idea that appeared to many patriots to encapsulate the essence of the political drama that had unfolded in 1859–60: that, irrespective of human intentions and actions, there was a force, a hidden hand, which was directing the course of history towards predetermined goals. Was this not the best explanation for how the country had been unified in the teeth of so many seemingly insurmountable obstacles? There had been the indifference or outright hostility of much of the Italian population, the bitter antagonism between the moderate and democratic wings of the national movement, the existence of deep-rooted regional divisions, the absence of strong economic, cultural and linguistic bonds, and the vehement opposition of the three greatest powers on the continent: the Roman Catholic Church, Austria and France (the emperor Napoleon III had been happy to see an enlarged Piedmont, but the last thing he had wanted was to bring about a united Italy that might rival France in southern Europe).

That the unification of Italy had been in large measure fortuitous had been underlined for many Italians by the sudden death in June 1861, just a few weeks after the formal proclamation of the new kingdom, of Count Cavour, the man who more than any other had appeared to have a sense of the direction in which affairs in the peninsula were moving and some degree of mastery over them. Verdi had called him 'the Prometheus of our people'; and when news came through of his demise, he wept, he confessed, 'like a child'.[2] The impression that the country now faced an extremely precarious future was reinforced by the rapid deterioration of law and order in the south of the peninsula in the second half of 1861, mounting insolvency and a slide towards civil war. And when, shortly after completing the score of *La forza del destino*, Verdi accepted a commission for a work to mark an international concert for the London Exhibition in the spring of 1862, he produced a cantata, entitled *Inno delle nazioni* (*Hymn of the Nations*), in which a 'bard' calls for a world of peace and invokes divine aid for the completion of Italy's political and moral resurrection – but in terms that were far more redolent of uncertain yearning than confident expectation:

> O Italy, O Italy, O my fatherland betrayed,
> May the benign heavens be propitious to you still,
> Until that day when you rise again, free, to the sun!
> O Italy, O Italy, O my fatherland!

From the moment when the French revolutionary forces of Napoleon Bonaparte crossed the Alps into Piedmont and Lombardy in the spring of 1796 and brought with them the idea that the people of Italy might constitute a free and independent nation, the struggle to determine the character of a new unitary state in the peninsula proved immensely difficult. Even more problematic was how to transmit to millions of illiterate peasants, most of them scattered in isolated mountainous settlements, the idea that their primary loyalty should henceforth be to something called 'Italy'. Ever since the collapse of the Roman Empire in the West in the fifth century, the peninsula had been subjected to a succession of invaders; and amid the chaos it was the Church and the network of largely autonomous towns in the north and centre of the country that had emerged as the most enduring focal points of political authority. Often, though, it was a smaller unit – a faction, a party, an urban district, a confraternity or a family – that had developed as the principal focus of an individual's allegiance. How to graft 'the nation' onto this intensely fractured political landscape – and in the teeth of the countervailing universalism of Roman Catholicism – was to be the main task confronting those who were drawn to the ideology of patriotism created by the French Revolution.

This book seeks to examine how, under the impact of the Napoleonic invasion and the mixture of optimism and resentment that this engendered, an initially small group of educated men and women began to promote the idea of an Italian nation and consider why a country that in the past had boasted the civilizations of classical Rome and the Renaissance had fallen behind other parts of Europe so conspicuously in recent centuries – economically, culturally and politically. Much of the discussion focused on the problem of the Italian character, using concepts that had been made familiar by writers of the eighteenth century (and earlier) who had endeavoured to account for the rise and fall of states and empires in essentially moral terms. The task of what came to be known as the Risorgimento (literally 'resurrection' or 'revival') was not just to secure the independence of Italy from foreign rule (French, initially, and Austrian after 1815), but more fundamentally to eradicate the vices that centuries of despotism and clerical rule had allegedly engendered – for example, subservience, indiscipline, excessive materialism and a lack of martial ardour. This approach to the country's problems retained a powerful allure long after unification in 1860, fed by repeated disappointments in domestic and foreign policy. It reached its apogee with fascism.

The restoration of absolutist government throughout the peninsula after 1815 forced patriots to look above all to secret societies to further their cause; but as the young Genoese conspirator Giuseppe Mazzini came to recognize in the early 1830s after a series of failed insurrections, the crucial issue was not so much revolutionary leadership and organization as education – reaching out to the mass of the population, 'the people', and persuading them to support the cause of progress and national unity. And the key to success in this domain, he believed, lay in appropriating the language and practices of the most powerful framework of reference for the majority of Italians, Catholicism, and harnessing them to the cause of the nation. Hence his emphasis on the centrality of God, faith, duty, doctrinal purity, preaching, martyrdom and blood to the attainment of a new united Italy. The interpenetration of religion and politics, the sense – part instinctual, often quite calculated – that political movements needed to make use of the paradigm of the Church if they were to win an enthusiastic popular following, was to remain an enduring theme of Italian history deep into the twentieth century.

The decades leading up to the unification of Italy laid down the principal terms of the debate about the nation; and many of the issues that had so preoccupied patriots in these years of the Risorgimento – the questions of character and education, the desire to recover former greatness, the problem of how to engage the masses, the search for a common history, the balance between freedom and unity, regionalism and centralization, and the place of the Church – were carried over into the new kingdom and continued to inform much of the political and cultural life of Italy down to the Second World War (and in certain significant respects beyond). And one important reason why these concerns remained as pertinent and vital after 1860 as they had been before was because of a widely shared sense that the national movement had only succeeded in bringing about the material unification of the country – and that largely as a result of foreign intervention. 'Moral unification', as it was frequently referred to, had yet to be achieved. Relatively few of the peninsula's 20 million or so inhabitants felt emotionally engaged with the new state; and many were overtly hostile. As the Piedmontese politician Massimo d'Azeglio observed in a remark that became famous, Italy had been made, but the task of making Italians had still to be accomplished.

The fortuitous manner in which unification was achieved gave rise after 1860 to a complex amalgam of hopes and fears. There was an acute sense of the precariousness of the new kingdom and of the fragility of the institutions – neither parliament nor the monarchy could claim significant moral authority; and the fact that the most influential organization in the peninsula, the Church, was hostile – refusing to recognize Italy's existence formally until 1929 – widened the gap between the masses and the state. The rapid emergence of revolutionary socialism from the 1870s further accentuated the division between what was referred to as 'real Italy' and 'legal Italy'. In these circumstances the country's rulers felt impelled to adopt a variety of strategies, some of them mutually conflicting, in an effort to create moral unification and thereby, it was hoped, 'make Italians'. The realization that many of the policies pursued – including centralization, suffrage reform, military service and education (understood in broad terms, and distinct from 'instruction') – were either ineffective or counter-productive led increasingly to a view that the best means of healing the country's inner fractures and giving the state the prestige that it lacked was through war. After all, had not every major nation in the world – whether Britain, France, the United States, or (in 1864–70) Germany – been forged in the crucible of military success?

But the impulse towards war did not only derive from concern at the country's lack of internal cohesion. It was also fed by the rhetorical legacy of the Risorgimento, and the often extravagant claims made by the likes of Mazzini and Vincenzo Gioberti about Italy's glorious future destiny. Admittedly such claims were intended in large measure as tools for mobilizing popular support for the cause of unification, but they inevitably clung to the image of the resurgent nation, and after 1860 disillusioned patriots were quick to denounce what they saw as the prosaic character of the new kingdom and contrast it with the 'poetry' of the Risorgimento. Failures in foreign policy and the frequently disparaging attitudes displayed by foreign governments towards Italy created a growing antipathy to cautious parliamentary liberalism and an increasing receptiveness to the language of bellicose nationalism. The chasm between expectations and the reality of the country's limited material resources, already a feature of the Risorgimento, grew more pronounced, causing the German Chancellor, Otto von Bismarck, to remark on one occasion: 'Italy has a large appetite, but poor teeth.'

The drift towards hyperbole, evident in the writings of the 'national bards', Giosuè Carducci and Gabriele D'Annunzio, and in the politics of Francesco Crispi in the 1880s and 1890s and subsequently of the Nationalists and Mussolini, owed much to the strength of the idealist tradition within Italian elite culture – the belief, in part of religious provenance, that it was spirit rather than matter that shaped the course of history. If Italians learned to think in ambitious terms and eschewed their former cynicism and passivity, what was to stop the country emerging once again as a dominant force in Europe? But the extraordinary manner in which Italy had come into being in 1859–60 also cast its shadow over later generations, prompting the likes of even sober-minded politicians such as Giovanni Giolitti to throw caution to the wind on occasions and embark on some unpredictable venture – as he did on the fiftieth anniversary of unification in 1911, with his sudden invasion of Libya. If providence had come to the rescue of Cavour and Garibaldi, why might it not do so for others prepared to take similar risks? But to live dangerously was to risk falling prey to the intoxication of hubris; and hubris could bring nemesis in its wake, as the 1940s showed.

Once unleashed in the 1790s, the idea that 'the people' constituted the nation and that the nation should be coterminous with the state was a genie of ferocious power. As the case of Italy suggests, the imperative inherent in the concept of unity could be as disruptive and coercive as it was liberating. Mazzini dreamed of a world composed of free nations living in contentment and universal peace. But as his own career amply demonstrated, it was one thing to ordain the existence of a God-given community and quite another to persuade millions of disparate men and women that this was the unit of humanity to which they naturally belonged. Furthermore, it was far from self-evident that nations would ever reach the point where they felt sufficiently secure and internally cohesive to pass from a condition of 'becoming' to one of being 'made'. Mazzini himself was a quintessential Romantic, inclined to value the pain of pursuit above the joy of attainment, and he often stressed how moral identity was inseparable from 'mission' – a category that did not augur well for harmonious international co-existence.

This book seeks to explore how the national idea unfolded in Italy during the last two centuries and examines some of the initiatives that politicians, intellectuals and others undertook in an effort to bridge the gap between the imagined community and the reality (though what was regarded as reality was itself often the product as much of imaginative interpretation as of objective description). Inevitably, given the countless rivulets that feed into all thoughts and feelings, a work of this kind can only ever hope to provide a very partial picture of the complex inter-action between the moral and material worlds; and the fact that no two human beings can harbour exactly the same outlooks or responses means that many dimensions of the debates have necessarily been overlooked or underplayed. What I hope to indicate, though, in the course of the narrative is how the problem of the Italian nation has been formulated in terms that recur throughout the country's recent history; and while these terms should not be seen as having had any teleological force, they might legitimately be regarded as constituting one of the patterns in the carpet that it is the task of the historian to identify.

The nation-state has not enjoyed a particularly good press during the last few decades, certainly in continental Europe, and historical writing has tended to reflect this by seeking to highlight the persistence of local or regional identities deep into the modern era and stressing how for most people a plurality of loyalties was a reality of life. But the fact of multiple layers of attachment is not an argument for placing the nation-state in the dock and claming that it per se was to blame for the tragedies of the twentieth century. Human beings from time immemorial have felt the need to owe primary allegiance to a collective body of one kind or another – be it a tribe, a city, or some alternative ethnic, geographical or cultural unit; and the impulse to assert the identity of the group, however large or small it may be, can easily lead – especially when feelings of insecurity are involved – to aggression and intolerance. There is no reason to suppose that a supra-national structure such as Europe would be any less prone to the same uneasy dynamics of self-definition – particularly if the latest ideological cleavages in the world were to result in a concept such as Christendom being plucked from the historical locker and held up as a possible solution to current anxieties.

In Italy, the political earthquake of the early and mid-1990s that led to the collapse of the First Republic has sparked fierce debates about the merits and demerits of unification and a protracted argument about which elements of Italian history should be celebrated and which con-demned. The Northern League has declared that the south of the country should properly be regarded as a separate nation and has criticized the

Risorgimento for having imposed the straitjacket of unity on the country. And in the south voices of protest have been raised against what have been seen as the persistent colonialist and racist attitudes of northerners and the perpetration during the 1860s of what some have claimed was tantamount to genocide. The parties of the right have looked to rehabilitate fascism and have condemned the left for its inability to face up to the political crimes that were committed by anti-fascists during (and immediately after) the war, while the left has retaliated by defending the work of the Resistance and highlighting the illiberal, undemocratic and inhumane aspects of Mussolini's regime.

The acrimonious character of these debates, and the fact that they have been linked closely to current party political battles, has created a difficult climate in which to discuss Italy's modern history: exaggeration, omission and distortion have been common features of much recent discussion. No historian can expect to remain uninfluenced by these polemics, even when writing from a distance; and some of the central themes in this study – among them the question of why Italy has failed to acquire a strong sense of either the nation or the state – have been thrown into sharp relief largely as a consequence of the turmoil following the breakdown of the 'First Republic'. But it has not been my intention in writing this book to engage systematically with any one point of view. I have tried to see events in Italy during the last two centuries as far as possible from the standpoint of the participants, and such issues as whether or not unification was an error make little sense historically. This does not mean that the past should be viewed with moral neutrality: understanding may attenuate blame, but it cannot absolve those who have the advantage of hindsight, and are able to see what particular lines of thought and action ultimately led to, from rejecting political systems and ideas that resulted in so much human suffering and damage.

In writing this book I have incurred a number of debts. During the last ten years a group of outstanding Italian scholars have revitalized the study of the Risorgimento by examining how the national message was generated and transmitted. I owe an enormous amount to their work, and especially to the pioneering studies of Alberto Banti. I am particularly grateful to the British Academy for the award of a two-year Research Readership in 2003–5, which freed me from university commitments and enabled me to undertake much of the necessary reading and reflection. My colleagues in the Department of Italian Studies at Reading have been a source of support as well as intellectual stimulation over the years, and I would like to thank them for their forbearance during my absence. Richard Bosworth read almost the entire typescript and his comments were invariably highly perceptive, saving me from stylistic infelicities as well as factual inaccuracies. Francesca Medioli offered some very astute observations on the early chapters. Others who generously helped with specific points include David Laven, Lucy Riall, Stephen Gundle, Chris Wagstaff, John Foot, Linda Risso and Grazia De Michele. Naturally any errors that remain are entirely my responsibility. I would also like to thank Elena Gianini Belotti, whose excellent novel *Prima della quiete* first introduced me to the case of Italia Donati. I am very grateful to my agent, Felicity Bryan, for her encouragement and belief in the project from the outset, and to Simon Winder at Penguin Books for his unfailing enthusiasm and consummate editorial wisdom. Mark Handsley has been an excellent copy-editor. My greatest debt is to my family. This is the second large volume that Amy and Tom have grown up with, and no writer could ask for a better salve for the pessimism often engendered by studying the crooked timber of humanity than being continually reminded of what is important and good in life. My heartfelt thanks to them – and to Jennifer, to whom the book is dedicated.

I have not included a bibliography: the sources for a book of this kind and scope are inevitably somewhat eclectic (and mostly in Italian). Those wishing for guidance on further reading in English could usefully begin by consulting D. Beales and E. Biagini, *The Risorgimento and the Unification of Italy* (London, 2003), D. Mack Smith, *Modern Italy: A Political History* (New Haven and London, 1997) and P. Ginsborg, *Italy and Its Discontents 1980–2001* (London, 2001).

In order not to burden the text with Italian, I have in general given the titles of books, poems and paintings in English – unless the original is well known, significant or suggestive. I have not anglicized Italian names of kings and princes except in the cases of Victor Emmanuel and Ferdinand.

Italy before 1796

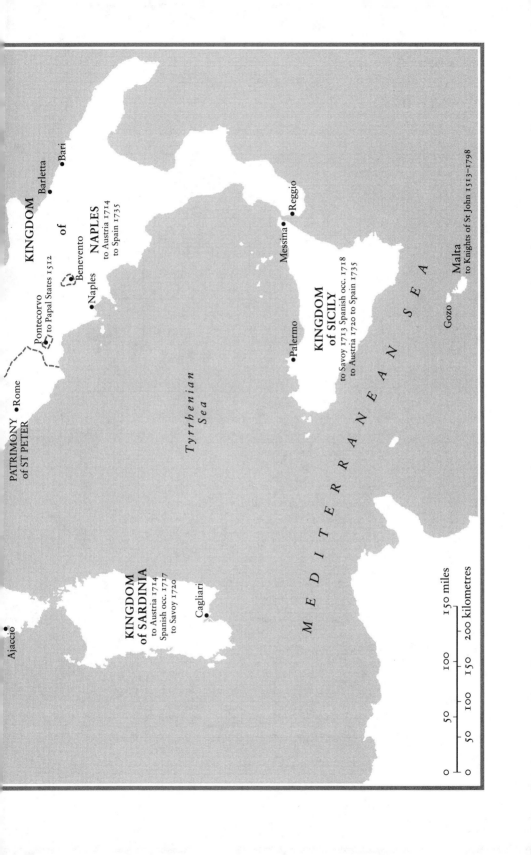

KINGDOM of NAPLES
to Austria 1714
to Spain 1735

PATRIMONY of ST PETER

KINGDOM of SICILY
to Savoy 1713 Spanish occ. 1718
to Austria 1720 to Spain 1735

KINGDOM of SARDINIA
to Austria 1714
Spanish occ. 1717
to Savoy 1720

Pontecorvo to Papal States 1512

Malta to Knights of St John 1513–1798

Barletta

Bari

Benevento

Naples

Rome

Reggio

Messina

Palermo

Cagliari

Ajaccio

Gozo

Malta

Tyrrhenian Sea

MEDITERRANEAN SEA

0   50   100   150 miles

0   50   100   150   200 kilometres

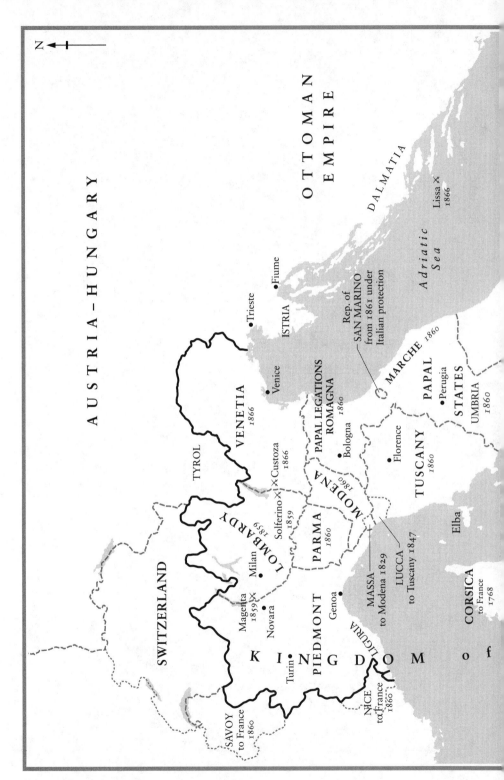

The unification of Italy 1815–70

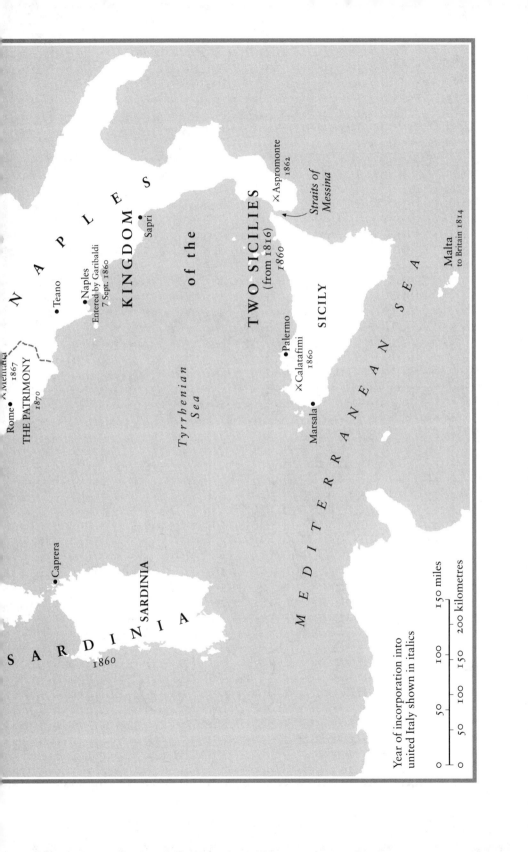

N A P L E S

KINGDOM

of the

TWO SICILIES
(from 1816)
1860

SICILY

Rome ●
×Mentana
1867
THE PATRIMONY
1870

●Teano

●Naples
Entered by Garibaldi
7 Sept. 1860

●Sapri

×Aspromonte
1862

*Straits of
Messina*

●Palermo
×Calatafimi
1860

●Marsala

●Caprera

SARDINIA

SARDINIA
1860

*Tyrrhenian
Sea*

M E D I T E R R A N E A N   S E A

Malta
to Britain 1814

Year of incorporation into
united Italy shown in italics

0	50	100	150 miles
0	50 100	150	200 kilometres

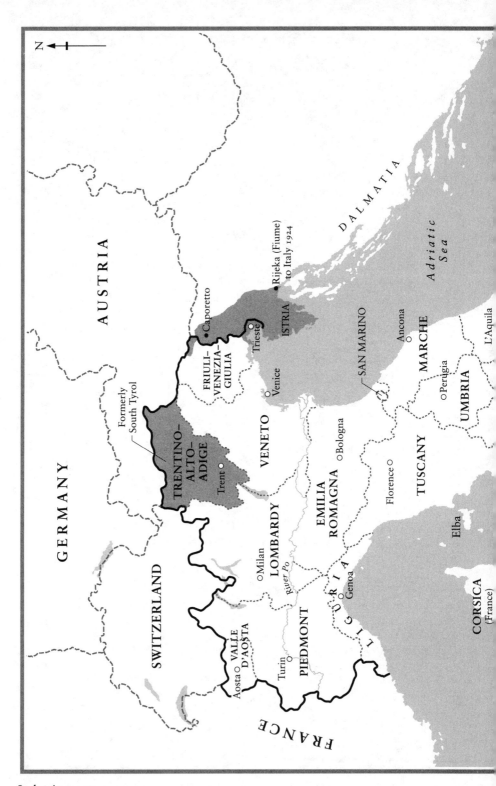

Italy since 1919

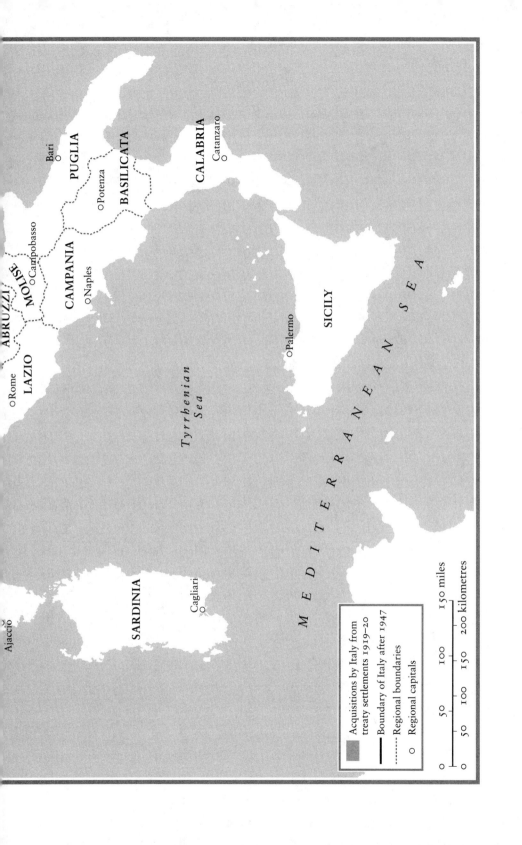

ABRUZZI

MOLISE

LAZIO

oRome

oCampobasso

CAMPANIA

oNaples

PUGLIA

Bari
o

BASILICATA

oPotenza

CALABRIA

Catanzaro
o

Ajaccio

SARDINIA

Cagliari
o

*Tyrrhenian
Sea*

Palermo
o

SICILY

M E D I T E R R A N E A N   S E A

Acquisitions by Italy from
treaty settlements 1919–20

Boundary of Italy after 1947

Regional boundaries

o   Regional capitals

0   50   100   150 miles

0   50   100   150   200 kilometres

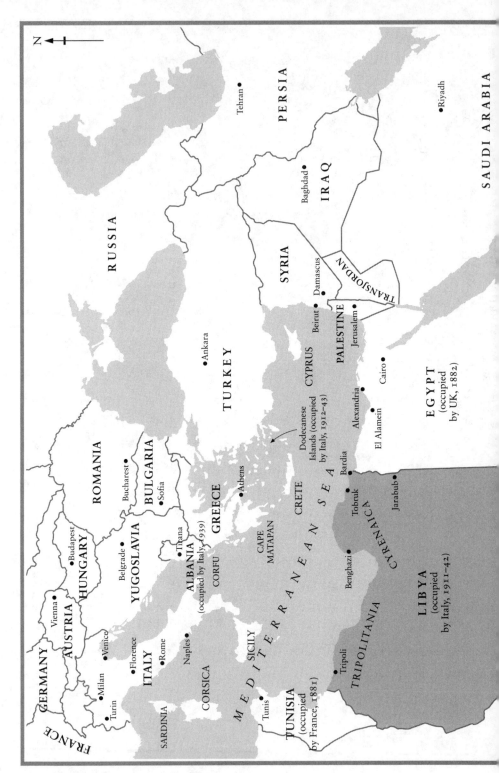

Italy and the Mediterranean basin in the inter-war years

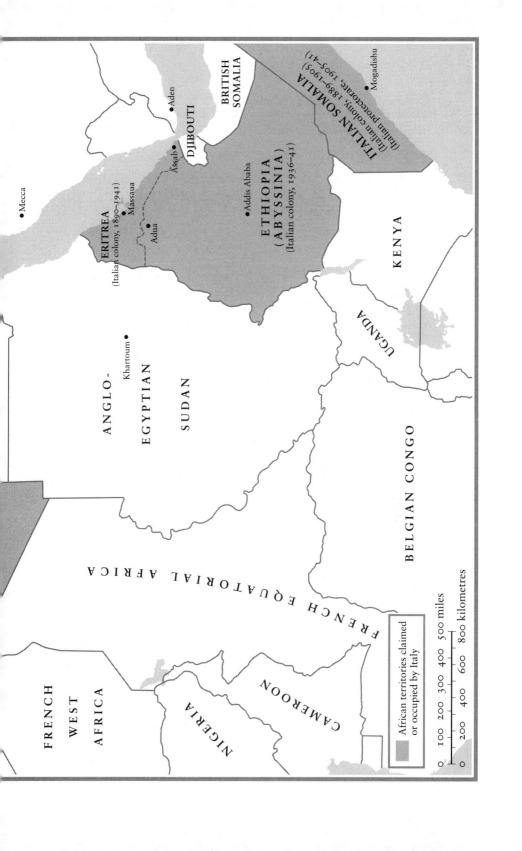

Mecca

Aden

Adua

Massaua

Āsab

Addis Ababa

Mogadishu

Khartoum

ERITREA
(Italian colony, 1890–1941)

DJIBOUTI

BRITISH
SOMALIA

ITALIAN SOMALIA
(Italian colony, 1889–1905)
(Italian protectorate, 1905–41)

ETHIOPIA
(ABYSSINIA)
(Italian colony, 1936–41)

ANGLO-
EGYPTIAN
SUDAN

UGANDA

KENYA

BELGIAN CONGO

FRENCH EQUATORIAL AFRICA

FRENCH
WEST
AFRICA

NIGERIA

CAMEROON

African territories claimed
or occupied by Italy

0   100   200   300   400   500 miles
0   200   400   600   800 kilometres

PART ONE

Awakening
1796–1815

the Enlightenment ideals of moral and material progress, to herald a new era of freedom and regeneration for both the city and Italy. And he hurried to show his enthusiasm for the revolutionary order, constructing a curious tree of liberty in front of his villa of Malgacciata: a massive oak with a Phrygian bonnet of polished bronze tied to its top-most branch, and two enormous sails of canvas hanging below that swelled and flapped in the wind. Angiolini had a similar tree of liberty set up in the piazza of a nearby village, summoned the local peasants and delivered a speech to them about the importance of what was taking place. Their response, it seems, was one of intense bemusement and anger.[7]

Milan must have seemed to Angiolini in the next three years a vibrant city – the city 'awoken from its slumbers' described by the great French romantic writer Stendhal in the opening pages of his novel *The Charterhouse of Parma*, where the height of ambition was no longer 'to print sonnets upon little handkerchiefs of rose-coloured taffeta on the occasion of the marriage of some young lady belonging to a rich and noble family', but altruistically to serve 'the nation'.[8] Though ill and gout-ridden, Angiolini put his wealth and considerable talents at the disposal of the new regime, hoping to spread the gospel of revolution to the people. He produced pamphlets and jotted his political thoughts down in notebooks, which he had printed and distributed to his friends. He became involved in the setting up of the National Theatre, and almost certainly contributed to the production of such popular (and educational) musical dramas as *The Dream of a Democrat*, *The Republican* and *Silvio, or the True Patriot*. But his revolutionary ardour was in due course to cost him dear.[9]

Italy in 1796 was not a single state and in no obvious sense a 'nation'. Ever since the collapse of the Roman Empire in the west in the fifth century, the peninsula had been contested by a succession of invaders – Huns, Goths, Lombards, Byzantines, Arabs, Normans, Hohenstaufens, Aragonese, Angevins – who had left the country politically, culturally and economically fragmented. In the Middle Ages the prosperous urban communities of the north and centre – towns such as Genoa, Milan, Verona, Padua, Bologna, Pisa, Florence and Siena – had rebelled against the nominal sovereignty of the German emperors north of the Alps and established self-governing city-states. But they had fought bitterly with one another and so added to the legacy of disunity. The ambitions of the popes in Rome to have their own independent state in the centre of Italy had created a further element of division. In the sixteenth century the Spanish had established supremacy over much of the peninsula after several decades of devastating wars; in the early eighteenth century they were replaced by the Austrians. But the political fragmentation remained, and by the time Napoleon's armies arrived there was still a kaleidoscope of discrete states in Italy. They included the Republic of Genoa, the Kingdom of Piedmont–Sardinia, the Republic of Venice, the Duchy of Modena, the Duchy of Parma, the Grand-Duchy of Tuscany, the Papal States and the Kingdom of Naples. The Duchy of Milan formed part of the Austrian empire.

However, the idea of 'Italy' as, potentially at least, a single political unit had acquired far greater significance than before as a consequence of the French Revolution, a movement that had injected fresh meaning and extraordinary dynamism into the terms 'nation' and 'fatherland'. In the past the words *nazione* and *patria* had been used rather loosely in Italy (as elsewhere). They might denote simply the region or the city where someone had been born; or (more commonly) they could indicate a collection of people with what appeared to be a shared cultural heritage. Hence the frequent references to the 'Venetian nation', the 'Lombard nation', the 'Piedmontese nation', the 'Neapolitan nation' and the 'Sicilian nation'. From the early eighteenth century, talk of an 'Italian nation' grew more common, but again the sense was mainly cultural – a people possessed of a shared language and literature. There was no suggestion of Italians abandoning their political allegiances to the existing states.

A good example of this idea of the Italian nation is an essay published in a journal edited by Pietro Verri, *Il Caffè*, in 1765. Entitled 'Of the fatherland of the Italians', it takes the form of an imaginary conversation with a stranger who on entering a coffee shop in Milan is asked whether he is a 'foreigner'. The stranger says he is Italian, 'and in Italy an Italian is never a foreigner'. But he is told that this claim has little meaning, as in Italy it is 'the universal practice to call anyone who has not been born but who lives within the precincts of a city wall a foreigner'. The stranger goes on to argue that Italy is a nation dating back to the time of the Romans, and that it is precisely because Italians have failed to put aside their differences and recognize that they have a common fatherland that so much damage has been done to the cause of progress in the peninsula. However, he draws a clear distinction between cultural and political patriotism: while Italians need to work together to increase 'national glory' in the sciences and the arts, they still have a duty to obey the laws of the state they live in.[10]

The outbreak of the French Revolution changed the terms of the debate. Self-styled 'patriots', like Pietro Verri, who followed events in France with enthusiasm, began to wonder whether the 'Italian nation' might not form a political as well as a cultural unit. The most important figure in the development of this line of thinking was a young Tuscan called Filippo Buonarroti, a distant descendant of the great Michelangelo. Buonarroti had embraced the radical democratic 'Jacobin' ideas of the revolution and was worried on the eve of Napoleon's invasion of Italy that the French government might be looking to pursue a policy of conquest rather than 'liberation' in the peninsula. To forestall this danger, he urged Italian patriots to prepare insurrections ahead of the French army in the name of the 'freedom of Italy':

We cannot wait to see that joyful moment when our fatherland shall be free. And above all we want the frivolous distinctions of having been born in Naples, Milan or Turin to disappear among patriots. We all belong to the same country and the same fatherland. Italians are all brothers . . . and must make common cause and consult one another about the best course of action.[11]

In May 1796, shortly before Napoleon reached Milan, Buonarroti was arrested for his part in a plot – the 'conspiracy of the Equals' – to overthrow the government in Paris. But the idea that Italy should form a single state continued to gain ground among Italian patriots and was aired in the myriad newspapers, pamphlets and political clubs that sprang up in northern Italy in the wake of the victorious French armies. Napoleon himself encouraged such talk. Though in private he was extremely sceptical about Italian unity – he told a senior diplomat in 1794 that it was 'a beautiful idea', but that he could see no way in which Piedmontese, Lombards, Genoese, Romans and Neapolitans could all be turned into 'one people'[12] – in public he spoke of his admiration and liking for the 'descendants of Brutus and Scipio' and his hopes that the Italian people might be roused from their torpor after many centuries of enslavement.[13]

*

Napoleon was almost certainly a moving spirit behind the famous competition that was launched by the French-controlled administration in Milan in September 1796 for an essay on the subject 'Which form of free government is most conducive to the happiness of Italy?' This competition was remarkable for airing many of the themes that were to dominate the debates about Italian unity and the Italian nation in the decades to come. The organizing committee felt that the essays should serve an educational purpose: for centuries Italians had been kept in ignorance by their tyrants, which was the main reason why they had so far failed to display the 'signs of energy' that were required for winning freedom. The learned were therefore invited to reveal to 'the people' the ideals of liberty and equality, show them the blessings that these principles would bring, and remind them of Italy's ancient glories. Entries could be written in French, Italian or Latin, and the prize would be a gold medal worth 200 *zecchini*.[14]

Most of the fifty-seven essays submitted to the competition argued that Italy should have a unitary republic similar to that of France. According to the winning entry by a young philosopher from Piacenza, Melchiorre Gioia, the principal factor behind the failure of Italy over the centuries to win freedom was not, as was often claimed, its climate (the great French writer Montesquieu had famously argued in his *The Spirit of the Laws*, 1748, that hot climates engendered sloth and servility, cold ones energy and independence) but its political fragmentation. This lack of historical unity demanded that Italy should become a centralized state and not a federation. Italians were 'weak' in character and prone to quarrelling and, if the country remained divided, they would fight each other for local dominance and generate 'a thousand ferocious discords'. In the meantime foreign enemies would 'avidly watch the growth of factions and the increase in national hatreds' and seize the opportunity to invade. With the introduction of liberty and equality, bonds of brotherly affection would be created, and there would no longer be 'Sicilians, Florentines and Turinese, but Italians and men'.[15]

Not all of the essayists were quite so confident. One Venetian writer felt that the divisions that had plagued Italian history were so deeply entrenched that the democratic government of a new unitary republic would have to work extremely hard to fuse Italians into a 'single people' imbued with a 'national spirit and national character'. Reason was to be the principal tool of education. To prevent any possible jealousy, the capital of Italy was to be located in the middle of the peninsula in a purpose-built city (as in the United States of America), and administrative boundaries would be drawn up on rational rather than historical lines. Local capitals would be selected so as to avoid generating rivalries, and public buildings would be of equal size and conform to a standard template. In this way, Italians would gradually lose their old corrupt habits and be reborn as 'citizens', with the good of *la patria* their sole concern.[16]

The majority of entrants to the competition agreed that a unitary republic was the best way to ensure that Italy overcame its historical divisions and had sufficient strength to deal with a foreign invasion, but a few thought that such an arrangement was unrealistic. According to the former priest and passionate Piedmontese democrat Giovanni Ranza, the regional differences in Italy were so pronounced that unity stood as much chance of success as the search for 'perpetual motion or the philosopher's stone'. He suggested a federal republic made up of eleven states with a General Congress in Pisa (and the construction there of a giant monument to 'our mother', the French Republic).[17] Other writers supported federalism on the grounds that the climatic differences between north and south, the mountains and the plains, had resulted in very different character types, with the south being largely mercurial and 'Greek' in spirit, the north stolid, sober and 'German'. 'The blunt and well-fed Lombard does not need the same laws as the crafty Genoese and the clever Tuscan. And what Ligurian or Venetian dolt would ever respect the lordship of Naples?'[18]

The problem of the Italian character loomed large in many of the essays. Most writers believed that the Italians had become corrupt and enervated, and lacking in those virtues that had helped to create the Roman empire and the free city-states of the Middle Ages. Some entrants, like Melchiorre Gioia, believed that the vices of Italians would be made good simply through the salutary effects of liberty, but others claimed that more would be needed. One writer proposed 'a vigorous campaign of public education' to make Italians aware of just how much damage had been done to them by centuries of tyranny and Roman Catholicism. Only in this way would they be roused from their current inertia, and recover 'that bellicose and free genius' that had once made them the rulers of the world.[19] Nor was this education to be narrowly conceived. Clubs, associations, newspapers, schools, laws, public ceremonies, plays, poetry and music could all be channels for the creation of a new patriotic spirit in Italy.[20]

The Milan competition had as its theme what kind of government Italy should have, and in the circumstances it is hardly surprising that most of the writers took the French Republic as their model. Apart from a general recognition that Italians had suffered from centuries of division and might need to be educated to democracy and freedom, there was little discussion of exactly what the Italian nation was. Even its geographical parameters were unclear. Some writers seemed instinctively to equate Italy with the 'Lombard nation' and assumed the new republic would be limited to the regions in the north, while others saw Italy as embracing the whole of the peninsula, but with Sicily excluded. At least one writer wanted Italy to include Corsica and Malta together with the Italian-speaking provinces of Switzerland. Nevertheless there was an assumption behind the competition that Italy was a nation, and this view acted as a powerful spur to further reflection and debate among the educated in the years to come.

From Milan, Napoleon swept southwards and eastwards with his army, occupying the territories of Bologna, Ferrara, Modena, Reggio and the Papal Legations in the summer and early autumn of 1796. In the course of the next months the young general dabbled in constitutional experiments – the first of a string of political arrangements that were to punctuate the history of Napoleonic Italy. In December representatives of the cities of Bologna, Ferrara, Modena and Reggio assembled at a congress and proudly proclaimed the formation of the Cispadane Republic ('one single people, one single family'). Elections were staged, a new constitution drawn up, and a white, green and red tricolour (in horizontal bands – vertical bands were introduced only in 1805) adopted as its flag; but in May 1797 Napoleon decided to abolish it and create a new republic, the Cisalpine Republic, comprising Lombardy, Reggio, Modena, Massa and Carrara. At the same time the Republic of Genoa was replaced by a new Ligurian Republic.

The French government's attitude to Italy was highly ambivalent. Despite all the talk of liberation, the principal motive behind the invasion of northern Italy was harshly pragmatic. Italy was a diversion from the main theatre of war in northern Europe, and any conquests were intended as bargaining counters with which to try to persuade Austria

The Last Letters of Jacopo Ortis, published in 1802, tells the story of a young man who is forced to flee his native Venice after its surrender to Austria. He takes to the Eugenean hills, and falls in love with a girl called Teresa. But Teresa is already betrothed to a marquis. Tormented by his love for Teresa and his lost fatherland (both Venice and Italy), he sets out in pursuit of solace, but neither the beauties of Italy's landscapes nor the vestiges of its past glories console him. Everywhere he is reminded that Italy is suffering under the yoke of foreign domination, and, like Teresa, is not free. He returns home after two years to find Teresa married, and kills himself.

Foscolo's racked romantic hero was to furnish a powerful model for many Italian patriots. Suffering and self-sacrifice as a consequence of exile – and exile could be emotional as well as physical: 'all Italians are exiles in Italy', Foscolo later wrote[27] – now took on an aura of nobility. Moreover the linkage between sexual longing and Italy's condition of enslavement was to be an important ingredient in the appeal of the national cause in the years to come, especially to educated young men imbued with the romantic precept of self-realization through struggle. Italy – imagined either as a violated mother, or sister, or fiancée – had to be fought for and freed and her honour avenged. However, the very elusiveness of the object of pursuit – Teresa/the fatherland – in Foscolo's novel was also to find an echo (and a dangerous one) in the national movement: those who struggled for Italy should not expect to be satisfied. Italy would always exist as an ideal – to be made and remade, morally if not materially.

Foscolo's disillusionment with the French was shared by another important writer who, like Foscolo, played a major role in shaping the cultural parameters of the national question in Italy. Born in Piedmont in 1749, Count Vittorio Alfieri travelled around Europe indulging his twin passions for racehorses and women before deciding to dedicate himself to literature. As for many other Italian émigrés of the period, the experience of living abroad gave him a strong sense of cultural patriotism; but as a Piedmontese aristocrat he had been brought up to speak and write French. For Alfieri language was the principal determinant of nationality, and in 1776 he went to Tuscany to (as he put it) 'un-French' himself – foreshadowing another famous patriotic pilgrimage to the cradle of the Italian language, that of the novelist Alessandro Manzoni fifty years later. Thereafter Alfieri turned his hand to playwriting and produced a string of successful tragedies, mostly on classical subjects, whose central theme was the struggle of the heroic individual for freedom against oppression and tyranny.

A central theme of Alfieri's work was the celebration of virility. This was partly because he disliked what he saw as the flaccid cosmopolitanism of French-inspired *politesse*, but also because he wanted to rouse Italians from their decadence and recover the primitive, even barbaric, energy of the Italic race that had once produced Scaevola, Brutus, and the Gracchi, and the glories of ancient Rome. As a writer he saw it as his duty to inspire: indeed he cast himself in the role of the vatic poet of national resurrection – the first of a long line of such figures from Foscolo to Giosuè Carducci and Gabriele D'Annunzio – who would impart 'boiling passion to hearts and minds . . . and an insatiable thirst for great deeds and glory'.[28] He believed that Italy had a mission to lead the world out of decadence and into a new era of liberty.

Having settled in Paris with his mistress, Louise, Countess of Albany, wife of the dissolute and alcoholic Charles Edward Stuart ('Bonnie Prince Charlie'), Alfieri was at first enthusiastic about the French Revolution. But his enthusiasm evaporated with the onset of the Terror, and in 1792 he fled the French capital for Italy, where he spent the last years of his life in Florence excoriating France for its hegemonic ambitions and inciting Italians to hatred of 'those barbarians from across the mountains'.[29] Alfieri's anger was heartfelt – especially after Napoleon's invasion in 1796 – but it was also instrumental. He believed that Italy would only become a nation capable of great achievements if its people came together and learned to bury their differences; and there was no more effective and energizing national glue than a shared enemy. As he wrote in his posthumously published work, *Il Misogallo* (*The Anti-Gaul*):

O Italy, hatred of the French, under whatever ensign or mask they present themselves, must be the single and fundamental basis of your political existence . . . May the word MISOGALLO from now on be accepted into your language as signifying . . . FREE ITALIAN. Then before long the time will return when the French no longer possess such overwhelming resources and numbers, and you will have shed all the vileness of your customs, divisions and opinions. Then you will be great in your own right; and from having hated and despised the French in fear, you will move majestically to hating and despising them in scorn.[30]

Alfieri was a preacher of sentiment and morality rather than thought. But that made his influence on future generations all the greater. According to the literary critic Francesco De Sanctis, a future Minister of Education in unified Italy who himself believed passionately in the need for Italians to bury their differences and become a morally integrated nation, Alfieri was 'a gigantic and solitary statue wagging an admonitory finger'.[31] Alfieri sought to teach Italians that they shared a common *patria*, and they should work together in loving and defending it; that they had a glorious past, which should serve to shake them from their current lethargy and drive them to throw off the yoke of foreign domination. He called for 'strong feeling' and 'masculine virtue'; and he prophesied in the concluding poem of *Il Misogallo* that the day would come when 'now resurrected, Italians [would] stand bravely on the field of battle, and defeat the French, no longer cravenly defended by another's arms'.[32]

The patriotic exhortations of Foscolo and Alfieri could not easily eradicate the legacy of history. The arrival of Napoleon and the collapse of Austrian rule in northern Italy opened the floodgates to old municipal rivalries, and once liberated the cities of the Po Valley hurriedly sent deputations to Paris to appeal for as much territory as they could as independent republics. Milan had a particularly large appetite: it claimed Genoa, Mantua, the Venetian terra ferma, even Venice and Dalmatia. Modena wanted Ferrara; Ferrara wanted Cento and Pieve, but preferred to be ruled by Milan rather than Bologna. Bologna angled for the Romagna, Ferrara and Ancona; Ancona wanted the Marche, but when this looked impossible it asked to be included in the Cisalpine Republic – anything but be ruled by Rome again. Ironically municipalism often fuelled the calls for Italian unity at this time: Brescia and Reggio saw unity as a means of throwing off the baleful yokes of their old capitals of Venice and Modena.

The strength of these municipal rivalries greatly hampered government of the Cisalpine Republic, and made something of a mockery of calls for an Italian nation 'one and indivisible'. Napoleon, who by temperament as well as by education liked centralization, found the constant spats between the Italian cities deeply frustrating. In France, he commented ruefully, everything was centred in Paris, but in Italy Milan's claims were bitterly contested by Bologna, Pavia, Padua or

Venice.[33] He tried juggling, but with scant success. In 1797, and again a few years later, he sought to create a National Institute along French lines and offered to locate it in Bologna as compensation for Milan being made capital. But the Milanese dug their heels in, and the plan had to be aborted. (He eventually found a solution in 1810 with the establishment of a Royal Institute of Sciences, Letters and Arts in Milan, but with four additional sections meeting at regular intervals in Bologna, Padua, Verona and Venice.)

These rivalries were not just a question of local pride and historic memories. Utilitarian considerations of jobs, contracts and taxes also came into play. Melchiorre Gioia, the winner of the 1796 essay competition, who had argued for a unitary Italian state precisely because he hoped that it would stop municipal and factional quarrels, watched with dismay in 1798 as the Cisalpine Republic became hamstrung by fiscal revolts and disputes over the assignment of public contracts and the location of state institutions:

[One politician] wants the guns to be bought in Brescia, whereas the interest of the Republic demands that they be put up to tender open to all sellers; [another] wants the Mantua lottery to be introduced into Milan in defiance of all justice and good faith; the inhabitants of Reggio want the court of appeal to be located in Reggio, the Bolognese struggle against the excise on foodstuffs as if it did not exist in their department.[34]

But even more damaging than divisions between city and city was the division between the cities and the countryside. During the early 1790s peasants in some parts of Italy had occasionally voiced their discontent at taxes, or high food prices, or feudal burdens, using ideas that had filtered through to them from across the Alps ('What payments, what taxes, what Royal Court! We want to do it like the French!', an angry mob had cried in the piazza of a small southern Italian town in December 1793 when the council was discussing the payment of communal taxes to the king);[35] but in general the Italian peasantry had adopted the views peddled by their parish priests and saw the Revolution in terms of rampant godlessness (as well as requisitions and more onerous demands from the state – not least military service). The writer Stendhal's bucolic description of French soldiers standing at cottage doors in the spring of 1796 'dandling the housewife's baby' and dancing the *monferrina* and *saltarello* with local girls was largely a figment of his imagination.[36]

Napoleon's army met with fear and at times vicious opposition as it advanced through the northern countryside.

Peasant fears and anger found an outlet in an explosion of religiosity. In the Romagna and the Marche priests led their congregations in public prayers, calling for divine mercy against the sacrilegious 'beasts' that had invaded the Papal States. Mass pilgrimages were staged to the shrine of the Holy House at Loreto. In Ancona the eyes of the Virgin Mary were seen flickering in a painting, and as word spread, crowds flocked to the church from all over the Marche, and the miracle was repeated time and again in front of the ecstatic onlookers. At Monte Santo, the church bells were heard ringing in the middle of the night when the building was empty, and a succession of remarkable cures were reported at the shrine. 'It is quite incredible how many images were declared to be miraculous in those days in Rome and a hundred other places across the State,' recorded the father of the great poet Giacomo Leopardi, 'and how many prints were made of these images, and how many works were published describing the miracles, and how many sensible people were convinced of their authenticity.'[37]

Popular hostility to the French descended into violence in many places. In May 1796 some 5,000 peasants and artisans stormed into Pavia and forced the garrison to surrender. A month later in Lugo, news that the French had seized a silver reliquary of the patron saint of the town, Saint Illaro, sparked off an orgy of rioting, with the heads of murdered soldiers being paraded through the streets in triumph.[38] In April 1797 Verona erupted into five days of vicious street fighting, and some 200 French soldiers were butchered, to cries of '*Viva San Marco! Viva San Marco!*' Very often it was the clergy who played a leading part in inciting the violence. Among those arrested and shot by the French in their brutal suppression of the Verona rising was a priest called Luigi Franzini. The text of a sermon he had preached, urging the Veronesi to kill 'these savage men' ('let their blood be a sign of our salvation, for liberty is never secured without blood'), had been discovered in his house.[39]

Some of the worst instances of bloodshed occurred in central Italy. In a bid to strengthen its position in Italy and minimize the chances of an attack on the Cisalpine Republic from the south, the French government decided in January 1798 to invade the Papal States. As the French army led by General Berthier arrived at the outskirts of the Eternal City, several hundred Roman patriots gathered in the ruins of the Forum and

of Padua. By now they numbered some 40,000 men. At an open-air mass, Ruffo placed them under the protection of Saint Anthony – San Gennaro had shown his unworthiness by liquefying for the French – and the following day the assault on the city began.

It was a brutal affair, worse than the slaughter in January, and it seared itself on the collective imagination for decades. It lasted for over two weeks. The *lazzaroni* joined in, roaming the streets with the Calabrians to cries of 'Long live the king', hacking down Trees of Liberty, ransacking and burning the houses of the rich, looting monasteries and churches, and murdering anyone who looked like a supporter of the Republic. Many republicans attempted to conceal their distinctive flowing 'Jacobin' haircuts by sticking on false pigtails, but to little avail. 'If a Jacobin you want to find / Pull his pigtail from behind / If it comes off in your hand / That is a true Republican', ran a popular verse at the time.[51] The diarist Carlo De Nicola watched the horror of severed heads and mutilated bodies with mounting nausea, a disgust that reached a peak on 2 July when the corpses of two Jacobins were burned, and chunks of their charred flesh were sliced off by the angry mob, passed round 'even to children', and consumed. 'Here we are in the middle of a city of man-eating cannibals who eat their enemies.'[52]

Ruffo did his best to limit the carnage by agreeing to a treaty with the French and republican garrisons holding out in the city's forts, but his orders were ruthlessly countered by Nelson – who arrived in the Bay of Naples with the British fleet on 24 June, declared Ruffo's treaty invalid, and promptly proceeded to have a leading rebel hanged from the yard-arm of one of his ships, and his body flung into the sea without Christian burial, as a sign that no quarter should be shown to the enemy. The king and queen were equally set on revenge. Ferdinand returned to his capital on 10 July, greeted by rapturous crowds shouting: 'We want to see our father', and in the weeks that followed dozens of patriots were tracked down and then hanged or decapitated. Among them were distinguished intellectuals such as Domenico Cirillo, professor of botany at Naples university, friend of Linnaeus and fellow of the Royal Society in London. Another was Eleonora Fonseca Pimentel. She went to the scaffold on 20 August, her brown skirt tucked modestly around her legs, and uttering the words of Virgil: '*Forsan et haec olim meminisse juvabit*' – 'Perhaps one day even these things will bring pleasure.' Oblivious to such erudition, the crowd cheered loudly as she hanged.[53]

2

Searching for the Nation's Soul

'I am Italian,' Corinne interrupted. 'Forgive me, my Lord, I think I see in you the national pride which is so often characteristic of your compatriots. In this country we are more modest; we are neither self-satisfied like the French, nor proud of ourselves like the English. All we ask of foreigners is a little indulgence, and as, for a long time, we have been denied the lot of being a nation, we are often greatly at fault, as individuals, in lacking the dignity which is not permitted to us as a people. But when you know the Italians, you will see that in their character they have a few traces of ancient greatness, a few scanty, half-obliterated traces which might, however, reappear in happier times.'

Madame de Staël, *Corinne, ou L'Italie* (1807)

I do not believe that all good institutions came from Egypt, Greece, Thrace or anywhere else you care to name. They arise wherever there are men. Nature has given us life, and it would be absurd to think that, needing to breathe in order to preserve it, we had been forced to draw breath from another people.

Vincenzo Cuoco, *Platone in Italia* (1804–6)

PLATO IN ITALY

The fall of the Neapolitan Republic was part of a more general collapse of French power in Italy in 1799. Northern Italy was overrun by Austrian and Russian forces in the spring, with Milan being taken in April and Turin in May. Tuscany, which had been hastily occupied by the French early in the year, had to be abandoned in the summer. The Roman Republic held on for a while, but it too fell in September. Everywhere the progress of the coalition troops was assisted by popular risings. In Piedmont a peasant army known as the 'Massa cristiana' roamed the countryside pillaging and rooting out sympathizers of the French to cries of 'Long live the king! Long live the emperor! Long live Jesus and Mary!', while in Tuscany a similar army, led by an ex-dragoon officer, his wife and his wife's lover, an English diplomat, and supported by numerous priests and monks, terrorized the countryside to cries of '*Viva Maria!*'

By contrast to these huge popular movements, the opposition to the French of those Italian patriots who hoped for a unitary republic was of very limited impact. A number of Jacobins responded to the events of 1797–8 by seeing in unity the best, perhaps the only, means of ensuring independence from foreign control, and a shadowy secret organization appeared in northern Italy called the Society of Rays, with cells in Bologna, Modena, Reggio and Milan. This aimed to 'irradiate' the message of unity and resistance to French aggression throughout the peninsula, but it lacked coordination and its leaders were unclear as to whether they wanted a single republic or a federation.[1] In 1799 Italian patriots addressed several petitions to the government in Paris urging it to pursue a policy of Italian unification as the best way of ensuring France had a strong ally on its southern flank. But these petitions fell on deaf ears.

The lack of patriotic sentiment in Italy was deeply galling to those, like the choreographer Gasparo Angiolini, who had had such high hopes of better things in 1796. Following the collapse of the Cisalpine Republic, Angiolini was arrested by the Austrians and questioned about the Tree of Liberty that he had erected outside his villa (and which the peasants had chopped down and burned in 1798). He was imprisoned and then deported to Dalmatia, before being released and returning to Lombardy a broken man. Shortly before his death in 1803 he wrote an impassioned memoir, in which he lamented the failure of Italians to prevent the French behaving as conquerors and keeping the peninsula divided. 'All this occurred because we do not know how to act together, because we have no national spirit . . . O Italy, O Italy, to what level of baseness have you been reduced? . . . O Italy, when will you awake? . . . You were the first in Europe, now you are the last, the last because everyone subdues you . . . Only when Italy again recovers its warrior spirit will it avenge and humiliate its enemies.'[2]

Another despondent observer of the situation in Italy at this time was a young writer called Vincenzo Cuoco. Cuoco had been born into a provincial middle-class family in the Molise region of southern Italy in

1770, and had moved to Naples to study law. He had never graduated: his real passions were for history and philosophy, and he had got caught up in elite intellectual circles, befriending such men as Mario Pagano and Vincenzo Russo – both of whom were executed in 1799 for their roles in the Neapolitan Republic. Cuoco himself played only a minor part in the Neapolitan Republic, but he was nonetheless sentenced to exile and had his property confiscated on the return of King Ferdinand. While in exile he reflected on the tragic events he had witnessed in Naples, and published his conclusions in 1801 in his *Historical Essay on the Neapolitan Revolution of 1799* – a work that was to prove extremely influential.

According to Cuoco the fatal flaw in the Neapolitan revolution was the chasm separating the leaders from the mass of the population. Naples in recent decades had lost all sense of its cultural distinctiveness, with the government and the court being packed with foreigners – men like John Acton, or the queen's confidante Emma Hamilton – and intellectuals keenly flaunting the latest ideas from north of the Alps. 'We became by turns French, or Germans, or English; we were no longer anything.'[3] The revolution of 1799 was a 'passive revolution', transplanted from France onto Neapolitan soil, with a French constitution and French ideas; and not surprisingly it meant absolutely nothing to the great majority of ordinary Neapolitans:

Our revolution was passive, and the only way it could have been successful was if we had won over the opinion of the people. But the views of the patriots and those of the people were not the same: they had different ideas, different ways of doing things, and even two different languages . . . The Neapolitan nation could be considered as divided into two peoples, separated in time by two centuries and in climate by two degrees.[4]

Cuoco may have been influenced by the conservative writers Edmund Burke and Joseph de Maistre, but his principal debt was almost certainly to the great early-eighteenth-century Neapolitan philosopher Giambattista Vico. Vico had elaborated a general theory of the cyclical decline and regeneration of nations, and had argued that nations, like individuals, had unique characters that were moulded by events and expressed in different languages and cultures. For Cuoco, as for many other patriots in the early years of the nineteenth century grappling with the problem of how to bring the Italian nation into being (assuming that it existed, and most took it for granted that it did), a crucial question was whether and how this historically shaped national character could be changed. In his *Essay* Cuoco suggested that the revolution in 1799 might have worked if the leaders had focused more on the needs of the masses, for example by creating representative local bodies and concentrating on bread and butter issues such as taxation and land. But he also felt that the masses had to be reformed. They lacked necessary civic qualities such as 'love of the fatherland and military virtue'.[5]

Cuoco talked about the 'Neapolitan nation', but he also referred quite freely to the 'Italian nation', and when he settled in Milan after the French had retaken the city in 1800 following Napoleon's victory over the Austrians at the Battle of Marengo in June, his interest in the 'Italian nation' grew stronger. This development was partly (and rather ironically) because he felt that he and other southern exiles were treated as complete foreigners in Lombardy.[6] In 1803 he launched a newspaper, *Il Giornale Italiano*, the main aim of which was to help form a national spirit in Italy and educate Italians to the ideals of unity and independence. Italians needed to celebrate their past greatness, he said. They should study their own country and stop believing that foreign things were always better. The state should take charge of education, and give it a strongly religious inflection (the people were instinctively religious), create citizens, and teach them to have pride in their nation and strive for its glory. And Italians must be taught to fight: like Machiavelli, Cuoco saw military strength as the foundation of political life.[7]

Cuoco was the first Italian writer to state clearly that the national problem in Italy was above all one of education, of how to turn a population of *lazzaroni* and peasants, vitiated by centuries of foreign domination, priests, political division and ignorance, into a patriotic, independent, united and disciplined people. It was a view of the national question that was to have enormous resonance in the decades to come. It is no coincidence that the most important ideologue of the Italian nation, Giuseppe Mazzini, who came to regard it as his God-given mission to educate Italians to their national duty, as a young man copied out and assiduously annotated Cuoco's articles in *Il Giornale Italiano*.[8] But if Italians needed to be educated and their character changed, what was the end product to be? What sort of nation should Italy aspire to become?

For some patriots at this time, such as the dramatist Alfieri, republican

Rome offered a template. But it was a vague and rather problematic one. Alfieri could admire the raw energy, heroism and altruism of ancient Romans who thrust their hands into braziers or had their sons condemned to death for treason (and his own autobiography was in part written to show how he had transcended the dissolute ways of his youth and refashioned himself as a 'new man', resolute, independent and duty-driven), but it was hard to push the paradigm too far. After all, if Alfieri condemned the French for their imperial ambitions, how could he urge Italians to imitate their ancestors, who had ended up by being masters of almost all of the known world, Gaul included?

For Cuoco there was much to admire in the Romans, not least their patriotism and military valour, but his philosophical temperament led him to hanker after a less sanguinary model for the Italian nation. He found it in a mythical civilization that had flourished before ancient Rome and Greece, and was, in his eyes, superior to both of them. His case for this remote origin for Italy was set out in an abstruse and rambling (but highly successful) novel called *Plato in Italy*, which describes the journey made by the philosopher Plato and a certain Cleobolus from Greece to Italy, their talks with local wise men, and their discovery of a once mighty 'Etruscan' state, whose people had 'prospered in laws, agriculture, war and trade', but who had, as a result of moral degeneration, been overrun by foreign invaders and lost their independence and unity:

When this was, I cannot tell you ... All I can say is this: that in those times all the Italians formed one single people, and their imperium was called 'Etruscan' ... Today only the smallest part of Italy survives with that name. I know that industry and trade generated wealth, and wealth generated sensual pleasure and easy living, and that these sapped first the strength of the people and then the strength of the government, too. The state collapsed, the arts were neglected and forgotten, and vice produced oppression and poverty ... and Italy again became a desert in which men returned to living like beasts.[9]

Cuoco published his novel in 1804–6, as the French were tightening their grip once again over the entire peninsula, and he intended it as a paradigm for Italy's present condition. He had high hopes for its impact. He told Napoleon's stepson, Eugène de Beauharnais, that reminding his readers of Italy's former greatness would 'foster the public morality of Italians, and inspire in them that spirit of union, that love of the fatherland, and that love of military service, that till now they have lacked'.[10] His ambition was clearly overstated; but it was an ambition that in the decades to come was to fire many other Italian patriots, alarmed at what seemed the paucity of civic virtue around them and eager to regenerate their nation. In 1843, for example, the Piedmontese priest Vincenzo Gioberti looked to inspire nationalist feelings among Italians by making similar claims to Cuoco's for Italy's cultural pre-eminence (and for the nation's pre-Roman origins) in his bestselling book *On the Moral and Civil Primacy of the Italians.*

Not that the idea of a primordial Italian civilization was regarded by Cuoco as simply mythic. Giambattista Vico had argued in 1710 for the existence of a highly sophisticated pre-Greek society in Italy on the basis of a philological study of Latin, and in 1723–4 the posthumous publication of a monumental history of 'Etruria' by an eccentric Scottish adventurer and professor of law at Pisa called Thomas Dempster fuelled what soon became a veritable industry of 'Etruscology'. An academy was set up in Cortona in 1726 to propagate knowledge of the Etruscans, and archaeological finds of elaborately painted tombs, funerary sculptures and other imposing works of art in central Italy encouraged scholars such as Mario Guarnacci (author of *The Italic Origins*, 1767, whose huge bequest of Etruscan artefacts and 50,000 books to the city of Volterra in 1761 created one of the first public museums in Europe) to claim that Etruria was the source not just of Roman civilization but of world civilization as a whole.[11]

IN THE BED OF PROCRUSTES: NAPOLEONIC RULE

The idea of a free and unitary ancient Italian civilization that had been overrun by the Romans had strong patriotic resonances after the French reimposed their control over the peninsula from 1800. Napoleon's second invasion of Italy in the spring of that year, following his coup of 18th Brumaire and the creation of the Consulate, led to a fresh round of constitutional experiments, with borders once again being rubbed out and redrawn almost at will. The Cisalpine Republic was reconstituted in Lombardy and Emilia, with the addition in 1801 of sections of the

Veneto, and later of Modena, the Romagna and the Marche. In 1802 it was restyled the Italian Republic, and in 1805 the Kingdom of Italy. Piedmont was made a 'French military division' in 1801 before being annexed to France the following year (Sardinia remained in the hands of the House of Savoy, under the protection of the British fleet). Tuscany became the Kingdom of Etruria under a member of the Bourbon family (and was then annexed in 1807). The former republic of Lucca was made a principality and given to Napoleon's sister Elisa in 1805. The south of Italy was conquered in 1806 and became a kingdom ruled first by Napoleon's brother, Joseph, and then by his brother in law, Joachim Murat. The Papal States were annexed in 1809 and the Pope, Pius VII, carried off to France.

The main hopes of Italian patriots were pinned on the Cisalpine Republic, and from 1800 Milan was again the centre of discussions about an independent state. There was talk of a possible federation for the whole of Italy (Napoleon's foreign minister, Talleyrand, favoured such an arrangement) or of a separate northern Italian kingdom. But Napoleon had little time for these ideas. Napoleon's principal lieutenant in the Cisalpine Republic, the widely respected moderate Count Francesco Melzi d'Eril, accepted the constraints imposed by Paris, but himself harboured patriotic ambitions. He hoped that the Republic might, if it was administered efficiently and produced a good army, become the natural kernel of an Italian nation, irradiating patriotic virtue and gradually drawing to itself other territories of the peninsula: 'No, we are not yet a people; and we must become one and form ourselves into a nation, strong through unity, happy through wisdom, independent through true national sentiment.'[12]

As in 1796–7 Napoleon was very uncomfortable with talk of Italian unity – *divide et impera* was more to his taste – but politically it suited him not to crush patriotic hopes altogether. Having drawn up a constitution for the Cisalpine Republic, which gave its President near absolute powers (despite article two stating that sovereignty resided with 'the universality of citizens'), he summoned a consultative assembly of 441 notables to Lyon at the end of 1801 to approve the text and secure his appointment as President. Many of the delegates were clearly not happy at what they felt was an affront to the Republic's independence and, in an attempt to mollify them, Napoleon convened a final plenary session on 26 January, in which, surrounded by a glittering array of generals and ministers, he delivered a speech, in Italian, setting out his plans and justifying his acceptance of the presidency. Every time he uttered the word 'Cisalpine', however, there were cries from the delegates of 'Italian'. And when he ordered the final version of the constitution to be read out, there was a chorus of 'Italian, Italian, Italian' from all sides of the hall. Napoleon bowed to the delegates' wishes, and amid rapturous applause the Cisalpine Republic became the Italian Republic.[13]

But in political terms the victory amounted to little. Francesco Melzi d'Eril was appointed Vice-President, and over the next three years he managed to carve out some autonomy for the Republic (despite Napoleon insisting on almost daily reports), creating a relatively efficient, conservative, state committed to the maintenance of law and order, sound public finances, fiscal and administrative rationalization, and support for the landowning classes. But on crucial matters it was Napoleon who dictated terms. Thus d'Eril's attempts to furnish the Republic with distinctive Italian penal and civil codes failed: Napoleon insisted on the French ones instead. D'Eril also failed to expand the borders of the Republic, despite interest from territories such as Lucca, Parma and Liguria in annexation. Nor would Napoleon allow the Republic to have separate diplomatic representation: all of its foreign policy decisions were taken in Paris.

When in 1805 the Republic of Italy became the Kingdom of Italy, and a new Viceroy, Eugène de Beauharnais, was appointed, there was even less freedom for manoeuvre. In part this was because the growing demands of war required that Italy be compliant and obediently supply money and men to support the French army. In part, too, it was because Napoleon now felt less obliged than before to temper the prejudices that he, like many of his compatriots, harboured towards Italians. 'You are wrong to think that the Italians are like children,' he told Eugène in July 1805. 'There is evil in them. Do not let them forget that I am the master and can do whatever I wish. This needs to be drummed into all peoples, but especially the Italians, who only obey the voice of a master. They will respect you only if they fear you, and they will fear you only if they realize that you understand their false and deceitful character.'[14] Eugène took the message to heart, remarking to his new subjects that if Milan were in flames, 'you must ask for orders to extinguish them'.

Napoleon was conscious of the power of spectacle to awe and impress, and he hankered after a grand coronation in Milan. He ordered the hapless Melzi d'Eril to lead a deputation offering him the crown of Italy. Melzi at first hesitated, then agreed, and then tried to soften this fresh blow to Italy's independence by seeking to have Lombardy made a separate monarchy. But to no avail. Early in April 1805 Napoleon set off from Fontainebleau, crossed the Mont Cénis pass, and descended into the Lombard plain, stopping at Marengo to recall the battle and inaugurate a monument to the dead. On 9 May he entered Milan amid delirious scenes, and for three weeks received a steady stream of admiring ministers, councillors, generals, judges, prelates, writers and scientists, who filed past him amazed at his affability, his knowledge and grasp of detail. On 23 May, in a dazzling ceremony in the cathedral, he was invested with the title of King of Italy, placed the Iron Crown of Lombardy (which had been used in medieval imperial coronations: it was in fact made of gold, but contained a thin band of iron said to have been beaten from a nail used at the Crucifixion) on his own head, and proclaimed the ancient Lombard formula: 'God gives it to me. Let anyone who touches it beware.' Popular enthusiasm was said to be almost boundless.[15]

Melzi d'Eril was bitterly disillusioned at this loss of any remaining autonomy, but he and other high-minded patriots were in a small minority. The middle classes were for the most part satisfied with the opportunities for jobs and the purchase of former feudal or ecclesiastical lands opened up by the Napoleonic regime, and served it loyally. Members of the old aristocracy were less comfortable with the new order, and often retreated sullenly to their estates, like the Marchese del Dongo in Stendhal's *The Charterhouse of Parma* (who repeated darkly, 'It is ideas that have been the ruin of Italy');[16] but in general their attitude was one of acquiescence rather than of overt hostility. Intellectuals and artists were courted assiduously by Napoleon and Eugène and encouraged to celebrate the Empire. And many obliged. Thanks in part to the enthusiastic patronage of the Bonaparte family, Antonio Canova became the most celebrated sculptor in Europe (the painter David said he could write to him using as an address 'Antonio Canova, Europe'),[17] while Gaspare Spontini triumphed in Paris with grand operas such as *La Vestale*. The poet and close friend of Ugo Foscolo, Vincenzo Monti, enjoyed enormous success as the laureate of the Napoleonic regime in Italy.

Napoleon had a passion for uniformity, and what had worked in France was deemed good for others. Throughout continental Italy (Sicily and Sardinia never came under his control) French rule led to the imposition of nearly identical administrative structures and constitutions. Everywhere departments (or provinces) were created, run by government-appointed prefects (intendants in the south), with below them districts and communes, also with centrally appointed officials. Consultative councils were set up, composed of 'respectable' members of society; but they were purely consultative: elective democracy was anathema. The judiciary was restructured into three tiers; the fiscal system was rationalized (with four categories of direct tax); internal customs barriers were removed; and weights, measures and currency were standardized. The French penal, civil and commercial codes were introduced, and the remaining vestiges of feudal tenure and privilege (considerable in southern Italy) were abolished. Relations with the Church followed those of the 1801 concordat between France and the Pope.

Such uniformity appealed to rational minds, and the gains were often palpable. For contemporaries the spirit of progress enshrined in the new administrative order found a potent symbol in the introduction of street lighting. 'At night [Naples] – formerly so dark that it concealed thefts and obscene crimes – was now lit by one thousand, nine hundred and twenty brilliant lamps,' recalled the historian and enthusiast for the new order Pietro Colletta.[18] But in many parts of Italy, especially in the south, the writ of the new legislation simply did not run: communities were too cut off and communication too difficult to allow for enforcement. There was also popular resistance to change, a conservatism compounded by aversion to a system whose main features for the masses were higher taxes, military conscription and the closure of monasteries. As Colletta noted indignantly, 'the people' rejected the metric system and 'remained with the ancient barbarism of an infinite number of different weights and measures'. Similar opposition greeted attempts to control gambling and prostitution.[19]

EVOKING NATIONAL MEMORIES

Although the young poet Ugo Foscolo had talked operatically of plunging a knife in Napoleon's heart after the Treaty of Campoformio in 1797, he forgave him. He fought alongside the French army in 1799, was wounded at the siege of Genoa, fled Italy in the wake of the Austrian victories, and returned to Milan after the Battle of Magenta. In 1801, between military assignments and intense love affairs, and at the request of the Cisalpine Republic, he penned a passionate appeal to Napoleon urging him to respect Italy's independence and freedom. In this *Oration to Bonaparte for the Congress of Lyon* he took up Cuoco's central thesis about the need to match political institutions to the culture and character of the nation. 'Any constitution that is not based on the nature, arts, strengths and customs of its people is useless and dangerous.' He wanted Napoleon to create a republic based on sound administration and economic prosperity; but it had to be Italian: 'I, along with the entirety of the people, describe our liberty as being: to have no magistrate (except for Bonaparte) who is not Italian ... There is no freedom ... where national independence is in chains.'[20]

Exactly what this nation was, and who felt part of it, he (like Cuoco) was not inclined to discuss. In the next few years, though, posted on the sunless north French coast with the Napoleonic army, translating Laurence Sterne's *Sentimental Journey* and fathering a child by an English woman, his sense of emotional attachment to an imagined Italian community deepened and bore fruit in his most celebrated work, *On Tombs*. This long ode took its cue from a decree that extended to Italy a French law banning burials inside churches, for reasons of hygiene. For Foscolo such a ban threatened to sever the link between the living and the dead – above all the glorious dead – that was essential to the spiritual health of a society. He reflected on the impact that seeing the graves of Machiavelli, Michelangelo and Galileo in Santa Croce in Florence had had on his own imagination (and on that of Vittorio Alfieri), and how recollection of past greatness could spur strong spirits to 'noble deeds'. Would the Greeks at Marathon, he wondered, have found 'the courage and the anger' to resist the Persians had Athens not made a cult of its heroes and raised sacred monuments to them?[21]

Foscolo was naturally prone to dyspepsia, but the craven and supine behaviour of his compatriots particularly incensed him. As he wrote in the *Last Letters of Jacopo Ortis*: 'Where then, [Oh Italy], are your sons? You lack nothing except the strength that derives from concord ... Wretches! We are constantly recollecting the liberty and glory of our ancestors, whose splendour is all the more magnificent in so far as it lays bare our present abject slavery.'[22] By recalling 'the Italian glories' of the illustrious dead, celebrated in tombs such as those in Santa Croce, Foscolo hoped that Italians might be inspired to take a more robust stand against their French overlords. And sadly these 'glories' were virtually all that was left of greatness in Italy ever since foreign invaders had breached 'the ill-defended Alps' and stripped Italians of 'their arms, patrimony, fatherland and altars, everything except memory'. It was now up to 'strong intellects' (presumably self-appointed vatic poets such as Foscolo himself) to act as priests of national redemption, and, 'when hope of glory should once again shine upon Italy', to 'take auspices' at the tombs of the great, and urge Italians to action.[23]

For the most part 'the Italian glories' were literary: Foscolo refers in his ode to Dante, Petrarch and Parini as well as Alfieri and Machiavelli. Such a focus was hardly surprising given that the Italian language had for long been the main foundation of Italy's claims to nationhood. And it was precisely because the national question was so closely tied up with a literary tradition that Italian writers, from Alfieri and Foscolo onwards, were to feel that they had a prerogative to act as guardians of the nation's conscience. But Foscolo was also keen to parade other glories before his compatriots, especially military glories, as one of his most pressing concerns was with the decline of military valour in Italy. A year after writing *On Tombs* he began publishing a lavish edition of the works of the great seventeenth-century Modenese general Raimondo Montecuccoli – the most highly regarded military theorist of the time. His aim, Foscolo said, was 'more than literary': he wished, 'by the example and precepts of an illustrious fellow citizen, to inspire the Italians with a portion of his martial spirit . . .'[24]

Partly on the strength of his edition of Montecuccoli's works, Foscolo was elected to the Chair of Eloquence at the University of Pavia, and on 22 January 1809, to a packed and expectant audience of students, academics and political dignitaries, he delivered his inaugural address. The post was an official one, and to underscore his independence and his reputation as an Italian patriot Foscolo refused to include the customary eulogy of Napoleon (though this did not prevent the lecture being accepted immediately for publication). His theme was, 'Of the Origin and Office of Literature'. Drawing heavily on his detailed knowledge of ancient Greek culture, with occasional nods towards Renaissance Italy, he set out, in carefully honed Italian, his belief in the civil mission of literature. He maintained that literature's original purpose was to preserve the value system and traditions of a community, by 'lending grace to those opinions that contribute to civil concord' and condemning vigorously any ideas that would 'erode social bonds' and expose a society to factionalism, disorder and foreign invasion.[25]

Turning to Italy, Foscolo grew impassioned. He lamented the fact that it was foreign academics who were now the leading authorities on classical civilization, and he berated Italian intellectuals for their hermetic aloofness and inability to emulate the brilliant examples set by Machiavelli and Galileo and present their ideas in a style that was elegant and accessible to the general public. He decried the moral shortcomings of the educated class and their failure to impart a civic morality that was grounded in patriotism and public virtue. After all, what other nation could boast a history that had so many lessons for the present? And yet who had followed in the footsteps of Livy and Machiavelli?

Oh, the virtues, misfortunes and errors of great men cannot be written in cloisters and ivory towers! We have chronicles, genealogies and municipal annals . . . but where is a history of Italy? . . . O Italians, I exhort you to the study of history, as no other people can claim more disasters to be lamented, more errors to be avoided, more virtues to be respected, and more great spirits worthy of rescue from oblivion . . .[26]

What most concerned Foscolo was the education of the (largely urban) middle classes, those 'located by fortune between the idiot and the littérateur'. Such people were crucial to the future well-being of the nation: they had 'houses, land, social status and security of inheritance, and when possessed of civil and domestic virtues they ha[d] the resources and energy to impart these to the masses and to the state'. At present, though, they were wallowing in ignorance. Ignored by the merchants of high culture, they were feeding on a diet of newspapers, novels and popular verses, which left them with little sense of the beauty of their language and literature and prey to all manner of 'stupidities and vices'. It was up to the men with education and principles to set aside their disdain for the common herd, and make it their mission to teach the mass of the population how to live virtuously and love Italy, and so rescue the nation from its decadence – a nation whose spirit and essence were timeless and immortal:

My fellow citizens! How meagre is the comfort to be had from being pure and enlightened if you cannot defend our fatherland against the ignorant and the immoral! Love your nation and love literature openly and generously, and you will at last know one another and have the courage that stems from unity . . . [L]ove your fatherland, and you will not allow the native purity, richness and grace of our tongue to be polluted with foreign terms . . . Visit Italy! O adorable land! O temple of Venus and the Muses! How have you been portrayed by travellers who claim to celebrate you! How have you been humiliated by foreigners who presume to teach you how to behave! But who can describe you better than he who is born to behold your beauties all the days of his life? . . . Neither the barbarism of the Goths, nor the disputes between provinces, nor the devastations of countless armies, nor the fulminations of theologians, nor the usurpation of scholarship by monks, have extinguished in these lands that immortal flame that inspired the Etruscans and the Latins, inspired Dante in the nightmares of exile, Machiavelli in the agony of torture, and Galileo amidst the terror of the inquisition . . . Prostrate yourselves on their tombs, ask them about how they were great and unhappy, and how love of their fatherland, of glory and of truth increased their courage, the strength of their spirit, and the blessings they have bestowed on us.[27]

This peroration elicited prolonged and rapturous applause. But Foscolo's hope that a love of the nation and its literature would create a community of intellectuals proved illusory: 'Italy' was a word charged with powerful emotions, but it belonged chiefly still to the sphere of rhetoric. Foscolo's scorn for most of his fellow writers, mere lackeys in his view of the Napoleonic establishment, embroiled him in increasingly ugly feuds and cost him the friendship of among others Vincenzo Monti. When in 1811 his tragedy *Ajace* was staged at La Scala in Milan his enemies turned the occasion into a fiasco, and the play was banned after one performance. Foscolo was forced to leave the Kingdom of Italy. He withdrew to Tuscany, where in relative seclusion he turned his hand to rarefied works, including a satire on Milanese society written in biblical Latin. The role of Old Testament prophet, caustic and aloof, suited him. It was also to appeal to other self-appointed priests of the national cause in years to come.

'BEAUTIFUL ITALY': SONS
AND LOVERS

When Vittorio Alfieri died on 8 October 1803, his lover, Louise, Countess of Albany, was determined he should have a grand monument in the church of Santa Croce in Florence. The choice of artist seemed obvious: Italy's greatest poet should be commemorated by Italy's greatest living sculptor, Antonio Canova. At the time Canova was inundated with commissions from princely courts around Europe, but the Countess of Albany was strong-willed and well connected. So too was her new lover, the French painter François Xavier Fabre. And together, and with the support of the papal Secretary of State, Cardinal Consalvi, they persuaded Canova to undertake the memorial.

Progress was slow. The countess was not happy with Canova's original design of a stela with genii and a bas-relief portrait of the writer: for 10,000 *scudi* she felt entitled to at least one three-dimensional sculpture. There was also the problem that Canova was busy at the time with other major commissions, such as the colossal statue of Napoleon, naked, as 'Mars the Pacifier': the monument to the author of the *Anti-Gaul* had to wait. However, by early 1807 the final composition had been settled on: a large sarcophagus on a two-tiered elliptical base, with lyres, masks, festoons, garlands and inscriptions, and at the front a majestic woman, personifying Italy. To make room for the monument next to the tomb of Niccolò Machiavelli the countess elicited the help of the ruler of Tuscany, Elisa Baciocchi, in having a number of older, if historic, tombs cleared out of the way. She had also used her powerful contacts to overcome the opposition of the clergy of Santa Croce to her own name figuring prominently on the plinth: her relationship with Alfieri had after all been somewhat scandalous.[28]

The monument was inaugurated in September 1810 and the general response was overwhelmingly enthusiastic. Canova had gone to considerable lengths to ensure that the composition was 'grave and majestic', 'to correspond', he wrote, '. . . to the fieriness of the pen of this supreme poet' (he had allegedly read Alfieri's works and Foscolo's *On Tombs* to gain inspiration). In particular it was the figure of Italy – the first ever depiction of the nation in a monument – that attracted the greatest plaudits. Adapted from Canova's statue of Temperance on the tomb of Pope Clement XIV and from his image of Venice on a projected memorial to Francesco Pesaro, the tall and graceful woman, with a coronet of crenellated towers, and a flowing high-waisted classical dress and cloak, her head bowed in grief, and dabbing tears from her eyes, almost immediately established itself as a powerful icon for Italian patriots: Italy as the collective mother weeping for a lost son, and by extension weeping at her own sorry plight over a lifeless, unresurrected nation. When Foscolo paid a visit to his 'holy friends and masters' in Santa Croce in 1812 he came away ecstatic at Alfieri's memorial: 'Oh, how beautiful Italy is! Beautiful! And yet, for all that, she stands over a grave.'[29]

The personification of Italy as a woman with a crown of towers and city walls on her head – symbolizing the country's strong municipal traditions – was Roman in origin. It reappeared occasionally in eighteenth-century allegorical paintings, such as Martin Knoller's fresco of *The Apotheosis of Alberic the Great* (1777–82) in the Palazzo Belgioioso d'Este in Milan, where an Amazonian warrior with large bare breasts (foreshadowing French revolutionary representations of liberty, democracy and the nation as a mother suckling her children), a long spear and a star above her coroneted head, points to a Roman legionary standard bearing the inscription 'Italy liberated from foreigners'. But it was during the Napoleonic period, when there was a concern to make politics into a secular religion, that the iconography of Italy began to flourish.

The images of Italy in the Jacobin years of 1796–9 were in the main pale reflections of their French counterparts: a young woman, usually with one of her breasts naked, in a Greek or Roman tunic, carrying a spear, Phrygian bonnet and a bundle of lictors' rods or *fasces*. Iconographic innovation came with a competition launched by the Cisalpine Republic in 1801 for a painting on the theme of Italy's gratitude to Napoleon for its liberation to be hung in the projected Bonaparte Forum in Milan (whose monumental buildings were never completed). An exhibition of the submitted works was held at the Brera Academy and attracted huge public interest, with troops being deployed to control the crowds. The winning entry by Giuseppe Bossi was especially striking. While other artists showed Italy passively restored to life and liberty by Napoleon, Bossi's canvas, suffused with neoclassical dignity and grandeur, depicted a strong, statuesque woman, dressed in green and white, with a red girdle, a crown of walls and towers round her head, standing proudly before the seated Napoleon, one arm outstretched to receive from him branches of olive and oak leaves (symbols of peace and constancy), the other clasping a copy of the constitution of the Republic.[30]

Further images of Italy appeared at this time, some of which achieved wide circulation as prints. For example, an allegorical drawing by the most famous Italian artist of his day, Andrea Appiani, showed Hercules (symbolizing the French people) scattering the forces of reaction with his club, while the figure of the Italian Republic, a woman crowned with towers, is presented by Minerva to Napoleon, who is ordering Victory to close the door of the temple of Janus (as a sign of peace).[31] Appiani also produced an image of the Cisalpine Republic as a somewhat dishevelled woman, again crowned with towers, surrounded by a throng of naked children imploring Napoleon for help, in the cycle of paintings known as the *Triumphs of Napoleon* in the Royal Palace in Milan – the most important single work of artistic propaganda of the period.

And high art was not the only medium through which ideas and images of the Italian nation were generated. Following the lead of revolutionary France, civic festivals were organized in Italy after 1796 in a bid to mobilize ordinary people and create enthusiasm for the new political order. Often the focus was some famous local figure: Dante in Ravenna, Ariosto in Ferrara. In Mantua in 1797 a day of celebrations was staged for Virgil, and statues of the poet and assorted other luminaries, among them Columbus, Galileo, Rousseau and Petrarch, were paraded through the streets. To save money – and, as far as the city's republican elite was concerned, also to score a political point: though whether the mass of the population shared their glee seems unlikely – statues of saints were taken from the city's churches and turned into secular icons.[32]

Some of the most elaborate festivals were held in Milan, where a large arena, begun in 1805, staged gymnastic games, horse and chariot races, and mock naval battles, with participants and spectators often decking themselves out in Roman costume for the occasion, while a vast tract of open land near the Sforza castle, designated the Bonaparte Forum, was home to spectacular *mises en scène*. The festival of 26 June 1803 was especially lavish, with the artist Appiani having a major hand in its design. Among the key works were a giant statue of the Italian Republic, erected by the Naviglio canal, with a bas-relief on its pedestal of the

Departments as young women holding hands in a joyous dance, and two statues of the French and Italian Republics 'amorously embracing . . . in the most beautiful green bower', with beside them four figures of Fame, 'announcing this happiest of unions to all the world'. In the centre of the Bonaparte Forum, amid a sea of smoking altars and tripods, rose a massive column, surmounted by a figure of Napoleon, with a relief around the drum showing the French army crossing the Great St Bernard. Near to it were two slightly smaller columns bearing representations of the French and Italian republics.

Ceremonies and symbols were tools of the new civic religion of patriotism. They were instruments for engendering, channelling and focusing popular enthusiasm around the cult of the nation. But in the case of the most important and probably most influential literary personification of Italy in this period, that of the supremely beautiful, talented and sibylline figure of Corinne in Madame de Staël's 1807 novel, *Corinne, or Italy*, the inspirational power of the symbol was undercut by disquieting strains of criticism (all the more disturbing for their being largely implicit and almost casual) towards those who had failed to make the heroine happy and prevent her tragic early death. This was no doubt one reason why the novel (which went through over forty editions in the course of the nineteenth century)[33] was never as popular in Italy as it was in Britain, France or the United States. Italy as a beautiful and dignified matron or grieving mother was an invitation, without criticism, to comfort and support; as a radiant young woman who could not find a worthy partner among her compatriots, the call to help and action was interlaced with aspersions cast on Italian masculinity – though the response might be all the more vehement as a result of wounded *amour propre*.

Corinne, or Italy was the fruit of a trip that Madame de Staël made to Italy in 1805 in the company of her children's tutor, the distinguished German academic and translator of Shakespeare, August Wilhelm von Schlegel, and the great Swiss scholar Simonde de Sismondi. Sismondi was then engaged in writing the first volume of his monumental history of the Italian medieval republics, a work whose celebration of the raw energy, military prowess and independence of the city-states in the centuries before the Renaissance helped to inspire a generation of Italian patriots. Born to Swiss Protestant parents, brought up in a highly cosmopolitan environment in Paris – her father was Jacques Necker, Louis XVI's eminent finance minister, whose sacking in July 1789 triggered the storming of the Bastille – and married when young to a Swedish aristocrat, Madame de Staël was fascinated by questions of national identity and in particular by the institutional and environmental forces that went into shaping the characters of different peoples. Before 1805 her opinion of Italians had been low: her emotional and intellectual centre of gravity had been located firmly in the north of Europe. But the influence of Sismondi, a passionate love affair in Rome, and anger at Napoleon's despotic callousness towards both herself and the peninsula softened her prejudices.

In print, at least. In private, her behaviour on her trip to Italy was characteristic of the impatience and condescension shown by many northern travellers at this time, an attitude that she herself caricatured in *Corinne* in the figure of the frivolous and philistine Frenchman, the Count d'Erfeuil ('as nations, I like only the English and the French . . . It is just a prejudice to admire those thorn-covered ruins . . . There is not a monument intact in Europe today which is not worth more than those stumps of columns, than those bas-reliefs blackened by time . . .').[34] De Staël hurried through the north and centre of Italy, dismissive of most of the monuments and works of art, quarrelling continually with Schlegel, who wanted to do sightseeing properly, irritated by the sycophancy of the local *érudits*, who everywhere turned out to shower her with tributes in verse and prose, and declaring that there was nobody worth talking to apart from the poet Vincenzo Monti. Only when she got to Rome did things change. There the statuesque 39-year-old *salonnière* and enthusiast for Rousseau and free-love encountered the handsome Dom Pedro de Sousa Holstein, a future prime minister of Portugal, fifteen years her junior; and Italy suddenly acquired a much more appealing air.[35]

Madame de Staël wrote *Corinne* in Switzerland and France between 1805 and 1806 at the time when Napoleon was extending his despotic control over almost the entire peninsula; and this backdrop, together with the republican Sismondi's patient and no doubt insistent tutoring of de Staël as she dashed through the peninsula, ensured the novel had a sharp political undertone (as Napoleon immediately saw: he was enraged, and renewed de Staël's ban from Paris). On the surface, though, the novel was little more than a rather melodramatic romantic tale. Lord Nelvil, a young, handsome and world-weary Anglo-Scottish aristocrat, goes to Italy to restore his health and meets a vivacious and emotionally liberated poet called Corinne, just as she is being crowned with laurels on the Capitol in a brilliant ceremony in honour of her genius. They fall in love and travel together around Italy, drinking in the country's beauties and admiring its artistic treasures. But Nelvil is increasingly troubled by his late father's wish that he should marry a suitably demure English girl, and returns to England to try to resolve the conflict that he feels between love and duty. Corinne secretly follows him, believes Nelvil has abandoned her for someone else, goes back home, distraught, and enters into a long decline, losing her good looks and her talents, and eventually dies; but not before she has seen Nelvil again and been reconciled to him, after he explains that he had never ceased to love her, and had only deserted her because he was under the misapprehension that it was she who had in fact deserted him.

Corinne, though, is also a highly intellectual novel, whose imagery and plot are heavily informed by the conversations that were taking place at the time among the educated about nations and nationality (this latter word was invented by Madame de Staël's circle and appears for the first time in European literature in *Corinne*).[36] The figure of the heroine is de Staël's attempt to encapsulate the soul of the Italian nation (and this is Italy as a whole, irrespective of regional diversity, for wherever Corinne goes, whether Rome, Naples, Florence or Venice, she is immediately recognized and feted by all classes). Physically she is made to resemble one of Domenichino's exotic and sensuous Cumaean Sibyls ('An Indian turban was wound round her head, and intertwined with her beautiful black hair . . . Her arms were dazzlingly beautiful; her tall, slightly plump figure . . . gave a keen impression of youth and happiness; her eyes had something of an inspired look'); in character she is represented as artistic, creative, intellectual, spontaneous, emotional and unaffected. But Corinne is the timeless essence of Italy, a kind of Platonic ideal, and not its historical reality, for political decadence and fragmentation have produced moral decline. As Prince Castel-Forte, the acme of contemporary Italian manhood, says:

We say to foreigners: 'Look at her, she is the image of our beautiful Italy; she is what we would be but for the ignorance, the envy, the discord, and the indolence to which our fate has condemned us.' We delight in gazing at her as an admirable product of our climate and of our arts, as an offshoot of the past, as a harbinger of the future. And when foreigners talk ill of this land which gave birth to the great minds that have enlightened Europe, when they have no pity for our failings which arise from our misfortunes, we say to them: 'Look at Corinne.'[37]

If Corinne is Italy, the quintessence of the sun-soaked south with its perpetual proneness to lethargy and sensuality, Lord Nelvil is the northern soul, rational and intrinsically active, but inclined by cold, damp and fog to gloomy introspection. But as an Anglo-Scottish peer he is also a symbol of the political freedom and vigorous self-governance that de Staël and her circle so admired; and the question that nags through the novel – and it is one that is made all the more pertinent by the recent suppression of the Italian Republic – is how a successful marriage between Italy and liberty could be achieved. That Italy is suited to freedom and flourishes in its presence is affirmed in the radiant nature of the love affair (and Corinne wastes away and dies once she is deserted by Nelvil); and that the country has the potential to recover its former greatness is explicitly stated (and for both these reasons Sismondi regarded *Corinne* as 'a noble defence of a people that everyone else has long treated with ingratitude').[38] But who is to bring about Italy's regeneration given that Italians, or at least Italian men, have been rendered so corrupt, decadent and effete by centuries of servitude?

Clearly not the French, who were incapable of love or sympathy for Italy; and implicitly not the British either (though with the early chapters being conceived around the time of Nelson's victory at Trafalgar, it is possible that de Staël initially entertained the hope of British armed support; and some English liberals of a romantic disposition, such as Lord William Bentinck, would certainly have relished the challenge of supporting Italian nationalism). Corinne speaks of two former lovers who had both turned out to be inadequate, 'a great German nobleman' and a Roman prince (representing, presumably, the medieval Empire and the Papacy): the first had brawn, but insufficient intellect, and did not want to live in Italy, the second 'shared all [her] tastes, and liked [her] way of life', but lacked the strength to protect her when things got difficult.[39] By default, then, the responsibility for protecting Corinne ('Corinne's . . . eyes sought the protection of a man friend, a protection no woman, however superior she may be, can ever dispense with')[40] would seem naturally to lie with Italian men. But how were they to find the necessary vigour and determination for the task?

This was a question that in the years to come was to trouble many Italian patriots as well as foreign observers. And it was a question that had already taxed the minds of some of the most astute historians and philosophers in Italy since the end of the fifteenth century, when the humiliating conquest of the peninsula by Spanish, French and German troops had led Machiavelli and others to speculate on what had gone wrong and why a land that had produced such great citizens and warriors in ancient Rome could have become so conspicuously lacking in civic and military virtues. Catholicism was one much favoured culprit. But in that case, why had the French, who were also Catholics, ended up conquering almost the whole of Europe to cries of 'Vive la patrie!'? Madame de Staël's preference was to attribute Italy's plight to its despotic political institutions and the cynical rapaciousness of foreigners. As Corinne tells Lord Nelvil, after he has disparaged Italian men for their weakness and lack of purpose in life (like Madame de Staël herself in private: in her travel notebooks she was utterly scathing about the 'feminine' character of Italian males):[41]

What you say about the Italians is what all foreigners say . . . But you must probe more deeply to judge this country, which at different periods has been so great. How comes it then that this nation was the most military of all under the Romans, the most jealous of its liberty in the medieval republics, and in the sixteenth century the most famous for literature, science, and the arts? . . . And if now it is no longer distinguished, why would you not blame its political situation, since in other circumstances it has shown itself to be so different from what it is now? . . . In every age, foreigners have conquered and torn apart this beautiful country, the goal of their permanent ambition; and yet foreigners bitterly reproach this nation with the failings of nations that have been conquered and torn apart![42]

The degenerate behaviour of Italians is thus due to their having been subjugated and divided for centuries. But there was a problem with this line of argument, for if, as de Staël says, 'governments make the character of nations',[43] how can a people which has become deeply corrupted find the moral resources needed to throw off the yoke of tyranny? And if by some accident of history that yoke is thrown off for them (by, say, a foreign power), what is to stop the vices of the people then vitiating the institutions and destroying them before those institutions have had time to work their pedagogic effect?

Here was another conundrum for Italian patriots to wrestle with, particularly those of a democratic persuasion who believed in representative government and an Italy made by and for 'the people'. How could there be a guarantee that those who were elected to an assembly would not simply mirror the behaviour and values of the unregenerate masses? It is a thought that seems to have troubled Madame de Staël towards the end of her novel. When Lord Nelvil returns to England he is struck by the dignity, order and prosperity of his native land, and the 'poetic impressions' that had filled his heart when he was with Corinne gave way to 'the deep feeling of liberty and morality'. He now has nothing but pity for Italy, where there is no society or public opinion, and where 'the institutions and social conditions only reflect confusion, weakness, and ignorance'.[44] There was always the hope, of course, that a virtuous minority might succeed in educating Italians, using the medium of literature in particular to evade the censors ('There is so much feeling in our arts that perhaps one day our character will equal our genius,' says Corinne, after quoting a patriotic line from Alfieri). But here, too, de Staël was aware that a similar circularity of cause and effect risked nullifying the impact of the written word on Italian society. For, as Corinne acknowledges, one of the consequences of centuries of enslavement had been that Italian writers had 'lost all interest in truth, and often even the possibility of expressing it'. Rhetoric and artifice had come to replace serious thought and genuine feelings.[45]

The personification of Italy as a beautiful woman – whether a grieving young mother in search of consolation, or a sister or fiancée whose honour had to be safeguarded against predatory foreigners (or avenged), or, as in the case of Corinne, a nubile and poetic creature longing for the embrace of a strong protector – was to develop into a major theme in the patriotic literature and art of the next few decades and helped to inject into the movement for national redemption a note of sexual frisson. And particularly when mixed with religious sentiment it made for a cocktail powerful enough to inspire young men to risk their lives in conspiracy or on the barricades. Recalling his youthful infatuation with the cause of Italian unity, the Tuscan democrat Giuseppe Montanelli wrote in 1853 of how he and his friends absorbed 'the religion of the fatherland' from books, and how 'Italy became for us a cherished mother, a mother in chains, and we loved her as one loves one's mother': 'And we came to look upon the day when it would be given to us to fight the battle for national redemption as the most beautiful day of our lives.'[46] Another leading democrat, Goffredo Mameli, described in January 1849 his frustration at the betrayal of Italy, his metaphors slipping waywardly between the realms of the sexual and the religious: 'Italy had arisen most beautiful after centuries in her tomb, armed with her faith; and she was surrounded by countless lovers. But many only loved her to disarm her, and many only kissed her on the face for Judas' thirty pieces of silver. And our poor fatherland was crucified.'[47] Six months later, Mameli achieved his own martyrdom, dying on behalf of his beloved Italy from wounds he had received defending Rome against the French.

3

Conspiracy and Resistance

The idea ... behind this society came from a Bolognese of exceptional intellect, and was called Platonic Astronomy ... The solar circle was divided into two hemispheres, one based in Bologna, the other in Milan. These hemispheres only communicated with each other orally, not in writing, and the words were carried from one hemisphere to another by one of the planets, who while carrying out his mission was known as a comet. Every member of the hemisphere was also the president, or first star, of a segment and directed its operations. Each star in a segment constituted a ray, of which it was the source of light. Each member of a ray was called a line; and whenever a ray got too big, the most active lines broke away and formed new rays ... [By 1802] the society had 30,000 lines.

G. Breganze, description of the Society of Rays, c.1830

I wish, Lord, that you could feel fully the truth of what I have the honour of telling you: that we are no longer the people we were twenty years ago, and it is not possible for us to return to how we were except by renouncing ways and feelings that are too dear to a nation that has the desire, the means and the energy to be such.

Count Federico Confalonieri to Lord Castlereagh, 18 May 1814

RURAL REVOLTS

On the evening of 29 November 1807 Napoleon crossed the lagoon to Venice. It was his first and only visit to the city. It was cold and wet, but the Venetians had gone out of their way to make the man who had ended their independence and then handed them over to the Austrians feel welcome, constructing a huge triumphal arch across the entrance to the Grand Canal between the churches of San Simeone and the Scalzi.

For ten days the Emperor of the French and King of Italy was feted by the nobility and middle classes. A splendid regatta was staged in his honour, and there was a glittering gala at the theatre of La Fenice (where a royal box had been built specially for him), with the performance of a newly commissioned cantata entitled *The Judgement of Jove*. In return for this hospitality Napoleon passed a series of decrees, founding academies, opening San Marco to the public (and making it a cathedral), and ordering the demolition of the west end of the Piazza and the construction in its place of a ballroom.[1]

From Venice, Napoleon travelled to Milan, where on 17 December he was the guest of honour at a mock naval battle laid on for him in the newly finished arena. A nautical theme was not without relevance, for on that same day he issued a decree reinforcing the blockade of the ports of continental Europe against British shipping – a policy that he had launched the previous year in a bid to bring the British economy to its knees. Three days later he addressed the electoral college of Milan. As often, he was careful to flatter his audience with patriotic rhetoric, recalling the past glories of Italy and highlighting the damage that had been done to the nation over the centuries by regional rivalries and divisions. But precisely because there was still so much to be done to restore the country to its former greatness, he said, the French and the Italians should see themselves as brothers, and the Iron Crown of Lombardy be united with the imperial crown of France. Italy, in other words, was to remain subordinate to France.[2]

There was certainly resentment among the upper classes at French rule; but it was muted. Nor did a burgeoning sense of patriotism necessarily mean hostility to the Napoleonic order. Vincenzo Cuoco was perfectly happy to occupy administrative posts in Milan while urging the civic and political education of Italians; so, too, was Melchiorre Gioia, who became a respected civil servant. Foscolo's snarls of anger and frustration were the exception rather than the rule. Much of the explanation for this acquiescence lay in Napoleon's deliberate policy of seeking to win the backing of the propertied classes; and in the last years of his regime this *ralliement* gathered pace, with even the old nobility dropping its surliness towards the Napoleonic order in many places and gracing the courts of Naples and Turin, Florence and Milan with its presence.

The sale of former feudal 'national lands' was one important way of winning support. In contrast to France, where the peasantry benefited heavily from such sales, in Italy it was mostly existing landowners and the urban professional classes who gained. In Piedmont typical beneficiaries were major aristocratic families such as the Cavours, the d'Azeglios and the Balbos (all of whom were later to play a major role in the national movement). In southern Italy, where feudalism was abolished in 1806 in the wake of the French occupation, there were attempts to ensure that the peasantry received something. The key issue here was the common lands, on which local people had enjoyed ancient rights, for instance, of pasturage or wood gathering, and which had been critical to their livelihood. A special commission was set up to explore the often complex competing claims of feudatories and the commune to such lands, and where rights were established, part of the land was supposed to be given to the poorest peasants. In practice, however, the barons were often able to thwart the endeavours of the state officials, and the issue of the distribution of the common lands was to remain a running sore in many areas of the south well into the twentieth century.

Ecclesiastical lands also flooded the market in these years and helped to keep the middle and upper classes happy. A concordat of 1803 between the Pope and the Cisalpine Republic declared Catholicism the state religion and guaranteed the Church against control by the civil authorities in many important areas. But once it was signed, Napoleon proceeded to ignore both its spirit and its letter. Religious orders were tightly regulated by the state, Church property continued to be confiscated, civil marriage and divorce were imposed, and parishes were reorganized. The situation got even worse after French troops annexed the Papal States in 1809 and arrested the Pope. In the countryside especially it was often priests who took the lead in opposing the government and stoking popular unrest. For the propertied classes, though, the material benefits of Napoleon's anticlerical policies allayed most of their spiritual qualms.

Though taxes on property certainly went up sharply under Napoleon, the burden for landowners was offset by the steep rise in the prices of wheat, rice, wine and other goods. The introduction of the Continental Blockade from 1806 damaged Italian ports badly, but Italy now became a major supplier of raw materials to France, and this trade gave a powerful boost to agricultural production as well as to the manufacture of silk. The merchant classes benefited from the removal of internal customs barriers, the unification of coinage, the new commercial and civil codes and the vigorous road-building programme that was under-taken, especially in the north of the country (the great Simplon road, built over the Alps in 1802–5, was emblematic). Italian manufacturing was already weak and may not have been damaged much by French industrial imports. Indeed it may have gained from supplying matériel to the army.

While most of the peasantry probably resented military conscription, for the upper classes – or at any rate for those who did not purchase exemptions – the experience of serving in the Grande Armée was often a source of pride and (paradoxically) of patriotic sentiment: Italians, after all, could fight, and fight well. When it came to the army Napoleon was typically ambivalent in his attitude to the national question. On the one hand he did not want the Italian units to develop an independent identity: they were thus incorporated into the main body of the French forces. On the other he was quite happy for patriotic feelings to be nurtured among the Italian regiments as a way of promoting *esprit de corps*. The Italian language was declared the common medium of communication, and dialect discouraged; and officers were told to foster bonds of fraternity among the troops by appealing to the idea of an Italian 'patria': 'The concept of an Italian army, in name and practice, is to be drummed into the conscripts as often as possible,' ran a directive from the Italian Minister of War in 1809. 'They are to be told that they serve for the splendour of Italy.'[3] Efforts were also made to celebrate an Italian military tradition. For example, the Neapolitan exile and patriot Francesco Lomonaco (who was a doctor: among his patients were his friends Vincenzo Cuoco and Ugo Foscolo) followed up his successful *Life of Dante* and *Lives of the Illustrious Italians* with a three-volume work, *Lives of the Famous Captains of Italy* (1804–5), written for the military academy of Modena.

There was a particularly strong cult of the flag in the army. The first time the Italian tricolour was used was on 6 November 1796 when Napoleon presented a red, white and green standard, embroidered with a wreath of oak leaves and the republican symbols of a Phrygian cap, the daggers of Brutus and Cassius, and the inscription 'Equality or death', to the first cohort of the Lombard Legion. Two months later at the congress of Reggio, the tricolour was adopted as the flag of the Cispadane Republic, and thereafter it was employed by all Italian army units throughout the Napoleonic period. In the campaigns fought on foreign soil in Germany, Spain and Russia, where the Italian losses were huge (only 13,000 of the 85,000 who set out returned alive), the tricolour became a powerful symbol of collective identity and suffering. And it is hardly surprising that in the spring of 1814, when, under the terms of the armistice of Schiarino-Rizzino, Italian units were supposed to become incorporated into the Austrian army, there was widespread resistance, and rather than hand over their flags troops preferred instead to burn them, divide up the ashes, and sometimes eat them in soup.[4]

The writer Stendhal – admittedly not always the most reliable witness – was convinced that military service under Napoleon was an important means of reducing regional divisions and countering the bourgeois effeteness of many Italians. He recalled in 1817 how before the arrival of the French 'the aristocracy of Bergamo used to feel an inexpressible contempt for the peaceable ways of the Milanese, and would invade the masked balls held at La Scala, firmly intending to offer provocation to anyone they met. "Let's go to Milan and slap a few faces!" was a common cry in Bergamese society.' However, the Napoleonic wars had 'refashion[ed] all these diverse regional idiosyncracies, and the gentlemen of Milan, whether on the field of Raab or in the Peninsular War, fought fully as valiantly as their brother officers from Bergamo or Reggio'.[5]

Whether the experience of army life had the permanent nationalizing effect that Stendhal believed is unclear, though it is certainly the case that patriotic sentiment remained strong in the ranks of Italian officers after 1815 and was an important ingredient in the insurrections that broke out during the first years of restored Austrian rule. It is also true that the idea of the army as the 'school of the nation' was a powerful legacy to united Italy, and served to shape many aspects of political life after 1860 in far-reaching (and sometimes dangerous) ways. However, there seems little doubt that educated Italians frequently felt they were helping the cause of 'Italy' while they were in the Napoleonic army, not least by acquiring martial skills and making good some of the damage that had been done by centuries of servitude. As a Venetian lieutenant wrote to a Milanese friend from Calais in July 1804:

As an Italian, I attach great significance to this expedition for the fortunes of my country, because it is certain that if the Italian Republic is ever mentioned in the general peace, it will be because of these two wretched divisions . . . Our main aim is to learn about war, as this will be the only means by which we can make ourselves free . . . We are still too young to think of getting liberty. Let us think about being soldiers, and when we have got one hundred thousand bayonets, then we will be able to talk.[6]

If the Napoleonic regime in Italy was on the whole successful in winning over the middle and upper classes (albeit, at times, at the cost of fanning potentially dangerous patriotic flames), it was far less fortunate when it came to the mass of the population. The gulf between the educated and the illiterate, the rich and the poor, the town and the countryside, that Vincenzo Cuoco had identified as the Achilles' heel of the Neapolitan revolution of 1799 remained an enormous problem after 1800, and continually threatened to undermine the authority of the state almost everywhere in mainland Italy. In the absence of a workable policy to distribute land to the poor, there was nothing to mitigate the feelings of anger that many peasants felt at rising prices, spiralling indirect taxation, the loss of common lands, military conscription and the suppression of the monasteries (which, apart from the offence done to their religious sensibilities, deprived them of an important source of charitable welfare and jobs).

Unrest in the countryside grew particularly acute in northern Italy at the end of 1805, when Austria ceded Venice and Dalmatia to the Kingdom of Italy under the Peace of Pressburg. This change meant peasants could no longer slip across the border as before to escape conscription. Typical of the revolts at this time – and characteristic of the severity with which Napoleon dealt with them – was an incident at Crespino near Rovigo. It began in October 1805 as a protest against taxes, with some fifty local workers sacking the town hall and destroying registers. Support for the rebels arrived from nearby villages, and the local militia was disarmed and the gates of the town thrown open to Austrian soldiers. When news of these events reached Napoleon, he was incensed, and on 11 February he signed a decree in the Tuileries declaring that the people of Crespino should henceforth be stripped of their citizen rights and be treated as 'people without a fatherland'. They were to pay double taxes, and be punished by floggings rather than imprisonment. And over the entrance to the town hall he ordered the following inscription to be set in marble: 'Napoleon I, Emperor of the French and King of Italy, has decreed: the inhabitants of Crespino are not Italian citizens.' The town was eventually pardoned – at the price of one fishmonger being shot.[7]

Napoleon's relative leniency on this occasion was not always repeated. The commander in charge of putting down a rising in the mountains near Piacenza in January 1806 was ordered 'to set fire to one large village and shoot a dozen rebels'.[8] No less harsh was the government's response to a huge wave of revolts that swept across much of northern Italy in 1809-10. These were triggered by tax rises and an invasion of the Austrian army, but were often fuelled by deep-seated tensions between town and countryside. In the Veneto 8,000 insurgents besieged Vicenza, while Schio, Feltre and Belluno were captured, taxes abolished and the return of Venetian laws proclaimed. In Rovigo the houses of Jews and wealthy merchants were sacked and public documents burned, and in the Romagna a series of tax revolts culminated in a full-scale assault on Bologna. Often it was public officials who were the main targets of peasant wrath. The traumatized mayor of Crespellano wrote to the prefect in October 1809 of 'these monsters, speaking different languages, terrible in appearance, but more terrible still in their deeds', who had sacked his town hall and raped his wife.[9]

But it was once again southern Italy that saw the worst violence. Here popular anger at French rule after 1806, with its heavy taxes, its confiscations of Church property, its failure to resolve ownership of the common lands and (from 1809) its imposition of conscription, was compounded by old patterns of conflict – between rival towns, between factions within towns, and between landlords and peasants (Joseph Bonaparte described the violence as 'a war of the poor against the rich'). The British and the Bourbons (in exile in Sicily) added a further dimension to the turmoil by giving military and financial support to bandits and rebels. The result was five years of brutal guerrilla warfare, much of it concentrated in Calabria and the Abruzzi, in which some 20,000 French soldiers were killed. There was little that was 'patriotic' about this violence, certainly in the sense of fighting for some idea of 'Italy'; though some of the rebels undoubtedly felt inspired by feelings of loyalty to the king and the Church.[10]

Appalling atrocities were perpetrated on both sides. Only one of the peasant leaders, or *capimassa*, Geniale Versace, had a reputation for being in any way merciful to captives, and prisoners were quite regularly castrated, flayed, impaled, crucified or burned alive. Giuseppe Rotella was justly nicknamed 'the executioner', while Capo Scapitta was reputed to dine on flesh from the freshly severed heads of his enemies. The French replied with a similar ruthlessness. In July 1806 Napoleon told his brother Joseph Bonaparte: 'Grant no pardons, execute at least 600 rebels . . . Let the houses of at least thirty of the principal heads of the villages be burned and distribute their property among the troops. Disarm all the inhabitants and pillage five or six of the villages that have behaved worst . . . Confiscate the public property of the rebellious villages and give it to the army.'[11] Joseph complied, and by December 1806 some 4,000 rebels had been killed on sight in the three provinces of the Abruzzi alone.

The most famous rebel was an irregular soldier and bandit, Michele Pezza, known as Fra Diavolo (Brother Devil). Born in 1771, the son of a carter and trader from the small town of Itri in the region of Lazio, Pezza had apparently earned his nickname while still a child as a result of his unruly character and a vow that his mother had made to San Francesco di Paola (which she had kept) to dress her son as a monk if he ever recovered from a serious illness. After murdering two men in the mid-1790s in a dispute over honour (the classic starting point for many a brigand *curriculum vitae*), he had fled to the hills and formed a bandit gang, but had been given a pardon in return for enrolling in the Bourbon army. In 1799 he had joined Cardinal Ruffo's Christian Army, leading a force of several thousand notoriously bloodthirsty volunteers, and he had played a prominent part in the overthrow of the Neapolitan Republic and the subsequent attack on the French garrison in Rome. As a reward for his services King Ferdinand had given him 2,500 ducats and promoted him to colonel.[12]

When the French invaded the Kingdom of Naples at the beginning of 1806 Pezza emerged once again at the head of a force of irregulars, harrying the French mercilessly and conducting a reign of terror in the towns and villages of Campania (all in the name of King Ferdinand). He was supported by the British, who in July landed a force in Calabria and defeated the French at the Battle of Maida (an encounter bucolically commemorated in Maida Vale, London). In the wake of this victory Pezza tried to start a rising in southern Italy, but with little success. A huge bounty of 17,000 ducats was now on his head. The French were bent on capturing him, and by an appropriate twist of historical fate, given the fascination that he (and his moniker) were to exert on the romantic imagination, the officer entrusted with hunting him down was Sigisbert Hugo, father of the great poet, Victor. Pezza and his men were routed near Campobasso. Pezza himself escaped, but he was caught soon after and turned over to the French (after being wounded by rival bandits). He was promptly put on trial. British requests to have him considered a prisoner of war were rejected, and on 11 November 1806 he was executed in Naples as a common criminal.[13]

The king and queen of Naples hurried to show their gratitude to Fra Diavolo and celebrate his achievements – despite his highly chequered career. A solemn mass was held for him in the church of St John the Baptist in Palermo, attended by numerous political dignitaries and a detachment of British soldiers, and with the archbishop officiating. Inscriptions proclaimed Pezza's noble virtues and glorious deeds, and the joy he had experienced in 'dying for [his] fatherland'.[14] The support of the authorities for criminal figures such as Pezza was to be an alarming feature of political life in southern Italy for years to come and was to make the imposition of the rule of law hard to achieve. And the fact that Pezza's life, like that of many other bandits after him, quickly became wrapped in romantic myths, added further to the difficulties the state faced in making private violence morally repugnant. Indeed, Pezza was soon swept into the pantheon of musical immortality with Daniel Auber's hugely successful comic opera, *Fra Diavolo* (1830), where he appears as a dashing figure, masquerading as a marquis, who dupes Lord and Lady Cokbourg (Eugène Scribe's rendering of 'Cockburn') and filches Lady Pamela's diamonds from around her neck.

The campaigns of Sigisbert Hugo and other Napoleonic officers had an effect, and for a couple of years after Pezza's death the violence in southern Italy abated. But in 1809 it flared up again following the introduction of conscription by the new King of Naples, Joachim Murat. As before, the clergy were often key figures in the unrest, sometimes leading local rebellions in person, more generally inciting the peasants to take the law into their own hands and defy their godless masters: rebels were said to cut crosses on their musket balls before shooting at the 'French devils'.[15] Monasteries frequently acted as bases for the insurgents, providing them with food and shelter and serving as depositories for arms and ammunition. In general, however, the unrest lacked coordination and systematic leadership, and though it remained a serious problem for some time, especially in Calabria (where the British secretly channelled weapons and money to rebel gangs), by 1811 much of it had been brought under control by the French.

SECRET SOCIETIES AND OPPOSITION TO NAPOLEON

Secrecy was a necessary political tool in a climate of oppression. Under Napoleon, and during the restoration after 1815, opponents of the existing order were forced to try to evade the police and the censors with subterfuge. One way of doing this was by coding their dissent: for example, by disguising opposition in cultural debates (about language, literary styles or the study of history), or in poetic, artistic and musical symbols, or even in fashion statements (hair and beards were a particularly rich source of political expression from the 1790s). Alternatively recourse could be had to clandestine organizations, with oaths and rituals being used to protect members from infiltration or betrayal. However, secrecy was not just a utilitarian commodity. It had also become charged with an intellectual frisson in the eighteenth century: access to secret knowledge was the key to revelation and enlightenment, and brought with it membership of a new elite, one that was based on intellect rather than wealth or social class.

The Italian secret societies for the most part evolved from Freemasonry, which had apparently first been introduced into Tuscany from Britain during the 1730s. Despite papal bans, Freemasonry had gradually spread through the peninsula, and by the 1780s it had secured aristocratic and royal patronage and with it a measure of respectability. But with the outbreak of the French Revolution it came to be seen as subversive, and lodges were closed or forced deeper underground, often assuming in the process a more radical political character. The Society of Rays, which appeared in parts of Lombardy and Emilia Romagna in the late 1790s, with a vague programme of national independence and opposition to France, almost certainly had Masonic roots. This society resurfaced for a while after 1800, and may have been behind a rebellion that broke out in Bologna in July 1802. But like so many of the sects of these years, it suffered from municipalism and a lack of clear goals and leadership, and soon fizzled out.

A number of Catholic secret societies operated in these years, spear-heading reactionary opposition to Napoleonic rule, and their roots were probably more in the various associations that had been created by Jesuits after the suppression of the Society of Jesus in 1773 than in Freemasonry. They derived their support from the anger felt at the anti-clerical and anti-papal policies of the French, from loyalty to the old order, and from the conservative strand of romanticism that emerged around the start of the nineteenth century with its celebration of religion, mystery, authority and aesthetic traditionalism. Christian Amity, an association founded back in the early 1780s, operated in Piedmont, while the Society of the Heart of Jesus was active under the Italian Republic (and caused Melzi d'Eril and his government much anxiety). In the south there were the sects of the Trinitari and the Calderari. These were nurtured by agents of the Bourbons and drew inspiration from Ruffo's Holy Faith movement of 1799.

But the most important of the secret societies was that of the Car-boneria, or 'charcoal burners'. Exactly when and where it began is uncertain. Some accounts suggested it began in Scotland, some in the Jura, some in the forests of Germany. It may first have infiltrated Italy in the 1790s, but it only began to grow significantly after 1806 in the Kingdom of Naples, in part thanks to support from the British. The members of the Carboneria – Carbonari – were broadly united in their opposition to Napoleon (the 'fat wolf' who had 'killed the republic')[16] and to French rule, and in their desire for Italian independence, but as with the Society of Rays there was a good deal of uncertainty about exactly what they wanted instead – whether a federal republic or some form of constitutional monarchy. There were also problems with the society's social goals. Initiates into the highest grade were apparently expected to embrace radical egalitarian ideas of the kind that Filippo Buonarroti and his followers had espoused back in the 1790s. But many rank and file members – typically smaller landowners, professional men, soldiers and civil servants, and clergy – would have bridled at such extremism, and this part of the Carboneria's programme was played down.[17]

The Carboneria was heavily Masonic in both structure and style. The basic unit was a local cell called a *vendita*, with a group of *vendite* being controlled by a *vendita madre* (mother *vendita*), which in turn answered to an *alta vendita* (high *vendita*). Initially there appear to have been just two grades, those of Apprentice and Master, but at some point a third grade was added, that of Grand Master; and this tier was subsequently replaced by an additional scale of a further seven grades, perhaps after 1815. With each grade came a new initiation ceremony, rituals and catechism, and access to a new level of knowledge: apprentices were taught general philanthropic, moral and religious precepts, while those higher up were given political instruction in how to set about overthrowing tyrants. All Carbonari were required to be armed with a musket and bayonet and to pay a monthly due to their *vendita*. To minimize the risk of being betrayed by police spies or informers, organization was tight. Affiliates were allowed access to only a small circle of other affiliates, and recognition signs and passwords were changed regularly on the instructions of the *alta vendita*.[18]

In an uncertain world of political upheaval, peasant unrest and fresh economic opportunities, the Carboneria was able to provide useful networks of support and solidarity; and the benefits to be gained from the connections it generated must have compensated for the risks that the initiates ran of being arrested and imprisoned. These social benefits were no doubt a major part of the sect's appeal. But another important aspect of the Carboneria, and one that characterized the life of almost all the secret societies at this time and later spilled over into the ethos and imagery of the movement for national unification, was its religious character. The language and rituals of the Carboneria drew heavily on Christian liturgy and symbolism, and this, too, must have been a reason for its appeal, emotionally, and probably intellectually as well.

Central to the teachings of the Carboneria were the ideas of steadfastness in the face of adversity, dedication to truth and virtue, and opposition to tyranny. The patron saint of the society was Saint Theobald, an eleventh-century hermit from a noble family who had spurned worldly goods and honours and retreated to the forests of Germany and northern Italy along with his friend Walter (and later his mother) to live a life of austerity. Another key figure for the Carbonari was Jesus Christ, as both man and God. The instruments of the Passion – the crown of thorns, the nails and the cross – were important symbols for the sect. And there were many allusions to the life of Christ in its rituals. In the most common version of the initiation ceremony for the grade of Master candidates were told how Jesus, 'Grand Master of the Universe', was the perfection of humanity, and how he had become the 'victim of the cruellest tyranny' for having tried to educate the people and free them from slavery. The candidate then had to take the part of Jesus in an elaborate re-enactment of his trial before Pontius Pilate, and at the climax of the crucifixion swear loyalty to the Carboneria.[19]

At the highest levels the rituals became more political (and more gothic) but they were still shot through with religious and liturgical allusions. A Carbonaro catechism of 1818 described the initiation ceremony for the grade of Grand Master conducted by the 'Lieutenant of the Patriarch' in the presence of the *alta vendita*. The candidate, carrying an acacia branch (a Masonic symbol of purity and constancy) and a skull, was brought into a blue room, decorated with white, red, black and green festoons and the image of an acacia tree, with on either side of it the letters L and E, standing for liberty and equality, and at its base a lump of coal, an axe and a dagger, tied together with a white, red and black ribbon. The Lieutenant, standing at a table, drew back a cloth to reveal a vessel containing a red liquid, and said: 'Behold this blood. It was gathered from the severed veins of the tyrant in the last moments of his criminal existence. Pour some of it into his skull, and drink it to seal your union with us.' The candidate knelt, declared his 'undying hatred of tyrants', and swore to devote all his strength to destroying them. He was then taught the greeting sign: the right hand, with the fingers crooked, on the left shoulder, drawn down diagonally to the right hip. Finally came the baptism of admission. Dipping a cloth into the red liquid and touching the candidate's eyes, ears, nostrils and mouth, the Lieutenant said: 'Your ears hear only the groans of tyrants and the cries of joy of the liberated peoples . . . The corpse of your enemy always smells sweet. Your lips are sealed with the blood of tyrants.'[20]

While the Carboneria was the most important secret society in the south of Italy, in the north the main liberal sects were those of the Fildadelfia and Adelfia. These were probably first introduced from France by disaffected army officers, and their ranks then swelled by former Italian Jacobins, angry at the growing social conservatism of the Napoleonic regime. The leading patriot and conspirator, Filippo Buonarroti, became active in the Adelfia after he was released from prison in 1809 and soon gave it added vigour and direction (over the next twenty-five years he was to establish himself as the guiding force in Italian sectarianism). Another secret society in northern Italy was the Guelfia, founded in Rome in October 1813 but most active, it seems, in the Romagna, where it probably picked up the remnants of the Society of Rays. The elusiveness and protean character of these sects served to magnify the fears of the Napoleonic police, and often pushed them to the brink of paranoia, but the indications are that they only began to attract significant support and present a serious threat to the authorities from the end of 1812, when news of the disastrous conclusion of the Russian campaign made it clear that the Napoleonic empire was beginning to crumble.

The propaganda of the secret societies helped to give the idea of liberating 'Italy' increased emotional force, and the explicitly sexual imagery that was sometimes used injected notes of honour and revenge (not to mention outright prurience) into the already religiously charged domain of national redemption. A catechism of the Guelfia of 1817, divulged by a dying affiliate to a priest in his confession, was particularly graphic. It took the form of a dialogue:

Q: Are you a Guelf?
A: My mother is married to the sea and her breasts are high mountains.
Q: Who is your mother?
A: The woman with black locks and fine bosom, the most beautiful in the universe.
Q: What are the qualities of your mother?
A: Beauty, wisdom and, once, strength.
Q: How has nature endowed her?
A: A delightful garden, graced with flowers, where fruitful olives and vines grow and a soft breeze blows.
Q: What is your mother doing now?
A: She is groaning, wounded.
Q: Who has wounded her?
A: Her neighbours helped by her degenerate sons.
Q: Why did they wound her?
A: Because they were jealous of her beauty.
Q: Where did they wound her?
A: In her breasts and her vagina.
Q: How did she come to be wounded?
A: Through the neglect of her guardians.
Q: How long has she been wounded?
A: For fourteen times one hundred years.

Q: Where are you going?
A: To find a remedy for my mother . . .
Q: How will your mother be after she is cured?
A: She will come back more beautiful, strong and feared.

The affiliate also revealed that the two recognition signs of the Guelfia were a hand placed on the forehead and an index finger struck on the palm or wrist six times to signify each of the letters of 'Italia'. A further revelation – and a good indication of just how intellectually rarefied the world of the sectarians could be – was that a true Guelf was expected once a month to dine on milk alone, sipped in the light of the moon, in honour of Saturn and 'the great mother' – an allusion to the poet Virgil's description of Italy as 'Saturn's land, great mother of the harvest, great mother of men'.[21]

An important source of support for the sectarians was Sicily, which had been occupied by the British after the Bourbons had fled there in 1806 to avoid the French. The island had for some time enjoyed close commercial ties with Britain thanks to the development of the Marsala wine industry by English entrepreneurs since the 1770s. And these ties were greatly strengthened during the Napoleonic period as the fashion for fortified wines grew in Britain in the absence from tables of French clarets and burgundies. By 1814 four English firms were operating in Marsala, with several others further down the coast at Mazara. Such, indeed, was the extent of the British interests in Sicily at this time that there were some thirty consuls or vice-consuls dotted around the island. The close-knit and for the most part very rich landowning Sicilian aristocracy relished these links, seeing in them a way of realizing their long-held dream of independence for the 'Sicilian nation' from much-hated Naples. In Palermo salons it even became fashionable to speak Italian or Sicilian with an English accent.

King Ferdinand did not enjoy being in Palermo and did not trust the Sicilian nobility: all the principal posts in his government in exile went to Neapolitans. His main concern seemed to be milking the island for money to help pay for the war with France (as well as the extravagant lifestyle of his court), and when, after various clashes with the nobility, he tried to go behind the back of parliament and raise taxes by decree, the opposition forces raised the banner of revolt. Ferdinand (or more precisely his queen, the redoubtable Maria Carolina, sister of Marie Antoinette: as in 1799 Ferdinand preferred to save most of his energy for hunting – and botany – in the woods around Palermo) responded by having five of the ringleaders, all of them princes, arrested and deported to penal islands. At this point it looked as if the constitutional tussle between the king and the Sicilian nobility would be won by Ferdinand. But on 22 July 1811 a new British commander, Lord Bentinck, landed in Palermo.

Bentinck was a tall patrician-looking soldier of impulsive character and robust Whig views who had recently returned from acting as governor of Bengal. He had a firm belief in Britain's civilizing mission (as governor general of India he was later to outlaw the practice of suttee) and an equally firm belief, derived from Edmund Burke, that nations were primordial, almost mystical, entities that needed to find expression in appropriate civil and political institutions. The tyranny of Napoleonic France, he thought, could best be fought by promoting the causes of freedom and independence ('Bonaparte made kings, England makes nations,' he is reputed to have said shortly after arriving in Palermo).[22] He certainly considered Italy to be a nation, but he saw no reason why Sicily should be part of it. Geography, history and the hostility of the barons to Naples all suggested that the island could be seen as a nation in its own right.

On reaching Sicily Bentinck quickly sided with the parliamentary opposition, forced the king to accept a government of Sicilian ministers (among them three of the deported princes), and had the meddlesome queen banished from Palermo. Then in the summer of 1812 he sanctioned the introduction of a British-style constitution that abolished feudalism, affirmed the sovereign independence of Sicily, and created a two-chamber parliament, with a House of Commons and a House of Peers, which had sole powers of legislation and taxation, and to which the executive was answerable. Bentinck was not altogether comfortable with this extraordinary demonstration of Anglophilia. Apart from anything else he saw no reason why the British constitution should work if transplanted to the very different cultural environment of Sicily. And some of the most level-headed Sicilians were similarly minded: 'Too much liberty is for the Sicilians, what would be a pistol, or a stiletto in the hands of a boy or a madman', one of the island's most intelligent reformers, Paolo Balsamo, warned Bentinck.[23]

Their fears were soon realized. In the absence of firmly established traditions of compromise and trust, and without any clear sense of a higher collective good to which private interests should be subordinated, a series of bitter power struggles flared between the nobility, the Crown and middle-class radicals in the House of Commons. Just ten days after meeting under the new constitution parliament was prorogued, and Bentinck was ruefully forced to admit that his hopes for Sicily had been wildly misplaced. The nation, he said, was still in its 'infancy and weakness', and was not ready for freedom; and the islanders had to be governed with 'bonbons in one hand and il bastone [the stick] in the other'. For nine months from the autumn of 1813 he ruled Sicily as a dictator, seeking to lay the foundations of 'civil liberty' with economic and institutional reforms. In this way 'the general character of the people' might begin to change and Sicilians learn the habits and practices needed for 'political liberty'.[24]

Bentinck had hoped that the example of constitutional government in Sicily would inspire mainland Italians to rise up and throw off the yoke of Napoleonic oppression. There was also the model of Spain to look to. Here a huge popular revolt had broken out against the French army in 1808, culminating, after several years of vicious guerrilla warfare, and with the support of British forces, in the introduction in 1812 of a radical liberal constitution. Germany, too, was stirring. At the so-called 'Battle of the Nations' at Leipzig in October 1813 a colossal army of Austrians and Prussians, assisted by Russians and Swedes – in all nearly 400,000 men – overcame some 200,000 Napoleonic troops, and in so doing laid the cornerstone of German nationalism: the moment when 'the German people' had come together to assert its identity.

From Sicily Bentinck established contact with members of the secret societies in northern and southern Italy and urged them to action. And revolts led by Carbonari did break out in late 1813 and early 1814 against Joachim Murat in parts of Calabria and the Abruzzi. However, they were local in character, lacked strong mass support, and were quite easily extinguished. Propaganda was also funnelled into Italy from printing presses in London, where in 1813–14 a Milanese exile called Augusto Bozzi Granville took the lead in exhorting his fellow Italians to unite and free themselves from the ignominy of foreign domination in the pages of a patriotic literary journal, L'Italico.[25]

In the turbulent climate of early 1814, when it was clear that over twenty years of convulsive war were coming to an end and that the fractured map of Europe would soon have to be haggled over and pieced together again amid competing strategic, dynastic and perhaps even national claims, it could seem to many with power at their disposal that almost any throw of the dice might be worth the gamble. Bentinck set his sights on a national rising in Italy. Like many Englishmen of his background, he harboured feelings of nostalgic sympathy for the land of Augustus and Virgil. But there were also pragmatic geo-political considerations to his concept of Italian independence. If, he told the Foreign Secretary, Lord Castlereagh, in January 1814, 'the national energy' of the Italians could be roused, as in Spain and Germany, 'this great people, instead of being . . . as formerly the despicable slaves of a set of miserable petty princes, would become a powerful barrier both against Austria and France . . .'[26]

But was there any 'national energy' in Italy? The British government did not think so; nor, probably, did Bentinck himself. In October 1812 he had told Archduke Francis of Austria that the Italians had become 'passive' under French rule, that they had none of 'the character of greatness of soul shown by the Spaniards', and that their protests, such as they were, were 'the complaints of slaves rather than the murmurs of a magnanimous people who want to conquer or die for liberty and independence'.[27] However, he was willing to see if any insurrectionary spark existed, and on 9 March 1814 he landed a small Anglo-Sicilian force on the Tuscan coast at Livorno. A few days later he issued a proclamation calling on Italians to put their trust in Britain, take up arms and fight the French. There was no response. He then marched up the coast and 'liberated' Genoa, and suspecting (quite rightly) that the British government had plans to hand the city over to the fiercely reactionary King of Sardinia once the war was over – an idea that horrified him – he decided to try and forestall this by restoring the old Republic in keeping with what he felt were 'the general wishes of the Genoese nation'.[28]

Meanwhile Austrian troops had occupied the Veneto and pushed back Eugène de Beauharnais. In Lombardy there was feverish talk about salvaging an independent state from the wreckage of the Kingdom of Italy, but the Milanese nobility could not agree on whom to propose as their new ruler. A group of so-called 'Pure Italians' led by Count Federico Confalonieri wanted almost anyone provided he was not French, and looked to the British to save them from the clutches of the Austrians; but others hankered after Joachim Murat of Naples, or even Eugène de Beauharnais, and still others had their eye on the Archduke Francis (an Austrian, but born in Milan). On 17 April 1814 the elderly Francesco Melzi d'Eril tried to force the issue in favour of Beauharnais, but this action so incensed the Pure Italians that they unleashed a mob on the city, which lynched the Finance Minister and overturned the government. Beauharnais threw in the towel and handed Lombardy to the Austrians, who entered Milan on 28 April, eighteen years to the day after Napoleon had signed the armistice of Cherasco, which had opened the way to the occupation of northern Italy by the French.

Confalonieri and his Pure Italians were in reality much more concerned with having an independent Lombard state that they could dominate than with anything truly 'Italian', and this line seems to have been generally shared. According to the writer Ludovico Di Breme, the Milanese would happily have ruled the whole of Italy, 'but when it comes down to it, Italy does not extend very far beyond the [suburb of] Borgo degli Ortolani, in their view'.[29] But in the spring of 1814 talk of nations and their rights was very much in fashion, and in a desperate bid to prevent Lombardy being relegated once again to the status of a province of the Austrian Empire, Confalonieri begged Lord Castlereagh to realize how much had changed in the past twenty years, and how Italians now had 'the desire, the means and the energy' to be a nation. Rule from Vienna would be a travesty: 'No land is more divided from Germany by natural barriers, linguistic differences, and divergence of character, temperament and habits.' Castlereagh was impervious to such appeals. The Lombards, he said, had absolutely nothing to fear from the 'kindly government of Austria'.[30]

During the years of Napoleonic rule the idea of an Italian political nation had become imbued with new inflections, feelings and energy, but an enormous gap still separated rhetoric from reality, thought from action, and the mental universe of the educated from that of the mass of the population. For millions of peasants scattered about the countryside of the peninsula 'Italy' was still devoid of any significance or resonance: their world was one of survival, bounded emotionally by ties to the family, village and local saints, and by hostility to tax collectors, recruiting officers and, often, local landowners. For most members of the middle and upper classes the restoration of the old ruling dynasties in 1814–15 was met with emotions that ranged from resignation to enthusiasm. Outright anger and hostility were rare. Some of the more high-minded did experience problems, though. After several years of devoted service to Joachim Murat, Vincenzo Cuoco found the return of the Bourbons hard to stomach, and suffered a mental breakdown from which he never fully recovered. He died in 1823. Ugo Foscolo was for a time tempted to throw in his lot with the Austrians, but could not bring himself to swear an oath of loyalty to the Emperor. He went into exile, first in Switzerland and then England, where he stayed till his death in 1827.

Even the most stirring appeals failed to have any impact on the general mood of scepticism and acquiescence that seemed to have descended on the peninsula. On 30 March 1815, a few days after his brother-in-law, Napoleon, had re-entered Paris, amidst scenes of wild jubilation – the start of the Hundred Days that were to culminate in June at the Battle of Waterloo – Joachim Murat issued a proclamation from Rimini calling on Italians to rise up and join him in fighting for their independence and unity:

Italians! The hour has come in which the great destiny of Italy must be fulfilled. Providence is summoning you at last to be an independent nation. From the Alps to the straits of Sicily one cry can be heard: 'The independence of Italy!' . . . Was it for nothing that nature erected the Alps as your barrier? Was it for nothing that you were given an even greater barrier in differences of language and customs and a unique and distinctive character? No! No! Away with all foreign domination! You were once masters of the world, and you have paid for that perilous glory with twenty centuries of subjugation and slaughter. Let it be your glory now to break free from your masters . . . I appeal to you, noble and unhappy Italians of Milan, Turin, Venice, Brescia, Modena and Reggio, and all the other illustrious and oppressed regions . . . Form a strong and binding union with a government of your choice, a truly national representation, and a Constitution worthy of the century . . .[31]

Some Italian patriots were moved by Murat's appeal. Alessandro Manzoni, a young Milanese writer of great promise and future distinction, a friend of Cuoco and Foscolo, began to write an ode praising Murat and extolling the cause of Italian unity ('we shall not be free if we are not one'). After fifty-one lines, though, he heard that Murat had been defeated by the Austrians at the Battle of Tolentino on 13 May, and abruptly stopped, leaving the poem (fittingly) as a mere fragment.[32] But Manzoni had picked up his pen, not his sword; and in all only about 500 volunteers had responded to Murat's patriotic proclamation. After Tolentino, Murat fled to France, but in October he returned to southern Italy with a band of 250 faithful followers in a last desperate bid to recover the throne of Naples. He found nothing but hostility among the local Calabrians, and after being cornered by Bourbon troops on the coast, he was taken to the fort of Pizzo, and on 13 October was executed by firing squad. The last words of this innkeeper's son from a little village in southern France, who in the tempestuous world of passion, ideals, opportunism and seemingly endless possibilities thrown up by the French Revolution had risen to become a general, a marshal, a grand-duke and a king, were: 'Spare my face. Aim for my heart!'[33]

PART TWO

Preaching
1815–46

4

Restoration, Romanticism and Revolt, 1815–30

Italia! Oh Italia! Thou who hast
The fatal gift of beauty, which became
A funeral dower of present woes and past,
On thy sweet brow is sorrow plough'd by shame,
And annals graved in characters of flame.
Oh, God! That thou wert in thy nakedness
Less lovely or more powerful, and couldst claim
Thy right, and awe the robbers back, who press
To shed thy blood, and drink the tears of thy distress.

Lord Byron, *Childe Harold's Pilgrimage,*
Canto IV, xlii (1818)

O Italy, take care to honour the dead . . .
Turn around and look, my fatherland,
At that endless crowd of immortals,
And weep and feel ashamed;
For without shame grief is now foolish:
Turn, feel shame and rouse yourself,
And let the thought of our ancestors
And posterity for once spur you on.

Giacomo Leopardi, *Sopra il*
monumento di Dante che si preparava
in Firenze (1818)

PUBLIC DUTIES

Francesco Hayez was the most distinguished north Italian painter of his generation. There was not a great deal of competition, it is true. After the death of the leading Milanese neo-classical artists Giuseppe Bossi in 1815 and Andrea Appiani in 1817 there was something of a dearth of talent. Neither Bossi nor Appiani had produced any pupils worthy of note, and the only other artist of major stature was the Bolognese Pelagio Palagi, an architect, ornamentalist, sculptor and furniture designer, as well as portraitist, with a penchant for archaeology (he built up a huge collection of ancient Roman, Etruscan, Greek and Egyptian marbles, bronzes, gold, silver and glass, and liked incorporating motifs derived from them into his work).[1] But Palagi was an accomplished painter, not a great one – an academic, conservative air hovered about many of his canvases, and they lacked spark and passion. And like Bossi and Appiani Palagi suffered from having been rather closely identified with official Napoleonic Italy.

In 1820 Hayez created a sensation in Milan with his exhibition at the Brera Academy of a historical painting showing an obscure fifteenth-century military captain being implored by his family to stay with them and refuse a request to go and fight for the Venetian Republic. Hayez was twenty-eight years old. He had been born in Venice in 1791 of humble parents, and in 1809 had won a scholarship to study classical and Renaissance art in Rome under the tutelage of the sculptor Antonio Canova. He was not a particularly political animal (love affairs were his primary pursuit after painting), and the momentous events sweeping Europe in the last years of Napoleon's empire do not seem to have touched him deeply. He was enormously relieved to find a way out of military service (as was the young composer Rossini, just then bursting onto the operatic scene, whom Hayez met and befriended in Rome in 1812),[2] and with the return of the Austrians to northern Italy, and after completing a papal commission, Hayez went back to Venice to pursue his career, before moving to Milan in 1820.

Hayez's early works had been largely classical in inspiration, but for his 1820 Brera picture he decided to delve instead into the Middle Ages. He recalled in his memoirs how he spent his evenings reading Simonde de Sismondi's history of the Italian medieval republics (a work that was soon to establish itself as a canonical text for Italian patriots), looking for a suitable subject, but his real source was almost certainly the less politically illustrious *Histoire de la République de Venise* (1759–68),[3] by the Frenchman Marc-Antoine Laugier. When the painting was exhibited Hayez underlined its historical credentials with a detailed, if less than pithy, title: *Pietro Rossi, lord of Parma, stripped of his dominions by the Della Scalas, lords of Verona, while receiving an invitation in the castle of Pontremoli, whose defence he is conducting, to take command of the Venetian army that is about to move against his enemies, is besought by his wife and two daughters, with tears, not to accept the commission.*

The painting was immediately hailed in Milan as revolutionary. It was seen as an endorsement of the superiority of romanticism over classicism. Critics praised its emotional pathos, its attention to historical detail (evident in the architecture of the castle, the costumes and the knights' armour – clearly inspired, as were the colours and the interplay of gestures and tilted heads, by Hayez's recent study of works by Venetian Renaissance artists such as Giorgione, Cima and Carpaccio)[4] and the unconventional poses of the figures, with backs turned and faces hidden or half hidden, generating tension and mystery and inviting viewers to use their imaginations to work out the narrative and the expressions. Patriotism, *hommage* and prescience of death were neatly blended in the weeping daughter to the right, modelled on Canova's statue of Italy on Alfieri's tomb in Santa Croce.[5] Hayez's depiction of the dilemma confronting Rossi also earned the admiration of critics. Rossi's face and pose, with their air of calm, dignity, sadness and reflective uncertainty, seemed to encapsulate well the gravity of the choice before him: whether to heed the siren calls of love and domestic duty, or go and fight his enemies, the Della Scalas (he chose the latter, and was killed in the process). But the success of Hayez's painting in 1820 was not due simply to its championing of the new vocabulary of romanticism. Political factors were also at work.

When Europe's statesmen gathered in Vienna in November 1814 to sort out the new political order their main concerns were to create stability and peace, hold France's imperialist inclinations in check, and prevent any recurrence of revolution. The idea of popular sovereignty – the chief culprit, it was widely believed, of much of the turmoil in the previous twenty-five years – was cast aside in favour of the principle of 'legitimacy': the upholding of the legitimate rights of sovereigns and states such as had existed prior to the conquests of Napoleon. In general terms this approach meant restoring the borders of 1789; but there was some elasticity in the application of the principle. The ambitions of the main victors – Britain, Austria, Prussia and Russia – together with the need to ensure a balance of power and to contain France, resulted in the sacrifice of some smaller states, including, in Italy, the republics of Genoa and Venice.

As for the 'nation', the idea was now stripped of the revolutionary apparel with which the French Revolution had clothed it and returned to the safe conservative sphere of historical pragmatism. Nations were not to be regarded as timeless mystical entities that needed to find expression in the liberated wills of their people. Nations existed only in so far as they had demonstrated their capacity to maintain political independence over time. Italy, accordingly, was not a nation. It was, as the Austrian Chancellor Prince Metternich brutally put it in 1847, 'une expression géographique'.[6] And Italian nationalism was no more than a pipe-dream of a handful of sectarians and intellectuals who felt they had a right to threaten the existing political and social order and unsettle the tranquil existence of the great mass of the population. What, after all, did ordinary people want beyond material well-being, sound administration and good laws?

In the conservative climate of the Congress of Vienna the sympathy of English liberals such as Lord Bentinck for Italian nationalism wilted in the face of old-style dynastic politics. It was agreed that Austria should be compensated for losses of territory in Germany and the Belgian provinces by receiving control of the whole of Italy. Lombardy, the former Venetian Republic, Trentino and the Valtellina were merged into the Kingdom of Lombardy–Venetia and became part of the Habsburg Empire, ruled, through a viceroy, from Vienna. The grand-duchy of Tuscany was restored to the Emperor of Austria's younger brother, Ferdinand III of Lorraine, while the duchy of Parma was assigned to his daughter, Maria Luisa. Modena was to be ruled by Francesco IV of Austria-Este, Lucca by the Bourbons of Parma. In central Italy and the Romagna the Papal States were reconstituted in full, but the Austrians were permitted to station garrisons in the fortresses of Ferrara, Piacenza and Comacchio, so enabling them to intervene swiftly in the Pope's dominions should any trouble arise there. In the south the Bourbon Ferdinand IV was restored to his old kingdom (now restyled the Kingdom of the Two Sicilies in a token gesture towards the Sicilians for their loss of independence), but only after agreeing to a permanent defensive alliance with Austria. Because it was regarded as a strategically important buffer between France and Austria, Piedmont–Sardinia was the one Italian state that was allowed to keep formal independence. Its ruler was the arch reactionary, King Victor Emmanuel I.

But the Restoration did not mean a wholesale turning back of the clocks. The administrative, legal and other reforms that had been introduced under Napoleon were in large measure retained after 1815. After all, the new more centralized machinery of government, the abolition of feudalism, and the elimination of many of the ancient privileges of the nobility and the Church strengthened the powers of the monarchy and seemed finally to have resolved the secular struggle between the king and his barons, centre and periphery, in favour of the Crown. If the growth in state power caused resentment – and it was bound to in some quarters – it was hoped that this would soon melt away as subjects came to appreciate the benefits to be had from a more efficient bureaucracy and justice system, improved schools, roads and public works, and a lower (at least in comparison to the Napoleonic period) and fairer tax burden.

However, if the broad principles of the 'administrative monarchy', as the new form of government was called, were similar throughout much of Italy, there were important variations in practice. In Sardinia feudalism continued until the late 1830s, and only in 1848 were the legal codes in operation in Piedmont and in Liguria extended to the island. In southern Italy King Ferdinand was quite happy to keep (perhaps from inertia as much as prudence) the new French-style structures of the judiciary and the Napoleonic codes (with a few obeisances to the Church, as with the abolition of divorce) – a move that enabled Neapolitan lawyers to argue with good reason in the next few decades that they had the most sophisticated legal system in Italy – but in Piedmont the curmudgeonly Victor Emmanuel, who rode back into Turin in 1814 after eight years of exile in Sardinia pointedly wearing an old-fashioned peruque and pigtail, reinstated much of the pre-Napoleonic legislation. He abolished equality before the law and gave himself the right to overturn court rulings. Jews and Protestants were faced with discrimination once again, and the aristocracy recovered many of its old privileges, as well as its monopoly of boxes at the opera house. In the former Republic of Genoa, however, such conservatism was intolerable, and here Victor Emmanuel was forced to let his new subjects retain many of the Napoleonic reforms.[7]

Similar variations were to be found in central Italy after 1815. In the small duchy of Parma, the new ruler, Maria Luisa, refused to make concessions to the Church, promoted the economy and public education, and retained the French laws (not surprisingly, perhaps, given she was Napoleon's second wife). But next door in Modena, the ambitious duke, Francesco IV, was in thrall to reactionary romanticism and looked to carve out a personal fiefdom based on the close alliance of throne and altar. He restored the old administrative practices of the House of Este, swept away almost all the Napoleonic legislation, welcomed back the Jesuits and other religious orders, and forged contacts with a mysterious secret Catholic sect called the 'Consistorials' (which some contemporaries alleged was conspiring to drive the Austrians out of Lombardy–Venetia and make Francesco ruler of much of northern Italy).[8] In Tuscany Ferdinand III remained true to the grand-duchy's strong traditions of enlightened reformism, but in the Papal States the Pope refused to have truck with anything that smacked of the French, or indeed of modernity: street lighting and vaccination were both banned.[9]

The rulers of the Restoration wanted to rebuild a world in which hierarchy and order were respected, and they hoped, with the moral support of the Church, that they could win the hearts and minds of the common people and bind them to their regimes. But they faced serious economic problems. The costs of administration, not least the charge on the exchequer of maintaining large garrisons of Austrian troops, meant they were unable to keep taxation as low as they would have liked. The reintroduction of tariffs and customs barriers affected agriculture and commerce badly and food prices and supplies were dangerously volatile. Famine continued to be a perennial threat (tragically so in 1815–17), and poverty was widespread: according to a survey in 1829, there were over 400,000 beggars, vagrants and unemployed in the Papal States out of a population of some 2.5 million.[10] There was also the problem of land hunger, especially in southern Italy, where attempts by the Bourbons to get the former commons distributed among the peasantry were hampered by rapacious local landowners who blocked settlements with court cases that dragged on sometimes for decades.

Conscription was another source of popular discontent. The Napoleonic era had transformed the character of military conflict between states, turning it from what was little more than a princely pursuit of limited dimensions into something whose logic was towards what the Prussian general Karl von Clausewitz called 'total war'. Mass armies were now inescapable (something that made the pursuit of the active loyalty of subjects considerably more important in the nineteenth century than the eighteenth). In Lombardy–Venetia conscription was introduced in August 1815 to the widespread dismay of the peasantry; and in 1820 the period of service was raised from four to eight years (with much of this time often being spent outside Italy).[11] In Piedmont the standing army was increased from 12,000 to 30,000 in 1817, and conscripts were enlisted for eight years. In the south, the period of service was less, six years; but fear of domestic unrest led the Bourbons to fix the peace-time army at 60,000.[12] Sicilians were exempted from military service: their loyalty was considered too suspect.

The masses were certainly a worry for the Restoration governments, but there were good grounds for hoping that a re-energized Catholic Church, with its religious orders, missions, jubilees and pilgrimages, and panoply of new or extended popular cults – those of the Virgin Mary in particular: the rosary, Our Lady of Sorrows, the Marian month – would help keep the peasantry quiet. The real problem, though, lay with the educated classes. For years they had been exposed to ideas that were often diametrically at odds with those of absolutism, and many of those who had risen to positions of influence under Napoleon now found themselves pushed aside and replaced by members of the old aristocracy – particularly in the Papal States and Piedmont (though a dearth of skills among the nobles soon forced a partial volte-face).[13] In the south of Italy King Ferdinand kept on the majority of the Napoleonic civil servants and army officers, but here there was a major problem with an education system that turned out too many graduates, lawyers especially, for the jobs available.

But the biggest source of friction with the upper classes lay, paradoxically, in the failure of the restoration states to be more restorative. The Napoleonic regime had come as a severe shock to most of the old aristocracy, who had found the local powers and privileges, on which they and their families had often prided themselves for generations, swept away. This loss of local influence had been partially offset by the creation of provincial and communal councils, in which nobles and professional men took the lion's share of the posts; but these councils had never had much muscle. There were certainly those in the civil service and the army who had become strong supporters of centralization, but the majority of the old guard were desperately hoping in 1814–15 that many of their old powers would be reinstated.[14] They were bitterly disappointed; and in their frustration they began to look with growing fondness at constitutional liberalism and even at some form of national unity as ways to undermine the Restoration settlement and give themselves once again positions of influence.

In the light of the cultural dynamism of Milan under Napoleon and all the memories of the Italian Republic and the Kingdom of Italy, the Austrian viceroy, Count Heinrich Bellegarde, knew it would be hard to incorporate Lombardy and the Veneto successfully into the Austrian Empire. Bellegarde was a fine soldier with a good political brain who had spent many years serving the emperor loyally; but he was not convinced that Vienna was right in pushing for centralization (his family origins in Savoy may have inclined him to be more sympathetic than many of his colleagues to Italian wishes). He thought that a large measure of autonomy would be wise, and he told Metternich in July 1815 that the best way for Austria to secure real influence in Italy would be by making the administration of Lombardy–Venetia as independent and as 'national' as possible. And since dreams of Italian national unity had begun to materialize under Napoleon (and Milan was 'saturated with this unitary spirit', he complained), any arrangements that might bring together the different peoples of Italy along the lines of the German Confederation 'would be extremely pleasing to all parties'.[15]

The emperor was fond of Italy and admired its culture – he had been born and brought up in Tuscany – but his overriding concern was with the well-being of his empire as a whole. The Italian provinces were important to him as a source of revenue and conscripts. But they were above all vital for Austria's security against France, for it was on the plains of Lombardy that French–Habsburg rivalry had for centuries been fought out. As Metternich succinctly remarked, 'It is on the River Po that we defend the Rhine.'[16] This was why Vienna was so determined to keep Lombardy–Venetia on a tight rein and not to pander to autonomist sentiment. Metternich, too, liked Italy greatly – but for what it was and for what it had been, and not for what it might become. When he visited the peninsula in 1817 he came in the deliberate guise of a wide-eyed tourist and not a political observer, marvelling at 'the ridiculous cheapness of an enormous alabaster vase' and delighting in the relative sophistication and charm of Tuscan peasants. Italy had about it, he felt, a serene beauty, which was not to be disturbed ('The basis of contemporary politics, I would venture to say, is and must be *sleep*').[17]

There was much resentment at Austrian rule in Milan. Levels of taxation were thought to be unduly high – though it was hard to prove this, given that the authorities kept the kingdom's budgetary accounts secret. Merchants were frustrated by the erection of high protective barriers against Piedmont and France, which forced them to direct their trade towards the rest of the empire and away from the lucrative outlets of Genoa and Lyon. And civil servants and lawyers became aggrieved as posts in the bureaucracy and the judiciary were assigned to native German-speakers. The emperor, it is true, tried to channel away the simmering discontent by introducing a measure of representation (something that Napoleon had not allowed), instituting a Central Congregation composed of deputies drawn from the propertied classes. But these deputies were centrally appointed; and their powers were merely consultative. An attempt was also made (vain as it happened) to defuse the deep rivalry that had long existed between Lombards and Venetians by making the two regions into discrete administrative units with their own governors (and separate Central Congregations). But this arrangement hardly compensated Milan for losing its position as capital of a kingdom.

So when the Austrian authorities attempted to win over the educated elite and simultaneously dampen down Italian national sentiment by opening Milan up to the latest developments in European culture, they quickly found that the experiment back-fired. They tried to get Ugo Foscolo to edit a new government-subsidized literary journal, the *Biblioteca italiana*. But after some hesitation he refused, and set off for exile. And when the journal came out in January 1816 it contained an article by Madame de Staël on the innocuous-looking subject of literary translations, but which very soon descended into a pitched political battle between pro- and anti-Austrian intellectuals over the respective merits of classicism and romanticism. The authorities ran for cover, and the

Biblioteca italiana soon abandoned any attempts to promote the new romanticism and became instead the standard-bearer of conservative culture in Milan.

De Staël had not said anything particularly provocative, but her liberalism and known sympathies for the cause of Italian independence ensured that the views she expressed in the article acquired added political significance. She suggested that Italian literature was rather insular and would benefit from being more open to contemporary trends in other countries, especially England and Germany. There was too much artifice and not enough truth and directness in Italian writing, and exposure to European romanticism through the medium of translations would be salutary. What gave her comments more than just literary value, however, was her suggestion that the arts in Italy were failing to fulfil their civic mission to educate the public; and coming from de Staël, the clear implication was that this education should be liberal and patriotic. She wanted theatre especially to acquire a more elevated tone, as it had in Germany under the influence of Schiller and Schlegel. At present, she said, Italians were renowned for chatting during performances rather than listening, and this habit did nothing to improve 'the intellect of the nation'. Literature should aim to combine pleasure with 'public education' and thereby aspire to true greatness. For what, after all, could Italy claim distinction in if not the arts? And if the arts languished, Italians 'would sink into a deep sleep from which not even the sun would be able to wake them'.[18]

Inspired by de Staël, Milan's patriotic liberals threw their weight behind the cause of romanticism. Art must be direct and simple. It must be true to nature and its subject matter drawn from real life, whether contemporary or historical. It must seek to portray human emotions and experience in all their richness and complexity. And, as the poet Giovanni Berchet said in 1816 in what became in effect the manifesto of Italian romanticism, it must endeavour 'to improve the behaviour of men'. This aim meant reaching out beyond the narrow confines of traditional aristocratic audiences (whose culture was so rarefied and cosmopolitan, according to Berchet, as 'to lose every trace of a national imprint') and addressing 'all those other individuals who are able to read and listen', in other words, 'the people' (the uneducated masses, or 'Hottentots', were a lost cause). Berchet was one of a new class of professional writers in Lombardy who endeavoured to make a living from their pens, and his hope of creating in Italy 'a common literary fatherland' made up (somewhat fancifully) of 'millions' of readers had a self-interested material side to it as well as an idealistic one.[19]

From September 1818 until October 1819 – when the Austrian censors finally got tired of striking out passages with their blue pencils and forced it to close – the Lombard liberal romantics had a mouthpiece in a distinguished journal called *Il Conciliatore*. Its contributors included some of the leading Italian intellectuals of the day, among them the patriotic aristocrat Federico Confalonieri, the lawyer Gian Domenico Romagnosi, and the writers Silvio Pellico, Ludovico Di Breme, Ermes Visconti and Berchet. The journal was eclectic in tone, and its articles covered a wide range of subjects, from economics, geography and law, to science, religion, education and literature. History featured prominently, thanks in part to the direct involvement of Madame de Staël's friend Simonde de Sismondi, whose *magnum opus* on the Italian medieval republics reached its final volume in 1818 and appeared in translation from the French the same year. Indeed it was from the pages of the *Conciliatore* that a clarion call first went out for Italians to turn their attention to the Middle Ages – not just because the Middle Ages were in vogue among romantic writers in northern Europe, notably Walter Scott, but more importantly because there was now a growing conviction that the roots of the Italian nation were to be located in the medieval period, where the energy, civic pride and warrior virtues of the city-states had produced independence, freedom, economic prosperity and cultural glory for the peninsula.[20]

But how many people were there to share the ideas of the *Conciliatore*? The editors certainly hoped for a big readership. For long, they said in their programme, knowledge in Italy had been restricted to a handful of scholars, 'scattered in cloisters and academies', who argued with one another about abstruse points of grammar and similar unworldly issues. But all that had now changed. The reluctance of 'the Public' to engage in discussion of serious matters (the result of 'the sleep caused by prolonged peace' and 'the lack of communication between the various peoples of Italy') had been ended by the cataclysmic events of the previous twenty years. 'Stung by the spur of misfortune', people had now been taught to think and were open to fresh ideas; and it was to assuage their appetite that a group of Milanese writers had 'resolved to offer a new journal to the ITALIAN PUBLIC', driven by a fervent commitment to 'the common good'.[21] Their optimism was not well founded, though, and the writings of this virtuous minority scarcely circulated beyond the plush salons of the liberal aristocracy. In its brief life the *Conciliatore* managed just 240 subscriptions, almost all of them in the city of Milan. The overwhelming majority of the country's 20 million inhabitants lay far beyond its reach. How to connect to a larger audience was one of the biggest problems facing Italian patriots in the decades to come.

In the summer of 1820 (when Hayez exhibited his canvas of Count Pietro Rossi torn between domestic happiness and fighting) revolution was in the air. A mutiny among troops in Cadiz at the beginning of the year had sparked off a revolution in Spain, and in March the king had been forced to restore the democratic constitution of 1812. Inspired by this example, sectarians in southern Italy had begun to prepare for a rising of their own, and early in July a group of thirty Carbonari from the town of Nola supported by soldiers from the local garrison marched through the countryside to Avellino to the sound of blaring trumpets and cries of 'Long live liberty and the constitution'. There they were joined by two regiments from nearby Naples led by Guglielmo Pepe, a former Napoleonic officer who had fought in Spain and witnessed at first hand the potential power of guerrilla warfare. King Ferdinand quickly bowed to the insurgents' demands and agreed to introduce the Spanish constitution, and on 9 July the victorious mutineers paraded through the streets of Naples with bands playing and black, red and blue Carbonaro banners waving, led by the proud members of the 'Mucius Scaevola' *vendita* from Nola. A few days later the revolution spread to Sicily, though from the start there were bitter divisions here about which constitution to invoke (the Spanish or Sicily's own of 1812) and how far to push for independence from Naples.

The ripples of revolution also spread northwards up the peninsula. In Piedmont the reactionary policies of Victor Emmanuel I had irritated the liberal aristocracy, and during the second half of 1820 demands began to be formulated for the granting of a constitution and for a war to liberate Lombardy–Venetia and establish a Kingdom of Upper Italy under the House of Savoy. The growing belief (justified as it turned out) that Austria would soon be forced to send troops to put down the revolution in southern Italy, thereby greatly reducing its capacity to defend its northern possessions, gave these proposals an air of practicality. In the autumn contacts between the Piedmontese and Lombard liberals intensified, and in Milan the members of the *Conciliatore* group, most of whom belonged to a recent transmutation of the Adelfia secret society called the Italian Federation, took the lead in preparing the ground for an insurrection. Their plans, though, hinged on the willingness of the Piedmontese king to allow the bitter pill of constitutionalism to be sugared by a dynastic war of expansion against his old enemy, Austria. And that was far from being a foregone conclusion.

The Austrian response to the unrest in Italy was to solicit the support of the major powers for armed intervention. France and Russia would happily have seen Austria's influence in the peninsula reduced; but neither was comfortable with the fact that the democratic Spanish constitution had been introduced in Naples. In Britain there was plenty of support for the cause of Italian liberalism and independence; but while London was reluctant to sanction military repression of the revolution, it had no wish to fall out with Metternich so soon after the Congress of Vienna. Accordingly, when a congress was convened at Troppau in Silesia in October to try to resolve the situation in Italy, Austria was able to secure a declaration that would allow it to intervene in the Kingdom of the Two Sicilies to restore absolutism. Britain and France did not sign it – a foretaste of their future orientation towards Italian independence – but neither was prepared to veto Austrian action. Out of respect for their sensibilities Metternich agreed to invite King Ferdinand to another congress at Ljubljana in January 1821 so he could explain what steps he intended to take to put his house in order.

In Naples news of the Troppau declaration led to consternation in liberal circles, but Ferdinand made a solemn pledge to parliament and to 'the Nation' that if he went to Ljubljana he would make sure his people enjoyed 'a wise and liberal constitution'. But as soon as he was out of his kingdom he let his mask slip, telling Metternich that the constitution had been forced upon him and entreating Austria to intervene. Early in February Austrian forces crossed the Po into Papal territory and began the march south. In Naples, there was little prospect of serious resistance. The army was badly split between former supporters of Joachim Murat and more democratic Carbonari elements, and no proper plans had been made for the defence of the revolution. Indeed the best Neapolitan troops were in Sicily, where they had been sent the previous summer to stop the island pushing ahead with plans for independence (and also to help the nobility, who having hoisted the flag of revolt quickly found themselves in danger of being engulfed by urban and rural workers out to settle old scores, abolish taxes and seize land). Nor was there any realistic chance of the peasantry rising en bloc as they had in Spain under Napoleon: as in 1799 the liberal intelligentsia in Naples had failed to win over the rural masses. Consequently the Austrian forces were able to advance rapidly, and despite a spirited show of resistance by one commander, Guglielmo Pepe, the patriotic veteran of the Peninsular War, they entered Naples on 23 March.

Meanwhile a revolution had broken out in Piedmont. Tension had been growing since the start of the year. In January the army had opened fire on rioters in Turin university angered by the arrest of two students for wearing red berets at the theatre, and in the weeks that followed preparations gathered pace in liberal circles for a possible rising and a war against Austria. A key figure in the sectarians' plans was the future heir to the throne, Carlo Alberto, a young man of austere religious character, riddled with insecurities (he was to be dubbed the 'Hamlet of the monarchy' by Giuseppe Mazzini),[22] whose upbringing in France during the Napoleonic period was supposed to have left him sympathetic to liberal and patriotic ideas. He certainly welcomed the attention of aristocratic sectarians in these months and did nothing to disabuse them of their hopes that when the rising broke out he would support them and work to persuade King Victor Emmanuel to grant a constitution and invade Lombardy–Venetia. On 6 March the main architects of the conspiracy visited Carlo Alberto and told him that everything was ready and that 'the most glorious epoch in the history of the House of Savoy' was about to begin.[23] They asked for his assent, and he apparently gave it, shaking hands with the idealistic leader of the coup, Count Santorre di Santarosa. Three days later a tricolour flag (probably the green, white and red of the Kingdom of Italy)[24] was hoisted over the fortress of Alessandria, and the insurrection was under way.

It did not go according to plan, however. Though the revolt spread rapidly to a number of other garrisons in Piedmont, who followed Alessandria's lead in running up tricolours and proclaiming the introduction of the Spanish constitution (though in some cases the tricolour was that of the Carbonari), King Victor Emmanuel was too frightened of Austrian wrath to back the rebels' programme and dealt the insurrection a fatal blow at the outset by abdicating. He nominated Carlo Alberto as temporary regent, as the new sovereign, Carlo Felice, Victor Emmanuel's grimly reactionary brother, was at that moment absent from the kingdom in Modena. Carlo Alberto was caught. Forced to treat with the rebels he agreed on 15 March to introduce the Spanish constitution, but added as a codicil to his oath the words: 'I swear to be faithful to King Carlo Felice. So help me God.'[25] Two days later he received a delegation of Milanese liberals, who urged him to send the Piedmontese army into Lombardy: he refused.

From Modena, Carlo Felice sent Carlo Alberto a proclamation (pointedly in French: he scorned anything that savoured of Italian patriotism) stating that he would not tolerate a constitution or anything else that infringed 'the plenitude of royal authority'. But Carlo Alberto persisted in his ambivalence for a few days: he failed to publish the proclamation, strung the rebels along by appointing Santorre di Santarosa as Minister of War, and then secretly left Turin on the night of 22 March and headed for the safety of Novara, where the garrison was loyal to Carlo Felice. Abandoned to his fate, and with many of the conspirators disheartened by Carlo Alberto's defection, Santarosa strove valiantly to mobilize what troops he could for the liberation of Lombardy and defence of the revolution, issuing a series of appeals containing ringing declarations of loyalty to the king and wordy references to 'honour', 'glory', 'virtue', 'brothers', 'the fatherland' and 'the nation' – though quite what this 'nation' was, and how far it extended beyond northern Italy in his mind, is unclear.

Santarosa, though, was preaching to the unconverted. The revolution had been confined almost entirely to the army, and then mainly to sections of the officer class; and now that defeat seemed likely, the rank and file troops began melting away. The great mass of the population remained utterly indifferent to talk of constitutions and the freeing of their 'brothers' in Lombardy, even more so when Carlo Felice issued an appeal to the powers still assembled in Ljubljana for help and the Austrians responded by preparing to send an army into Piedmont. The remnants of Santarosa's followers advanced east towards Novara, desperately hoping that the troops there might yet be won over to their cause ('Soldiers of Novara! Will you soon make common cause with the cruellest enemies of your fatherland? . . . No, brothers! Come and embrace us, come!).[26] But with 15,000 Austrians now on the west bank of the Ticino river, their cause was hopeless, and in a skirmish outside the walls of Novara on 8 April they were soundly defeated. The Austrians then proceeded to occupy Alessandria (as a gesture of humiliation they sent the keys of the city to the Emperor) and installed garrisons across the kingdom, while the commander of the Novara soldiers marched into Turin.

As in Naples and Sicily, the Piedmontese revolution had come to an inglorious end. Around a thousand rebels managed to escape into France or Switzerland or found a ship to carry them to Spain. Santarosa took refuge in Paris, where he lived under an assumed name, writing his memoirs. The young philosopher Victor Cousin befriended him and for a time shielded him from the police. But he was tracked down, imprisoned and then expelled. He went to England and stayed with Ugo Foscolo in Chiswick, before moving to Nottingham, where he tried to make a living teaching French and Italian. In November 1824 he set off for Greece to fight for the cause of independence; but the presence of Italians was not particularly welcome, as they were seen as potentially embarrassing to the international community. On 8 May 1825 Egyptian troops launched an attack on the island of Sphacteria, and Santarosa was killed: he allegedly looked too wretched to be worth sparing. His body was never found.[27]

The fate of Santarosa and the other exiles of 1821 greatly moved a serious-minded teenager with a passion for the novels of Walter Scott and romantic literature in general, a deeply religious sensibility, and a slight tendency to self-dramatization. Giuseppe Mazzini was just fifteen and a university student when in April 1821 he and his mother ran into some of the fugitive rebels wandering along the quayside at Genoa desperately seeking a passage to Spain and asking passers-by for help. As he recalled years later:

A man with a stern and fierce expression, dark, bearded, and with a piercing look which I have never forgotten, called out from a distance and stopped us. He held out in his hands a small white handkerchief and uttered simply the words: for the exiles of Italy. My mother and her friend put some money into the handkerchief . . . That day was the first on which there took shape confusedly in my mind . . . the thought that we Italians *could* and therefore *ought* to struggle for the liberty of our fatherland . . . The memory of those refugees, many of whom became my friends in later life, pursued me wherever I went by day, and mingled with my dreams by night . . . Upon the benches of the university . . . in the midst of the noisy tumultuous life of the students around me, I was sombre and distracted, and appeared like one suddenly grown old. I childishly determined to dress always in black, imagining myself in mourning for my country . . . Matters went so far that my poor mother became terrified in case I should commit suicide.[28]

In the wake of the revolutions of 1820–21 governments throughout Italy became fiercely repressive. The influence of the Church spread into almost every sphere of public life as rulers looked to smother subversive liberal ideas under a blanket of official piety. Education and censorship in particular felt the full weight of Catholic morality and intolerance. In the south sweeping purges were carried out of the army, the civil service and the judiciary, and the Carboneria was reduced to a shadow of its former self, surviving only as countless scattered fragments, often with new names and rituals. In the Papal States the Jews were confined once again to ghettoes, and hundreds of political suspects were arrested, especially in the Romagna, where the activities of the sectarians had been strong. In Piedmont Carlo Felice felt vindicated in his reactionary instincts and his mistrust of intellectuals ('the bad are all educated and the good are all ignorant'),[29] and while the courts passed dozens of death sentences on the rebels (almost all *in absentia*), the administration was systematically cleansed of dissidents.

In Lombardy a series of high-profile trials involving nearly a hundred members of the Italian Federation, Carbonari and other sectarians culminated in November 1823 in the sentencing to death of Federico Confalonieri, Luigi Porro-Lambertenghi (the co-founder of *Il Conciliatore*), Giorgio Pallavicino-Trivulzio, Francesco Arese and a dozen other leading figures of Milanese intellectual and social life. At an earlier trial the writer Silvio Pellico had also received a death sentence. Many of the accused had unfortunately broken down under interrogation and betrayed the names of fellow conspirators (and despite what later propaganda alleged, the Austrian authorities behaved with rectitude and did not resort to torture), and as a result the sectarian movement was all but destroyed in Lombardy. Most of the condemned had earlier found safety in exile, and in the case of others the emperor agreed to commute the death sentences into various terms of imprisonment, but this did not stop the victims acquiring martyr status – especially after 1832 when Silvio Pellico published a widely translated account of the eight years that he spent in the prison fortress of Spielberg, a work that did enormous damage to Austria's reputation in the eyes of the international community.[30]

With tightened censorship making it much more difficult for liberals to voice their ideas openly in print, other media were to acquire increasing importance in the 1820s and 1830s as vehicles for patriotic sentiment. Paintings necessarily had a restricted audience, but many of the most acclaimed works of Hayez and his contemporaries could reach a very wide public in the form of engraved reproductions. Images such as that of Pietro Rossi sadly relinquishing the joys of family life in order to go and fight his enemies thus helped to disseminate and celebrate key aspects of public morality and so give them enhanced stature and force. Furthermore, in a society that was attuned through Catholicism to graphic depictions of the torments endured by saints as tests of their holiness, pictures of secular suffering had a marked capacity to move and sanction. When Francesco Arese returned to Milan after serving three years in the Spielberg fortress, he commissioned Hayez to paint a portrait showing him sitting in his bare stone cell with chains on his feet (he may have been partly motivated by an uneasy conscience: he had been one of the freest in his revelations to the police). The contrast between Arese's aristocratic dress and bearing and his grim and servile circumstances was calculated to produce the maximum emotional impact.

When the subject of the painting was taken from Italian history, something else was also achieved: a link to the past that was not only inspirational and instructive, but which also helped map out the contours of a common 'national' tradition to which contemporaries could see themselves as heirs. After purchasing Hayez's acclaimed canvas of Pietro Rossi (and having his death sentence commuted into twenty years in prison, most of which he served), Giorgio Pallavicino-Trivulzio decided while he was in the Spielberg prison to commission a pendant to accompany it. He turned to Hayez's friend and rival, Pelagio Palagi, and the subject that he chose was again one that focused on the sacrifice of domestic happiness to a higher calling: Cristoforo Colombo bidding farewell to his two small sons as he prepared to set sail from the port of Palos to discover the New World. As a native of Genoa, Colombo could reasonably be accommodated in the pantheon of illustrious Italians whose character and achievements were worthy of celebration, and in

Restoration Lombardy there was something of a cult of the explorer, with a major biography appearing in Milan in 1818, a verse epic in 1826, additional paintings by Palagi and other artists, and several operas, including one in 1829 by the promising young Neapolitan composer Luigi Ricci.[31]

But depicting the Middle Ages in Italy raised some awkward problems. If Vico, Cuoco and others had challenged the view of most Renaissance and Enlightenment scholars that the roots of modern Italy lay in the Roman world, positing instead a pre-classical civilization of united, peace-loving and cultivated Etruscans, the growing belief of historians after 1815 that the origins of the European nations were to be found in the bloody era of barbarian invasions after the fifth century AD meant turning the spotlight onto a period fraught with ambivalent patriotic messages. Columbus was a man of undoubted vision and energy: but why had he been forced to rely on Spanish patronage for his voyages of exploration? Pietro Rossi, too, was evidently somebody endowed with ambition and fine martial virtues, ready to wreak vengeance on his enemies. But who were his enemies? Not foreign invaders or foreign oppressors, but the lords of Verona and their followers; in other words, fellow Italians.

5

Fractured Past and Fractured Present

When the whole of Europe was moving towards centralized monarchical government, Italy continued to be feudal . . . In Italy there has never been a period of industrialization or of revolution for the benefit of the bourgeoisie . . . The yoke that weighed on the different states of Italy [from the sixteenth century] was neither equal nor general. There are some provinces of Italy that from the time of the Greek emperors to the present have only known government by hear-say . . . [and] rule themselves according to their own customs and laws. Calabria, Basilicata, the Abruzzi and large parts of Sicily are cases in point. On the other hand Tuscany has never experienced the total loss of political rights that its neighbours have.

Alexander Herzen, *Lettres de France et d'Italie*, 4 February 1848

The fundamental and radical difficulty facing Italy is that it does not exist . . . It is not a question simply of resurrecting a nation, but rather of creating *one . . . I have spent many years searching through the past for an Italy; I have found towns, glorious communes, splendid atoms, but nowhere anything that resembles that organism that we call a people.*

Edgar Quinet, *Les Révolutions d'Italie* (1848–51)

'UNITED . . . IN MEMORIES': HISTORY AND THE NATION

Italy's past was to remain thorny terrain for patriots throughout the Risorgimento – and indeed well beyond. While it was widely accepted that history had a vital role to play in fashioning a national consciousness and (rather more questionably) in teaching Italians how to be good citizens, the difficulty lay in locating a common thread. 'The history of Italy is the history of a single nation composed of a mass of separate states,' asserted Pasquale Villari, a young Neapolitan scholar and a future Minister of Public Instruction, confidently in 1849. And he added that a detailed examination of the individual states would reveal to a determined enquirer the collective national fabric.[1] But many thought such optimism misplaced, indeed dangerous. As Giuseppe Ferrari, a Milanese republican whose awareness of the historic strength of the divisions in Italy led him to a passionate advocacy of federalism, wrote in 1858: 'Where then is Italy? What does it consist of? What bond is there that links the republics, the *signori*, the popes, the emperors and the invasions? What connection is there between individuals and the masses, sectarians and wars, wars and revolutions? Scholarship does not help shed any light. Indeed, far from instructing us, it simply underlines the chaos . . .'[2]

The desire to locate the historical roots of the Italian nation had developed a new urgency after the 1790s. The traditional idea that Italians were the descendants of the Romans (culturally, if not racially) was felt to be increasingly out of place as the cosmopolitanism of the Enlightenment gave way to a new era of nationalism. Apart from any-thing else, Rome had been far too broad in its geographical reach and too universal in its legacy (had not the French revolutionaries and Napoleon felt it quite natural to appropriate aspects of its civic morality and iconography?) to provide a viable model for Italy. The growing interest of Romantic scholars in unearthing the origins and character of the peoples of Europe gave the study of history fresh momentum in the first decades of the nineteenth century, and after 1815 many of the most influential Italian patriots – among them such brilliant figures as Alessandro Manzoni, Massimo d'Azeglio, Cesare Balbo, Vincenzo Gioberti and Giuseppe Verdi – looked to Italy's past, and especially the Middle Ages, for material with which to educate the public, foster enthusiasm for independence, and justify their vision of the nation-to-be.

For much of his long life, the great Milanese writer Alessandro Manzoni was too plagued by anxieties to work quickly. He suffered from frequent panic attacks. He was terrified of thunderstorms, frightened of crowds, and often fearful when out walking that a house might collapse or the ground open beneath his feet. He could not stand puddles, and the sound of sparrows drove him to distraction. He felt at times that he would end up completely insane, like his good friend Vincenzo Cuoco. As he grew older, though, he learned to keep many of his neuroses at bay by sticking to a strict regimen. He would walk for twenty-five minutes before lunch, eat the same food every day, go to bed at precisely the same time, and always ensure that his clothes were exactly the right weight and thickness for the temperature. If anxieties did assail him, he would leave the house and set off briskly through the streets or countryside until he felt calm, sometimes covering twenty or even thirty miles in a day.[3]

Manzoni had a difficult upbringing. He was born in 1785 into an aristocratic Milanese family (his mother was the daughter of the great jurist Cesare Beccaria, and rumour had it that Alessandro was the product of a liaison she had with the younger brother of the eminent Enlightenment scholar Pietro Verri), but his parents separated when he was just six, and he saw very little of them thereafter. He found solace in intense study, and his precocious literary talents brought him to the attention of Foscolo, Monti and other leading figures in Milanese society. Marriage in 1808 to a young Swiss girl, Enrichetta Blondel, and a growing family, created some emotional stability in his life. So too did his intense re-conversion to Catholicism in 1810, and stays in Paris, where he became part of the liberal intellectual circle around Madame de Staël, with its passion for romanticism and historical study. After 1815 he rapidly emerged as a dominant figure in Milanese literary life, and though he did not contribute directly to the *Conciliatore*, he promoted the cause of romanticism strongly, and his tragedy, *The Count of Carmagnola* (1816–19) (the subject of a major painting by Hayez), established itself as one of the key works of the new movement. He also became close friends with Berchet, Visconti and others of the *Conciliatore* group.

Freedom from oppression and the comforting embrace of a united community – family and friends in the first instance and beyond them the nation and Christendom – were among Manzoni's cherished ideals, and when in March 1821 it looked as if the Piedmontese revolution might spread to Lombardy, and from Lombardy to the rest of the peninsula, Manzoni was fired with patriotic hope, and dropping his customary slow rate of composition, he quickly wrote an ode. In it he imagined that the rebels were already on the east bank of the Ticino river and were taking a solemn oath to liberate the whole of Italy, and Italians everywhere were responding in kind, raising their newly sharpened swords to the sun, shaking hands with one another in fraternal joy, swearing to be 'companions on our deathbeds or brothers on free soil'. The poem called on the Austrians to depart from a land 'that did not bear them', and to remember how God had destroyed the Egyptian army when Pharaoh had tried to keep the Israelites enslaved; for at last, after long years of suffering and looking idly to others for redemption, Italy's sons, a people 'one in arms, language and faith, memories, blood and heart', had risen up to fight for their own freedom, united around the 'holy colours' of their flag and strong in their sense of shared pain.[4] Not surprisingly, given the course of events in March and April 1821, Manzoni did not feel he could publish the ode. Only after the Milanese had launched a successful insurrection against the Austrians in 1848 did he feel the moment had come to release it.[5]

Of the six elements that Manzoni listed as being shared by the Italian people – arms, language, faith, memories, blood and heart – the only one that in fact had much commonality in 1821 was 'faith' (and ironically this was the one that was ruled out of the national equation when political unity was finally achieved). This ingenuousness was of course partly due to artistic licence and the demands of political rhetoric, but Manzoni was also suffering, like many northern Italian intellectuals of his generation who crossed the Alps far more readily than the Apennines, from a degree of ignorance. He knew next to nothing of the mass of the population, certainly in central and southern Italy where the levels of illiteracy and general ignorance were most marked. He makes one allusion in the poem to the extreme south of the peninsula (significantly using a mythological reference point, 'the cave of Scylla'), but otherwise the geography is all northern; and when as a metaphor for the remorseless fusion of all Italians he talks of tributaries mingling their waters to form one mighty torrent, the rivers he names are those that flow down through Piedmont and Lombardy into the Po. Manzoni's Italy, like Santarosa's, was in reality restricted primarily to the north.

The failure of the 1821 revolution and the subsequent arrest of many of his friends left Manzoni deeply saddened, but it also gave him a renewed sense of purpose, and the next few years were to be the most creative of his life. History fascinated him; and in a recent visit to Paris his interest in Italy's past had been stimulated by discussions with the brilliant young French historian Augustin Thierry.[6] But a problem that he and other Italian writers of his generation faced was how to portray that past in a way that avoided ambivalent or even conflicting messages. In his verse tragedy *The Count of Carmagnola*, published in 1820, Manzoni had focused on the career of an early-fifteenth-century mercenary captain executed for alleged treason by the Venetians after they had hired him to fight the Milanese. In the play a chorus is used to provide an ethical commentary on the action, and in the central episode, the Battle of Maclodio in 1427, the Venetian troops are rebuked for rejoicing in their victory. For in reality what was there to celebrate? 'Brothers [had] killed brothers', and 'heaven [was] filled with abomination at the hymns of thanksgiving that were issuing from their murderous hearts.'[7] Nor was the offence simply one of fratricide. It was also a crime directed against Italy as a whole, for waiting in the wings, observing the piles of dead on the battlefield with obvious glee, were rapacious foreigners ready to descend and enslave a country weakened by civil war.

Manzoni's message was clear enough, but in training the spotlight on a typical passage of Italian medieval history he risked underlining just how deep-rooted and bitter (and thus, in the view of many commentators, foreign especially, indelible) the internal divisions were. As was well known, in England, France, Spain and other European countries the domestic conflicts of the Middle Ages had gradually been resolved within the framework of a nation-state. But in Italy this process had not happened, and to hold up to audiences a mirror that showed their present weaknesses reflected vividly in their past (albeit with a wag of the finger) might aid the cause of the conservatives as much as of the patriotic liberals. And Manzoni faced another problem: his Catholicism. If Italians were to shake off the foreign yoke they would not only have to unite as brothers but also fight; and war meant setting aside those pacific Christian values that were widely seen as having sapped the martial energy of Italians. Carmagnola is a warrior, but a Christian warrior, who refuses to capitalize on his victory and magnanimously releases his prisoners after the battle. Charged with treachery and sentenced to death, he is consoled by the belief that justice is not to be had on earth but in heaven – an idea that points logically towards resignation and inaction.

Herein (from a patriotic point of view) lay the Achilles' heel of Manzoni's vision of Italian history; and herein, ironically, may have lain one important reason for his great popular success in the 1820s and

1830s (and later). Delving back into the shadowy era of Lombard domination in the seventh and eighth centuries, and poring over the fragmentary documentation that had been gathered by antiquarians such as Ludovico Antonio Muratori, Manzoni thought he could discern the existence of an Italian 'race' and 'nation', an 'immense multitude of men . . . passing unnoticed over the land, its land', oppressed by foreign rulers and suffering in silence.[8] But was that silence good or bad, a sign of abjectness or of Christian fortitude? When in 1820–22, against the backdrop of the failed revolutions in northern and southern Italy, he composed a verse tragedy about the defeat of the Lombards by the Frankish king Charlemagne in 774, he included a stirring patriotic chorus in which he imagined the Italians, 'a scattered crowd that has no name', roused to action from their servile condition.[9] But the central message of the play pointed in a different direction: that injustice on earth should be seen as something that tempers and tests the Christian soul and paves the way for happiness in the afterlife, rather than as a springboard to expiation.

By the time he wrote his most famous work, the historical novel *The Betrothed* (1821–5), Manzoni's retreat from martial rhetoric and heroic posturing was complete. The silent, suffering generations who had peopled the peninsula in the Dark Ages under Lombard and Frankish rule and formed the backbone of the 'Italian nation' found their spokesmen in the humble characters of Renzo and Lucia, two village lovers in seventeenth-century Lombardy who are thwarted in their plans for marriage by war, famine and the machinations of an aristocratic overlord. The book certainly has its patriotic aspects: the oppressiveness of Spanish rule, for example, is suggested by the iniquitous and tyrannical behaviour of Don Rodrigo. But national redemption is not at the heart of the novel (indeed the word 'nation' appears only once in the 1827 edition).[10] What really interests Manzoni is how the main characters respond to suffering. And his celebration of passive Christian fortitude was not surprisingly uncongenial and frustrating to more militant patriots who were desperate to shake Italians out of their lethargy. Where, asked Giuseppe Mazzini in a review of 1835, was the book's spark?

The fact is that passion, the burning tempestuous passion that plants heaven or hell in your soul, that makes you into a saint or a criminal, a giant or a pigmy, that ordains you for martyrdom or for victory, is banished from these pages . . . Its joys are the joys of the family, its sufferings do not lead on to revolt, its expiations are always achieved through submission and prayer . . . and its constant refrain is: Turn your eyes towards heaven![11]

Other patriots were even more scathing. Luigi Settembrini, a Neapolitan liberal who played a leading role in trying to educate southerners to the national ideal in the 1830s and 1840s (and suffered with imprisonment), said the novel's perpetual preaching of forgiveness and resignation to the will of God encouraged 'submissiveness to slavery and negation of the fatherland', and thereby made *The Betrothed* into 'the book of reaction'.[12]

Yet the work proved enormously popular, going through over seventy editions and reprints between 1827 and 1870, and selling in excess perhaps of a quarter of a million copies – a huge figure given the restricted size of the reading public in Italy at this time. Some of the book's appeal may have been due indirectly to patriotic factors. Here for the first time was an Italian novel that could stand comparison with the best that was being produced in Britain, France or Germany. And the fact that it was widely translated and generally well received abroad added to its cachet in Italy ('one of the three or four books which I have read with most pleasure in my whole life,' said the French romantic writer Lamartine).[13] Manzoni gave a further patriotic inflection to the novel by setting out after 1827 to make it a model for 'correct' written Italian everywhere in the peninsula, taking as a yardstick contemporary spoken Tuscan, on the grounds that this dialect was closest to the language of Dante, Boccaccio and Petrarch, and gradually purging the text of archaicisms and Lombard usages (an elderly Florentine governess employed in his house in Milan allegedly had a decisive influence on the final edition of 1840-42). But much of the appeal of *The Betrothed* undoubtedly lay in its quaintly reassuring vision of Italian history, with priests, local politics, family, unscrupulous landlords, intrigue and sexual honour at its heart.

It took the Protestant historian Simonde de Sismondi to provide a more robust patriotic vision. His achievement was two-fold. In the first place he provided a genuinely 'national' reading of Italian history, one that could offer justification for concerted political action in a way that the local histories of the Enlightenment period – for example Pietro Verri's of Milan or Rosario Gregorio's of Sicily – could not do. He maintained that in the ninth and tenth centuries Italy had been swept by what he called 'a celestial fire', which had shot through 'the entire nation' and stirred the Italian people to political action (contemporary interest in the electrical sources of life and energy, of which the Bologna physicist Luigi Galvani had been a pioneer, affected Sismondi's vision, as it did that of other observers concerned with the problem of how to rouse Italy from its 'sleep'). The second important element in Sismondi's interpretation was that it shifted responsibility for Italy's decline away from areas such as character and climate towards institutions. Italians had become degenerate, certainly; but it was bad government, lack of education and the pernicious influence of the Church that were among the chief culprits. The solutions were thus not hard to discern.[14]

In contrast to Manzoni, Sismondi saw the barbarian invasions of the early Middle Ages as having benefited Italy. The Goths and the Lombards intermarried with the natives, and their rough northern energy fused with the refined patriotism of the indigenous population to create a powerful cocktail that resulted in the communal movement of the eleventh and twelfth centuries, the Lombard League and the defeat of the German emperor Frederick Barbarossa at the Battle of Legnano in 1176. The late twelfth century marked the apogee of Italian history, and the emergent nation, according to Sismondi, should have capitalized on its success by cementing the alliances made between the city-states in the campaigns against Barbarossa with a federal constitution. In other words the Italians should have done what the Swiss did. In this way they would have stayed free.[15] But the moment was allowed to pass, the bonds of friendship slipped, and Italy fell back into a state of fragmentation and civil war, paving the way for Spain's eventual conquest of the peninsula in the sixteenth century.

Sismondi had originally intended to bring his history to an end with the fall of the Florentine republic on 28 October 1530, but he in fact continued it down to the late eighteenth century, when the last flickers of republicanism were snuffed out by Napoleon. As a passionate Italophile, Sismondi hoped that the example of an earlier age, one possessed of 'more virtue and energy than our own', would stir the embers of patriotism that still glowed beneath the ashes and inspire Italians to action.[16] What was needed, though, was leadership, for with the exception of Alfieri (whose widow was a close friend) nobody, in his view, had yet pointed Italians in the right direction. And good leadership could pay handsome political dividends for those of a democratic persuasion, since, like a growing number of romantically inclined foreign travellers who viewed Italy through the lens of Rousseau, Sismondi believed that the ancient qualities of the Italians survived still in the ordinary people, particularly the peasants, who had remained untouched by the effete hand of society.[17] In another age and environment might not a bandit like Fra Diavolo have been a freedom-loving William Tell?[18]

Sismondi's celebration of the medieval republics provided Italian patriots with much historical ammunition, and from the 1820s episodes such as the oath of Pontida (1167), the Battle of Legnano (1176), the Battle of Benevento (1266), the Sicilian Vespers (1282), the duel of Barletta (1503), the siege of Florence and the Battle of Gavinana (1530) were established as sites of national memory. So were the careers of such men as the twelfth-century religious reformer and scourge of the papacy, Arnaldo da Brescia, the fourteenth-century tribune of the Roman republic Cola di Rienzo, and the early-sixteenth-century military captains Ettore Fieramosca and Francesco Ferruccio. But it was elements of Sismondi's monumental work rather than the totality of his vision that Italian patriots latched on to. For the problem, once again, was that the positive messages that the author hoped to impart risked being undercut by the general tenor of the historical narrative. It was all very well for Sismondi to say that Italians could have formed a federal state in the twelfth century, but the fact is they did not; and what is more they proceeded thereafter to tear at each other for several hundred years until the Spanish stepped in and imposed stability. The impulse to freedom that Sismondi wanted to emphasize could also be seen as an impulse to anarchy.

This was the difficulty with Italian history: it always seemed to be pulling in different directions and offered little *prima facie* support for the idea of an Italian nation. The result was that the most influential works of patriotic literature in the Risorgimento were those that took single episodes (the Battle of Legnano, the Sicilian Vespers, the siege of Florence) and turned them into metaphors for national redemption in ways that were not justified on strictly historical grounds. Thus the victory against Barbarossa in 1176, or the slaughter of the French in Palermo in 1282, or Ferruccio's struggle with the imperial forces in 1530 were used to suggest that there had been a deep-seated sense of 'Italian' nationhood, a desire for independence from foreign rule, that the ensuing centuries of decadence had managed to stifle. These episodes were also chosen to demonstrate that Italians had once been fiercely military and could fight and fight well, and that the common taunt of foreigners (which many patriots found deeply insulting) that Italians were by nature cowardly was historically unfounded.

Viewed as a whole though, Italy's history offered little comfort for patriots. Ancient Rome undoubtedly had its glorious aspects, but as far as its civil politics were concerned the Republic seemed largely a chronicle of factionalism and civil war, the Empire of civil war and licentiousness. A few scholars, like the great Milanese economist and republican Carlo Cattaneo, managed to derive a positive message from the turbulence of the Middle Ages, seeing in the vigour and prosperity of the city-states a vindication of some kind of federal structure for the future nation (but given the wretched relations that had existed between most cities, and between most of the cities and their surrounding countryside or *contado*, he not surprisingly felt unable to spell out exactly what this would mean in concrete political terms). For most patriots, however, the search for a holistic vision of Italy's past ended either in fiction, or in the invisible undergrowth of history (as with Manzoni), or in the realms of myth (as with Cuoco).

The alternative was to see the past as something to be transcended, an object lesson in what a new Italian nation-state should try to avoid. This, broadly speaking, was the approach taken by Carlo Botta, the historian of Italy whose works aroused most enthusiasm among patriots during the Risorgimento (Michele Amari and Pietro Colletta were also hugely admired, but they wrote about Sicilian and Neapolitan history). Botta was a Piedmontese doctor whose anti-clericalism and strong support for the French Revolution forced him to seek asylum in France after 1814. In exile he produced three major narrative works on Italian history: like much of the patriotic literature written at this time they had to be printed abroad, in France or in Switzerland, or else in Tuscany where the censorship was relatively light. The first covered the years 1789–1814 (in six volumes, 1824), the second continued Francesco Guicciardini's Renaissance history, and went from 1534 to 1789 (in ten volumes, 1832), and the third surveyed the entire course of Italian history from Constantine in the fourth century down to the fall of Napoleon (in five volumes, 1825–7).

According to Botta, the Romans were vitiated by conquest and unmanly foreign customs; the rule of law gave way to the imperium of the sword; and 'the soil of Italy . . . was bathed in blood shed by Roman hands'.[19] Christianity then sapped the martial spirit of the Italian people and pagan tribes swept into a land that was divided and without patriotism. The Middle Ages were an inglorious era. Political factions prevailed: 'and nothing so easily produces corruption and decay'.[20] There was a frenzy of warfare, as city fought against city, showing that it was 'more difficult to organize liberty than overthrow tyranny'.[21] And 'Italy' now meant nothing to anyone: even the much-vaunted Lombard League was just an extension of the Guelph–Ghibelline struggles. The one bright spot was the literary revival begun by Dante and Petrarch, which precipitated the glories of the Renaissance. But Italy remained politically decadent, and the divisions in the peninsula opened the way to foreign conquest from 1494. Thereafter Italy slid into a prolonged period of lethargy, redeemed only by the achievements of a few artists and scientists. The Enlightenment was a period of significant improvements, but the cosmopolitan culture of the eighteenth century eroded the national spirit ('cosmopolitans . . . are not patriots').[22] Napoleon brought material benefits, but overall the impact of French rule on Italy was negative: it led to 'distasteful adulation, a servile literature, an enslaved press, a total abasement of character, the loosening of all patriotic bonds and the complete loss of the prestige of the name of Italy. Italy under [Napoleon] was no longer Italy. It was France.'[23]

Factionalism, division and an absence of patriotism: Italy's fractured and discordant past aroused feelings of deep anxiety in patriots of the Risorgimento. 'Have you not heard, my great and good Lamartine, that no harsher insult could have been hurled at [Italy] than *diversity*, . . . a word that sums up a long history of misfortune and humiliation?' wrote Manzoni in the spring of 1848.[24] And the sorry spectacle of centuries of weakness and conflict created a sense of insecurity that had a profound influence on the way the Italian nation was imagined in the Risorgimento and also on the trajectory of Italian politics after 1860, with their pursuit of integration and 'moral unity' as prophylactics against a slide into a seemingly imminent abyss of chaos. Since the old Italy had been plagued by internal discord, the new Italy must be a land of fraternal (and sisterly) love, strength, and unity of purpose. As the young democrat

Goffredo Mameli put it in verses written in 1847 (and which, as a jaunty marching song, became Italy's unofficial national anthem after 1860, and in 1946, with some irony following three years of occupation and civil war, the official anthem of the new Republic):

> Brothers of Italy
> Italy has awoken
> And has placed on its head
> The helmet of Scipio . . .
> For centuries we have been
> Downtrodden and derided
> Since we are not a people
> Because we are divided;
> Let us gather round one flag
> United in one hope
> For now the hour struck
> For us to come together . . .
> Let us unite, let us love;
> For union and love
> Reveal to the peoples
> The ways of the Lord.
> Let us swear to make free
> Our native soil:
> And united in God
> Who can ever defeat us? . . .
> From the Alps to Sicily
> Every place is Legnano
> Every man has the heart
> And the hand of Ferruccio . . .
> The sound of every bell
> Has sounded the Vespers.
> Let us form a tight cohort,
> We are ready for death:
> Italy has called![25]

THE MATERIAL MOSAIC

In a celebrated chapter of *The Duties of Man*, published in 1860, Giuseppe Mazzini explained to Italian workers what obligations they owed to their nation, and why. God, he said, had granted to no other country of Europe such sharply defined borders:

To you who have been born in Italy, God has assigned, as if he wished to single you out, the most clearly demarcated fatherland in Europe. Other countries have borders that are more uncertain or broken, and here doubts may arise . . . But in your case there can be no doubts. God has stretched around you sublime and irrefutable boundaries: on one side, the highest mountains in Europe, the Alps; on the others, the sea, the immense sea . . . As far as [the Alps] people speak and understand your language; beyond them you have no rights. Yours without question are Sicily, Sardinia, and Corsica and the smaller islands that lie between them and the mainland of Italy . . .[26]

Mazzini's conviction was based on faith rather than direct experience. Apart from some brief visits to Tuscany and a short spell in Rome in 1849, he had no first-hand knowledge of Italy outside his native Genoa. The great majority of his adult life was spent abroad in exile, mostly London, where he was able to enjoy the benefits of tarmac roads, a fast-expanding rail network, horse-drawn buses, national and local newspapers (foreign as well as British), bookshops, libraries, clubs and an efficient postal service. A glance at the map of Europe might indeed have suggested that God had intended the Italian peninsula (and perhaps all its neighbouring islands as well) to be one and indivisible, but had Mazzini travelled as much in Italy as many English, French and German tourists did in the decades after 1815 (or the occasional intrepid north Italian, such as the distinguished Piedmontese artist and politician Massimo d'Azeglio, who unusually for someone of his generation and background had a good knowledge of Sicily – which he quite liked – and Naples – which repelled him), he might have been less confident about the connection between geography and the nation.

Internally, Italy was riven by mountains, and while the broad flat plain of the Po valley had long been traversed by a good network of roads and canals, much of the peninsula was still all but inaccessible to the outside world in the first half of the nineteenth century, certainly during the autumn and winter months when heavy rain turned the mule tracks and sheep runs into glutinous mires. While all roads may once have led to Rome, in the 1820s only two did, and neither was very safe. And beyond Rome there were only two proper arteries heading southwards, one going through the malaria-ridden Pontine marshes, the other through Sulmona and Isernia. Both of these finished at Naples, thus leaving the regions of Calabria, Basilicata and Puglia in effect severed from the rest of the peninsula. Crossing the Apennines from west to east was particularly difficult, and it was far quicker and cheaper to get from Rome to Ancona (some 200 kilometres as the crow flies) by boat, via Naples, Reggio Calabria, Brindisi and Pescara, than by road. Most small towns and villages in the mountainous interior were beyond the reach of all but the most determined travellers: of the 1,828 communes in the mainland south 1,431 had no roads to serve them in 1860.[27]

Engineering difficulties as much as a lack of capital or initiative were to blame for this parlous state of affairs. And the same was true for railway building – though here the concern of the Church that dark tunnels could pose a threat to morality also came into play. Italy's first stretch of railway was opened in Naples in 1839, and significantly its function was more one of dynastic security than general utility: when completed its eighty-four kilometres connected the royal palace of Caserta to the military bases of Castellammare, Nocera, Capua and Nola. During the 1840s other Italian states embarked on railway building, but progress was very slow, and by the end of the decade there were only 620 kilometres of track in operation (at this date Britain had nearly 10,000, Germany 6,000 and France 3,000). Except in Piedmont, almost no serious thought was given to how railways might benefit the domestic economies; and until 1846 there were no plans to link the networks of the different states.[28] The material integration of the peninsula was clearly not high on government agendas.

This state of affairs was hardly surprising, and not just because the Austrians were reluctant to do anything that might give momentum to national unification. Italy had a weak economy, and most of the axes of trade radiated outwards from the peninsula. Exports of grain and olive oil from southern Italy, for example, shifted in the course of the eighteenth century from Genoa and Venice towards the wealthy industrializing economies of northern Europe. Britain became a particularly important trading partner as demand for 'cloth oil', used in the production of textiles, increased. Sulphur, of which Sicily had almost a world monopoly, also had important industrial uses, and most of it went overseas. Citrus fruit was exported to grace the tables of wealthy urban families in England, Austria and Germany, and soon further afield in Russia and the United States – which from the early nineteenth century became the main market. In 1855 just 11.8 per cent of exports from the Kingdom of the Two Sicilies were directed to other Italian states (excluding the figure for the Austrian Empire). And imports showed a very similar picture, with only 8.5 per cent coming from within the peninsula.[29]

Matters were made worse by the protectionist policies that the Italian states adopted after 1815. The one exception was Tuscany, where Ferdinand III decided to keep faith with the free-trade policies of his forebears, hoping thereby to benefit from the grand-duchy's good market position, its relatively strong agricultural sector, its abundance of raw materials, including marble, mercury and iron, and its commercially minded land-owning aristocracy: the Marquises Ginori had produced high-quality ceramics at Doccia, near Florence, since the mid eighteenth century, while from the 1830s Baron Bettino Ricasoli perfected the particular blend of red and white grapes that made Chianti into one of the world's great wines. Yet, for all its openness Tuscany, like the Kingdom of the Two Sicilies, ended up trading primarily with non-Italian partners, with much of its produce passing through the cosmopolitan and bustling free port of Livorno. Elsewhere the erection of numerous tariff barriers acted as a major disincentive to commercial life. Goods travelling the sixty kilometres from Mantua to Parma had to pass through seven barriers, while on the river Po boats could be stopped and searched at up to eighty different points. In 1839 traffic moving between Florence and Milan could take up to seven weeks to cover the 300 kilometres.[30]

However, these obstacles did not produce any significant pressure for the formation of a national market. Only towards the middle of the 1840s did serious calls begin to be made for greater economic integration in Italy, and then the leading proponents – aristocratic liberals such as Cesare Balbo and Camillo Cavour in Piedmont – were motivated much more by political than by strictly commercial considerations.[31] Most Italian producers appear to have been highly wary of anything as unpredictable and dangerous as a single Italian market, and their complaints were targeted at internal excises and duties rather than protectionist tariffs between states. This insularity was reflected in the exclusive character and fiercely local focus of the relatively few agricultural and commercial associations that existed in Italy in the 1820s and 1830s. One of the oldest and most famous, for example, the Accademia dei Georgofili of Florence, had a governing body of fifty members, and according to the statutes all of them had to be resident in Florence. Only in 1870 was this requirement relaxed.[32]

Italy's commercial and manufacturing classes were still relatively small in size, certainly compared to those of Britain, Germany and France, and even in the major cities their presence was limited. In Naples, for instance, which had a population of 430,000 in the early nineteenth century, trade in agricultural goods, public works contracts, insurance and tax-farming was controlled by a tiny group of around 300 merchants and bankers.[33] The industrial sector, textiles and engineering especially, saw some growth after 1815 thanks largely to government support (and secured notable successes: the first steamship in Italy was launched at Naples in 1818 and the first iron suspension bridge was constructed over the Garigliano river in 1828–32), but it still amounted to no more than a few dozen entrepreneurs running a few dozen workshops. And many of them were foreigners, Swiss and British capitalists with names such as Vonwiller, Egg, Pattison and Guppy, enticed by the Bourbons into investing their money in Naples in exchange for guaranteed state contracts. Given their heavy dependence on court patronage and protection it is hardly surprising that these manufacturers were in general opposed to liberal reforms and an open national market.[34]

Even in the economically most advanced city in Italy, Milan, the business sector was small. In 1838 there were just 42 bankers, 25 money changers and 196 textile manufacturers in a population of nearly 150,000 (and silk and cotton were Lombardy's main industrial products). In addition there were several hundred wholesale merchants dealing in a variety of agricultural and industrial goods such as cereals, sugar, leather and cloth – all told, perhaps, little more than a thousand people – as well as 4,700 landowners (3,000 of them nobles) and a professional middle class that included just 170 lawyers and 500 engineers.[35] The horizons of this economic elite were again, as in Naples, more local than national. Though there was certainly a good deal of grumbling at the Austrian tariff system that forced producers to trade within the empire, the fact was that the commercial life of Lombardy (and the Veneto) looked inwards, or at best northwards over the Alps, and had little reason to orientate itself 'nationally'. This insularity was evident in the agricultural and industrial societies of Milan, which, like the Georgofili in Florence, were exclusive in character and largely provincial in focus, something that even unification found extremely difficult to break down. When in 1862 a group of Piedmontese farmers tried to inject a more national note into agriculture by setting up an Italian Agrarian Association, Milan's leading landowners responded by establishing their own Agrarian Society of Lombardy.[36]

If there was little pressure for greater economic integration in Italy coming from the country's elites, there was none from the mass of the population. The many thousands of artisans and shopkeepers, domestic servants and clerks, who typically made up the middle ranks of urban society (the 'popolo' or 'people' of contemporary parlance) catered primarily to the needs of the local moneyed classes and tourists. Below them lay the 'plebe' or 'plebs', a teeming sea of poor, of no fixed occupation, who eked out a living on the streets, hawking chestnuts and offal, opening carriage doors and carrying bags, taking patients to doctors and clients to lawyers, offering their services as casual labourers on building sites, or simply thieving or begging. Their ranks were swollen by temporary migrants from the countryside, especially when there was little work on the land or food was unusually scarce. This huge underclass of destitutes was particularly large in the southern cities – Rome, Naples, Palermo – and it seems to have been growing in the early decades of the nineteenth century as population pressure, poor harvests and falling prices drove peasants out of agriculture.

In the countryside the population consisted mainly of subsistence farmers and day labourers, who had relatively little contact with urban markets, especially in the south, where the journey to the major towns and cities was on average far greater than in the Po valley. There was a strong tradition of migration, both seasonal and more permanent, especially in northern Italy, where the expansion of large agricultural estates from the late eighteenth century led to a decline in smallholdings and an increase in underemployed and landless workers. But much of this migration was directed outside Italy – to the cities of eastern France (the great silk-manufacturing city of Lyon, for instance) or further afield to Spain and even South America. Argentina was a particularly favoured destination for seasonal workers known as 'golondrinas' or 'swallows', who spent the winter months harvesting in the southern hemisphere and the summer back in Italy. This transatlantic migration rose steadily in volume in the first half of the nineteenth century before becoming a torrent after the 1870s.

Money, of course, and the prospect of a better lifestyle were what mainly drew Italian peasants abroad. But the willingness with which so many settled in foreign lands and frequently became assimilated as Argentinians, Brazilians or Americans says something about the inhospitable conditions that they happily left behind. Extreme poverty was accompanied by poor diet and diseases such as malaria, pellagra and cholera (average life expectancy at birth in the mid nineteenth century was about thirty years; in England it was over forty; in Europe probably only Russia was worse). But in addition to their terrible material conditions most of them faced brutal treatment from landowners or their agents, for outside Tuscany, where there was a strong tradition of paternalism linked to share-cropping contracts that encouraged good relations between proprietors and peasants, there was little to temper the crude force of the market. Southern landowners sometimes incorporated a measure of feudal benevolence into the workings of the great estates or *latifondi*, but not often it seems.[37] In general the peasantry were regarded with a mixture of contempt and fear by the propertied classes, especially in the cities, where for centuries town walls had been seen as a barrier, both psychological and real, between the dark and menacing rural world, with its ignorance, squalor, banditry and jacqueries, and civilized urban culture.

Italy's economic fragmentation was underlined by the enormous variety of currencies, weights and measures that continued to be used in the peninsula after 1815. Napoleon's attempts to achieve a degree of standardization had apparently borne very little fruit. In Lombardy–Venetia the main coins were the *fiorino* and the Austrian *lira*; Piedmont had its own version of the *lira* (uniquely based on the French decimal system), the Papal States had the Roman *scudo*, Tuscany the Lucchese *scudo* and the *lira*, Naples the *ducato*, and Sicily the *onza*. More localized and disparate still were the myriad units that were employed for length and distance, liquid and dry weights, and surface areas. Even within individual states there could be considerable diversity. For instance, in the Kingdom of Piedmont–Sardinia each region had its own separate system. In Piedmont the main units of length were the *trabucco*, the *piede*, the *oncia* and the *raso*; in neighbouring Liguria, the *cannella* and the *palmo*; and in Sardinia the *trabucco* (which was six centimetres longer than the Piedmontese *trabucco*), the *canna* and the *palmo* (a centimetre and a half longer than the Ligurian *palmo*).[38]

Such differences did not of course stop, or necessarily even hamper, business transactions being conducted between the regions, but they were an indication of how circumscribed and local much of the peninsula's economic activity was at this time. Even an energetic and enterprising farmer like Camillo Cavour, whose horizons were quite exceptionally broad for a Piedmontese aristocrat of his generation (he imported guano from Liverpool and sold merino sheep to the pasha of Egypt), operated mainly within a narrow economic corridor in eastern Piedmont, and his paramount ambition was to make his estate at Leri 'more prosperous than any other in the province of Vercelli'.[39]

If the economic life of the peninsula was local and fractured, so too was the linguistic map. Italian – in other words the vernacular Tuscan of Dante, Petrarch and Boccaccio – had been established since the Renaissance as the standard medium for written (and if need be oral) communication among the educated. Exactly how many people spoke Italian at the time of unification has long been debated, but recent estimates suggest that perhaps 10 per cent of the population used it as their first language, with especially heavy concentrations in Tuscany and Rome (whose strongly cosmopolitan environment necessitated a lingua franca).[40] In addition it would be reasonable to suppose that most of those who had received some formal education and were officially classified as literate – 22 per cent in 1861 – understood and read Italian, even if they could not write or speak it very well. But even with this higher figure nearly 80 per cent of the population still would have been conversant with dialect only and would have struggled to understand or even recognize Italian. When the Milanese aristocrats Giovanni and Emilio Visconti Venosta took the unusual step of visiting inland Sicily in 1853, the locals could not work out where they came from and assumed they must be English.[41]

Of course multilingualism was the norm in much of Europe in the nineteenth century, and it was generally taken for granted that one language would be used at home, another at work, and yet another perhaps when writing or carrying out official business. Nobles in the

Hungarian diet in the 1820s and 1830s conversed with each other in Croat or Magyar, but switched to Latin when they got up to address the assembly.[42] Nor was the prevalence of patois in the countryside all that unusual, as the case of rural France under the Third Republic would suggest.[43] But Italy's dialects were remarkable in their diversity, reflecting centuries of foreign conquest and settlement – Greek, Arab, Norman, Catalan, Spanish, Albanian, Slav – as well as the deliberate pursuit by many competing cities of distinct local identities. As a result even relatively near neighbours might find it difficult to comprehend each other. Ugo Foscolo claimed in the early nineteenth century – though perhaps with an element of the exaggeration to which he was prone – that somebody from Milan 'would need many days of lessons' before understanding somebody from Bologna, and vice versa.[44]

For many patriots in the Risorgimento, the Italian language and the glories of its literature were the biggest single source of national pride, but as Foscolo and Manzoni frankly confessed, Italian was no longer a living tongue by the early nineteenth century.[45] All classes, from the aristocracy and the highly educated to artisans and peasants, used dialect. In Piedmont sermons were delivered in dialect; in Venice judges and lawyers deliberated in dialect; and in Naples dialect was used at court.[46] And since the middle of the eighteenth century the status of dialect had been underpinned by a thriving literary tradition: the brilliant comedies of Carlo Goldoni in Venice, the lyric poetry of Giovanni Meli in Palermo, and the immensely popular comic and satirical verses of Carlo Porta and Giuseppe Belli in Milan and Rome. In Piedmont the king and his ministers generally spoke dialect and wrote French (much of Cavour's correspondence relating to the unification of Italy was in French); and though Carlo Alberto himself had uncommonly good Italian, he was amazed if he came across anyone of similar competence. A patriotic Piedmontese noblewoman recalled a conversation with the king in 1840 in which he complimented her on her Italian:

'You speak Italian very fluently. Were you at college in Florence?'

'No, Your Majesty. I've never left Turin.'

'I'm astonished, as our ladies only speak Italian like French people speak it.'

'That is because French is the language of court. Were you to talk Italian to them in the way that you can, Your Majesty, everyone would love you for it . . .'

'Everyone, yes, if everyone was like you.'[47]

STENDHAL'S ITALY: MUNICIPALISM
AND IGNORANCE

The great French writer Stendhal adored Italy. Like Madame de Staël he saw it as a land of art, beauty and imagination, a place where the absence of social constraints and convention allowed for the spontaneous expression of passion and emotion. It seemed the antithesis of the chilly, drear and oppressive world of his childhood in Grenoble. Like Madame de Staël, too, he longed for Italy to recover its former glory and become a great nation; and though he was aware that centuries of despotism and clerical rule had sapped Italians of much of their ancient civic and military virtue, he nonetheless believed there was energy still lurking beneath the ashes of their cynicism and apparent resignation, waiting to be fanned into life and surprise the world ('who would have guessed, in 1815, that the Greeks, so docile and so obsequious to the will of their Turkish masters, stood poised upon the very brink of heroism?').[48] But unlike Madame de Staël, Stendhal was a great admirer of Napoleon and believed that fifteen years of French rule had given the peninsula a salutary jolt; and while the Swiss writer fretted over how to restore liberty to a society that had grown decadent, Stendhal had little doubt that democracy would only take root after another period of benevolent dictatorship.[49]

What struck Stendhal so forcibly as he travelled around northern and central Italy in 1816 and 1817 was the strength of what he called *patriotisme d'antichambre*, the fierce and inordinate pride that local people felt towards their home town or village. Some aspects of this patriotism were charming, he thought; but it was often accompanied by an insularity of outlook and a resistance to any criticism or change. Milan was a wonderful city – his favourite – and the Milanese were right to be fond of their newly completed cathedral with its forest of spires, their fine opera house, large *palazzi* with superbly efficient tin guttering, and clean streets. But their values were still those of a medieval republic ('indeed the whole of Italy today is nothing but an extension of the Middle Ages') and their horizons restricted. They were passionate about their patron saint, Carlo Borromeo; about the productions at La Scala; about the mock naval battles, chariot races and sack races for dwarves staged in the Circus of Napoleon; about the Sunday *corso*, when the populace thronged the main streets to gaze at 'its aristocracy' parading in carriages. But they were indifferent to politics and despised the government as 'predatory vermin', unworthy of their support. And they were broadly indifferent to literature (there was no appetite for novels) and to the few dozen intellectuals who frequented the salons of Confalonieri, Pellico and their friends.[50]

Had this intense local patriotism been wedded to fraternal feelings towards neighbouring Italian towns and cities, then national sentiment might have been more in evidence, but as it was the peninsula was scored with hostilities ('Italy is quite as much the native home of hatred as of love').[51] One of Stendhal's informants told him of the bitter animosity that Bergamo, Pavia and Novara harboured towards Milan, and added that there was not a single Italian city that did not loathe its neighbour, with the exceptions of Florence (which no longer had the energy to keep up its old feud with Siena, he said) and Milan (whose inhabitants were too concerned with 'keeping a good table and acquiring a warm overcoat' to indulge in hatred):

You do not need telling that these different peoples are very far from forming a homogeneous nation . . . [and] it follows that our rulers have no difficulty in the fulfilment of their aim: *divide ut imperes*. This unhappy people, shattered by hatred into fragments as fine as dust, is governed by the several courts of Vienna, Turin, Modena, Florence, Rome and Naples.[52]

As Stendhal travelled southwards from Milan, through Emilia Romagna and Tuscany, he became increasingly disturbed by the levels of prejudice and ignorance that he encountered, which gave the local *patriotisme d'antichambre* an almost surreal quality. Each town, each village, seemed like a closed universe, impervious to criticism and the outside world, where the humblest talent and the meanest public building were extolled to the skies. There was also a great deal of superstition, and the emotional life of the poor was dominated by the clergy, whose intercessions were continually sought to ensure good harvests, avert natural disasters and keep evil spirits at bay. The extent of the cultural gap separating the mass of the population from the educated elite alarmed him. After reporting how one village had been terrorized for days by the appearance in the sky of a 'dark spectre' (which turned out to be simply an eagle), he wrote: 'I am afraid for the future of Italy. The nation will continue to bring forth philosophers like Beccaria, poets like Alfieri, soldiers like Santarosa; but the trouble is that these illustrious individuals are too isolated from the masses of the people.'[53]

For these masses life was hard and precarious, and the main source of comfort came from the Church, whose capacity to engage the hearts and minds of ordinary people through colour, music and spectacle was remarkable. Stendhal observed this in Rome on 18 August 1817, when he watched the 77-year-old Pope Pius VII being carried triumphantly through the city on a dais before a sea of adoring faces, 'stamped with the profound belief that the Pontiff . . . is the sovereign arbiter of their eternal felicity or damnation'. The procession began with five orders of friars bearing huge torches and singing hymns. Then followed the regular clergy from the great basilicas, divided into seven bodies by huge banners of scarlet and yellow (the traditional colours of the city), 'and each of these banners, of wholly oriental aspect, was preceded by a weird and wondrous instrument surmounted by a bell, from which, at regular minute intervals, there was extracted a high and solitary note'. Next came the cardinals:

Then, all at once, the multitude made genuflexion, and there, mounted upon his advancing dais swathed in draperies fashioned of the richest and rarest stuffs, I beheld a figure, pale, inanimate and proud, likewise shrouded in vestments reaching high above the shoulders – a figure which seemed to me to merge into a single entity, a *whole*, one and indivisible, together with the altar, the swaying dais and the golden sun, before whose orb the figure was bowed down, as though in adoration. 'You never told me that the Pope was dead,' complained a child who stood beside me to its mother. And no words can better convey the utter and motionless fixity of this unearthly apparition. At that instant, amongst the multitude which encompassed me on every side, there was not a single unbeliever, and even I was to be numbered among the faithful, if beauty be counted a religion.[54]

How could a new secular religion of the Italian nation hope to compete with the old faith?

LEOPARDI'S ITALY: THE
ABSENCE OF SOCIETY

Perched on a hill to the south of Ancona, a few miles from the great pilgrimage shrine of Loreto, Recanati was not untypical of many small provincial towns in the Papal States. Its medieval towers and walls bore witness to its importance as a military stronghold in the Middle Ages, while its broad streets and substantial houses attested to a degree of commercial prosperity in the sixteenth and seventeenth centuries. But by the time the poet Giacomo Leopardi was born there in 1798 much of its affluence had vanished, and Recanati was little more than a cultural and economic backwater, dominated by the sound of bells from its seventeen churches and awash with signs of its former wealth and distinction: a thirteenth-century bishop's palace, a fine cathedral with the sarcophagus of the saintly fifteenth-century pope Gregory XII, towers and monasteries, a piazza, on one side of which stood the substantial *palazzo* in which the Leopardi family had lived for over 500 years, and many important Renaissance sculptures and paintings, including four works – one of them a bizarrely dramatic Annunciation, complete with startled cat – by the maverick Venetian genius Lorenzo Lotto.

Giacomo Leopardi's father, Monaldo, was a conservative nobleman, who dressed austerely in black and wrote religious, philosophical, literary and historical works attacking the errors of the French Revolution and defending Christianity as the necessary bedrock of society. He hoped to shield his son from the dangers of the modern world and had him educated privately by Jesuit tutors, surrounded by the vast personal library he was amassing in Palazzo Leopardi with what little remained of the family fortune. Giacomo displayed precocious intellectual gifts, and by the age of eighteen he had mastered Latin, Greek and Hebrew and several modern languages, written a history of astronomy and a treatise on the scientific errors of the ancient world, and composed two tragedies, poems and numerous verse translations. But he was far from happy. He suffered from a spinal condition that left him deformed; and he longed to escape from his family and Recanati, the 'uncivilized town of my birth', where his scholarly aloofness and disdain for his fellow townsmen made him less than popular.[55]

Romanticism had made suffering and personal growth the material of art; and like Foscolo, Manzoni and Stendhal, Leopardi found an outlet for his emotional discontent in an idealized vision of the Italian nation – a vision that was made all the more powerful by its being vague and ill-defined and shot through with sexualized imagery and exhortations to revenge and war. In a series of brilliant odes written between 1818 and 1821 he contrasted the greatness of the past with the 'mediocrity' and 'mire' of the present, portraying contemporary Italy as a beautiful woman, covered in blood and wounds, her clothes torn and hair dishevelled, with chains on her arms, sitting on the ground, weeping. He appealed to the young men of Italy – 'her sons' – to take up arms and rescue her, and so emulate the ancients, 'who rushed in droves to die for the fatherland'. And he hoped that scholars and writers, by recollecting the achievements of great men such as Dante and Tasso, and laying them before the public, would prise Italians out of their 'lethargy' and inspire them to 'illustrious deeds'. For since the sixteenth century only one man had arisen worthy of Italy (but 'unworthy of his craven age'), Alfieri; and his fierce energy, 'masculine virtue' and hatred of tyrants had come to him, 'not from this arid and weary land of mine', but from north of the Alps.[56]

Leopardi finally managed to break away from Recanati in 1822, and went to Rome, and later Milan, Bologna and Florence, where he met Manzoni and other leading writers. But travel did little to improve his estimation of his fellow countrymen, and he remained disturbed by their deep cynicism, resignation and lack of ambition. He was also alarmed by just how little national sentiment there was, and this at a time when other countries – Britain and France principally, but also Germany, and latterly Spain and Greece – seemed flush with patriotic feelings that were inspiring soldiers, politicians, engineers, businessmen, writers and artists to new heights. On reflection, it struck him that there was a close causal connection between the state of the Italian character and this absence of any clear sense of the nation, and he set out to analyse the relationship between the two in an essay entitled 'On the Present State of the Customs of the Italians' written in 1824 (but not published till 1906).

Italy's fundamental problem, he argued, was that there was no 'society', no national community, to which the disparate peoples of the peninsula felt bound, and which regulated conduct and tastes and gave rise to sentiments of honour and shame. And in the modern world such a community was indispensable, as the Enlightenment had left a vacuum by kicking away the religious pillars on which societies had rested for centuries (here Leopardi was taking issue with his father, who was doggedly looking to stem the tide of change by defending the alliance of throne and altar). For various reasons, not least the absence of a capital city like London or Paris, Italians had no consciousness of a broader moral collectivity, beyond their family or their town, that would generate ideals and prevent cynicism – the besetting vice of Italians that led them to disparage everyone and everything. Italians were individualists, and were proud of it; and 'every Italian city, indeed every Italian, has his own style and way of doing things'. And the problem was particularly acute in the smaller provincial centres. The only forums in which most Italians looked to be judged were those of the '*passeggiate*, festivals and Church'. No other society existed. 'They promenade, go to shows and entertainments, sermons and masses, sacred and secular festivals. That is all . . .'[57]

Leopardi's eye may have been jaundiced by his life in Recanati, but his view of Italy was shared by many patriots of the Risorgimento – well-educated young men (and some women) of middle-class and aristocratic backgrounds, conscious of the gap that separated themselves from the mass of the population, and their poetic ideal of a resurrected, glorious Italy, vigorous and unified, worthy of its great past, from the humdrum and fractured reality. Leopardi died in 1837 in a villa on the slopes of Vesuvius, a lonely and frustrated figure. But he left an enduring legacy of some of the most beautiful lyric poetry of the nineteenth century, poetry that he hoped would educate his fellow countrymen as well as entertain them. As he wrote in his diary in 1821: 'To arouse my poor fatherland . . . I will seek to deploy the weapons of emotion and enthusiasm, eloquence and imagination, in the poetry and prose that it will be given to me to write.'[58] Many of his more overtly pedagogic projects remained incomplete on his death: 'On the Education of Italian Youth', 'Letters of a Father to his Son', 'Moral Instruction for the Use of Children'. It was to be left to others to try to find ways of creating that sense of a national community that Italy so manifestly lacked.

6

Apostles and Martyrs: Mazzini and the Democrats, 1830–44

God does exist. But even if he did not exist, there exists the universal belief in him: there exists the universal need for an idea, *a centre, a single principle . . . Superstition, intolerance and priestly despotism have up till now fed on this impulse to believe. Let us deprive them of this support, based on a false interpretation. Let us seize that idea, that symbol of Unity: let us show God to be the author of liberty, equality and progress. The masses will ignore men, not God. Our people, as a result of many centuries of servitude, have been rendered cold, deathly cold; and to rouse them we need a religious enthusiasm, the cry of the Crusades:* God wills it!

Giuseppe Mazzini, Corrispondenza con Sismondi (1832)

Reverend father . . . We know and follow the religion of Jesus Christ like you, or, if you will permit me, better than you . . . Because the charity and love that are the hallmarks of that religion are precisely what lead us to this most cruel of ends . . . So, Father, rest assured that just as our death is certain, so tomorrow, despite the terrible anathemas of Pope Gregory, we will be up above (pointing to the sky). *But we will not find Dominic there.*

Anacarsi Nardi to a Dominican monk on the eve of his execution, 1844

'ITALIANS CANNOT FIGHT'

In a field outside Florence on 19 February 1826 the nephew of Vincenzo Cuoco, Gabriele Pepe, fought a duel with the distinguished French poet Alphonse de Lamartine. Pepe, a soldier, scholar and writer who had supported the Neapolitan Republic in 1799 and served with Napoleon's armies in Italy and Spain, had settled in Tuscany in 1823 and become part of the literary circle of Gian Pietro Vieusseux, a Swiss merchant who had recently founded a high-profile liberal journal called the *Antologia* to follow in the footsteps of the suppressed *Conciliatore*. Pepe had been angered by a poem of Lamartine in memory of Lord Byron, in which the Frenchman had described Italy as a land 'of the past' and of 'ruins', where everything 'sleeps' ('a land of the dead' as it was famously summarized), devoid of military virtue and given over to 'perfidious sensual pleasures'. Pepe denounced Lamartine as 'a trivial poet'; and Lamartine, mistaking him, it seems, for his more illustrious namesake Guglielmo, issued a challenge. Pepe won, wounding Lamartine seriously in the arm and gallantly staunching the flow of blood with his own handkerchief. He became the cynosure of patriotic circles in Florence.[1] In 1913 a large statue in his honour was inaugurated in his tiny home town of Civitacampomarano in the Molise, in the presence of the king's cousin.

Lamartine's claim that Italians were too indolent and pleasure-loving to be capable of fighting was an old slur, dear to French and German writers especially, dating back to the late fifteenth century at least.[2] But coming as it did from one of the most widely read European writers of his generation, it stung Italian patriots, and stung them badly – especially those, like Pepe, who had served with distinction in the Napoleonic campaigns, or later, in the 1820s and 1830s, in the wars of liberation in Spain, Greece and South America. The patriotic novels of Massimo d'Azeglio and Francesco Domenico Guerrazzi, written in the 1830s and 1840s, with their accounts of Italian military heroism in the Middle Ages, were intended to remind foreigners (as well as Italians) that Italians were far from being congenitally supine. The great guerrilla leader, Giuseppe Garibaldi, whose brilliant military career was to culminate in 1860 in the conquest of the Kingdom of the Two Sicilies and the unification of Italy, saw his life almost as an extended riposte to Lamartine. As he wrote in his memoirs:

How proud I was to be born in Italy! In that land of the dead! Among those people that do not fight, as our neighbours say . . . Where a generation of young men arose who scorned danger, torture and death, and marched fearlessly to fulfil their duty and throw off the shackles of slavery . . . The fatherland of the Scipios and the Gracchi, the nation that boasts the Vespers and Legnano, . . . may for a moment be trampled on by the bullying foreigner, but it can never be wholly without sons who can astound the world.[3]

The ease with which the Austrians put down the revolutions of 1820–21, and the purge of sectarians from the army and the civil service that followed, focused the minds of patriots on military problems. How could Italy generate an effective national rising of the kind that Spain had seen in 1808–12? The enduring status of Spain as a beacon of liberal nationalism was shown by the enthusiasm with which hundreds of Italians went off to fight for the constitutional regime there in 1821–3. But it was the Greek war of independence, waged by fierce mountain klephts dressed in kilts and by bands of peasant guerrillas, that most captured the imagination of Italian liberals in the 1820s. Philhellenism, indeed, became an important cultural movement in Italy, with 'Greek Committees' appearing in Piedmont and Tuscany from 1823 and a thousand or so volunteers crossing the Ionian Sea to help the Greek freedom fighters.[4] Dozens of articles appeared in the press and periodicals such as the *Antologia* supporting Greece; Foscolo, Berchet and others produced poems in honour of the insurrection; and one of Hayez's most successful paintings, *The Exiles of Parga* (1826–31), was on a Greek theme. It depicted an episode in 1818 when the inhabitants of a small town near Epirus were forced into exile after the British had misguidedly sold their land to the Turks. A crowd of men, women and children (among them Hayez himself, looking, somewhat immodestly, like Raphael) were shown in the (revolutionary) light of dawn, distraught but suffused with patriotic ardour, clutching at clods of earth and branches from a willow tree beneath which their forefathers lay buried – an instance of the poeticization of the ancestral landscape that Verdi was to give supreme musical expression to a decade later in his celebrated chorus of the Hebrew slaves in the opera *Nabucco*.

The fact that Greek independence was finally secured only with the diplomatic and military support of Britain, France and Russia provided an important lesson for Italian patriots, and certainly many of those who took the road to exile after 1821 and ended up in Paris or London – where Foscolo remained an important point of contact until his death in 1827, welcoming among others Berchet, Guglielmo Pepe, Gabriele Rossetti (father of the poets Dante Gabriel and Christina) and Antonio Panizzi (creator of the British Museum Library) – had some of their insurrectionary ardour softened by the pragmatic liberalism of their new political surroundings.[5] But the mythic appeal of a Spanish-style popular rising remained strong, and buoyed by the achievements of the Greek insurgents, revolutionary sectarian networks continued to operate in Europe, coordinated by the elderly Filippo Buonarroti, who in the 1820s modified his organization of the Sublime Perfect Masters into a new and less intricately Masonic society, 'The World', with affiliates in France, Belgium and also Italy.

Among the sectarians in Buonarroti's orbit was Carlo Bianco di Saint-Jorioz, a Piedmontese officer who had participated in the Piedmontese revolution of 1821 and fought in Spain. While in exile in Malta, Saint-Jorioz wrote a treatise about guerrilla warfare, in which he argued that the Spanish model of a popular national insurrection might be applicable to Italy. He envisaged ruthless bands of peasants in the countryside, conducting lightning attacks on the Austrian forces and harrying them pitilessly, cutting their lines of communication, wearing them down and bringing about their demoralization, dispersal and eventual destruction. Perhaps deliberately he minimized certain features that had been crucial to the Spanish experience during the Peninsular War, notably the leading role played by the local clergy and the support given to the guerrillas by the British army. But despite these oversights, Saint-Jorioz's book was eagerly seized upon by Italian exiles, especially in France, after it was published in 1830.[6] Among those who took firmly to heart its central idea of 'insurrection by armed bands' was a young supporter of Buonarroti called Giuseppe Mazzini.

There was a weak link in Saint-Jorioz's thesis, however, and one which he himself acknowledged: Italian peasants, unlike their Spanish (or Greek) counterparts, had to date shown no evidence of national patriotic feelings, or even any serious signs of disliking the existing governments. Years of servitude had made them cowed, conservative and materialistic, he said; and while it was undoubtedly ignominious for a man to fight for the formation of his fatherland from any motive other than duty, the sad fact was that the masses would only be roused to action by 'personal financial gain'.[7] He accordingly felt it necessary for there to be a social dimension in the national revolution, and proposed that once the war of independence was over the government should distribute state land and property confiscated from the enemies of the new order to the peasantry. Whether such inducements would ever be sufficient to outweigh the counter-revolutionary pressures of local priests and landowners, though, was unclear.

The issue of motives – economics versus ideals – was an important theme of the Risorgimento and one of the main sources of contention and debate before (and after) 1860. The great majority of patriots, certainly those of a democratic persuasion, disliked materialism, and maintained that action should spring from unsullied faith and not from any desire for personal gain. They were influenced in this view by the emphasis that Romantic culture placed on the sphere of the spirit as the highest arena of human development and achievement and as the principal motor of history, driving men on to fight and die, build vast cathedrals, compose great poems or cover the ceilings and walls of churches with masterpieces. They also had an acute sense that material-ism was a particular problem in Italy. It was often argued that the peninsula had begun to decline when the pursuit of worldly goods permeated Italian culture in the Renaissance, making men (and women) more concerned with how they looked and what they owned than with collective ideals such as freedom or independence. Mazzini was a particularly stern critic of materialism. Central to his crusade for Italian unity from the early 1830s was the belief that Italians must fight for their nation from a sense of religious duty, and he repeatedly fell out with those fellow patriots of a more pragmatic turn of mind who wanted to emphasize instead economic and social issues.

For, as Mazzini was well aware, the issue was not whether Italians *could* fight or not: individually they were clearly every bit as brave and aggressive as others – according to some even more so, if the bloody history of banditry, revolts and jacqueries in the peninsula was anything to go by. The key question was *what* they would fight for. And here the great dream of patriots was to divert Italians from thoughts of personal honour and private or factional feuding towards collective action, and so achieve the supreme expression of modern nationhood, the 'nation in arms', a mass citizen army willing to sacrifice everything for the fatherland. As the leading Tuscan democrat Giuseppe Montanelli wrote in his memoirs in 1853, the mission of the Risorgimento was to make Italy one in both war and peace: 'Our wish is to free ourselves from the foreign yoke, and give the nation a civil and warrior "I".'[8] More moder-ate patriots harboured similar hopes. The Piedmontese Catholic his-torian and politician Cesare Balbo said that he would have given three or four Alfieris, Manzonis or even Dantes 'for one captain who could lead behind him 200,000 Italians, to win or die'.[9] And at the other end of the peninsula the Sicilian historian Michele Amari – who was continually scanning Italy for signs of military revival – told a friend of his sadness when he heard of the assassination of a leading politician in Rome in November 1848, not so much on account of the victim, but 'because people will start crying out again about our stiletto knives; and because, to be honest, it is high time that Italians threw away their daggers and wielded the bayonet more manfully'.[10]

The key patriotic texts of the Risorgimento struggled to impart the right military message; and it was a struggle, because so many of the historical episodes chosen for their 'national' significance were clearly open to very different, 'non-national' readings. This was the case with the Sicilian Vespers of 1282 – the subject of two paintings by Hayez, an opera by Verdi (though his libretto was in fact adapted from a story set in Holland) and a major historical study by Amari. The popular rising which broke out in Palermo on Easter Monday 1282 and which led to the slaughter of some 5,000 Frenchmen was commonly seen as an instance of 'Italian' patriotism; but the traditional strength of Sicilian separatism and the deep-seated hostility of many islanders towards Naples suggested that it was more likely to have been fuelled by much narrower, local feelings. Indeed when his work was first published in 1842 Amari had to defend it against charges that it was 'municipal', saying that 'provincial patriotism' was not damaging to the interests of 'the great Italian family' provided it was 'sincere and enlightened'. He was also taken to task for having referred at one point to mainland Italians as 'foreigners', but he hurriedly changed this slip in later editions.[11]

Another military episode that had to be shoe-horned with some difficulty into a national patriotic mould was the 'duel of Barletta' of 1503, the subject of Massimo d'Azeglio's best-selling novel *Ettore Fieramosca* (1833) and of half a dozen operas between 1839 and 1848 (Verdi was asked to do a version in 1849, but declined: it was 'a beautiful moment' in Italian history, he said, but had already been overworked).[12] The duel was an obscure event in the Franco-Spanish campaigns fought in Italy at the beginning of the sixteenth century and seems to have been occasioned by a French taunt about the good faith or courage of Italians. Thirteen Italian knights did battle with thirteen French knights somewhere in the countryside near Barletta in Puglia to resolve the point of honour, and the Italians won. In reality the 'duel' was probably little more than a joust to help while away the winter months prior to the resumption of serious fighting; and it is not even clear that anyone was killed. But d'Azeglio seized on the episode in the hope that it would 'put a little fire in the bellies of Italians'. He at first thought of doing a painting or a poem, but decided on a novel instead, 'so as to be heard in the streets and piazzas and not just on Mount Helicon'. He was concerned with 'national regeneration', he said, and not with historical veracity, and accordingly made the 'duel' into a metaphor for Italy's liberation from foreign oppression, casting the leading Italian soldier, Ettore Fieramosca, as a heroic and selfless patriot and his fellow knights as symbols of 'Italy', natives of different regions standing shoulder to shoulder against the enemy.[13] A love affair and a traitor added piquancy to the story. The novel, not surprisingly, played down the fact that the Italian knights had in reality been mercenaries in the Spanish pay.

REVOLUTIONS, 1830–31

On 27 July 1830 a revolution broke out in Paris. Tricolours and trees of liberty appeared in the streets, barricades went up, and after three days of fighting the conservative King Charles X was forced to abdicate in favour of Louis-Philippe, who, in good liberal fashion took the title 'King of the French' rather than King of France. The waves of unrest fanned out across Europe. In Brussels on 25 August the long-standing grievances of Catholics and French-speakers against their Dutch Protestant rulers in The Hague came to a head in mass rioting after a performance of Auber's opera about the Neapolitan revolt of 1647, *La Muette de Portici* (which ended in suitably explosive style with the eruption of Mount Vesuvius), and a few weeks later, with the support of Britain, France and Prussia, an independent Belgian state was proclaimed. In November the Poles rose against Tsar Nicholas I, but with far less favourable results. Here there was no foreign assistance forthcoming, and after nearly a year of often savage guerrilla and regular fighting, the insurrection was crushed by the Russian army and tens of thousands of Poles killed, imprisoned or driven into exile.

These events in Europe gave heart to Italian liberals and sectarians. For a number of years the focus of conspiratorial activity had been the Duchy of Modena; and oddly enough it was the duke himself, Francesco IV, a reactionary prince with a Romantic penchant for intrigue and grandiose ambitions of becoming king of a much larger state, who pulled many of the strings. He hoped to exploit the tensions that had arisen in Europe as a result of the Greek war of independence to get Austria to withdraw from the Italian peninsula, possibly in exchange for Turkish territories in the Balkans; and his main agent was a mysterious figure called Enrico Misley, a young law graduate and son of a distinguished professor of veterinary studies in Milan, who had close connections with the Carboneria and other secret societies. Misley spent several years travelling round Europe, forging links with Italian exiles, French liberals, and Greek and Russian emissaries, and preparing the ground for an improbable-sounding rising, centred on the Papal States, that would have as its final aim the creation of an independent and unified Italy with Francesco IV as its constitutional ruler.

The July revolution in Paris frightened Francesco and he began to back away from Misley's intrigues; but Louis-Philippe's accession gave the Italian sectarians enormous encouragement, as they now believed that a rising directed against the Austrians in Italy would naturally be supported by a new liberal French king. Plans for an insurrection accordingly assumed a momentum of their own towards the end of 1830, with the duchies of Modena and Parma, the city of Bologna and the Romagna (in the northern part of the Papal States) serving as the focal points of conspiratorial activity. Here the liberals could count on high levels of discontent among the propertied classes, particularly those who had lost in the post-1815 settlement or who had been adversely affected by tariffs and other impediments to trade. There was particular anger in the Romagna, the most affluent part of the Papal States, where the wealthy laity resented the stranglehold of the Church on the administration, the tax immunities of the clergy and their ownership of the best land, the byzantine complexity of the legal system, and the generally obscurantist culture emanating from Rome.

The death of Pope Pius VIII at the end of November 1830 and a period of two months' interregnum that followed intensified the insurrectionary atmosphere, and early in February risings broke out in Modena, Parma and Bologna, and quickly spread throughout the Romagna and the Marche and down Umbria. In Paris, Filippo Buonarroti and other leading democratic exiles proclaimed their support for their 'friends and brothers . . . from the Alps to Etna', and urged them to take up arms, overthrow their rulers, expel the Austrians and create an Italy that was 'independent, one and free'. A column of volunteers was assembled in

Lyon and set off to attack Piedmont: but it was halted by the French government, which quickly showed itself to be much less sympathetic to the cause of revolution in Italy than the sectarians had hoped. Meanwhile in Bologna an assembly of delegates had convened and declared the Pope's temporal power to be at an end. It had also proclaimed that those provinces that had risen up would form 'one single state, one single government and one single family' – an indication as much of insecurity as of intent, given the fierce municipal rivalries that had long beset this part of Italy and which would soon undermine the revolution.[14]

Louis-Philippe watched the events in Italy with growing alarm. Apart from fears that the revolution might take on a dangerously republican complexion, he was also concerned by the presence in Italy of various members of the Bonaparte family, including Napoleon's nephew, the future emperor Napoleon III, a former Carbonaro serving with antipapal volunteers in the Marche. Accordingly he indicated to Vienna at the end of February that France would not intervene to stop Austria reasserting its control in Italy. On 4 March Francesco IV – who had fled from Modena in the face of the revolution a month earlier – crossed back into his duchy accompanied by Austrian troops, and in the space of the next three weeks the insurrections in both the duchies and the Papal States were suppressed. Protests were voiced in France by opposition deputies and sections of the public who maintained that the dignity of the French nation had been compromised by its failure to halt the Austrians, but by then it was too late.

The ease with which the Austrians regained control made clear the weakness of the sectarians in Italy. The faith of Misley in Francesco IV was shown to have been misplaced – just as Santarosa's hope in 1821 that Carlo Alberto would back a constitutional movement in Piedmont and Lombardy had been exposed as naive. With the Austrians so entrenched in the peninsula, was it realistic ever to expect anything of an Italian prince? Belief in the assistance of revolutionary France was also shown to have been misguided. Even more disappointing was the absence of any serious sign of national sentiment. Most of those who supported the insurrections in 1831 wanted internal political and economic reforms: not independence, and certainly not national independence. And almost nobody was prepared to fight the Austrians. Indeed there was only one significant clash between volunteers and Austrian troops, near Rimini on 25 March, and even this engagement was minor.

Finally provincial and municipal rivalries were as pronounced as ever. The cities of Emilia, Romagna and the Marche displayed little willingness to make common cause, and the leading role played by Bologna in particular aroused strong suspicion. The frustration that this gave rise to was evident in a letter that a Lombard liberal wrote to a fellow sectarian in April 1831:

Ten years of shame and suffering have still not taught our people that there is no strength without union, and that in order to be united we need to have respect for one another. Many secret societies were formed in an effort to stop certain personal vendettas and extinguish provincial rivalries. But what was the upshot of some of these societies? Unbridled ambitions were encouraged, the hatreds got worse, malicious gossip increased and provincialism acquired greater strength than ever . . .[15]

MAZZINI AND THE DEMOCRATS

The events of 1831 were a major turning point in the national movement in Italy. Many liberals now came to look on secret societies and conspiracy with deep suspicion. There was simply not enough support at a grass roots level – let alone from any foreign governments – to sustain an insurrection. Far better, they thought, to concentrate on improving economic, political and moral conditions within the existing states and play down talk of independence and unity. Newspapers, journals and books were the way ahead, to mould public opinion and gradually pressurize rulers into conceding reforms. And during the next decade and a half this was the course that the so-called 'moderates' adopted. The more radical liberals, by contrast, drew a very different lesson. They believed that nothing good should now be expected of princes and their governments, and certainly nothing that would help the cause of Italy. The 'people' would have to act, and act alone. But in order to do so they needed to feel stirred by passion, and that meant shifting the focus of conspiratorial activity away from secrecy and ritual towards overt education and incitement – by word and by deed.

It was no coincidence that Giuseppe Mazzini – who was to dominate the democratic wing of the Italian patriotic movement over the next three decades – regarded Hayez's painting *Peter the Hermit Preaches the Crusade* as one of the most brilliant works of the new school of what he called 'the Precursors of National Art'.[16] The painting was first exhibited at the Brera in 1829, and generated enormous interest among the public, who immediately sensed its daring political symbolism: according to one commentator the viewers crowding in front of it seemed (quite appropriately given the 'civil' mission that the Italian Romantics had set themselves) like an extension of the work itself.[17] What excited Mazzini in particular was the totality of the religious feeling that permeated the canvas, from the cloud-capped mountains in the background, through the figure of Peter on horseback, contorted with energy and brandishing a crucifix ('pale and gaunt, but venerable in his enthusiasm and conviction'), to the small crowd of ordinary men, women and children gathered around him in enthusiasm and rapture: 'Everywhere we are in contact with the infinite . . . [E]veryone is driven on by a single, true and binding force, the thought that pervades each mind: "God wills it, God wills it" . . . Unity is *felt* here, without being *seen*.'[18]

Through his passionate preaching Peter the Hermit had incited thousands of peasants across Europe at the end of the eleventh century to abandon their homes and risk hardship and death in order to liberate the Holy Land from the Turks. The potent mixture of religion and politics that Peter and the crusading movement of the Middle Ages had embodied fascinated Mazzini and many other radical-minded intellectuals of his generation searching for an elixir to convert aimless individuals into a single-minded army of progress. The Crusades, indeed, became one of the major themes of Italian patriotic art and literature from the mid-1820s, beginning with Tommaso Grossi's epic poem, *The Lombards on the First Crusade* (1826) (which his friend Hayez illustrated with an important series of lithographs)[19] and Massimo d'Azeglio's painting of the same year of *The Death of Count Josselin de Montmorency*.[20] In the 1830s and 1840s Hayez undertook two further works inspired by the Crusades, *Urban II Preaching the First Crusade* (in which the Pope is shown in the main square of Clermont surrounded by a seething crowd – a response to criticisms that *Peter the Hermit* had been too restrained) and a massive canvas, inspired by Grossi's poem *The Thirst Suffered by the First Crusaders outside Jerusalem*, commissioned by King Carlo Alberto and promptly hidden in a corner of the royal palace in Turin after the collapse of Carlo Alberto's personal crusading hopes on the battlefield of Novara in 1849.[21]

The central position that Mazzini assigned to religion in his idea of the Italian nation emerged in the wake of the 1831 debacle. As a patriot and law student in Genoa in the 1820s and an enthusiast for romanticism Mazzini had been naturally drawn to the world of sectarianism, and in 1829 he became a Carbonaro. Betrayed by a companion to the police, he was imprisoned for three months and forced into exile, and in March 1831 he settled in Marseille. Here he encountered a lively community of Italian liberals, many of whom were followers of Filippo Buonarroti. Among them was Carlo Bianco di Saint-Jorioz, the theorist of insurrection by guerrilla warfare and leader of a recently formed paramilitary secret society, the Apofasimeni, whose declared goal was to make Italy 'one, independent and free'. Mazzini entered this organization with the rank of 'centurion' shortly after his arrival in Marseille; but a few months later he decided to set up his own society, Young Italy (*Giovine Italia*), not, it seems, to supplant the Apofasimeni and the other societies linked to Buonarroti, but rather to secure greater cooperation between them and establish an agreed agenda, particularly now that the collapse of the revolutions in Italy and the 'betrayal' by France had left the sectarians confused about the way ahead.[22]

But Mazzini's initiative aroused suspicion, and in 1831–3 he found himself facing growing criticism from the older sectarians and was forced to define the position of Young Italy increasingly in opposition to them. On the face of it Young Italy did not pose a threat to sects like the Apofasimeni. It had the same goal of a united, independent and free Italian republic, and looked to similar means to achieve it – 'education and insurrection'. Moreover Mazzini's programme for the insurrection was taken straight from the pages of Saint-Jorioz's treatise, with guerrilla bands being set up to wage war on the enemy and furnish the nuclei of an eventual national mass army. But in certain crucial respects Mazzini differed from the older sectarians. First, his focus was unequivocally on the national redemption of Italy by Italians. Italy was not to be subordinate to France in any way and not to look to Paris for its cue. For ardent Francophiles like Buonarroti this line was difficult. Secondly, the republic that Mazzini aspired to was very different to that envisaged by the older sectarians. For the latter 'equality' was to be crucial in any new regime, and this meant material equality, with the property of the rich being expropriated and distributed to the poor. Mazzini was certainly passionate about improving the economic lot of the masses, but through mutual aid societies, welfare, universal suffrage and schooling, and not class warfare. Mazzini was no Jacobin; and all his life he was to be an unremitting enemy of socialism.

But it was the religious dimension of Young Italy – a dimension that was to cast a long and in many ways problematic shadow over the national question in Italy for more than a century – that distinguished Mazzini most from the other sectarians. Not that the earlier secret societies had been godless. Far from it: the rituals, symbols and language of the Carboneria had been heavily imbued with Christianity. But this religious freight had been largely formal in character, a mechanism chiefly for giving the sects an air of gravity and ensuring that the affiliates took their oaths and duties seriously. What Mazzini aimed to do was to fuse God, the people and the nation into a sacred trinity and make the pursuit of unity, liberty and independence itself a religion. God, he claimed, had ordained Italy to be a great nation with a great mission in the world; and it was accordingly incumbent upon Italians to unify Italy and implement his will, and be prepared, as true believers, to sacrifice everything, if need be their lives, for the holy cause. As Mazzini wrote some years later, looking back to 1831 in terms tellingly reminiscent of a Damascene conversion (in reality his 'conversion' to the new religion of Italy was more gradual than he cared to suggest):

At that time even the immature conception inspired me with a mighty hope that flashed before my spirit like a star. I saw regenerate Italy becoming at one bound the missionary of a religion of progress and fraternity, far grander and vaster than that she gave to humanity in the past. The worship of Rome was a part of my being ... Why should not a new Rome, the Rome of the Italian people – portents of whose coming I deemed I saw – arise to create a third and still vaster Unity; to link together and harmonize earth and heaven, right and duty; and utter, not to individuals but to peoples, the great word Association – to make known to free men and equal their mission here below?[23]

Mazzini had come from a deeply religious family: his mother was a passionate if unorthodox Catholic, of an austere and anti-hierarchical persuasion, who was convinced that her only son had been sent by God to raise humanity to new heights.[24] But it was the writings of the French philosopher and social reformer the Comte de Saint-Simon (1760–1825) that appear to have been decisive in shaping Mazzini's central ideas, informing his belief in progress, in the transition of modern society from an age of individualism to one of collective action or 'associationism', and in the need for a civic faith to heal the eighteenth-century fracture between reason and religion. Such a faith was vital, for mankind advanced, according to Saint-Simon, only when there was a guiding principle in which men believed fervently ('Remember that to do anything great you must be impassioned,' he told a friend shortly before he died). Many of the key terms in Mazzini's lexicon – words such as mission, apostolate and faith – were common currency among the Saint-Simonians in the later 1820s and 1830s.[25]

The nation for Mazzini was a community willed by God; and each nation had a particular mission assigned to it. Exactly what these missions were he never made entirely clear, though like Madame de Staël he saw the 'historic' peoples of Europe as possessing distinctive character traits that could indicate the special role providence had ascribed to them. Germans, for example, were by nature given to speculation and philosophy. Nor was he altogether clear about what the political map of Europe should eventually look like. He did not favour Irish nationalism; and he suggested on occasions that Spain and Portugal should merge, and Holland and Belgium be absorbed into Germany and France. He found Danish claims to nationhood hard to swallow, and he thought that the Scandinavian countries might form a single unit. But he was not dogmatic on these points, partly because he accepted that practical politics might require states to be grouped differently at different times.[26] However, on one issue he was absolutely clear: the centrality of the national question to the modern world. Each nation had to find its own voice and assert its freedom through the will of 'the people'. And only when every nation had been set up on an appropriate political footing would God's designs for humanity be finally fulfilled and universal peace achieved.

The vagueness of much of Mazzini's thinking (not to mention what often seemed his arrogance and self-righteousness) annoyed many of the older sectarians and fostered the increasingly bitter wrangles that plagued the democratic camp in the 1830s. But the vagueness was largely deliberate. Mazzini's aim was to generate faith; and faith was a natural instinct ('remember that religion is a desire, a need of the people')[27] founded on hope and simple precepts, not prosaic blueprints. Christianity had triumphed by holding out to all the prospect of justice and happiness in the afterlife; and this message had been spread from country to country by men and women using the power of the written and spoken word and the example of their own suffering and martyrdom. The believers in the new gospel should do likewise. Their dogmas should be clear – unity, independence, freedom – and their preaching and actions radiate unshakeable conviction. They should be willing to shed their blood for the cause ('the tree of liberty grows stronger when watered by the blood of martyrs';[28] 'for in sacrifice there is something sublime, that compels man born of woman to bow his head before it and adore; because somehow he senses that from that blood, as from the blood of a Christ, will come forth sooner or later the second life, the true life of a people').[29] And the particular focus of their national faith, Italy, should be made into an ideal onto which men and women of all regions and classes could project their longings.

Mazzini's eclectic mixture of religion and politics was at one level a natural outgrowth from European romantic nationalism, which contained numerous mystical and messianic strands (in the 1830s and 1840s the great writer Adam Mickiewicz preached the cause of Polish independence in similarly messianic terms, seeing in the country's sufferings a sign of divine favour and imminent resurrection: Poland as the 'Christ of nations'). But Mazzini also had his eye firmly on the specific situation in Italy, and his programme was in important respects deliberately tailored to fit the particular needs of Italian nationalism. Italy had been fragmented since the fall of the Roman empire some 1,400 years earlier: this disunity was to be rectified by means of a strong unitary state (he was firmly opposed to federalism) and a capital city whose symbolic power would give rise to cohesion and identity: Rome. Italians were by nature individualistic and prone to factionalism: this problem would be remedied by encouraging the establishment of associations and the drawing up of clear agendas that could be agreed on by everyone. The educated classes held France and French culture in awe, while at the same time resenting deeply French arrogance: such subservience would be countered by emphasizing Italy's magnificent past and its brilliant future, for according to Mazzini the nineteenth century had been ordained by God to be the century of Italy, just as the eighteenth century had been the century of France.

But it was the nation as the focus of a new secular religion that was the most important element for Italy in Mazzini's programme. This was partly because Mazzini believed that God was now addressing humanity through the medium of 'the people' and nations, and that the Church's mission on earth, so important once, was at an end. Italy, as the centre of Catholicism, accordingly had a mission to bring to a close the Middle Ages by destroying the Papal States and inaugurating on their ruins the age of nations: 'Only from Rome, for the third time, can the word of modern unity come, as only from Rome can the final destruction of the old unity begin.'[30] However, precisely because Italy was the seat of the Church, and Italian unity, it seemed, would only ever be secured in the face of fierce Catholic opposition, any popular national movement would have to neutralize the moral power of the Pope and the clergy by creating a rival religion powerful enough to win over the hearts if not the minds of the masses.

Mazzini knew that this task would be Herculean. The Church was rooted in the affections of most ordinary Italians, and had at its disposal a formidable army of secular and regular clergy. It was strongly supported by the various governments in the peninsula, who guaranteed it a stranglehold over education and censorship and punished mercilessly anyone who dealt in dangerous ideas ('Where verbal apostolate leads to the gallows, you cannot hope to find apostles,' Mazzini lamented to a friend in 1834 about the difficulties of reaching out to the common people).[31] The Church also had in its armoury a powerful tradition of ritual and spectacle, not to mention some of the greatest art and architecture in the world. And the emotional hold on the masses that this great aesthetic tradition afforded gave the Church a huge advantage over its competitors.

The magnitude of the Church's power was brought home to Mazzini forcefully when he went to Rome for the first time in his life in March 1849. 'Rome was the dream of my youth, the idea that had guided and nurtured all my thoughts, the religion of my soul; and I entered the city on foot in the evening . . . timidly, almost in adoration. Rome was – and remains for me . . . the Temple of humanity.'[32] But despite his hopes that a new age would soon be born, he could not ignore the fact that Catholicism was still a supreme moral force, and as one of the rulers of the Roman Republic during the spring of that revolutionary year, he felt unable to oppose it. On Easter Sunday he stood in front of St Peter's, with Michelangelo's great dome above him, watching as a priest blessed a sea of thousands of faithful gathered between the colonnades of Bernini's piazza. He turned to the painter Nino Costa beside him and said: 'This religion is strong, and will remain strong for a long time to come, because it is so beautiful on the eye.'[33]

Thanks to his strangely magnetic personality, which for many of those who came into contact with him seemed to conform to Romantic notions of a heaven-sent genius – passionate, single-minded and somewhat tortured, by turns saturnine and mercurial, with an almost mesmerizing facility with words (already in Marseille devotees could describe him as 'the most beautiful being, male or female' they had ever seen, or refer to his 'divine eloquence such as never before shone over Italy')[34] – and thanks, too, to the clarity of his message, with its national focus and its elimination of social egalitarianism, Mazzini quickly established Young Italy as the most successful secret society. Like the older sects it had an initiation ceremony and passwords, and pseudonyms to protect the identity of its members, but it did away with the tiers of Masonic grades that had in the past separated the enlightened elite from the benighted rank and file. Its structure was simple, with central and local committees, and it had a periodical, also called *Young Italy*, mostly written by Mazzini himself, which was smuggled into Italy by sympathizers. By early 1833 the society claimed, probably accurately, to have over 50,000 members, mostly drawn from the middle classes but reaching out in the cities to shopkeepers and artisans, and even to sections of the poor. The main areas of strength were in Liguria, Lombardy, Emilia and Tuscany. Piedmont remained primarily Buonarroti's domain. There was virtually no penetration in the south.[35]

Mazzini's immediate goal was insurrection, and his frenetic conspiratorial work quickly had the authorities in Italy worried. By 1833 police reports regularly referred to him as the 'famous' or 'infamous' Mazzini, and from Vienna the Austrian chancellor, Metternich, repeatedly urged the French government to hunt him down and expel him. Perhaps deliberately, Metternich exaggerated the strength and democratic appeal of Young Italy, saying it had over 100,000 recruits, mostly from among 'the lowest classes of the population and dissolute young men'; but such talk did as much to raise Mazzini's already formidable standing in sectarian circles as to induce greater vigilance and repression.[36] Among those drawn to Mazzini at this time were Vincenzo Gioberti, a priest who was to play a leading role in the development of a moderate Catholic programme for national unification in the 1840s, Luigi Carlo Farini, a future Italian prime minister, Luigi Melegari, a future foreign minister, and many others who as journalists, writers, academics, deputies and civil servants would ensure that much of the spirit if not the letter of Mazzini's teaching was carried over into united Italy after 1860.

Mazzini aimed to trigger a rising in Naples that would then spread into northern Italy. But the Italian governments sensed something was afoot and became acutely nervous, and when early in 1833 plans for a military coup were uncovered in Piedmont, the king, Carlo Alberto, insisted on exemplary punishments being meted out. Twelve conspirators were executed in public and a hundred others were sent to prison. Mazzini himself was condemned to death *in absentia*, and was now forced to leave France. He went to Geneva, from where he continued to correspond tirelessly with his followers and prepare for revolution. He was convinced that Italy was a powder keg and that a mere spark would unleash a general conflagration. One of his more desperate schemes was for an invasion of Savoy (then part of the Kingdom of Piedmont–Sardinia) by four columns of Polish, German and Italian volunteers led by Saint-Jorioz and by a former Napoleonic officer and veteran of the 1821 revolution in Piedmont. It proved to be a total fiasco. A simultaneous rising was supposed to break out in Genoa, but almost the only person who turned up for it was a young sailor from Nizza (Nice), who had recently joined Young Italy, called Giuseppe Garibaldi. He was sentenced to death, but not before he had managed to escape across the border into France.

The failure of this insurrection resulted in harsh crackdowns everywhere in the peninsula and the rapid break-up of Young Italy as a revolutionary organization, and for a time Mazzini had to accept that practical conspiracy was pointless. In the spring of 1834 he and a handful of other refugees founded a new association called Young Europe to coordinate the national movements in Poland, Germany and elsewhere; but it made little headway. Mazzini now experienced a growing sense of desperation. For two years, amid the snow and fog of the Jura mountains, living in poverty and on the run from the police, he went through a profound spiritual crisis, seeing all around him nothing but 'scepticism' and 'mistrust' and 'the disintegration of that moral edifice of love and faith within which, alone, I could achieve the strength to fight'. But one day he woke with his 'soul at peace . . . and the feelings of one who has been saved from an extreme danger'. His faith had survived – but in Italy rather than Italians. Indeed his disillusionment with his compatriots had seemed to intensify his love of abstractions (and animals): 'The company of a cat is much dearer to me than that of a man . . . I feel hatred towards men! If you could see the satanic smile I have on my lips for them! – and how they deserve it from me, my fellow citizens more than all the others – yet my country . . . I still love her; indeed I love her more truly, and with more nostalgia.'[37]

In 1837 Mazzini left Switzerland for England, and here he was to spend most of the remainder of his life, living like many exiles on whatever his family could send him, and on the meagre pickings to be had from journalism, translating and the occasional business venture. London was home to a large number of émigrés from Italy, some of whom, like Antonio Panizzi, had access to the drawing-rooms of the rich and powerful; but most of these Italians would not associate with a republican like Mazzini, nor Mazzini with them.[38] Of greater immediate benefit was the general current of sympathy towards Italy in England – less powerful, perhaps, than it had been in the 1820s, but still strong nonetheless, especially in radical circles. The philosopher John Stuart Mill was very excited to meet 'the celebrated Mazzini . . . the most eminent conspirator and revolutionist now in Europe', and promptly signed him up for the *Westminster Review*.[39] Other useful contacts soon appeared and, though Mazzini disliked socializing, there was no shortage of invitations from intellectuals and politicians. One of his closest associates during his early years in London was the writer Thomas Carlyle – and even more Carlyle's wife, Jane, the first of a number of strong-minded middle-class women who were drawn to this sensitive, passionate and rather solitary figure, who lived in near squalor, smoked heavily and played the guitar beautifully.

MISSIONARIES

The failed risings of 1833–4 and the police repressions that followed left the Italian democrats scattered and confused. Many sought refuge in France, Switzerland or north Africa. Some like the Piedmontese priest Vincenzo Gioberti settled in Brussels. Garibaldi departed for South America, where he formed a Legion of Italian Volunteers to fight for the independence of Uruguay, while a number of sectarians, among them such influential characters as the Modenese revolutionary Nicola

Fabrizi, went off to support the liberal cause in the civil war that had recently broken out in Spain. Economic hardship as well as disillusionment kept many of these exiles away from serious political activity. Saint-Jorioz became so burdened with debts that he took his own life, by gas, in Brussels in 1843. The patriarch of sectarian conspiracy, Buonarroti, attempted to maintain his influence in Italy by forming yet another secret society, the True Italians, with an unashamedly Jacobin and egalitarian programme. But his message was looking increasingly dated, and his Francophilia was unappealing to a younger generation of Italian patriots steeped in Romantic nationalism. By the time he died in Paris in 1837 he was a somewhat lonely and isolated figure.

While Mazzini's political stock fell sharply in the wake of the Savoy invasion fiasco, Young Italy had undoubtedly struck a powerful chord in democratic circles. Over the years many of even the most radical patriots were to find Mazzini's dogmatism and stress on 'God' excessive, often intolerable, but they agreed with his general premise that they should regard themselves as the missionaries of a new religion and shape their thoughts and actions accordingly. Though Francesco Hayez was primarily a professional artist, willing to accept commissions wherever they came from – and in the 1830s and 1840s he happily worked for the Austrian Emperor, painting among other things a huge allegory for the Royal Palace in Milan (destroyed by an aerial bombardment in 1943) depicting the peace and prosperity that imperial rule had brought – he was attuned to the mood of the patriotic elite in northern Italy. In 1825–7, several years before Mazzini burst on the scene, he executed a double portrait of Filippo and Giacomo Ciani for their father, Baron Ciani, one of the wealthiest bankers in Milan. The brothers had been involved in the 1821 risings and had gone into exile in Switzerland, France and England. In the canvas they were shown as the Apostles Saint Philip and Saint James, dressed in red, white and green robes, sitting on a rock while 'on their travels, preaching'. In his memoirs Hayez said that he had wanted to suggest that the two men were missionaries who were endeavouring to 'convert the people into working to liberate their fatherland from the foreigner'.[40]

This sense of being apostles of a new faith influenced the mindset of the democrats strongly. They saw themselves as members of a tight-knit family and spoke of each other as 'brothers' and 'sisters' (and not as 'cousins' as the older sectarians did). Their correspondence was often pious in tone and full of fraternal sentiments, and a typical salutation was 'health and brotherhood'. If they quarrelled, as they very frequently did, they would nevertheless pull together in adversity, and they made a point of giving emotional and material support to those who were in trouble or to their relatives. Charity, selflessness and forgiveness were highly regarded qualities, as were honesty and frankness (though not of course to the police), disdain of money and worldly goods, and stoicism in the face of adversity. Suffering was viewed almost as a virtue in itself, and it found its supreme expression in a willingness to die for the cause. A number of the most famous democrats – among them the Bandiera brothers, Carlo Pisacane and Felice Orsini – effectively took their own lives by throwing themselves into hopeless ventures. Suffering was also linked to a vision of politics as struggle towards an ideal, and this attitude had as an important consequence a tendency to be permanently dissatisfied with the status quo and unwilling to compromise with it. After 1860 the democrats were to fuel a culture of disparagement of united Italy and a belief that the mission of the Risorgimento had still to be fought for.

The bonds between the democrats were strengthened by the fact that they came from similar backgrounds. Almost all (not surprisingly) were from landowning or urban middle-class families. A few, like the Sicilian revolutionary Rosalino Pilo, belonged to the aristocracy (mostly younger sons); a handful, among them the Sardinian firebrand Giorgio Asproni, had peasant origins. But class was not in itself particularly significant, and did little to determine friendships or alliances. And only occasionally (and usually as a result of contact with French socialist ideas) did democrats think of themselves and their politics in class terms: 'the people' was a much more potent category for them, by which they meant anyone in the nation who was politically aware. What was crucial to the formation of democrats was the cultural environment in which they had been brought up. Almost all belonged to families with Jacobin or liberal Napoleonic traditions, where talk around the table would have been of constitutions and Carbonari. And almost all were highly educated – often because they were shouldering the burden of family expectations of upward mobility.

The democrats might fall out over the means, but they all agreed (as did most moderates) in seeing the final goal as an independent, strong and united Italy. More problematic, though, was the extent to which 'freedom' should stand as a primary aim. Freedom from foreign rule, certainly; but internal political freedom presented serious difficulties given the ignorance of the mass of the population ('the plebs' as opposed to 'the people') and the anticipated strength of opposition that any new state would face from reactionary landowners and in particular the Church. The democrats all subscribed to popular sovereignty; but they also believed (as they had to in the absence of any empirical alternative) that the Italian nation had an existence that was prior to and independent of the will of the people. Accordingly they could argue that the rights of the individual might have to be sacrificed to the rights of the nation; and Mazzini's political theology, with its emphasis on the divine origin of nations, made this position easier to justify. Many democrats foresaw a period of dictatorship after unification had been achieved. How long this situation would last was inevitably not specified.

The main battleground for the democrats, and also the main source of division between them and the moderates, was over exactly how independence, strength and unity would be secured. Some, like Giuseppe Ferrari and Carlo Cattaneo, argued that Italy would only ever be strong if the historical reality of regional differences was recognized in a federal structure. Many others followed Mazzini in accepting that a centralized state was necessary precisely so as to minimize the weakness that local feelings would cause (though a degree of administrative autonomy was certainly possible). Supporters of republicanism claimed that national unity was incompatible with monarchy, given that princes only ever had the interests of their dynasties at heart and would not support 'the people' or oppose the Papacy. But some democrats, like Vincenzo Gioberti, broke with Mazzini over republicanism on the grounds not only that it was politically unrealistic but more importantly (and *pace* Sismondi) that it would resurrect the communal chaos of the Middle Ages and prevent Italy from emerging as 'one, strong, powerful, devoted to God, harmonious and at peace with itself'.[41]

These divisions in the democratic camp became more pronounced from the mid-1830s as rival organizations to Young Italy and Buonarroti's True Italians began to appear. In Naples, Giuseppe Ricciardi attempted to mobilize local radicals around a somewhat shadowy body called the Central Committee, while from his base on Malta the Modenese conspirator Nicola Fabrizi ran a paramilitary association known as the Italic Legion, which aimed to make the extreme south of the peninsula and Sicily the springboard for a national guerrilla war. In

Calabria, Benedetto Musolino, a young and highly idealistic intellectual, formed a secret society, the Sons of Young Italy, whose goal was a great military republic with a supreme dictator in Rome. Its members were armed with a carbine and dagger and wore black clothes like those of the local peasantry; and they had a flag: a white skull on a black background.[42] The great importance that Musolino attached to social and economic issues led Mazzini to dismiss him as a 'materialist' and a 'communist'. Musolino retaliated by describing Mazzini as a corrupt and sinister figure who was only interested in himself and not the poor.[43]

The problem that all these democrats faced was how to reach out beyond their various organizations to a wider audience. They could communicate with each other well – in some ways too well: they were generally prolific letter writers, eager to stay in close touch with the members of their friendship group and nervous about their standing with their peers and fearful of being cast out into the cold. Mazzini's surviving correspondence runs to some 10,000 letters, all of them written in a crabbed microscopic hand; but his total output was probably over 50,000. But communicating with the uneducated was quite a different issue: they spoke (very often literally) a different language. The aspiration of the democrats was to turn 'plebs' into 'people'. As the novelist and politician Guerrazzi put it: 'If a blacksmith . . . can write verses or prose, is a fine son, husband and father, has genuine love for his country, abhors any kind of tyranny, and shuns idiotic superstition, he is no longer plebs, but people.'[44] But to reach this situation, and so create the popular force needed to destroy the existing order and unite Italy, the masses would have to be receptive to the teachings of the democrats, and currently, precisely because they were 'plebs', they were not. Furthermore, until 'Italy' was made, the democrats would not have the political space required to tackle the task of education seriously. The paradoxes were well put by the leading Tuscan democrat, Giuseppe Montanelli, in the mid-1850s (criticizing Mazzini):

We needed freedom to educate the masses; we needed the masses to win freedom. In order to make the divided peoples of Italy conscious of their nationality they needed to be mixed up so that they formed a *de facto* Italian reality, and to achieve this *de facto* reality the peoples needed to feel they wanted it as a result of being conscious of their nationality. How were we to get an insurrection without the people? How could we have the people without having had an insurrection? The obsessive preachers who from their land of exile thought it right to cry out, 'If you wish to be free, rise up', sounded exactly like somebody saying to a sick man, 'If you want to get better, be cured.'[45]

THE DEATH OF THE
BANDIERA BROTHERS

In 1839 Mazzini set out to regain the conspiratorial initiative and re-launched Young Italy. He was concerned that the appearance of rival organizations would result in a dissipation of revolutionary energy; and with the outbreak of Chartist agitation in England he sensed that Europe might be about to enter a new phase of popular unrest. Southern Italy seemed a likely site for insurrection – a particularly brutal revolt, largely social and economic in character, had swept through Sicily in 1837 in the wake of a cholera epidemic – and Mazzini tried to persuade Nicola Fabrizi, the commander of the Italic Legion, to work with him in preparing a concerted plan of action. He was afraid that a southern rising might be too provincial – and too material – in focus; and he was particularly worried that an insurrection in Sicily would end up being directed towards the independence of the island and not of Italy. However, Fabrizi was less than enthusiastic about collaborating with Mazzini, and when minor revolts broke out in the Romagna in the spring of 1843 and in Calabria a year later, they owed rather more to the initiative of local conspirators than to Mazzini or Fabrizi.

The rising in Calabria centred on the remote and mountainous district of the Sila in the far south-west of the peninsula, an area long known for its lawlessness and banditry. It had been planned for some months with a number of liberals in Naples. At dawn on 15 March 1844 around a hundred armed men descended on the town of Cosenza waving a tricolour flag and shouting 'Long live liberty!' They sought to break into the palace of the provincial governor, but a posse of police appeared and shooting broke out, and the captain of the gendarmes (the son of a famous Neapolitan philosopher, Pasquale Galluppi) and four of the rebels, among them the leader, were killed. The remaining insurgents managed to flee, but in the days that followed dozens were rounded up, and under pressure from the government the courts handed down exemplary punishments. Nineteen conspirators were sentenced to death in public by firing squad. In concrete terms the rising had achieved nothing; but it had (and this was always one of the intentions) shown that Italians could act bravely ('better act and fail than do absolutely nothing,' said Mazzini).[46] It had also secured a lot of coverage abroad, especially in France and Britain, where the exile community did its best to ensure that the press reports were exaggerated. It was even suggested that the rebels had sparked off a general insurrection and that much of southern Italy was in arms.[47]

Among those who read these inflated newspaper accounts were two young Venetian noblemen and brothers, Attilio and Emilio Bandiera. They had founded a secret society called the Esperia in 1842 to spread Mazzinian ideas in the Austrian navy, but had fled abroad after being betrayed to the authorities, ending up on the island of Corfu. Here they fell in with an ardent republican from Forlì and member of Young Italy called Giuseppe Miller, who in the spring of 1844 convinced them that an armed expedition to Calabria stood a good chance of success. Eighteen other exiles were also persuaded to take part, most of them from the Romagna, the Marche and Emilia (including the splendidly named Anacarsi Nardi, a lawyer whose uncle had been 'dictator' of Modena during the 1831 revolution). There was also a Calabrian with a rather fearsome reputation called Giuseppe Meluso, a former seller of packed snow (hence his nickname, 'Snowy') who had taken refuge on Corfu and opened a bar there after having committed a murder. He agreed to accompany the expedition as a guide.

Dressed in military-style uniforms with red, white and green cockades, and armed with muskets, sabres and daggers, the twenty-one landed at night on a beach near Crotone on 16 June. As day broke a number of peasants came down to begin harvesting. They were understandably alarmed by the presence of this exotic band of 'foreigners',[48] and in a bid to reassure them and get their support Miller suggested that Attilio Bandiera should give them the jewel-encrusted sabre that he had been presented with by Sultan Abdul Majid as a reward for his part in the Syrian campaign of 1840. Bandiera thought this gesture excessive and instead handed over a Persian dagger, urging the locals to go and collect men and arms (which they would pay for) and telling them that they were honest men, not bandits. This did little to allay the peasants' suspicions, it seems. The rebels heard to their intense dismay that there was no insurrection in Calabria, and that foreign accounts of an insurgent force of 600 men up in the mountains were unfounded. After taking refuge in a wood a little inland they resolved to get a boat back to Corfu as quickly as possible. But they were worried about retracing their steps to the coast in case they had been reported to the police, and decided to cross over to the other side of the peninsula and embark there. On the evening of 17 June they set off and walked through the night. The next morning they discovered that one of their number, Pietro Boccheciampe, had gone missing.

Many Risorgimento accounts of key patriotic episodes – the Sicilian Vespers, the duel of Barletta, the siege of Florence – included a traitor in the narrative; not simply so as to provide added drama, but also to deflect blame from others, offer a clear-cut explanation for failure, and, by analogy with betrayals in popular folk tales, epics and Bible stories (most obviously that of Christ by Judas), to underline the heroism and saintliness of the protagonists. And Boccheciampe was cast in this role for the Bandiera expedition. Mazzini was later to be especially outspoken in his accusations of treachery.[49] But there is little to suggest that Boccheciampe deserved such vitriol. He had decided to give himself up to the authorities, and had gone to a café in Crotone, had a meal, paid for it, and then walked into the local governor's office. But he never compromised his companions by divulging the real purpose of the expedition; and the chief of police in Naples eventually got so frustrated with his reticence that he had wanted him sent back to Calabria to stand trial along with the others.[50]

Meanwhile the remaining band of twenty men approached San Giovanni in Fiore, a town high on the densely wooded Sila plateau cut off from the outside world for five months of the year by snow and dominated by the clergy and a handful of wealthy landowners. Among the latter was Domenico Pizzi, the commander of the local police guards, who summoned everyone to the main piazza, ordered the women into church to pray for the salvation of the king, armed the able-bodied men, priests included, and led them out to cries of 'Long live the King Our Lord. God save him!' They headed for Stragola, where the rebels had found an inn and fountain and were refreshing themselves and filling up their water bottles. On hearing the cries of the posse from San Giovanni they rushed out into a hail of bullets. Miller and another man were killed. Several others were wounded. A few escaped but surrendered later in Crotone. The remainder waved white handkerchiefs and were arrested without resistance. They were bound, robbed of their possessions (including 75,000 lire in gold they had brought to pay for the expedition), and led off to prison amid abuse and insults. The bodies of Miller and the other dead man were left to rot in the sun and their remains never found. The king rewarded the townspeople of San Giovanni for their great loyalty by handing out eighteen knighthoods, forty-three gold medals and eighty-six silver medals of the Royal Order of Francis I, pensions, and a blanket exemption from land and mill taxes (all of which caused some embarrassment after 1860).[51]

The trial of the remaining rebels was a foregone conclusion. The defence of the Bandiera brothers was that they had not committed treason, because they had come to Calabria believing reports they had heard in émigré circles that King Ferdinand was secretly planning to use the revolt in the south as a springboard for a campaign to unify Italy. Their expedition was thus intended to help, not overthrow, him. Rumours (quite unfounded) of Ferdinand's Italian ambitions had indeed been doing the rounds, but the judges surmised, no doubt correctly, that the rebels had not taken them seriously and were simply using them now to try to avoid the death penalty. Their case was not helped by a violently republican proclamation, found on Miller's body, which the Bandiera brothers had signed. In line with government instructions nine of the accused were sentenced to death by firing squad. Their bravery at the last was by all accounts exceptional and sealed their reputation as martyrs of the national cause, both in Italy and abroad, much to the annoyance (and alarm) of the authorities. As they were taken through the streets of Cosenza to the place of execution on the morning of 25 July 1844, bare-footed, dressed in black, their heads hooded, they sang in firm voices a chorus from Saverio Mercadante's opera *Donna Caritea*:

> Who dies for the fatherland
> Has lived long enough
> The leaves of the laurel
> Will never fade away
> Far better to perish
> In the prime of life
> Than languish for years
> Under a tyrant's yoke[52]

After the executions (at least according to an account by a follower of Mazzini), the humble people who had been watching collected the blood-soaked musket balls and divided locks of the victims' hair among themselves, 'as if they were sacred relics'.[53]

7

Educators and Reformers:
The Moderates

A confederation is the arrangement that is most suited to nature and the history of Italy. Italy, as Gioberti has rightly observed, includes, from north to south, provinces and peoples that are almost as different from one another as the most northerly and southerly peoples of Europe. Consequently, it always has been, and always will be, necessary to have a separate government for all, or almost all, of these provinces.

Cesare Balbo, *Delle speranze d'Italia* (1844)

Scene 2
The banks of the Euphrates

Hebrews (in chains, at forced labour)

Fly, thought, on wings of gold;
Go settle on the slopes and hills,
Where, soft and mild, the sweet airs
Of our native land smell fragrant! . . .
Oh my fatherland, so beautiful and lost,
Oh, remembrance so dear and so fraught with despair!

Giuseppe Verdi and Temistocle Solera, *Nabucco* (1842)

PROGRESS

By the early 1840s there was a growing sense everywhere that political and economic change was unstoppable. Georg Hegel's *Lectures on the Philosophy of World History*, published in 1840, proclaimed the inevitable progress of society towards greater subjective freedom, while in the same year Alexis de Tocqueville issued the second volume of his

144

study of *Democracy in America*, with its central premise that the world was moving remorselessly towards an era of the masses and egalitarianism. In England the Chartists were organizing huge demonstrations in favour of broader political representation, while the mood of nervous and at times almost apocalyptic optimism (epitomized in the utopian schemes of Charles Fourier and Robert Owen) was well caught by the young Alfred Tennyson in his 1842 poem 'Locksley Hall', with its 'vision of the world and all the wonder that would be', where airships thronged the skies with commercial traffic, steamships and railways acted as material counterparts to the 'march of mind', and 'the nations' airy navies' fought each other in the clouds, with 'the standards of the peoples plunging thro' the thunder storm', till universal and enduring peace was finally sealed 'in the Parliament of man, the Federation of the world'.[1]

In Italy the sensation that the pace of change was accelerating in Europe caused anxiety as well as excitement: conservatives were fearful of the political consequences, while the liberal-minded were worried that Italy might again miss its appointment with history and be left behind. By 1843 the small state of Belgium had more than 300 miles of railways: Italy had less than fifty. The manufacturing sector was showing signs of progress, with the silk and cotton mills of Lombardy and the textile and engineering workshops that the Bourbon government was promoting in Naples. But these developments were as nothing compared to the huge advances, quantitative and qualitative, taking place in Britain, Germany and France. Agriculture was a source of some pride, especially in Tuscany and parts of the north, but as a whole the sector was backward compared to most of northern Europe, with yields per hectare in the south of the peninsula barely one-tenth those in England.[2] The cultural gap was similarly broad. The Habsburgs had developed a good system of primary and secondary schools in Lombardy and the Veneto, but elsewhere the situation was dire. Associations were widely seen as a benchmark of modernity ('The need for associations to neutralize the individualism that works to undermine the bonds of society is one of the most important features of our age,' wrote a Venetian publicist in 1843),[3] but Italy was making little headway here, even in the major cities, and those societies that did exist were mostly just recreational circles for the aristocracy.[4]

Progress meant the dissemination of knowledge and new ideas, and in the years around 1840 there was a proliferation of journals in cities such as Palermo, Florence, Bologna and Milan devoted to the study of the economic, cultural and moral conditions of the peninsula. For some years liberal debate in Italy focused largely on Tuscany, where a group of enlightened landowners, led by Gian Pietro Vieusseux, had taken advantage of the relatively lax local censorship laws to produce such distinguished periodicals as the *Antologia*, the *Giornale agrario* and the *Guida dell'educatore*. Milan had also had an important forum of intellectual discussion in the *Annali universali di statistica, economia pubblica, storia, viaggi e commercio*, edited until his death in 1835 by the brilliant lawyer and philosopher Gian Domenico Romagnosi. Among the contributors to this publication was a young economist, Carlo Cattaneo, who in 1839 founded his own periodical, the *Politecnico*, arguably the most influential of the new crop of journals that did much to shape the cultural landscape of the educated classes in the decade leading up to the 1848 revolution.

Cattaneo was heir to the empirical and rationalist tradition of Pietro Verri and the Milanese Enlightenment, and he abhorred what he saw as the rhetorical and mystical excesses of much romantic nationalism. His patriotism was pragmatic and sober, and it was informed by the reassuring knowledge that he came from the most prosperous region of Italy (and indeed of the Austrian Empire). He believed progress should be gradual, and should take place if possible within the framework of the existing states, with governments being pressurized by informed public opinion into making reforms. The main architects of change were to be the urban middle classes, for it was principally through trade and industry that the cause of 'civilization' (as Cattaneo envisaged it) was advanced. Above all progress should be grounded in diversity, for history moved forward through the healthy and invigorating clash of competing ideas: 'Variety is life and inscrutable unity is death.'[5] Like many of his contemporaries, Cattaneo was an avid student of history; but while others saw the fragmentation of medieval Italy as having led to decadence, individualism and loss of independence, Cattaneo believed instead that the rivalry of the 'hundred cities' had resulted in the glories of commercial prosperity, well-planned streets and double-entry bookkeeping. Not surprisingly he was to become a passionate advocate of Italian federalism.

Academic debate was helping to create a national community (or 'society' to use Leopardi's term) for Italian intellectuals. And the process was furthered by the inauguration in 1839 of a series of annual congresses of Italian scientists to encourage reforms and the exchange of knowledge along the lines of similar initiatives in Britain and Germany. The first congress was held in Pisa with the blessing of Grand Duke Leopold, and attracted a good deal of hostility (the Pope banned his subjects from participating): only 421 scientists turned up, of whom about half were from Tuscany itself. But the ensuing congresses in Turin, Florence, Padua, Lucca, Milan and Naples were much better attended, with a peak of 1,613 registrations in 1845. The meetings took care to maintain a strictly academic profile: they concentrated on discussing specific economic and social issues and then took forward their work by setting up commissions to gather information. But it was hard to avoid patriotic inflections altogether. In Florence in 1841 the Marquis Cosimo Ridolfi could not refrain from winding up proceedings (in which the main theme had been the education of the rural masses) with an invitation to the delegates to go home and tell their compatriots 'that mountains and seas no longer exist . . . [and] that the various peoples now form a single family'.[6]

While economic arguments did not contribute significantly to the development of the national debate in Italy, the establishment of the German Zollverein (tariff union) in 1834 encouraged some discussion about the possible advantages of increased commercial integration in the peninsula. A leading Tuscan intellectual declared in 1843 that the future of Europe lay with countries that were 'great both politically and economically', and he called for a customs confederation to increase the 'wealth and power' of Italy.[7] The potential of the railways to promote economic progress also attracted attention, first in a study of 1845 by a leading Piedmontese economist, Count Ilarione Petitti di Roreto, and then, more provocatively (hence its publication in a French journal), in an essay the following year by the young Count Cavour. Cavour's arguments were only in part economic. An extensive railway network, he said, would bring in tourists who wanted 'distraction from the boredom fostered by the fogs of the north', and more importantly would make Italy into the fulcrum of international trade flowing between Europe and the East, and so enable it to 'regain the brilliant commercial position that she held throughout the Middle Ages'. But it was the moral and political benefits that most interested Cavour. The railways would further 'the progress of Christian civilization and the spread of enlightenment', and this would necessarily bring about 'the best possible future ... and one for which we long with all our heart ... namely the national independence of Italy'.[8]

Like many moderates at the time Cavour had no clear sense of how, or when, national independence would be secured, but he was adamant that it should be the result of peaceful and not revolutionary means. 'The people' needed to be educated morally, within the framework of the existing social and political order, not incited to violent action as Mazzini and his followers wanted. To this end enlightened conservatives in the 1830s and 1840s produced a steady stream of 'popular' journals, especially in regions such as Tuscany, Piedmont and Lombardy where a strong tradition of Catholic paternalism was accompanied by higher than average levels of literacy. Their aim was to promote good economic practices and a better lifestyle among the poor, encouraging the virtues of hard work, honesty and sobriety, and attacking superstition, poor hygiene and diet, and alcoholism. There was always the fear that any kind of instruction, however restrained and moral in tone, might undermine the docility of the masses and unleash demands for radical social and economic changes; but it was hoped that unrest could be avoided through the creation of strong bonds of mutual affection between employers and employees. And anyway, if nothing was done, the risk was that the field would be left open to the revolutionaries, and their gospel of redemption through a mass insurrection in the name of Italy might fall on receptive ears.

Most of these publications adopted the almanac style of popular literature that Benjamin Franklin had pioneered in the United States a century earlier. Practical information about feast days, local markets, lunar cycles, sowing and harvesting, of a kind that had long circulated in rural areas, was mixed with poems, stories and articles extolling the benefits of industry, self-reliance and religiosity. Some of the journals, such as Enrico Mayer's *Educatore del povero* (*Educator of the Poor*, 1833) in Tuscany and Lorenzo Valerio's *Letture popolari* (*Popular Reading Matter*, 1836) in Piedmont, apparently reached quite large audiences, at least among smallholders and artisans – though to what extent the political and social message was absorbed is another matter. Such publications certainly attracted more readers than Mazzini's forays into popular literature. *Giovine Italia* was only ever intended for the educated middle classes, but in 1833 Mazzini produced three numbers of a newspaper called *Insegnamenti popolari* (*Popular Teachings*), which employed the question and answer form of Catholic catechisms to try to get across his message about Italian unity and independence. But sixteen pages of abstractions about duties, rights and the glories of the nation were not calculated to strike a chord with most peasants and workers. He tried again in the early 1840s with the *Apostolato popolare*, this time placing the accent on the social gains a national revolution would bring, but again he had little success.[9]

Some of the pedagogic initiatives undertaken by the moderates aimed to be more enduring. In 1835 a commission headed by two of Florence's most eminent liberals awarded the first prize of 1,000 lire for a book to 'provide children with moral instruction as well as practice in reading' to a former Austrian censor from the Veneto, Luigi Alessandro Parravicini. His *Giannetto* (revealingly described as being 'for the use of children and the people') was to prove enormously successful and went through sixty-nine editions down to 1910.[10] Cesare Cantù and Giovanni Prati, both from Lombardy, were prolific patriotic authors of prose and verse works intended for largely popular audiences in which the virtues of rural life, work, resignation and love of one's fellow men were celebrated. Paternalism was a major theme in the fiction of Caterina Percoto, 'the peasant countess', a strong-minded woman who ran the family estates in Friuli, smoked pipes and large cigars and from 1844 produced a string of highly regarded stories about the local peasantry, in which the sufferings of the main characters are always relieved with the intervention of a benefactor or virtuous priest.[11]

The printed word was bound to have limited impact in a society where there was so much illiteracy, and some moderates preferred more visual media to try to bridge the gap to the masses. One such was Niccolò Puccini, an energetic Tuscan landowner and patron of the arts, who from 1824 used his considerable fortune to turn his eighteenth-century villa at Scornio near Pistoia into a beacon of patriotism and a meeting point for the educated elite and the working classes. The famous gardens – which were open to the public – were an eclectic celebration of Italy's past glories and an exhortation to its future greatness. Set amid avenues of trees, in bowers, small piazzas and temples, were statues of distinguished figures, including Dante, Columbus, Raphael, Machiavelli,

Michelangelo, Tasso, Galileo, Muratori, Vico, Alfieri, Botta and Canova. A mock-Gothic castle (intended as a reminder of how the Italian republics had built fortresses to defend themselves against foreign oppressors)[12] housed memorials to such 'Italian' warriors as Castruccio Castracani, Carmagnola and Giovanni delle Bande Nere, while outside on a column stood a large statue of Francesco Ferruccio fighting his last battle. The main building was a Pantheon dedicated to 'illustrious men', containing the busts of fourteen eminent Italians (among them Napoleon) and an empty niche reserved for 'the future benefactor of Italy'. On the wall Puccini placed an inscription warning any Italian who did not 'tremble with vendetta and love for Italy' as he passed through the temple that he would be 'cursed on the day of its glory' and deprived of the 'sanctifying robe of citizen'.

Puccini was a close friend of many leading Italian patriots of the 1830s and 1840s, and among those who came to his villa were Guerrazzi, Vieusseux, Gioberti, Leopardi and Botta. On 25 June 1836, the anniversary of the Peace of Constance in 1183 between the emperor Frederick Barbarossa and the cities of northern Italy, he was host to the elderly Sismondi, who wandered around the garden, inspecting the statues, reading the inscriptions and chatting to the distinguished playwright Giovanni Battista Niccolini, while crowds of admirers cheered 'the historian of our Italian republics'.[13] Like Sismondi, Puccini was keen to highlight episodes from Italy's past that could serve as inspiration for the present generation, and among the numerous paintings he commissioned were works depicting the sixteenth-century Florentine republican leader and martyr Niccolò dei Lapi (which the artist and writer Massimo d'Azeglio promised him, but never delivered), the death of Ferruccio, the Sicilian Vespers, the revolt of the Genoese against the Austrians in 1746 (in which the instigator of the rising, the boy 'Balilla', is seen urging the frenzied mob forward like Delacroix's *Liberty Leading the People*), and the death of Filippo Strozzi (to show 'how a beautiful death can cancel out a life of infamy').[14] Puccini's pictures (and the monuments in his garden) were often reproduced as engravings and widely circulated.[15]

Puccini devoted huge amounts of energy to his friendships with the liberal intelligentsia, but he also found time for other initiatives. He promoted public works in the Pistoia area to improve agriculture, set up welfare institutes, and took a particularly keen interest in education, establishing a school in the grounds of his estate to provide free instruction for local poor children (with a characteristically strong emphasis on religious and moral teaching). In 1842 he launched a series of carefully choreographed annual fairs called the Festivals of the Ears of Wheat, held in the garden of his villa, which brought together peasants and landowners in a mutual celebration of the harvest. The first day was devoted to sermons by priests, extolling the joys of work, family life and agriculture, while the second and third had a more bucolic tone, with games, music, singing, eating and drinking, and the awarding of prizes to the most successful farmers.[16] There were also lectures by guest speakers. In 1846 the distinguished Sicilian exile Giuseppe La Farina gave a passionate address on how the future progress of humanity depended on the moral elevation of the people:

Oh! The masses are worth far more than those that calumny them think! Speak to them of the fatherland, of religion, and their hearts will swell with generous feelings. But who is to blame if the border of their fatherland is the hedge that girds their plot of land or at best the cross that marks the end of their village, if they often feel that justice and prejudice are the same thing, and if religion dissolves for them into a chaos of materialism, superstition and errors? Who is to blame?[17]

The turbulent events of 1848–9 and the collapse of the hopes of a national revolution were to leave Puccini deeply disillusioned. The Festival of the Ears of Wheat was allowed to lapse, and Puccini withdrew into the world of art and literature and comforted himself with memories of Italy's former glories. He spent the summer of 1851 at Gavinana, the small town in the hills high above Pistoia where in 1530 Francesco Ferruccio had fought his last battle trying in vain to defend the Florentine republic. The following year he died.[18] In the 1860s his villa and gardens were sold off and soon fell into ruins, and his art collection was scattered. As a final humiliation a railway, the ultimate symbol of nineteenth-century materialism, was driven through what remained of the estate. By the end of his life Puccini had grown pessimistic about the potential of the people for virtue, and his pessimism was shared by many moderates and became an important point of difference between them and the democrats. As the Tuscan democrat Francesco Guerrazzi told Puccini in September 1848:

You have no faith in the masses and you are wrong . . . When I think about the masses I am always reminded of that charming picture of Albano, of Love riding a lion and playing a lyre to spur him on. Certainly much thought and much chiselwork will be necessary to sculpt this marble to perfection; but one day a god will spring from it.[19]

OPERA

One of the most potent vehicles for the spread of the national idea in the early 1840s was music. Opera was a passion throughout Italy, and attracted all classes, and the evening performances of the latest works by Donizetti, Mercadante or Ricci were the only occasions on which the authorities would regularly permit the public to manifest collective feelings. Theatres were microcosms of urban society. The boxes belonged to the aristocracy, and, like salons, had a strong female presence. The stalls resembled the piazza: almost exclusively male, and thronged with students, soldiers, merchants and middle-class professionals. At the top, in the gods, almost out of sight, were the poorer classes: the artisans, small traders, shopkeepers and servants. The noise and bustle were constant, and there was no sign of the reverential silence that was starting to become the norm at symphony concerts in northern Europe. The German composer Otto Nicolai was shocked to find that the music and singing were almost drowned out by the chatter, while Berlioz observed how members of the audience argued and shouted and clattered their sticks on the ground as freely as if they were on the stock exchange.[20]

The Restoration governments had been keen to encourage opera- and theatre-going, and more than 600 new playhouses were built in Italy in the decades after 1815, mainly in the north and centre. The motive was partly civic, a continuation of the Napoleonic idea that public entertainment was a good way of fostering social ties in a controlled environment, and also of keeping young men off the streets and out of the taverns at night.[21] The censors made sure that the works contained no subversive material, while the police patrolled the stalls and upper galleries to prevent disorder. Moreover the fact that the main theatres were usually dedicated to members of the royal family and were patronized by the ruler and his court was seen as politically beneficial: the prince united with his subjects in pleasure. The problem was that an environment that encouraged displays of public loyalty and obedience when times were good, might just as easily in a less favourable climate become a forum for protest.

Such an inversion occurred in the 1840s, when the growing mood of confident and assertive patriotism in Italy was perfectly caught by the young Giuseppe Verdi. There is not much to suggest that Verdi himself felt very strongly about 'Italy' – his main attachment all his life was to the dull flat farmland around the village of Busseto near Parma, where he had been born in 1813 (technically, at that time, a French citizen) – but he and his publishers had an acute sense of what the public wanted and were accordingly wily in the strategies they used to try to circumvent the censors. *Nabucco* (1842), with its theme of an enslaved people yearning for freedom and its great patriotic chorus of 'Va pensiero' ('Oh my fatherland, so beautiful and lost'), was spared the blue pencil partly by being given a 'safe' religious setting; and the same probably also applied to Verdi's next, and almost equally successful, opera, *I Lombardi alla prima crociata* (*The Lombards on the First Crusade*, 1843), which he dedicated to Maria Luisa of Austria, perhaps to make doubly sure that he was not thought to be subversive.[22] In the case of *Ernani* (1844) the seemingly inflammatory story of a band of high-minded conspirators setting out to assassinate Charles V ('We are all one single family ... unavenged and neglected slaves we will be no longer') was carefully tempered by portraying the emperor as a magnanimous and noble figure.[23]

It was not always easy to predict what the censors would or would not allow. One problem was regional variations: Naples and Rome tended to be more stringent than Lombardy and Tuscany, especially when it came to issues of religion. Sometimes an opera would be permitted if it was transposed. Thus Rossini's last and only seriously political opera, *William Tell* (1829), which he wrote for the French stage, could only ever be performed in Italy in a cut version set in Scotland and called *Rudolph of Stirling*.[24] Verdi's *Giovanna d'Arco* (*Joan of Arc*, 1845) was problematic on two counts: first, its heroine was officially a heretic, and second, it dealt with a people (the French) fighting for freedom against a foreign oppressor (the English). In much of Italy it had to be relocated to fifteenth century Greece with a heroine called Orietta of Lesbos. Sometimes the problem was not so much the censors as the local theatre directors and their sensibilities. Thus the nobles on the executive committee of La Fenice in Venice refused to première Verdi's 1844 opera *I due Foscari* on the grounds that it showed two of their fifteenth-century predecessors in an unfavourable light.[25]

An important feature of Verdi's early operas – which both reflected and fed the charged political climate of the mid-1840s – was their novel use of the chorus. In an essay of 1836 Mazzini had lamented the lack of truly passionate and spiritual music in Italy that would further the 'religious and national education of the masses' and inspire young men to take up arms (Donizetti had made a start with *Marino Faliero*, he said; but Rossini had simply portrayed 'man without God'); and he suggested that composers should elevate the operatic chorus from its present largely passive role into a dynamic embodiment of 'the people', united, spontaneous and assertive.[26] It is not known if Verdi was aware of Mazzini's ideas, but the chorus certainly assumed an increasingly central position in his work from *Nabucco* to *La Battaglia di Legnano* (1849), with the theme of popular struggle for freedom at the heart of the most successful of them – even *Macbeth*, where the main adversaries of the king and his wife are the chorus of Scottish men, women and children rather than Macduff.[27]

But what made operas such a powerful vehicle for the diffusion of national feelings in the 1840s was not so much the intentions of composers as the willingness of audiences (or sections of them) to impose political readings on librettos and turn performances into occasions for patriotic demonstrations. And there was little the censors could do about this situation, especially in 1846–8 when governments everywhere in Italy were being forced to bow before a tidal wave of liberal euphoria. Already at the first performance of *I Lombardi* in 1843 the line with which the crusaders were incited to battle against the infidel – 'Today the Holy Land will be ours' – was greeted with cries of 'Yes! Yes!' and loud cheering. And virtually any allusion to 'the fatherland' or 'war' in the mid-1840s risked triggering similar responses, even in works that had not previously been seen as political – as with Bellini's *Norma* (1831), which in 1846–7 suddenly became a 'patriotic' work (and in particular its Druid chorus of 'War! War!'), despite the fact that the oppressors were Romans. On occasions enthusiasm could spill out of the opera house onto the streets (probably with prior planning), as happened in Palermo in November 1847, when an aria containing the words 'you deprived me of heart and mind, fatherland, gods and liberty' in Donizetti's *Gemma di Vergy* (1834) provoked a storm of applause and violent clashes with the police. The censors had probably overlooked the line because the context was one of love, jealousy and revenge, and on the face of it not remotely political.[28]

MODERATE PROGRAMMES

Until 1843 the moderates lacked a clear programme to pit against Mazzini and the democrats, but in that year Vincenzo Gioberti published in Brussels a prolix hymn to Italian intellectual and spiritual superiority called *On the Moral and Civil Primacy of the Italians*. It proved an astonishing success, despite being banned in parts of Italy, selling 80,000 copies in five years. In a thousand pages of dense adjectival prose Gioberti ranged over centuries of cultural and religious life in Italy, which demonstrated, he said, how the peninsula had been ordained to dominate the world through the power of its moral leadership. The impact of the book was as much psychological as political. As the Neapolitan liberal Luigi Settembrini recalled:

We were slaves, divided, shattered, scorned by foreigners who said we were a decadent race and that Italy was a land of the dead . . . And we too saw ourselves as inferior to everyone else, having over centuries of wretched servitude lost all sense of our own being. This man then says: 'You Italians are the world's leading people.' 'We Italians?' 'Yes, you have civil and moral primacy over everyone' . . . The effect of the book was extraordinary, and raised the spirits of a prostrate people.[29]

At one level the book was a total repudiation of Mazzini. Gioberti suggested that independence should be secured not through a popular revolution and a republic, but by making the existing Italian states into a federation under the presidency of the Pope. And while Mazzini regarded the papacy as an insurmountable obstacle to Italy's rebirth, Gioberti saw it as integral to the nation's identity, its chief glory, and a guarantee of its future greatness. But Gioberti's differences with Mazzini were less pronounced than at first sight appeared. Both saw the moral resurrection of Italy as their supreme goal; both wanted the new nation to be powerful and independent, and no longer culturally and politically subservient to other countries, above all France; and both saw a resplendent and regenerate Rome as the acme of their dreams. What principally divided them were the means for achieving the regeneration. Gioberti considered the Italian 'people' a mere abstraction, 'a desire and not a fact', and it was pointless to imagine they could somehow be conjured into being overnight and used as a basis for unification. Italy was united by religion and a common written language, but divided by 'governments, laws, institutions, dialects, customs, feelings and practices', and any programme of moral revival had to start from this harsh empirical reality.

But the appeal of Gioberti's book was not just that it offered a conservative model of Italian unification: the princes, under his programme, would keep most of their absolutist powers, diluted only by local consultative bodies and a central Diet to decide on national issues.[30] It was also and quite deliberately mythopoeic, an attempt to shake Italians from their lethargy by 'stirring their imaginations, inflaming their hearts, entrancing their spirits with the beauty and magnificence of the picture that I set before them'.[31] Gioberti firmly believed that political redemption could only come about after moral redemption had been achieved; and the starting point for moral redemption was to make Italians aware of what they had once been, and thus who they were today: 'Italy cannot be resurrected to new life unless it searches for the seeds within itself; and its modern form must arise out of its past, and be its own and national.'[32] Hence his celebration of Italy's glorious intellectual and cultural traditions and his assertion that these were historically quite inseparable from the papacy and Rome.

Underpinning this vision of Italy's past was a suggestion of ethnic continuity. Like Vico and Cuoco, Gioberti claimed a remote origin for the Italian nation; but in contrast to their secular classicism Gioberti preferred a foundation story that was rooted in the Bible, thereby reinforcing his notion that the Italians were a chosen people. Italy, he said, had begun with the 'Pelasgians', a population descended from Japhet, son of Noah, which had colonized the central regions of Italy and given rise to the Etruscan, Roman and Italian civilizations. The defining characteristic of this 'race' (*stirpe*) was energy, as was suggested by the ancient name for Italy, 'Vitellia', or 'land of bulls'. Three times in the course of world history the Italians had shown their exceptional 'creative potency': under the Romans (politically and militarily), with the papacy (spiritually), and during the Renaissance (culturally). Now, however, the natural 'virile sexuality' of the Italians had become wasted. In recent centuries Italy had been 'feminized by lax education, leisure and softness', and was treated as a 'woman', 'honoured by poets ... but in reality walked over and regarded as a cipher'. Gioberti's aim was to rekindle in his fellow countrymen a desire for assertion and dominance.[33]

On the face of it Gioberti's programme stood little chance of success. The general assumption among patriots had always been that the papacy would never back such a dangerously modern and progressive idea as Italian national unification; and certainly, in 1843, the 78-year-old Pope Gregory XVI seemed far too reactionary to have any truck with the views of an exiled priest who had once flirted with Young Italy. But the possibility of the Church taking up the cause of progress did not seem totally far-fetched. Inspired by the likes of Lamennais and Montalembert in France, a number of Italian intellectuals had since the 1820s been trying to reconcile liberty with Catholicism, among them the writer Alessandro Manzoni and the philosopher Antonio Rosmini. In 1835 a well-known scholar from Dalmatia, Niccolò Tommaseo, had published (in Paris) an important book calling for the liberation of Italy by the people in the name of a new evangelical and democratic Catholicism. In the field of history various so-called 'neo-Guelph' studies by the Neapolitan Carlo Troya and others had appeared, in which the medieval papacy had been depicted as the heroic defender of 'the freedom of Italy' against efforts by the German emperors to crush the communes.

One of the most important of these neo-Guelph historians was Cesare Balbo, a Piedmontese aristocrat and former Napoleonic official, who had spent the 1820s in exile for his liberal views. Like many of his background and generation Balbo cared deeply about Italian independence and even more passionately about Piedmont and its monarchy, and when *On the Moral and Civil Primacy of the Italians* appeared, his cousin, Massimo d'Azeglio, urged him to go into print with his own thoughts on the subject of Italy. This he duly did, and in 1844 his book *On the Hopes of Italy (Delle speranze d'Italia)* appeared, dedicated to Gioberti. It was a work that proved, if anything, to be even more successful than Gioberti's, though its popularity was probably due less to its contents, which were neither very hopeful nor particularly original, than to its succinct and upbeat title. Indeed, the satirical press dubbed

Balbo's book, and not without some justification, *On the Despair of Italy* (*Della disperazione d'Italia*).[34]

Even more than Gioberti, Balbo considered Italy totally unfitted yet for real unity, and he dismissed Mazzini's views as 'puerile' and contrary to history and to common sense. The sixteenth and seventeenth centuries had been times of terrible decadence, and while Italians (and the Piedmontese in particular) had made some advances in the eighteenth century 'in industriousness, civic virtue, national sentiment and the desire for independence', there was still a long way to go. Laziness was the most prevalent national vice – a consequence of the climate and years of despotic rule – and Italians needed to look abroad and gradually learn lessons from the 'Christian progress' made by other countries. Gioberti's idea of an outright Italian primacy was accordingly unrealistic, and it made more sense (and here, ironically, he was echoing Mazzini) to think of 'multiple primacies', with one nation taking the lead in industry, another in science, another in African colonies, and so on. Italy could recover its old eminence in the arts or in Mediterranean trade, but its supreme mission would always be to protect and glorify the papacy. But to achieve this position, it needed to be fully independent; and since it was impossible for any kind of insurrection to succeed, given the inability of Italians to work together successfully, and since, too, the princes were unlikely to cooperate with each other effectively, the best hope lay with international diplomacy.[35] Balbo's suggestion (and it was by no means a new one)[36] was that Austria might eventually be persuaded to give up its possessions in Italy in exchange for territories in eastern Europe taken from the disintegrating Ottoman empire.[37]

The obvious beneficiary of Austria's withdrawal from Lombardy–Venetia would be Piedmont, and one reason why Balbo's book was so important was because it indicated just how easily Italian independence could be squared with the old dynastic ambitions of the House of Savoy to dominate northern Italy. And Balbo provided further encouragement for this line of thought in his extended discussion of how Italians could be made 'virtuous'; for while diplomacy might remove the Austrians from the peninsula, the only way that Italians could remain independent in the long run was if they recovered the outstanding civil qualities (*virtù*) they had possessed in the twelfth century ('I can sum up all I have written ... in two words: one single goal, INDEPENDENCE; one single means, VIRTUE').[38] In particular they needed to learn once again how to fight, as the best remedy for the 'effeminacy', 'weakness' and 'corruption' that had taken hold of the Italian character as a result of prolonged peace and sedentary living was military training. And who better to educate Italians to martial virtue than the most military people in the peninsula, namely the Piedmontese?[39]

While Gioberti's book unleashed a fierce debate among Catholics about whether an institution as universal and timeless as the Church should identify itself with such a narrowly political and ephemeral issue as the Italian national question, Balbo's work helped to train attention on Piedmont. For many years this small state in the north-west of Italy had been doggedly reactionary, and its king, Carlo Alberto (who had succeeded his cousin, Carlo Felice, after the latter's death in 1831), had shown little inclination to break with the obscurantist traditions of his forebears. By temperament austere and almost insufferably religious (he would often turn up at court dinners flanked by two Jesuits for company), he made sure that throne and altar were kept bound together in a tight alliance. Ecclesiastical courts and religious censorship continued to operate, and writers such as Machiavelli and words such as 'nation', 'revolution', 'liberty' and even 'Italy' remained banned. But from the late 1830s the situation began to change. Under pressure from public opinion, the last vestiges of feudalism were abolished, new penal and civil codes were promulgated, and attempts were made to modernize the economy by reducing tariffs and promoting trade. As a result silk, cotton and wool manufacturing expanded fast, and by the mid-1840s Piedmont was emerging as a serious rival to Lombardy in terms of its general prosperity.

But what was crucial about Piedmont from the point of view of Italian independence was that it had an army. Piedmont was a buffer state wedged between France and Austria whose security had always been of paramount concern to its rulers, and with the development of the road (and rail) network in northern Italy the threat from Lombardy in particular was growing. Nearly half of total government spending went on defence from the early 1830s, and as a result of reforms the size of the army, reservists included, was gradually raised to around 150,000 men by the mid-1840s. In terms of training and equipment these Piedmontese forces were impressive. They were also loyal: after the threatened coup in 1833 Carlo Alberto took care to foster the cult of the monarchy within the army, creating among the officer ranks especially what one senior general described as a 'veritable adoration' of the royal family.[40] The only other state in Italy with substantial military forces (around 80,000) was Naples, but while technically good, they had none of Piedmont's fierce devotion to the ruling dynasty.

The pressure on Carlo Alberto began to mount. In the summer of 1845 one of the most distinguished Piedmontese aristocrats, Massimo d'Azeglio, broke off writing his latest historical novel (about the Lombard League in the twelfth century: 'the most beautiful and radiant period in our history')[41] to become actively involved in politics. He made a secret tour of the Romagna, talking to sectarians about their hopes for radical change in the Papal States now that Gregory XVI's pontificate was nearing its end, their disillusionment with conspiracy, and their dreams of possible Piedmontese help. On his return to Turin d'Azeglio had an audience with Carlo Alberto, and to his astonishment the king expressed a willingness to give his support: 'Let those gentlemen know that they should wait quietly and take no action, since as yet nothing can be achieved: but let them also know that when occasion offers, my life, the lives of my sons, my arms, my treasure, my armies – all will be spent in the Italian cause.'[42] A few months later d'Azeglio turned the heat up further with a brilliant pamphlet entitled *On the Recent Events in the Romagna* (dedicated to Cesare Balbo), a searing denunciation of the brutality and backwardness of papal government, in which he called for a halt to all attempts at popular insurrection – they stood no chance of success given the almost complete absence of 'civil education' among the masses – and instead urged right-minded Italians to embark on a vigorous campaign of peaceful protest ('conspiracy in the broad light of day') that would raise awareness at home and abroad of their oppression and of their firm desire to be liberated from foreign rule.[43]

Amid all the discussion about independence and how to expel the Austrians from Italy, issues of constitutions, representative government and individual rights took a back seat. In part this omission was practical. 'First independence, then liberty: first I want to live; afterwards I will think of how to live well,' said Giorgio Pallavicino-Trivulzio;[44] and his pragmatism was shared by many in both the moderate and democratic camps. But the failure to address questions of internal freedom betrayed more than just a fear of provoking serious rifts and fracturing the national forces before unification had been achieved. There was also a sense that 'nation' and 'freedom' could not in Italy's case automatically be combined, because national sentiment was still very rudimentary and representative institutions risked producing a babel of voices urging private, sectional or municipal interests that would make coherent government impossible. The 'nation' had to be imposed; it could not as yet easily be linked to the defence of personal interests and rights as most Italians understood them. There was also the spectre of history to contend with. Memories of the licentiousness unleashed by the Jacobin experiments of 1796–9 and of the chaos of the city-states during the Middle Ages hovered over the idea of 'freedom'. Indeed, one reason why Italian liberals were to have so many problems coming to terms with the practice of parliamentary government both before and after 1860 was because parties were often seen as synonymous with the factions and sects that had so bedevilled the course of Italian history.[45] Nation implied concord; freedom almost suggested its antithesis.

These considerations, as much as a concern not to alienate the existing absolutist rulers in Italy, was why moderate writers such as Gioberti suggested that constitutional reform should be limited to consultative assemblies of 'men of truly outstanding character'.[46] And although the democrats were generally more interested in practical arrangements for safeguarding political freedoms, they too tended to focus on the revolution to win independence and unity and not on what might come after it ('to tell you the truth, I am not really fussed about matters of internal liberty, administration and laws,' Mazzini confessed to a friend in 1861).[47] Those liberals who did show an interest in constitutional problems had often developed their ideas as a result of engagement in debates and polemics while in exile or travelling abroad, particularly in France and Britain. But most of them accepted that the application of liberal constitutional government to Italy would be bedevilled by major practical difficulties.

One such was Giacomo Durando, a distinguished Piedmontese officer who had spent much of the 1830s fighting in the Carlist wars in Spain and witnessing at first hand the catastrophic regional tensions in that country. In 1846 he published a major study of the national question in Italy, arguing that the peninsula was much too diverse still to be pushed into a single political straitjacket. He suggested, on geo-strategic grounds, that it should be allowed to evolve into two federated states, one in the north ('Eridania') and one in the south ('Apennine'), with the papacy having control of Rome and perhaps of Sicily and Sardinia, too; but he stressed how important it was to compensate the 'sub-nationalities' of Lombardy–Venetia, Parma, Modena and the Romagna for their incorporation into an eventual enlarged Piedmontese kingdom by setting up representative institutions. Otherwise they would feel that they had simply 'exchanged being garrisoned by soldiers in white uniforms for soldiers in blue'.[48] For many observers, though, such an arrangement ran the risk of perpetuating or even fuelling the very divisions that had hindered the development of national sentiment – a sentiment that was arguably itself indispensable to any successful federalism. The conundrum of how to combine unity with freedom in Italy was clearly difficult. The revolutions of 1848–9 were to underline, brutally, just how difficult.

PART THREE

Poetry
1846–60

8

Revolution, 1846–9

If you return, I beg you, be the last to do so. We endure this harsh separation patiently: but honour and duty are preferable to everything else . . . If I followed my affections alone I would summon you back instantly to my side . . . But it is not for nothing that I have long made it my life's work to love Italy with faith, and to sacrifice everything to duty. Do not think that I love you the less for not asking you to return . . . But this is a time for sacrifices, and I find in sacrifices a melancholy and most holy delight.

Caterina Franceschi Ferrucci writing to her husband and son, volunteers in the Tuscan Battalion stationed in Brescia, from Pisa, 14 June 1848

We, though unworthy, represent on Earth Him who is the author of peace and the lover of charity, and Our Supreme Apostolate obliges us to love with equal paternal affection all peoples and all nations . . . We must reject the insinuations . . . of those who would wish the Roman Pontiff to be President of some new Republic to be created by all the peoples of Italy together. On the contrary . . . we passionately exhort [the peoples of Italy] . . . to remain faithful to their Princes . . . Were they to act otherwise, they would not only be failing in their personal duty, but would also run the risk of Italy ending up divided by discord and internecine factions. Allocution of Pope Pius IX, 29 April 1848

'O SOMMO PIO'

On 16 June 1846, after a conclave lasting just two days, Giovanni Maria Mastai-Ferretti, bishop of Imola, was elected Pope and took the name of Pius IX. The election had been rushed partly out of fear that sectarians might take advantage of a lengthy interregnum to launch another rising in the Romagna. The new pope had been a compromise candidate and was something of an unknown quantity. He came from an aristocratic family in the Marche and had a reputation for amiability and good works, but as bishop he had kept a low political profile, and had avoided taking sides publicly with either liberals or conservatives on the issue of reforms in the Papal States. His elevation to the throne of St Peter accordingly received a rather muted reception. But a month later he issued an amnesty for political prisoners – a not unusual act for a new pope, but one which in the febrile political climate of the time resulted in an extraordinary explosion of excitement. On the evening of 17 July crowds swarmed into the piazza in front of the Quirinal Palace. As the democrat Giuseppe Montanelli recalled:

At that solemn hour, as if between two firmaments – between the brilliant stars of a summer sky and the thousands of torches blazing in the huge piazza – we saw the Pope come out onto his balcony dressed in a white tunic to address the vast and prostrate multitude. The spirits of those present dissolved into an ocean of love; and every face was etched with intense emotion; and for the first time the cry was heard that was later to accompany popular insurrections: 'Long live Pius IX.'[1]

That evening of 17 July 1846 was for Montanelli an epiphany. A young and idealistic professor of law at the university of Pisa, strongly influenced, like Mazzini, by Saint-Simon, he had for some time been racked by the problem of how to draw the masses emotionally into the campaign for Italian unity and independence. Suddenly with the election of Pius IX such an involvement seemed possible, for whatever Pius may have felt or believed in private, there was every reason to imagine now that a frenzy of popular enthusiasm could sweep the pontiff ineluctably down the path of reform, injecting the national cause with religious fervour. Gioberti's vision of Italy and the papacy rising together in unison, like phoenixes, gloriously regenerate from the ashes of their decadent pasts, appeared more than just an intellectual fantasy:

The utopia of a reforming papacy opened up before me as a marvellous prospect ... An Italian, I at last saw the scattered limbs of my nation reunited in a single body, a body whose soul was in Rome, and whose capital was capital not just of Italy but of the whole of Christianity. In this way Italy would once again occupy the first seat in Europe, and would emerge as the high-priestess of nations ...[2]

The excitement generated by Pius' amnesty spread swiftly through the Papal States – and beyond – and jubilant crowds poured into the streets to applaud the new pope. Special performances were staged of Verdi's *Ernani*, with the opening words of Charles V's aria of tribute to Charlemagne in the third act changed from 'O sommo Carlo' to 'O sommo Pio' ('O, supreme Pius'), and with the conveniently appropriate line 'perdono a tutti' ('pardon to all') eliciting wild cheering and cries of 'Evviva'.[3] In the months that followed the sense of anticipation was kept simmering, as Pius, quite unprepared for the furore that his election had generated, and caught between liberal and conservative factions within the Vatican, nervously edged his way forward with liberal reforms. In November he set up special commissions to examine the judiciary, education and the economy and confirmed plans to build a rail network linking Rome to the outside world, while the following spring he relaxed the censorship laws and established a governmental consultative assembly, with representatives drawn from across the Papal States. Such was the continuing air of expectation around Pius that in September 1847 Mazzini wrote to him and urged him to assume the lead in uniting Italy ('with you at its head ... the struggle would take on a religious aspect and free us from many risks of reaction and civil war'),[4] and a few weeks later another erstwhile enemy of the papacy and Catholicism, Giuseppe Garibaldi, offered his services and those of his Italian Legion to 'the man who serves the Church and the fatherland so well'.[5]

The atmosphere in Italy throughout 1847 was tense and unsettled. As in other parts of Europe, the agricultural sector was in serious crisis. The poor harvests of 1846 had been followed by catastrophic crop failures and widespread famine, and as food became scarce, prices rose and armies of starving peasants drifted into the cities. Industry, too, was facing severe difficulties, as overproduction caused factories to close and unemployment to increase. Everywhere public order was under threat, and there were frequent riots and demonstrations; and even without the example of the Pope to contend with, governments would have faced enormous pressure to introduce reforms. Tariff barriers were lowered and demands for free trade grew (flush from his victory over the Corn Laws in Britain, Richard Cobden toured Italy triumphantly in the spring of 1847); and in November the Papal States, Tuscany and Piedmont signed a preliminary agreement on a customs league, similar to the Customs Union that had been established by various German states in 1834. Press laws were relaxed and steps were taken to liberalize the judiciary, the police and public administration – even in Piedmont, where a new local government law in the autumn allowed for elected town councils.

Amid the unrest, moderates and democrats jockeyed for position. Like many observers Mazzini sensed that revolution was brewing throughout Europe, and while his supporters on the ground in Italy – young men, often students, who flaunted their radicalism by openly defying government strictures on facial hair with thick beards 'Ernani style' and flowing 'Nazarene' locks[6] – formed secret 'committees', wrote inflammatory pamphlets, and agitated on the streets, he himself worked from his base in London to focus public opinion on the national question and on the need to expel the Austrians from the peninsula. Many moderates, on the other hand, feared that the mounting chaos would spiral out of control and end in a bacchanal of popular terror, as in the 1790s, and their goal was to keep the turmoil in constitutional channels by ensuring that governments pressed ahead with the necessary reforms. In July Massimo d'Azeglio published a pamphlet calling on the princes of Italy to work together in a 'tight union', move towards a common political programme, and draw behind them all the 'progressive moderates', who were now so numerous as to form 'Italian national opinion'.[7]

But the chances of keeping the unrest peaceful and reformist looked slim. The Austrian Chancellor Metternich showed no willingness to pander to Italian patriotic feelings. In April he referred to Italy dismissively as simply a 'geographical expression', and when in July he sent troops across the Po to garrison Ferrara in the Papal States (as he was entitled to do under the Treaty of Vienna), the response was a wave of ugly demonstrations in many cities with anti-Austrian chanting and tricolour flags. Early in September the mood of growing belligerence in the peninsula reached new heights following the brutal suppression of an attempted rising in southern Italy and clashes in Milan between the Austrian police and crowds celebrating the arrival of a new Italian archbishop in the city. Tuscany, the most liberal of the Italian states, saw the largest outpourings of patriotic fervour. A huge rally was held in Florence on 12 September in favour of a national federation attended by thousands of liberal delegates from all over northern and central Italy, with banners bearing slogans such as 'Long live Pius IX', 'Constitution', 'Italian League', 'Arms' and 'War against the foreigner'.

There was often a strongly dramatic dimension to the rallies held in these months – in part perhaps a spontaneous overspill from the opera houses, where in the second half of 1847, as censorship grew more relaxed, medleys of favourite 'patriotic' music were in demand: Act Three of *Ernani*, the oath scene from *Orazi e Curiazi* by Mercadante, arias from *Ettore Fieramosca* by Antonio Laudamo.[8] But theatricality was also quite deliberate, a means of reaching out to the urban masses, for in Italy, according to Montanelli, the imagination of the people was by instinct 'poetic', and 'it is not right to omit from political calculation the flights of the popular soul'.[9] He himself first experienced the power of 'poetry' when he stood on the steps of Pisa cathedral on 6 September 1847 addressing a crowd that was gathered to inaugurate the local Italian federation, and felt 'intoxicated' as the last words of his speech, 'Italy has risen again', echoed back to him across the piazza from an ecstatic audience. And later in the day he went further, administering the 'national oath' to the new members of the federation from the terrace of his house in a scene fully worthy of an opera:

The sky was stormy, and that magnificent amphitheatre of the Lung'Arno, in the midst of which I lived, was completely festooned with banners. I had with me a black-bordered national flag, which the Lombards had adopted as a symbol of mourning. I asked if we would meet again in danger, just as we were now gathered in celebration. I asked the mothers and fathers if they would send their sons to battle. And the answer came back: 'Yes!' I asked the priests if they would bless the armies as the bells were pealing out. And again I received that sacred promise: 'Yes, yes, we swear!' Then I said: 'We will all be there!' And with arms raised, hands outstretched and cheeks streaked with tears, the vast crowd answered in unison, three times, with a mighty cry that still echoes inside me: 'All.'[10]

REVOLUTION

January the 12th 1848 was a public holiday in Palermo. It was the king's birthday and people were out strolling in the streets or gathered in the piazzas smoking and talking. Tension had been running high in Sicily for months. Pamphlets and posters had been appearing denouncing Bourbon rule and calling for the introduction of sweeping reforms and the establishment of an Italian federation. Doves dyed green, white and red had been seen flying around the city, and rumours that secret revolutionary committees were at work had been rife – and young men like the aristocrat Rosalino Pilo and his lawyer friend (and a future prime minister of Italy) Francesco Crispi had indeed been making plans with liberals in Naples for an insurrection in Sicily. At the end of November a series of patriotic demonstrations had taken place in the local theatres, with cries of 'Long live Pius IX' and 'Long live Italy', and women in the boxes had tied their scarves together to form a chain symbolizing the union of Italy. Rioting had broken out, which the police had brutally suppressed. So when on the morning of 12 January a popular preacher stood up in the market square of the old quarter of the city and began haranguing the crowds, it did not take much for a fracas to snowball into street fighting and then into an all-out revolt, with barricades and pitched battles with police and soldiers. The following morning gangs of crudely armed peasants descended on the city from the small hill towns above Palermo, just as they had done in the revolution of 1820, eager to join in the melee and become the sans-culottes of any new political order, or more often simply to loot, kidnap and pillage.

From Sicily the revolutionary waves rippled up the peninsula. On 29 January, following huge demonstrations in Naples and a peasant rising in the Cilento, the well-meaning but staunchly conservative King of the Two Sicilies, Ferdinand II (whose passions were for his thirteen children and food far more than politics), reluctantly granted a constitution ('O sommo Carlo' became 'O sommo Ferdinando' in a performance of *Ernani* the next day). In Piedmont, Carlo Alberto quickly declared his readiness to introduce a 'statute' (he bridled at the term 'constitution') and Leopold of Tuscany made a similar announcement on 11 February. Pius IX set up a commission to prepare institutional reforms and issued a proclamation calling for calm and obedience which concluded with the electrifying words: 'Grant thy blessing, great Lord, on Italy.' Then the initiative passed to the rest of Europe. At the end of February a revolution broke out in Paris forcing King Louis-Philippe to abdicate, and this sent shock waves travelling east, rapidly engulfing the whole of Germany and central Europe. Metternich fled Vienna in mid-March (and settled peacefully in a fine house overlooking the Thames at Richmond in Surrey), leaving the way open for risings to break out in Lombardy and Venetia. The Milanese took to the streets on 18 March and drove the Austrians out in five days of fierce fighting, while the Venetians followed suit and proclaimed the re-establishment of the Republic of St Mark on 22 March.

The insurrection in Milan immediately brought the spotlight to bear on King Carlo Alberto. Demonstrations in favour of war against Austria broke out across Piedmont, and in Genoa the agitation risked turning democratic and republican. On 23 March Cavour published a portentous article urging the king to action: 'The supreme hour for the Sardinian monarchy has sounded ... one path alone is open to the nation, the government and the king. War! Immediate war, without delay!'[11] But Carlo Alberto, the 'Italian Hamlet', was racked with doubts: to invade Lombardy would mean violating the treaties of 1814–15, not to mention the Austro-Sardinian alliance of 1831. Yet it was fast becoming clear that the only alternative was to be swept from his throne. On 24 March he announced his intention to intervene, and identified himself grandly with the cause of Italy; but in the diplomatic notes that he sent the great powers he claimed that he was acting primarily to prevent the revolution in Milan from becoming republican – which was almost certainly much closer to the truth.

Unfortunately no preparations had been made for the campaign. The general staff was riven with rivalries and disputes, which was one reason why there were no plans. There was also the problem that the king insisted on acting as commander-in-chief, and his inveterate indecisiveness transmitted itself downwards. The army advanced only slowly into Lombardy (the absence of maps did not help) and no attempt was made to open a front in the Veneto or to occupy the Trentino and cut off the Austrians' principal line of communication over the Brenner Pass. This failure meant the enemy forces were able to retreat safely to the powerful group of forts in the lower Po valley known as the Quadrilateral. When the king reached Milan (having at the last moment ordered seventy tricolours, after the Milanese indicated that they did not want to see Savoy flags in their city), it quickly became apparent that he was more interested in securing the annexation of Lombardy and the Veneto than pursuing a war of national liberation. Old dynastic ambitions were clearly uppermost in his mind, as many democrats had feared. He cold-shouldered the more radical Milanese patriots, who had borne the brunt of the fighting, and gave a lukewarm reception to soldiers arriving from other parts of Italy. And throughout April he remained almost inactive, allowing the Austrians to regroup and bring reinforcements down into the Veneto.

Carlo Alberto's declaration of war on Austria produced a rush of excitement in patriotic circles. Exiles hurried back from abroad to lend their support, and across Italy volunteer units assembled and set off for Lombardy. There was a great deal of suspicion on the part of the other Italian rulers about Carlo Alberto's real ambitions, but neither Leopold of Tuscany nor Ferdinand of Naples felt strong enough to resist popular clamourings to go to his aid, and both dispatched small contingents of regular troops. Even Pius IX authorized the formation of an expeditionary force. Led by a Piedmontese general, Giovanni Durando (brother of Giacomo), it was supposed only to defend the northern part of the Papal States against a possible Austrian incursion (or an internal revolt) and not cross the frontier into the Veneto, but Durando and his principal lieutenant, Massimo d'Azeglio, had higher hopes. They were aware of how crucial papal support was for the success of the national cause and were determined to manipulate public opinion to try to drag Pius into a war, even though there were clear signs that he was bridling at the prospect of conflict with Austria, a Catholic power.

Durando and d'Azeglio overplayed their hand. As the troops advanced north from Rome, dressed like crusaders, with crosses sewn on the front of their uniforms, a series of highly rhetorical orders of the day (written by d'Azeglio) were released to the press corralling Pius into the national camp. The first was bold: 'Militiamen and soldiers! . . . The glorious souls of those who fought at Legnano smile upon you from heaven: the great Pius gives you the blessing of the Almighty: Italy trusts in your courage . . . Long live Pius IX! Long live Italian independence!'[12] The second, issued on 5 April after the Piedmontese had crossed into Lombardy, was reckless, and when Pius read it he was incandescent with fury at its violent and presumptuous tone:

Soldiers! . . . We are blessed by the right hand of a great Pope . . . [who] has had to recognize that Italy . . . is condemned by the government of Austria to pillage, rape, the cruelty of a savage army, arson, murder and total devastation . . . The Holy Father has blessed your swords, which, united now with those of Carlo Alberto, must move in concord to annihilate the enemies of God, the enemies of Italy, and those who have insulted Pius IX . . . and assassinated our Lombard brothers. Such a war of civilization against barbarism is accordingly not just a national war but also a supremely Christian one . . . Let our battle cry be: GOD WILLS IT![13]

Just over three weeks later Pius issued an allocution repudiating the war: the Pope was the head of all of Christendom, not just Italy, he said. The hopes of those who had wanted the Italian nation sanctioned, if not created, by the Church, were irrevocably dashed.

Pius' defection was a body-blow to the national movement. Many of the volunteers returned home disconsolately, while the princes withdrew their support from the war against Austria and concentrated instead on domestic political problems. In Naples Ferdinand felt emboldened to fight back against the reformers, and on 15 May he sent troops into the streets to clash with democrats. He then dissolved the new parliament and revoked the constitution. Everywhere from the early summer of 1848 the revolution began to splinter into local protest movements, with regional rivalries and economic and social grievances pushing to the fore. Sicily became obsessed with its old aim of independence from Naples, and turned its back on the rest of Italy, while in Lombardy mistrust of Carlo Alberto developed steadily into deep resentment of Piedmont. And everywhere rural workers agitated for land and lower taxes, while urban workers went on strike and called for lower rents, shorter hours and better pay. D'Azeglio, who had been so optimistic at the start of the year, became increasingly frustrated with his fellow countrymen: 'God save Italy, not from foreigners but from Italians!'[14]

Carlo Alberto's plans for creating a north-Italian kingdom under Piedmontese control took shape slowly in May and June. Despite profound misgivings, Lombardy, Parma, Modena and the Venetian mainland all voted with plebiscites in favour of annexation (hoping thereby for military help). Only Venice held out. Resurrected memories of former glories encouraged the Venetians, led by the lawyer Daniele Manin, to dream of independence within an Italian federation. But by the beginning of July the Austrians were reasserting control across north-eastern Italy and the Republic of St Mark had to swallow its pride, accept Piedmontese military support and agree to be annexed. Three weeks later, after several days of fighting around Custoza, near Verona, Carlo Alberto's overstretched forces were defeated by the Austrians. It was not a major reverse, but his army was too demoralized to carry on. Carlo Alberto was frightened that Milan might declare a republic, and he was keen to fall back on the city as quickly as possible. The only military bright spot that summer came with Giuseppe Garibaldi, who had arrived in Italy from South America at the end of June aboard the aptly named *Hope*, fourteen years after being sentenced to death. He enjoyed some success against the Austrians around Lake Maggiore at the head of a column of volunteers (Carlo Alberto would not allow such a dangerous man to fight alongside the regular Piedmontese troops) before taking refuge across the border in Switzerland.

The Pope's allocution and now Carlo Alberto's defeat took the wind out of the moderates' sails, and in the last months of 1848 the initiative passed to the democrats. In other parts of Europe, though, the tide of revolution was flowing in the opposite direction, as disorder in the towns and countryside in the summer of 1848 frightened middle-class liberals and pushed them into the arms of the conservatives, who did not hesitate to suppress the working-class movements brutally. As a result the drift towards republicanism in Italy was out of kilter with events elsewhere, and any hopes that the democrats might have had of securing foreign support for Italian unity proved illusory. In Tuscany a wave of riots and demonstrations in the early autumn led Giuseppe Montanelli to call for an Italian constituent assembly (the people had so far fought 'as Piedmontese, Tuscans, Neapolitans and Romans, not as Italians');[15] and in late October he and the writer Guerrazzi were carried to power at the head of a radical government. In Rome Pius tried to keep the radicals at bay by appointing as his chief minister Pellegrino Rossi, a liberal law professor of international distinction; but on 15 November Rossi was assassinated, a knife thrust in his carotid artery as he entered the parliament building for the first session of a new Chamber. A few days later Pius slipped out of the Quirinal Palace disguised as a priest and fled to Gaeta, leaving the way open for Mazzini and all the most passionate Italian patriots to flock to the Eternal City. On 9 February a newly elected constituent assembly proclaimed the formation of the Roman Republic and with it the end of the temporal power of the Pope.

In Turin the upsurge of republicanism in central Italy was looked on with horror. Gioberti, who had become prime minister in December, hoped to salvage his dreams of an Italian federation by invading Tuscany and Rome, restoring Pius and Leopold (who had fled his capital just before the Roman Republic was declared) and then waging a united war of independence against Austria. But Carlo Alberto, who had never had much time for such grandiose national programmes, wanted to concentrate instead on recovering Lombardy – which he had abandoned altogether the previous summer after deciding it was best to sign an armistice with the Austrians and return to Piedmont – and towards the end of February he dismissed Gioberti, replaced him with a nondescript general, and made ready to resume hostilities and advance again on Milan.

For the leading moderate, d'Azeglio, the victory of the republicans in central Italy was yet another sign of the democrats' total lack of reality. Mazzini's ideas, he said in a pamphlet published towards the end of 1848, were typical of an exile who had no grasp of the appalling reality of the situation on the ground.[16] Republics were for politically mature peoples with an overwhelming sense of the public good and a deep respect for the law. For 90 per cent of Italians politics meant at best either the Pope and the Austrians or Freemasonry and the Carbonari, and until the country had been through a profound process of moral and civil education it was madness to think of entrusting the nation to 'the people'. How much patriotism was there in a country that could produce only 50,000 volunteers in a population of 25 million?[17] 'We need to change ourselves . . . extricate ourselves from the mud in which we are drowning, escape from our current profound ignorance of political affairs, become, for God's sake, a people with qualities, with good qualities and virtues, and not a degraded, despised race, made the laughing stock of the civilized world, as sadly we are!'[18]

On 20 March Carlo Alberto resumed the war with Austria, but most of his troops were suffering from severe demoralization, unconvinced of the merits of the campaign and mindful of the disasters of the previous year, when they had been beaten by the Austrians and treated by the Lombard population as foreign invaders. Nor did the king's decision to entrust overall command to a Polish general called Chrzanowski inspire confidence: Chrzanowski's knowledge of the terrain was almost as bad as his Italian (and his eyesight). On 23 March, after a day of heavy fighting around Novara, the Piedmontese were defeated by well-ordered Austrian forces under General Radetzky. When it was clear that the day was lost Carlo Alberto threw himself into the thick of the fighting hoping to be killed. He had no luck, and later that evening he abdicated in favour of his son, Victor Emmanuel, and set off for exile in Portugal, where he died four months later in a villa in Porto. Meanwhile in Genoa news of the defeat at Novara led to fears of an imminent Austrian attack, and egged on by republicans the city erupted into a full-scale revolt at the beginning of April. A leading Piedmontese general (and future prime minister of Italy), Alfonso Lamarmora, arrived swiftly with three columns of troops, and perhaps feeling the need for some success after the humiliation of Novara bombarded the city into submission. For thirty-six hours the soldiers were allowed to ransack the city and rape the local women almost at will.[19] As Lamarmora marched into the Ligurian capital with his men the Genoese retreated behind bolted doors and windows as a mark of protest.

Everywhere in Italy (and Europe) the momentum of revolution was dying out. After reasserting control in Naples, King Ferdinand had dispatched an army to Sicily to bring the island to heel. Messina had been captured after a particularly bloody siege early in September. In Palermo the moderate leaders had done very little to prepare to defend the revolution militarily, vainly imagining that Britain or France would intervene at the last moment to save them from the wrath of the Neapolitans. They had also, like Carlo Alberto, appointed a Polish commander-in-chief, hoping thereby to avoid disputes between rival Sicilian officers. But by the middle of April, Bourbon troops were in control almost everywhere in the island. In Tuscany the triumph of the democrats had proved short-lived. Leopold's flight from Florence had been followed by loyalist peasant risings and growing fears among the middle classes of social unrest, and the calls of Montanelli and his supporters for a republic and unity with Rome were rejected. On 12 April the moderates invited Leopold back; and Leopold promptly asked the Austrians to help him restore order. They obliged. The only vestiges of revolution were in Venice – where the Republic of St Mark under Daniele Manin held out resolutely against the Austrians until 24 August – and in Rome.

The brief but brilliant existence of the Roman Republic in the spring and summer of 1849 ensured that Mazzini and the democrats emerged from the year of revolutions with considerable credit. As in Venice, and also briefly in Brescia and Palermo, the determined resistance of the local population against the counter-revolutionary armies helped to sanctify the forces of the left and ensure they were given an honourable place at the table of the international working-class movement. In the 1850s many Italian exiles in London and Paris were viewed with a measure of benevolence that they had not previously received. The martial exploits of the democrats also served to allay the old cliché that Italians could not fight. As a leading figure of the Roman Republic said to Carlo Cattaneo: '[T]he royal armies are weak . . . It is we, and not Carlo Alberto's men, who have cancelled out those sinister words: *Les italiens ne se battent pas*.'[20] More troublingly, though, the Roman Republic gave the myth of Rome – a myth which both the neo-Guelphs and Mazzini had been trying with some success to harness to the national question – a powerful new momentum. Henceforward it would be almost impossible to separate Italian unification from the idea of the 'new Rome', with all its accompanying rhetoric of messianic regeneration and imperial glory.

And this rhetoric could not fail to move audiences deeply imbued with classical culture. Even those of quite modest learning had a mental landscape peopled with ancient heroes – the Horatii, the Scipios, the Gracchi – to whom they could feel heirs, and whose robust civic virtues offered a powerful template for political thought and action. For Giuseppe Garibaldi, who told the enthusiastic crowds that turned out to greet him on his arrival in the Eternal City on 12 December 1848 that he had never, during all his time in South America, 'given up hope of kissing [the] august relics of ancient Rome',[21] the aim of Italy's Risorgimento was to 'rejuvenate' the nation and restore it to 'the primitive era of Roman life'.[22] And it was Rome even more than the American or French revolutions that led him to believe, like many democrats, in the need for a dictatorship to accompany the national revolution. Indeed the rule of a single man of great strength and virtue, like Cincinnatus or Andrea Doria, brought in to help the country through a time of acute crisis, was 'the most glorious institution that had ever existed in Italy'. And given the moral decadence pervading Italian society after centuries of corruption he was firmly of the opinion that a dictatorship would be needed for a long time before any kind of parliamentary government could be risked.[23]

The Roman Republic was inaugurated amid huge emotional excitement. On 27 January, Verdi conducted the premiere of his new opera, *The Battle of Legnano*, in the Teatro Argentina. From its stirring opening chorus ('Long live Italy! A sacred pact binds all its sons') to its pathos-soaked final scene, in which the mortally wounded hero, who has personally slain Frederick Barbarossa in combat and thereby ensured Italy's liberation from the 'barbarians', kisses the tricolour and dies to the strains of a *Te Deum*, the work was rapturously received. A soldier sitting in the fourth tier was so overcome at the end of Act Three that he flung his sword, coat and epaulettes onto the stage, along with all the chairs in his box.[24] Verdi (who had hurried from Paris specially for the occasion – and returned there almost immediately afterwards) had to take twenty curtain calls. A few days later, following extraordinary elections in which 250,000 people had turned out to vote, the first session of the constituent assembly was held. In his inaugural address the veteran republican Carlo Armellini reminded the deputies of the huge weight of historical expectation that lay upon their shoulders as they prepared to create a new Italy, the Italy of 'the people': 'You are sitting between the tombs of two great epochs. On one side are the ruins of imperial Italy, on the other the ruins of papal Italy; it is up to you to build a new edifice upon those ruins.'[25]

The Roman Republic was a remarkable experiment in democratic government – though the fact that Austria, Spain, Naples and soon France all responded to the Pope's appeal for help by sending troops against it led in March to the establishment of a dictatorial (and suitably classical) 'triumvirate' for the duration of what was rather euphemistically called 'the war of independence'. The most authoritative of the triumvirs was Mazzini, and to the surprise of many he wielded power with tact and moderation, earning widespread respect and admiration, not least among foreign observers. The death penalty, censorship and tariffs were all abolished, and during the spring and summer a highly progressive constitution was drawn up which envisaged a democratic form of parliamentary government, based on universal suffrage and the principles of liberty, fraternity and equality and committed to the 'improvement of the material and moral conditions of citizens'. But such radicalism did not stretch, as had been widely feared, to attacks on the Church. Indeed everything possible was done to guarantee the safety and independence of Roman Catholicism: there was even an explicit ban on wood from confessionals being used in the construction of barricades.[26]

But it was the defence of the Roman Republic that did most to capture the imagination of contemporaries. From late April to early July some of the best-known patriots of the Risorgimento – Garibaldi, Pisacane, Bixio, Bertani, Medici, Nicotera, Saffi, Belgioioso – took part in a desperate struggle against 40,000 French troops sent to Rome by Louis Napoleon, the new president of the Second Republic, in a cynical gesture to win over Catholic opinion at home. Several thousand patriots lost their lives in the fighting, among them the young poet Goffredo Mameli, whose fervent wish it had always been that Italians would learn to die as martyrs for their nation (it had horrified him to think that just a few thousand Italians had been killed in all the wars of independence, 'less than Napoleon Bonaparte sacrificed in one day to win a battle').[27] But the odds were heavily stacked against the Republic, and on 2 July, with the French poised to enter the city, Garibaldi summoned his remaining troops to St Peter's Square and called on those who wished to continue the struggle to follow him into the countryside, where they might win the support of the rural masses: 'I can offer neither pay, nor shelter, nor food. I offer hunger, thirst, forced marches, battles and death.' Swords were brandished defiantly, and there were cries of 'We will all come! You are Italy! Long live Garibaldi!' That evening a column of over 4,000 men slipped out of Rome and headed north into the hills of Tuscany and the Marche; but the peasantry showed no desire to fight for a Roman Republic, let alone for Italy, and by the end of the month most of the volunteers had grown disheartened, and they melted away.

Amid the wreckage of defeat the memory of those euphoric days early in 1848 when it looked as if Italy might arise like some glorious new Venus from the seemingly unstoppable flood of patriotism was almost too painful to bear. 'How marvellous to behold those legions of volunteers,' recalled Giuseppe Montanelli of the time when he set off in March to fight the Austrians, 'in which doctors, lawyers, artisans, nobles, rich men, poor men, priests, masters and servants marched together with a common cult of Italy! O what joy to feel ourselves at last warriors of Italy!'[28] But the great hopes had faded, shattered by a papal allocution, military defeat, foreign indifference and hostility, rifts between moderates and democrats, and regional rivalries. Searching for a metaphor of Italy that would embody the feelings of disappointment experienced by many patriots after 1848–9, Francesco Hayez lighted on the image of a sensuous girl with long dark hair, sitting, slightly slumped, in an upright chair, gazing out at the viewer with a brooding, almost accusatory, expression. As with earlier revolutionary depictions of the nation and liberty, her white dress was pulled down off her shoulder to reveal a breast. But this was no confident mother figure ready to lead her sons on to victory. This was a woman who had been abused, perhaps violated: her dress was dishevelled, and her face blotched with patches of dark shadow, like bruises. In her lap was a large book. When it was exhibited at the Brera in 1850 the picture was entitled *Meditation on the Old and New Testament*. But a close inspection of the spine of the volume shows that it is in fact a 'History of Italy'. Hayez certainly wished to imply that the cause of independence was a holy and God-given mission. But as an avid student of Italian history was he also offering a somewhat melancholy reflection on the relationship between Italy's current desperate plight and the huge legacy of its past?

9

Piedmont and Cavour

Even in Piedmont, difference of language is our great difficulty: our three native languages are French, Piedmontese and Genoese. Of these, French alone is generally intelligible. A speech in Genoese or Piedmontese would be unintelligible to two-thirds of the Assembly. Except the Savoyards, who sometimes use French, the deputies all speak in Italian; but this is to them a dead language, in which they have never been accustomed even to converse. They scarcely ever, therefore, can use it with spirit or even fluency. Cavour is naturally a good speaker, but in Italian he is embarrassed. You see that he is translating; so is Azeglio; so are they all . . .   Marchioness Arconati to Nassau William Senior, 6 November 1850

This is to tell you that I have enrolled the very beautiful Countess of Castiglione in our diplomatic ranks and invited her to flirt with and, should it be expedient, seduce the Emperor [Napoleon III]. If she succeeds, I have promised to give her father the post of Secretary in Saint Petersburg.
    Count Camillo Cavour to Luigi Cibrario, 22 February 1856

If we catch Mazzini, I hope he will be condemned to death and hanged in Piazza Acquasola . . .   Count Camillo Cavour, 8 July 1857

CONSTITUTIONAL LEADERSHIP: PIEDMONT

As the revolutionary movement collapsed, everywhere in Italy except in Piedmont the clocks were turned back. The liberal reforms of 1847–8 had not brought the princes the respect and support of their subjects they had hoped. Instead the floodgates had been opened and a dangerous tide of social and political unrest unleashed. In Lombardy press censorship was now tightened and a huge collective fine of 20 million lire was imposed on those leading families who were thought to have favoured the revolution, while in the lower Po valley hundreds of peasants were hauled before military tribunals and condemned to death for crimes against property or persons. In Naples the liberals were harshly persecuted: a number of figures of international standing, including Carlo Poerio and Luigi Settembrini, were shipped to penal islands, clapped in irons, while anyone suspected of being unsympathetic to the Bourbons was subjected to police surveillance and debarred from public posts and some professions. Even in Tuscany there was no return to former tolerance. Guerrazzi was sentenced to hard labour (commuted to exile), press freedom was curtailed and centralization reinforced. In the Papal States, Pius IX had had his fingers badly burned by his flirtation with liberalism: never again would he have any truck with such godlessness. But one or two things did survive from the Roman Republic. The plan agreed by the constituent assembly in April 1849 to adorn the Pincio gardens with busts of great men was allowed to go ahead, but only after Machiavelli had been recut as Archimedes, Leopardi as Zeus, Savonarola as Pietro Aretino, and Gracchus as Vitruvius.[1]

In Piedmont the new king, Victor Emmanuel II – a bluff, coarse-mannered man, with a passion for the army and wild boar (and women) but none for politics – was eager after his father's defeat at Novara to revoke the constitution and return to the absolutist traditions of his forebears, but the Austrians were worried that this might strengthen the liberals and even invite the intervention of republican France. They therefore made him keep it. As it was, the constitution (*Statuto*), which in 1861 became the legal basis of united Italy, was a remarkably backward-looking charter that made only minimal concessions to the principle of popular sovereignty. In the preamble it was described as 'the fundamental law of the monarchy', not the nation (indeed there was only one fleeting reference to 'nation' in the whole text),[2] and throughout the monarch's powers were tightly protected. The king was head of state and of the executive, and appointed his own ministers (who answered to him, not parliament). He was commander of the army, and foreign policy was his exclusive domain. Justice was said, in an extraordinarily anachronistic phrase, to 'emanate from the king': he chose the judges and had the right to overturn sentences he did not like. The upper chamber, or Senate, was appointed by the king, and while the Chamber of Deputies was elected (with a very limited suffrage), it was not at all clear how much power it really had: the king could prorogue or dissolve it at will, and no law could be promulgated without his consent. On paper the *Statuto* thus gave the Piedmontese monarch the possibility to dominate and control almost any aspect of the state that he wanted.

Nevertheless Piedmont was the only state in Italy that was to preserve any form of constitutional government after 1849, and this was one important reason why in the course of the next decade it was able to present itself, both at home and abroad, as the logical standard bearer of the national question. The fact, too, that hundreds of exiles from all parts of the peninsula found a home here in the 1850s also helped its growing identification with the cause of Italy. Though many of these exiles struggled to make ends meet, were often subjected to police surveillance and even from time to time expulsion, some established themselves as respected journalists and academics and used their positions to encourage debate about unification. They also provided an important source of misinformation. Very few Piedmontese had first-hand knowledge of central or southern Italy, and refugees like the Sicilian Giuseppe La Farina were able to spread sometimes deliberately inflated accounts of the political, economic or moral conditions of their native provinces, and be believed. As Cavour, who came to rely very heavily on La Farina for advice about southern Italy in the later 1850s, confessed, he knew considerably more about England than he ever did about Naples.[3]

In national terms, though, Piedmont was not an obvious leader. As Vincenzo Gioberti confessed, this small kingdom straddling the Alps was the least Italian region in the peninsula. It had intensely insular traditions and the educated classes regarded it as a nation in its own right. But after the collapse of the neo-Guelph dream Gioberti was forced to admit that there was now no other Italian state that could spearhead the national movement. In his last major work, *On the Civil Renewal of Italy*, published in 1851, he ascribed the failures of 1848–9 to what he called the 'puritanism' of the democrats and the weakness of national sentiment in Italy. But he also believed that Italy needed to recover its martial spirit and, though Piedmont was deeply provincial, it could at least claim to be ethnically virile, as the etymology of Turin – from the Latin *taurini* or 'bull people' – suggested. It was thus Piedmont's role to furnish Italy with military leadership.[4] However, Rome was also needed for moral hegemony; but if the papacy were to fulfil this role it would have to be reformed and free itself of the burden of the Papal States. The Vatican did not take very kindly to this suggestion and placed Gioberti on the *Index* of proscribed authors. A year later he died in somewhat mysterious circumstances, in his room in Paris, where he had been living in self-imposed exile, copies of the *Imitation of Christ* and Manzoni's *I promessi sposi* (*The Betrothed*) on his bed – in ironic more than hopeful juxtaposition, now.

THE DEMOCRATS DIVIDED

While Piedmont had constitutional government (and an army), its ambivalent behaviour during the year of revolutions still rankled with the democrats, and for several years after 1849 many continued to believe in the possibility of bringing about unity and independence through a popular insurrection. But, as before, the problem was how to persuade the masses to act. 'Italy' meant nothing still to the great majority of peasants, but the social unrest that had been such a marked feature of the risings in 1848–9 – abroad as well as in Italy – showed that issues of land ownership, taxation and wages could be used to galvanize the poor in both town and countryside. Accordingly a number of leading democrats peeled away from Mazzini after 1849 and struck out in the direction of socialism. They included Montanelli and Pisacane and also the Milanese Giuseppe Ferrari, who tried to persuade his fellow Lombard Carlo Cattaneo to assume leadership of the democratic movement. But Cattaneo preferred to spend his time in exile in Switzerland quietly studying and writing, and declined – to the considerable detriment of the cause of federalism, which in the 1850s steadily lost ground as a practical alternative to the Mazzinian or Piedmontese options.

Another fault-line that became more marked within the democrats after 1849 was over the relative merits of north and south. In Sicily and in mainland regions such as Calabria, Basilicata and Campania, there were enormous social and factional tensions relating to land ownership, local resources and the control of communal government, and with the appropriate leadership and good organization it was widely believed that these could be converted into raw revolutionary energy. In Sicily there was the bonus of the paramilitary peasant squads, led by local *mafiosi*, from the hill-towns around Palermo, that could be mobilized in times of crisis. Mazzini was sceptical about using the south as a springboard for unification: the impulse to action had to be pure, not sordidly materialistic; but for those of a more pragmatic cast of mind such as Nicola Fabrizi or Pisacane the 'southern initiative' was highly appealing. One important incidental advantage was that it would allow the democrats to dominate the course of events without too much risk of the Piedmontese at the other end of the peninsula intervening to stop them. Already in 1850 the idea that a movement for national unification might be started by sending an expeditionary force of a thousand men led by a charismatic soldier such as Garibaldi to link up with a peasant rising in western Sicily – the winning formula in 1860 – was being widely discussed.[5]

The divisions within the democratic camp were to deepen sharply in the course of the 1850s, but for a while the glorious after-glow of the defence of Rome and Venice, together with the fact that France was still a republic – and might yet intervene in Italy against the Austrians – helped to keep the revolutionaries in a buoyant mood. But a series of disastrous local risings in Sicily, Lombardy–Venetia and elsewhere, followed by sweeping arrests and executions, dampened their hopes, while the dream of French support died with Louis Napoleon's *coup d'état* of December 1851 and his proclamation of an Empire the next year. Recriminations began to fly in democratic circles, and accusations of incompetence, of selling out to the moderates or of betrayal to the police became commonplace. The appalling poverty and insecurity in which so many of the émigrés lived added to the pressures and poisoned the atmosphere further. Exile could make Italy a mirage, a promised land of concord and brotherly love; but the day-to-day reality of living with fellow refugees was often a nightmare. As one émigré recalled: 'Sons of the same land, embittered by physical hardships, do not tolerate one another. On the contrary they come to blows, they tear one another apart, they detest one another with a vengeance.'[6]

Mazzini tried to keep the various democratic factions together. For eighteen months after the fall of the Roman Republic he remained in the relative safety of Switzerland, with occasional forays to France and England, corresponding with fellow exiles and preparing for what he believed would soon be a fresh round of revolutions. In the autumn of 1850 he announced the formation of an Italian National Committee, based in London and affiliated to another organization that he had set up with French, German and Polish friends called the Central Committee for Democratic Europe, through which he hoped to coordinate the activities of the exile groups around Europe. Its programme was deliberately vague, with no mention of republicanism, but despite this there was a great deal of reluctance among many Italian democrats to throw in their lot with a man who was widely seen as having an unhealthy obsession with religion and a dangerous proclivity to dogmatism. Former colleagues referred to him as 'a new Mahomet' or the 'tsar of democrats',[7] while the French writer George Sand, who had been in close correspondence with him for several years, found his intolerance of socialism too much to bear and denounced him as having 'the arrogance of a pope who proclaims: "Outside of my Church, there is no salvation!"'[8]

The Italian National Committee soon found itself up against a rival, the Latin Committee, which favoured a federal republic in Italy under French patronage, and Mazzini had to acknowledge that his moral hold over the democratic movement was limited. Partly for this reason, though, he pushed ahead with plans for insurrections: blood, he always believed, was one of the best ways of creating fraternal bonds. From his base in London he watched as the Austrian authorities tortured and executed dozens of liberal patriots, including priests, while reports suggested that 20,000 political prisoners were languishing in gaols in Naples and another 4,000 in Tuscany. In the Papal States the guillotine (a curious concession by the Church to modernity) was used to impress upon the Pope's subjects the wages of political sin (the poet Robert Browning was traumatized one day out riding near the Circus Maximus when he came upon a still bleeding decapitated corpse).[9] Such levels of persecution suggested to Mazzini that Italians would be seething with anger and ready to rise up, and in this misguided belief he gave his support to an insurrection planned to break out in Milan on a Sunday in carnival in February 1853 and then spread across Italy. It proved a fiasco: a handful of Austrian soldiers were killed in the first exchanges, but the ringleaders were swiftly rounded up and sixteen executed.

The Milanese disaster did as much damage to Mazzini's credibility in Italian revolutionary circles as the Savoy invasion nearly twenty years earlier, and many of his surviving followers now considered the time had come to abandon him for good. In England, though, his reputation remained remarkably high, at least for a while. He had returned to

London early in 1851 to great acclaim after his exploits as triumvir in the Roman Republic, and found a new enthusiasm for Italian independence among the British public. The appearance in the late spring of William Gladstone's searing letters to Lord Aberdeen, in which the brilliant young conservative politician denounced the Bourbon administration as 'the negation of God erected into a system of government', created a sensation at home and abroad, and added hugely to public support for Italy. Mazzini took advantage of this climate by setting up a society called the Friends of Italy to campaign for Italian independence. It attracted 800 members from all over Britain (200 from Scotland), and its central committee contained several leading politicians and newspaper editors and a host of eminent intellectual figures, including the poets Walter Savage Landor and Leigh Hunt, Samuel Smiles, Professor Francis Newman (the brother of the cardinal), the historian James Froude and the writer George Henry Lewes (the future partner of George Eliot, herself an enormous admirer of Mazzini).[10] As much as £20,000 was raised through subscription funds in less than two years, with a large part of it coming from ordinary factory workers and miners who were being encouraged at this time by their radical leaders to identify their own political aspirations with the emancipation of the oppressed peoples of Europe in countries such as Poland, Hungary and Italy.[11]

Mazzini's continued dabbling in ill-fated insurrectionary movements, even after the Milan fiasco, his public opposition to the Crimean War, and the emergence of Piedmont as the lodestar of the Italian national movement under its energetic and Anglophile new prime minister, Cavour, led to a drop in his popularity in Britain from 1854. But he still felt more at home in England, 'my second fatherland', than he ever did in Italy. In addition to pet projects such as the school he had founded in Holborn in 1841 to provide free education for the hundreds of poor Italian children who regularly roamed the streets of London with barrel organs or trained mice, begging, he enjoyed the unswerving friendship of what he referred to as his 'clan', a close-knit group of devoted supporters, many of them high-minded middle-class women, who met regularly at a house in Muswell Hill to dine, talk, sing and play chess. When not with this 'family of angels', he passed much of his time in small rented rooms in west London surrounded by piles of papers and books, writing, a cigar constantly in his mouth, and small birds flying freely about his head (he could not bear to see them caged).[12]

CAVOUR

Far from Italy, amid the fog of London (which he loved),[13] Mazzini could keep his patriotic dreams alive, but for many of those who had been caught up in the euphoria of the 1840s the chill encounter with reality in the early 1850s brought a sense of disquiet, guilt and even revulsion at the ease with which they had been deluded. Some, like the exiled Milanese economist Pietro Maestri, turned to hard-edged empirical scholarship in a bid to generate a more temperate outlook: statistics as an antidote to rhetoric. There was a dangerous chasm between real and imagined Italy, he thought:

[I]n every age Italians were condemned to have only an ideal fatherland. And that separation between idea and history, theory and social reality, has given Italian thought an anomalous and exceptional character. It is speculative and vague, lacks solid ground beneath its feet, and avoids the lessons and restraints of facts. It will not allow caution of any kind to intrude on the idealized destinies of the fatherland, and, as reality hurtles on its fateful path, hope turns to disillusionment, utopia to cursing.[14]

After the collapse of such intense hopes, many patriots found themselves wondering if history was not more powerful than they had previously thought, and as so often in the past (and future) they were inclined to see the root cause of their political problems as lying in the character of their fellow countrymen. D'Azeglio lamented bitterly to a friend in the spring of 1849 that the events of the previous year had convinced him that 20 per cent of Italians were 'headstrong, roguish imbeciles' and the remaining 80 per cent were 'good-natured, timid imbeciles', and that together they had got what they deserved.[15] Another leading liberal, Michele Amari, confessed ruefully in 1853 that he had been under the impression until quite recently that it was just the Neapolitans and Sicilians who were 'infinitely more fickle and quarrelsome than the ancient Greeks', but his experience of living in exile with northerners as well as southerners had persuaded him that history was right, and that the problem lay with Italians in general ('as we get closer to the Alps the snow does not cure us of that nervous instability').[16] For both these men the idea that Italy could trust to its own native energies and 'make itself' seemed wholly unrealistic. And many democrats were inclined to agree with them. A decade earlier Amari had looked to the Sicilian Vespers as a model for political redemption, but his interest was now in the tenth and eleventh centuries, when Sicily had been turned into one of the most prosperous and civilized regions in Europe under the enlightened rule of the Arabs. Virtue, it seemed, flowed from good (even foreign) government rather than from self-determination.

In 1853 Amari was beginning to pin his hopes of national unification on what many regarded as the least Italian state in the peninsula, Piedmont; and Piedmont now had as its prime minister a man who felt more at home in Paris, London and Geneva than he did in the austere and claustrophobic surrounds of his native Turin. Camillo Benso di Cavour was born in 1810 into an aristocratic family. His father, Michele, had done well during the years of direct French rule, rising to become Chamberlain to the governor-general of north-western Italy, Napoleon's brother-in-law, Camillo Borghese (after whom Cavour was named). His mother, Adèle, was Swiss, and the close ties that Cavour enjoyed with his relatives in Geneva were to be of enormous importance in his cultural and political development. As a young man Cavour served as an engineer in the army, supervising the construction of forts on the French border, but he was too much of an individualist, and too intellectual, to relish military life, and much of his spare time was spent studying economics (like Napoleon, he was an extremely good mathematician), reading Guizot, Constant, Bentham and other modern European writers, and gambling: all his life he was to remain a passionate card-player and was never happier than when sitting at a green baize-covered table enjoying what he called the *crispation* – thrill – (his first language was French, and he struggled to write and sometimes even to speak Italian) of games such as *goffo* and whist.[17]

After extensive travels in Britain and France, which left him with an abiding fascination with 'progress' (he loved looking around factories, gas works, prisons and schools) and a conviction that the best way to advance the cause of civilization was by steering a middle path between political extremes (the *juste milieu*), he returned to Piedmont, where he ran the family estates, helped launch an Agricultural Association and a Whist Club and wrote occasional learned articles. Only in the mid-1840s, following the furore generated by Gioberti's and Balbo's books on the national question, did he begin to get involved in active politics. Cavour does not himself appear to have had any clear thoughts or even strong feelings at this time about 'Italy'. In later life he claimed to have dreamed as a young man of a 'great, glorious and powerful Italy',[18] but his pragmatic cast of mind always led him to distinguish sharply between what was realistic and what was not, and unity, certainly of a Mazzinian kind, was in his view no more than a dangerous fantasy. He also, like most Piedmontese aristocrats, felt intensely loyal to his own state and regularly spoke of Piedmont as a nation and hankered after what he called its 'aggrandisement'. What chiefly drew him into politics in 1845–7 was his sense as a gambler that a major game was about to be played out in Italy, and probably also in Europe as a whole, with high stakes and potentially enormous winnings and losses. He did not want to be a mere spectator.

Piedmont lost in 1848–9, but not calamitously; and though Cavour was devastated by the defeat at Novara, railing in his anger at everyone from the king and his Polish commander to the rank-and-file troops and the democrats, he had the consolation that the republicans failed to capitalize on the disaster and also that the constitution was kept by Victor Emmanuel II and with it parliamentary government. Cavour had been elected to the Chamber of Deputies in Turin in June 1848, sitting on the right with the conservatives, and had quickly proved a very skilful debater. In October 1850 the prime minister, Massimo d'Azeglio, rewarded him with the portfolio of Trade and Agriculture and soon afterwards with that of Finance, and Cavour energetically set about stimulating the Piedmontese economy by lowering tariffs and drawing up commercial treaties. He also began manoeuvring against d'Azeglio, who had little zest for politics and was seriously hampered by a bullet wound in his knee he had sustained in 1848. Cavour aimed to build a new centrist coalition that would provide a more stable platform for reforms than the present parliamentary configuration and prevent Piedmontese politics from careering to the far right or the far left. Louis Napoleon's *coup d'état* in December 1851 greatly allayed the threat from the republicans, but it strengthened the hand of the reactionaries – a very powerful group – and a few weeks later Cavour revealed to his astonished cabinet colleagues that he had made an alliance (*connubio*) with the centre-left. The underhand character of this move caused ructions, and Cavour was forced to resign. But he knew he was too talented to be overlooked for long. He was right: in the autumn d'Azeglio had to step down and magnanimously recommended to the king that Cavour should succeed him.

Before he became prime minister Cavour went on a trip to Britain and France. He had toyed with the idea of travelling around Italy, but in the end considered he had more to gain by visiting the two countries that he loved and admired most. One point of interest to him was to get some sense of what the French President, Louis Napoleon, was planning to do: was it possible to be a nephew of the great Napoleon and not to have grandiose ambitions in Europe? In England d'Azeglio's success in keeping the constitutional experiment going in Turin had won Piedmont widespread respect, and Cavour had little difficulty in securing audiences with the leading politicians of the day, including Palmerston, Gladstone, Disraeli and Clarendon. He went on a tour of the Woolwich Arsenal, inspected the London slums, and travelled up to Scotland with a volume of Walter Scott to see the lochs and mountains and experience 'romantic emotions'.[19] His enthusiasm for Britain was greater than ever, and he thought of emigrating to London if the reactionaries came to power in Turin. Paris he found a little disappointing, but he saw Gioberti and Manin and had meetings with some of the key figures in the new administration; and on 5 September he went to Saint-Cloud to talk to the French President. With his reserved and languid manner and hooded eyes Louis Napoleon was notoriously inscrutable, but he revealed enough for Cavour to realize that if Piedmont played its cards right it could win the support of France in redrawing the map of Italy at Austria's expense. As Cavour wrote excitedly to a friend: 'Our destiny depends above all on France. Whether we like it or not, we have to be her partner in the great game that sooner or later must be played in Europe.'[20]

When, in December, Louis Napoleon proclaimed himself Napoleon III, Emperor of the French, there was inevitable nervousness in London, Berlin and above all Vienna about the prospects for the balance of power in Europe. For Cavour, though, France was henceforth to be one of the twin pillars on which his domination of Piedmontese politics was built – the other being the centrist coalition that he had constructed in parliament. Victor Emmanuel had little liking for his headstrong and energetic prime minister, who dressed, as he put it, 'like a lawyer', regularly threw fits, hurling abuse and kicking furniture, and who in 1854–5 pushed through a bill to nationalize Church property that led to the king's excommunication by the Pope (particularly embarrassing for a monarch one of whose proud titles was King of Jerusalem). But Victor Emmanuel was prepared to endure almost any humiliation in return for the prospect of making good on the field of battle the damage done to the prestige of the House of Savoy by the defeats at Custoza and Novara (though he came perilously close to fighting a duel with his prime minister when Cavour impugned his masculinity by claiming his long-standing mistress was engaging in orgies with other men).

The first opportunity for war came in 1854. Russia had given Austria a vital helping hand in eastern Europe during the revolutions of 1848–9, and as a return favour it felt justified in invading the Ottoman provinces of Moldavia and Wallachia (modern Romania). Russia's advance westwards towards the Mediterranean alarmed the British, who saw the Tsarist empire as the biggest threat to their global power, and in March 1854 Britain declared war on Russia and dispatched its fleet to the Black Sea. Russia had hoped Britain would be isolated, and so unwilling to act. But it had miscalculated, for Napoleon III was now on the lookout for ways of unstitching the Vienna settlement and reckoned that, if he allied with Britain against Russia, Britain would be obliged to support France against Austria in western Europe. On the face of it Piedmont had little to gain by involving itself in the Crimea, especially when the Austrians agreed, after much prevaricating, to refrain from going to the aid of Russia in return for a guarantee from France to preserve the status quo in Italy. But the king was desperate to prove the valour of his army, and secretly negotiated with the French behind Cavour's back to enter the war, forcing Cavour and his cabinet colleagues to forgo their (considerable) reservations, defy the hostility of much of parliament, and commit Piedmont to a campaign in which Austria was, nominally at least, now their ally.

Cavour had no expectation of any clear gain, but his hope was that the 18,000 Piedmontese troops would distinguish themselves sufficiently in battle to provide him with a strong bargaining counter in a future peace conference. Unfortunately General Lamarmora's soldiers were sidelined in Russia, and the only engagement of any note in which they were involved took place on the Tchernaya river on 16 August, and cost just fourteen lives. Two thousand others died from cholera during the campaign. Victor Emmanuel attempted to make amends for this rather desultory state of affairs by proposing to the French and British that he should take over as commander-in-chief of all forces in the Crimea, but his offer was not surprisingly declined. In an alternative, and more

1. The invasion of Italy by France in 1796. A contemporary allegory showing turreted Italy being assailed by Marianne while Gallic cocks run riot. On the left Italy's 'emasculated military genius' lies sleeping.

2. The bronze horses of St Mark's, Venice, being shipped off to Paris on Napoleon's orders in 1797. The horses were used to adorn the Arc de Triomphe du Carrousel – built to celebrate France's victories – before being returned to Venice in 1815.

3. Antonio Canova's monument to the poet and playwright Vittorio Alfieri, in the church of Santa Croce, Florence (1806–10). The figure of Italy grieving became an icon for patriots of the Risorgimento.

4. Francesco Hayez's painting of Pietro Rossi, lord of Parma, being implored by his wife and daughters not to take up command of the Venetian forces (1818–20). The figure on the right was modelled on Canova's sculpture of Italy in Santa Croce.

5. *Peter the Hermit Preaching the First Crusade* (1827–9), by Francesco Hayez. The depiction of 'the people' being inspired by religious zeal to undertake a great mission made this painting a particular favourite with Giuseppe Mazzini and the democrats.

6. A meeting of Carbonari – apprentices to the left, masters to the right – in a lithograph of 1821. Behind the Grand Master in the centre is a picture of St Theobald, the patron saint of the Carboneria.

7. An engraving celebrating Pope Pius IX's allocution of 10 February 1848 in which he invoked God's blessing on Italy (*Benedite Gran Dio l'Italia*). The hopes of Italian patriots were shattered shortly afterwards when Pius denounced the national movement.

8. Francesco Hayez's second version of his painting *La Meditazione* (*Meditation*, 1851). The female figure, representing Italy's abject condition after the revolutions of 1848–9, holds a history of Italy inscribed with the date of the Milanese rising of March 1848.

9. Giuseppe Mazzini in a photograph taken in the 1860s. From an early age Mazzini vowed always to dress in black as a mark of mourning for his enslaved country – and Italy, as far as he was concerned, was still enslaved after 1860.

10. Count Camillo Benso di Cavour in a photograph taken during the Paris peace congress in 1856.

11. King Victor Emmanuel II and Rosa Vercellana around the time of their morganatic marriage in 1869. The daughter of an army officer and barely literate, Rosa had become the king's mistress when she was only fourteen. Victor Emmanuel relished her simple peasant cooking.

12. North meets south following unification. A *bersagliere* posing beside the body of the bandit leader Nicola Napolitano after he had been captured and shot at Nola, near Naples, in September 1863.

13. Giuseppe Garibaldi, with a characteristically exotic hat, displaying the bullet wound he had received in his right ankle during an encounter with Italian troops at Aspromonte in August 1862. Parallels with Christ and his suffering were an important part of Garibaldi's appeal.

14. Francesco Crispi (right) meeting Bismarck at Friedrichsruh in October 1887. Bismarck was unreceptive to Crispi's suggestion of a war against France. Cartoonists made much of the physical resemblance between the two politicians.

realistic, bid to raise Piedmont's standing with his allies he visited Paris and London in the autumn in the company of Cavour. D'Azeglio went along, too, partly because his refined patrician bearing was guaranteed to go down well in courtly circles, and partly, too, because he could write and speak good Italian and so mitigate the embarrassment that might be caused by the leading members of a delegation claiming to represent Italy having a weaker grasp of the national language than did Gladstone or Lord Russell. The visit went well, though the king's brusque manners, coarse sexual remarks and lack of political tact ('Austria must be exterminated,' he told a terrified Queen Victoria at a banquet)[21] did cause eyebrows to be raised. Queen Victoria forgave him, and even found his directness refreshing, attributing his eccentricity, rather condescendingly, to 'the low level of morality' in Italy.[22]

Cavour went to the peace conference in Paris in February 1856 desperately hoping to win some territorial concessions for Piedmont – Lombardy, perhaps, or the duchies of Modena and Parma – but the British and the French were not prepared at this juncture to fall out with the Austrians, and Cavour's only success (though it was a considerable one) was to have the Italian question formally discussed by the delegates after the negotiations had been concluded. There was some criticism of the Bourbons and of the situation in the Papal States, but to Cavour's chagrin not much more. Before leaving Paris, Cavour had several meetings with Daniele Manin, the hero of the Venetian Republic, who was fast emerging as the leading spokesman for those exiled democrats who had lost faith in a popular insurrection as a means to unify Italy and were now looking instead towards Piedmont. Cavour said in a letter that he found Manin 'a little utopian' and too concerned with 'the idea of Italian unity and other such nonsense' (a remark that later had to be expunged from the official edition of Cavour's correspondence), but he could see how useful the Venetian might be for channelling Italian patriotic sentiment towards Piedmont – sentiment that Cavour could then manipulate and use as a further card in the increasingly strong hand he was accumulating. For his part Manin remained suspicious of Cavour's 'Piedmontese' ambitions, but he and his friends could see that Cavour might be useful to them, as well.

From the spring of 1856 the Italian national question gathered momentum. A series of forceful letters to the press from Manin and his friend, the distinguished exile Giorgio Pallavicino-Trivulzio, denounced

Mazzinian conspiracy ('the theory of the dagger') and proclaimed the support of many former republicans for the House of Savoy provided Victor Emmanuel committed himself unequivocally 'to the making of Italy and not the aggrandisement of Piedmont'. In a further attempt to shape public opinion Manin and Pallavicino launched what became known in 1857 as the Italian National Society, an organization that aimed to bring together all those who wanted the 'unification and independence' of Italy under the leadership of Piedmont. One of its most important early adherents was Giuseppe Garibaldi. The Secretary was the pugnacious émigré Sicilian Giuseppe La Farina, now living in Turin, and it was largely thanks to his drive that the National Society became a major force in Italian politics over the next three years, attracting several thousand members, turning out countless newspaper articles and pamphlets, and forging links with patriotic groups throughout the country. Cavour worked closely with La Farina: indeed La Farina was later to claim (rather improbably: he was prone to serious exaggeration) that he had a secret meeting with the prime minister every morning before dawn from September 1856.

The National Society was a major threat to Mazzini, in large measure because it stole so much of his clothing. The Italian nation was said to be a sacred entity, 'an immutable law of nature', before which everything, 'municipalities and provinces, individuals and sects, traditions and hopes, dynasties and liberties', had to yield. Patriotism was a religion, open to everyone ('no church is closed to him who recites the symbol of the faith'; whoever enters 'will find on the altar . . . that sacred image of Italy that he saw on the pediment'), and Italians had a duty to work and if necessary die for 'the independence and greatness' of the fatherland.[23] Where the National Society differed from Mazzini was in the much more ruthless approach it took to means and ends. Mazzini hoped to reconcile faith with freedom: to realize God's designs through the spontaneously expressed will of the people. For La Farina, Manin and Pallavicino such a hope was illusory. Italians were the product of centuries of division and decadence, and could not bring about unification themselves. Force was needed, which in practice meant the Piedmontese state and army. And unification, the National Society repeatedly stressed, was fundamental and had to take precedence over everything else, liberty included, because as history had repeatedly shown, it was the fragmentation of Italy that had led to its servile condition and hence all its ills.[24]

This uncompromising vision not surprisingly found plenty of supporters even among conservatives in Piedmont, for it offered a justification for the domination, and even conquest, of the rest of the peninsula
by Turin. But to what extent Cavour himself was convinced by it is
uncertain. Like many northern Italians he evidently thought that somewhere not far beyond Tuscany lay a different order of civilization,
more African than European in character, and that uniting the corrupt
impoverished south with upper Italy was probably not only unrealistic
but also undesirable. Far better concentrate on creating a compact and
homogeneous state in the north of the country.[25] La Farina did his best
to persuade Cavour that the south was less poor than he imagined, and
that the problems bedevilling the Kingdom of the Two Sicilies were
primarily the result of bad government – in other words that with good
Piedmontese rule the south would be restored to the luxuriance of
classical (and Arab) times. Conceivably such arguments helped to bring
Cavour round to the idea of unity in 1860; but if they did, they also
encouraged him to see a strong centralized regime as vital.

With Piedmont very much in the driving seat of the national movement, Mazzini and his remaining supporters desperately looked to regain
some initiative. Precisely because they suspected Cavour of having little
serious interest in the south, the Kingdom of the Two Sicilies became their
main target from 1856. They were helped by the fact that King Ferdinand
was suddenly looking exposed, for Russia had long been his close ally,
and now, in the wake of the Crimean War, Britain and France felt free to
turn against him. They urged him to make reforms, and when he refused
they broke off diplomatic relations in October 1856. Napoleon began
pushing the idea of getting his cousin, Lucien Murat, son of the former
king, Joachim Murat, onto the Neapolitan throne. Cavour could see
possible advantages in this move and indicated his support for the idea
(he was spinning an increasingly complex web, negotiating with the
different players in the 'great game' in ways that left them uncertain of
exactly where they – and indeed he – stood) – much to the alarm of the
members of the National Society and also of the British government,
which did not want a major extension of French power in the Mediterranean. Indeed it was partly in a belief that Britain might now support
an 'Italian' insurrection in the south to forestall the French that Mazzini
and his friends backed plans for a revolution in Sicily (where an abortive
rising broke out near Palermo in November 1856) and Naples.

Cavour, too, had good reasons for encouraging the democrats in the south – not because he wanted them to succeed, but because a visible threat from republicans would enhance his negotiating position as the respectable face of Italian nationalism – and there is every reason to believe that the disastrous expedition of Carlo Pisacane in June 1857 was planned and organized in collusion with the Piedmontese authorities.[26] The idea was for Pisacane and a handful of men to sail from Genoa to Ponza, release the political prisoners being held on the island, land in southern Campania, stir up the local peasantry and then descend on Naples, which, in the meantime, would have risen up. As ever with such ventures, there were too many things that could go wrong, and Pisacane knew that the chances of success were slim. But he was determined to act. The hardship of exile had induced in him, as in many democrats, a growing sense of desperation; and he believed that the only way the downtrodden masses would be sparked into life and achieve economic and political emancipation was if intellectuals abandoned their ivory towers, mixed with the people and provided them with resolute leadership. If he failed, he could at least feel he had provided a heroic example to others.

Pisacane landed at Sapri on 28 June with some forty companions and 300 prisoners liberated from the island of Ponza; but only a few of these had turned out to be political prisoners and most of the others proved to be unreliable and soon deserted. Of the thousand or more armed men who were supposed to have arrived from Naples to meet them, there was no sign. The small force marched north, reading out a proclamation as they went calling for the overthrow of the tyrant Ferdinand. But they received no support from the local population. On 1 July they ran into several battalions of government troops and gendarmes sent to intercept them, and over fifty of their number were killed. Pisacane and his remaining followers fled to the town of Sanza, and took refuge in a monastery. But here they were set upon by a furious peasant army, egged on by the local arch-priest, and a further twenty-seven were murdered. Two dozen others were arrested. Pisacane, it seems, took his own life.[27]

It was a fate that the rebels had predicted. Before landing at Sapri they had issued a declaration saying that if their expedition failed they would know how to die bravely and 'follow in the footsteps of our martyrs'.[28] In addition Pisacane had left behind a political 'testament', which was released to the press shortly after his death. In it he declared that the government of Piedmont was no better than that of Austria and that the unity of Italy could only be achieved by 'conspiracies, plots and attempted insurrections'. But most of the document was a pugnacious and rather ill-tempered defence of his peculiar political creed ('I believe in socialism, but in a socialism different from the French systems').[29] Of far greater value from a patriotic point of view was a poem about the expedition, 'The Gleaner', written towards the end of 1857 by Luigi Mercantini, which quickly became one of the most popular literary works of the Risorgimento. In this simple elegiac ballad a peasant girl standing on the seashore meets 'the three hundred' ('they were young and strong, and now are dead' – in fact none of the 284 who eventually stood trial for the rebellion was executed) as they land at Sapri and watches them kneel and kiss the soil. She goes up to their handsome young leader, with 'blue eyes and golden hair' (Pisacane was in fact dark; the same mistake was often made about Garibaldi), takes his hand and asks him where he is going: 'My sister, I go to die for my beautiful fatherland.' She follows the men as they march off and watches them as they die heroically at the hands of the gendarmes (the role of the local peasantry is obscured), all the while praying for their souls.[30]

10

Unity, 1858–60

The populations of the Provinces of Parma wish to be united with the Kingdom of Sardinia under the constitutional government of King Victor Emmanuel II
Plebiscite in Parma and Piacenza, August 1859
   Yes: 63,107   No: 504

Annexation to the constitutional monarchy of King Victor Emmanuel – or – separate kingdom
Plebiscite in Emilia, March 1860
   Annexation: 426,006   Separate: 756

Union with the constitutional monarchy of King Victor Emmanuel, or separate kingdom
Plebiscite in Tuscany, March 1860
   Union: 366,571   Separate: 14,925

The people desires Italy one and indivisible, with Victor Emmanuel, constitutional king, and his legitimate descendants
Plebiscite in the mainland south, October 1860
   Yes: 1,302,064   No: 10,312

The Sicilian people desires Italy one and indivisible, with Victor Emmanuel, constitutional king, and his legitimate descendants
Plebiscite in Sicily, October 1860
   Yes: 432,053   No: 667

Do you wish to be part of the constitutional monarchy of King Victor Emmanuel II?
Plebiscite in the Marche and Umbria, November 1860
   Yes: 232,017   No: 1,520

In practical political terms, the Sapri expedition may have underlined the futility of insurrection as a method of achieving unification and further convinced many Italian patriots to trust instead to Piedmont and diplomacy. But the propaganda value of heroic failure was considerable, and Pisacane's sacrifice helped to sanctify the cause of Italy in the eyes of much of the liberal international community – especially in Britain, where enthusiasm for Italian independence was fanned by hostility to the Catholic Church and a belief that Austria had become the epitome of a brutal and autocratic power. Another desperate gesture by a leading Italian democrat a few months later raised the moral temperature still higher. In January 1858 Felice Orsini, a disaffected Mazzinian and author of a well-known memoir about his escape from imprisonment in Mantua (published in English under the portentous title *The Austrian Dungeons in Italy*),[1] attempted to assassinate Napoleon III, hoping the emperor's death might trigger a revolution in France that would then spread across the Alps. Three powerful pear-shaped grenades ('Orsini bombs') were hurled towards the emperor's carriage as he drove to the Paris Opéra (appropriately enough to see a performance of *William Tell*), killing eight people and wounding more than a hundred others, but leaving Napoleon himself unharmed. Orsini used his ensuing trial to air the cause of Italian freedom and even wrote an impassioned appeal to Napoleon urging him to liberate the peninsula. Orsini's calm dignity as he went to the guillotine was widely admired.[2]

Cavour was worried after the Sapri affair that Napoleon III might think (with justification) that he had been in cahoots with the insurgents and withdraw his sympathy for Piedmont; but a close friend of Cavour's taking the waters at the spa of Plombières in the Vosges was informed in the strictest confidence by the emperor that he needed a popular war to strengthen his own position at home and that of France internationally. It was simply a question of waiting for the most appropriate moment. Cavour was exhilarated: 'The emperor is our best friend, the one important person in France who supports the cause of Italy, the only sovereign in Europe who has a genuine interest in the aggrandisement of Piedmont. If we march in step with him we will reach our goal.'[3] There was a considerable price to be paid for this friendship, however: firmer measures against the democrats in Piedmont and a reduction of constitutional liberties. Cavour did what he could to maintain his independence, but following Orsini's assassination attempt the emperor insisted that if

Cavour did not comply with French wishes fully, he would terminate his friendship and ally with Austria. Cavour now felt he had no choice, and in the course of the next few months many political refugees were expelled from Piedmont and press and jury freedoms curtailed.

With Britain heavily committed in the Far East following the outbreak of the Indian Mutiny in 1857, Napoleon considered the time right to embark on a campaign against Austria, and in the late spring of 1858 he sent his private doctor to Turin to inform Victor Emmanuel and Cavour of his plans for Italy (which were to be part of a broader struggle between the 'Latin races' and the Germans for dominance in Europe) and to invite Cavour to talks in Plombières. The two men met on 21 July, and in the course of a long drive through the countryside of the Vosges in the emperor's phaeton they worked out the future of the peninsula. The Austrians were to be expelled from Lombardy and Venetia and Italy would become a loose confederation under the presidency of the Pope, with France as its protector. Victor Emmanuel would acquire all northern Italy, including Modena and Parma, and possibly the Romagna and the Marche as well. There would be an enlarged Tuscan state (with a ruler yet to be decided); King Ferdinand would be deposed in Naples and replaced with Lucien Murat, if possible; and the Pope would lose all his territories except for a small area around Rome. As for a convincing pretext for war, one idea was that they should instigate a revolt in Massa and Carrara and get the rebels to appeal to Piedmont for help. Turin would then decline, but in terms that were sufficiently critical of Austrian rule to provoke Vienna into a retort out of which a quarrel and then a conflict could arise.[4]

France would of course gain hugely from the war by replacing Austria as the controlling power in Italy, but Napoleon also wanted a marriage alliance between the king's fifteen-year-old daughter, Clotilde, and his cousin, Prince Jérôme Bonaparte. Victor Emmanuel found this very hard to swallow, not least because Clotilde was a shy and deeply pious girl, Jérôme a dissolute and middle-aged philanderer, but Cavour eventually managed to cajole the king into agreeing ('to achieve our holy objective I would confront greater dangers than the hatred of a little girl and the anger of the court').[5] A potentially far more difficult problem was Napoleon's insistence that two of the historic heartlands of the Piedmontese state, Nice and Savoy, should be ceded to France. Cavour knew that any agreement on this point would not only be technically unconstitutional but also hugely unpopular in nationalist circles. Nice especially was widely regarded as much more Italian than French, and it had been the birthplace of the most popular and famous Italian patriot, Garibaldi. When the treaty committing France to a war in alliance with Piedmont was signed in January 1859, Cavour had to make sure that the clause relating to Nice and Savoy remained totally secret.

Engineering a conflict with Austria turned out to be much more difficult than Cavour had imagined. As Piedmont embarked on a programme of rapid rearmament and diplomatic initiatives to isolate Austria intensified, rumours of an impending war escalated. In January, Victor Emmanuel opened the new parliamentary session with a belligerent speech in which he spoke of 'the cry of anguish' that was reaching him from across Italy. This provocative phrase had been suggested by Napoleon, and accepted by Cavour and his cabinet colleagues after much nervous deliberation, and as expected it raised the temperature – but rather more than intended. At La Scala cries of 'Viva Verdi' – standing for 'Victor Emmanuel king of Italy' (Vittorio Emanuele Re D'Italia) – were heard,[6] and in a performance of Bellini's Norma members of the audience leapt to their feet and enthusiastically joined in the Druids' chorus intoning 'War, war!'[7] Cavour had needed to create an atmosphere out of which a conflict could arise but with Austria appearing the aggressor and Piedmont the innocent victim and peace-loving defender of Italian rights and liberties. It was a supremely difficult juggling act, requiring the nerves, the instincts (and luck), of a born gambler; and it was an act that subsequent Italian politicians were to be tempted to emulate in a bid to realize the dreams of grandeur created by the Risorgimento. More and more, though, it was looking to the outside world early in 1859 as if Piedmont and France were the real warmongers, not Austria.

Had there been signs of popular enthusiasm in Italy for a war, the position of Cavour and Napoleon would have been much easier. As it was, 'the cry of anguish' that Victor Emmanuel had spoken of was turning out to be almost inaudible, and the attempts made by La Farina and the National Society during the winter of 1858–9 to organize revolutionary movements in accordance with the plans made at Plombières met with little success. One reason for this was that the instructions coming out of Turin were necessarily very ambiguous, for what Cavour and La Farina wanted were controlled risings that they could use as pretexts for a quarrel with Austria and not full-blooded insurrections that might be hijacked by the democrats and used to launch a popular war of liberation. In these circumstances the various clandestine committees dotted around Italy with whom La Farina was in touch were uncertain what to do, especially when, as was often the case, they were also in secret correspondence with exiled Mazzinians who had a very different agenda.[8] The absence of grass-roots initiatives was particularly disappointing to Napoleon, who had been under the impression that discontent was much more widespread in Italy than it actually was, and without a moral shield to hide behind he was looking more and more to the outside world like an unprincipled and dangerous aggressor. To make matters worse his attempts to isolate Austria diplomatically were not working out well, as the Prussians were threatening to support Vienna in the event of any conflict with France. With the cards stacking against him, Napoleon decided early in March to postpone the war.

Cavour was furious, and when a few days later the Russians proposed that a congress should be convened to sort out the problems with Austria peacefully, and Britain and France agreed, he was beside himself. He hurried off to Paris to see if there was anything to be done, but found Napoleon deeply dejected and no longer interested in war and most of the diplomats and politicians he met angry with him personally and with Piedmont for having got Europe into such an awful mess. He returned to Turin in despair, and during the first two weeks of April there was a flurry of diplomatic activity by the great powers designed to bring about the disarmament of Piedmont and Austria and stop what the British Foreign Secretary described as Cavour's 'violent policy which threatened all Europe with war'.[9] As international pressure on him mounted, Cavour became increasingly prone to severe mood swings, and when on 19 April he was finally forced to accede to disarmament, he declared that there was now nothing left for him to do except blow his brains out. He wrote to his nephew with instructions about what to do after his death and shut himself in his study with orders for nobody to enter and began burning his private papers. Only the intervention of his oldest friend, it seems, stopped him from carrying out his threat of suicide.[10]

What Cavour did not know was that Austria had in fact settled on war. Convinced that Napoleon had now withdrawn his support from Piedmont, but equally convinced that he was going to fight Austria at some point soon; and convinced, as well, that Austria's prestige in Italy could not survive further provocations from Piedmont, Vienna dispatched an ultimatum to Turin on 23 April. It could not have been better timed. By agreeing to disarmament Cavour had overnight made himself the toast of British liberals. Suddenly Austria had cast itself in the role of the bullying aggressor. It was, as Massimo d'Azeglio told him, a remarkable piece of gambler's good fortune, 'one of those lottery jackpots that occurs once in a century'.[11] Cavour was euphoric. Piedmont was given three days to reply, during which time final preparations were made with the army and full emergency powers granted to the king. Cavour was nervous in case Britain tried to use its good offices to restrain Vienna, but his luck held, and on 26 April he was able to hand a formal rejection of the ultimatum to the Austrian envoys waiting in Turin. Turning to his colleagues he announced triumphantly: '*Alea jacta est*; we have made history, so now we can sit down to dinner.'[12]

History had indeed been made, but not quite as Cavour anticipated. One of his big concerns was that the Italian contribution to the war should be sufficiently large to ensure that the French did not dictate terms entirely. But the Piedmontese forces amounted to only about 60,000 men, less than half the size of the French army, which accordingly bore the brunt of the fighting that took place in the stifling heat of the Po valley in late May and June. Furthermore the organizational and structural problems that had undermined the performance of the Piedmontese army in 1848–9 resurfaced in 1859. There were still no good maps of Lombardy and no proper campaign plans, and it was extremely fortunate that the Austrian commander showed little initiative at the start of operations and failed to launch a serious attack on Piedmont, which could have been overrun before the French arrived. There were also difficulties once again with the army leadership, as Victor Emmanuel insisted on acting as commander-in-chief despite his lack of experience (and penchant for outdated cavalry charges) and resented taking advice from anyone, including his senior generals.[13] The upshot was poor communication and frequent arguments about tactics, which contributed to several major blunders during the campaign, including the failure of the Piedmontese forces to arrive until it was almost too late at the Battle of Magenta on 4 June and the unnecessarily high casualties inflicted on the Piedmontese in the one serious engagement in which they played a prominent role, at San Martino three weeks later.[14]

No less disappointing to Cavour than the minor part played by

Piedmont in the fighting was the relative lack of national sentiment on display during the war. This was politically very embarrassing, as the principal justification for Napoleon's intervention as far as the rest of Europe was concerned was the need to liberate the people of Italy from the oppressive and unpopular rule of the Austrians and their satellite princes. Demonstrations did break out in the streets of Florence on 27 April (instigated by eighty policemen from Turin dressed as civilians) which caused the grand-duke to flee, but even after the Austrians had been defeated at Magenta and the way opened for the occupation of Milan, Modena and Parma, the large-scale risings that La Farina and the National Society had confidently told Cavour would break out showed no signs of materializing. The northern part of the Papal States remained alarmingly inert after the Austrians withdrew their garrisons from Bologna and Ancona, leading Cavour early in July to complain to one of his confidants in the Romagna, who had assured him that the local population was enthusiastic in its desire for annexation to Piedmont, of 'the very meagre signs of patriotism displayed so far' and of the burning need that 'the masses do something' to show their hatred of papal rule.[15]

As with the campaign against Austria in 1848-9, part of the problem was a widespread suspicion that Piedmont was more interested in conquering than in liberating. The traditional mistrust felt by many Lombards towards their ambitious neighbour was evident in the cool and sometimes overtly hostile reception given the advancing Piedmontese forces (in contrast to the French, who were warmly received in Milan); and these old regional rivalries were no doubt a factor in the conspicuous courage displayed by the Italian-speaking units from Lombardy–Venetia that fought on the Austrian side in the war (Cavour had hoped 50,000 Italians would desert the Austrian colours; very few did).[16] A similar wariness about Piedmont's motives may well have acted as a deterrent to volunteers. In the months leading up to the outbreak of hostilities thousands of young men arrived in north-west Italy to fight the Austrians, but many were given a lukewarm reception by the Piedmontese authorities, not least for political reasons, and in the end only about 3,500 enrolled in the battalion of irregulars that was placed under the command of Garibaldi. Not until Napoleon complained bitterly that 'showing you are ready to fight is the sole way to prove your worthiness to become a nation' did Cavour begin to take a more positive attitude towards volunteers, but by then it was too late as the war was nearly over. Karl Marx noted at the time that the small state of Prussia had generated more enthusiasm and more volunteers against France in 1813 than the whole of Italy against Austria in 1859.[17]

The battle fought at Solferino, a few miles to the south of Lake Garda, on 24 June was a major victory for the French and Piedmontese armies, but it was immensely bloody. One chance observer, a Swiss businessman called Jean Henri Dunant, was inspired to found the Red Cross after witnessing the horrific spectacle of the 30,000 dead and wounded lying strewn under the blazing sun.[18] The Austrians, however, were not decisively beaten, and with little prospect of an immediate end to the war in sight, Napoleon decided to press for peace. He was already alarmed by Cavour's attempts to engineer the annexation of Tuscany and the Romagna to Piedmont, and he was worried that Prussia might be about to enter the war on the side of Austria. He was also facing opposition from Catholic opinion at home. The Austrians, for their part, were concerned that any prolongation of the war might unleash a wave of revolutionary nationalism in their empire. On 11 August, Napoleon and the Austrian emperor met at Villafranca and agreed that most of Lombardy, but not Modena and Parma, should be given to Piedmont, and that an Italian Confederation should be established, with Austria as one of its members. Napoleon was prepared to renounce his claim to Nice and Savoy, but insisted that Piedmont should shoulder the full costs of the war. The terms were then shown to Victor Emmanuel, who agreed to them. When Cavour was told of this rather ignominious settlement he lost his temper completely, hurled every manner of abuse at the king, who sat quietly smoking a cigar, and resigned.[19] Victor Emmanuel had never forgiven Cavour for humiliating him over his mistress, and was delighted to see the back of him.

THE THOUSAND

The war in northern Italy goaded the democrats into action. Napoleon's intervention was widely and largely correctly seen as a cynical move intended not to advance the cause of unification but simply to replace Austrian with French hegemony in the peninsula. In July 1859 one of Mazzini's more committed followers, Francesco Crispi, travelled from London to Sicily to teach bomb-making techniques to potential revolutionaries and pave the way for an insurrection in the island on 4 October.[20] Garibaldi still had a substantial force of volunteers under his command near the papal frontier, and Mazzini hoped he could persuade him to launch a simultaneous attack on Rome. But Garibaldi would not proceed against the wishes of Victor Emmanuel; and the king would not act without the consent of Napoleon, who not surprisingly vetoed the idea. Meanwhile preparations for the Sicilian rising continued, but they were heavily undermined by conflicting messages coming from La Farina in Turin urging caution, and in the end the rising was called off. But the leaders of the peasant squads had been alerted to the possibility of a revolution in the island, and in the course of the next few months they and their contacts in Palermo began making plans and building up stashes of weapons in readiness for action. Francesco Crispi hurried off to Turin.

In central Italy the provisional governments that had been set up in Parma, Modena, Tuscany and the Romagna during the war proceeded to elect representative assemblies, which, in defiance of the terms of Villafranca, demanded annexation to Piedmont. Napoleon had no wish to see Piedmont expanded on such a scale, but by the autumn, with a new Whig government in London headed by Palmerston and Lord John Russell favouring an arrangement of this kind (precisely because it would help to curtail France's influence in the peninsula), it was becoming clear that the emperor's alternative scheme of an Italian Confederation was unrealistic. Napoleon now decided to agree to the annexations provided that he received Nice and Savoy as compensation, and when Cavour returned to power in January, his first task was to sort out the practical arrangements for this territorial resettlement. His chosen tool was the plebiscite based on universal suffrage, which, as Napoleon had shown at the time of his 'election' as emperor in 1852, could easily be manipulated to achieve the desired result. On 11–12 March 1860 the people of central Italy went to the polls in a staged carnival atmosphere with bands playing, flags waving and landowners escorting their peasants, and since voting was in public it was no surprise that very few ballots were cast in the 'No' urn. Before the elections Cavour had promised that the former states would be given a large degree of regional autonomy – a promise he did not keep – and this pledge probably helped to win over many conservative middle-class voters.[21] A few weeks later Nice and Savoy were handed to France with a similarly artificial plebiscite.

Meanwhile in Sicily preparations were being made for a rising. For months the island had been in febrile state, with subversive leaflets and posters appearing, acts of terrorism being perpetrated and countless rumours flying around, and when early in April a revolt broke out in Palermo, it quickly spread across the island, fuelled by peasant griev-ances over land and taxation, local factional struggles and the wide-spread hatred that many middle- and upper-class Sicilians felt for rule from Naples. On 10 April a leading Mazzinian exile and a close friend of Francesco Crispi, Rosalino Pilo, landed near Messina carrying a clutch of hand-grenades and sporting an exotic beard and long hair (trademarks of the international revolutionary), and travelled west from town to town announcing as he went that the most famous Italian soldier, Giuseppe Garibaldi, 'the man who does not lose battles', was about to land in Sicily.[22] His news was greeted with extraordinary excitement: Garibaldi's achievements in South America, in the Roman Republic and in the war of 1859, his flamboyant good looks (studiedly similar to those of Christ: a point underlined in many prints and paint-ings) and unconventional modest lifestyle, his simplicity of manner and immense personal bravery, and his seeming invulnerability on the battle-field had all combined to make him a cult figure with unprecedented popular appeal.[23]

In fact Garibaldi had made no such agreement to land in Sicily. Pilo and Crispi had been writing to him in February and March urging him to 'save the cause of Italy' and head an expedition to the island, but Garibaldi had refused to commit himself.[24] The intention was clearly to try to force Garibaldi's hand by generating an atmosphere of expec-tation. The news at the end of March that Cavour had consented to give Garibaldi's home-town of Nice to Napoleon certainly increased Garibaldi's desire to do something to embarrass the Piedmontese prime minister (whom he had always suspected of not having the interests of Italy at heart), but even then he was reluctant to act until he had clear proof that the Sicilian rising was so extensive as to make success almost certain. Throughout April, Crispi and the other exiles gathered in Genoa made it their task to convince Garibaldi to lead an expedition, using what were often deliberately exaggerated newspaper reports and anything else they could lay their hands on to suggest that the Bourbons had totally lost control in Sicily. Garibaldi wavered and wavered, and only at the end of April (when in reality the rising had largely petered out in the island) did he make a final decision.[25] On 6 May two small steamers with just over a thousand men on board set sail from Quarto, near Genoa, for Sicily.

Cavour was on the horns of a terrible dilemma. Despite the fact that many of the volunteers with Garibaldi were Mazzinians or former Mazzinians, 'the Thousand' announced from the outset that their slogan was 'Italy and Victor Emmanuel'. How could Cavour possibly oppose openly an expedition, led by the most famous and popular of Italian patriots, whose declared aim was to unite all Italy under the king of Piedmont? Yet if Garibaldi succeeded in conquering Sicily, crossed to the mainland and marched up to Naples and then on to Rome, not only would there be a major risk of Napoleon intervening (though Britain would have worked to restrain him), but much more importantly Piedmont's (and of course his own) position as the guiding force in the Italian national question would be destroyed. Cavour had to endure many sleepless nights over the next five months, but no image would have disturbed him more than one of Garibaldi victoriously ascending the Capitol in Rome amid cheering crowds, to the acclaim of millions throughout the world, a new Bolívar or Washington.

On the face of it, Garibaldi's venture stood very little chance of success, and Cavour did what he could behind the scenes to make the odds longer still. He made sure, for example, that the volunteers did not have any decent weapons: they left with just a thousand rusty smoothbore converted flintlocks provided by La Farina (who admitted he could have given them much better arms had he wanted to) and no ammunition. But through a combination of extreme good luck and inspired leadership Garibaldi's men were able to land safely at Marsala on the west coast of Sicily, advance inland and defeat a force of Bourbon soldiers sent to block their route at Calatafimi. News of this success rekindled the stuttering rising in the countryside, and local administration everywhere began to crumble, with government officials and unpopular landowners being assaulted or even killed.[26] The victory also encouraged the local population, who up to this point had been reluctant to help the expedition, to give their support. At the end of May, Palermo was captured after three days of fierce street fighting and contrary to all expectations the expedition looked as if it might succeed.

Cavour needed to stop Garibaldi before he got any further, and early in June he sent La Farina to Palermo with several boxes of posters bearing the words 'We want annexation!' These were quickly pasted up around the city, and La Farina then set to work organizing demonstrations and pressurizing members of the local ruling classes into calling for speedy union with Piedmont.[27] He was greatly helped by the fact that law and order were breaking down across the island, which encouraged many among the propertied classes to feel that the sooner the Piedmontese arrived with some battalions of regular soldiers, the better. There was also a widespread desire for autonomy in Sicily, especially within the Palermo aristocracy, and the prospect of being able to negotiate a favourable package of self-rule for the island, under Piedmontese protection, was deeply appealing. But Garibaldi and his chief political adviser, Francesco Crispi, stood firm against La Farina, realizing that if they surrendered Sicily they would no longer have a base from which to launch the conquest of the rest of Italy. Early in July, La Farina was expelled from the island, and the next month Garibaldi crossed to the mainland and began a triumphal advance on Naples.

Cavour tried to seize control of the situation by staging an insurrection in Naples ahead of Garibaldi. Agents were sent to the city to make the necessary arrangements, and Piedmontese warships with soldiers concealed below their decks were stationed offshore, ready to land as soon as the rising broke out. But through a mixture of poor organization and mistrust of Turin nothing happened, and on 7 September, Garibaldi entered Naples, arriving by train well in advance of most of his army, amid scenes of extraordinary jubilation. He was careful to please the local populace by attending a *Te Deum* of thanksgiving in the cathedral and visiting the chapel of San Gennaro, and from a balcony he saluted the crowds that gathered to greet him in front of the Royal Palace, proclaiming the age of tyranny over, and holding his index finger aloft in a gesture to symbolize the unity of Italy.[28] Cavour was livid at the 'ignominious' and 'disgusting' conduct of the Neapolitans, calling them 'spineless chickens', with 'corrupt' characters, who were as 'incapable of rising up as they were of fighting'.[29] In a last attempt to gain the initiative, he was now forced to take one of the biggest gambles of his career: an invasion of the Papal States.

His pretext was that he needed to stop Garibaldi reaching Rome and thereby save the Pope from the clutches of an army of dangerous revolutionaries, and the fact that Mazzini, Cattaneo and a number of other leading republicans were assembling in Naples gave some added force to his case. He told Napoleon of his intentions; and the emperor consented, provided that an insurrection were staged in advance in Umbria and the Marche to make the attack on the Pope's dominions at least look like a war of liberation rather than one of conquest. But despite the best endeavours of the National Society, no rising materialized, and the Piedmontese army was forced to invade the Papal States in violation of international law without any obvious moral smokescreen. Meanwhile, Garibaldi was pinned down fighting the Bourbon forces on the Volturno river and as Victor Emmanuel advanced south it became clear that the political initiative was swinging decisively in Piedmont's favour. Crispi and a number of other democrats desperately tried to salvage what they could by demanding elected assemblies to lay down terms for the unification of the south with the north. But the pressure on Garibaldi to concede annexation was huge, and on 13 October he agreed to hold plebiscites. A week later the voters of Naples and Sicily went to the polls to answer the question: '[Do you want] Italy one and indivisible, with Victor Emmanuel, constitutional king, and his legitimate descendants?' 1,734,117 said 'Yes', 10,979, 'No'.

With the Bourbon army defeated Garibaldi crossed the Volturno river at the head of several thousand soldiers on a pontoon bridge that had been laid by British volunteers and rode north with members of his red-shirted general staff to rendezvous with Victor Emmanuel. At dawn on 26 October they encountered a column of Piedmontese troops marching towards the small town of Teano. Suddenly the cry went up, 'The King! The King!', and the strains of the Royal March were heard. Victor Emmanuel rode up, dressed in a general's uniform and mounted on a dapple-grey stallion, escorted by a retinue of officers and courtiers. Garibaldi took off his hat, but his head was still covered with a silk scarf knotted under his chin that he had put on to protect his ears from the chill and dampness of the autumn morning air. The king stretched out his hand. 'I salute you, my dear Garibaldi. How are you?' 'Well, Your Majesty, and you?' 'Very well!' Then turning to those around him Garibaldi cried: 'Behold the king of Italy!' 'Long live the king!' came the reply. The two men rode side by side for a short distance, and then went their separate ways.[30] A fortnight later Garibaldi delivered to Victor Emmanuel the results of the plebiscite in the throne room of the Royal Palace in Naples, and the next day, his authority in southern Italy now formally ended (and his request to remain in Naples for a year as Royal

Lieutenant declined), he sailed for his home on the small island of Caprera, off the north coast of Sardinia. He had been offered money, titles, a castle and even his own private steamer, but in true Roman republican fashion he had spurned them all, and he departed on the *Washington* with just a few packets of coffee and sugar, some dried cod and a bag of seeds. The following March with an act of parliament Victor Emmanuel was proclaimed 'King of Italy, by the grace of God and the will of the nation'.

Italy, with the exception of the Veneto, Trentino, South Tyrol and the city of Rome and its immediately surrounding territory, had been united into a single kingdom. But the new state was far from being the creation, or even expression, of a national will. Without the armies of Napoleon III, the fortunate conjuncture of diplomatic circumstances, the ambitions of Cavour and Piedmont, the desperation of the Sicilian peasantry, and the determination of Garibaldi and a handful of followers, unification would not have occurred. The Risorgimento as a political and cultural movement had been the work of a small minority of the population inspired by a vision of the nation that owed much to literary and artistic fantasy and to a willing suspension of disbelief in the face of the fractured reality of much of the peninsula. For the overwhelming majority of the twenty-two million people who suddenly found themselves 'Italians', 'Italy' had meant little or nothing. For many it had been a wholly unfamiliar term. Listening to the crowds cheering 'Viva l'Italia' in the streets of Naples in 1860 one French observer heard a man turn to his neighbour and ask bemusedly: 'What is Italy?'; and in Sicily it was apparently quite widely maintained that 'La Talia' was the name of the new king's wife.[31] A major challenge facing the country's rulers after 1860 was how to give 'Italy' resonance in the minds of a population that neither history, nor education, nor social and economic interaction had prepared for political unity.

But the attainment of what contemporaries often referred to as the country's 'moral unity' was necessarily a much more complicated process than the achievement of its 'material unity', and it required as a guiding template a set of assumptions, both negative and positive, by which the Italian nation could chart its course. Most of these assumptions were formulated in the Risorgimento and, with varying inflections and emphases, were transferred to the political and cultural life of the new state after 1860. They included a sense that Italy had a great past to live up to, and had a mission to fulfil in the world, and should not content itself with becoming merely 'a large Belgium without industry';[32] that the peoples of the peninsula had a legacy of decadence and corruption to shake off, and that national regeneration required the emergence of Italians purged of their old vices and weaknesses and educated to citizenship; that the abasement of previous centuries had been due in large measure to fragmentation and discord, and that the future of the country depended on creating internal cohesion – particularly necessary for survival in a Darwinian world where international conflict was inevitable and mass patriotic armies indispensable; and that for this integration to be truly strong and lasting Italians had to transfer a measure of faith and enthusiasm to the secular sphere and so fashion the communion of believers in 'Italy' that Mazzini and many other Italian patriots of his generation had longed for.

Among those who had been caught up in the feverish excitement of 1860 was a young student and passionate enthusiast for the cause of Italian unity from the Veneto called Carlo Tivaroni. He had joined a battalion of *bersaglieri* in Ferrara as a volunteer and saw action in the last stages of the fighting against the Bourbons. Tivaroni was in later years to become a prominent figure in radical journalism and a deputy in parliament. His principal allegiance was always to the democrats, and in particular to his great hero Garibaldi, but he came to accept that the moderates, too, had played a crucial part in securing the unification of Italy. And when in the 1880s and 1890s he turned to writing a grand narrative of the events in the peninsula since the French Revolution, he presented the Risorgimento as an almost miraculous synthesis in which the various contending forces had complemented one another perfectly (if unwittingly) in bringing about the goal of national unity. But like many of his background he regarded the attainment of material unification as merely one stage in the Risorgimento. As he said towards the end of his monumental work, in 1897:

Once material unity had been achieved, it remained to complete moral unity, without which there is no nation, but simply a collection of individuals, easily dissolved . . . This is a serious issue, as moral unity is a matter not of the form of the government . . . but of its very substance, and is essential to a modern state . . . When the conscience of the ruling classes is shared by everyone, when a sense of patriotism pervades the rural masses, when all the provinces of Italy have these attributes in equal measure, then, and only then, will Italy be able to look ahead with confidence and faith. Otherwise the work of the Risorgimento will have been in vain and will have served no other purpose than to demonstrate the physiological inability of Italy to be a nation.[33]

PART FOUR

Prose
1861–87

II

The New State

We have visited a number of towns in the province of Molise . . . Towns! More like proper pigsties! . . . It will take many, many years, to bring these places up to the level of civilization that we are familiar with. There are no roads, no hotels, no hospitals – in fact none of the things you would find today even in the most backward part of Europe! . . . What kind of government has God willed upon the people here? They have no sense of justice or honesty – they lie constantly – they are as timid as children . . . And then there are the terrible feuds. In these regions enemies or opponents kill each other. But you don't just murder an enemy: you have to butcher him . . . In short this is a land that needs to be destroyed or at least depopulated and its inhabitants sent to Africa to be civilized!

Nino Bixio, letter to his wife from San Severo, Puglia, 1863

What is the goal towards which we are all striving? To make Italy once again into one body, one nation. Which is easier to unite: divided cities and provinces or divided hearts and minds? In the case of Italy in particular, I think the second is far harder than the first.

Massimo d'Azeglio, speech to the Senate, 3 December 1864

PONTELANDOLFO, 14 AUGUST 1861

Prior to its annexation to the new Italian state with the plebiscite on 21 October 1860, the small walled town of Pontelandolfo, some forty miles to the north-east of Naples, had been part of the Duchy of Benevento, an ancient enclave of papal territory situated deep inside the Kingdom of the Two Sicilies and ruled over since the Middle Ages by the local archbishop. Like countless other settlements in the Apennines of central and southern Italy, Pontelandolfo (or Polfo as it was often affectionately known) was accessible only with difficulty. It was perched at a height of some 2,000 feet, with a steep precipice on one side and surrounded by tracts of dense woodland, with the sheer Matese mountains towering over it to the north and to the south rugged hills running away down towards the Volturno river. The great majority of its five and a half thousand inhabitants were peasants, many of them landless labourers, who before dawn would assemble in the Piazza del Tiglio with their tools hoping to be hired for the day by an agent of one of the small group of rich landowners or *galantuomini* who dominated the political and economic life of the community and who singled themselves out from the rest of the population with their smart tailcoats and top hats and carefully groomed beards and moustaches – the *mosca* or toothbrush up to 1860, thereafter the more flamboyant handlebar in imitation of King Victor Emmanuel.[1]

For most of the population of Pontelandolfo life was extremely hard, and since the abolition of feudalism in 1806 the indications are that it had been growing progressively harsher, as common lands were enclosed by unscrupulous *galantuomini* and demographic pressures resulted in local resources being spread ever more thinly and wages being kept low: Pontelandolfo's population rose sharply in the first half of the nineteenth century, perhaps by as much as 80 per cent, in line with much of the rest of southern Italy.[2] The average pay for sixteen hours of digging on parched rocky soil was about one-third of a lira, enough to buy half a kilogram of bread and a few vegetables; and since work was available for only a hundred or so days in the year, those peasants who could not supplement their incomes with produce from their own plot of land or with milk and cheese from a goat were forced to forage in the countryside, hunting for birds, hares, hedgehogs, wolves, wild boar and other livestock in which the woods were relatively abundant still, or simply stealing. Many families not surprisingly lived perilously close to the breadline and suffered from poor health and high death rates (life expectancy at birth was just over thirty for Italy as a whole in 1861)[3] and any additional financial demands that were made upon them – such as the local tax on land or the much resented levy on goats – were very sorely felt.[4]

But severe material deprivation was in part redeemed by a strong local patriotism that was to make it hard for many of the inhabitants to develop a parallel loyalty to any broader geographical entity, certainly one as unfamiliar and abstract as Italy. Pontelandolfo had a well-developed sense of its own past, retold in songs and epic poems chanted to large audiences by peasant bards and storytellers on summer evenings after harvest or during the many festivals that punctuated the year. It was a history in large part of a community that had suffered repeatedly at the hands of forces from an unpredictable and hostile outside world. According to legend the town had been founded in remote antiquity by the Samnites in honour of Hercules and had enjoyed great peace, prosperity and happiness until conquered by the Romans at the beginning of the third century BC. During the Dark Ages a Lombard bishop called Landolfo had constructed a bridge in the area, from which the settlement derived its modern name; but thereafter Pontelandolfo had suffered a succession of devastating attacks and natural disasters, including a raid by Arab invaders in 862, a terrible siege and fire at the hands of the Normans in 1138 and another at the hands of the Aragonese in 1461, and catastrophic earthquakes in 1349, 1456 and 1688. In 1806 it had been the turn of the French to pillage and burn. So when in September 1860 Garibaldi's troops arrived in the area, followed shortly by the Piedmontese, it was easy for the town's inhabitants to feel somewhat sceptical about the claims of their liberators that an unprecedented era of prosperity, justice and freedom was about to begin.

To make matters worse, it was soon quite clear that the cultural world of most peasants and even *galantuomini* in Pontelandolfo would not attract much sympathy or understanding from their new rulers. One obvious barrier was language: the local dialect was almost incomprehensible to outsiders, and the soldiers garrisoning the province of Benevento soon had a sense of living in a foreign land, linguistically as well as emotionally. Illiteracy was universal among the poor and knowledge of the broader world was restricted to what the *galantuomini* or clergy cared to pass on to them or to what could be gleaned from trips to neighbouring markets at San Lupo, Cerreto, Guardia or Campobasso.[5] Violence and murder were common, and seemed to be regarded virtually as part and parcel of everyday life, and the often close links that existed between bandit gangs operating in the mountains around Pontelandolfo and the townspeople (not least the landowners) was something that men who had been brought up in Piedmont or Lombardy with a fairly strong sense of the state found hard to stomach. Nor was it self-evident that these links were simply the result of fear: the rich used bandits to control their tenants and workers, police their estates and conduct feuds with enemies in return for money, food and most importantly protection from the law.

Religion might have been expected to provide some common ground between Pontelandolfo and the Piedmontese, but in fact many northerners were nauseated by what they regarded as the superstitious character of much southern Catholicism with its belief in demons, portents and miraculous interventions, its fertility ceremonies and unorthodox rituals, its pomp and theatricality, its veneration of relics and its cults of obscure local saints. The patron saint of Pontelandolfo was San Donato, whose badly mutilated arm preserved in a reliquary in a chapel on the outskirts of the town was the focus of lavish celebrations held for several days each year in the second week of August. The local archpriest, Don Epifanio De Gregorio, probably viewed the pagan aspects of popular devotion in his parish with some scepticism and alarm; and as the author of a panegyric to the Bourbon king published in Naples in 1852 with the title *The Star in the Darkness, or the Immortal Ferdinand II King of the Two Sicilies* he must have hoped that his career would have taken him to more elevated surroundings than this remote rural community. But he had a duty to keep in with his congregation, and his easiest course was to indulge them in their wishes, however unorthodox they might be. It was also prudent to turn a blind eye to witchcraft, which was as widespread in Pontelandolfo as it was in most other rural settlements in Italy. The Church had often condemned the use of magic charms and curses, amulets and potions by wise women, but local people regularly employed them to secure good luck or to ward off the effects of the evil eye or, in the absence of doctors, to cure illnesses.[6]

On the evening of 7 August 1861, as the annual celebrations in honour of San Donato were beginning, some forty bandits rode down from the mountains to the chapel on the outskirts of the town where the people of Pontelandolfo had gathered to hear Vespers. They were led by Cosimo Giordano, a former Bourbon soldier who had taken to the hills the autumn of the previous year to avoid being arrested by the Piedmontese and sent to one of the prison camps in northern Italy where thousands of supporters of the old order were being interned, often in atrocious conditions.[7] His followers included young men who had failed, either deliberately or because they had not been told about it in time, to respond to a government decree of December 1860 calling up all those in their early twenties for service in the new Italian army. Since the beginning of the year patrols of government troops had been scouring the towns and villages of southern Italy searching for draft-dodgers, and in some places, as at Agro di Latronico and Castel Saraceno in Basilicata, anyone who was thought to be between the ages of twenty and twenty-five had been arrested and summarily shot as a deserter.[8]

Giordano and his men (who had styled themselves the Fra Diavolo Brigade in honour of the famous Bourbon bandit from the beginning of the century) were warmly received by the peasants of Pontelandolfo, whose relations with the authorities had been deteriorating fast since the end of 1860 as it became clear that 'Italy' meant not just conscription but also higher taxes and the anger of the Catholic Church: in March 1861 the Pope had publicly denounced the 'unjust and violent theft' of his territories by Piedmont and had refused to continue negotiations with Cavour for a compromise settlement. It also meant an end to any hopes that former common lands, illegally enclosed since 1806, would be returned to the community, for the local *galantuomini* were now sporting tricolour cockades and sashes in a clear sign that the government in Turin had turned to them as its local representatives, irrespective very often of whether they had been supporters of the Bourbons or not. Indeed, one of the richest local landowners, Achille Iacobelli, whose family had a long tradition of fierce opposition to any form of liberalism stretching back to 1799, quickly established himself as a lynchpin of the new provincial administration (and secured a satisfactory solution to a long-standing lawsuit with a neighbouring town over the expropriation of land).[9]

Emboldened by the presence of Giordano the people of Pontelandolfo, perhaps 3,000 in number, marched up into the town and ordered Don Epifanio to go into the parish church and sing a *Te Deum* in honour of the deposed Bourbon king. They then ransacked the headquarters of the National Guard, smashing portraits of Victor Emmanuel and Garibaldi and ripping the Savoy crest from the national flag, and broke into the town hall, destroying the registers of births (to make it hard to enforce conscription), pulling down and burning the tricolour on the balcony and hoisting the golden lilies of the Bourbons in its place. The inmates of the local gaol were released, and the homes of the leading *galantuomini*, all of whom had fled Pontelandolfo the day before, were looted.

The tax collector, Michelangelo Perugini, who had ill-advisedly returned to the town hoping that he could save his skin (and his property) by making public declarations of loyalty to the Bourbons, was murdered and his house set on fire, and a man popularly regarded as a Piedmontese 'spy' was caught hiding under a pile of hay in a stable and shot. Other scores were settled violently in the course of the day, and by the time Giordano and his band slipped out of the town on the night of 7 August, Pontelandolfo was a torrid cauldron of opposition to the new state.

Matters might gradually have calmed down had a detachment of *bersaglieri* not been sent from Campobasso to investigate rumours that Pontelandolfo was in the hands of brigands. Unwisely and contrary to orders the troops entered the town, where they encountered the full force of local anger. After taking refuge in the precincts of the medieval fortress, they decided to withdraw and try to reach the safety of San Lupo, some three miles away, but as they crossed the open countryside in the neighbourhood of Casalduni they were set upon by armed peasants, and forty-one of their number were killed.[10] Who exactly was responsible for the attack is unclear, but there are good grounds for believing that the ringleaders were tenants of the powerful landowner Achille Iacobelli, who was apparently engaged in a devious double game, not uncommon in a world where the elites were used to manipulating local violence to bolster their own political and economic standing, stirring up unrest so as to discredit his opponents and allow himself to pose as the guardian of law and order. Indeed it was Iacobelli who drew up a lurid and apparently highly inflated account of the killings and lawlessness in Pontelandolfo, which he sent to the newly installed military and civil commander of southern Italy, the Piedmontese general Enrico Cialdini, urging him to make an example of the barbarous 'nest of bandits', and show it no mercy.[11]

As soon as he received the report Cialdini summoned one of his officers, Carlo Melegari (who had been enjoying an evening out at the opera), and told him to proceed immediately to Benevento. Here he was to join up with Colonel Pier Eleonoro Negri, a tough-minded soldier from north-eastern Italy who had distinguished himself fighting in the Piedmontese army the previous year, march on Pontelandolfo and Casalduni and reduce the towns to 'a heap of rubble'. Melegari and Negri set out from Benevento on the night of 13 August with 500 infantry and four companies of *bersaglieri*, and as dawn broke they came in sight of their targets. Word had got through to Casalduni of what was in store for them, and when Melegari's men arrived only three people were left. All were shot, including one man lying on his sickbed.[12] Pontelandolfo was less fortunate, and as Negri's *bersaglieri* raced through the streets smashing windows and firing their rifles, many townspeople were still asleep. The troops had been instructed to shoot everyone except women, children and the infirm: but this was retaliation for the murder of forty-one comrades, and the violence was allowed to degenerate into a frenzy and became virtually indiscriminate. One particular target was the priest, Don Epifanio, who was widely regarded as being the main troublemaker in Pontelandolfo. Negri gave instructions that he be hunted down and executed first. Exactly what happened to him is unknown: he may have been killed that morning; he may have succeeded in escaping and been shot later; or he may have got away altogether. At any event, he was not heard of again.

During the five or six hours that the troops terrorized Pontelandolfo many atrocities were committed. Quite how many is unclear. Some estimates put the number of those killed at between one and two hundred, others much higher. A likely figure is perhaps 400, with dozens more being arrested and shot in the weeks that followed.[13] Negri's men were encouraged to loot and pillage at will; nothing was spared, and the scene in Pontelandolfo that August morning rapidly came to resemble a kind of infernal Cockaigne, with houses blazing and bodies lying in the streets, and gorged and drunken soldiers grabbing money, jewellery and whatever else of value they could find, and raping any women or girls they could lay their hands on. It was the intense heat, the screams of the dying and the unaccustomed abundance of food that etched themselves most on the memory of one *bersagliere*, Carlo Margolfo, a conscript from a village high in the foothills of the Alps in northern Lombardy:

We entered the town and immediately began shooting the priests and any men we came across. Then the soldiers started sacking, and finally we set fire to the town . . . What a terrible scene it was, and the heat was so great that you could not stand it there. And what a noise those poor devils made whose fate it was to die roasted under the ruins of the houses. But while the fire raged we had everything we wanted – chickens, bread, wine, capons. We were short of nothing.[14]

Towards noon the order was given to withdraw, and the troops set off back to Benevento. The following day Negri sent a report to the provincial Governor: 'At dawn yesterday justice was done to Pontelandolfo and Casalduni. They are still burning.'[15] In the months that followed many of those who had managed to avoid the massacre on 14 August were rounded up and 573 were put on trial. Of these 146 were sentenced to life imprisonment or to hard labour. The bandit leader Cosimo Giordano succeeded in escaping justice thanks largely to the protection of local landowners and politicians, and after a few years spent in Rome he emigrated to Marseille with a forged passport, where he opened a greengrocer's shop. Negri continued his successful military career and went on to serve in the war against Austria in 1866, being promoted to the rank of major-general.[16] The towns of Pontelandolfo and Casalduni were for the most part razed to the ground and some 3,000 people were left homeless.

The events at Pontelandolfo formed part of what was euphemistically referred to as the 'war against brigandage', which scarred the experience of unification at the very outset for millions of Italians. Well into the twentieth century local memories of what happened in the early 1860s in communities throughout the mainland south and Sicily remained raw and on occasions flared into anger against the *galantuomini* and representatives of the state, or else lay dormant and fuelled that most common of peasant feelings, fatalistic resignation.[17] The massacre at Pontelandolfo was especially brutal and as such reverberated widely – though much of the press coverage was extremely partial, with the emphasis on what one Turin newspaper called the 'acts of the most ferocious barbarism' perpetrated against 'our troops', which had now been suitably punished.[18] One member of parliament, the Milanese democrat Giuseppe Ferrari, visited the town shortly after the events and reported to the Chamber some of the horrific details he had learned from the survivors. (Pontelandolfo found the courage to name a street in his honour in 1973.) But revelations of this kind were regarded as unpatriotic and potentially very damaging to the fragile new kingdom's international standing and when Ferrari went so far as to suggest that what was going on in southern Italy was tantamount to a 'civil war' he was angrily shouted down. The violence in the south, he was reminded sharply, was due to 'brigandage' and nothing else.[19]

For political reasons the new rulers of Italy had little choice but to present the unrest in southern Italy in the first years of unification as the result mainly of common criminality: what other form of opposition could there be to a regime that had been brought into existence by the will of the people and voted for overwhelmingly in plebiscites? But the sheer scale of the unrest belied such easy reductionism. By 1864 over 100,000 troops were deployed in the south trying to keep order, nearly half of the entire Italian army; and as the commanders on the ground repeatedly lamented (and as Pontelandolfo showed), attempts to draw a clear line between those who could legitimately be described as 'brigands' and other sections of the local population who were regularly in contact with the bandits or themselves committed acts of violence was extremely hard. To make matters worse, the army almost every-where had to contend with a wall of silence, and getting reliable infor-mation about the movements of the enemy proved virtually impossible. One reason for this was fear: peasants were often terrified of reprisals if they spoke to the authorities. But that was only part of the explanation, as a report on the entry of the bandit Nunziato Mecola and his numerous supporters into the small town of Orsogna in the Abruzzi in January 1861 suggested:

On the morning of the 4th Mecola entered Orsogna in triumph at the head of a horde of brigands and was received by ... four *galantuomini* and the clergy carrying the statues of San Nicolò and the Virgin and preceded by a band of musicians ... A hundred or so men were carrying rifles. More than two hundred were armed with pistols, knives, spits, sickles, axes, scythes and pitchforks ... But what really made the blood run cold was the disorderly crowd of whorish women who were also armed and carrying sacks, an ominous and evil sign of impending pillage. After assembling in the main piazza they went into the church of San Nicolò where a solemn mass was celebrated and pictures of the Bourbon king and his wife were displayed ... [20]

Such scenes convinced many northerners that what they were dealing with in the southern provinces was not simply a politically backward population but a different level of civilization. The idea that Africa began somewhere just beyond Rome was already a commonplace well before unification, but the sudden arrival of northern officials in the annexed south produced an outpouring of revulsion, with prejudice and intolerance giving rise to brutal judgements and these brutal judgements in turn widening the chasm of incomprehension out of which the preju-dice had grown. The Romagna politician Luigi Carlo Farini (who became Italy's fourth prime minister in December 1862) was one of many who found the situation in the south repellent when he came there in October 1860 as the new viceroy of Naples. 'But my friend, what lands are these!' he wrote to Cavour. '. . . What barbarism! This is not Italy! This is Africa: compared to these peasants the Bedouin are the very flower of civilization.'[21] Similar remarks about the 'barbarism', 'ignorance', 'immorality', 'superstition', 'laziness' and 'cowardice' of southerners peppered the reports sent to Cavour at this time, and Cavour himself not surprisingly concluded that the south was rotten to 'the very marrow of its bones'.[22] Nor was it just northerners who were disparaging. With a vehemence characteristic of converts, some of the most scathing judgements came from exiles – men such as Giuseppe Massari, a native of Puglia, who had fled to Turin after the 1848 Neapolitan revolution and now called for 'a major onslaught of Piedmontese morality' to cleanse the 'Augean stables' of southern corruption.[23]

Many of these near hysterical comments were fuelled by a mixture of self-interest and fear: self-interest in that by depicting the south as a land of backwardness and corruption the Piedmontese created a moral climate in which the imposition of their own constitution, laws and administrative system (not to mention personnel) on the rest of the country appeared wholly justified; and fear in case Italy, 'one and indivisible', was suddenly overwhelmed by contagion spreading up through the peninsula, like disease through a body. Indeed medical images abounded at this time in reports, speeches and correspondence (and remained common for many decades to come), with the south frequently being described as a 'wound' or 'gangrene' that required urgent surgery or as a sick patient that was in desperate need of a doctor.[24] Massimo d'Azeglio thought that unification with Naples was like getting into bed with someone with smallpox (he was thus opposed to annexation altogether), while Farini felt that although it would not be possible 'to make a clean, deep cut in the wound overnight' in Naples, everything should be done to ensure that the south did not become 'the gangrene of the rest of the state' and cause the 'moral break-up of Italy'.[25]

But if the south was sick and riddled with corruption, what should the remedy be? Cavour's north European faith in the therapeutic effects of liberalism apparently assailed him on his death-bed in June 1861 when he called for the Neapolitans to be ruled with freedom, not martial law ('I would show them what ten years of freedom can do for those lovely lands. In twenty years they will be the richest provinces of Italy').[26] And others, including Garibaldi and many of the democrats, echoed these sentiments, arguing that if southerners were backward then this was due to centuries of despotism, and that the way forward was not yet more repressive rule but education through the patient administering of free government. But the sense of deep insecurity that seized the country's leaders from the end of 1860 made such views seem mawkish or utopian, especially as there was evidence that the unrest in the south was being whipped up by agents of the deposed Bourbons (a Spanish officer called José Borjes toured the south in 1861 in the name of the ex-king in Rome) and by the clergy.[27] There were also fears that the democrats might take advantage of the chaos to launch another attempt to march on Rome and so complete the popular revolution out of which they had felt cheated in 1860. In such circumstances force and repression prevailed.

Given that one of the strongest cultural strands running through the movement for unification had been a desire to put an end to centuries of conflict and division and create a nation that was bound together by bonds of fraternal love and concord, it was bitterly ironic that Italy was established amid so much bloodshed and ill-will. Part of the problem – and it was a problem that was to unsettle many Italians in the decades to come, especially those whose background and upbringing predisposed them to look to an ideal, perhaps in some cases as a substitute for conventional religion – was the gulf separating the dream from the reality, or as contemporaries put it, the poetry from the prose. And disillusionment all too easily gave rise to anger. Carlo Nievo was a young democrat from north-eastern Italy whose passionate love of the cause of Italy drove him to join up with Garibaldi's forces in the summer of 1860, but as he marched through the squalid towns and arid countryside of southern Italy he found the absence of any vestige of civilization, as he understood it, almost too much to bear. In October he wrote to his brother, the distinguished writer Ippolito (who had himself sailed with Garibaldi's Thousand in May) from the town of Sessa, to the north of Naples:

I have been here since yesterday evening and have no idea when I will leave this appalling place . . . I need to stay in a city that merits at least in part such a name, as up until now I have only seen in the south towns that make you vomit simply entering them. Forget about annexations and popular votes, I would burn alive all the people living between the Tronto and where I am now. What a race of brigands![28]

How many died in southern Italy in the first years of unification is unclear and is still a subject of acrimonious and highly emotive debate. At the time governments were understandably deeply embarrassed by the situation and refused to allow any general discussion of what in private even the sober-minded Piedmontese moderate Quintino Sella admitted was a 'real civil war'.[29] A parliamentary enquiry was set up to examine the causes of banditry in December 1862, but its focus was almost entirely on the socio-economic conditions of the south, with little suggestion that the unrest was being driven by a widespread rejection of the new political order, and even then its findings were kept as secret as possible. One further problem was that the army resented any civil intrusion into its affairs and did not feel itself accountable to parliament (indeed under the constitution it was answerable only to the king) and as a result the scale and horror of episodes such as the sacking of Pontelandolfo went uninvestigated. Estimates based on official figures for those executed or shot in engagements between June 1861 and December 1865 suggest that around 5,200 were killed, but other sources, including local anecdotal testimony and reports in the foreign press, point to a much larger total, running to tens, perhaps several tens, of thousands. Recently claims have been made for 150,000 dead and even much higher.[30] These latter figures are unlikely but not impossible, for as at Pontelandolfo many of the killings arose from the frustration of soldiers who were operating in a world that eyed them malevolently and who in return regarded those they encountered as merely a 'race of brigands'. Killings of this kind by their very nature do not make the official record.

PIEDMONT VERSUS ITALY

Central to the Risorgimento had been the idea of resurrection, the revival of a glorious nation after centuries of decadence. But there was a paradox as most patriots saw it: Italians would find it hard to win independence until they had recovered some at least of their (alleged) past virtues; and yet without independence it was difficult to see how these virtues could be acquired. After the trauma of 1848–9 many democrats had accepted that Italy was unlikely ever to 'make itself' and had abandoned their faith in popular risings and turned to diplomacy, foreign intervention and war. Garibaldi's astonishing achievements in southern Italy in 1860 had allowed 'the people' to claim some credit for unification. But it was Piedmont and France that had been largely responsible for the collapse of Austrian power in the peninsula in 1859, not Italians as a whole; and it was Piedmont that had emerged as the victorious player in 1860, as Garibaldi's handshake with Victor Emmanuel at Teano and his cession of all the conquered southern provinces had shown. But Piedmont's success brought with it a fresh paradox: now that material unity had been completed (bar the Veneto, Rome and Trentino), how could 'moral' unity be secured and Italy turned from a geographical expression into a 'nation' if the country's new rulers were first and foremost Piedmontese?

One man who was particularly alert to this problem was Francesco De Sanctis, a literary scholar of great distinction and a towering figure in Italian cultural life in the 1860s and 1870s, who served as Minister of Education under Garibaldi and in four separate Italian governments between 1861 and 1881. De Sanctis had been born in a small town in the mountains to the east of Naples in 1817, and like many of his generation he had been captivated as a young man by romanticism and by the novels of Walter Scott in particular ('to us he seemed to open up a whole new world').[31] His liberal sympathies and his participation in the revolution of 1848 had earned him imprisonment by the Bourbons from 1850 to 1853, followed by periods of exile in Turin and Zurich, where he had held a chair in Italian literature. Absent-minded and unworldly, with ill-fitting clothes and a remarkable capacity to lose umbrellas, a shock of grey hair and a cigar stub (which he was forever trying to relight) protruding from beneath his unkempt walrus moustache, De Sanctis was widely admired for his immense learning, high moral principles and limpid character. Like Mazzini he loved to have his room filled with canaries flying freely around (and he gave them literary names such as Poliziano and Boccaccio, and chatted to them continually). But unlike Mazzini he had very few enemies. Indeed when Cavour was asked why he had made him a minister in the spring of 1861 he said it was because he was the only Neapolitan that he had come across about whom two compatriots did not have a bad word to say.[32]

The dream of De Sanctis was to teach Italians how to be free. For freedom, in his view, was not obtained simply with the introduction of certain institutions or legal arrangements; it was a moral condition, a set of beliefs, attitudes and practices that could only be acquired through the patient education of the intellect and emotions. It involved learning respect for the law, developing a sense of duty towards the state, harbouring feelings of sympathy and regard for all compatriots, and engaging actively and maturely in the political life of the nation. As for the German romantics, by whom De Sanctis had been strongly influenced, true freedom entailed the expansion of the self and a spontaneous identification with the broader collectivity, so that personal, family or local interests were willingly sacrificed to the greater needs of the nation. It meant shaking off the corrupt habits of the past, dissolving the old municipal and regional loyalties and becoming morally united as Italians. As he told the inhabitants of his native province of Avellino in October 1860, urging them (with strong echoes of Mameli and Manzoni) to vote 'Yes' in the forthcoming plebiscite:

What have we been until now? A people divided into small states, incapable of defending ourselves, invaded and trampled underfoot by the French, the Spanish and the Germans ... We will be a nation of twenty-six million people, one in language, religion, memories, culture, intellect and kind. We will be masters in our own home. We will be able to proclaim with Roman pride: 'We are Italians.' And foreigners who have ordered us around and despised us will say: 'This is a strong race. Twice it has been great, and when after so many centuries of oppression we had thought it dead and buried, look how it raises its head again, and is even greater than before.'[33]

For those, like De Sanctis, who saw the main task after unification as being 'to make Italians', the new kingdom got off to an inauspicious start. Mazzini and most of the democrats had never been certain about what constitutional and administrative arrangements they wanted, but they had been clear that 'Italy' must be the expression of the whole nation, a synthesis of all its constituent parts, and visibly different from what had preceded it. It must not be the imposition of one state on the rest. During the revolution in southern Italy in the summer of 1860, Piedmontese laws and the *Statuto* had been introduced by Garibaldi in the liberated provinces, but this had been essentially an emergency measure and a tactical ploy (to reassure Cavour and international opinion). Many imagined that once Rome had been taken a national assembly would be convened and collective decisions made on such key issues as the constitution, legal codes, regional autonomy and local government. But the failure of Garibaldi to reach Rome and the surrender of the south to Victor Emmanuel meant that the initiative passed entirely to Piedmont in the autumn of 1860. And the Piedmontese did almost nothing to allay the suspicions of those who had always felt that this ambitious state was more interested in its own aggrandizement than the cause of Italy.

In fairness to Cavour, there was a remarkable shift of opinion among liberals throughout Italy during the autumn and winter of 1860. Before the plebiscites in October it had been generally assumed that there would be a considerable degree of regional autonomy in any new Italian state; and in fact a commission had been set up in Turin in the early summer of 1860, with Cavour's approval, to look at plans for devolved power in the recently expanded Piedmontese state. But the growing chaos in southern Italy towards the end of 1860, with rural communities teetering towards anarchy and cities buckling under the pressures of economic and political dislocation, as armies of unemployed workers, disbanded Garibaldian volunteers, sacked Bourbon officials, disillusioned democrats and supporters of the former regime joined forces to riot and protest in the streets against the new government, persuaded Cavour and his allies (including many in the south) that decentralization could weaken the new edifice of Italy and bring about its rapid collapse.[34] Sicily was a particular worry: if autonomy was conceded here, might this not revive the island's old demands for independence?

But the introduction of centralization and the application of Piedmontese laws and institutions to the whole of Italy were carried out with so little consultation and such haste and insensitivity that many local sensibilities and interests were left badly damaged. Admittedly Piedmont was the only Italian state that had a constitution, and so could claim a degree of moral superiority on this score; but in many spheres – for example, education, local government and justice – Lombardy, Tuscany and even the Kingdom of the Two Sicilies could claim to have superior credentials to Piedmont, which had only very recently shed its reputation of being the most backward-looking part of the peninsula. In Lombardy the process of what quickly became known as 'Piedmontization' was pushed through by decree laws in the summer and autumn of 1859, without any parliamentary discussion, and Milanese business-men suddenly found themselves saddled with the Piedmontese lira and Piedmontese tariffs, lawyers with the Piedmontese legal codes and judicial structures, and teachers with the Piedmontese education system – and this despite widespread agreement that the Austrian system of schooling was quite outstanding, particularly at the elementary level.

Elsewhere in Italy 'Piedmontization' started in 1860 and gathered pace during 1861, culminating in the autumn in a series of decrees that transferred Piedmont's administrative and political structures almost in their entirety to the rest of Italy. As the prime minister of the time, Bettino Ricasoli, explained:

The supreme and most urgent need at this moment . . . is to unify . . . A universal and, it should be said, perfectly rational desire exists on the part of the Italian nation for a robust central power that is able to carry out its activities in all areas and can everywhere impress a uniform direction on public affairs . . .[35]

This was disingenuous, and was indicative of a dangerous capacity on the part of Italy's rulers to divorce the claims of the nation, understood in an abstract, almost Platonic, sense, from those of the people that constituted it; for the reality by the end of 1861 was that there was deep anger throughout Italy at the application of what one leading democrat called the 'straitjacket' of Piedmontese uniformity.[36] For example, in southern Italy the imposition of military service was causing huge prob-lems, especially in Sicily, which had no previous experience of the draft, while Piedmontese tariffs were resulting in thousands of people losing their jobs as workshops and factories that had depended under the Bourbons on high protective tariffs for their survival were forced to close down.

But in some ways even more damaging than the drive for uniformity and centralization (and as the chaos and discontent in the country grew, the government felt driven to tighten its grip from Turin, in what risked becoming a vicious circle) were a number of symbolic aspects of 'Piedmontization' that were harder to explain away on the grounds of political necessity. One concerned the first Italian parliament. This met in February 1861 in a hastily built structure housing 500 wooden seats (fifty-seven were left empty for the future representatives of Rome and the Veneto) in the courtyard of Palazzo Carignano in Turin.[37] It was officially described as the eighth legislature, not the first, thereby suggesting formal continuity with the Piedmontese state going back to May 1848. Equally insensitive was the title given to the new king. Many democrats in particular felt that Victor Emmanuel should show from the outset that 'Italy' was distinct from the Kingdom of Sardinia by changing his numeral. Francesco Crispi wanted the royal formula to be simply 'Victor Emmanuel, King of Italy', pointing out (in a remark that revealed something of his aspirations) that 'Charlemagne, Napoleon and all the founders of dynasties' signed their laws and decrees with their name alone.[38] But the new parliament meekly bowed to the king's wishes and agreed that he should remain King Victor Emmanuel II. Equally galling to many, certainly outside Piedmont, was the formula to be used on official documents after the king's name: 'by the grace of God and the will of the nation, king of Italy'. The first clause, 'by the grace of God', flatly contradicted the second clause and called into question the legal status of the plebiscite votes. Furthermore 'king of Italy' was archaic: 'king of the Italians' would have been more modern and liberal. Victor Emmanuel was clearly reluctant to break with the absolutist traditions of his dynasty and so did nothing to allay suspicions that he saw Italy as something he had in effect conquered.

Indeed the monarchy was to make little effort in the first decades of unity to identify with the nation and promote among the mass of the population a sense of 'Italy' in the way that De Sanctis and others wanted. Victor Emmanuel repeatedly made it clear that he expected the nation to identify with him and not vice versa. He resolutely refused to change his way of life, preferring to spend much of his time as before hunting in the Alpine valleys of Piedmont or consorting with his buxom mistress, Rosa Vercellana, rather than applying himself to politics or travelling around meeting his new subjects – which in some ways was just as well, as he often ended up causing offence with his impatience and bad language, or worse still inviting ridicule, as when the shoe polish with which he blackened his greying hair ran into his collar and shirt in the rain. In due course his earthy and eccentric behaviour probably won him a fair measure of popular affection, no doubt helped by stories of his sexual prowess (and attendant jokes about his being 'the father of the nation') and even by the rumour that he was in reality a butcher's son who as a baby had been swapped for the true heir to the throne.[39] But in the short term he did little to endear himself to the majority of Italians, especially in the south: the fact that the peasants of

Pontelandolfo went to the trouble of tearing out the Savoy crest from the Italian flags indicates how much of their anger following unification was directed at what was felt to be a usurping monarchy. Nor was he helped by the sobriquet that Massimo d'Azeglio had given him of '*il re galantuomo*'. If in the north *galantuomo* signified a gentleman of integrity, in the south it was generally synonymous with the reviled class of provincial landowners.[40]

Far and away the most popular national figure in 1861 was Garibaldi, and had Victor Emmanuel and Cavour been generous in recognizing the huge contribution that he and his followers had made to national unification, the new state would have been greatly strengthened at the outset. But the events of the summer and autumn of 1860 showed that the government in Turin looked on the volunteer army in the south as a threat, to be neutralized as quickly as possible; while Garibaldi, precisely because of his huge popularity, was regarded more as a rival than an ally, to be hustled into the wings at the first opportunity. And it was not just the scale of Garibaldi's popularity that alarmed Victor Emmanuel and Cavour. It was also its character, for Garibaldi was treated in southern Italy as a divinity, feted by ecstatic crowds, with people kneeling as he passed, straining to touch his clothes or stirrups or kiss his hand, and thrusting their children forward to be blessed or even baptized by the man who was frequently compared in songs and ballads to the Archangel Michael or to Jesus Christ.[41] Nor was this enthusiasm confined to Italy. In Britain during the summer of 1860 countless pamphlets, poems and books appeared celebrating Garibaldi's heroic achievements. Subscriptions were raised, and volunteers flocked from all over the country to join him – including a working-class brigade from Glasgow and London that got a bad reputation for unruliness and drinking and nearly shot Victor Emmanuel by accident.[42] And in other countries, too, Garibaldi quickly became a living legend: in Russia the great anarchist Bakunin heard Siberian peasants talking of being liberated one day by 'Gariboldov'.[43]

The ingratitude and hostility displayed by Victor Emmanuel and Cavour to Garibaldi and his volunteer army alienated many of the most committed patriots from the new Italy and gave rise to the enduring myth of a passive revolution. The nation had been severed at the outset from the lymph of popular enthusiasm; another march on Rome was needed to connect with the people and give the nation true life. Mazzini was particularly disappointed at the outcome of 1860. It was a triumph for Piedmontese self-interest and for materialism and force over faith, he believed: 'I had thought to evoke the soul of Italy; all I see before me is its corpse.' He returned to London, where he continued to work for a fresh revolutionary initiative that would lead to the capture of Rome and the Veneto. He could acknowledge that Cavour was a remarkable politician but he regretted the statesman's 'Machiavellian calculations of expediency' that had thwarted the country's spiritual regeneration and risked leaving a legacy of corruption to Italy.[44] And there were plenty in England who shared his concerns. The writer George Meredith produced a powerful defence of Mazzini and his views in his 1866 novel *Vittoria*, while George Eliot's remarkable parable about the two souls of Italy – the Machiavellian and the austerely moral – in *Romola* (1863) concluded with a thinly disguised lecture to the new nation about its future ('Mamma Romola, what am I to be?'),[45] in which she stressed the importance of choosing the path of real virtue over narrow hedonism and selfishness. Mazzini read and enjoyed the book.[46]

A number of other leading democrats followed Mazzini in turning their back on united Italy, retreating into private life or else conspiring in southern Italy against the new kingdom. But some felt duty-bound to fight their corner from within the state. One such was Francesco Crispi, who despite considerable government opposition managed to get himself elected to parliament in January 1861 for a constituency in his native Sicily. Crispi had spent more than a decade in exile for his beliefs and had risked his life for the cause of Italy, but that did not stop Cavour targeting him in the summer of 1860 as one of the dangerous 'red republicans' and 'socialist demagogues' around Garibaldi who needed to be 'thrown into the sea'.[47] Victor Emmanuel used far less polite language, and when the two men met near Naples in November the king refused to shake hands with this future prime minister of Italy. Crispi never forgot the snub. Cavour, too, would not look Crispi in the face after he arrived in Turin as a deputy.

This callous and impolitic lack of magnanimity extended also to the troops who had fought in southern Italy. While many regiments from the standing armies of the annexed territories in the north and centre were welcomed into the Piedmontese forces in 1860–61, those who had served under Bourbon or papal commanders were looked on with grave suspicion and treated very differently. Tens of thousands were taken prisoner and sent off to penal islands or to fortress camps in Lombardy and Piedmont (in one case high up in the Alps), where many – precisely how many is still unknown – died from disease, malnutrition and cold. The officers generally fared better, and over 2,000 were eventually admitted into the Italian army – though less out of a desire for integration and more from a concern to deprive the rebel population in the south of potential leaders. And once in the army these southerners had a difficult time, often facing severe discrimination from an institution that saw itself still as Piedmontese and insisted on monopolizing the upper ranks for many years to come. As the Minister of War explained to parliament, though, the south had for long been culturally and morally backward and therefore could not be expected to produce good soldiers.[48]

There was even greater mistrust towards the volunteers who had fought with Garibaldi. Undoubtedly the southern army was something of a rag-bag, with many of the 50,000 who had ended up on the pay-rolls having joined simply to get a job and boasting few if any military (or patriotic) credentials. There were also numerous irregularities, with soldiers listed as being in more than one regiment and so claiming multiple daily allowances (the full extent of the corruption is unknown as the southern army's chief administrator, the writer Ippolito Nievo, was drowned in mysterious circumstances, taking all the accounts with him, in March 1861). But from a political point of view Cavour's decision to liquidate the southern army in January 1861 and his reluctance to let the officers transfer to the Italian army was highly insensitive and resulted in the former commander of the volunteers, General Sirtori, declaring angrily in parliament in March that the Piedmontese had come to the south as enemies, 'in order to fight us who were Italy!'[49] And worse followed. On 18 April, Garibaldi turned up in the Chamber of Deputies, wearing a red shirt and poncho, for a debate on how the divisions in the country could be healed and accused the government of having provoked 'a fratricidal war'. Pandemonium broke out and the sitting was suspended, and despite the best efforts of the king at mediation, Garibaldi and Cavour refused to shake hands. A few days later Crispi wrote to a friend saying that he was planning to write an account of the revolutionary events of 1860 with the projected title: *The Civil War.*[50]

PARLIAMENT

The new Kingdom of Italy was a parliamentary monarchy and when Cavour decided in December 1860 to hold elections he was confident of securing a safe majority. He was not disappointed. According to the Piedmontese electoral law, which was hastily extended to the whole of Italy, only those who paid forty lire a year in taxes or who had a university degree or professional qualification were entitled to vote, and this resulted in an electorate of around 420,000, or about one in ten of males aged twenty-five or over (in Britain the figure was about one in five). The rationale behind such a restricted suffrage was not so much to defend 'property' as to ensure that the country was governed by people with sufficient education and financial means to enable them to make informed and independent political judgements. In practice, though, many voters, especially in small rural communities like Pontelandolfo that made up the backbone of Italy, were drawn almost instinctively into supporting the government from considerations of material advantage, especially when law and order was under threat or breaking down, as was the case early in 1861. Consequently, when the first national elections were conducted at the end of January and beginning of February 1861, more than 300 of the 443 deputies returned to parliament were supporters of Cavour.

Having, unlike most of his fellow countrymen, studied parliamentary practices in other countries, Cavour was able to dominate the Chamber almost effortlessly, and partly because of the commanding position he had secured for himself in Piedmont during the 1850s many new deputies were inclined to support him unquestioningly. One such was Giuseppe Verdi, whose uncritical romantic fondness for heroes led him to be a staunch admirer of the Piedmontese prime minister ('the Prometheus of our nationality') as well as of Mazzini, Garibaldi, Napoleon III and later Crispi.[51] In January 1861 Cavour asked Verdi to stand for the college in which his home town of Busseto was located; and Verdi agreed, wishing, as he said, to do all he could to help 'our country for so long a time divided and torn by civil discord'.[52] But once elected to Palazzo Carignano he felt rather out of his depth, and clung on to Cavour's coat-tails almost childishly. As he told a friend towards the end of 1861: 'As long as Cavour was alive, I watched him in the Chamber and stood up to approve or reject when he stood up, because I was certain I would not go wrong doing exactly what he did.'[53]

Verdi's jejune performance as a deputy (he soon stopped attending the Chamber altogether) was perhaps forgivable for someone who saw himself primarily as a musician (and increasingly as a gentleman farmer wrapped up in the running of his estates, autocratically, and quarrelling with the local town council),[54] but it was indicative of a more general problem facing Italy. Outside Piedmont, experience of parliamentary government had been very limited and there was little clear idea of exactly how national politics were to be conducted under such a system. The fact also that only 57 per cent of those eligible to vote in the 1861 elections actually did so was a further cause for concern, not least because it meant that in many places deputies were being returned to parliament for colleges of 50,000 inhabitants with just a few hundred or even a few dozen votes (Verdi got 339). Some of these abstentions were caused by ideological objections, which was worrying enough – Catholics angry at the invasion of the Papal States and governmental anticlericalism, or loyal supporters of the deposed rulers – but in many cases the main issue seems to have been one of indifference or scepticism towards an institution that had no resonance for most of the population.[55]

Parliament, indeed, carried none of the glamorous freight that it had in Britain, and even in Turin in the 1850s there had been a strong vein of hostility towards an institution that was widely seen as damaging to the prestige of the monarchy and as alien to Piedmontese traditions. Parliaments had certainly existed in Savoy and Piedmont in the Middle Ages (as one scholar noted in 1829 – only to find his book banned by the censors), but the founding fathers of the Piedmontese state were figures such as Emanuele Filiberto and Vittorio Amedeo II who were famous for having centralized power and reduced the authority of representative bodies such as the general congregations.[56] Elsewhere in Italy some fragmentary local memories existed of medieval assemblies and councils, but the only region in which these had crystallized into a serious historical tradition was Sicily, where the island's struggle for independence from foreign (usually Neapolitan) rule was seen as closely linked to the assertion of parliamentary freedoms from the time of the Normans down to 1848–9.

Another major problem facing representative government in Italy was that parliament had never featured prominently in the context of the 'nation'. The struggle for unification and independence had been viewed primarily in terms of ridding the country of foreign oppression; and the means for achieving this were personal sacrifice, education, solidarity, conspiracy, insurrection and war. Nowhere was it suggested that freedom was to be won either by or for parliament. Nor was there much room in the patriotic mythology surrounding key historical episodes such as the Battle of Legnano, the Sicilian Vespers, the duel of Barletta or the siege of Florence for assemblies or collective decision-making: the focus was on instinctive individual heroism and action. And even when it came to the events of 1848–60, the role of the Piedmontese parliament was entirely overshadowed by the campaigns of Victor Emmanuel, Napoleon and Garibaldi, the secret diplomacy of Cavour and the activities of the executive (which was responsible for the pivotal constitutional arrangements, including the *Statuto* and the decree laws of the autumn of 1859 which laid down the fundamental administrative and legal structures of the new Italian state).

One important reason why parliament did not figure in the national mythology was because it easily brought to mind discord, division and weakness. The communes of the Middle Ages had abounded in deliberative assemblies; but while such bodies had permitted an exceptional degree of democracy they had also been powerless to curb (indeed had arguably encouraged) the factionalism that was ultimately to make the city-states ungovernable and prey to foreign conquest. It was precisely to end the internal conflicts in his native Florence and other free Italian republics that Dante, the supreme 'patriotic' poet, had invoked the coming of an omnipotent emperor to crush the warring parties and impose unity and order. Given that for patriots of the Risorgimento concord was a supreme ideal, it is not surprising that they were often uncertain whether parliament would be able to provide appropriate leadership for the new unified Italy. The eminent poet and former Mazzinian Giosuè Carducci offered a model of how an assembly should behave – unanimously and not adversarially – in a poem written in 1876 to celebrate the seventh centenary of the Battle of Legnano. Entitled *Il Parlamento*, it described how the Milanese were summoned to a parliament to decide whether to resume war against Frederick Barbarossa or sue for peace. Amidst the thorn-covered ruins of the city, which some years earlier had been razed to the ground by the German emperor, the knight Alberto da Giussano reminded the crowds of the appalling humiliation and suffering that had been inflicted on them by the foreigner. Parliament's response to his speech was visceral and unequivocal. 'Through the whole parliament a spasm ran, almost as if of wild beasts.' On all sides the women stretched out their arms in supplication to the men and cried: 'Kill Barbarossa.'[57]

The issue of parliament also touched another sensitive nerve: that of the consequences of Italy's tradition of rhetoric on the national character. In their analysis of Italy's slide into decadence during the Renaissance, Francesco De Sanctis and other commentators had called attention to the corrosive effects of literary humanism, with its emphasis on style over substance and artifice over truth. Italians, they maintained, had become great talkers and wordsmiths, adept at florid speeches and well-crafted sonnets, but prone to passivity and scepticism – with fatal consequences after 1494. As De Sanctis put it, the cultivation of rhetoric had resulted in a separation of thought and action, thereby producing 'that thinking which is not feeling, that feeling which is not doing, that are characteristic of the Italian race and its shame'.[58] He argued repeatedly that Italians needed to learn to reunite thought and action, and so produce the passion that had inspired Alberto da Giussano and the people of Milan to go into battle against the Germans and defeat them. From the outset, Italy's parliament, where speech and debate were inevitably paramount, risked being viewed through this filter of patriotic anxieties and disparaged as weak, lacklustre and ineffective. Already in 1862 a leading democrat published a collection of pen-portraits of the new deputies in Turin under the revealing title *The Moribund Men of Palazzo Carignano*.[59]

One final problem confronted the parliamentary system from the start. If, as was widely accepted, 'Italians' had still to be made, how could an institution that by its very nature was representative hope to remedy the country's defects? Would it not simply mirror them? This was to be an issue of growing concern from the 1870s, but already in the 1860s the tendency of deputies to cluster along regional lines and to see parliament as a tool for securing jobs, subsidies and contracts for their friends back home was causing alarm. Ironically, one reason why there had been relatively little opposition in the end from the propertied classes to rigid centralization was probably because they could see in the Chamber a way of safeguarding their local interests – and this despite article forty-one of the *Statuto* specifically stating that deputies represented 'the nation in general' and not their constituency and their voters. And again rather ironically, the fact that the formation of parties was positively discouraged in the interests of fostering a disinterested 'national' spirit – 'party' still had very negative connotations of factionalism – meant that deputies were accorded freedom in parliament to allow their instinctive regional loyalties to surface and find expression.[60]

All this was deeply distressing to those patriots who had hoped that parliament would be a major source of national education. De Sanctis came to believe that the aversion to parties had to be overcome and two powerful blocs formed, as in Britain, of left and right (currently the labels 'left' and 'right' were applied loosely and did not correspond to coherent groupings in the Chamber), each with a clear and distinct national programme to which deputies and ministers would be committed. In this way, he felt, politicians (and hence voters) would start thinking in terms of 'major political battles' fought on behalf of 'Italy' and stop the 'sordid personal squabbles and petty rivalries' that were currently lacerating the Chamber. As he said in a speech in 1864:

Today Italians see Italy through the prism of their province. It is thus not enough to shout 'Long live Italy!' and think that Italy has been made. I can see that everyone still carries inside them something of their past, of their memories, of their traditions. Each of us, though Italian, nevertheless still feels in some measure Neapolitan, or Lombard or Tuscan.

Could the legacy of the past be effaced, he asked: '*Hoc opus, hic labor*' ('That is the task, the labour').[61]

12

The Road to Rome, 1861–70

On the night of 30 December [Victor Emmanuel] arrived in Rome . . . No Roman emperor ever made an entrance that was as great in its simplicity! . . . The whole city grew excited and rejoiced at seeing him, and expressed its enthusiasm and gratitude in a thousand different ways. The city council and the officers of the National Guard came to offer him their thanks; and Victor Emmanuel addressed the following . . . forthright and moving words to them, words that fully reveal his spirit: 'We are finally in Rome, as has been my heartfelt wish. No one will ever take it from us.'

I. Ghiron, *Il primo re d'Italia. Ricordi biografici* (1878, popular biography)

Never did such a momentous event attract so little attention. The king arrived in the evening, and hardly anybody turned up to greet him outside the station. Those that had gathered were poor wretches rather than respectable citizens . . . When the king got down from his carriage in the atrium of the Quirinal Palace, he turned to Lamarmora in the fashion of a traveller bored by the journey and muttered, in Piedmontese: 'We are finally here.'

A. Oriani, *Lotta politica in Italia* (1892, eyewitness account)

ASPROMONTE

Rome had not been taken in 1860: the horrific prospect of Garibaldi and his followers – no doubt joined by Mazzini – celebrating on the Capitol together with the risk of French intervention had persuaded Cavour that the city should stay in the hands of the Pope. But Rome had been at the heart of the national question for nearly two decades, elevated into a potent symbol of regeneration and unity by Gioberti and Mazzini, and with patriotic fervour at fresh heights after the remarkable events of 1860, it was almost unthinkable that the Eternal City should not be proclaimed 'Italian' by the new state. Apart from anything else, to renounce Rome would be to split the moderates and democrats irreparably. So when in March 1861 the issue was debated in the Chamber, Cavour got up and announced that Rome had to be Italy's capital for 'great moral reasons', as it was the only city whose importance was much more than simply geographical and whose memories were not 'exclusively municipal'. In return, as befitted a liberal state, the kingdom would guarantee the Church in its spiritual mission: 'We are ready to proclaim this great principle in Italy: a free Church in a free state.'[1]

Pope Pius IX could not accept such a solution; and given the fury of French Catholic opinion at what had happened to the Papal States – the Marche and Umbria had both been annexed, leaving the Church with Lazio – nor could Napoleon III. As a result a large garrison of French troops remained stationed in Rome and the Italian government was forced to defer occupying the city until a suitable opportunity arose. But not everyone believed that Rome should become the capital of Italy. Massimo d'Azeglio argued that a city 'impregnated with the miasmas of 2,500 years of material violence and moral pressure inflicted on the world by its successive governments' was a bad choice for a modern liberal state.[2] His preference – not surprising, perhaps, for an urbane artist and writer – was for Florence. D'Azeglio's father-in-law, Alessandro Manzoni, was similarly repelled by the grandiose and sanguinary images that Rome summoned up, and though he came to accept that for political reasons the city had to be the capital, he never wanted to set foot there.[3] The leading Neapolitan moderate Ruggero Bonghi felt that an 'intoxicating breeze' would inevitably waft from Rome across Italy and that the new nation would do better to forget its past and concentrate instead on the mundane problems that confronted it in the present.[4] For such reasons some people suggested that Italy should follow the example of the United States and build a new capital city from scratch, for example in the centre of the peninsula, in Umbria, where it would be largely free from the deadweight of unwelcome historical memories.[5]

But such views belonged to a minority, and even those who were largely unmoved by the Eternal City's past could nevertheless feel drawn to it for what it might become in the future. Mazzini's vision of a Third Rome with a universal mission resonated far beyond democratic circles

and often in quite surprising quarters. The Piedmontese wool manufacturer and economist Quintino Sella, who as Finance Minister in the
1860s and 1870s wrestled sternly with the country's massive public
debts, was not normally given to rhetoric or poetry, but even he confessed that his old bones became 'electrified' when he heard talk of
Rome.[6] He dreamed of making the new capital into a great international
centre for science – raising the banners of positivism and progress triumphantly over the ruins of the Pope's temporal power – with a string of
academies and schools, institutes of chemistry, physics and biology,
botanical gardens and centres for the arts. Rome would thus become a
formidable moral and material symbol of the nation, uniting Italians
in a common purpose, with 'the struggle for truth against ignorance,
prejudice and error' giving rise to 'the same unanimity as is to be found
in the days of fighting to defend the fatherland'.[7]

Garibaldi shared Sella's secular vision, and he too saw the acquisition
of Rome and its elevation into a great and modern capital city as
necessary to the moral unity of Italy. After his clash with Cavour in the
Chamber of Deputies in April 1861, his sense that the cause of Italy had
been betrayed by the opportunism of the Piedmontese prime minister
intensified, and he returned home to the island of Caprera determined
to resume the march on Rome at the earliest opportunity. The satis-
factions to be gained from leading the life of a modern Cincinnatus,
fishing, farming, building walls and reading, albeit interspersed with a
steady stream of tourists arriving by boat and seeking a lock of hair or
some other souvenir of 'the hero of the two worlds', were necessarily
rather paltry after the heady poetry of the previous year. For a while
he contemplated accepting an invitation from the US government to
serve as a general with the Unionist forces in the Civil War ('tens of
thousands of American citizens would glory in serving under the Washington of Italy'),[8] but only on the unlikely conditions that he was made
commander-in-chief and that President Lincoln declared the complete
abolition of slavery. In reality his sights were still firmly set on Italy.

By the end of 1861 Garibaldi and his democratic friends were toying
with the idea of using the growing chaos in southern Italy as the basis
for a renewed march on Rome. Throughout the country political associations sprang up to mobilize public opinion and provide Garibaldi with
a pretext for a fresh initiative and hopefully too – and this was crucial –
give the government grounds in the eyes of the international community

for standing aside and letting the 'will of the people' prevail. In June 1862 Garibaldi sailed from Caprera to Sicily. He may not have known exactly what he was going to do there, but such was the reception he received, with vast crowds cheering him wherever he went and calling for 'Rome and Venice' and 'Rome or death', that the pressure to act soon became overwhelming. Volunteers began assembling – though for the most part not the well-educated students who had made up the backbone of the Thousand, but rather the unemployed and the hungry, desperate for food and pay; and with rumours rife that Garibaldi had a secret understanding with the king (and possibly Victor Emmanuel had intimated something),[9] the insurrectionary momentum in Sicily fast became unstoppable. On 24 August two steamers crammed with volunteers crossed to the southern tip of Calabria, and Garibaldi began marching north.

Meanwhile the government in Turin had come under strong pressure from the French to intervene. Already on 3 August the king had issued a proclamation urging Italians not to support Garibaldi and warning them of the dangers of civil war. But the hope had been that this was merely a ploy to keep Paris happy and that Victor Emmanuel was secretly planning to repeat the trick of 1860: let Garibaldi advance and then step in at the last moment, take Rome and 'save' the Pope from the clutches of the rebels. In reality, though, the government was too frightened of Napoleon to risk such a dangerous game. And perhaps just as importantly the Piedmontese generals who were in charge of the regular army in the south, Lamarmora and Cialdini, had no wish to see Garibaldi and his loathsome volunteers win yet more plaudits. On 20 August martial law was declared in southern Italy, and a few days later a column of 3,500 troops under Colonel Pallavicini was dispatched to halt the rebels.

Garibaldi and his 2,000 men had wandered up from the Calabrian coast onto the thickly wooded slopes around Aspromonte, hoping to avoid a clash with the Italian army. On the morning of 29 August, tired and hungry after two days of marching, they came in sight of Pallavicini's troops and took up a defensive position at the edge of a pine forest. Strict orders were given to hold fire: Garibaldi had no wish to shed 'fraternal blood'. But Pallavicini was a professional Piedmontese officer with instructions to treat the volunteers as insurgents, and without pausing to parley he sent his *bersaglieri* into action, shooting as they raced forward. A few of the volunteers lost their nerve and returned fire, and in the course of the next ten minutes a dozen or so men were killed. Garibaldi was hit twice: once, lightly, in his left thigh, a second time, far more seriously, in his right ankle. Pallavicini approached and found Garibaldi lying under a tree smoking a cigar. He asked him to surrender. The Hero of the Two Worlds was then taken on a stretcher to a nearby port. He asked to embark on a British ship, but General Cialdini would not hear of it. He was conveyed to La Spezia and imprisoned in a nearby fort, before being amnestied in October. Colonel Pallavicini was promoted, and seventy-six of his men were awarded medals for their gallantry.[10]

Garibaldi's wounded foot was to cause him immense pain for years to come and left him severely incapacitated. Doctors from all over Europe hurried to offer him their services, and it was one of them – the celebrated French physician Auguste Nélaton – who located the bullet deep in the arthritic bone of his ankle. Once extracted the lead ball quickly became the target of souvenir hunters willing to pay huge sums for such a relic. As far as the international community was concerned Aspromonte did nothing to diminish the remarkable esteem in which Garibaldi was held. If anything it reinforced his reputation as a simple, brave and selfless patriot willing to risk all for his nation, even against the chicanery of professional politicians. Gifts poured in (Lord Palmerston sent an invalid's bed), subscriptions were launched, and prints, cartoons and tributes, in verse and prose, rolled from the presses, with Italy (or at least official Italy) almost invariably cast as the villain of the piece. One popular lithograph in France showed Garibaldi as the crucified Christ with members of the Italian cabinet standing at the foot of the cross brandishing the tools of execution and casting lots for his clothes, with Napoleon III and the Pope merrily dancing a jig together in the background.[11]

In Italy, Aspromonte weakened the already tenuous position of the authorities in the annexed regions, above all in the south. In Sicily the imposition of martial law led to thousands of arrests and dozens of summary executions. Demonstrations in favour of Garibaldi, and even the singing of the eminently patriotic 'Garibaldi hymn', were banned. Subversive violence escalated, and the forces of law and order were left feeling ever more beleaguered and paranoid – a paranoia fuelled by mysterious episodes such as that of the *pugnalatori* in October 1862, when thirteen people were stabbed on a single night in different parts of Palermo. Terms such as *camorra* and *camorristi* were deployed in an attempt to explain such lawlessness and invest it with a strongly criminal image (and so conceal its political dimensions); and in 1865 a new word appeared in government reports from Palermo: the mafia. While there was no evidence for the existence of any formal association with this name – which allowed Sicilians subsequently to claim with some justification that the mafia had been 'invented' by northerners – the idea of a large-scale secret organization certainly gave the authorities the conceptual ammunition they needed to persist with emergency measures.[12]

The heavy-handed methods used by the government in the south put the democratic deputies in parliament in an awkward position. Some felt that they should show their disgust by resigning their mandates, but others like the Sicilian Francesco Crispi argued that they should do all they could to support constitutionalism, stay put, and fight their corner from within Palazzo Carignano. Matters came to a head in December 1863 with a speech to the Chamber by a senior Piedmontese general, Giuseppe Govone. Govone had been sent to Sicily the previous summer with twenty battalions to round up draft-dodgers and had used particularly brutal (and technically illegal) means, including besieging towns, cutting off water supplies, and seizing women and children as hostages. In an attempt to defend his actions he foolishly let slip some remarks about the uncivilized character of Sicilian society and the 'barbarity' still prevailing in the island. Pandemonium broke out on the benches (Crispi challenged one leading northern deputy to a duel – although this too was technically illegal)[13] and twenty-one democrats ended up resigning. Among them was Garibaldi.

The government urgently needed to try to regain some moral credibility, and the prime minister, the distinguished Bolognese patriot Marco Minghetti – whose great erudition and urbanity had not stopped him from wounding a former prime minister in a duel in June 1863 following an altercation in the Chamber – looked to do this by moving the kingdom's centre of gravity away from Turin. As Massimo d'Azeglio said, the biggest challenge facing the country was to find ways of making the rest of Italy hate Piedmont less.[14] After hurried negotiations a convention was signed with Napoleon III in September 1864 under which the French would withdraw their troops from Rome in return for a guarantee of the Pope's remaining territories and the transfer of the capital to Florence. On the face of it this looked like a renunciation of the Eternal City, but the government hoped that Italians would see it as a step in the right direction (at least geographically). Unfortunately for Minghetti the 'September convention' unleashed a storm of anger in Turin with three days of rioting in the streets, and he was forced to resign. A new government was installed with the Piedmontese general Alfonso Lamarmora as prime minister and with five of the nine cabinet portfolios also assigned to Piedmontese (two of the others went to Lombards).

Under Lamarmora's direction the drive towards centralization was intensified. A series of laws in 1865 led to the unification of Italy's civil and commercial codes, though the extension of the Piedmontese penal code to the rest of the peninsula proved problematic, as Tuscany was proud of its enlightened traditions and was deeply unhappy about introducing the death penalty. Some regional variations in the criminal law were accordingly allowed to persist, and uniformity was only finally achieved in 1889. The Piedmontese administrative system had already been applied to the annexed territories in 1859–61, but a law of 1865 made a number of important modifications and clarified the role of the pivotal figure in the system, the prefect. Prefects were appointed by the Minister of the Interior and controlled the sixty or so provinces into which the new kingdom was divided. They had wide-ranging powers, including responsibility for public order, censorship of the press, the monitoring of town councils (mayors were also centrally appointed) and the conduct of elections – which in practice meant doing everything possible to help government candidates. Not surprisingly, a high percentage of prefects in the first decades of unity came from Piedmont, or at least from the north of the country, and in the case of key posts such as Milan, Florence, Naples and Palermo they were almost invariably friends of the minister.[15]

Administrative and legal unity, however, could not obscure the deep moral fault-lines that ran through the country and made something of a mockery of the idea of Italy 'one and indivisible'. Moderates and democrats were bitterly opposed; the old municipal and regional rivalries were as pronounced as ever; north and south were riven by mutual antipathy and virtual civil war; and Catholics were being urged to boycott the new state (in December 1864 the Pope racked up the tension further by condemning the central tenets of liberalism in the so-called

'Syllabus of Errors'). Surveying the somewhat desolate scene a year before he died Massimo d'Azeglio could not but conclude, as he told the Senate, that it was far easier to unite 'divided cities and provinces' than 'divided hearts and minds'.[16] He felt that if the nation were ever to become truly strong then Italians would have to undergo a process of profound re-education. As he said in his memoirs, written towards the end of his life with the intention of helping his fellow countrymen to understand the great task that lay ahead of them:

The struggle against the foreigner is largely completed. But this is not the principal challenge . . . The most dangerous enemies of Italy are not the Austrians but the Italians . . . as they have wanted to make a new Italy while remaining the Italians of before, with all the infirmities and moral weaknesses that have been their undoing for centuries. For Italy . . . will never become a well organized and properly governed nation, strong both against the foreigner and internal sectarians, free and independent, until everyone, humble, middling or great, each in his own sphere, carries out his duty and carries it out well . . . Italy's most pressing need is to mould Italians who are capable of doing their duty . . . Sadly we are each day travelling in the wrong direction . . .[17]

D'Azeglio longed for a race of new Italians possessed of 'virile qualities', with 'good blood' flowing in their veins instead of the present 'cream of vanilla'; Italians made of 'strong and robust material, not rags whose stitches fall out' – like the British, whose resolute national character had been forged in the crucible of war in the seventeenth century. 'Perhaps we will have such virtues in the future. As for the present . . . Just look!'[18]

CUSTOZA AND LISSA, 1866

D'Azeglio died in Turin on 15 January 1866, and six months later war broke out between Austria and Prussia, giving the young nation a chance to put behind it the disappointments of the previous few years and affirm itself on the battlefield. Tension between Berlin and Vienna had been mounting for some months, and had it wanted to Italy could have acquired the Veneto peacefully in return for giving the Austrians a simple pledge of neutrality. But the mood in the country was too bellicose for such an inglorious and mercenary transaction. In February a former

republican and follower of Garibaldi, Antonio Mordini, had declared
in parliament that Italy would never be considered a great nation until
it had fought and defeated Austria with its own forces: 'We must endure
many sacrifices and shed much Italian blood if we are to secure the place
in the world that we deserve.'[19] And two months later Francesco Crispi
had called for 'a baptism of blood' in order to demonstrate to the major
powers of Europe that 'Italy too is a great nation, with sufficient strength
to ensure that it can make itself respected in the world.' His words were
greeted with loud applause by his fellow deputies.[20]

One of the attractions of war was the prospect of the rifts and animos-
ities disappearing in the face of a common enemy and bonds of solidarity
and brotherly love arising – as they had briefly in the first months of
1848. At the end of May, Francesco De Sanctis was sailing on a ship
full of volunteers and reservists, and experienced a moment of joyous
epiphany, a deep sense of romantic self-realization, as the prospect
of fighting for Italy bound men of different regions and backgrounds
together:

I have never felt 'Italy' so intensely as I do now. We were standing on the deck
towards midnight. The sky was starry . . . All of a sudden everyone linked arms.
There was an artillery captain from Turin, a lieutenant from Parma, two Neapolitans, eleven Sicilian volunteers from distinguished Palermo families travelling at
their own expense, and a Florentine. And we were all there together, before the
vastness of the sea, singing 'Farewell, my lovely, farewell!' And after we had
finished that historic song, we sang others – all the songs of '48 revived . . .'[21]

Three weeks later, with hostilities imminent, De Sanctis was thrilled to
see how the Chamber and the Senate were burying their differences,
'sacrificing all for concord'. It was deeply reassuring: 'When it comes to
fighting the foreigner encamped on our soil, Italy is able to set aside
personal and party interests and form into one solid phalanx.'[22]

The declaration of war against Austria on 20 June was greeted
throughout Italy with extraordinary excitement. The writer Edmondo De
Amicis recalled the crowds milling excitedly in the streets, the carnival-
like atmosphere and the air of exultant patriotism that seemed to have
gripped almost everyone ('These are great days for Italy! A great war!
. . . This is how nations are made!).[23] A young Tuscan student, Sidney
Sonnino, who nearly fifty years later as foreign minister was to negotiate
Italy's entry into another much larger conflict, wrote in his diary: 'What

a magnificent day for Italy! For the first time in its entire history the whole country is rising up, on its own, to assert its rights! Never, never before has anything similar been seen. How lucky we are to witness it!'[24] For Sonnino, as for so many others, defeat seemed unthinkable – and not just because the consequences were too awful to imagine ('We must win, for a new nation like ours cannot continue in a state of tension for so long without disintegrating ... We should remember how in 1793 an old nation, as France was, came close to disintegrating as a result of the factionalism of the Girondins and Jacobins – and how much more united they were than we are!').[25] The Austrians, after all, were fighting on two fronts; their fleet was half the size of Italy's; and their forces in the Veneto were heavily outnumbered by the 400,000 or so men that Italy could mobilize. On paper at least Italy had every right to expect a victory.

These expectations made the events of the next few weeks deeply painful. The lessons of 1848–9 had manifestly not been learned and again no adequate preparations had been made. Lamarmora had rejected Bismarck's request in the spring for a military convention, and the Italian general staff were accordingly left in the dark as to their Prussian ally's battle plans. There was a hopelessly muddled command structure, with Victor Emmanuel insisting on acting as commander-in-chief but with *de facto* command divided between Cialdini and Lamarmora (who was anyway thoroughly ill-prepared for such a responsibility after serving for two years as prime minister and foreign minister – he only stood down as prime minister on 20 June). Garibaldi was given a separate command as head of the volunteers. Cialdini and Lamarmora failed to communicate with Garibaldi; worse still they hardly communicated with each other, as both, it seems, were secretly hoping to take the lead role. Consequently when they met at Bologna on 17 June to sort out operational plans they did not clarify exactly what they would do with their respective halves of the army.

The consequences were devastating. On 23 June Lamarmora crossed the River Mincio seemingly unaware that the Austrians would be waiting for him on the other side, as he had failed to get hold of proper reconnaissance reports. The next day, with his troops strung out across a broad front near Custoza, he came under attack. When the king telegraphed Cialdini to say that serious fighting had broken out, Cialdini was utterly incredulous: 'Lamarmora had promised me he would confine himself simply to a feint.'[26] Cialdini was too far away to come to Lamarmora's aid. With no plans and no general staff, Lamarmora raced along the lines muttering to himself 'What a defeat! . . . What a disaster! . . . Not even '49 was this bad', desperately trying to locate his senior colleagues, and as a result nobody, not even the king, knew where to find him. By the early afternoon he had ended up quite bizarrely at the town of Goito, about twenty kilometres from the battlefield, something which subsequently he was unable to explain satisfactorily, and in the absence of anyone to provide coherent leadership, the confusion among the Italian forces rapidly resulted in chaos. Had the king possessed tactical ability, he might have rallied the troops and saved the day. But he did not, and the army was allowed to fall back towards Cremona in disarray. Cialdini still had his forces encamped to the east on the River Po, but he too decided to retreat – despite an explicit request from Lamarmora not to do so. The rout was complete.[27]

For a couple of weeks after the defeat at Custoza the army remained inactive as the king and his generals sought to recover their nerve and decide what to do. In the meantime the Prussians inflicted a major defeat on the Austrians at the Battle of Sadowa, and, backed by Napoleon, Austria now tried to get Italy to pull out of the war in return for being given the Veneto. But this was felt to be too demeaning without a victory. On 14 July, Victor Emmanuel, Lamarmora, Cialdini and other senior generals and politicians met at Ferrara and decided that the navy should be pressed into action. The only problem was that nobody had much faith in the admiral, Count Carlo Persano, who with characteristic insubordination had already defied instructions to hunt down and attack the Austrian fleet. Persano was well liked at court, which was the main reason why he had risen so high; but he was not very competent and had a track record of blunders to his name, including on one occasion having run aground a ship carrying the king and the royal family and nearly drowned them. It was suggested that he should be replaced, but no address could be found for his successor. So he was left in command and ordered to engage the enemy on pain of immediate dismissal.[28]

The government had invested heavily in the navy since 1861, and as a result Persano had an impressive fleet, with thirty-two warships, including twelve ironclads. The Austrians by contrast had just seven ironclads. But even more than the army, the navy was torn by fierce internal rivalries among the officers, mostly along regional lines; and there was also a severe shortage of trained crew, with three of the largest Italian vessels having just nineteen gunners instead of the more than 230 they should have had.[29] It was partly because of these problems that Persano had been reluctant to engage the enemy, but faced with the threat of dismissal he felt he had no choice now but to act. He decided to attack the island fortress of Lissa, to the south-east of Ancona, where his fleet was currently based. But there were no maps to hand and he failed to agree an operational plan in advance; and when he unexpectedly encountered the Austrians on the morning of 20 July his fleet was badly scattered (largely as a result of orders being disobeyed). To make matters worse he had unaccountably decided at the last moment to transfer ship, and since there was no admiral's flag on board to indicate the vessel's changed status, confusion reigned over who was in charge. During the battle – the first of any significance to involve ironclads; the last in which battering rams were deployed – one Italian ironclad was rammed and sunk, another exploded and caught fire, and though it was not a heavy defeat, it was a defeat nonetheless, and Persano was subsequently tried and found guilty by the Senate of incompetence, negligence and disobedience. Many others might have faced similar charges for their part in the events of 1866, but it was politically convenient to have one scapegoat to draw the fire of public anger and indignation.[30]

The humiliation of Custoza and Lissa was made worse by the armistice that followed between Austria and Prussia. The Austrians agreed to give up the Veneto, but not to Italy. Instead they handed it to Napoleon III, who, in truly imperial fashion, then passed it on to Italy as a gift. It was all highly galling. Italy had hoped to emerge from the war as a powerful and respected nation, able to assert itself independently on the international stage, but instead found its face being rubbed in the dirt. 'To be Italian was something we once longed for; now, in the present circumstances, it is shameful,' wrote Francesco Crispi to a friend.[31] The catastrophic events of 1866 cast a long and deep shadow over the next few decades – much longer and deeper than has generally been recognized – not just because they left a painful military insult to be avenged at the earliest opportunity but also because they placed a major question mark over the manner in which the settlement of 1860–61 had been achieved and over the men who had been its principal architects – the supposedly tough and competent Piedmontese. Writing more than

forty years later one of Italy's most passionate and influential intellectuals, Giustino Fortunato, told a veteran of the Thousand just how much
he longed to talk to him about what had gone wrong since the glorious
events of 1860:

For then I will make you realize what kind of dull-minded cretins they were who
in 1866 wasted the most marvellous moment that history had presented to Italy,
the moment in which for the very first time since the dawn of its existence all the
sons of Italy, from all of its regions, were fighting *for the Fatherland* under one
single banner . . .[32]

Custoza and Lissa also had the effect of destroying most of the remaining vestiges of optimism generated by the events of 1859–60. The idea,
so central to the national movement from the time of Napoleon, that
Italy needed to undergo a fundamental moral transformation in order
to shake off the legacy of centuries of corruption and decadence, resurfaced and caused many to argue that the Risorgimento, far from being
concluded, had in reality yet to begin. These sentiments were well
expressed by the Neapolitan historian Pasquale Villari in a famous
article entitled 'Who is to Blame?' published immediately after the war,
in which he said that the defeats had laid bare in brutal fashion the
shortcomings of the unification process. Had Italy been brought into
existence through a genuine national revolution, engineered entirely by
its own people, then a 'new, young and warlike' ruling class would have
emerged 'out of the crucible of a long and bloody struggle', to replace
the *ancien régime* elites and provide the nation with vigorous leadership.
But this had not happened, and instead Italy had been left ill-governed
and prey to all its ancient weaknesses: 'In the heart of the nation there
lies an enemy more powerful than Austria: our colossal ignorance,
the illiterate masses, the dumb bureaucrats, the stupid professors, the
infantile politicians, the insufferable diplomats, the incompetent generals, the unskilled worker, the authoritarian farmer, and the rhetoric
that eats our bones.'[33]

As if to underscore the point, an insurrection broke out in Palermo in
the middle of September just as the war ended, and for a week the city
was in the control of some 40,000 insurgents, many of them belonging
to the same peasant squads that six years earlier had poured down from
the hills in support of Garibaldi. The rising was as much social as
political in character, and lacked clear organization, with republicans

and separatists rubbing shoulders incongruously with Bourbonists and clericals; but the government was extremely jittery after the recent defeats and the army leadership keen to highlight what it saw as one of the main sources of contamination of the country's moral fibre, and a large force was dispatched to Sicily under the Piedmontese general Raffaele Cadorna, and Palermo bombarded into submission. Martial law was declared, and there were sweeping arrests and numerous summary executions (including of women). To justify the severe measures, Cadorna drew up a list of atrocities that had allegedly been committed by the Sicilians, including policemen being burned alive and bitten to death, a soldier being crucified, and *carabiniere* flesh being sold publicly in the streets; and the government went ahead and published these claims, even though Cadorna later confessed they had been based on little more than hearsay.[34] The Minister of the Interior further stoked the flames by talking publicly for the first time about a deadly secret society called 'the mafia' which he alleged had been largely responsible for the horrors in Sicily.[35] The demons within Italy were rapidly emerging as every bit as menacing as those without.

THE TAKING OF ROME

The costs of unification had been very high, and Italy's public finances had been in a precarious condition for some time. The war of 1866 was the last straw, and it left the country financially as well as morally prostrate. During the next four years the government was forced to concentrate heavily on the prosaic business of staving off bankruptcy, raising loans, issuing vast amounts of paper money, selling off ecclesiastical property and increasing taxes. The first of the country's major parliamentary scandals broke out in 1868–9 in relation to the sale by the state of its tobacco monopoly to a consortium of bankers for a seemingly paltry sum, with widespread rumours that many deputies (and even the king) stood to make huge personal gains from the transaction.[36] On the left in particular there were angry accusations that Italy was being dragged into a moral morass, and metaphors of 'mire' and 'mud' began to be bandied about freely in reference to the Chamber of Deputies. The image of Italy as a modern-day 'Byzantium' – effete, corrupt and decadent – also began to circulate, and soon became common currency. To add to the growing sense of despondency serious rioting broke out early in 1869 – this time in the north rather than the south, in the Romagna – following the introduction of a highly unpopular new grist tax, and again martial law was declared and General Cadorna sent in with the army.

The idea of a march on Rome to complete the country's material and moral unification remained in the air, and in the autumn of 1867 the elderly Garibaldi embarked on one last desperate bid to seize the Eternal City. The prospect of a war with France did not worry him. Indeed he welcomed it: it would be the making of Italy. 'A few days of energetic action will serve to sort everything out and win over the entire nation,' he informed his friend Francesco Crispi. '. . . The whole population would rise up, women and children included, and the world would see a demonstration of the will of the people such, perhaps, as had never been witnessed before.'[37] But his hopes proved unfounded. Thousands of volunteers assembled in Florence and again there were rumours of a secret understanding between Garibaldi and the king; but the rising that was supposed to have broken out in Rome to provide a pretext for armed intervention failed to materialize, and although Garibaldi advanced into papal territory, the government lost its nerve and refused to send in the army to support him, thereby allowing the French to land an expeditionary force at Civitavecchia unopposed. Without assistance from the local population, the venture was doomed to failure and on 3 November, demoralized by the cold and the rain, Garibaldi and his supporters were defeated in a minor engagement at Mentana. Far from being erased the humiliations of Custoza and Lissa the previous year had been compounded.

Rome was finally acquired only in September 1870, and the event was not the glorious culmination to the national movement that many patriots had hoped for. The outbreak of war between France and Prussia obliged Napoleon III to withdraw his garrison of troops from the city in July, but the Italian government under the eminently worthy but lacklustre Piedmontese doctor Giovanni Lanza remained wedded to the idea that Rome should if possible be secured peacefully, with the consent of France and the papacy, and hesitated to use military action. It continued to hesitate even after Napoleon had been defeated at the Battle of Sedan early in September and been forced into exile; and it was largely only fear of republicans seizing the initiative and increasing pressure from public opinion, whipped up in the main by the patriotic democratic press (even the king's mistress got excited: she vowed never to sleep with Victor Emmanuel again if he did not take the city),[38] that persuaded the government to move. On the morning of 20 September, Italian artillery punched a hole in the walls of Rome near Porta Pia. The Pope had asked his soldiers to put up token resistance – just enough to show that he was yielding to force – and there were only a few casualties. A white flag was soon flying over St Peter's, and within a day all that remained of the temporal power of the popes was the Vatican.

For those who had grown up under the influence of Mazzini and the other patriotic writers of the Risorgimento, the half-hearted manner in which Rome was taken was frustrating. It seemed to indicate a lack of faith in Italy as a nation: for if Italy had been providentially ordained, as so many had wished to believe, then surely it was entitled to seize what rightfully belonged to it, if necessary by force, without having to worry about diplomatic niceties? And if the country's leaders displayed so little confidence in the national principle, what hope was there that the rest of the population would acquire any sense of patriotism? Even after the city had been captured, the government remained nervous, almost as if it was embarrassed by what had happened and was worried about upsetting the Pope more than it already had done. Victor Emmanuel only travelled to Rome for the first time on 30 December, arriving discreetly in the middle of the night and staying for just a few hours; and even then the official reason for the visit was to offer sympathy to victims of a recent flood of the Tiber and not for the king to set foot in his new capital. The gulf between the poetry and the prose was horribly apparent; and in the decades to come the anxieties and frustrations that this gulf engendered were slowly to gnaw away at the moral foundations of the liberal state and foster among the country's leading intellectuals desperate, and sometimes wholly unrealistic, schemes for rectifying the situation.

The writer Giosuè Carducci – the former Mazzinian who dominated the Italian literary scene in the 1870s and 1880s – voiced the sense of disappointment at the stark contrast between what might have been and what was brilliantly. In a poem written in 1871, which conflated the city's capture with Victor Emmanuel's fleeting visit of three months later, he imagined 'Italy' creeping up to the Capitoline Hill at night:

Be quiet! Be quiet! Why this commotion in the moonlight?
Geese of the Capitol, be quiet!
I am Italy, united and great.
I come in the dark because Dr Lanza
Is afraid of the rays of the sun . . .
Please, geese, make less noise
Lest [the Pope's minister] hears . . .
Forever on my knees . . .
Daughter of Rome
I plant my kisses on one foot after another
And down in the mud
I drag my turreted locks
With the star attached . . .[39]

In another poem, written to commemorate his friend the Romagna democrat Vincenzo Caldesi, who had died in 1870, Carducci provided what quickly became the literary *locus classicus* for frustrated patriotic hopes – Italy as the new Byzantium:

Sleep my Vincenzo, sleep, furled in your cloak of glory:
We are living in an age of weak and devious men
When the strong are forgotten . . .
I would not wish to cry the name of Rome
Above your holy tomb
Yet, if I were to lean over your secluded grave
And say with heartfelt pride:
Vincenzo, we have ascended the Capitol once more . . .
You would spring from the earth
To behold and defend again that Rome
Whose liberty you invoked
And to which you sacrificed the best portion of your life.
But sleep on . . .
The burden of sin still weighs us down:
Italy, unprepared, demanded Rome –
They have given her Byzantium.[40]

How to turn 'Byzantium' into 'Rome' was to be the main problem facing Italy's political class now that the material unity of the nation was to all intents and purposes complete.

13

The Threat from the South, 1870–85

I want to speak of the mafia. You say to me: what is the mafia? Perhaps it is something that cannot be defined, but all the many documents that we have gathered indicate that it is a powerful and massive association, it is a solidarity in evil, an association of the guilty for enjoying the fruits of crime and ensuring that law remains beyond their reach.
Stefano Castagnola (Ligurian), speech to the Chamber of Deputies, 8 June 1874

The co-existence of Sicilian civilization and that of central and northern Italy in the same nation is incompatible with the prosperity of the nation and, in the long run, with its very existence, for it produces a weakness that makes the nation vulnerable to disintegration at the slightest push from outside. One of these two civilizations must therefore disappear . . .

Leopoldo Franchetti (Tuscan),
Condizioni politiche e amministrative della Sicilia (1877)

The mafia is neither a sect nor an association, it has no regulations or statutes. The mafioso is not a thief or a criminal. And if the word's recent change in fortune has meant that the term mafioso has been applied to thieves and criminals, this is because the ill-informed general public has not had time to consider the meaning of the word properly or bother to find out that . . . a mafioso is simply a brave and assertive man who does not tolerate insults.

Giuseppe Pitrè (Sicilian),
Usi e costumi, credenze e pregiudizi, del popolo siciliano (1887)

'EXAMINING ITALY IN THE SPIRIT OF MACHIAVELLI'

In the summer of 1870 Francesco De Sanctis was working on a monumental history of Italian literature. Since the disasters of Custoza and Lissa he had turned away from parliamentary life in order to concentrate on academic studies. Not in any spirit of escapism or reclusiveness: scholarship, in his view, needed to be politically engaged and should seek to educate hearts and minds to the responsibilities of citizenship in a modern state. As he ranged over the vast corpus of Italian writings from the Middle Ages to the present, he identified two archetypes of the national character, which he wanted to hold up to his fellow countrymen as exemplars of what to avoid and what to emulate. The first was that of the early-sixteenth-century historian Francesco Guicciardini, who had viewed the world with scepticism and detachment, aware of what was morally desirable but unwilling to do anything to achieve a higher goal if this required personal inconvenience or suffering. The spirit of this 'Guicciardini man', he believed, had infiltrated Italian society since the Counter-Reformation and brought about the country's decline. The second archetype, and Guicciardini's moral antithesis, was represented by another early-sixteenth-century writer, Niccolò Machiavelli. He had looked the world squarely in the face, had analysed ruthlessly the weaknesses of the Italian people, and (crucially) had believed that their vices should and could be rectified. 'Machiavelli fights the corruption of Italy without despairing of his country . . . With Guicciardini we have the emergence of a more resigned generation.'[1]

As he sat writing in his small house in the centre of Naples on 20 September 1870, just a stone's throw from where the great philosopher Giambattista Vico had been born 200 years before, surrounded by cigar smoke and papers, De Sanctis could hear the church bells ringing out to celebrate the taking of Rome, and he hoped fervently that the collapse of the Pope's temporal power would usher in a new age for Italy – one grounded in the spirit of Machiavelli, simultaneously scientific and idealistic, in which the polestars of both thought and action were nation, state, fatherland, liberty and equality.[2] But if Italy were to enter fully into the modern world, it would first have to undergo a process of rigorous self-examination and discovery:

[Italy] now has to look into its heart and search for itself . . . Its life is still too external and superficial. It must search with unclouded gaze, free of all filters and distortions, exploring reality in the spirit of Galileo and Machiavelli . . . We must examine . . . our ways of behaving, our ideas, our prejudices, and our qualities, both good and bad, and make the modern world our world, studying it, adapting to it, and moulding it . . . We live to a large extent in the past and rely heavily on the achievements of others: we have yet to fashion our own life and our own achievements. And in our boastful claims can be glimpsed a sense of our inferiority . . .[3]

The need to examine closely the moral and material reality of Italy appeared all the more pressing in the light of developments elsewhere in Europe. The Paris Commune of the spring of 1871, with its mixture of socialism and insurrectionary violence, sent shock waves through conservative circles, for it was widely regarded as the work of the International Working Men's Association ('the International'), an organization that had been founded in London in 1864 to coordinate the demands and activities of the working-class movements of Western countries. On one level Italy seemed much less vulnerable to socialism than more industrialized states: its rural economy and mass of illiterate peasants meant that it was historically still too immature for revolution, at least according to the theories of Karl Marx and his followers. But the great poverty of the countryside and the strong traditions of rural disorder – well over a thousand people had been killed or wounded in the Romagna riots of 1869 – led many to fear that the message of the International might fall on receptive soil in Italy, particularly as the poor had almost no national sentiment and little sense of loyalty towards the institutions that could serve as prophylactics against the new subversive doctrines.

Somewhat ironically, the introduction of liberalism in 1860 had meant that the great majority of the population were economically more vulnerable than they had been under absolutism. The *ancien régime* rulers had sought to safeguard the poor against the uncertainties of the market place and the rapaciousness of local landowners with price controls, protectionism, low taxes, laws to promote land distribution and charity from the Church – whose vast network of monasteries, hospitals, schools, orphanages and charitable foundations and endowments afforded a crucial source of welfare (not to mention employment).[4] United Italy had brought with it the chill winds of free trade, with particularly devastating effects on the fragile manufacturing sector in the south. It had also given the propertied classes an unprecedented degree of power, for town councillors and parliamentary deputies were elected by the wealthiest social groups, and answered to them, and in effect to them only, rather than (as formerly) to a paternalistic monarch. And in the absence of a strong national ethos to counter the moral imperatives of self-interest, the ruling elites were able to use their privileged position to feather their own nests, often quite shamelessly.

The difficulty the government faced in trying to legislate in favour of the working classes was evident time and again in the early decades of unity. Despite, in the 1860s and even more in the 1870s and 1880s, a number of major inquiries which revealed the appalling scale of urban and rural deprivation in Italy, attempts to introduce a fairer tax system, or increase the number of peasant smallholdings or constrain employers to behave responsibly towards their tenants and workers were blocked in parliament by ad hoc coalitions of deputies eager to protect their interests. If a measure did make it to the statute book that might in theory have helped the poor, the realities of local life often served to hamstring it. This was the case, for example, with the massive sale of more than 2 million hectares of ecclesiastical and ex-feudal property by the state during the late 1860s and 1870s. Despite a stipulation that it should be sold off in small units in order to allow peasants to make purchases, the absence of credit facilities, especially in the south, together with the government's desperate need for ready money meant that in the end it was only the already well-off who were in a position to benefit. Moreover the auctions were frequently rigged by the *galantuomini*, who used intimidation to ensure that nobody dared bid against them.[5]

The state's need to raise revenue quickly in order to deal with the huge public debt was one important reason why the burden of taxation fell disproportionately on the poor after 1860. Piedmont had run up a huge overdraft in the late 1840s and 1850s, well over 1,000 million lire, fighting the Austrians and constructing railways; and when to this were added the debts that the new kingdom inherited from the other Italian states at unification, the costs of fighting banditry in the south and of the war of 1866, and the expenditure incurred in setting up three capital cities in the space of a decade, it is little wonder that united Italy imposed abnormally high levels of taxation on its new subjects.[6] By 1870 the national debt had reached the dizzy heights of more than 8,000 million lire. Revenue from direct taxes went up by 63 per cent between 1865 and 1871, but the difficulties involved in getting accurate returns for private income forced the government to fall back more and more on easily levied consumer taxes – on salt, on tobacco, and most notoriously on the grinding of wheat and other grains – which hit the working classes particularly severely. Receipts from indirect taxation rose by 107 per cent between 1865 and 1871.[7] Local councils were also entitled to impose taxes, for example on food and livestock, and again it was the poor who were disproportionately affected. When the young Tuscan liberal Sidney Sonnino visited Sicily in 1876 he found that mules and donkeys – which the peasants owned – were much more heavily taxed than cattle, which belonged to the large landowners.[8]

Not surprisingly these enormous fiscal burdens were a source of widespread popular resentment towards the state, and there were growing fears that the gap between rulers and ruled – or what was commonly referred to as 'legal' and 'real' Italy – might prove fatal to the new kingdom. Already in the early 1870s great alarm was caused by the presence of anarchist agitators among the peasantry, especially in the Romagna (where an armed insurrection was attempted in 1874) and in southern Italy. Fears for the future of Italy were most acutely felt by those whose involvement in the democratic movement since the 1840s had given them a sense of responsibility towards 'the people' and a strong awareness of the weakness of patriotic sentiment among the mass of ordinary Italians. One such was Francesco Crispi, who in October 1873 travelled to Tricarico, the constituency in the mountainous interior of Basilicata that he had represented since 1870 and not visited before: it was common for leading politicians to be returned in a college *in absentia*. He was deeply shocked by what he found.

The journey involved a two-day trek inland by carriage from the nearest railway station at Eboli over steep and ill-made roads. Of the thirteen towns and villages that comprised the electoral college, only two were connected to the outside world by road: the rest were accessible by rough tracks that turned to quagmire in the winter rains. The extent of the poverty was almost indescribable. The peasants lived on a diet of beans or barley ground up into a coarse flour. But they were being bled dry by the grist tax, which the government's agents levied remorselessly;

and in several places Crispi was assailed by crowds of angry women protesters. The landowners could not market their produce because of the high costs of transport, and as a result their crops were being left to rot. The levels of ignorance were dire, and in most places the welcoming party had to consist largely of priests, who at least spoke Italian. Crispi was pleased that in one town the streets had been given 'Italian' names – Plebiscito, Vittorio Emanuele, Garibaldi, Mille and even Pisacane – but overall he had a sense of an angry and subversive world that was still outside the confines of the nation. As he told his friend, the doctor and social reformer Agostino Bertani:

What has the national government done to bring civilization here and win over the masses? Nothing. What it has done has been counter-productive ... I will not tell you of the cries, the abuse and the tears. I will tell you only that the Italian government is cursed and hated. And if brigandage were to break out again, how could the government complain? And if they threatened unity, would we dare to punish them? It is enough to drive you mad.[9]

The indications are that in the first forty years of unification the standard of living of the Italian population as a whole did not improve at all – indeed in many cases it seems to have fallen – and this at a time when almost everywhere else in Europe experienced at least modest rises in prosperity.[10] The 1880s did see a significant expansion of industry, with the creation of state-sponsored iron and steel production (a considerable achievement given the near total absence of coal and other minerals), the establishment of new engineering plants and sustained growth in the main manufacturing sector, textiles (cotton, wool and above all silk, of which Italy was the world's leading producer after China). But these developments were confined almost entirely to the three north-western regions of the peninsula and did not result in an industrial 'take-off' of any kind. Nor was it clear that factory workers were better paid than their rural counterparts: the massive labour pool ensured that wages were kept depressed. As it was Italy remained an overwhelmingly agricultural country, with around two-thirds of the labour force employed on the land in the 1870s and 1880s; and here the general picture in the last two decades of the nineteenth century was bleak, with low investment and falling prices leading to rising unemployment and a general decline in living standards. Millions of Italians voted with their feet and emigrated.

THE 'SOUTHERN QUESTION'

It was the economic and social conditions of the south of Italy that attracted most attention after 1870. The civil war that had raged in the first years after unification died down during the second half of the 1860s, and though banditry remained an intermittent problem, the main focus of government and academic concern moved away from law and order towards examining the root causes of the backwardness and poverty of the southern provinces. For in almost every sphere the gap between north and south was wide, and despite hopes that the introduction of political and economic liberalism would soon reduce the deficit, the disparities in fact showed every sign of growing. Apart from certain pockets of intensive cultivation, as on the eastern seaboard of Sicily or the coastal plains of Puglia, where citrus fruit, vines and olives abounded, southern agriculture was characterized by poor yields, limited investment and outdated farming methods. Income was generally much lower and unemployment greater; mortality and birth rates were higher; and illiteracy levels were nearly double those of Piedmont and Lombardy. There were also major discrepancies in the quality of civil society, with the north having a far more vigorous and developed cultural life than the south. Naples, for instance, had just five bookshops in 1881, despite being the largest city in Italy (Florence had twelve, Turin ten). Some of the most striking differences were to be found in the economic infrastructure. In 1869 there were twenty-five banking houses in the north, and only three in the south; and a decade later the imbalance had become if anything more pronounced: 193 as against thirty-one.[11]

The problem was that the 'southern question', as it came to be called in the 1870s, was from the start clouded by resentment and prejudice, much of it fuelled by the highly insensitive fashion in which unification had been imposed after 1860. This not only made it extremely hard for discussions to be conducted in 'the spirit of Galileo and Machiavelli', as De Sanctis had wanted, but also influenced the terms in which many of the arguments were framed. Indeed the very idea of a 'southern question' derived more from an old belief in a deep cultural and moral cleavage between the two halves of the peninsula than from any self-evident fact: 'the south' was after all never a homogeneous entity.[12] When northerners attributed the south's problems largely to the shortcomings of the local landowners – their feudal attitudes, their ignorance, their lack of entre-preneurial spirit – they were often drawing on long-standing stereotypes. When southerners, by contrast, blamed the region's continued poverty on the new state – on free trade, on centralization, on an inequitable tax system – they were often reflecting resentment at what had seemed a Piedmontese 'conquest' (and forgetting that the south's relative back-wardness in fact long predated unification).

The problem of prejudice in relation to the southern question was nowhere more evident than in the question of 'the mafia'. Sicily had been the most disturbed region in Italy during the 1860s, and talk of a sinister criminal organization had begun to surface in official circles in 1865–6, especially in the wake of the Palermo rising. Quite what the mafia was, was unclear, and there was a strong suspicion in some quarters that the idea of a dangerous secret society was little more than a canard being used to explain the unrest and justify severe repressive measures. When in 1874, following renewed fears of an insurrection, the government announced that it would introduce exceptional measures to deal with 'the mafia', there was an outcry in the island and accusations began to fly that the reputation of Sicily was being besmirched by hostile and uncomprehending northerners. The issue was debated in parliament in the summer of 1875, bringing 'the mafia' to international attention for the first time, but from the discussions it was evident that nobody knew exactly what the phenomenon was – and even if it existed. Indeed the prevalent view seemed to be that 'the mafia' was best understood not as an organization but as a form of behaviour involving exaggerated notions of personal honour and a willingness to deploy private violence.[13]

It was partly to find out the truth about 'the mafia' that in the spring of 1876 a young Tuscan intellectual, Leopoldo Franchetti, travelled to Sicily with his friend Sidney Sonnino. The study that he published later that year of the administrative and political conditions in the island was at once brilliantly penetrating and profoundly disturbing, for it revealed a world where the state had failed almost entirely to establish its moral authority, leaving power in the hands of men who could threaten and kill with impunity. 'The mafia', he discovered, was not a secret society. There certainly were criminal associations in Sicily with initiation rites and statutes; but these were usually quite small in scale and tended to operate in niche economic markets. The reality was that *mafiosi* – men with a reputation for violence – did not need a formal organization, for they were operating in an environment (much of western and central Sicily) where their authority was respected almost without question and where nobody would think of denouncing them to the police. They were pivotal to almost every aspect of life: they dominated the land and labour markets, mediated with the authorities, settled disputes, protected property and ran elections. And since they were so pivotal, everyone (including state officials) ended up having dealings with them, whether they liked it or not, and became in effect their accomplices.[14]

Franchetti was deeply patriotic – he was to commit suicide in November 1917 after learning of Italy's disastrous defeat at Caporetto – and he longed to see Sicily fully integrated into the nation. But he found it immensely hard to see how this process could be achieved. The problem was that the men who used private violence, the *mafiosi*, were deeply woven into the texture of society and this made it impossible to find a clear-cut answer to the 'eternal question' haunting the mind of those who studied the island 'like a nightmare': 'Who is to blame?' Everyone – from police and politicians, to landowners and peasants – was in some degree implicated and culpable. 'When a drop of oil falls on a marble table-top, it remains unchanged and can be easily wiped off, but if it lands on a piece of paper it begins to soak in and spread, and becomes as one with the material itself and inseparable from it.'[15] The only hope for Sicily was for the state to acquire sufficient moral ascendancy to deprive the *mafiosi* of their authority. But he could not see how this would be achieved, as there was no social group in the island with sufficient independence and influence to spearhead the task of regeneration. And if no solution could be found, he concluded rather desperately, Italy should abandon Sicily 'to its natural forces and let it proclaim its independence'.[16]

One man who was rather more confident that he had the answer to Sicily's – and indeed humanity's – problems was a young Jewish doctor from Verona called Cesare Lombroso. After graduating in medicine from the university of Pavia in 1858, Lombroso had travelled with the army in southern Italy during the campaign against brigandage and had become fascinated by the issue of crime. He had measured and examined some 3,000 conscripts and in 1864 had published a study of the links between soldiers' tattoos and deviancy. But his moment of epiphany came one day in 1870 when he was carrying out an autopsy on a 69-year-old Calabrian thief and arsonist, suspected of banditry, called Giuseppe Villella. While examining the skull he noticed an anomaly: where the occipital ridge should have been, close to the junction with the spine, there was a depression, 34 mm long, 23 mm wide and 11 mm deep, whose profile suggested a deformation of the brain caused, per- haps, by arrested foetal development. Similar occipital depressions were known to occur in various species of monkey and lemur: 'When I saw that depression,' wrote Lombroso a number of years later, 'I suddenly saw unfolding before me, like a vast plain stretching off endlessly towards the distant horizon, the problem of the nature of the human criminal, who in the modern age was driven to replicate the behaviour of primitive man and of animals right down to carnivores.' Lombroso preserved Villella's skull all his life, regarding it, he said, as 'the totem, the fetish of criminal anthropology'.[17]

Lombroso was to be the founder of a hugely influential school of criminology that attracted to its ranks some of Italy's best-known scien- tific or 'positivist' intellectuals of the last quarter of the nineteenth century, including several of the country's leading socialists. His most famous work, *Criminal Man*, first published in 1876, went through five editions in twenty years (expanding in the process from 250 to more than 2,000 pages) and was widely translated in Europe and the Americas. Though he never denied the impact of environment and social conditions on criminal behaviour (which was one reason why many socialists were happy to embrace his teachings), Lombroso's central contention was that the most hardened and violent offenders were almost invariably the product of a genetic throw-back or what he called 'atavism'. And from the start he saw the main determinant of atavism as race. Writing the same year as his seminal dissection of Villella's skull, and inspired by the recent appearance of Charles Darwin's ground-breaking *The Descent of Man*, Lombroso argued that the different levels of civilization in the world were to be explained in terms of degrees of evolutionary develop- ment away from primates, with white Europeans at the peak (their crania were perfectly proportioned) and Mongols, bushmen and blacks at the base. Black people, he claimed, resembled monkeys in the small size of their skulls, their dark skin, curly hair, eye membranes and 'particular odour'.[18]

It was a very small step from here to a racial reading of Italy's 'southern question', for though criminal statistics only began to be collected systematically from 1879, the overwhelming impression given by the south from 1860 was of a region beset by crime, especially violent crime – banditry, kidnapping, feuding and armed robberies. And violence, according to Lombroso and his followers, was a good indicator of barbarism, and barbarism of racial degeneracy. Thus the high rates of murder around Palermo were to be explained by the settlement there in ancient times of the 'rapacious Berber and Semitic tribes', while the generally lower incidence of killings in the eastern half of the island was the result of the richer mixture of 'Aryan blood'.[19] The existence of criminal organizations such as the Neapolitan camorra and the Sicilian mafia was also evidence of a greater level of atavism in the south, for secret societies, he said, were frequently to be found among primitive peoples – as, for example, the Mumbo Djembo of Senegal.[20] Lombroso was dismissive of claims by certain Sicilian ethnographers and others that *mafiosi* were in fact 'men of honour' who embodied a distinctive set of traditional local values: *mafiosi* were just 'vulgar criminals', as was clear from their jargon, their clothes and their liking for expensive rings.[21]

Lombroso held a number of distinguished academic posts at the universities of Pavia and Turin, and the school of criminal anthropology that he built up influenced Italian intellectual life heavily in the last quarter of the century – and continued to do so for many years after his death in 1909. He believed strongly that he was engaged in a patriotic mission, writing in 1879 of how he felt inspired 'not by love of a sect or a party, but of the nation', and was thus driven to do everything in his power to combat 'the tide of crime that is always rising and rising, threatening to submerge as well as disgrace us'.[22] And his contention that criminality posed a deadly and growing threat to the country was widely accepted (despite the problems of getting hold of any reliable statistics) and became something of a national obsession in the course of the 1880s, with the prominent Neapolitan jurist Raffaele Garofalo claiming that Italy had sixteen times as many murders as Britain and a prison population that was twenty times greater, and with a young Milanese lawyer and future leader of the Italian Socialist Party, Filippo Turati, announcing in 1882 that the country enjoyed a 'real primacy' in Europe, but unfortunately not that 'dreamed of by Gioberti', namely in crime.[23]

Lombroso had no doubt that he and his followers were acting in the 'spirit of Machiavelli': his numerous books (more than thirty) and articles were packed with data drawn from a huge array of sources, and studded with statistical tables, charts, photographs and diagrams. And it was their voguish scientific quality, as much as the fact that they seemed to offer an answer to the nagging question of who or what was to blame for Italy's ills, that helps explain their remarkable appeal to contemporaries. In reality, though, their use of evidence was extremely crude, with the taxonomy of features of 'born criminals' – narrow foreheads, thick black hair, hirsute limbs and torso, wispy beards, prominent jaws, large canine teeth and jug ears – providing an object lesson in the power of prejudice to shape 'impartial' observation (Lombroso, though, was proud that his findings tallied with popular stereotypes: 'the knowledge of a criminal physiognomic type . . . is often instinctive in the common people').[24] And the idea that the north–south divide in Italy could be accounted for largely in genetic terms, with northerners descended from a European Aryan race, southerners from a Semitic or Mediterranean race that had emerged from Africa, had even less empirical substance.

Yet racial explanations for the southern question proved surprisingly enduring, despite the obvious fact that they risked creating a permanent fault-line through the nation. One reason for this was that they dovetailed with the old preoccupations about the degeneracy of the Italian character. Another was that they provided ammunition for those – and they were fast growing in number in the 1870s as the full extent of the country's economic, social and political problems became apparent – who felt that the existing political and legal structures were ill-suited to Italy's needs. Lombroso himself believed that the basis of the entire judicial system had to be shifted away from the classical liberal concern with the offence to dealing with the offender if the nation were to protect itself adequately against the corrosive effects of atavism: punishment had to be fitted to the criminal rather than the crime, with 'born criminals' facing the death penalty (to hasten evolution through natural selection) and lesser felons being subjected to the appropriate corrective and educational measures. And since there were major disparities in the levels of atavism between north and south, Italy needed to be less centralized and have penal codes more finely attuned to local conditions.

The danger that investigations into the southern question, whether from the angle of crime or of socio-economic underdevelopment, might weaken the credibility of liberalism became increasingly apparent in the 1880s and 1890s. While some of the most eloquent spokesmen for the south – such as the distinguished politician and scholar from the Basilicata region Giustino Fortunato – argued passionately that progress could only be achieved if Italy remained strong and fully united, with parliament legislating to rectify the disparities between the two halves of the peninsula, others came to the conclusion that much more radical and authoritarian approaches were needed. And the fact that successive governments failed from the 1870s to come up with laws that made any serious difference to the south, despite numerous inquiries and reports (a commission created in 1877 to look into agricultural conditions in Italy delivered its findings in fifteen weighty volumes in 1885),[25] added to the growing stridency of the debate. Indeed most observers found it hard to see what material improvements, if any, there had been in the south during the first decades of unity, apart from in railway building: thousands of kilometres of new track were laid down, though the government's motives here were as much military as economic.

A good example of how discussions about the nature of the country's socio-economic problems and fears of racial degeneracy began to call liberalism into question is provided by an important book, first published in 1882, by a Neapolitan sociologist and former follower of Garibaldi, Pasquale Turiello.[26] The central thesis of his lengthy study, *Government and Governed in Italy*, was that the political and administrative system that had been introduced in Italy after 1860 had been much too doctrinaire and foreign (French) and had failed to take sufficient account of the Italian character. Race, climate, geography and history had all combined over the centuries to make Italians strongly resistant to authority and prone to intense individualism, or what he called *scioltezza* ('in their decisions and actions the "I" is more apparent than the "we"').[27] And these traits were especially pronounced in the southern half of the country, as the high levels of crime, especially violent crime, there indicated. Although the fundamentals of the Italian character could not be altered they could be modified with the appropriate external controls, and in the Middle Ages institutions such as guilds, citizen militias and navies had been used by the city-states to keep Italians on a tight rein. This was why they had managed to achieve great things. But after 1500 the external controls had dwindled and Italians had slipped back into *scioltezza*.[28]

The mistake in 1860, according to Turiello, was to give Italians too much freedom and to believe that progress went hand in hand with a relaxation of central controls by the state. As a result *scioltezza* had been allowed to flourish as never before, especially in the south, and the new liberal institutions had simply encouraged selfishness and individualism. He felt that parliamentary government was highly problematic, as deputies were forced to pander far too much to the local interests of their electors; but it was not necessarily irredeemable, provided that the nation was subjected to a process of education that forced Italians to think less of their private needs and more of the collectivity. Among the various educational measures he proposed were the creation of distinctively 'Italian' institutions to foster social and political cohesion, an increased presence of the monarchy in public life, the building of gymnasia, the introduction of compulsory fitness programmes in every town and village, and the promotion of group and military activities among children ('from parades to target shooting, our schools, from primary to university level, are totally without attractive structures for encouraging Italian youth to feel "we" rather than "I"').[29]

But it was the army that Turiello looked to most to overcome *scioltezza* and restore the moral fibre of the nation. Schools were too poorly funded and ill-attended to have very much impact on the national character; and parliament, with its 'sordid disputes between the petulant egos of deputies', offered no guide to behaviour in the new Italy. It was military service that would do most to correct the indiscipline of Italians; and the spectacle of serried ranks of well-drilled young men parading through the streets would provide an uplifting model for the values that citizens should aspire to, while simultaneously raising the prestige of the state (how much, he wondered, of the dispute with the Pope would be resolved by the sight of several thousand students marching silently and austerely at public ceremonies through Rome, 'consciously re-enacting the [military rallies] of their forefathers in the Campus Martius'?).[30] But for the army to realize its full educational potential it needed to be invested with the glory of success. And a great national military victory was accordingly the key to Italy's future:

[A] new, mighty and virile offensive, a second test of arms and blood, [will] restore to Italy the strength that it now seems to lack . . . From 1866 until today we have returned a third time to a period of prolonged peace, which, as history shows, can only be endured by Italians at the cost of their being ruined . . . Our character, which becomes weak in peacetime and is only strengthened in the crucible of war . . . compel[s] us today to accept any opportunity to fight . . . Italy can continue to be at peace, but only at the price of gradually slipping back to the moral condition into which the protracted periods of peace had led us in 1494 and 1792 . . . When the army and the nation have been reinvigorated by a great and glorious war, well planned in advance, the damage that is being done [to the state by its enemies] will be reduced to almost nothing.[31]

14

National Education

When he had stretched his legs out, Pinocchio began to walk by himself and to race round the room; until he slipped through the door, leapt into the street and took to his heels . . .

'Catch him! Catch him!' shouted Geppetto: but when the people in the street saw this wooden puppet running like a racehorse, they stopped in amazement to watch him, and laughed, and laughed and laughed, such as you could not imagine.

In the end, as luck would have it, a carabiniere turned up . . . who seized him cleanly by the nose (and it was an enormous nose, that seemed to have been made specially to be grabbed by the carabinieri) and handed him back to Geppetto. And Geppetto straight away wanted to give him a good tweak of the ears by way of a punishment. But imagine his surprise when he looked for the ears and could not find any. And do you know why? Because in his haste to carve him, he had forgotten to give him any. Carlo Collodi, *Le avventure di Pinocchio* (1883)

I know, too, that Italy has been reunited for only ten years and is not firmly established; our common people are ignorant . . . and the army remains the great crucible in which all the elements are fused into Italian unity . . . I have always said that even if it had no other purpose, the army would always be a great school of Italian-ness. Nicola Marselli, *Gli avvenimenti del 1870–71* (1871)

PRIMARY SCHOOLS

It was not just the educated elites who had had such high hopes for unification. One reason, presumably, why there was so little grass roots support for the *ancien régime* states in 1859–60 was because some of the aura surrounding 'Italy' had spilled over from the towns and cities into the countryside. Patriotic landowners, schoolmasters, local *érudits*, travelling musicians playing snatches of Verdi, former volunteers from the campaigns of 1848–9 and even parish priests were among the many possible conduits through which Risorgimento rhetoric could trickle into rural backwaters. Popular expectations attaching to the national movement were echoed in baptismal registers. Names such as Italia and Roma enjoyed a certain vogue among the peasantry in the 1860s. Variants of Garibaldi – Garibaldo, Garibalda, Garibaldino, Garibaldina – were also quite common, especially, it seems, in parts of central Italy. Anita (after Garibaldi's first wife) and even Mentana featured, too. In regions such as Liguria and the Romagna, where republicanism had struck a chord with sections of the working classes, Mazzini left a nominal imprint in Mazzino, Mazzina and Mazzinia.[1]

It was probably in Tuscany where the poor had been most exposed to the language and sentiments of patriotism, for this was a region that had long been proud of the paternalistic bonds between landlord and peasant fostered by the agricultural system of sharecropping and the educational initiatives of enlightened reformers such as Vieusseux, Capponi, Montanelli and Guerrazzi. So when on 1 January 1863 a daughter was born to a humble brush-maker called Gaspero Donati, in a crowded two-storeyed farmhouse on the outskirts of the village of Cintolese in the marshy countryside between Florence and Lucca, a few miles to the south of Pistoia (where Niccolò Puccini had built his famous villa and garden), it was not altogether surprising that she should be baptized Italia. About Gaspero very little is known, but he must have had some hopes that his children would rise in the world, as both Italia and her elder brother, Italiano (born in 1851), received a sound education (though Gaspero's other son, Gabbriello, remained illiterate, and after years of struggling to make a living as a labourer he emigrated to America, like so many others, abandoning his wife and two small daughters). Italia showed sufficient academic promise to aspire to the position of a teacher, and in 1882, at her second attempt, she passed the necessary qualifying examination and was awarded the title of 'primary schoolmistress, lower grade'.[2]

She was appointed to a post in the hamlet of Porciano, some ten kilometres to the south-east of Cintolese and a short distance from the little town of Vinci, where more than 400 years earlier one of the most learned men of the Renaissance had been born and educated. Her annual salary (in keeping with national guidelines) was 550 lire, about as much as an agricultural labourer or an artisan might hope to make in a year, and out of this she was expected to pay all her living costs, including her accommodation. Such a situation was quite normal. A recent reform of 1877, the Coppino Law, had endeavoured to raise the profile of primary education and teachers in Italy; but it had left responsibility for the hiring and remuneration of staff in the hands of the local councils; and even in a region of relatively progressive traditions like Tuscany the landowners who typically comprised the councils were rarely willing to spend more than the bare minimum on educating the peasantry. To make matters worse, schoolmasters, and even more schoolmistresses, had almost no protection against their employers (as Italia was soon to discover to her terrible cost), and requests for improved pay, a bigger classroom, or even basics such as chalk, inkwells or a blackboard would be greeted with a deaf ear or sometimes with a contract being terminated.

When Italia arrived in Porciano, a naïve and vulnerable 23-year-old, she immediately came under enormous pressure from the mayor, Raffaello Torrigiani, an autocratic man and notorious womanizer who was living openly with his mistress as well as his wife, to accept an offer of free accommodation in one of his houses. The prospect of avoiding rent and being able to send a larger part of her salary back to her elderly parents in Cintolese was attractive; but what drove her to accept in the end was the realization that a refusal would lead to her being forced out (as had happened with the two previous schoolmistresses), for Torrigiani ruled the town as if it were a personal fiefdom and had a majority of the councillors firmly under his thumb. But once she had taken up the offer Italia not only had to fend off the mayor's advances – which she succeeded in doing – but much more insidiously she had to contend with the maliciousness of a community that now regarded her as not much better than a whore.[3]

Like many elementary schools, the school at Porciano consisted of a single room, ill-lit and poorly furnished, rented by the council, into which some fifty boys and girls ranging from six to twelve (or sometimes older) were expected to squeeze. A map of Italy and a portrait of the king were probably the only hangings on the wall. Under the Coppino Law education was free and compulsory up to the age of nine, and strict provisions were in place for enforcing attendance. Article three, for instance, said that parents who kept their children at home and could not provide the mayor with a satisfactory explanation were to be fined

50 cents in the first instance and up to 10 lire for subsequent infractions.[4] But as with so many Italian laws the gulf between intent and practice was huge and this measure was largely unenforceable. Even if the mayor bothered to chase up offenders, few would have been able to pay the fines; and anyway peasants needed their children to work in the fields, especially in the spring and summer months, and almost nothing would make them forgo this. A survey of a province in the Romagna in 1886–7 found that in only three out of the forty communes had attempts been made to impose fines for truancy; and in only five had proper lists been drawn up of those who were absent.[5] In these circumstances it is hardly surprising that attendance in primary schools in Italy was patchy and that most children, certainly in places like Porciano, emerged at the age of nine still functionally illiterate.

A difficulty that Italia Donati did not have to face was a communication barrier with her pupils. During the 1860s the government had embarked on intensive discussions about what form of Italian should be adopted as the national language, and the view that came to prevail was one championed by the elderly writer Alessandro Manzoni, namely that it should be contemporary spoken Tuscan. There was a strong feeling in official circles that linguistic centralization was needed to complement political unity, and Manzoni wanted the authorities to use schools to stigmatize dialect. He and his followers even went so far as to suggest that teachers should be recruited from Tuscany only.[6] But there were huge practical problems with such a draconian approach – not least the fact that the vast majority of the population, certainly outside Tuscany and the principal cities, had almost no contact with 'Italian' in their daily lives, and to try to impose it in such circumstances was virtually impossible. In the early 1870s a prominent philologist called Graziadio Isaia Ascoli made a passionate plea for dialects to be respected and for any standardization of the spoken idiom to be allowed to occur spontaneously as communication and culture gradually spread. And some influential figures, including Francesco De Sanctis, were inclined to agree with this sensible view. But the official line remained that Italian should as far as possible be enforced, with 'Italian' texts being used in schools and dialect literature (of which there was a distinguished tradition in many regions) being discouraged.[7]

But the linguistic problems facing teachers in primary schools were as nothing compared to the moral difficulties that they frequently encountered. If they were local (and the government's initial policy of trying to ensure that schoolmasters came from outside regions soon had to be relaxed for practical reasons) they could always fall back on dialect to get their message across: a national enquiry in 1908 found that half of all teachers regularly did so. Much more difficult to bridge was the huge cultural gap separating the 'priests of the new Italy', as Agostino Bertani optimistically called them,[8] from the mass of the peasantry. Over the centuries the Catholic Church had learned to adapt its teachings and practices to the everyday needs of the poor, and the clergy had thus managed in most places to secure a position of considerable authority and respect. Schoolmasters, with their new doctrines of secular positivism, faced a harder task. As a primary schoolteacher working in rural Romagna explained in 1872:

The teacher tries to destroy the errors, prejudices and superstitions regarding the rotation of the sun around the earth, the unlimited powers of the moon, witches, Fridays, spirits and so on. But when the child goes home and relates what the teacher has told him at school, these truths are refuted with false arguments and a string of facts that appear to be correct because they are backed up with the names of the family members who witnessed them, and the circumstances, place and time when they are said to have occurred.[9]

Equally problematic, as Italia Donati found, was that teachers were dependent on the mayor and his councillors, and could thus seem to many peasants to be part of the intimidating world of the state, with its tax collectors, recruiting officers and policemen. And ironically the fact that Italia was herself of very humble origins may have added to her difficulties, depriving her of authority and making her appear in the eyes of the poor something of an opportunist, even a traitor. Certainly in the months after she arrived in Porciano the whispering campaign against her among the villagers gathered pace, despite every indication that she was a conscientious and efficient teacher, and in the summer of 1884 an anonymous letter was sent to a magistrate in Pistoia alleging that she had procured an illegal abortion with the assistance of the mayor. The author of this attack was never unearthed, but in all likelihood it was one of the mayor's political opponents, who saw in Italia's increasingly equivocal position a good means of discrediting him; and Torrigiani was in fact eventually forced to resign.[10]

But for Italia the consequences of the allegation were devastating.

Though the police found not a shred of evidence against her, the hostility of the townspeople was now unbounded. She begged to be allowed to undergo a medical examination to prove her innocence, but neither the judicial authorities nor the town council would give their permission. She appealed to the regional inspector of schools, the well-known writer Renato Fucini, but he handed the matter over to the sub-prefect, who then took no action. She moved into a new house, but the campaign against her continued unabated; and as the strain took its toll on her health, the rumour spread that she was again pregnant – her sweats and pallor were proof. She asked to be moved to another school in the neighbourhood, and in the spring of 1886 the town council agreed. But her reputation had proceeded her, and the new community made clear its anger at having such a shameless woman foisted on them. Those that could sent anonymous hate-mail.[11]

On the evening of Monday, 31 May, Italia penned a brief note of apology to her parents, protesting her complete innocence. To her brother, Italiano, she wrote:

I am totally innocent of all the accusations made against me . . . I beg you, on my knees, with all my heart, my only brother, to do whatever it takes to bring back my honour. Please do not be alarmed by my death, and be comforted by the thought that it will restore the honour of our family. I am the victim of public vilification and my persecution will end only with my death. Take my corpse and with an anatomical inspection clear up this mystery. Let my innocence be proved . . .[12]

She told him she wanted to be buried in her native village of Cintolese, but knew that her family would probably not be able to afford the costs of transporting her body there: 'If it cannot be done, leave me in this wretched place and on my tombstone write these words: Here lies the unfortunate victim Italia Donati, schoolmistress of Porciano.'[13]

She walked in the dark to the race of the old watermill on the Rimaggio river, a little way out of the town, secured her skirts tightly with two safety pins (she did not want the humiliation of being found with her legs uncovered), and jumped. The autopsy confirmed that she had died a virgin. When the press got wind of the suicide, a reporter from the leading Milanese newspaper, the *Corriere della Sera*, was sent to investigate and published a detailed account of all that had transpired. There was a public outcry. The Neapolitan writer Matilde Serao wrote an impassioned article, denouncing the terrible plight of schoolmistresses in Italy and chronicling other recent instances of suicide. A subscription was launched to pay for the expense of reinterring Italia in her native village, and on 4 July her coffin was exhumed and transported to Cintolese in great solemnity, with a cortege of dignitaries, and amid huge crowds of local men, women and children, standing by, silent and contrite. An elegant black stone, inscribed with gold lettering, and costing 110 lire, paid for by the *Corriere della Sera*, was placed on her grave: 'To Italia Donati, municipal schoolmistress of Porciano, as beautiful as she was virtuous, forced by vile persecution to seek in death peace and proof of her honesty.' The stone, along with the grave, has long since vanished.[14]

At the heart of the Italian government's approach to primary schooling was a huge dilemma. Should the masses be instructed or educated? A degree of instruction was clearly desirable in a modern state – though quite how much was debatable given that the great majority of Italian men and women found little need for literacy or numeracy in their adult lives. Moreover if they did learn to read and write, what was to stop them using such skills to air their political and social grievances or to imbibe and pass on the dangerous ideas of the Internationalists, anarchists or republicans? The real requirement, it was generally believed, was education – to mould the character of children so that they grew up obedient, respectful, truthful, hardworking, patriotic and accepting of their station in life. As the author of the 1877 education reform, Michele Coppino, stated, primary schools should ensure that the masses were 'content to remain in the condition that nature had assigned to them, and not encourage them to abandon it'. And he added that the general aim of elementary education should be to 'create a population that is instructed as far as can be, but which is first and foremost honest and industrious, useful to the family, and devoted to the fatherland and the king'.[15]

This preoccupation with morality was reflected in the texts used in primary schools. In the first few decades after 1860 there was an outpouring of books devoted to the formation of the Italian character, many of them modelled on the Englishman Samuel Smiles's immensely popular work, *Self-help* (1859); and the pedagogic principle behind most of these texts was that of 'example': models of good behaviour, it was believed, would help train the will and encourage the poor to make virtuous choices in life. Supporting the search for an Italian version of *Self-help* in 1867, the prime minister, Luigi Menabrea, spoke of the enormous benefits that such a work would bring, 'for once this book was distributed among the masses it could not fail to excite emulation and drive them to follow the examples that are set before them'.[16] The most widely read imitation of Samuel Smiles was Michele Lessona's *Volere è potere* (*Will is Power*, 1869), whose thirteen chapters offered potted biographies of distinguished Italian men (no women) from all over the country – artists, musicians (among them Verdi and Rossini), writers, soldiers, industrialists and academics. Another of the same genre was Paolo Mantegazza's *Glories and Joys of Work* (1870), whose gallery of illustrious men to be imitated (again women failed to secure a mention) included Galileo, Alberti and Melchiorre Gioia. It went through thirty-four editions.[17]

Probably the most famous writer of educational books for children was Carlo Lorenzini, a former Mazzinian and volunteer in the campaigns of 1848 and 1859 (and 1866) who adopted the pen name Collodi after the little town in Tuscany, near to Cintolese and Porciano, where he had spent much of his childhood. Lorenzini was acutely conscious of the vast gap separating the ideals of the Risorgimento from the realities of united Italy, and of the pressing need to transform the rough and ill-educated peasants that he had known well when he was young into mature, dutiful citizens of a modern state; and in the 1870s, after many years of journalism and humdrum work in local government offices in Florence, he decided to turn his hand to children's fiction. In 1876 he published the first of seven volumes of stories about a boy called Giannettino, a picaresque, red-haired, blue-eyed character whose rumbustious comic adventures were interlaced with suitably improving pedagogic maxims ('for every school that opens there is a prison cell that closes'). But it was the tale that he began writing rather grudgingly for a magazine in 1881 ('Do what you like with this infantile piece,' he told the editor, 'but if you print it, pay me well so that I'll have an incentive to carry on with it')[18] that proved to be by far his most successful work.

Pinocchio works on numerous levels, which helps to explain its universal appeal, but the story of an ill-disciplined puppet-child, hewn from a coarse piece of wood, who abjures the restraints of duty, education and hard work for a life of pleasure reflects many of the anxieties of Italy in the early 1880s: the Italy of Turiello's *Government and Governed*, with its central theme of how to curb the natural tendency of the Italian people to unruliness. Collodi's message is bleak: the path to redemption lies through toil and self-sacrifice, and those who fail to appreciate this risk ruin ('Everybody, whether they are born rich or poor, is obliged to do something in this world, to be employed, to work. Do not fall prey to idleness! Idleness is a dreadful illness that must be cured immediately, when you are young . . .').[19] But Pinocchio does not gain salvation from self-growth alone. He also needs the love and guidance of his father and surrogate mother, the good fairy – an implicitly monarchical arrangement of a kind that many on both right and left were coming to embrace as their disillusionment with parliament grew. Indeed in 1882, a year before *Pinocchio* first appeared as a book, the one-time republican Giosuè Carducci wrote a famous tribute to the new Italian queen, the young and beautiful Margherita, hailing her as the 'regal eternal feminine' and Italy's hope for the future.[20] Collodi's fairy, 'the lovely girl with blue hair', is endowed with similarly charismatic (and redemptive) qualities.

The torrent of pedagogic literature in the decades after 1860 bore witness less to any well-thought-out educational agenda for the masses and more to the concerns of the patriotic middle classes at the weakness of the new national edifice. The obsession with work and self-improvement was of course common to many European states at the time, but it acquired additional urgency in Italy from the belief that the country's backwardness was essentially moral in character and that the process of regeneration started by the Risorgimento had only just begun. As Lessona (a leading exponent of Darwinism) explained in *Will is Power*, a major reason why the British had been so successful was because they had learned self-sufficiency, whereas the Italians had developed the fatal habit of blaming the government for everything and not taking personal responsibility themselves. But this was one of many vices to be purged:

We are still a long way from having fulfilled all our duties. We have other more difficult victories to win – and this cannot ever be emphasized enough. Ignorance, superstition, horror of work, glorification of idleness, errors, lack of concern for personal dignity and good reputation, discord, envy, partisan anger and municipalism are all much more dangerous and terrifying enemies than Austria ever was.[21]

The chances of this pedagogic literature having much impact on working-class children were slight: most pupils did well in the short time they spent in a cramped schoolroom with an ill-paid (and sometimes incomprehensible) teacher to secure basic numeracy and literacy, and the prose of Collodi or Lessona was in all likelihood far beyond them. Nor was it probable that any of these books would find their way into peasant homes given that on average about 80 per cent of rural income in the later nineteenth century went on meeting essential food needs: clothes (heavily recycled, rarely, if ever, new) and other basic requirements accounted for most of the rest.[22] If anything was left over for leisure it would probably be spent at a local inn – there were growing concerns about the levels of alcoholism among the poor in the 1870s and 1880s, especially in northern Italy, where cheap spirits and strong and often adulterated wines were becoming increasingly available.[23] Books extolling the virtues of hard work and holding up the lives of Galileo, Rossini or Melchiorre Gioia as models of where diligence and study might take you were unlikely to be high on most peasants' wishlists.

MILITARY SERVICE

Since education was more important than instruction, and since schools could have only a limited impact on the masses, it was to the army that politicians of both right and left principally looked to 'make Italians'. As a well-known writer and devoted friend of Garibaldi, Giuseppe Guerzoni, explained at a conference in Padua in 1879, the army was 'the main primary schoolmaster of the nation' and its 'chief educator':

The ambition of the army is this: to take a man from society and leave its imprint on him for his entire life. To turn a ruffian into a gentleman . . . an anarchist into a citizen, a coarse peasant or uncouth worker into a person of breeding, honesty and civility . . . Living continually with men who all dress identically, all obey the same rules, and all answer to the same superior . . . who gradually instils in him a sense of discipline, a respect for hierarchy and a feeling for true equality; moving periodically from one end of the peninsula to another; . . . enjoying the constant comradeship of people speaking different dialects from every region of Italy; . . . seeing just one flag, the revered symbol of the fatherland and the king –

... everything works to engender a universe of new and better feelings and affections and so create a different man. And in this way the by now proverbial saying is becoming a strict reality: having made Italy the army is making Italians.[24]

The elderly Francesco De Sanctis was in agreement. The previous year he had decided to mark his third term as Minister for Public Instruction by introducing a bill that would assist the army's educational mission. For the biggest problem with Italians, he told the Chamber, was not their lack of knowledge – indeed they often knew too much – as their inability to convert knowledge into action. It was a matter of character. 'We must educate the will,' he announced to cheers from his colleagues: '. . . To regenerate the country properly, we need to mould the imagination, train the will, and ensure that everything that is in our brains exercises a beneficial effect on all our faculties.' This was why he had decided to make gymnastics compulsory in primary schools. A strong physique would not only induce physical bravery, but also, and more importantly, give rise to moral courage, to open and honest behaviour, and to a hatred of those 'sly and underhand practices . . . that darkened the history of Italy in its decadence'. He quoted with approval the remark of the great Prussian general Helmuth von Moltke that learning on its own did not prepare a man to lay down his life for an idea or the honour of his nation. And the reason, he said, why the German and the Anglo-Saxon races had been so successful in recent decades was because of their physical training programmes: 'A virile education from early childhood creates the moral energy out of which springs a sense of initiative, tenacity and seriousness of purpose . . .'[25]

Parliament gave almost unanimous backing to De Sanctis's bill and the only serious note of dissent came from a deputy on the far left who suggested that a better way to improve the physique of the masses would be to get them to eat more and pay less in taxes.[26] But improving the health of the nation was not the underlying purpose of the new law – though the fact that 28 per cent of army recruits had to be rejected in the early 1880s because they were too short (under 1.56 metres) or had a disabling illness showed that there was a major problem that badly needed to be addressed.[27] What really concerned politicians was that since the Franco-Prussian war of 1870 it had become clear that modern armies had to be mass armies, the 'nation in arms', and that success on the battlefield depended on having huge supplies of well-trained and patriotic citizen-soldiers of the kind that had beaten the French so decisively at Sedan. Gymnastics in schools would be a step in the right direction. As the parliamentary commission reporting on the bill said, Italians had to be prepared from an early age for military service, particularly as the country had a long and dangerous tradition of prizing intellectual and artistic achievements over physical ones: 'What happens to peoples who are refined in spirit and forget the rigours and disciplines of military life is shown by the fate of the ancient Greeks when confronted by the Romans, the Greek empire when faced by the Turks and Italy itself from the seventeenth century to the present.'[28]

Getting Italians to think positively about military service was difficult. Though a series of reforms in the early 1870s reduced the amount of time most conscripts spent in the army from five to three years (with a longer stint in the reservists – in line with the Prussian model), the *naja*, as the draft was commonly called, remained something to be avoided if possible. Selection was by lottery. The military authorities decided each year what percentage of the eligible young men would have to serve the full term, and the higher the number drawn out of an urn the better the chances of securing exemption. Charms, amulets and prayers (particularly to St Michael and St Sebastian) were regularly used to bring good luck, while those who wanted to evade the draft at all costs resorted to self-mutilation: rubbing caustic materials into the eyes, burning the scalp to simulate the effects of ring-worm, applying tight ligatures to the toes. A doctor observed in 1875: 'The majority resign themselves to carrying out the most holy of duties that the law demands, but they try every means they can to escape it.'[29]

Propagandists did their best to endow military service with a romantic aura, and their writings certainly touched a chord with middle-class audiences, particularly in northern Italy, where the army was for the most part held in high esteem. Probably the most famous of these publicists was the prolific Piedmontese author Edmondo De Amicis, whose best-selling *Military Life* (1869) painted a glowing picture of patriotic peasant soldiers bound together in fraternal comradeship, of indulgent and fatherly officers, of proud parents, adoring sweethearts and an admiring and grateful general public. 'The life of the camp is sometimes tough, sometimes uncomfortable, but always beautiful and heart-warming. Does anyone who has experienced it not love it, not recall it with delight, not long for it passionately?'[30] This theme was continued by De Amicis in several other works written in the 1870s and 1880s, culminating in his phenomenally successful novel *Cuore* (*Heart*), which sold a million copies in thirty years. The book was set in a primary school in Turin, and its central message was that the army was the paragon, crucible and embodiment of the nation, mixing men of all classes and regions into a harmonious, caring family. As such it was to be revered and cherished:

Yesterday an infantry regiment went past, and fifty boys began skipping and dancing around the military band, singing and beating time with their rulers on their packs and satchels. We stood in a group on the pavement watching . . . The soldiers marched by, four by four, covered in dust and sweat, their rifles glinting in the sun. The Headmaster said: 'You must love the soldiers, boys. They are our protectors, men who would lay down their lives for us, if a foreign army threat-ened our country tomorrow. They are boys, too, not much older than you. And they also go to school. There are poor and rich among them, as with you, and they come from every part of Italy. Look, you can almost recognize them by sight: there are Sicilians, Sardinians, Neapolitans and Lombards . . . Do something for me, my sons. When the three colours go by, raise your hand to your forehead and give a child's salute.' The flag, carried by an officer, passed in front of us, torn and faded, with medals hanging on the staff, and we put our hands to our foreheads and saluted, all together. The officer looked at us, smiling, and returned our salute . . . Meanwhile the regimental band turned the corner at the end of the street, surrounded by a throng of children, and a hundred joyful cries accompanied the blasts of the trumpets as if it were a battle song.[31]

Quite possibly such celebrations of the army and army life filtered down and gave the *naja* positive connotations in the eyes of the poor, and certainly from the 1870s the draft came to acquire something of the status of a rite of passage for those who happened to be chosen. As one peasant recalled: 'You had to do what you could to avoid becoming a soldier, but if you couldn't, you had stories to tell, because it was man's stuff!'[32] Selection for military service was widely regarded as an affirmation of virility ('Who is no good for the king is no good either for the queen' was a common bawdy saying), and while there were many popular songs expressing sorrow at leaving behind loved ones and going off to a life of hardship, there were others that spoke of the joys of male comradeship and of the sexual conquests that lay in store.[33] It was apparently a standard practice for new recruits to mark their first day as soldiers with a visit to a brothel in the nearest town – for many of them their first experience of sex.[34]

Life in the barracks was certainly not easy and many found it difficult to adjust to the harsh discipline, to being thrown together with men from different regions, and to being largely isolated from the rest of society. On average military tribunals had to deal with between 3,000 and 4,000 cases of insubordination each year (twice this figure in the 1860s), while a survey in the 1870s found that suicide rates in the army were running at nearly ten times the national average.[35] In the 1880s several particularly high-profile episodes underlined the sometimes grim realities of the *naja*, most notably in the case of a Calabrian, Salvatore Misdea, who on Easter Sunday 1884 barricaded himself in his dormitory in the Pizzofalcone barracks in Naples and let off some fifty rounds from his rifle, killing five soldiers and wounding seven others seriously. A commission of psychiatrists headed by Cesare Lombroso found that he had been reduced to insanity by repeated abuse and bullying, and was not responsible for his actions; but a military court thought otherwise and called for the death penalty. The king ignored appeals from the public for clemency and Misdea was shot.[36]

The general tenor of military life was probably no harsher than in many other countries, but the policy of sending recruits outside their native region does seem to have generated particular problems of social isolation, at least for the rank and file. While officers regularly enjoyed close links with the leading local families, attending receptions, giving riding lessons, and going to theatres and clubs, ordinary soldiers found very little to do outside the barracks except head straight for the nearest brothel. (Venereal disease was a constant concern for the military authorities, with average monthly infection rates running at more than one per cent in the 1860s.) Middle-class conscripts probably fared better than their working-class and peasant counterparts, as they could often get themselves posted close to home in return for paying for their upkeep.[37] For the great majority, though, the *naja* must have been a far cry from the rich and rewarding experience that De Amicis described, and for many the principal consolation was probably the kudos (not least sexual) that they acquired on going back to their native village – like the character Turiddu Macca in Giuseppe Verga's celebrated short story 'Cavalleria rusticana', who every Sunday 'strutted in the piazza in his *bersagliere* uniform and red beret, with all the girls eating him up with their eyes'.[38]

Was the army the 'school of the nation' as was widely claimed? The evidence suggests that its impact on Italian society was much more limited than hoped. Recruits often acquired the rudiments of reading and writing (especially after 1873, when a ministerial note said soldiers were not to be discharged until they were literate); and many no doubt absorbed at least some patriotic ideas regarding the flag, the monarchy, and the history and politics of Italy. But teaching in the barracks was hampered by a lack of central planning and support from the Ministry of War, and also by a marked anti-intellectual culture.[39] And the officers were generally not of much help. They were often sharply divided from the rank and file by language and a rigid sense of hierarchy (Lamarmora claimed that the absence of mutual trust between officers and men was one of the main reasons for the disasters of 1866)[40] and most seem to have believed it was not their business to provide conscripts with anything other than basic technical training. As an institution rooted in the old Piedmontese state and answering to the king, the army did not always feel obliged to do what civilian governments wanted.

One of the peculiarities of the Italian army was the obsession with trying to minimize municipal or provincial loyalties by shifting regiments around the country (on average every three to four years in the 1870s and 1880s), posting recruits outside their native region and making sure that each regiment was made up of troops drawn from all over the peninsula. The intention, it seems, was twofold: to 'nationalize' the conscripts and to try to make certain that they would not fraternize with the enemy if called on to sort out local unrest of the kind that had blighted the south and the Romagna in the 1860s. Whether soldiers really did feel more 'Italian' as a result of being thrown together with men from other provinces is extremely questionable. There are good grounds for believing, indeed, that the policy had exactly the opposite effect, with soldiers from the same region ganging together and 'whiling away the boredom and tedium of barracks life by persecuting, harassing and tormenting . . . soldiers from another region', as one observer noted, with 'quarrels, brawls and bloody scenes'[41] (Salvatore Misdea was apparently the victim of such behaviour). Nor is it clear that stationing recruits outside their native regions did very much to 'nationalize' them given the limited contact that most of them had with the local population.

Nevertheless the army remained for virtually all members of the ruling classes the 'great crucible' that would fuse Italians into one unit,[42] 'the steel thread that had sewn Italy together and was keeping it united', as the veteran Risorgimento patriot Luigi Settembrini told the Senate in 1876.[43] And as parliament became ever more tarnished with decadence, corruption and factionalism in the 1870s and 1880s, so the army's reputation as the school of the nation grew ('The army remains . . . the most Italian institution we have, much more than parliament,' a leading conservative politician confided to his diary in 1877).[44] The armed forces, it was felt, embodied those qualities that the nation lacked and needed to learn: discipline, cohesion, patriotism, respect for authority, selflessness and a willingness to die for an ideal – thought and action blended perfectly. And until these qualities had been instilled into the people it seemed to a growing number of observers that liberalism might be a luxury that the country could ill afford, certainly in an age of growing international rivalry. For as one of De Sanctis's most influential students, the writer and politician Nicola Marselli, said, Italy had introduced freedom before it had educated the masses, ignoring the lesson of nations such as Britain where the process of education had come first. He argued that the present political system was failing to provide 'the force of cohesion needed to turn Italian society into an organic body'; and like others, he looked to the army to 'make Italians' and 'militarize' society.[45] He also wanted a much stronger state, educative and ethical; and a different kind of representative assembly: one that was less fractured and better qualified, both morally and technically.[46]

It was somewhat ironic that in being looked to as the 'school of the nation' the army was rendered less effective as a fighting force. The fear of having regiments of local soldiers meant that in the event of war mobilization would be slow, as reservists had to criss-cross the country to link up with their companies. Furthermore, the disparate composition of regiments almost certainly reduced their potential cohesion and morale: revealingly the two most famous and highly decorated Italian units of the First World War were made up almost exclusively of regional troops: the Sassari from Sardinia and the Alpini from the mountain valleys of the far north.[47] Nor, despite the best endeavours of the propagandists, does the army seem to have been held in much esteem or affection by the mass of the population. Certainly the involvement of troops in aid work during cholera epidemics and natural disasters helped to bridge the gap to the masses; but in general the armed forces appear to have been looked on as remote and as inhabiting a different sphere, that of the state (doing military service was sometimes referred to as 'going off to Italy') – and the state had been responsible for the violent suppression of many riots and disturbances, not to mention the brutal operations in the south in the 1860s. It also had the fiascos of 1866 hanging round its neck. For these reasons there was a growing feeling in many quarters from the 1870s that the best hope both for the army and for Italy lay in a great military victory that would expunge the past, heal the rift between government and governed, cement the prestige of the monarchy and the institutions, and finally secure the moral unity of the nation.

SYMBOLS AND FESTIVALS

One of the awkward legacies of the Risorgimento was that the cult of Italy had been most closely identified with Mazzini and his democratic followers. This created a problem after 1860. Should Italians be encouraged to focus their loyalty first and foremost on 'the nation', with the risk thereby of highlighting the role that had been played by the far left in the unification process, or should they be steered towards the safer conservative ground of 'the king'? It was not a clear-cut dichotomy, of course, in so far as the monarchy could always allege (and an army of propagandists worked hard to support the claim) that it had been in the vanguard of the national movement, at least since 1848. But it was not a position that would stand up to too much scrutiny, and the fact was that 'Italy' conjured up more images of conspiracies, republican martyrs and barricades than it ever did of the House of Savoy. The conflict between 'Italy' and 'the king' was rarely, if ever, openly addressed, but it hovered in the background and from the start weakened attempts to forge a strong iconography of the nation.

In contrast to Marianne in France or the figure of Germania, the female image of 'turreted Italy' that had been given currency in the Risorgimento by the likes of Canova was never strongly encouraged after 1860. Instead it was the head of the king and the cross of Savoy that dominated sites such as postage stamps and coins: not till 1908, amid growing pressure from nationalists for a more aggressive foreign policy, did the personification of Italy feature on a coin, standing on a chariot and wearing the helmet of Minerva (but clutching a suitably emollient olive branch as well).[48] Even public monuments celebrating the architects and martyrs of Italian unification were surprisingly bereft of images of Italy. The main exception was the imposing figure of 'turreted Italy' on the memorial inaugurated in Milan in 1880 to those who had died fighting with Garibaldi at Mentana in 1867 to liberate Rome (significantly, though, its sponsors came largely from the far left). Not even the monument to Victor Emmanuel in Piazza Venezia in Rome (the so-called Vittoriano), the most colossal and ambitious of all the national memorials constructed after 1860, had a representation of Italy. The central female figure below the equestrian statue of the king is the goddess Roma, not Italia.

No less striking was the absence of any new national holidays after 1860. Just as Victor Emmanuel remained Victor Emmanuel II and the parliament that convened in 1861 was officially the eighth legislature – to underline the formal continuity of Italy with the Piedmontese state – so the only public holiday after unification was one that had been introduced in Piedmont in 1851 to celebrate Carlo Alberto's concession of a constitution, the 'Festival of the Statuto'. Though its title was extended by law in 1861 to 'Festival of the Statuto and of National Unity', this was, quite predictably, too much of a mouthful to have any chance of sticking and it quickly reverted in general parlance to 'Festival of the Statuto'. The one lasting change was to move it from the first Sunday in May to the first Sunday in June, primarily so as to ensure better weather for the parades and fireworks.[49] The failure to establish a genuinely national holiday in Italy comparable to Memorial Day in the United States (1868), Sedan Day in Germany (1871) or Bastille Day in France (1880) was a reflection of the deeply contested character of unification and the resulting impossibility of reaching any consensus among politicians and the general public over which particular episode to celebrate.

There was also a big fear after the events of 1848–9 and 1859–60 of crowds in public spaces: what could be more humiliating than to have tens of thousands of angry Italians in Naples, Palermo or some other southern city using a national holiday as an opportunity to protest against the new regime under the gaze of foreign tourists and reporters?

This was one reason why the Festival of the Statuto was kept to a Sunday, when church-going and other traditional social and leisure activities would dispose people to calm. Indeed the whole character of the festival was such as to avoid exciting political passions, keeping the public firmly in the role of spectator and eliminating opportunities for popular enthusiasm (in Piedmont in the 1880s the holiday was ironically known as the Festival of the *Staciuto* or 'Be quiet!').[50] And what was on display was essentially the authority of the state. In the morning there would be artillery salvoes and military parades with plenty of martial music and renditions of the national anthem, the old-fashioned, jaunty Royal March. Dignitaries would process in carriages along streets lined with *carabinieri*, and there would be a prize-giving ceremony for local schoolchildren with the mayor distributing money, medals, bank saving books or whatever was deemed appropriate (in the south often shoes and clothes).[51] Only in the evening were the proceedings less formal, with races, regattas, bands, gas illuminations, lotteries and firework displays, which in Rome, where the population had been used to lavish spectacles under papal rule, were often quite dramatic, with the Castel Sant'Angelo decked out in lights and with giant images or allegories of the king and Italy, and patriotic slogans, projected against the sky.[52]

Otherwise, though, the state did little in the way of celebrations or festivals to etch the reality of the new Italy into the hearts and minds of the public. The two most important 'national' events of the 1870s and 1880s both involved the monarchy: the funeral of Victor Emmanuel in 1878 and the 'pilgrimage' to his tomb six years later. Only in 1895 was a second official holiday instituted, 20 September, to commemorate the taking of Rome in 1870. As a result the way was left open for the Church to continue its traditional domination of public spectacles – with its galaxy of feast days and the elaborate processions and ceremonies that accompanied them – and for local initiatives to outstrip national ones. Many of the most lavish celebrations, indeed, were narrowly communal, whether for patron saints (Santa Rosalia in Palermo, San Gennaro in Naples, San Giovanni in Florence) or (rather ironically) for episodes from the Risorgimento, such as the revolutions of 1848: 12 January in Palermo, 11 February in Padua, 29 May in Florence, 8 August in Bologna. Even the twenty-fifth anniversary of the expedition of the Thousand in 1885 became a predominantly Sicilian event.

For those many Risorgimento patriots who had imbibed the central lesson of Mazzini that the nation, to be strong, needed to become the focus of a secular religion, the failure of the liberal state to capture the popular imagination through spectacle, imagery and display was a source of deep disappointment. It was also, from the late 1870s, a cause of rapidly growing anxiety as Catholicism embarked on a vigorous campaign to mobilize Italians behind the Church and as socialism started to percolate through regions such as Lombardy and Emilia Romagna with its heady doctrines of emancipation. As a leading article in a newspaper owned by the man who was to dominate Italian politics in the last years of the century, Francesco Crispi, said in 1882:

We need to make this religion of the Fatherland, which must be our principal if not only religion, as solemn and as popular as possible. We all of us, servants of Progress, have gradually destroyed a faith that for centuries sufficed our people, precisely because through the ritualized forms of its displays it appealed to the visual senses, and through the visual senses to the minds of the masses, who are impressionable, imaginative and artistic, eager for shapes, colours and sounds to feed their fantasies. What have we substituted for this faith? As far as the masses are concerned, nothing. We have closed our new Gods of Reason and Duty within ourselves . . . without adorning them with the external trappings of religion that still today, in the absence of an alternative, draw to church people who are nostalgic for beauty at a time when beauty is tending to disappear. We must address this, as the character of a people is not changed overnight . . .[53]

The Risorgimento ought to have provided the principal foundation myth for the new Italy, but the bitter divisions that had been created between the various strands of moderates and democrats in the 1840s and 1850s took time to heal, and it was only in the 1880s and 1890s that passions abated sufficiently for a degree of consensus to be reached. The winning formula was a providential one: that whatever their declared differences republicans and monarchists, federalists and unitarists, conservatives and radicals had all contributed to the remarkable alchemical mix out of which unification had miraculously sprung in 1860. The two poles around which this new synthesis came to rotate were Victor Emmanuel and Garibaldi, whose deaths in 1878 and 1882 respectively marked the beginning of an extraordinary cult, with a torrent of hagiographic literature and a proliferation of public statuary. The deep fractures of the unification movement were eased from the official record, and the

Risorgimento was reborn as a serendipitous coming together of state (Victor Emmanuel) and nation (Garibaldi), diplomacy and popular initiative, war and conspiracy, monarchy and people.

The cult of Garibaldi was not hard to foster given the remarkable reputation that he had enjoyed in his lifetime, but after 1882 it received massive official encouragement, with towns and cities across the country vying with one another to provide tributes to the Hero of the Two Worlds. Some 300 statues and 400 busts and commemorative inscriptions were unveiled in the years following his death, and any place he had visited or building he had slept or eaten in or stopped at was graced with a suitably solemn memorial plaque (though bathos was not always absent, as at Casamicciola: 'Returning from Aspromonte – in this chamber – Giuseppe Garibaldi – took a bath').[54] His image circulated freely through a huge variety of media – postcards, prints, magazines, paintings, banners, medals, cups, plates, figurines, posters, banknotes and food-packaging (Garibaldi biscuits were first manufactured in England in 1861) – and his heroic qualities and achievements were celebrated in countless speeches, poems, memoirs, biographies and newspaper articles.

One of the most striking features of the cult was the extent to which Garibaldi was invested with saintly, even divine, attributes. This had already been an important aspect of his appeal at a popular level during his lifetime, but after 1882 it was strongly encouraged by exponents of high culture as well. Sometimes market forces may have been at work: books portraying a radiantly handsome (often blue-eyed and blond-haired) and infinitely virtuous hero were probably guaranteed to sell better than more sober and judicious accounts. But among democrats in particular there was also a desire to capitalize on popular credulity to strengthen the political position of the left. Thus when Giuseppe Guerzoni published a serious biography of Garibaldi in 1882, his colleague, the republican journalist and deputy Achille Bizzoni, criticized it for being too refined and quickly wrote an alternative short version 'for the people', full of fantastic legends, in which Garibaldi featured as a Christ-like figure, simple, courageous and just, a martyr to his cause and a long-suffering victim of ingratitude, jealousy and betrayal.[55] Another prominent figure of the left who like Bizzoni had known Garibaldi well (and who in private had often been critical of his all too human failings) was Francesco Crispi. He, also, could see the enormous political value of a sanctified patriotic hero – the nation desperately needed secular saints – and after 1882 he became one of the leading exponents of the Garibaldi cult. And as he told a student audience at Bologna university in 1884, the preservation of this cult was a sacred duty:

It would seem there was something divine in the life of this man. He was superior to Heracles and Achilles in the ancient world. If he had been born in Athens or Rome, altars would have been raised to him . . . [I]n certain periods of history . . . it happens that Providence causes an exceptional being to arise in the world, whose deeds and qualities are out of the ordinary. His marvellous exploits capture the imagination, and the masses regard him as superhuman. I have said it already and I say it again: if Garibaldi had been born in Athens or in Rome, the people would have made him a demigod and erected temples in his honour. In our times we are more modest: the altar of Garibaldi is in the heart of every patriot, without distinction of party or class. Those who wish Italy to be united from the Alps to the two seas, in accordance with the plebiscites, and those who love the fatherland, strong, great, prosperous and respected – all these hold the hero in veneration and harbour his cult.[56]

The apotheosis of Garibaldi was part of a broader attempt in the 1880s to celebrate all aspects of the Risorgimento. During the 1860s and early 1870s Italian governments had been dominated by men of the right, who had encouraged a 'moderate' and Piedmontese view of unification centred on Cavour and Victor Emmanuel. In 1876 the left came to power, bringing to office those like Agostino Depretis and Francesco Crispi who had been active in the democratic world of conspiracy in the 1840s and 1850s, and this opened the way to a more ecumenical reading of the national movement as well as to a new determination to reach out to the masses. In 1881, as part of the planning for the building of the Vittoriano in central Rome, a questionnaire was sent out to every province enquiring how many statues had to date been erected to Victor Emmanuel 'and the principal figures of the Italian Risorgimento'. Fully a quarter said that none had been built or were even projected.[57] With official encouragement this situation was remedied in the course of the next twenty years, with monuments to the architects of national unity springing up all over the country. In Florence, for example, six statues were unveiled in the 1880s and 1890s (to Victor Emmanuel, Garibaldi, Daniele Manin, Bettino Ricasoli, Ubaldo Peruzzi and Cosimo Ridolfi) and in Rome five (the Cairoli brothers, Terenzio

Mamiani, Cavour, Minghetti and Garibaldi). The most striking omission was Mazzini, whose republicanism and opposition to the new state after 1860 still made him largely anathema. Crispi secured agreement from parliament in 1890 for a monument in Rome to Mazzini (who had died, incognito, in a friend's house in Pisa in 1872, lonely and demoralized), but it was to be more than fifty years before it was finally completed.

National exhibitions were another vehicle for disseminating the sense of a shared past. The most famous of these in the first decades of unity was the General Italian Exhibition held in Turin in 1884, which was primarily intended as a showcase for the country's scientific and industrial achievements since 1860 but also contained five rooms dedicated to the Risorgimento. In between official documents, flags and posters were such eclectic relics as the socks Garibaldi wore at Aspromonte, Gioberti's dog-collar, Cattaneo's hat, Cavour's handkerchief, Mazzini's guitar, a lock of Mameli's hair and the embalmed hand of a young female patriot, Colomba Antonietti, killed by a cannon-ball while defending Rome in 1849. The aim, as the president of the organizing committee said, was to induce feelings of reverence and dispel all spirit of factionalism among visitors ('Before the majesty of this spectacle parties do not exist').[58] Whether this was achieved is not known, but the authorities certainly strove hard to encourage popular attendance, providing discounts on rail tickets and offering a major prize for the best description of the exhibition by a 'worker'. A foreman from the Naples dockyards said that he felt 'proud of our past' when he visited the Risorgimento rooms, and was 'overcome by a sublime and religious awe'. Perhaps he was, or perhaps he guessed what the judges wanted to hear.[59]

In schools the government hesitated to allow Risorgimento history to be taught, not least because priests were often employed as teachers in many small towns (particularly before the Coppino Law); and they were unlikely to speak well of those who had worked to destroy the Pope's temporal power. In 1867 a decree stated that Italian history should not be studied beyond 1815, at any level, secondary or primary; and only in 1884 was this relaxed for secondary schools and the date moved down to 1870. When Francesco Crispi was prime minister in the late 1880s a major drive took place to 'nationalize' school curricula, and the Risorgimento now featured much more heavily than before. In the third year of primary school children were to be given a simple 'narrative of certain key facts relating to the formation of the Kingdom of Italy', while in the fourth and fifth years they were to be introduced to the whole gamut of Italian history from the founding of Rome to unification. In the *scuole normali* trainee teachers were to study the Risorgimento for a full year; and were told to make sure that their future charges absorbed from Italy's history a 'love of the fatherland'.[60]

Potentially, of course, the history of the Risorgimento was a minefield and great care was needed over how it was presented in school texts and other books. The reputations of the main characters had to be carefully safeguarded: to suggest that Cavour, or worse Victor Emmanuel, had been anything other than a selfless patriot was unacceptable. For this reason access to documentary material was very carefully controlled after 1860, and though the study of Italian history was encouraged through the establishment of a network of national archives in 1875, the creation of numerous local institutes and academies, and the publication of learned journals such as the *Rivista storica del Risorgimento* (1895), no official papers were available for consultation after 1815. Particular pains were taken to shield the monarchy, and when a major political figure died his papers were generally searched and his private correspondence with the king and anything else that might be compromising removed to the safety of the royal library. Occasionally a trusted scholar was allowed into the Savoy archives and given permission to publish a documented (but carefully vetted) history of recent political events. But this was exceptional. A similar near paranoid approach was taken to Cavour's reputation, and only heavily expurgated versions of his correspondence were published with his sceptical comments about unification, his vicious hostility to Garibaldi and his democratic followers in 1860, and his often deeply offensive remarks about fellow Italians all carefully excised from the public record.[61]

15

Sources of Authority: King, Church and Parliament, 1870–87

I wish the Pope would leave Rome, because I can't look out of the windows of the Quirinal Palace without seeing the Vatican in front of me. And it always strikes me that both Pius IX and I are prisoners.
        Victor Emmanuel II to the Queen of Holland, November 1871

The vast majority of the population, more than ninety per cent, . . . feels entirely cut off from our institutions. People see themselves subjected to the State and forced to serve it with their blood and their money, but they do not feel that they are a vital and organic part of it, and take no interest at all in its existence or its affairs.   Sidney Sonnino, speech to the Chamber of Deputies, 30 March 1881

The Chamber of Deputies no longer has the slightest popular support. On the contrary, it is generally laughed at and despised.   Corriere della Sera, 1879

CHURCH AND STATE: THE QUESTION OF ROME

After the capture of Rome in September 1870 Italy's leaders had two choices. They could confront the Catholic Church head on and affirm the lay values of the state aggressively, or be conciliatory and hope that tact and implicit contrition would draw papal anger. In practice they chose the latter course. In the spring of 1871 the Law of Guarantees was passed by parliament, which laid down the prerogatives of the papacy and the relationship of Church and State. It was highly generous. The Pope was given the full status and honours of a sovereign and his person was declared inviolable. He was allowed to keep armed guards and have his own diplomatic representation; and he was guaranteed freedom of the postal and telegraphic services. The state renounced many of its rights of control over the appointment of higher clergy, and bishops were no longer obliged to swear an oath of loyalty to the king. As critics pointed out, this in effect established a state within a state, and left Italy disarmed in the face of the most powerful moral force in the peninsula; for the Pope could now legally fulminate against the liberal regime and deploy his vast panoply of priests, monks, nuns, congregations, private schools, colleges, hospitals and welfare foundations to spread his message. And the hostility was real: the hopes of many moderates that the Pope would accept that he was better off without the burden of his temporal power proved unfounded, and on the same day the new law was published Pius IX issued an encyclical rejecting the settlement scornfully and demanding the restoration of his dominions.[1]

In the years that followed, the Church remained resolute in its opposition to the Italian state, and though informal accommodations and compromises often occurred at the local level it was only towards the end of the century that the Vatican began to soften its line, realizing that with the spread of socialism liberalism was the lesser of two evils and might be a useful ally in the war against godless materialism. In the meantime it set out to strengthen its already massive presence in Italian society, encouraging the faithful to be active in local government (Catholics were formally debarred by the Pope from national not municipal politics) and promoting mutual aid societies, rural banks and cooperatives as instruments for maintaining the loyalty of the masses and countering the doctrines of individualism and class conflict. In 1874 it created a major organization, the Opera dei Congressi, to coordinate these initiatives at a national level.[2] Every now and then there was talk of a possible conciliation, and secret negotiations sometimes took place, as in the summer of 1887, but the Pope was fully aware of the mobilizing power of conflict and the propaganda value of his being 'the prisoner of the Vatican', and felt under no great pressure to come to terms with the state.

But it was at the level of symbols that the Church tended to be most inflexible, and it was here that much of the friction with the state occurred – and here, too, that the weakness of the state following the Law of Guarantees was often highly visible. A typical episode was described to parliament by the distinguished democrat Agostino Bertani in 1877. It concerned a young patriotic Roman student whose dying request had been that a tricolour should be carried in his funeral cortege. However, when the parish priest saw the flag he announced that he would not accompany the body as long as 'that thing [was] there'; and despite earnest appeals from friends and relatives of the deceased he remained adamant, repeatedly referring to the tricolour as 'that thing'. A university professor stepped in and declared: 'Our standard will not be hidden or lowered in front of any cardinals or popes or tyrants. It will stand firm and triumph with that patriotism that the Catholic clergy knows nothing of.' But it was to no avail and the priest got his way, with the cortege split in two and the tricolour carried along a different route to the church by the student's friends, apart from the coffin.[3]

The Minister of the Interior confirmed that no action could be taken against the priest – only 'moral force' could be used, he said – and Bertani was left to voice his frustration at the huge damage that he felt was being done to the authority of the state:

I ask the Government and the Chamber: is it tolerable that there should exist in Italy a class of citizens, who occupy positions of intimate, exceptional and widespread influence, who use every subtle art to place themselves between heaven and earth, at one moment accommodating, at another aggressive, but always conspiring against the national institutions, and who remain subject to two powers, the one infallible and absolute, the other the political and civil authority sanctioned by the plebiscites?[4]

Given the fragility of national sentiment in Italy, Bertani's anger was understandable, but relatively few politicians after 1870 displayed any stomach for a fight: many, especially on the right, were themselves conscientious Catholics; and many feared that a tougher line against the Church would only alienate the masses still further from the state. Their preference – perhaps like the 'Guicciardini man', excoriated by De Sanctis, who failed to act resolutely on issues of principle – was for a quiet life: not to flaunt 'Italy' in the face of the Pope and thereby keep to a minimum the chances of friction.

Victor Emmanuel, too, had no wish for a fight – certainly on this front. As a member of a staunchly Catholic dynasty he had always been uncomfortable about attacking the Church. And it was probably his Catholic sympathies as much as his Piedmontese loyalties that kept him (and the court – itself a bastion of deeply conservative religiosity) out of Rome. He felt extremely uneasy about staying in the Quirinal Palace, which had formerly belonged to the Pope (he would have preferred Palazzo Barberini, but it was not for sale);[5] and after his first brief visit to the Eternal City at the end of 1870 he returned only intermittently, usually just for the state opening of parliament in November or when his mistress was in town (he bought a villa for her outside Porta Pia and could often be seen driving back dressed in rough outdoor clothes, with a couple of gun dogs, looking for all the world it was said like 'a good country merchant').[6] In November 1871 the government arranged for the purchase of a large hunting estate at Castel Porziano, for the huge sum of 4.5 million lire, hoping that this would encourage him to spend more time in the city. But to no avail.

The absence of the king and the court weakened the symbolic power of Rome as the kingdom's new capital, and despite the hopes of men like Quintino Sella that it might become a great modern metropolis, the city struggled after 1870 to emerge from the shadow of the papacy and establish a new identity for itself. It was almost, as Carducci scathingly suggested, as if Italy felt embarrassed to be there. The Chamber of Deputies was housed in Montecitorio, a large but undistinguished seventeenth-century building with few historical resonances tucked in the heart of Rome, out of sight of the Vatican; and though some patriotic politicians called for something grander and more conspicuous like the Capitol in Washington or the Palace of Westminster in London, nothing was in fact done. Garibaldi thought that a fitting way for the new kingdom to stamp its mark on the city would be to divert the course of the River Tiber and bring an end to the floods and miasmas that had for centuries plagued Rome – a massive engineering project that would simultaneously alter the capital's physiognomy and trumpet the superiority of science over superstition. But again, and despite enormous efforts by Garibaldi in the last years of his life, the idea came to nothing.[7]

The 1870s witnessed a frenzy of property sales in Rome, as dozens of monasteries, convents and other religious houses were taken over by the state and sold off. The financially hard-pressed government managed to raise nearly 13 million lire in this way. Among the principal purchasers were members of the Catholic or 'black' aristocracy – distinguished families such as the Odescalchi, Barberini and Doria Pamphili – who no doubt felt entitled to 'save' the property from the hands of godless liberals. There were also rumours that the Pope had authorized a leading Belgian prelate to acquire land and buildings, on the understanding that they would be returned to the ecclesiastical authorities once the Papal States had been restored.[8] Though the physical presence of the Church in Rome was reduced by these measures, the city remained heavily clerical in character, with many of the religious orders managing to secure exemption from closure or surreptitiously reconstituting themselves after they had been shut down. A survey conducted for the government in 1895 found that there were still 160 Catholic monastic communities and nunneries in the city – only about forty less than there had been in 1870 – housing nearly 4,000 members, male and female.[9]

After the left came to power in 1876, the pressure to transform the face of Rome increased, and banks poured huge sums of money – often given, with very few questions asked, to anyone claiming to be a property developer – into building projects. By the mid-1880s the city was awash with some 80,000 construction workers, and everywhere there was scaffolding and the sound of hammering and falling masonry as old streets, palaces and classical ruins made way for new public buildings and residential quarters. To the west of the River Tiber the Prati district was converted into a strident symbol of the Third Rome, with the massive Palace of Justice, government offices, barracks, up-market housing, and broad streets and piazzas with suitably pagan, anticlerical and liberal names – Seneca, Cicerone, Gracchi, Cola di Rienzo, Risorgimento, Cavour – intended, as the planners said, to engulf the neighbouring Vatican and 'bury' it.[10] A major thoroughfare, the Via Nazionale, was driven into the heart of Rome, while to the north and east of the old city famous villas and gardens, such as those of the Ludovisi and Capranica families, were sold off to developers and destroyed. The city council did what it could to control the banks and private speculators with planning schemes, but to little avail, and in many areas, especially the suburbs, building went ahead without any regulation.

From an aesthetic point of view the consequences were deeply dispiriting to many observers. The distinguished travel writer Augustus Hare claimed in the early 1880s that 'twelve years of Sardinian rule [had] done more for the destruction of Rome, with its beauty and interest, than the Goths and Vandals',[11] while the brilliant young poet and novelist Gabriele D'Annunzio was horrified by the barbaric disfigurement of the city by sordid profiteers in the years after he arrived there in 1881. Looking back in 1893 he wrote: 'Along with clouds of dust a kind of building madness spread . . . Everywhere seemed infected by a contagion of vulgarity at that time . . . The struggle for riches and power was waged with implacable ferocity, with no respite, and the weapons were the pick-axe, the trowel and bad faith.'[12] Francesco Crispi, whose Mazzinian background had given him an acute sense of the symbolic importance and potential of Rome, felt that the city resembled a 'cheap hotel' – second-rate and tawdry; and he called repeatedly in parliament for a capital worthy of the new nation: 'We must build Italy in Rome if we wish to remain in Rome, and in such a way that the third life of this great city should be commensurate with its past.'[13]

It was perhaps only inevitable that the city of Rome should fail to match up to the Risorgimento's grandiose dreams of regeneration, but this did not help to assuage the anger of disenchanted patriots, who turned the shortcomings of the capital into a potent symbol of all that was wrong in their eyes with united Italy. The constant wrangles between clericals and anti-clericals, moderates and democrats, centralizers and de-centralizers over the identity and status of Rome, the inability to enforce any coherent plan for urban redevelopment, the ugliness of many of the public buildings, and the anarchic speculative boom that ended in a hideous crash in the late 1880s served to underline for them the fractured, unprincipled and materialistic character of the new society. The poet Carducci, who was a central figure in the culture of dissatisfaction in the last decades of the century, repeatedly compared the sordid and petty character of the present ('the farce of the infinitely small', as he put it in a speech in 1886)[14] with the glorious ideal of 'Rome'. As he wrote in a famous poem of 1881 – with a sarcastic swipe at two of the most important political figures of the day, Agostino Depretis and Quintino Sella (and implicitly, thereby, at parliament as a whole):

> Rome, into your air I release my lofty spirit:
> Receive my spirit, O Rome, and envelop it in light.
> I come to you with no interest in little things:
> Who looks for butterflies beneath the arch of Titus?
> What do I care if the spectral bearded vintner of Stradella
> Blends Gallic pleasantry with inertia in Montecitorio?
> And if the long-toiling weaver of Biella gets entangled

In his own webs – a spider spinning in vain?
Surround me, O Rome, with blue, with sun illumine me, Rome:
The sun that shines through your broad heavens is divine.[15]

Aesthetic repugnance and a longing for some poetic ideal to raise what was disparagingly referred to as 'Italietta' out of the mire of mediocrity developed into a powerful theme in late-nineteenth-century Italian literature. 'Oh, God! The kingdom of Italy ushered in the reign of universal ugliness,' wrote Carducci in 1881. 'Ugly even are the over-coats and caps of the soldiers, ugly the coat of arms of the state, ugly the postage stamps. You could contract a jaundice of ugliness.'[16] And the following year he called for some noble enterprise, however desperate, to prise the Italian masses from their wretched, uninspiring lives: 'Oh, take them at least to die with glory against the cannon of Austria or France or whoever the devil brings!' Another leading writer, Carlo Dossi – who in the late 1880s, as a private secretary of the prime minister Francesco Crispi, was to be closely involved in schemes for the spiritual regener-ation of Italy through a major European war – felt that the prosaic designs on Italy's coins revealed something of the country's profound moral decadence, recalling as they did the debased currency of the Byzantines, with their 'gangling figures, all the same'. And this was particularly regrettable, he thought, given that the Italian soul was highly artistic by nature and required little more than a 'tiny spark to burst into flame'.[17]

The 'Third Rome' failed to establish itself as a potent and integrating symbol of the new Italy. It was the centre of national administration and government – and of the Church; but Milan claimed to be the country's 'moral' capital, the pre-eminent city of business, finance, pub-lishing, journalism and in due course industry; while other cities clung to their historic status and remained powerful cultural and political hubs in their own right. Rome grew fast after 1870, more than doubling in size to over half a million by the First World War, but it remained smaller than Milan and Naples. Furthermore its population lacked cohesion and a strong sense of civic identity, and there were marked divisions between Catholics and liberals, indigenous inhabitants and northern (and later southern) immigrants – dismissively referred to by locals as 'foreigners', 'Piedmontese' or 'chestnut sellers' (*buzzurri*). As a result the city found it hard to fend off the images of corruption and decadence that were applied to it with mounting frequency from the 1870s – as in the playwright Luigi Pirandello's description of the political life of Rome in the 1890s: 'Slime was pouring everywhere; and it seemed that all the sewers of the city had broken open and that the new national life of the Third Rome would be drowned in that dark putrescent flood of sludge . . .'[18]

KING UMBERTO

At the end of December 1877 Victor Emmanuel learned that Alfonso Lamarmora was dying. He had never forgiven the old general for the disaster of Custoza and for over ten years had refused to have any contact with him. Painful memories of the summer of 1866 no doubt came flooding back to him, and when a deputation of politicians came to salute him on New Year's Day he was in a particularly bullish mood and told them that Italy needed to be 'strong, feared and respected' (though according to the *Times* his exact words were too extreme to be reported).[19] The news of Lamarmora's death on 5 January visibly shook him, and though he was feeling unwell – he had a fever and was shivering – he summoned up the strength to send off a telegram of condolence. He then took to his bed. The fever – which was probably malarial in origin – worsened dramatically, and it soon became apparent that his life was in danger. Victor Emmanuel wanted to die a good Catholic – his wife would never have forgiven him if he did not, he said – and after much resistance the Church authorities agreed to administer the last rites. The king's mistress wanted to visit his bedside, but the government ordered she be stopped: scandal had to be avoided at all costs. On the morning of 9 January, with the end approaching, a steady stream of dignitaries filed silently in front of the king, propped up semi-conscious on pillows. Every now and then a faint smile flickered on his lips. At two-thirty the royal doctor placed his ear to the chest of the 57-year-old monarch and pronounced the first king of Italy dead.[20]

In life Victor Emmanuel had been a rather poor national symbol; in death he was to make amends. He was to be buried in Rome: the delegation from Turin asking that his body be laid to rest with his ancestors was given short shrift, and the capital of Piedmont had to be content with his sword, helmet and medals. The funeral was a magnificent public spectacle, carefully designed by the Minister of the Interior, Francesco Crispi, as a moment of supreme national synthesis. Huge crowds poured into Rome – perhaps as many as 200,000 – attracted by the heavily discounted rail tickets, and the gilt funeral carriage drawn by eight crape-covered horses wound its way slowly through the streets from the Quirinal Palace down to the Pantheon amid a sea of onlookers, with flowers and wreaths falling silently on the coffin. The martial note was pronounced: thousands of troops headed the procession, and every minute from dawn to dusk a cannon boomed out across Rome. Victor Emmanuel's aide-de-camp rode in front of the funeral carriage, bearing his sword; behind walked the old charger that he had ridden at the Battle of San Martino in 1859. But great care was also taken to underline that Victor Emmanuel had been a constitutional monarch and the embodiment of the entire nation. The coffin was flanked by the four most senior figures from the Chamber and the Senate, and the cortège included representatives from almost every section of the state and civil society: deputies, senators, prefects, policemen, mayors, town councillors, judges, doctors, engineers, businessmen, landowners, academics, artists, teachers, students, artisans, workers and even Alpine guides.[21]

The funeral marked the beginning of the apotheosis of Victor Emmanuel – his elevation into the immortal 'father of the fatherland' – and the process continued with a great torrent of tributes and commemorative books, pamphlets and prints, and a magnificent performance of Cherubini's *Requiem* in the Pantheon on 16 February. Some 300 deputies packed the interior, along with ministers, ambassadors and numerous other dignitaries, including members of the court and foreign royalty (there were three empty seats for the deposed king of Naples and his family). The great cupola had been transformed into a shimmering firmament, with 140 star-shaped boxes covered with white muslin set into the coffers and lit by gas jets, while on the walls were the arms of the nation's principal cities and inscriptions glorifying the king and his role in uniting the Italian people: 'Healer of Italian discords'; 'Son of the Martyr King – who took holy vengeance for his father – and founded the union of Italy'. A massive star of Italy had been placed over the central aperture; and below it towered the catafalque, covered in gold and black and flanked by four lions and statues of faith, hope and charity. The coffin itself was now empty as the embalming process had gone badly wrong, requiring the body to be interred hurriedly in a side chapel.[22]

The death of Victor Emmanuel was something of a watershed for liberal Italy. Many politicians felt grave forebodings for the future: who would now have the moral authority to save Italians from their factiousness, hold back the clerical and socialist tides, and prevent the fragile edifice of the new state from crumbling? Victor Emmanuel had had his faults – many of them – but at least he had possessed the prestige that came from securing national unification and fighting (if not always winning) battles; and though he could be rude, undignified and politically inept, he had had a certain simplicity and earthy panache that had probably endeared him in the end to the majority of his subjects. Would the new king, his eldest son, be able to fill his shoes? The signs were not good. Umberto (who wisely chose to be Umberto I, resisting pressure from the Piedmontese lobby to be Umberto IV) was a colourless and physically unimpressive man, of limited intellect, who was to find consolation for his deep feelings of inadequacy in serial philandering. His main asset was his wife (and cousin), the fair-haired and blue-eyed Margherita, a woman of strong character and cultural interests. And it was to her (and the dead Victor Emmanuel) that royal propagandists were mainly to turn in a bid to invest the Italian Crown with a suitable aura.

And the need for mystique was great. Most Italian politicians, including many former republicans, recognized after 1860 that the crown offered the best hope of safeguarding Italian unity. 'The monarchy unites us, a republic would divide us,' Francesco Crispi declared in parliament, to loud applause, in 1864. And the reason lay chiefly in the yawning abyss that was felt to divide the mass of the population from the ruling classes. As the philosopher Angelo Camillo De Meis argued in a well-known essay of 1868, the spheres of the educated ('those who think') and of the uneducated ('those who feel') were poles apart in modern society, and particularly so in Italy, where the credulous Catholic poor could not be expected to identify with the godless abstractions of liberalism. The only way of bringing the two camps together and preventing a bloody civil war from tearing the country apart – as had happened in southern Italy during the Napoleonic period and again in the early 1860s – was through 'a glorious national dynasty' that would embody simultaneously 'the religious and conservative instincts of the people' and the constitutional aspirations of the elites.[23]

But the Savoys were not particularly glorious, and the limit of their mystique was underlined on 17 November 1878, when a young anarchist tried to assassinate the new king in Naples. Umberto was saved in part thanks to his prime minister, the former republican Benedetto Cairoli, who lunged at the assailant, grabbing him by the hair and parrying the knife blow. 'The poetry of the House of Savoy is destroyed,' commented the queen ruefully.[24] In the days that followed, a series of terrorist bombings in Florence and Pisa, in which several people were killed, reinforced the general feeling that the nation's institutions were in jeopardy, threatened by subversives, and more generally by the resentment and anger of millions of poor Italians. As the authoritative and usually restrained *Nuova antologia* commented in the wake of the attacks:

How can one not reflect that if this Italy, hitherto protected by providence, had been unlucky, and the blow aimed at the king had not missed, we would immediately have found ourselves engulfed in the flames of a great conflagration, which only a miracle has prevented from breaking out, but which is smouldering hidden beneath our feet![25]

Many, including confirmed democrats like Francesco Crispi, felt that the time had now come to curtail political freedoms. Italy, he told parliament, could not afford to be as liberal as Britain, 'where respect for the monarch and religious sentiment are so deeply rooted in the hearts of the people that nobody dares to insult them or puts up with their being insulted. Every meeting ends with the celebrated anthem, "God save the Queen!"' In Italy, by contrast, patriotism and loyalty to the monarchy were skin-deep.[26]

In the course of the 1880s and 1890s enormous efforts were made to turn the monarchy into an authentic symbol of national cohesion. In Rome the massive marble monument to Victor Emmanuel, the Vittoriano, began to rise slowly above Piazza Venezia, alongside the Capitol (after some initial delays: the international competition for the design, launched in 1880, was won by a Frenchman; there was an outcry and the competition had to be re-run on a strictly national basis).[27] In January 1884 a 'pilgrimage' (as it was officially termed) was staged to mark the sixth anniversary of Victor Emmanuel's death, and tens of thousands of visitors flocked to the Pantheon to pay their respects to the late king, whose body was exhumed for the occasion and placed on a large catafalque beneath the rotunda. The event was accompanied by a fresh wave of commemorative literature with Victor Emmanuel, the bringer of 'concord', as the main theme.[28] Politicians, writers and artists glorified the monarchy in speech, print and paint, trumpeting the devotion of Victor Emmanuel and his father, Carlo Alberto, to national unity and claiming the dynasty had for centuries been committed to the Italian cause. Musicians, too, played their part. When Verdi revised his opera *Simon Boccanegra* he added a new section in which the fourteenth-century Doge of Genoa calms his unruly subjects and halts their inveterate factional and class struggles with the exercise of his regal authority: 'Fratricides! Plebeians! Patricians! People with a savage history . . . While brother tears brother apart in civil strife . . . I cry: peace!, I cry: love!' The scene was rapturously received at its premiere in March 1881.[29]

There were serious limits, though, to the capacity of the monarchy to serve as a symbol of cohesion in Italy. Umberto certainly adopted a less forbidding and martial image than his father – though he loved army manoeuvres and military parades. He was described as 'the good king', and toured the country with his glamorous wife, handing out prizes to schoolchildren, meeting the poor, and offering comfort and support to victims of natural disasters and epidemics (as with his acclaimed visit to Naples at the time of the cholera outbreak in 1884). But the Crown was not above politics, and this made it vulnerable. The king chose the prime minister, and if he so wanted he could on occasions go against the wishes of parliament – as happened with the appointment of Giovanni Giolitti in 1892 – with potentially embarrassing results. More importantly the monarch was seen as having an intimate relationship with the army and this meant that controversial measures, such as the introduction of martial law in times of civil unrest – Sicily in 1894, Milan in 1898 – could rebound against him personally. More generally the prestige of the dynasty was very closely linked to the conduct of foreign policy, which was one important factor behind Italy's increasing bellicosity and assertiveness on the international stage from the 1880s. The rewards of military success could be huge for Italy's fragile and lacklustre monarchy – which is why prime ministers, like Crispi, were willing to play with fire, egged on by Umberto. But it was a high-risk strategy and the price of failure could be no less great.

PARLIAMENT

The cult of the monarchy during the 1880s and 1890s was in part a response to the waning prestige of parliament. Representative assemblies had never been viewed with unalloyed enthusiasm by Risorgimento patriots: for democrats especially they had often seemed instruments for the furtherance of selfish sectional interests by the propertied classes, and thus inimical to 'the people' and 'the nation'. Universal suffrage was a possible solution, and many on the left certainly aspired to this in principle. In practice, though, it hardly seemed feasible to give the masses the vote while they were under the thumb still of priests and oppressive local landowners. Parliamentary government thus began in Italy amid considerable scepticism, and it was perhaps not surprising that as soon as evidence surfaced of corruption or abuse of privilege – as with the great tobacco monopoly scandal of 1868–9 (when a number of deputies were accused of fraudulently lining their pockets) – pessimism should quickly turn into generalized disdain and disgust. 'Parliament,' wrote a leading member of the far left to a friend in 1873, 'is a sordid pigsty, where the most honest man loses at the very least all sense of decency and shame.'[30] And another influential democrat published a major study of Italy's political system the same year dismissing the Chamber as just a collection of 'angry sects fighting one another for control of government ... factions, not parties, secret camarillas, motivated solely by personal interests'.[31]

The advent of the left to power in 1876 did not alter the negative assessments of parliament. Indeed they soon intensified, as conservatives became afraid that the extension of the suffrage promised by the governments of Agostino Depretis and Benedetto Cairoli would open the doors to the unruly masses. Already, before the passing of electoral reform in 1882, many on the right claimed to detect a coarsening of the parliamentary fabric, as Montecitorio became crowded with new men – a third of those returned in the elections of 1876 had never sat in the Chamber before – with few party ties and limited political experience whose support for the left had been motivated more by a desire to be spared the austere fiscal policies of the moderates, it seemed, than any genuine concern for greater democracy or freedom. No doubt there was much snobbery and prejudice in the scorn of many older liberals for the new intake; but the perception of a qualitative decline may have been well-founded. A Tuscan, Ferdinando Martini, was horrified by the ignorance of his fellow deputies and recalled an occasion when the Minister of the Interior, Giovanni Nicotera (a southerner and a former Mazzinian revolutionary), repeatedly referred to 'King Teodoro' of England in a speech after misreading a note that had been slipped to him about 'the Tudors'.[32]

Worries about parliament in the age of the masses were common to many Western democracies in the late nineteenth century, but in Italy they gained particular momentum by feeding on a dark hinterland of anxieties. Indiscipline and division had dogged the past: very little, it seemed, had now changed, despite all the hopes of the Risorgimento. And if Italians were still beset by the vices that had brought them centuries of decadence, how could a political system founded on representation do other than reflect back those vices and produce a degenerate assembly? 'Today Italy is like a ship in a mighty storm,' wrote a leading moderate with a characteristically Dantean note, surveying the situation in parliament in November 1876. 'Where is the pilot? I cannot see one.'[33] And many other observers on both the right and the left similarly found themselves viewing the present through the disquieting filter of history. The growing anarchy in parliament, De Sanctis told an audience in 1880, recalled the chaos of the Middle Ages, when factionalism had led to endless turmoil. 'How many ministries have fallen since 1860, how much passion and private ambition has been fomented, how many dissident and personal groups have arisen! Ah! This tale of groups and crises is not new; it is the ancient illness that gnaws at Italy . . .'[34]

Finding remedies for the shortcomings of parliament was very difficult, as problems seemed to beset almost every level of the political system, beginning at the base with the electorate. As De Sanctis pointed out, it was normal for voters in all liberal regimes to give their backing to a candidate from a mixture of private interests and general political concerns; but it was the balance between the two that was crucial, and in countries such as Italy where people had had little experience of freedom the claims of the collectivity were widely regarded as little more than 'a passport to personal ends'. People, he said, pledged their support to whoever offered the best prospect of securing money, jobs or assistance with some court case for themselves or their local community, and as a result they voted 'not for the most honest and talented man, but the man who is deemed to be most influential'. Fine principles were all very well where such principles were generally respected and upheld; but if lip-service alone were paid to the rules of the game, who would be so foolish as to put the requirements of something so remote as 'Italy' ahead of the interests of his family and friends? It was the old problem of thought and action. Everyone, according to De Sanctis, solemnly proclaimed that deputies represented the nation, but each then added quietly to himself: 'This ought to be the case; but between what ought to be and what is, there is an enormous gap. And so we are back to square one.'[35]

Local influence was a problem. The great majority of rural communities were dominated by a few wealthy individuals or families, who used their prestige, contacts, and social and economic muscle to control the elections. Bribery of all sorts was commonplace – money, food, offers of jobs, loans – and in many parts of the south men with a reputation for violence – bandits or *mafiosi* – were widely deployed to intimidate the voters. Election days were frequently turned into carnival occasions with landowners marching their supporters, as if they were a feudal army, off to the polling station accompanied by musicians, priests and dignitaries. And if there was some uncertainty as to whether the electors would actually vote as expected of them – ballots were after all secret – there were a variety of mechanisms for ensuring the desired outcome. Ballot papers could be procured in advance, filled in and handed to the voter (who would then bring back the blank ballot paper as a form of receipt). Individuals might be instructed to write a version of the candidate's name, perhaps with a spelling mistake, on the ballot paper in a way that would 'personalize' it and enable checks to be made later. And the tellers could be pressurized into nullifying votes cast for an opponent on a technicality. Francesco Crispi was incensed to find that he had lost in the college of Castelvetrano in western Sicily in 1870 after all the ballot papers with 'Francesco Crispi', 'Crispi' or 'Grispi' ('C' and 'G' were often interchanged in Sicily), rather than his full name and lawyer's title, were declared void.[36]

When De Sanctis travelled back to his home town of Morra Irpino in 1875, for the first time in forty years, to fight an election that had to be rerun after the initial result was contested, he did so with the full confidence that his fame and national standing would cause factional disputes to melt away and bring him a near unanimous vote. But to his intense disappointment all his passionate speeches about concord and unity seemed to fall on deaf ears and he picked up just twenty fresh votes as a result of his campaigning. The trouble was, as a local priest explained to him, that his talk about transcending petty municipal disputes for 'Italy's' sake meant nothing to most townspeople:

You see, in these small places, the world begins and ends here. The church tower is the brightest star in their little firmament. And there is as much passion in these rivalries and squabbles – what you call local tittle-tattle – as there is, let us say, between France and Germany. Everyone has his own personal epic. The epic of a child is his house of cards. And their epic is the campaign to win control of the town hall. You call this tittle-tattle, and want to be the deputy of everyone: but that means being the deputy of no-one . . . Moral enthusiasm is just *ignis fatuus*. Brute passions and interests are the stuff of mankind, and that is where your campaign must start.[37]

Nor were irregularities in elections the product simply of unbridled local influence and factionalism. The government, too, played its part, with the prefects and sub-prefects who were its agents in the provinces intervening in often blatant fashion to help friendly candidates and damage opponents. This could be done in a variety of ways, including harassing or arresting opposition supporters, banning opposition rallies, sequestrating opposition newspapers, and instructing state officials, the police included, to use their authority to secure votes for the government. A particularly powerful tool of manipulation lay in the drawing up of the electoral registers. Literacy and a tax threshold were the two principal criteria of eligibility for the vote, but literacy in particular was hard to define, and this led to a great deal of blurring at the edges. Until 1894 town councils were responsible for compiling lists of voters (with all the attendant risks of partisan interference) and the prefect then vetted them and added or subtracted names at will. Thus in 1867 the prefect ensured the election of a certain Ippolito Masci in the run-off for the twelfth college in Naples after removing 204 names from the list submitted by the local council and adding 187 entirely new ones.[38]

Appeals against irregularities could be made, and a parliamentary commission would investigate; and it was not uncommon for elections to be quashed and re-run (though sometimes parliament upheld elections even when the irregularities had been transparent: an indication of yet another tier of impropriety in the system).[39] But despite such checks there remained a widespread feeling that the electoral process in Italy was deeply flawed and increasingly unworkable, and by the early 1880s writers and journalists were denouncing it with at times near hysterical vehemence. The popularity of anti-parliamentary novels (several dozen appeared in the late nineteenth and early twentieth centuries), high-profile journals, including the *Cronaca bizantina* and *Nabab*, and news-papers such as the *Forche Caudine* – a broadsheet written almost entirely by one man, Pietro Sbarbaro, whose splenetic denunciations of political scandal and malpractice earned it sales of around 150,000 in the mid-1880s – bore witness to the general public's appetite for a negative and often scabrous vision of Italian liberalism. Political theorists also joined in the attacks. In 1884 the Sicilian Gaetano Mosca wrote a scathing denunciation of parliamentary government as the tyrannical imposition of a self-serving minority on the majority after witnessing the 'thousands of iniquities, abuses and brutal acts' that regularly attended Italian elections.[40]

Why were governments unable to curb electoral corruption? In part because they thought they could not. While commentators happily denounced parliament and politicians, often in the harshest terms, they conveniently overlooked the part they themselves played in generating and sustaining the system ('It is you who are responsible for your problems, electors,' said De Sanctis in 1880, with rare frankness. 'It is you who are making the new history of Italy').[41] Governments also believed that they had a right, a duty even, to intervene on behalf of their own candidates (and here they were following the model of French liberalism), not least because they had no permanent party machinery that they could fall back on. Paradoxically, though, one of the biggest reasons for governmental interference in elections derived from an acute sense of the fragility of liberalism in Italy: given the threat posed by reactionaries and subversives (clericals, republicans, radicals and in due course socialists), how could the values of constitutional freedom be upheld if the authorities did not do everything in their power to ensure that their men were returned to parliament? Of course they risked shooting themselves in the foot with their high-handed behaviour: but as long as the rules of the liberal game were widely ignored, they faced an almost impossible dilemma.

*

The new electoral law of 1882 was the product of several years of difficult deliberation. For the right in particular extending the suffrage did not seem the answer to the problem of how to bridge the gap between government and governed, 'legal' and 'real' Italy: to enfranchise those who had not yet acquired a 'sense of the state' was simply to 'endanger the institutions and the monarchy', according to Ruggero Bonghi.[42] The main fear for conservatives was radicals, republicans and socialists – which was why a few of them went so far as to argue for universal suffrage, on the grounds that the illiterate rural masses would provide a ballast of safe, Catholic docility. But the left was more concerned about the pernicious influence of the Church and was thus wary of giving the vote to the peasantry. And though worries about the ignorance and lack of patriotism of the working classes were almost as pronounced on the left as the right, there was a general feeling that the social question was now so insistently discussed throughout the Western world and so pressing that it would be political suicide to hold out against democratic reform. Furthermore, could the masses ever be educated to a 'sense of the state' if they were not entrusted with political responsibility?

The man who dominated Italian parliamentary politics from 1876 to 1887, Agostino Depretis, was a reluctant reformer. Cautious, affable and Piedmontese, with a long white beard periodically dyed grey for added *gravitas*, he entered office on a platform of free and compulsory primary education, increased local self-government, administrative decentralization and an extended suffrage. But he did not embrace change out of conviction or principle – indeed his lack of strong views meant that most people came away from talking to him feeling that he agreed with them – but rather from a sense that something needed to be done (and preferably the less the better) to prevent discontent boiling over in the country. In 1879 he brought in a measure that would roughly double the electorate. But this was widely considered inadequate, and two years later he submitted a more radical proposal to the Chamber giving the vote to all males over twenty-one who had completed two years of primary schooling or military service, or who paid at least 19.80 lire annually in direct taxes. This bill was passed, and the Italian electorate more than trebled from 620,000 to over 2 million. Education rather than wealth now became the principal criterion for enfranchisement: previously about 80 per cent of all voters had qualified on the basis of taxation.

Central to the new law was the introduction of the electoral system of *scrutin de liste*. Instead of 508 constituencies, each with a single deputy, there were to be 135 larger colleges with between two and five deputies chosen by preference voting from competing lists. The aim was partly to ensure that urban working-class districts were diluted with conservative rural votes. But the main hope of the scheme's proponents – principally Francesco Crispi – was that larger territorial units and lists of candidates would break the stranglehold of local interests on elections and encourage the creation of organized parties appealing to voters with 'national' programmes. As Crispi said:

I believe we must compel voters to look beyond the confines of their town and study the country on a broader basis . . . It is possible to suborn 400 voters, but not thousands; it is possible to intervene within the limits of a small constituency, but not of a province . . . I want *scrutin de liste* in order to nationalize the Chamber, by which I mean, gentlemen, . . . that those who in future enter this hall should forget where they were born, their parish pump, their local ties, and the wishes, the needs and the demands of the region of their birth, and should instead be inspired by a single idea, a sole concept, that of the good of the nation.[43]

The hopes surrounding *scrutin de liste* were not realized, and Italy was to revert to a system of single-member constituencies in 1891. Bribery and corruption continued unabated, and far from reducing the predominance of local interests in elections, the expanded suffrage simply meant that candidates (and deputies) now had to devote more time than ever to satisfying the demands of their key constituents. As in the past, offers of jobs, promotions, medals, pensions, loans, licences and contracts were the staple of a politician's life; and huge amounts of effort had to be expended answering the constant stream of 'letters of recommendation' that poured in from local supporters. Fulfilling promises was not imperative; but keeping clients in hope was. Nor did the enlarged electoral colleges encourage politicians to compete on the basis of rival programmes, as had been anticipated: instead candidates looked to avoid the lottery of an open contest by negotiating with rivals, carving up the territory and the votes in an often complex process of horse-trading. As one leading newspaper lamented in 1891, the short-comings of the parliamentary regime were evidently due more to the fact that united Italy had failed to reform Italians than to any structural problems with the state: 'These defects in our country can only be resolved through the furthering of our political education, which, to be honest, shows no sign of taking place.'[44]

With politicians heavily dependent on meeting the demands of constituents, parliament became weighed down with often petty local business, and rather than give their allegiance to a government on the basis of the merits of its programme, many deputies preferred to 'trade' their vote, moving between ministers and would-be ministers, seeing who would offer them the most favourable terms. As a result parliamentary votes were unpredictable, which was one important reason why governments fell so often: Italy had thirty-five administrations between 1861 and 1900. It also helps explain why it was so difficult to get major reforms through parliament, and, once passed, why they frequently showed signs of incoherence: they were usually the product of a good deal of convoluted bargaining. One deputy described the frenetic cattle-market atmosphere of parliament in a speech in May 1886:

You should see the pandemonium in Montecitorio when the time approaches for an important vote. Government agents run through rooms and up and down corridors trying to secure support. Everything is promised: subsidies, decorations, canals, bridges, roads; and sometimes a long-withheld legal decision is the price of the parliamentary vote.[45]

The magnetic pull of constituency interests – discernible, for example, in the unnecessarily circuitous paths followed by many railway lines built in these years – was not just the result of electoral expediency. The fact was, most deputies felt emotionally rooted in their home territory in ways that constantly cut across their national obligations. There was widespread absenteeism from the Chamber, as the press continually lamented, and in the first decades of unity barely half of those elected to parliament ever bothered to turn up. As a result the Chamber was frequently inquorate (under 50 per cent plus one of all deputies) and many of the votes taken were technically invalid (this was the case with 90 per cent of the decisions made in the 1870–71 legislature).[46] Some deputies may have stayed away from the capital as a gesture of protest, and some may have had financial reasons for not attending given that there was no parliamentary stipend; but most seem simply to have felt little inclination to bother themselves with affairs outside their home province – like Marco Miniscalchi Erizzo, whose meagre contributions to the life of parliament in the 1880s and 1890s consisted of suggesting to the Minister of Public Works that the question of the trunk line from his home town of Verona to nearby San Giovanni Lupatoto needed to be examined, and that any further development of the station at Porta Vescovo in Verona might be shelved until plans for the station at Porta Nuova had been studied more thoroughly.[47]

For some high-minded politicians such as De Sanctis and Crispi the answer to deputies' lack of commitment, rampant municipalism and horse-trading lay in the creation of disciplined parties, and periodically they issued impassioned pleas for Italy to emulate the British parliamentary model and give the labels of 'left' and 'right' real political substance. But their calls fell largely on deaf ears. One reason for this was that parties continued to be seen, as in the Risorgimento, as inimical to national unity and synonymous with the violation of individual and collective liberty by factions. There was a widespread (and well-founded) fear that organized parties in Italy would simply fragment the constitutional terrain, give voice to anti-system forces – clerical, regional, republican, socialist – and return the country to the chaos that had bedevilled it in the past. As the eminent constitutionalist Domenico Zanichelli said in 1900, parties ran the risk of 'reproducing in the new Italy that sad and distinctive feature of medieval Italy, paid for with centuries of martyrdom and oppression'.[48] But it was also the case that most politicians could not see what they stood to gain from being subjected to party restraints, as their power rested heavily on having their hands free to manoeuvre within the Chamber in order to meet the clientelistic demands of their voters.

In the early 1880s the situation appeared to be getting worse. The introduction of electoral reform aroused much anxiety on both sides of the Chamber, and there was talk of the need to 'transform' the old groupings of left and right and create a broad centrist alliance that would protect the institutions from the rising tide of 'seething demagogy' (as Marco Minghetti called it in a letter of 1881).[49] What came to be called 'transformism' was certainly not new (Cavour had done something similar with his *connubio* in the 1850s), nor was it confined to Italy: 'opportunism' in France was comparable. Nor, initially, did it have negative connotations: the distinguished Swiss political scientist Johann Kaspar Bluntschli had made centrism theoretically fashionable in the 1870s arguing that it was inherently progressive, like evolution.[50]

But the problem in Italy was that it coincided with a general revulsion towards parliament and growing anxieties about the country's 'decadence' – hugely fuelled by the government's failure in the spring of 1881 to stop the French occupying Tunis. 'Transformism' thus quickly became sucked into the vortex of execration and used as a further stick with which to beat the ruling classes. As Carducci wrote early in 1883:

Transformism is an ugly word and even more ugly thing. To transform oneself from left into right, and yet not become fully right nor remain fully left. As in Dante's infernal circle of thieves, where men are neither men nor serpents, but unquestionably reptiles, and monstrous reptiles in which the two forms are merged into one and which instead of uttering rational speech suffer from dyspepsia and spit.[51]

The blurring of party lines and the sense that the Chamber was dissolving into a quagmire of unprincipled factions held together only by the bargaining skills of the pliable but personally honest Depretis (one leading contemporary compared him to an English water closet that stayed clean despite the filth passing through it),[52] led a string of leading intellectuals and politicians – Bonghi, Minghetti, Jacini, Lombroso, Orlando – into anguished analyses of Italy's parliamentary system. In the 1880s there was a feeling that the shortcomings might yet be rectified; but by the 1890s residual optimism was fading fast as new and disturbing ideas about the nature and evolution of society gained widespread currency, fuelled by Darwinism and influential studies such as Hippolyte Taine's history of contemporary France. What if nations evolved only slowly, like natural organisms, in a realm beyond human reason? Could a state that had been drawn up largely in accordance with abstract principles and imposed on a population, as in France in the 1790s or Italy in the 1860s, be expected to function? Should not institutions be adapted to suit the particular character and psychology of a people? Parliament, with its 'anaemic, pointless and pernicious existence', as one leading newspaper put it,[53] was proving incapable of educating Italians and creating the new Italy that had been dreamed of in the Risorgimento. But what might be put in its place?

PART FIVE

War
1887–1918

16
Francesco Crispi and the 'New European Order', 1887–91

The eyes are piercing, intelligent, expressive and changeable; the eyes of a man who is very strong, very wily, very cunning. But they are missing something! M. Crispi has no eyebrows. And as soon as you realize what his physiognomy lacks, you discover whom it is M. Crispi resembles: he resembles Bismarck without eyebrows . . . Very refined . . . very Italian and very much a lawyer, he does not need the eyebrows that give his counterpart a very strong, very brutal, very German and very military appearance! M. Crispi strikes me as wanting to charm his interlocutors; Bismarck wants to terrorize them.

Jacques Saint-Cère, Le Figaro, 29 September 1890

The great ambition of Signor Crispi, and perhaps the mainspring of his actions, is to obtain a military success for Italy, no matter where or how . . . He believes himself now to be acting in Italy the part undertaken by Prince Bismarck in Germany before the events of 1866 and 1870. If once victory should crown the Italian army, Signor Crispi would feel sure of maintaining the dictatorship which he has assumed but which has not yet been assured him by his fellow countrymen.

British chargé d'affaires to Lord Salisbury, 24 December 1888

DOGALI

On 26 January 1887 a column of some 500 Italian soldiers was surprised by a force of 5,000 Ethiopians in the rocky hinterland of Massaua on the shores of the Red Sea and annihilated. News of the disaster took a week to reach Rome, and when it did the Secretary-General of the Foreign Ministry could not make out from the telegram the site of the battle. He suggested it was something like 'Dogali', and though no such place could be found on the map, the name stuck. When the prime minister, Depretis, walked into the Chamber (carrying an old atlas) to report the tragedy he was visibly shaken: according to one observer he had aged ten years.[1] The announcement was greeted with uproar. 'Persons not familiar with the energy of Italian rhetoric,' wrote the British politician Charles Wentworth Dilke, 'would imagine that a dozen duels next morning must be the result of a heated debate in the Chamber, unless indeed they were anticipated by a free fight on the floor of the House. The scenes which took place on the reception of the bad news from Massowah were of this description . . .'[2] Similar scenes were repeated across the country as demonstrators took to the streets in anger.

The Italian government had been lured to Massaua two years earlier after a succession of setbacks in foreign policy. In 1878 at the Congress of Berlin it had failed to win compensation for Austria's occupation of Bosnia–Herzegovina: Britain by contrast had picked up Cyprus, while France (though this was still secret) had been given a free hand in Tunisia. 'Victor Emmanuel would not have allowed this if he had lived. We are truly decadent,' Crispi wrote indignantly to a friend.[3] Three years later the French duly invaded Tunisia, a region in which Italy had powerful economic (and strategic) interests, and the government fell amid a torrent of censure and anger at its inability to prevent this fresh humiliation. There were fears now of 'encirclement' in the Mediterranean, and in 1882 Italy abandoned its traditional policy of neutrality and entered a defensive alliance with Austria and Germany, the Triple Alliance. And when at the end of 1884 London indicated that it would be happy to see Italy installed in Ethiopia (mainly to avert a possible French challenge in the upper Nile valley), the Foreign Minister, Pasquale Stanislao Mancini, seized the opportunity to send a contingent of troops to Massaua, without telling parliament. He later tried to justify his decision by declaring enigmatically that 'the keys of the Mediterranean' lay in the Red Sea, but in truth he appeared to have acted precipitately (and contrary to his earlier aversion to colonial ventures) in a desperate attempt to make up for the recent reverses.

Dogali was a disaster: but it was converted into a glorious disaster. The fact that the Italian troops had apparently fallen in a straight line facing the enemy was quickly seized on, and comparisons were drawn between the bravery and discipline of the dead in Africa and the craven irresponsibility and inertia of parliament. Ruggero Bonghi suggested that the heroes of Dogali were worth far more than his 500 fellow deputies, while a popular verse ran: 'This mourning garb you wear / Signals life not interment / The five hundred dead / Are sitting in parliament.'[4] An obelisk that had recently been unearthed near the church of Santa Maria sopra Minerva was converted into a large monument to the fallen in front of the central railway station in Rome and inaugurated in a lavish ceremony in the presence of the king (it was removed in 1925: the fascist government preferred to celebrate victories, not defeats). The piazza was renamed 'Piazza of the 500'. The artist Michele Cammarano was commissioned by the Minister of Education to paint a huge canvas of Dogali to 'record in the Gallery of Modern Art the heroic virtues of Italian soldiers'. Cammarano set off for Massaua, where he spent five years working on the picture, at great government expense, in a specially constructed studio. The finished piece, more than nine metres by four, was unveiled in 1896, unfortunately a few months after another, more calamitous defeat in Africa.[5]

The disappointments in foreign policy, the plummeting prestige of parliament, the sense that Italians were still profoundly vitiated, and mounting fears of popular unrest (a revolutionary socialist party appeared in Lombardy in 1885 – soon suppressed – and strikes and violent clashes with the authorities were becoming ever more common as the agricultural recession bit deeper) resulted in a growing belief that only something drastic – a great military success, perhaps – would cement the nation morally. And the idea was common to both left and right. In 1881 the brilliant young radical poet and deputy Felice Cavallotti told the Chamber that 'some bloody baptism' was needed to give Italy the 'position among the nations appropriate to its new destiny',[6] while the following year a well-known journalist, politician and former Garibaldian, Rocco De Zerbi, called famously for a 'warm steaming bath of blood' to sort out the country's problems. The well-connected conservative Marquis Alessandro Guiccioli wrote in his diary in 1882: 'When will we be able to celebrate a great victory won by the valour of Italians? ... That day I would happily breathe my last. A new nation can only be properly consecrated with a baptism of blood.'[7] And in May 1883 another leading conservative, Ruggero Bonghi, told parliament how he longed to see Italy militarily victorious so as to expunge the dreadful memories of Custoza and Lissa, which 'were, and remain, the principal reasons for our weakness'.[8] A left-wing deputy, Abele Damiani, wrote to his close friend Francesco Crispi (also in May 1883) about the 'decadence' into which the country was sliding. But he was hopeful that this situation would not last, 'above all if the guardian spirit of our fatherland should bring us swiftly into a new and heroic period, or else into a war'.[9] Damiani was to be Crispi's Under-Secretary at the Foreign Ministry from 1887 to 1891.

CRISPI AND THE 'NEW EUROPEAN ORDER'

The disaster of Dogali catapulted Crispi back into power. Ever since his resignation as Minister of the Interior in 1878 on a (well-founded) charge of bigamy, the former Mazzinian and Secretary of State of Garibaldi had been calling vigorously from the back-benches for a more assertive foreign policy and rearmament. He claimed that Italy faced a major external threat from France: the French had never forgiven Italy for achieving unity and destroying the temporal power of the papacy, he said, and since their defeat by Prussia they were looking to dominate the Mediterranean – at the expense, inevitably, of Italy. Domestically, Crispi was deeply worried about the challenge of the Church and the far left and the absence of national sentiment in the country; and he repeatedly spoke of the urgent need for 'moral unity' to complement 'material unity' and finish the work of the Risorgimento. Although he believed passionately that political and social reforms were required to help draw the masses inside the framework of the state, he had come increasingly to recognize that these would be ineffective in themselves without an accompanying process of 'political education'.

Crispi entered Depretis's eighth and final government in April 1887 as Minister of the Interior; and when Depretis died less than four months later he assumed the mantle of prime minister almost without discussion, retaining the interior ministry and adding the foreign ministry as well. For over two decades he had been a major figure on the Italian political stage, excluded from the highest office on account of his strongly demo-cratic views, his background (he was a Sicilian) and his irregular private life. But the country was now demanding energy and a change of direc-tion; and though some Piedmontese and Lombard politicians were alarmed at the prospect of a southern prime minister and tried to block his appointment, Crispi was adamant that his premiership would be 'national' as no other before it. As he told Ferdinando Martini:

To exclude me, who had already been designated as prime minister, simply because I was a southerner would have been a mistake. We must put a stop to this regionalism. From the Alps to the sea there are only Italians. And, to be honest, is there anyone who could claim to be more of a unitarist than me? To my mind, my whole life is proof of it, from Palermo to Turin. I am here to work for the country, to give it all my time, all my remaining energy. I hope that I will be able to do something good. I belong entirely to Italy, believe me. I feel as if I am back in 1860.

Crispi's eyes, according to Martini, were glistening with tears as he spoke these words.[10]

His first task was to sign a military convention with Germany. The situation in Europe was deeply unstable and there was talk in many quarters of an imminent conflagration. Austria and Russia were locked in dispute in the Balkans, while relations between Germany and France, irreconcilable enemies since the events of 1870–71 and the annexation of Alsace and Lorraine, had grown severely strained of late as a result of the inflammatory rhetoric of General Georges Boulanger and his bellicose nationalist supporters. The elderly German Chancellor, Bismarck, had no real stomach for any hostilities: as he informed the Italian government early in 1888 he had engaged in two major campaigns in 1866 and 1870 out of a sense of necessity – to secure German unification: 'But what could Germany gain from a war now? We have more Poles than we need, and more Frenchmen than we could ever digest.'[11] However, he faced strong opposition from the young Prince, and soon to be Kaiser, Wilhelm, and from a powerful group of senior generals who believed that Germany would have to fight a preventive war quickly before the rearmament programmes of France and Russia gave them a decisive advantage over the combined forces of the Triple Alliance. Crispi, too, was keen on a war, but not so much for reasons of security: he wanted a glorious victory over France to consolidate the Italian nation and establish it as a great power, much as Sedan had done for Germany. The first step that he needed to take was to strengthen the hand of the so-called 'war party' in Berlin.

At the end of September he set off for Friedrichsruh to see Bismarck. He travelled with his three private secretaries: young men he could trust who shared his ambitions for Italy (one of them a distinguished writer, Carlo Dossi); he had no confidence in the cautious bureaucrats of the Foreign Ministry. The visit was kept secret until the last moment, and when news of it broke there was a flurry of speculation in Europe and consternation in Paris: Crispi had been an outspoken critic of France in recent years, claiming repeatedly that it was incorrigibly aggressive and bent on crushing Italy in the Mediterranean. Why, then, such a baldly provocative gesture at the start of his premiership? Crispi claimed that he was simply paying a courtesy visit to an ally: in fact, aside from cranking up tension with France, he wanted to sort out practical arrangements for a war. Italy could not afford to repeat the disastrous mistakes of 1866, when nothing had been coordinated in advance with Prussia.

Bismarck was hoping for peace, but he was not inclined, particularly given the precarious situation in Europe, to turn down something as practical as a military convention with an ally. Moreover the German General Staff were very keen on the idea. Field Marshal Moltke ('the strategist before whom the whole world bows', as Crispi described him)[12] was invited to draw up the first draft, and after a month of negotiations the agreement was signed in Berlin on 28 January 1888. The main aim of the convention was to make a war as attractive as possible to Germany, and under its terms Italy agreed to send more than 200,000 men (six army corps and three divisions of cavalry) by train over the Brenner Pass and through Austrian territory to link up with the German left flank on the Rhine. This was a huge undertaking and it was premised largely on fears that an Italian offensive in southern France – which was still planned to take place – had little prospect of succeeding given the strength of the French Alpine fortifications. Better instead to concentrate on the principal front. And of course Crispi could not risk the humiliating scenario of France being overrun by Germany while Italy was pinned down or even defeated in the Alps (as happened in 1940).[13]

Crispi calculated – and it was a fair calculation – that, if it came to a war with France, Britain would not allow Italy, Germany and Austria to be beaten by France and Russia, especially if France had appeared the aggressor. Accordingly from the end of 1887 he embarked on a programme of systematic provocation, helped by the heightened mood of nationalism in France resulting from General Boulanger's bellicose posturing and the forthcoming celebrations for the centenary of 1789. He regarded the French as incorrigibly arrogant, and believed that with sufficient needling they could be induced to react: as they had, fatally, in 1870. Hence a succession of carefully orchestrated quarrels over trade tariffs, rearmament, army manoeuvres, espionage, consular rights, the taxation of French subjects in Massaua, plots with the Vatican, the future of Tunisia; and these, inflamed by the press (on both sides of the Alps), produced a state of mounting tension and mutual suspicion. Lord Salisbury explained the situation to the new British ambassador in Rome at the end of 1888:

If there could be war, Crispi hopes for Albania certainly, Nice possibly, and perhaps Tunis and Tripoli. There is some promise as to the two first, I am pretty certain . . . If there is to be war at all, it is Italy's interest to have it as quickly as possible. I am told that . . . Damiani, the Under-Secretary, [has] been heard to say as much. The consequence is that Crispi has been perpetually getting up little quarrels with the French . . . We have . . . declined to pronounce ourselves in his quarrels with the French; or to give him any assurances as to the future . . . My impression is that if France attacked Italy gratuitously by sea, the English would be in favour of going to her assistance, but that if a war were to arise out of one of Crispi's trumpery quarrels, England would certainly stand aloof. I confess I should be very glad to see Crispi disappear – spite of the German fondness for him . . . Of course we are externally the best of friends – and you will give him the most loving messages on my behalf.[14]

Crispi pressed hard for war in the early spring of 1888, but at the last moment he pulled back, telling Germany that it might be wise to wait until Italy had completed a further round of rearmament (spending on the army and navy was subsequently raised to over 560 million lire in 1888–9, higher than at any other time since 1860, and this despite the country facing a severe economic recession). In the meantime Crispi sent an emissary, Lieutenant-Colonel Goiran, to Berlin to put to Bismarck an idea of the Chief of General Staff, Enrico Cosenz, a Garibaldian veteran of 1860 with military ambitions similar to those of the prime minister. The following year at the time of the celebrations and Exhibition to mark the centenary of the French Revolution, the Kaiser should send a sudden invitation to the Italian king to review troops in Strasbourg, in annexed Alsace. The prime minister would advise the king to go. News of the visit would cause alarm in Paris, 'just as excitement at the Exhibition was reaching fever-pitch, and spark off the gunpowder'. Goiran added that General Boulanger wanted war and should be given a chance to declare it and that the Russians would be reluctant to mobilize their army during the revolutionary celebrations. 'The idea is not a bad one, but it needs to be thought about,' said Bismarck.[15]

In truth, Bismarck was as averse as ever to a war, and the Austrians did not seem very keen on one either ('In Vienna there exists . . . a kind of sentimental and philanthropic love of peace,' noted Goiran ruefully); and Goiran's general conclusion was not particularly comforting: 'It seems to me that it will be very difficult for us to be able to provoke a war simply for our own interests.'[16] But the accession of Wilhelm II in June tipped the balance in favour of the 'war party' in Berlin and offered renewed hope, and when in October the young Kaiser paid a state visit to Italy he was in a brazen and bullish mood, touring barracks, arsenals and ports, expressing pleasant surprise at the preparedness of the Italian army and navy and telling Umberto that they would meet again in Paris at the heads of their triumphant armies. 'Then you will return to Italy with your 300,000 victorious men and kick parliament out of the door. Crispi is a man with energy: he could help you.' Umberto professed to be rather shocked by the Kaiser's high-handed view of parliament, but admitted to a friend that he might have a point, given that Italy's current political system was not working: 'If we carry on as at present, in twenty years' time it will be very difficult to govern.'[17]

In the spring of 1889 Umberto paid a return state visit to Germany. He reached Berlin on 21 May, and the following evening, at a court banquet, the Kaiser turned to him and asked if he would like to review some troops in Strasbourg. Umberto accepted. The news was leaked to the press and a furore erupted. But it quickly became clear that the gesture was too baldly provocative to achieve the intended effect, and with the value of Italian stock plummeting on the exchanges and pro-French demonstrations breaking out, Bismarck moved to calm things down, announcing on the 25th that the Kaiser had 'spontaneously' decided to give up on the idea. In a speech at a Reichstag dinner that evening Crispi talked of the common destinies of Germany and Italy, of how they had been united under the leadership of 'two strong warrior dynasties', and of his lifelong commitment to the 'independence and brotherhood' of nations; and he dismissed the allegations that were circling that he was deliberately looking to start a war as 'calumnies' on the part of his enemies:

Nothing could be further from the truth. I want peace and peace alone. I strive for nothing else. There have been necessary wars, holy wars. But we have fought these, and the prize for them has been this Italy of ours and this Germany. Any other war would be a crime. Whoever provoked it would be committing an offence against humanity.[18]

Crispi was growing impatient: he feared that the French government would remain impervious to his provocations. But he had another card to play, this time involving the papacy – an inflammatory topic for millions of Frenchmen. On 9 June a statue to the sixteenth-century heretic Giordano Bruno was inaugurated in the Campo dei Fiori in Rome amid huge Masonic and anti-clerical celebrations, and as expected Pope Leo XIII was mortified. It was the latest of a string of insults deliberately directed by Crispi at the Vatican; and at a consistory summoned three weeks later Leo told the cardinals that this 'naked challenge by the Italian government to the Holy See' made it almost impossible for him to feel safe any longer in Rome. Most observers agreed that Leo had no intention at all of leaving the Eternal City and that his *cris de coeur* were merely histrionic and intended simply to rally Catholic support and sympathy throughout Europe. But Crispi looked to exploit the charged atmosphere to trigger a conflict, this time to coincide with the centenary of the storming of the Bastille.

On 13 July, Crispi told the king that he had received unequivocal intelligence of a French plot to remove the Pope from Rome and attack Italy by sea. He urged immediate defensive measures. A council of war was set up and mobilization begun. And in the next few days Crispi did all he could to rack up the tension, dispatching alarmist telegrams to ambassadors around Europe, sending a special emissary to Lord Salisbury ('Tell [him] . . . if war comes I will be drawn into it against my will'),[19] getting the king to leave Rome hurriedly for northern Italy, and insulting the Pope with accusations that he was recklessly endangering the peace of Europe. Critical was the response of Berlin. Crispi had already sent one agent to the German capital at the end of June; and on 14 July he sent another. And it seems that the offer of a *casus belli* on a plate split the German leadership badly, with the newspapers full of speculation in late July of a serious rift between the Kaiser and the 'war party' on the one hand and Bismarck on the other. But it was Bismarck and the 'peace party' who prevailed. In all likelihood what tipped the balance was the flimsiness of the pretext, for as Bismarck told Crispi's agent it was just not credible that France would bring about a European war (and its own destruction) with 'an action worthy of bandits'. He added that from a purely pragmatic and military point of view he almost wished the French would indulge in 'such a mad act of aggression': 'The upper tiers of the army in Germany would prefer a war right now, or next spring, rather than in two years' time when France will have filled its officer cadres, and completed its armaments and fortifications.'[20]

So, despite Crispi's best endeavours, the situation in Europe remained calm. The French government refused to rise to the bait and the French public continued to focus on the centenary celebrations. To make matters worse Italy's military machine barely moved during the crisis. Crispi had always been acutely conscious of the weakness of the Italian state and of the tendency of ministers, diplomats and other senior civil servants to pursue their own political agendas. This was why he relied on a secretariat of committed supporters and kept his cabinet colleagues in the dark as to what he was up to. And the army was particularly resistant to executive control, as it was largely a royal preserve and was staffed with the king's friends and relatives – many of whom had no wish to help someone like Crispi (a radical southerner). Those that did cooperate with the government, like the Chief of General Staff, Cosenz, could find themselves marginalized by their colleagues. When Crispi bumped into Cosenz outside Rome railway station on the evening of 18 July and asked him how mobilization arrangements were coming along, Cosenz said that he had no idea as the Minister of War only talked to him about such matters when he believed there was a threat.[21]

'THE CRISPI PHENOMENON'

Crispi was not to get his war in Europe and thereby fulfil 'the destiny assigned to Italy within the projected new European order', as a senior colleague put it.[22] At its best that new order would have seen a territorially enlarged Italy replace France as the dominant power in the Mediterranean, with Germany and Austria supreme on the continental mainland and Britain the ruler of the high seas (and much of the rest of the globe). It would also have created an Italy that was securer at home, for apart from the prestige accruing to the institutions from victory Crispi would certainly have seized the opportunity to tear up the Law of Guarantees and strengthen the state against the Church. But it was not to be, and though Crispi continued to try to engineer diplomatic and military openings – including in the summer of 1890 using a rumour of French plans to annex Tunisia as a pretext for a general war or an Italian invasion of Tripoli – he had to accept that Italy could not hope to achieve anything without greater support from its allies. He felt resentful towards Britain and bitter towards Germany, and in 1890 he put out feelers secretly to France, offering to abandon the Triple Alliance in return for the concession of Tripoli. This alarmed the king greatly and was one of the principal reasons why Crispi was forced out of power early in 1891.

But Crispi's assertiveness on the international stage earned him many plaudits. The hopes of greatness that the Risorgimento had engendered were resurrected, if only briefly, and old friends and colleagues were effusive in their praise. Antonio Mordini, one of the architects of the revolution in southern Italy in 1860, wrote to him in July 1889 of the 'honour' and 'glory' that his foreign policy had brought the nation, while another well-known elderly democrat, Luigi Orlando, spoke in the same year of Italy's new-found 'dignity and power'. For some the foreign policy simply underlined the prime minister's status as a great patriot. Giuseppe Verdi told Crispi in November 1889 of the pride that he felt in 'the man who controls the destinies of our beloved country with wisdom and so much energy. Glory to you!'; and in 1893 he sent him a photograph inscribed with the simple dedication, 'To Francesco Crispi. The great patriot.' The poet Carducci was lavish in his praise. In an open letter of February 1889 he called Crispi 'the grand old patriot' who had salvaged the dignity of Italy, and a few years later in another open letter he described him as 'the only truly Italian minister since Cavour', a man who, like Mazzini, Victor Emmanuel and Garibaldi, had wanted Italy to be 'strong and respected': 'For otherwise, what was the purpose of unification?'[23]

Crispi dominated the Italian political scene for nearly a decade, re-turning for a second term as prime minister in 1893–6, and though he faced fierce opposition from some quarters, particularly on the far left, his popularity in the country was quite astonishing. No other prime minister, not even Cavour, had succeeded in exciting the public imagination to such a degree. The distinguished sociologist Guglielmo Ferrero

– whose own sympathies were with socialism, not Crispi – was fascinated by the 'almost regal aura' that surrounded this elderly energetic man with a huge walrus moustache (the resemblance to Bismarck was striking and far from accidental), immaculate dress sense, colourful domestic life, and penchant for rings and jewellery (and a small horn of coral to ward off the evil eye). Writing in 1895 he said:

The Crispi phenomenon will remain among the strangest and most curious aspects of Italian history this century; and his dictatorship will be one of the problems that will most occupy historians in the future. No man this century has ever enjoyed as much power in Italy. Nobody has been able to impose his own personality on the entire country as he has, or stamp the political life of the nation so forcefully with his character, or arouse such enthusiasm, such hopes, such hatred. Nobody has so completely eclipsed the political world around him.[24]

Like many other contemporary observers Ferrero sought to explain Crispi's success in terms of the immaturity of Italian society and the failure of parliament to provide leadership for a population that was still vitiated by centuries of servility and unsuited to the rigours of freedom. Crispi was authoritarian and conducted politics 'as a poet writes or a musician composes, through impulses and flashes of inspiration'. Everything about him was emotional. 'Suffice it to see him when he makes a speech: his face grows bright, his eyes blaze, his gestures become taut, his curt and unadorned language bursts into flashes of true eloquence . . .' He appealed to the primitive 'messianic illusion' of ordinary people, with their longing for salvation in times of difficulty ('that tendency to trust to miracle-workers'), and he had a particular attraction to the country's middle classes, who lacked independence and strength and were prone to throw themselves into the arms of someone who could save them from their fears, real or imaginary. And at the root of Crispi's success lay the fact that he was unrepresentative: he was energetic, passionate and resolute where most Italians were lazy, indifferent and sceptical. Above all he had 'will': the average Italian was 'listless'.[25]

Crispi's towering stature and huge following in the country, together with the febrile anticipation that surrounded his high-wire foreign policy, guaranteed him a huge majority in parliament between 1887 and 1891 and enabled him to push through a remarkable programme of political, administrative and social reforms. After several years of inertia, the Chamber suddenly acquired new energy; and with the prospect of momentous international developments as long as Crispi was at the helm politicians were inclined to relax their usual obsession with horse-trading and pandering to their leading constituents in order to keep him in power. Among the landmark reforms in these years were a law that nearly doubled the number of local government voters to 4 million and allowed mayors of larger towns to be elected (formerly all mayors had been centrally appointed); a new penal code that abolished the death penalty and recognized the right to strike; a public health law that greatly increased the state's responsibility for controlling disease and monitoring local hygiene; a law setting up an independent tribunal to protect citizens against abuses at the hands of public officials; and a law that brought the country's 20,000 or more independent charitable bodies (*opere pie*) under local government control – a major step towards a welfare state.

For all his authoritarian instincts Crispi was a democrat who believed strongly in the need to defuse the social question by making sure that the masses had a stake in the life of the nation. But like many of his background he had lost his old Mazzinian faith in a decentralized liberal state as it became increasingly apparent that the threat of subversion was great – and growing. The Italian state needed to be strong in order to control, curb and educate. Hence the law extending the local government suffrage – which many considered to be a terrifying gamble, in that it opened the door to extreme left-wing and Catholic adminis-trations – was accompanied by an increase in the tutelary powers of the authorities, with prefects being given the right to dissolve town councils that were felt to be acting irresponsibly or incorrectly. Crispi was apolo-getic, but as he explained: 'People are as they are and not as they must be the day the education we are planning has been completed.'[26] And soon the new powers were being widely invoked, above all in regions such as the Romagna and Lombardy where socialist and republican administrations started to mushroom from the early 1890s.

AFRICA

Without a successful war in Europe, Crispi turned somewhat reluctantly to Africa. He had initially been swept into power on the back of public calls for revenge for the massacre of the five hundred at Dogali, but he had skilfully allowed Ethiopia to slip into the background after he became prime minister, so enabling him to focus instead on a possible conflict with France. However, during the course of 1889 Africa began to offer new and exciting opportunities, following the death in battle of the Ethiopian emperor at the hands of a local warlord called Menelik, whom the Italian army had been supporting. Menelik assumed the imperial title and promptly signed a treaty with Italy (the Treaty of Uccialli) recognizing its right to large swathes of territory inland from Massaua and agreeing – or so article 17 seemed to state – to an Italian protectorate over Ethiopia. In return Menelik was guaranteed Italy's assistance in bringing the empire fully under his control. King Umberto enthusiastically wrote to Menelik to confirm the alliance, informing him that a new cache of arms was on its way.[27]

Excitement over Africa began to soar in Italy. Former opponents of Italian colonialism such as the upcoming Piedmontese deputy Giovanni Giolitti changed their tune. So, too, did the poet Carducci: he had been unmoved by Dogali, but by the time he published his ode 'La Guerra' ('War') in 1891 he had grown almost exultantly jingoistic. The king and his senior army generals were excited by the prospect of cheap and (seemingly) easy victories; while a swelling chorus of economists and sociologists argued that colonies would provide a solution to the country's grave agricultural problems, and in particular create an alternative outlet for the tens of thousands of impoverished southern peasants who were currently crossing the Atlantic each year in search of a better life. Even the radical and republican far left was divided, with Giovanni Bovio and others trumpeting the virtues of Italy's civilizing mission in the Dark Continent.[28] When in October 1889 Crispi delivered a major speech in Palermo, it was the section on Africa that won some of the loudest applause:

Like the human body, nations need air that they can breathe in order to survive. Without it they would grow weaker and eventually perish. And as far as we are concerned we have understood this, and have secured the air for Italy's lungs . . . Today Italy is on the march and is asserting itself. Listen to the voice that rises from our colonies: they are exultant! 'Italy!' is the cry that comes from the shores of the Mediterranean and echoes back from the most distant oceans . . . Africa, mysterious and awesome, opens up to us, trusting and friendly . . . Ethiopia, now almost entirely pacified, reaches out its hand to us in the person of a sovereign desirous of civilization . . .[29]

But Menelik turned out to be less eager for Italian 'civilization' than Crispi hoped. Ethiopia was an ancient state with a long and proud history, and glib assumptions about the country's barbarism and backwardness proved misplaced. In the second half of 1889 Italian forces advanced inland from the Red Sea and early in 1890 a royal decree proclaimed the formation of a new Italian colony of Eritrea. Crispi wanted to push further west towards Sudan and take the town of Kassala and thereby get access to the lucrative trade of the upper Nile valley; but this was in the British sphere of influence, and after all the headaches that Crispi had caused him in the last three years Lord Salisbury was in no mood to concede anything to Italy. After being rebuffed by the British, Crispi was promptly upstaged and humiliated by the ambitious Menelik. According to the Italian version of the Treaty of Uccialli signed the previous year the Ethiopian emperor had 'agreed to use' the Italian government in all his dealings with foreign powers; but in the autumn of 1890 Menelik announced that the original Amharic text in fact said 'could' and not 'agreed to'. Ethiopia was therefore not an Italian protectorate. Crispi's African plans for the time being lay in ruins.[30]

17

The Fin de Siècle Crisis

The situation in Sicily is becoming ever more alarming. In Monreale, Giardini, Lercara and Valguarnera people are looting, burning and killing. Town halls are being ransacked. The watchword is: Long live the king, down with taxes! But those behind the violence are after something very different. They are probably being driven by French money. It is a new kind of cut-throat war that is being waged against us by our beloved Latin brothers!

Domenico Farini, *Diario di fine secolo*, 26 December 1893

Crispi: *We have fallen far, and I do not know if we will be able to pick ourselves up again . . . The morphine of cowardice has been injected into every citizen, and nobody believes any more in the power of the nation . . . A country of 32 million people has been brought lower in Europe than San Marino . . . The king must be a king, and correct what his ministers do.*
Queen Margherita: *And parliament?*
Crispi: *It is just a rudderless crowd . . . The parliamentary system is not suited to the Latin peoples after the levelling of classes brought about by the French Revolution.* Francesco Crispi talking to the queen, 2 January 1897

THE SICILIAN FASCI

Crispi was replaced as prime minister by a refined Sicilian nobleman, Antonio di Rudinì, but neither he, nor his successor, Giovanni Giolitti, could prevent the country lurching into what was generally considered the worst crisis the state had faced since 1860; and by the time Crispi returned to power in December 1893, Italy appeared to many on the brink of collapse. Writing to the Foreign Secretary early that month the British *chargé d'affaires* in Rome said the nation was gripped by a

338

'feeling of almost despair' – though he thought that this despondency and the accompanying desire to look to a miracle-worker for salvation were themselves a large part of the problem:

[F]ollowing their tendency to exaggeration which is so compatible with their excitable and somewhat weak temperament, many Italians are to be found, belonging to all classes of society, who are ready to prophesy the not far distant disrupture of the Kingdom ... The eyes of ... all [are] turned now to Signor Crispi, as the one man willing to undertake the task of guiding the country through her difficulties and possessing sufficient abilities to justify the universal hope that he would succeed.

He regarded Italy's political and economic problems as undoubtedly very serious; but he suggested, with characteristic British moralizing, that Italians might do well to examine their own conduct rather than heap all the blame on the king or parliament, as they tended to do. He had heard it said, for example, that 75 per cent of all taxes went unpaid as a result of 'false declaration and corruption of tax gatherers', and though this was probably an exaggeration it was certainly true that tax avoidance 'is not considered in this country to be a dishonest action nor even an evasion of a patriotic duty'.[1]

Since the late 1880s the Italian economy had been sliding into deep recession. A raft of new tariffs had been introduced in 1887 on a variety of agricultural and industrial goods, and this had been followed by a vicious trade war with France, which had damaged Italian commerce badly – not surprisingly given that nearly half of the country's exports (for the most part primary commodities such as raw silk, wine and food) were destined at the time for French markets.[2] Many farmers, especially in southern Italy, suffered severely as a result. Industry, such as it was – and it was still confined chiefly to small and medium-sized workshops in Lombardy, Piedmont and the Veneto, with textile production predominant – was also in serious difficulty from the late 1880s after enjoying several years of significant growth in sectors such as engineering and chemicals (Milan had become the first European city to have a central electricity generating plant in 1883, while the rubber manufacturer Giovan Battista Pirelli had pioneered the production of submarine telegraph cables in 1886). Construction had experienced a similar fate with a major boom followed by a disastrous crash, and rioting in the streets of Rome by laid-off workers in 1888 and 1889.

But the biggest crisis involved the banking sector. Italy had six banks of issue, all regionally based, privately administered, and closely tied to powerful local interest groups, which in the course of the 1880s had got sucked into dangerously speculative ventures. The most compromised was the Banca Romana, which had loaned huge sums, with far too few questions being asked, to a string of property developers only to be left with a mass of worthless bits of paper once the housing market crashed. It had also lent enormous amounts of money to politicians and journalists, often with no guarantees of repayment, in order to help them with the soaring costs of elections and running newspapers. The king had been a major beneficiary of the bank's largesse, too.[3] A government inspection, carried out in 1889, uncovered a mass of irregularities. The findings were known to Crispi and his Treasury Minister, Giovanni Giolitti, but otherwise they were kept secret. In May 1892 Giolitti was appointed prime minister, at the king's (not parliament's) instigation, and a few months later he tried to get the governor of the Banca Romana appointed a senator (which would have given him immunity from prosecution). But before he could do so a copy of the 1889 report was leaked to a republican deputy, who promptly divulged its contents to a stunned Chamber. This unleashed the Banca Romana scandal, which over the next few years threatened to discredit the entire political establishment in Italy, the monarchy included.

To make matters worse the country seemed to be slipping towards revolution. Encouraged by the establishment of a new nationally based socialist party in 1892, militant labour organizations were springing up across northern Italy among the agricultural workers of the Po valley, while in Sicily a movement known as the *Fasci* (from the word *fascio*, meaning 'bundle', indicating strength through solidarity) was mobilizing the peasantry and staging increasingly unruly strikes and demonstrations. In August 1893 a wave of rioting spread through the country. Initially triggered by the murder of a number of migrant Italian workers in the salt-pans of Aigues-Mortes in southern France (in Genoa and Naples trams owned by a French firm were set on fire; in Livorno the same fate befell Belgian vehicles), it quickly escalated into a more generalized working-class revolt, fanned in many places by anarchists. In Rome three days of turmoil culminated in the occupation of the Trastevere, and barricades soaked in petrol were thrown across the Ponte Sisto and set on fire when the cavalry arrived. In Naples the chaos continued for five days, and it needed 12,000 troops to restore order.[4]

Against this backdrop money began to pour out of Italy, and the banking sector entered free fall. In Sicily clashes between the security forces and the peasant *Fasci* became increasingly violent and there was talk of the island being 'in flames' and dissolving into anarchy. There were even allegations, widely believed, that the disorders were part of a general plan to spread socialist revolution throughout the peninsula. On 20 December, Crispi announced to the Chamber the formation of his new government and appealed to deputies to bury their differences and unite behind him in resolving this unprecedented crisis. 'To this end we ask of you the truce of God!':

When danger threatens we must all be united in the collective work of defence (*Hear! Hear!*) . . . Between 1859 and 1870 we endeavoured to secure the material unity of the fatherland. Now we must endeavour to bind it together morally and ensure that the edifice, for which the blood of our martyrs was shed, is made strong . . . The hour has struck to ask the country to make some sacrifices . . . Today I remind you that the fatherland is superior to all . . .[5]

At the beginning of 1894 martial law was declared in Sicily and 40,000 troops were despatched to the island. Military tribunals were instituted, and by the end of the month over a thousand suspects had been sentenced to deportation. Public meetings were banned, press censorship was introduced and weapons were confiscated. To use repression on such a scale against his native region was deeply distressing to Crispi, not least because he had begun his own political career in 1848 struggling for freedom on the barricades of Palermo. But he felt he had little choice. And anyway, he could claim that he was still fighting for 'Italy'. 'Who loves, fears. I love Italy greatly and my fear is that it could break up.' The problem, he told parliament, was that the nation had not been fused into a proper unit, and the 'seams' were showing from where the old states had been stitched together in 1859–60. And in reply to those on the far left who claimed that the use of martial law in Sicily was illegal (as technically it probably was), he said that Italy had a duty to protect itself against its enemies, within or without, and that he could always justify the harsh measures by appealing beyond human law to a higher law, 'an eternal law, the law that demands that the existence of nations be guaranteed'. His old friend Mazzini would have struggled to disagree with him.[6]

It was crucial for Crispi to try to get the country united behind him. The far left was a source of major concern for, although the radicals, republicans and socialists were a relatively small force still in the Chamber – some fifty deputies – they had a large and growing popular following, especially in the Romagna and Lombardy. And their leaders included men of cult status, such as the hard-drinking poet, playwright and inveterate dueller Felice Cavallotti, the so-called 'bard of democracy', whose pugnacious and often highly abusive rhetoric generated enormous enthusiasm in audiences. Lombardy was a particular worry: not only was it the centre of the new socialist party led by an able young lawyer, Filippo Turati, but it was also home to Italy's leading manufacturers and industrialists, who were growing resentful that the fruits of their success were being siphoned off in taxes by a corrupt political establishment in Rome led by an elderly Sicilian with expensive tastes in foreign policy. Milan had never been very enthusiastic about united Italy, and in the 1890s it became even less so; and calls for federalism and even for outright secession became insistent.[7]

Crispi knew that the disorders in Sicily were essentially socio-economic and spontaneous in character, but politically it suited him to suggest that they were the result of a conspiracy – and preferably a foreign one. Nothing was likely to engender national solidarity better than an external threat, and in the wake of the Aigues-Mortes murders there were plenty of people willing to believe that France had had a hand in the unrest.[8] Crispi claimed that the leaders of the *Fasci* had been in league with French republicans and radicals; that French gold and weapons had been smuggled into Sicily; that a French vessel, the *Hirondelle*, had been spotted making secret night-time signals off the coast; that the final preparations for the rising had been drawn up in Marseille; and even that the revolution was planned to coincide with a French invasion of Piedmont, followed by a Russian invasion of Sicily, and finally a French attack on Rome. The far left repudiated these allegations vehemently, and in the Chamber there were heated and increasingly disorderly exchanges; but in the country as a whole many were quite prepared to subscribe to them, it seems, and Crispi won great support for his handling of the crisis. The *Times*' correspondent in Rome claimed in March 1894: 'If he wanted to make himself Dictator for life, this country would vote it readily in its present mood. Anarchism, revolution, chaos in government and out, has created a longing for stability which no-one knows where to look for except in him.'[9]

Against this backdrop Crispi and his Treasury Minister, Sidney Sonnino, were able to push through a series of major tax rises to stabilize the economy and plug the massive budget deficit of more than 150 million lire. German banks were also induced to help, and thanks to their intervention the value of Italian government stock rose steadily in 1894 and the banking sector began to be successfully reorganized. Other measures were taken to deal with the threat from the far left. Although claims of revolutionary conspiracies were exaggerated, political violence by anarchists and other extremists was a frightening everyday reality, with assassinations and assassination attempts common (Crispi sustained two – and carried a revolver) and bomb attacks frequent (a large device exploded outside Montecitorio in March 1894). Laws were passed tightening press censorship and giving prefects powers to ban associations or meetings that seemed subversive and arrest anyone 'who had shown the deliberate intention of committing acts of violence against the social order'.[10] And in a move intended to weaken the electoral base of the socialists the literacy test for voting was tightened up and the electoral registers (which were widely known to be fraudulently inflated) were revised and some 800,000 names struck off, mostly in the south.[11]

But opposition to Crispi in parliament began to mount. A radical bill to tackle the agricultural problems of Sicily by distributing land to the peasants was denounced by conservatives as 'socialist' and blocked; and with discontent increasing on the right of the Chamber, Crispi's enemies manoeuvred against him. Among them was the former prime minister, Giolitti, who had been made to fall on his sword in 1893 (with a strong push from Crispi) in order to deflect blame from the king over the Banca Romana scandal. He soon sought to turn the tables, and on 11 December 1894 he melodramatically walked down from his seat in Montecitorio and placed before the President of the Chamber a file of documents purporting to show that Crispi himself was implicated in the scandal (and that his wife was immoral: there were 102 stolen private letters from her to a male confidant). The far left, headed by the 'bard of democracy', Felice Cavallotti, clamoured for a debate. But Crispi promptly asked for parliament to be prorogued on the grounds that the Chamber was being sabotaged by 'a handful of rabble rousers' and that the prestige of the institutions needed to be protected.[12] The king happily signed the decree: he did not want Cavallotti and his republican colleagues probing and insinuating. Giolitti, meanwhile, was indicted on fourteen counts, including defamation, but fled to Germany before he could be arrested.

Outside the radical heartlands of Lombardy and the Romagna, the proroguing of parliament met with little surprise or opposition. The reputation of the Chamber had been sinking in the 1880s; by the early 1890s it had reached its nadir. 'Parliament is a real cesspit of baseness and immorality,' a distinguished historian, senator and former Education Minister, Pasquale Villari, admitted to a friend in September 1892, 'and if the head of state were to kick out the occupants of the filthy stable of Montecitorio tomorrow, the whole nation would applaud.'[13] There were calls from a number of authoritative figures for a return to the letter of the *Statuto*, with the executive answering to the king, not parliament; and Crispi even suggested abolishing the Chamber altogether and replacing it with the non-elective and purely consultative Senate. 'The parliamentary system is not suited to the Latin peoples,' he told the queen, echoing fashionable sociological views about the tendency of assemblies and crowds to accentuate the excessive individualism and emotionality of southerners.[14] And foreign observers were inclined to agree. The British ambassador in Rome felt the proroguing of parliament was 'thoroughly justified' given the 'scandalous scenes' taking place in the Chamber, while the *Times*' correspondent was so disgusted by the 'wrangles and intrigues . . . and want of all principles and patriotism in Italian politics' that he thought the only hope for the country was 'ten years of a dictatorship' under Crispi.[15]

Elections were held in May 1895. In a bid to weaken the far left Crispi had opened up secret channels of negotiation with the Vatican, and had even called on the 'civil and religious authorities' publicly in a speech to close ranks in the face of socialism and together fight the 'villainous sect' that was leading the masses astray.[16] He had also made a point of staging a magnificent church wedding for his daughter in January, with two cardinals present. But the Pope had refused to relax the ban on Catholics voting, at least formally, and the support of the Catholic hierarchy for liberal candidates was therefore negligible. Nor did the heavily pruned electoral lists generate the desired outcome. Though the government secured more than 300 seats, the radicals won some forty-five, only slightly less than before, while the socialists went up from five to fifteen.

And when parliament reopened in the summer of 1895, the far left was more confident than ever and the personal attacks on Crispi, led by Cavallotti, intensified. Barracking, shouting and suspended sessions were the order of the day.

THE BATTLE OF ADUA

Shortly before he died in 1901, despondent and growing blind, Crispi scribbled down his reflections on what had gone wrong with Italy on hundreds of small scraps of paper. In the absence of any memoirs he probably intended them as his intellectual legacy. Time and again in these jottings he returned to the theme of Italy's failure to produce a genuine national revolution of the kind that Britain had achieved in the seventeenth century, or France in 1789–1815 or Germany, much more succinctly, in 1870–71:

Italian unity was the result of a mere aggregation of seven states, and not of a revolution. Apart from the wars of 1859 and 1866, fought to drive out the enemy princes, there was no violence, no change. The people remained as they were prior to the constitution of the new kingdom, with their former practices and their faults, tenaciously holding on to their local traditions, with no fusion or mingling of races . . . without any hope of nationalizing those characteristics that act to keep the peoples of the peninsula divided.[17]

In the autumn and winter of 1895–6 he pressed, as he had in 1887–90, for something cataclysmic: a military victory to furnish the 'baptism of blood' he had longed for in 1866.

The Eastern question provided one opportunity. By the late summer of 1895 there were growing fears that Russia was about to seize Constantinople. Crispi wanted Britain and the Triple Alliance to make a stand, and began pressing for a joint naval operation in the Dardanelles. The Italian fleet was readied and emergency measures taken to defend the Alps against a possible French attack. On 15 November one of the navy commanders made an appeal to deputies in Montecitorio: 'Give the ministry your firm support. With Crispi in power we feel confident, and if war breaks out we will win. Avenge 1866.'[18] The following day Crispi instructed the fleet to seize Tripoli immediately if it came to hostilities and a scramble for the remaining pieces of the Ottoman Empire. But

Britain again contrived to dash Crispi's hopes, with Lord Salisbury saying that he would only breach the Dardanelles with a firm guarantee of French neutrality. Crispi became increasingly impatient and at one point summoned the Navy Minister and ordered him to send the Italian fleet to Trebizond. The minister said that this would instantly mean war with Turkey and probably Russia, too, and refused.[19]

As in 1889–90, Crispi had to be content with seeking in Africa the military success that eluded him in Europe. In the course of 1894 Italian forces had been pressing south and west from Eritrea, capturing the town of Kassala in July; and by the beginning of 1895 there was a possibility that the whole of the province of Tigré might be taken ('If only we could win! To turn this Italy, sunk in gossip, sordidness and partisan hatreds, towards an ideal of glory and power!' wrote the Prefect of Rome, Alessandro Guiccioli, in his diary. 'For that I would sacrifice many years of my life').[20] But Italy's growing ambitions in the region drove the local warlords into the arms of the emperor, Menelik, and by the end of 1895 Italy found itself facing an all-out campaign against a powerful and united African state with a huge army at its disposal – and one that was being supplied by the French, who were shipping in large consignments of weapons for Menelik through the port of Djibouti. The warning signs were clear in December when a column of 2,000 Italian and native troops was massacred by a force perhaps twenty times its size. But Crispi was now too committed to back down. The commander in Africa was General Oreste Baratieri, a former member of Garibaldi's Thousand, and Crispi wanted to have him replaced, as he was clearly not up to the task of heading large-scale operations. But the king intervened, and Baratieri stayed.[21]

Crispi craved a victory, and not just to save his government and help the beleaguered monarchy. As his newspaper, *La Riforma*, explained in January 1896 in a leading article entitled 'L'Italia nuova' ('New Italy'), Italians had to be educated, and shake off the pusillanimous behaviour of the past and become a strong, disciplined and united people. And there was no better way of achieving this than through war:

In the meantime we should register the great victory we have secured over ourselves . . . When we remember how Italy seemed yesterday and how it appears today, we cannot avoid repeating just once – and let it be only once – the hymn that was raised to war one day in the Reichstag by Marshal Moltke, like the priestly evocation of the cult of Odin in the depths of the forests of Germany. 'War,' said the marshal, 'has been instituted by God, and is a principle of order in the world. In it, and through it, the noblest human virtues are enhanced: courage, selflessness, devotion to duty, love of sacrifice. Without war, the world would slide into putrefaction and drown in materialism.' And look, indeed, at how many cubits the Italian people has grown by since the war in Africa began ... No, this people is no longer the starving eunuch, forced or condemned, as some would have liked, for ever to watch over the harems of French policy ... Rather, this is a people of mature political conduct, conscious of its rights and duties ... Oh, what good blood, good blood that does not lie, is Latin blood! And so it is that ... the primal and essential element of our race has triumphed ... and the new Italy has begun to be formed ... When the moment of truth, the supreme test, arrives ... we find ourselves ... a serious and mature people, a truly superior people ... May victory soon shine on the heroes of Africa ... But in the meantime let us note that, thanks to them, the old wish, too often made a mockery of since 1860, can now be said to have been fulfilled. With pride, we can now claim that not only Italy, but also Italians, have been made!![22]

Six weeks later, driven to the brink of nervous collapse by a ceaseless barrage of telegrams from Rome pressurizing him into action, Baratieri ordered his troops to advance towards Menelik's army. He had heard that a large part of the Ethiopian forces were away, foraging, but this turned out to be quite untrue, and his three columns of some 17,700 soldiers marched towards as many as 100,000 men. To make matters worse, his orders had been unclear, and the sketch map he had made of the terrain was incorrect. As a result one of the three columns got completely separated from the rest of the army and blundered into 30,000 Ethiopian troops deployed on higher ground. The Battle of Adua, on 1 March 1896, was the worst defeat ever inflicted on a colonial power in Africa. Around 5,000 Italians and 2,000 native auxiliaries were killed, including 289 officers. Many more were wounded. The dead and some of the prisoners were castrated. Casualties on the Ethiopian side were estimated at 12,000–14,000. Baratieri himself survived the engagement. With appropriate symbolism, he was unable to see very much of what happened as he had lost his pince-nez in the confusion. He had to be led from the field of battle on a horse.[23]

ASSASSINATION AT MONZA

Crispi resigned in the wake of this disaster, and the new government made peace with Menelik and scaled down Italy's military presence in Ethiopia. But the change of direction in foreign policy did not lead to greater stability at home. On the contrary, the humiliation of Adua, and the well-founded suspicion that the king had been in some measure to blame for it (he, like Crispi, had been desperate for a victory and had ill-advisedly protected Baratieri), gave the far left fresh ammunition; and as the socialists and radicals gained rapidly in strength in regions such as Lombardy and the Romagna, Italy's leaders resorted nervously to repression to try to stem the tide. The Socialist Party, reconstituted after its dissolution in 1894, faced severe persecution in 1897; and when early in May 1898 major rioting broke out in Milan, triggered by high food prices and the recent outpouring of popular grief following the death of Felice Cavallotti – killed fighting his thirty-first duel, caught in the carotid artery by his opponent's sword – the government responded brutally. The army was sent in and opened fire with artillery, and according to official estimates eighty people were killed and 450 wounded – though the real figures were probably more than twice these. Thousands of arrests were made; newspapers were closed down; and 'subversive' associations were dissolved. And as if to underscore the huge chasm that now, more than ever, divided political and real Italy, the king decorated the general commanding the troops in Milan for 'the great service . . . rendered to our institutions and to civilization, and to attest to my affection and the gratitude of myself and the country'.[24]

In the wake of the disorders the government tried to pass a series of bills to tighten up on public security and curtail the freedom to strike. But in parliament the far left embarked on a campaign of filibustering, delivering interminable speeches and raising countless points of order, and in the summer of 1899 the prime minister, a Piedmontese general, Luigi Pelloux, attempted to force some of the measures through by royal decree. This was blatantly unconstitutional. Unruly scenes erupted on the floor of the Chamber with the voting urns at one point being knocked to the ground. The following spring Pelloux looked to solve the impasse by introducing a 'guillotine' motion: this was passed but only after the radicals and socialists had walked out of parliament in protest. Pelloux now appealed to the country, and in the elections that followed the radicals, socialists and republicans together won nearly 100 seats, some thirty more than in the previous parliament. The message was clear: repression alone could not stop the forward march of the far left. But there was a further message, too: that by operating within the framework of parliament and the law, and seeking to block the unconstitutional behaviour of Pelloux, the far left could win support in the country.

On 29 July, some six weeks after the elections, King Umberto was attending a display by the 'Forti e liberi' ('Strong and free') gymnastics association in a stadium in Monza, north-east of Milan. In the crowd was a tall, smartly dressed, thirty-year-old man who had recently arrived back in Italy from the United States. Gaetano Bresci was a skilled textile worker who in 1895 had been deported to the penal island of Lampedusa after becoming involved with anarchist groups in his native Tuscany. Early in 1898 he had emigrated to the United States, where he had set up home with his young Irish wife in Paterson, New Jersey, a silk-manufacturing town with a large community of Italian émigrés, many of whom, like Bresci, were anarchists.[25] Bresci had been deeply shocked by the repression of the Sicilian *Fasci* and horrified when in 1898 the king had 'decorated the authors of the slaughter of May, instead of hanging them'.[26] The spirit of the Risorgimento, embodied by warriors of freedom such as Garibaldi – the inauguration of whose statue in Bologna he had attended shortly before travelling to Monza – had been betrayed. At 8.20 in the evening, after the presentation of prizes to the athletes, Umberto stepped into an open carriage, ready to return to the royal villa. He saw a friend in the crowd and stood up to wave. Bresci fired four shots. 'I don't think it is serious' were the king's last words.[27] Bresci was sentenced to life imprisonment, but according to official reports he hanged himself in his cell in May 1901. The files that could confirm that it was indeed suicide are missing.

18

Rival Religions: Socialism and Catholicism

The great error ... relates to the idea that class is naturally hostile to class, and that the working men and the wealthy are intended by nature to live in mutual conflict. So irrational and false is this view that the precise opposite is the truth ... Capital cannot do without labour, nor labour without capital ... [and] the Church, with Jesus Christ as her Master and Guide ... seeks to bind class to class in friendliness and good feeling ... God has not created us for the perishable and transitory things of this world, but for things heavenly and everlasting ...

Pope Leo XIII, *Rerum Novarum*, 1891

For us, ideas are not abstractions but physical forces. When the idea seeks to become reified in the world it does so through manifestations that are nervous, muscular and physical ... The idea of Christianity, the liberation of the Holy Sepulchre, expressed itself in the gigantic military expeditions of the Crusades and in a prolonged period of warfare. In the same way the socialist idea – in other words the new form of society based on a radical change in the current relationships of property – will be realized through violent and revolutionary manifestations.

Benito Mussolini, *La Lima*, 11 April 1908

SOCIALISM

Like Felice Cavallotti, the writer Gabriele D'Annunzio was an inveterate duellist. He admired Nietzsche, and self-consciously strove throughout his life to make himself the embodiment of an *Übermensch*: unconventional, unpredictable, combative, cruel, artistically prolific and sexually predatory. He had fought his first duel in September 1885, at the age of twenty-two, outside the railway station at Chieti, near his home town of Pescara in the Abruzzi, with a part-time local journalist who had referred to him teasingly in a newspaper article as 'the small Gargantua of Italian poetry'. Despite his reputation as a skilled swordsman, D'Annunzio had managed to get himself slashed on the head by his opponent's sabre, and the attendant surgeon had poured a bottle of iron perchlorate over the three-inch gash to staunch the flow of blood. D'Annunzio later alleged (implausibly) that this had been the reason for his premature baldness – a baldness of which he became fiercely proud, claiming that it was a sign of a higher stage of evolutionary development, as hair no longer served a useful function in modern civilization. When a French woman once asked him if his lack of hair troubled him, he replied: 'Madame, the beauty of the future shall be bald!'[1]

In the 1890s D'Annunzio enjoyed prodigious literary success, with a string of novels, poems and plays in which the themes of heroism, love, decadence and death were interwoven with a characteristic *fin de siècle* obsession with aestheticism and cruelty; and on the strength of his fame he stood for parliament in 1897 as the so-called 'candidate of beauty', delivering florid electoral speeches decrying the decadence of the new Italy, its failure to avenge the massacre of Adua, its inability to live up to the glorious legacy of ancient Rome, and the reduction of the heroic ideals of the Risorgimento through anti-intellectual materialism to a 'thick grey slime where an ignoble multitude tosses and turns and traffics as in its natural element'.[2] Quite what the provincial voters of the Abruzzi constituency of Ortona a Mare made of D'Annunzio's often obscure rhetorical flights is not clear, but newspaper reports spoke of large crowds and copies of his speeches being stuck on poles and carried in triumph through the streets to cries of 'Long live D'Annunzio! Long live the Abruzzi poet!'[3] He was elected, and took his seat on the far right in the spring of 1898, surviving attempts by his opponents to get his election quashed on the grounds that he was an adulterer. But he was not a conscientious deputy: indeed the only word he uttered in the Chamber in the next two years was *giuro* ('I swear'), when taking the parliamentary oath.[4]

On the evening of 23 March 1900, after one of the many stormy debates over General Pelloux's public order measures, D'Annunzio made a dramatic gesture. He walked into the Red Room in Montecitorio, where the radical and socialist deputies were gathered in an emergency meeting, and delivered a carefully prepared statement:

I convey my congratulations to the far left for the fervour and the tenacity with which they are defending their ideas. After the spectacle witnessed today, I know that on the one side there are many dead men who shout and on the other a few who are alive and eloquent. As a man of intellect I go towards life.[5]

Cynics maintained that D'Annunzio's 'conversion' was little more than a publicity stunt to help the flagging sales of his latest novel, *Il fuoco*. But there was no question that it was an enormous coup for the far left, a confirmation of their greatly enhanced status in recent years among Italian intellectuals in particular but also in the country as a whole. The statement was greeted with loud applause, and the socialist leaders Filippo Turati and Leonida Bissolati came forward and embraced D'Annunzio warmly.

Socialism, anarchism, radicalism and republicanism, in a variety of forms and with differing degrees of organization and militancy, had been growing in strength in the peninsula for several decades. During the 1870s it was anarchism that had made most of the running. The great Russian revolutionary Mikhail Bakunin had identified Italy as a potential powder-keg, with its millions of impoverished peasants and its deep-seated traditions of rural violence, and in the years immediately following unification he had built up a substantial following among a younger generation of intellectuals disenchanted with Mazzini's remorseless insistence on progress and redemption through God, national unity and class collaboration. Freedom for the masses, Bakunin had argued, in language often no less messianic than Mazzini's own, could only come with a social revolution that would sweep away the bourgeoisie and overthrow the oppressive state. Talk of the 'fatherland' and the 'nation' was sentimental moonshine:

Mazzini is frightened of civil war and the destruction of national unity . . . [He] claims that the 25 million people who form the Italian nation are 'brothers' with the same faith and common aspirations. Do I need to prove to you that this is a brazen or stupid lie? . . . 'Fatherland bequeathed by God! Holy historical mission! Cult of tombs! Solemn memories of martyrs . . . Ancient Rome! Papal Rome! . . . Dante! . . . Rome of the people!' It was all so nebulous, so beautiful, and at the same time so absurd, that it was enough to deceive and hoodwink young men whose minds were more inclined to enthusiasm and faith than to reason and argument . . . Today, dear friends, it is your duty to organize a campaign of intelligent, honest, caring and above all persistent propaganda . . . to explain [to the masses] the programme of the International . . . And if, in order to achieve this, you organize yourselves throughout Italy, and do it in harmony and fraternity . . . I swear to you that in the space of one year there will no longer be any Mazzinian and Garibaldian workers, but all will have become revolutionary socialists . . . You will thus have laid the indestructible foundations for the forthcoming social revolution, which will save Italy and restore to her the life, the intelligence and all the initiative she is entitled to as one of the most advanced and humane nations in Europe.[6]

Such language, not least because it echoed much of the redemptive idealism of the Risorgimento, had fallen on receptive soil, and anarchism had begun to spread swiftly in regions such as the Romagna and Campania, especially after the Paris Commune of 1871 and the Spanish revolution two years later had indicated the insurrectionary potential of the International. In 1874 a band of 150 anarchists had set out from the town of Imola, hoping to stir up a rising among the local peasantry (who had recently been involved in agricultural strikes and food riots) and capture the city of Bologna. But the police had stopped them with little difficulty.[7] In the spring of 1877 two of the most prominent young anarchists, Errico Malatesta – a diminutive former medical student from the province of Caserta – and Carlo Cafiero – a wealthy Apulian landowner, with a deeply mystical and religious turn of mind who was later to die incarcerated in a lunatic asylum agonizing about whether he was getting more than his fair share of sunlight through the window – had tried to lead a rising in the Matese mountains to the north of Naples. Twenty-six anarchists had gone to the small town of Letino, burned the tax records, proclaimed the social republic, and handed out a few old guns to the bemused peasants (though one local priest had apparently tried to help by explaining that socialism and the teachings of Christ were much the same thing). But nothing had happened, and the insurgents had quickly been rounded up by troops.[8]

The failure of the Matese rising and the governmental crack-down that followed had severely weakened anarchism, and during the 1880s and 1890s it was 'legalitarian' socialism that had flourished, with the emphasis not on immediate insurrection but on preparing the ground peaceably for a working-class revolution through education, organization, and economic, social and political reforms. In 1881 a charismatic former anarchist, Andrea Costa, had founded the Revolutionary Social-ist Party of Romagna to help spread 'socialist consciousness' in the region, and a year later he had become the first socialist deputy in parliament.[9] In 1885 an Italian Workers' Party had been launched in Lombardy to press for universal suffrage, the creation of trade unions and the right to strike. And in 1892, in an effort to pull together the various strands of the Italian labour movement, a congress of more than 200 delegates representing 324 left-wing associations had convened in Genoa (taking advantage of cheap rail fares that were being offered as part of the city's celebrations of the 400th anniversary of Columbus' discovery of America) and created a national Party of the Workers. Three years later this became the Italian Socialist Party.[10]

By the time D'Annunzio made his dramatic move 'towards light' in 1900, the Italian Socialist Party had grown into a powerful political force in the country. Its main strongholds were in the Po valley, where the protracted agricultural crisis of the 1880s and 1890s had resulted in worsening conditions for many rural workers as landowners cut back ruthlessly on their labour costs – but it also enjoyed significant support in the central share-cropping regions of Tuscany and Umbria and in parts of the south (Puglia and Sicily especially). It had its own daily newspaper, *Avanti!*, a string of party offices, run typically by a local teacher, lawyer or journalist, and a dense network of economic organiza-tions including cooperatives, mutual-aid societies and Chambers of Labour. Trade unionism developed swiftly from the turn of the century, and by 1902 there were nearly a quarter of a million industrial workers enrolled in socialist-affiliated craft federations. In 1906 these unions and the Chambers of Labour came together to form the General Confeder-ation of Labour (CGL). The party also advanced rapidly in the polls in the first decade of the century: in the general election of 1900 it gained 216,000 votes and thirty-two deputies; by 1913 the tally had gone up to seventy-nine deputies and nearly a quarter of all votes cast.[11]

The spread of socialism was partly due to economic developments. Between 1896 and 1908 Italy enjoyed its first period of substantial growth since unification. A number of factors combined to produce this boom: the end of the world agricultural depression and the consequent upturn in prices and demand; protectionism and state support for sectors such as steel and shipping; the overhaul of the financial sector and the introduction of 'mixed' banks, with German and Austrian capital, specializing in entrepreneurial investment; the creation of hydro-electric plants in the Alps and the provision of plentiful supplies of energy (so helping compensate Italy for its relative disadvantage in coal); and the huge sums that were being sent back as remittances from overseas – the United States especially – by the hundreds of thousands who emigrated in these years, mostly from the south. Between 1896 and 1908 the value of industrial output in the country almost doubled, with especially strong levels of growth in such 'newer' areas as engineering, rubber, chemicals and metal-making: production of steel, for instance, rose from 140,000 tonnes in 1900 to 930,000 tonnes in 1913. However, textiles (silk in particular: Italy accounted for about a third of the world's silk market still on the eve of the First World War) remained the bedrock of Italian manufacturing, with one quarter of all the jobs in industry in 1911 in this sector.[12]

One striking indication of Italy's sudden flirtation with economic modernity was the emergence of the automobile industry. The combination of Piedmontese and Lombard engineering traditions with the establishment of electrical, steel and rubber manufacturing (Pirelli had founded his cable and tyre firm in Milan in 1872) led to a surge in car production from the turn of the century. After a period experimenting with motorized tricycles, a young Piedmontese cavalry officer called Giovanni Agnelli helped in 1899 to set up the Fabbrica Italiana Automobili Torino (FIAT); and his example was followed by a host of other entrepreneurs, who established such well-known companies as Isotta Fraschini (Milan, 1904), Lancia (Turin, 1906) and ALFA (Milan, 1906). By 1907 there were sixty-one companies, turning out 18,000 vehicles a year; and though recession forced many of these to close soon afterwards, there were still six major car producers in Turin alone in 1911, employing more than 6,000 workers. By 1914 FIAT was the clear market leader, accounting for about half of Italy's vehicles. But the Italian domestic market remained weak and would not support the dramatic levels of output – half a million cars – that the USA achieved at this time. It was only after the Second World War that FIAT could begin to contemplate mass production.[13]

The economic developments of these years – the growth of industry and the enormous surge in transatlantic migration in particular – had a marked effect on popular aspirations. After centuries of eking out a precarious existence in small rural settlements, beholden to local land-owners and priests, and constrained by geography and climate, millions of peasants could suddenly glimpse the hope of change. Many moved into the cities – net annual immigration into Milan stood at around 14,000 in these years and its population nearly doubled between 1880 and 1914 to 600,000 – and the encounter with a modern industrial environment was often quite exhilarating. The young Benito Mussolini was deeply struck by the iron railway bridge that spanned the River Lamone when he arrived in the town of Faenza in the 1890s from his native village of Predappio (understandably, perhaps, given that his father was the local blacksmith);[14] and when in 1902 the Neapolitan socialist Arturo Labriola moved to the Lombard capital, he was thrilled by the city's economic dynamism. 'For me, coming from an area of old-fashioned artisan production ... that class of industrial entrepreneurs, especially in Milan, with its business sense and audacity, was hugely attractive.'[15]

Overseas emigration, whether seasonal or permanent, had long been a notable feature of Italian economic life, but the combination of agricultural recession, cheap fares on steamships and relatively well-paid work on South American farms or North American construction sites led to a rapid rise in the volume of emigration from the end of the nineteenth century. Prior to the 1880s most emigrants had been small farmers or artisans from the northern regions crossing the Alps or sailing to Argentina or Brazil; thereafter it was southerners who made up the backbone of the emigrants, young men, usually rural labourers, fired by the possibility of earning as much in a few weeks in *La Merica* as they could back home in a year. Between 1900 and 1915 more than 8 million Italians went overseas, nearly half of them from the southern regions. Most set off with the intention of staying for a few years and then returning to their native village, paying off their debts, and buying a plot of land; but many ended up settling permanently in the United States. Sadly the dreams of most of those who came back remained unfulfilled, as the few hectares of soil that they managed to acquire with their savings often turned out to be little more than a barren handful of dust.[16]

Nevertheless the industrial boom and mass emigration of the early years of the century did much to erode the secular fatalism of the poor, and this, far more than any structural changes in the economy, encouraged support for socialism as the movement for working-class advancement. One sign of growing expectations at this time was an increase in school attendance, as it became clear that education was a valuable instrument for upward mobility and not just a hallmark of membership of a state that was still widely seen as redundant or hostile. In Sicily primary school attendance went up from 54.5 per cent in 1901–2 to 73.5 per cent five years later; and the decline in illiteracy levels (more than 10 per cent nationally between 1901 and 1911) was especially pronounced in areas of high migration, such as the Abruzzi, Basilicata and Sicily.[17] Literacy was very useful for securing work in big cities or getting through the immigration controls on Ellis Island; it facilitated dealings with banks or post offices when remittances were sent home for deposit in savings accounts; and it opened up channels of communication – writing letters to relatives or talking with Italians from other regions. And beyond this there were possibilities for the most talented of landing jobs in the civil service or within the ranks of the Socialist Party and its affiliated organs – for the Italian Socialist Party was first and foremost a party for intellectuals.

The widespread sense of despondency among intellectuals at the character of the Italian state – the persistent gap between the masses and the institutions, the pervasive corruption and materialism of the ruling classes, the shortcomings of parliament, the high levels of poverty and crime, especially in the south, and the inability of Italy to assert itself as a major power on the international stage – left many of those who had been inspired by the patriotic idealism of the Risorgimento searching, often somewhat desperately, for a new faith. While some, like the poet Carducci or the talented novelist Carlo Dossi, turned to the monarchy or to Francesco Crispi for inspiration, it was to socialism that virtually all the best minds in the 1890s were drawn. A survey of 105 writers, 63 academics and 26 artists in 1895 found that 110 supported socialism 'without reserve' and a further 41 'with reservations', and among them were such distinguished figures as the criminologists Cesare Lombroso and Enrico Ferri, the historians Gaetano Salvemini and Ettore Ciccotti, the writer Edmondo De Amicis, and the artist Giuseppe Pellizza da Volpedo, whose monumental canvases of serried crowds of rural workers, women as well as men, advancing confidently out of the darkness into the bright sunlight, with a dream-like calm, provided powerful visual icons for the new faith (not least thanks to their deliberate echoes of such traditional Christian iconography as the Holy Family, the Annunciation, and the Virgin and Child).[18]

The transition from frustrated Risorgimento idealism to socialism is well illustrated by the man who was to dominate the moderate or 'reformist' wing of the Italian Socialist Party down to the First World War, Filippo Turati. Turati was born in 1857, the son of a Lombard prefect and a deeply Catholic mother, but like many well-educated young men of his background he rejected the Church and gravitated towards the democratic currents of Mazzinianism and republicanism that were still powerful in parts of northern Italy in the 1870s. As a student at Bologna university he came under the spell of Carducci, who was teaching literature there: Turati later recalled how the passion and intensity of Carducci's verse and thought 'tore at [him] internally' and gave him and many of his fellow students (among them another future socialist leader, Leonida Bissolati) a sense of 'renaissance'. For some time Turati wrote and published poetry, and contemplated a literary career; but his graduation in 1877 coincided with the onset of a debilitating spiritual crisis – a crisis that was deepened the following year by Carducci's apostasy and conversion to the cause of the monarchy:

All my hopes, my goals, my ambitions, my noble dreams, all the happiness of my youth, everything came to an end, disappeared and dissolved into an abyss of the darkest misery, like a mirage melting; and I felt I was stumbling around in a night of the most unspeakable, agonizing neurosis. I was constantly exhausted, as if I had come back from an orgy . . . and acquired the reputation of being one of the biggest loafers in this wastrel country of ours, dosing myself with opium, bromides and chlorites to dull the pain . . .[19]

His distraught parents toured Europe with him for several years, no expense spared, searching for a cure. But their travels, certainly around Italy, did little to lift him out of his dejection: Turin seemed spiritually dead and cravenly 'on its knees before the monuments of the House of Savoy', while Rome left him feeling totally 'annihilated'. Only Genoa, with its 'chiaroscuro' architecture and unexpected vistas, enchanted him; and there was the bonus of a visit to the Staglieno cemetery and the tomb of Mazzini, where he 'tossed [his] visiting card through the gate like an infatuated disciple, and meditated on Foscolo's On Tombs like a student of rhetoric'. Among the many doctors he visited were Cesare

Lombroso, who administered electro-therapy, and the eminent Viennese psychiatrist Max Leidesdorf. In the summer of 1882 he went to Paris to consult the great neurologist Jean-Martin Charcot – who diagnosed 'cephalic and spinal neurasthenia' and told him that his only hope of recovery lay in complete abstinence from work. And it was while in the French capital that he learned of the death of Garibaldi: the news, he said, 'made me weep: I had not wept in years'. But in the end the solution to his illness came not from the medical profession, but rather from his growing absorption in Italy's social question and his conviction, which hit him with almost Damascene intensity, that the nation's moral problems could only be solved by radically transforming the material base of society. He also found therapeutic relief in climbing mountains (like another tortured late-nineteenth-century idealist, Nietzsche), and the Alps remained a lifelong passion.[20]

For Turati, as for many other intellectuals who got caught up in the ferment of progressive ideas in the 1880s and 1890s, socialism provided not just a new faith but also an agenda for action; for however much they wanted to believe that history was moving irresistibly towards the triumph of the proletariat as a consequence of the iron laws of dialectical materialism, the fact was the class war stood a much better chance of succeeding if the masses knew what they were supposed to do. Hence the vital importance of education and propaganda; and this was felt to be all the more necessary given that most Italian workers, certainly in the countryside, were, as Turati wrote in 1895, still profoundly ignorant and stuck in a medieval world of 'putrefied barbarism' and oblivious to the 'first signs of the modern age, the industrial phase, that is dawning in the most civilized and advanced regions, especially of the north'.[21] The leaders of socialism should turn themselves into 'new beings, a new and superior race', mingle with the masses, 'animate them, incite them and help them clarify their ideas'.[22] In this way, as the influential theorist of elite politics Vilfredo Pareto informed Turati, 'those creatures that are at present simply molluscs' would become 'men'.[23]

Buoyed up by missionary zeal, the socialist elites set about mobilizing the masses. Unlike their liberal counterparts they had few qualms about mixing with the poor – which is one reason why the new movement felt so threatening to the established order. A distinguished professor of ancient history, Ettore Ciccotti, was more criticized by his conservative colleagues for his habit of going to smoke-filled bars in Milan in the

evenings to address workers than for his subversive beliefs per se.[24]
Socialist activists staged public meetings, debates, conferences and lectures wherever they could: in clubs, halls, cafés and Chambers of Labour,
or out in the open air. They wrote pamphlets and contributed articles
to the countless local socialist newspapers that sprang up across northern
and central Italy from the 1890s; and in areas of high illiteracy these
could be read out to public gatherings. They encouraged school attendance – not least because a high proportion of primary school teachers
were socialists – and promoted 'popular libraries' to make books accessible to workers (a particular interest of Turati); though whether much
'socialist' literature was read is unclear: a survey of working-class readers
in Milan in 1905 found that Jules Verne was the most borrowed author,
followed by Zola and De Amicis. Karl Marx hardly figured.[25]

The crusading spirit that animated Turati and so many of his fellow
socialists helped impart a religious note to many of the educational and
propaganda initiatives. But as with Mazzini and the democrats more
than half a century before, there was also a strong measure of deliberate
political calculation, for the masses were widely seen as possessing
what Turati called a 'crude and semi-pagan religious idealism' that
predisposed them, he felt, to a 'higher social ideal'.[26] The influential
German-born socialist Roberto Michels referred more bluntly to their
'infantile psychology' and readiness to 'genuflect at the feet of mortal
divinities'.[27] (Michels was later to convert to fascism.) Accordingly
socialism needed to present itself, both in form and in substance, as a
parallel faith. 'When the people emerge from church, after the blessing,
stand on the steps outside or on a table in an adjacent inn and begin
your *sermon*' was the advice given by a senior party figure to activists
in 1893 for Sunday propaganda in small towns and villages.[28] And the
language and tone of the new preachers resembled, according to Michels,
the 'primitive era of Christianity':

Without doubt one of the most striking features of Italian socialism, ... which
distinguished it from socialism in every other country, was the extraordinary
abundance of *moral* precepts and demands that were circulated in thousands of
booklets and pamphlets written for the socialist propaganda of the masses. The
propagandists ... were moralizers, prophets, apostles, purifiers ... They railed
against the vices that infested the countryside, denouncing the murders, the
killings, the infanticides, the proneness to violence and the habit of drunkenness.[29]

The presentation of socialism as a new church struck a chord with many rural communities, and middle-class activists often found themselves feted as if they were saints ('angels descended from heaven' was how one peasant described the leaders of the Sicilian *Fasci*).[30] But there was a price to be paid for this popular fervour in the form of eclecticism and ideological inconsistency. The peasants in the Mantua countryside marched in the 1880s behind a tricolour flag with images of the poet Virgil (who had been born in the area), Cincinnatus and Garibaldi holding a hoe and a lamb,[31] while in western Sicily, where the socialists gained an enormous following in the early 1890s thanks in no small measure to their imaginative use of entertainments such as 'socialist' puppet shows and comedies, dances and family parties, and the introduction of Christmas trees, pictures of Karl Marx regularly appeared alongside those of the Virgin Mary and King Umberto.[32] Umberto, indeed, seems to have been quite popular, even in areas with strong republican traditions such as the Romagna, as a consequence, perhaps, of his charitable works and his carefully nurtured image as 'the good king'. The events of May 1898 may have tarnished this image but they did not destroy it. The provincial revolutionary socialist Alessandro Mussolini, father of Benito, publicly announced to the town council of Predappio his regret at the king's assassination in 1900, declaring that Umberto was at heart a 'gentleman'.[33]

For Turati and other socialist intellectuals the rapid spread of socialism among the peasantry was gratifying but also perplexing, for according to 'scientific' Marxism a revolution was only supposed to take place following the breakdown of capitalism in its most advanced phase. Yet as an elegant and highly strung Russian émigrée, Anna Kuliscioff, Turati's partner, told Frederick Engels in a famous letter of 1894, Italy was still 'two-thirds medieval' and its rural population both morally and materially impoverished, and until the country had gone through a prolonged phase of modernization there could be no serious talk of revolution. This consideration, together with the onset of rapid industrial growth at the end of the century, led Turati and his colleagues in parliament to announce that the Italian Socialist Party should defer the revolution and instead pursue a 'minimal' programme of economic, political and administrative reforms designed to 'organize and educate the proletariat . . . and prepare them for the assumption and successful running of the collectivized society'.[34] Or as Turati put it in more homely terms, they should seek to fatten up the bourgeoisie like a Christmas turkey, in order to have more to enjoy when the time arrived to cook it.[35]

What made 'minimalism' or 'reformism' seem practicable was a leftward shift in parliamentary liberalism after the reactionary crisis of 1898–1900 and the return to prominence (after having narrowly escaped imprisonment during the Banca Romana scandal) of Giovanni Giolitti, the man who was to dominate Italian politics until the First World War. Giolitti came from Piedmont, and like Cavour, Quintino Sella and other leading Piedmontese politicians he combined a pragmatic cast of mind with an Enlightenment faith in progress through material advancement. He had little sympathy with the idealism that had inspired so much of the Risorgimento and scant interest in metaphysics or the arts: there was an audible gasp of surprise on one occasion when he quoted Dante in a speech in the Chamber.[36] He tended to see discontent as rooted in frustrated self-interest and accordingly believed that most opponents had their price and could be transformed eventually into allies. This often smacked of cynicism: when asked why he condoned electoral corruption so readily, he replied that a tailor does not attempt to dress a deformed man in normal clothes. He displayed little liking for the south and visited it just once in the course of his long life.

Giolitti became Minister of the Interior in 1901 and prime minister two years later, and from the outset he made it clear that he was willing to do business with the socialists. If Turati and his colleagues wanted 'a great country that was genuinely and capitalistically modern' with a proper bourgeoisie and proletariat, he would help them;[37] but not to hasten the advent of a socialist revolution but rather to draw the masses within the framework of the state and thereby create a morally unified nation:

The Italian people does not have revolutionary tendencies; the Italian people has a long tradition of trusting in the Government; and perhaps no other people has suffered such appalling ills for so many centuries and with such fortitude as the Italian people. Were the Government and the ruling classes to furnish a period of serious social justice this would ensure that the population turned with love again to our institutions . . . We are at the beginning of a new era of history. Anyone who is not blind can see this . . . It is largely up to us, to the behaviour of the constitutional parties in their dealings with the working classes, to ensure that the advent of these classes provides a new conservative force, a new source of prosperity and greatness, and not a whirlwind that destroys the fortunes of the fatherland![38]

Under Giolitti's guidance, and with the support in parliament of the reformist socialists, a broad raft of progressive legislation was introduced in the early years of the century that laid the foundations of an Italian welfare state. There were laws to make a weekly rest-day compulsory, prohibit child labour, limit the length of the working day for women (to eleven hours), and institute sickness, old-age and maternity funds (ten lire per child paid by the state, with an additional thirty lire coming from employers' and workers' contributions). Spending on public works schemes rose sharply – by 50 per cent between 1900 and 1907 – with particularly large sums earmarked for the south: special development packages for the city of Naples and for the regions of Basilicata and Calabria (to provide roads, irrigation schemes, drinking water and reafforestation), subsidies to build aqueducts and railways, tax concessions and agricultural credit funds, and relief for Messina and Calabria after the earthquake of 1908.

But the biggest concession to the Socialist Party and the socialist-led unions of industrial and agricultural workers in northern and central Italy was a policy of strict governmental neutrality in labour disputes. As far as Giolitti was concerned this was a matter of economic growth as well as of social justice, for he claimed that the free operation of the laws of supply and demand afforded the best possible stimulus to production, as shown by the fact that 'the countries with the highest wages [were] at the forefront of industrial progress'.[39] The new laissez-faire attitude unleashed a tidal wave of strikes at the start of the century – on average nearly a thousand a year between 1901 and 1905, involving more than 250,000 industrial and agricultural workers, compared to just 200 and 40,000 workers in the 1890s. In 1906–10 the figures were higher still: over 1,500 strikes and nearly 350,000 workers.[40] Many of the strikes were successful and between 1901 and 1911 wages in industry and agriculture went up in real terms by about 2.5 per cent per annum, thereby allowing workers to enjoy some improvement in living standards: average daily calorie consumption, which had dropped to just 2,119 during the crisis years of the 1890s, increased in 1900–10 to 2,617.[41] But given the extremely low baseline from which such gains were made, most Italians would still not have experienced any dramatic change in their material circumstances, and certainly not enough to incline them to turn 'with love' to the institutions.

CATHOLICISM

If Giolitti hoped to defuse the challenge of socialism through liberal reforms and larger pay packets – and virtually every influential voice in Italy was soon decrying his pragmatism, his materialism and his failure to offer powerful inspirational ideals – the Church harboured no such illusions. Ever since the Counter-Reformation, when the papacy had dispatched cohorts of Jesuit missionaries into the remote interior regions of the peninsula to bring isolated pagan communities into the Christian fold, the Vatican had looked on the Italian peasantry as the bedrock of its support. The sight of socialist zealots preaching godlessness and staging secular weddings and baptisms ('I dedicate you, my child, to suffering humanity. You will be a struggler for the redemption of this class to which you belong by birth . . .')[42] was profoundly threatening, and priests such as Don Andrea Sterza responded militantly, appealing 'in the bowels of Christ' to his fellow clergy 'to raise their voices like trumpets against the most vicious of enemies, socialism, that is raging like a murderous hurricane . . . through the people of the countryside, meting out horrendous slaughter, people who were once so religious that a single word uttered by a priest was gospel!'[43]

The advent of liberalism and the loss of temporal power in the 1860s had been bad enough, and the Church had responded with characteristic vigour, issuing the Syllabus of Errors, promulgating the dogma of infallibility, trumpeting apparitions of the Virgin and other Marian miracles, and launching the movement of the Opera dei Congressi to 'unite and reorganize Catholics and Catholic associations from all of Italy in a common and coordinated action to defend . . . the sacrosanct rights of the Church and of the papacy and the religious and social interests of the Italians, in conformity with the desires and directives of the Holy Father and under the guidance of the episcopate and the clergy'.[44] It had also capitalized on its long-standing skills in choreography and spectacle, staging huge pilgrimages to Rome – such as for the Holy Year of 1875 or two years later for the fiftieth anniversary of Pius IX's consecration as a bishop, when massive crowds had flocked to celebratory services in St Peter's (deliberately scheduled to coincide with – and upstage – the national Festival of the Statuto) and filed through the Vatican, marvelling at the vast array of jewel-studded mitres, copes, chasubles, chalices, crosses, crosiers and monstrances that had been sent to the Holy Father as presents (most of which were distributed subsequently to churches and monasteries across the country, though the precious chalice sent by the king's younger son, the Duke of Aosta, was retained for the Sistine Chapel – in part as a trophy).[45]

As socialism began to spread, the Church stepped up its mobilizing efforts, using its network of parishes and dioceses and the organizational skills of the many devout members of the middle classes and the aristocracy who had remained hostile or indifferent to liberalism to establish a string of Catholic associations, circles, cooperatives, banks, newspapers and periodicals (principally in the north). These were monitored centrally by the permanent committee of the Opera dei Congressi, whose activities increased rapidly in the 1890s under the presidency of Giovanni Battista Paganelli, a vigorous Venetian with no sympathy for the liberal state ('In His Holiness we recognize not only the Pope but also the Father and supreme *Duce* [leader] of the Italians: the only man who can save them. To him we entrust the affairs of the Church and the fatherland').[46] By 1897 the Opera controlled 3,982 parish committees, 708 youth sections, 17 university circles, 588 rural cooperative banks, 688 workers' societies, 24 daily newspapers and 155 journals. And like the socialists, the Church aimed to use these instruments to penetrate civil society and build up grass roots support.

With socialism the principal enemy, the issue of the restoration of the Pope's temporal power, which had dominated Church–state relations since 1860, slipped quietly down the agenda, and during the 1890s a number of conciliatory gestures were made towards the Italian government. In 1896, for example, Cardinal Ferrari agreed to participate at the inauguration of a monument to Victor Emmanuel in Piazza Duomo in Milan.[47] And such gestures increased after the turn of the century, with Giolitti's tacit encouragement, and Catholics were even discreetly encouraged by the Opera dei Congressi to vote in national elections for a government candidate if that meant keeping a socialist out. But this easing of tensions was based on mutual convenience, not liking. There was still too much suspicion and bad blood around: only a few years before, Crispi had bullied and humiliated Pope Leo to the point where he had felt obliged to announce to the world that he no longer felt safe in Rome. Furthermore, as the Vatican's famous encyclical on the social question, *Rerum Novarum* (1891), made clear, Catholicism's core values of cooperation, inter-class solidarity, paternalism and charity were heavily at odds with those of liberal individualism.

In order to propagate its values, the Church had a powerful set of tools at its disposal to complement the traditional weapons of the sermon and the confessional. In regions such as the Veneto and Lombardy a huge amount of Catholic printed material of all sorts circulated in the countryside: diocesan and parish magazines, popular newspapers containing a mixture of Church news, parables, papal allocutions, serialized novels and rural sketches, bulletins from Catholic associations, and newsletters from religious orders and sanctuaries (the *Messaggero di Sant' Antonio* – Padua – begun in 1898, proved particularly successful: a century later it had global sales of over 1.5 million).[48] Catholic publishing houses were set up, among them the Tipografia dell'Immacolata Concezione in Modena and the San Bernardino in Siena, to distribute religious manuals, lives of saints and 'Catholic' novels – a growing genre, with such titles as *The Blasphemer's Family* (1904) by Father Giovanni Battista Francesia, intended as a corrective to the supposed immorality of realist literature, with its sympathetic depictions of murderers, prostitutes, thieves and drunks.[49]

The printed word could only have limited impact in a society where illiteracy was widespread, and accordingly the Church, even more than the socialists – who, as a party led by intellectuals, were particularly attached to 'high' culture – happily turned to other media in order to get its message across. Popular theatre was an especially important tool of propaganda in northern Italy in the late nineteenth and early twentieth centuries, with plays that highlighted Catholic family values and denounced the evils of liberalism, Freemasonry and increasingly socialism, with its attendant vices of sexual immorality, blasphemy and alcoholism.[50] One publishing house in Vicenza listed 5,000 'comedies, dramas, tragedies, farces, sketches and monologues' for use in 'Catholic seminaries, colleges, institutes, recreational circles and clubs' in its 1916 catalogue.[51] Sport, too, was widely promoted, with gymnastics particularly favoured for its capacity to foster discipline and self-control (football, by contrast, was apparently seen as too 'Protestant' in its encouragement of individual self-expression). The Catholic sporting federation FASCI (the fortuitous acronym of the Federazione delle Associazioni Sportive Cattoliche Italiane) claimed 204 affiliated societies by 1910.[52] Cinema was also used in the years immediately prior to the First World War, with the Oratory Fathers establishing a Cinemato-graphic Federation in Milan in 1909 and the Catholic production company Unitas turning out over thirty films in 1909–11 – for the most part documentaries about Jesus, the lives of saints and exemplary priests ('A true friend of the people'), or morality tales: 'How many bottles have you drunk?', 'Delirium tremens', 'The consequences of fashion', 'The bread thief'.[53]

Quite what impact these initiatives had is hard to know. In many cases they may have done little more than confirm the faithful in their devotion (and enmity) and sceptics in their indifference or anti-clericalism. However, the socialists often claimed that their propaganda was proving highly effective in eroding religious sentiment among the peasants of northern Italy, pointing to increased rates of 'suicide, sexual freedom and conversions to Protestantism' and falling levels of crime and drunkenness as evidence of a new – and higher – secular morality.[54] And official figures certainly suggested a rapid drop in belief in these years, with 874,000 Italians declaring they had 'no religion' in the 1911 census compared to just 36,000 ten years earlier. But the decline may have been due more to the unimaginative responses of the local clergy to the challenge of socialism than to a serious cultural shift – as in the village of Busati near Lucca, where the marble quarry workers were told by a Capuchin friar that if they joined a trade union they would no longer be allowed to receive the Eucharist. Not surprisingly, as the parish priest recorded sadly in his diary, 'only a few men' attended Easter communion in 1910, whereas in 1900 all had done so.[55]

It was in a bid to ensure greater centralized control over the fight against socialism that in 1905 Pope Pius X abolished the Opera dei Congressi and reorganized it as three 'unions' – dealing with propaganda, socio-economic affairs and elections – under the umbrella heading of Catholic Action. Part of the Vatican's concern was to curb what it saw as a dangerous slide among sections of the laity and clergy towards over-zealous engagement in social and political questions and heterodox 'modernism' – to the point, in certain cases, as with the energetic Romagna priest Romolo Murri (excommunicated in 1909), where Catholics could appear as radical as their socialist opponents. Pius also wanted to contain the pressure that was building from below for conciliation with the Italian state: he was a staunch traditionalist, an advocate of doctrinal purity, a lover of Thomas Aquinas, Gregorian chant and the cult of the Virgin Mary, and no sympathizer with liberalism. Catholic Action was placed under the immediate control of the bishops and thus of the Vatican, and although this led to greater cohesion and discipline at a grass roots level, it also tended to stifle much of the reforming enthusiasm that had inspired the progressive middle-class laity since the 1890s.

Giolitti was reluctant to make any formal public overtures to the Vatican. Indeed he described Church and state in 1904 as being like 'two parallel lines that should never meet'. If the Church wished to encourage Catholics to vote tactically in national elections in order to keep socialist candidates out, as it did in 1904, 1909 and (most conspicuously) in 1913, so be it. But he could not afford to give the *rapprochement* official sanction. His first priority was to bring the working classes safely inside the framework of the state, and any indication that he was willing to do deals with the conservative Catholics was likely to imperil his alliance with Turati and the reformist socialists and strengthen the hand of the revolutionaries. And, as he explained in his memoirs, depriving the revolutionaries of moral ammunition was absolutely crucial:

The elevation of the Fourth Estate to a higher level of civilization was the most pressing problem for us now . . . The exclusion of the working classes from both the political and administrative life of the country . . . necessarily has the effect of laying them open to the influence of the revolutionary parties and subversive ideas, for the apostles of these ideas have a formidable argument at their disposal when they see that the masses, on account of this exclusion, have no other means of defending themselves against the possible injustices of the ruling classes, whether particular or general, than with violence.[56]

Giolitti's strategy was on the face of it eminently rational, but it faced two huge and interrelated obstacles. The first was that the socialist movement contained a powerful revolutionary or 'maximalist' wing, which from the outset bitterly opposed Turati's reformism, fearing that a strategy of collaboration with the bourgeois state would corrupt the party leadership, domesticate the working classes and destroy any prospect of a proletarian victory. And while Turati believed that the masses were too prone to anarchic violence and required educating to restraint and maturity, the maximalists shared the view of many nineteenth-century Risorgimento democrats that Italians had been rendered overly passive by centuries of despotism and needed galvanizing through direct action and inspirational ideals. It is no coincidence that the distinguished French theorist of violence Georges Sorel enjoyed a larger following in Italy than in any other European country (his seminal *Reflections on Violence* appeared first in Italy in 1905–6), or that his views on the mobilizing power of myth strongly influenced the Italian revolutionary syndicalist movement (and through it, fascism).

The second obstacle confronting Giolitti was the immense aura of moral opprobrium that surrounded the liberal state, an opprobrium that allowed the puritanically minded maximalists to claim that their reformist colleagues were utterly misguided in believing that any good could come from an alliance with a degenerate political system – 'that Byzantium', as the young revolutionary Benito Mussolini called it, echoing Carducci, with its 'comedy of a parliament', dominated by a man who had 'the impoverished soul of a bureaucrat' and was lacking in all idealism and ethical substance, the 'worthy prime minister of what the English call ... the *carnival nation*'.[57] And the fact that this damning view was shared by nearly all of the most influential intellectuals of the day – among them the writers D'Annunzio, Pirandello, Corradini, Marinetti, Pascoli, Papini and Prezzolini, the sociologists Pareto, Mosca and Sighele, the philosophers Croce and Gentile, the artists Boccioni and Carrà, and the historians Volpe and Salvemini (who dubbed Giolitti 'The minister of the criminal underworld' in a damning exposé of electoral corruption published in 1910)[58] – reduced still further the chances of the reformists being able to convince the majority of their party that cooperating with the government was either politically expedient or correct.

As a result, and despite all the concessions and reforms, Giolitti's hopes of drawing the sting of subversion from the working-class movement proved illusory, and the revolutionary 'maximalists' remained a powerful and extremely vocal force within the Socialist Party, berating the reformists constantly for their tractability and seizing on inconsistencies in government policy to bolster their calls for intransigence. In particular they pointed to the fact that, notwithstanding the state's official policy of neutrality in labour disputes, workers continued to be killed and wounded in clashes with the police – some 200 between 1900 and 1904; and although this was not strictly the government's fault – strikes had a tradition of turning violent, especially in the south – the frequency of the 'proletarian massacres', as they were emotively styled, gave the extremists powerful moral ammunition. In September 1904, following a string of such 'massacres', they organized Italy's first general strike; and that same year they managed to win a majority at the party's national congress. The reformists regained the initiative at the 1908 congress, but lost it again, this time definitively, in 1912.

The ideological cleavage created in the socialist movement as a result of the reformists' alliance with Giolitti opened, as Michels ruefully recalled, 'a Pandora's box', and led to a state of protracted civil war, with individuals, factions, currents and tendencies vying with one another bitterly for supremacy: maximalists, minimalists, syndicalists, integralists, centrists, revolutionary intransigents, orthodox Marxists.[59] No quarter was given: in 1895 the party had voted piously to ban duelling among its members; but in the years that followed this ban was time and again ignored as leading socialists regularly resorted to sabres to resolve their differences. Passion and, with passion, violence became hallmarks of revolutionary faith, signs of being untainted by the abhorred sins of scepticism and materialism that had long been regarded as Italian vices, and which the 'arch corrupter' Giolitti seemed to embody so fully.[60] Thought and action needed to be demonstrably one. And in this tense climate a dangerous intellectual relativism began to emerge, a sense that ideas were to be judged more for their capacity to inspire to action than for their intrinsic merit. 'Life', as D'Annunzio had implied when embracing socialism, was about intensity not truth.

The allure of the ideal was evident in the early career of a man who was to become a dominant figure in revolutionary socialism on the eve of the First World War, Benito Mussolini. Born in 1883, in the small town of Predappio in the Romagna, the son of a self-educated blacksmith and a primary school teacher, he grew up in an environment where the poverty of the agricultural workers who made up the great majority of the local population was mitigated by ardent Catholicism, fervent socialism, alcohol and sex: adultery and *crimes passionnels* were common, and in later life Mussolini proudly recalled his youthful affairs with married women as well as his regular trips as a teenager to brothels (and one incident when he raped a girl).[61] Mussolini's mother was deeply religious, and some of the future dictator's earliest memories were of attending church services along with the rest of the community – but not his father: as a leading local socialist he made a point of staying away – and being excited (to the point of fainting) by the heady mixture of candlelight, incense, colours, music and singing.[62]

Mussolini was baptized, at his mother Rosa's insistence, but it was his father, Alessandro, who chose the names: Benito, in honour of the famous revolutionary and president of Mexico, Benito Juarez, Amilcare, after the distinguished local anarchist, Amilcare Cipriani, and Andrea, after Andrea Costa, the great Romagna socialist. And though Rosa continued to hope that her eldest son might remain within the Catholic fold, it was her husband's values of secular rebelliousness that proved most conducive to Benito. A period spent at a boarding school run by the Salesian Fathers in Faenza ended with his being withdrawn after a succession of episodes of disobedience and unruliness, culminating in his organization of a protest against ant-infested food and his wounding a fellow pupil with a knife during a fight on the feast of St John the Baptist. Thereafter he was sent to a lay college in Forlimpopoli run by Valfredo Carducci, brother of the poet, which he found much more congenial and where he trained to be a schoolteacher: his parents at least agreed on the merits of learning ('Either you study, or you learn to become a blacksmith' was Alessandro's repeated threat).[63]

Given his temperament and background it is hardly surprising that Mussolini gravitated towards the revolutionary wing of socialism. He was by instinct subversive and hostile to constituted authority, whether of the Church or the liberal state. He also shared the morbid fascination of many *fin de siècle* writers with violence and death: he wrote poetry in the style of Carducci ('The priest gazes darkly from afar at the blade bathed in the blood of plebeian arteries . . . In his dying eyes flashed the light of the Ideal, the vision of the centuries to come,' ran a sonnet describing the execution of the French egalitarian Gracchus Babeuf)[64] and he admired Dante greatly, not least for his moral vehemence, and was said to have walked the empty streets of Forlimpopoli at night declaiming passages from the *Inferno* and *Purgatorio*.[65] He liked Nietzsche, who filled him with 'spiritual eroticism', and whose glorification of the 'superman', disparagement of the masses, denunciation of Christian virtues and injunction to 'live dangerously' appealed to him greatly.[66] He also warmed to Sorel's ideas about myth and violence, and for a time identified with revolutionary syndicalism, leading an agricultural strike in Predappio in 1908 and inciting the peasants to destroy threshing machines and clash with the police. He naturally had no sympathy for the reformist socialists and their acquiescence in what he described as Giolitti's 'spineless socialoid ideology'.[67]

But as the leading anarchist Errico Malatesta observed, Mussolini gave the impression as a young man of being an instinctive revolutionary who ranged almost indiscriminately from one belief to another, apparently uncertain as to exactly what kind of revolution he wanted. And Mussolini himself confessed to a friend in 1912 that his view of socialism was essentially 'religious', implying that it was the power of the ideal that attracted him more than any specific content in the doctrines.[68] His father, too, had displayed a similarly emotional and somewhat eclectic approach to politics, combining a passionate support for internationalism, republicanism and anti-militarism with an idolization of the supreme Italian patriot, Garibaldi (whose portrait hung in the family home along with the Madonna of Pompei), sympathy for King Umberto, and admiration for the radical warmonger and vehement anti-socialist Crispi. According to a well-known story, when Mussolini was rejected for the post of secretary to the town council of Predappio in 1901, his father consoled him by shouting out in the central piazza: 'Do not be discouraged. You will be the Crispi of tomorrow!'[69]

And the ideal of national resurrection, which Crispi had embodied, was certainly one that hovered powerfully in the air during Mussolini's youth and without too much difficulty could be accommodated to the hopes and frustrations that lay at the heart of socialism. When Giuseppe Verdi died in 1901, 'comrade' Mussolini was selected by his fellow pupils at Forlimpopoli to deliver a tribute in the local theatre, and the young socialist gave a bravura impromptu performance in which, to loud applause, he recalled the great patriot of the Risorgimento who had lived to see his dreams shattered by the reality of united Italy and in particular by the persistent gulf between the ruling classes and the proletariat.[70] And in the next few years, as Nationalist ideology began to emerge as a powerful intellectual and political rival to socialism, Mussolini found the ideal of Italian regeneration at times too hard to resist. In 1909 he wrote to the editor of the influential journal *La*

Voce congratulating him on his attempts to 'forge the spiritual unity of Italians': 'A difficult task given our history and our character, but not an impossible one. The creation of the "Italian" soul is a superb mission.'[71] And in a newspaper article of the same year he elaborated on the importance of *La Voce*'s efforts in helping to raise the nation from the mire of mediocrity:

Education on its own cannot create a culture, . . . a glorious past cannot justify a present that is utterly vulgar and debased, and a nation's political unity cannot ensure it a historical mission in the world, unless there is the psychological unity to fuse wills together and direct energies . . . [*La Voce*] will help to resolve 'the terrible problem' that is confronting the national soul: 'either to have the courage to create the third, great Italy, the Italy that hitherto has not existed – the Italy, not of the Popes or the Emperors, but of those who think – or else to leave behind nothing but a trail of mediocrity to be blown away by the very first puff of wind'. This is the programme of *La Voce* . . . It is a superb endeavour . . .'[72]

19

Nationalism

Just as socialism taught the proletariat the value of the class struggle, so we must teach Italy the value of the international struggle. But is not international struggle war? Well, let there be war then! And let Nationalism arouse in Italy the will to a victorious war.

Enrico Corradini, speech to the first Nationalist Congress, 3 December 1910

Our aim is to establish . . . a religion that will link us to the deepest and most universal impulses of humanity and build the strong, ethical structure of the new history of Italy, which will secure our future in the world and extricate us from our current daily humiliation . . . If we had a way of influencing this profound transformation of the Italian spirit, we would be able to create the Italy of tomorrow, an Italy that would enable us to forget for ever the wretchedness of our past. Giovanni Amendola, *La Voce*, 28 December 1911

The word ITALY must prevail over the word LIBERTY
Electoral manifesto of the Futurists, 1913

Gabriele D'Annunzio's conversion to socialism did not endure: his instincts were far too aristocratic and aesthetic to allow any serious involvement with bread and butter politics. Nor did his parliamentary career last long: he was defeated in the elections of June 1900. Thereafter he resumed a self-consciously Nietzschean lifestyle, moving from one torrid sexual affair to another, fighting duels and pouring out poetry and plays dealing with themes of heroism, glory, myth, beauty, lust, violence, cruelty and death. He had always been fascinated by decadence; but whereas in the past much of his writing had focused on the struggle of the individual to escape from spiritual decay and sterility, increasingly it was the problem of national regeneration that concerned him. He wrote patriotic odes celebrating Dante, the medieval city-states and ancient Rome, and hailed the illustrious achievements of past Italians in war and the arts as spurs to action and harbingers of the country's future greatness ('Song of Augury for the Chosen Nation'). And in 'Song for the Mayday Holiday' he appealed to Italy's workers – 'rough spirits with vast heaving chests, sooty heroes whose smiling teeth gleam white in darkened bronze' – to ignore the sacrilegious teachings of the 'strident [i.e. socialist] tribune' and recognize that true strength and purpose came only from connecting with history, hearing 'the glorious song of the centuries' and acknowledging the 'fecund ancient Mother' that bore them: 'Let her sons feed at her breast.'[1]

The concern of D'Annunzio with national revival coincided with a new and aggressive response on the part of broad sections of the middle classes to the challenge of socialism, the timidity of foreign policy after Adua and (increasingly) Giolitti's perceived lack of idealism, and this enabled D'Annunzio to shed the remnants of his image as an *enfant terrible* and emerge as the darling of the Italian establishment. When Carducci died early in 1907 – a year after being awarded the Nobel Prize for literature – D'Annunzio was widely seen as the natural inheritor of his mantle, the bard of the nation and its spiritual conscience. Indeed the university authorities in Bologna hurried to offer him the Chair of Literature that Carducci had occupied for so long and with such distinction. D'Annunzio declined it – he had far too strong a sense of his own distinctiveness to risk being in another's shadow – but he was happy to acknowledge his affinity with the former Mazzinian and scourge of decadence and 'Byzantium', and in his 'Ode on the Tomb of Carducci' he celebrated the old poet's love of ancient Rome and all its attendant dreams of conquest, power and glory.

The work that set the seal on D'Annunzio's position as Italy's unofficial poet laureate was his play *La nave* (*The Ship*), which was first performed in January 1908 in the Teatro Argentina in Rome, to huge applause, in the presence of the king, Victor Emmanuel III. After the performance D'Annunzio was called to the royal box to receive the personal congratulations of the sovereign; three days later he was guest of honour at a banquet attended by senior politicians, including the Minister of Education. Set in Venice in AD 552, when the city was asserting its independence from the rule of the Emperor in Byzantium, it tells the story of two brothers, Marco and Sergio, who seize power by murdering the male members of the leading imperial family (the four brothers are blinded and have their tongues torn out). The beautiful Basiliola sets out to avenge her brothers by stripping, driving Marco and Sergio wild with desire, and inciting them to a duel, in which the jealous Marco kills Sergio. To atone for his sin Marco decides to take the great ship that the city is building, head off into the Mediterranean and perform heroic deeds for the greater glory of Venice ('Fit out the prow and set sail for the world', as the play's most famous line declared). At the last moment he realizes that he has been tricked by Basiliola and announces that she will be nailed to the front of the vessel in place of a figurehead as punishment. But she manages to struggle free from her captors and throws herself into the flames of an altar.[2]

The huge success of *La nave* (it toured the country extensively, and two films (1912, 1919) and an opera (1918) were made of it) was due in part to the fact that it echoed the growing campaign for the liberation of the so-called 'unredeemed' regions of Istria and the South Tyrol ('irredentism'), which had long been seen as rightfully Italian, and for an aggressive policy in the Adriatic against Austria (which dealt Italy a major strategic blow in the autumn of 1908 by formally annexing Bosnia–Herzegovina). But the play also mirrored the more general concern at the time with war as an antidote to national decadence, a major theme in Italian patriotic thought in the nineteenth century and one that was central to the doctrines of the new Nationalist movement. Indeed the struggle against Byzantium in *La nave* could be read as much as a moral metaphor (stemming corruption) as a political one (opposing Austria). For D'Annunzio the idea that war could save Italy from decline had already been evident in his youthful writings in the 1880s, and became a near constant refrain in his work from the beginning of the century, culminating in 1915 in his passionate appeals for the country's entry into the First World War. In June 1914, a fortnight before the assassination of Archduke Franz Ferdinand at Sarajevo, he explained to the French ambassador in St Petersburg just why he felt a conflict was so necessary:

We live in a loathsome epoch, under the domination of the multitude and the tyranny of the masses . . . The genius of the Latin people has never fallen so low. It has completely lost all sense of energy, pride and heroic virtues; it wallows in the mire and revels in humiliation . . . A war, a great national war, is the last remaining hope of salvation. It is only through war that peoples who have been turned into brutes can halt their decline, as it offers them a stark choice: either glory or death ... Consequently, this next war, that you seem to fear, I invoke with all the passion of my soul.[3]

Nationalism was a powerful current of thought and feeling in much of Europe from the turn of the century, but in Italy the increasingly beleaguered position of the state meant that it came to enjoy unusually wide resonance and appeal. Giolitti had tried to bolster the institutions through a conventional liberal programme of freedom and economic modernization; but as one leading conservative deputy, Antonio Salandra (who saw himself as an heir of Cavour and the traditions of the moderate right), noted sadly, a conspicuous consequence of this had been to allow the subversives to 'blaspheme against the fatherland' ('We must blaspheme!' the far left shouted back at him),[4] and lead the masses still further astray. 'Nation' and 'fatherland' needed to resonate with something more powerful, more passionate (and less dangerous and counter-productive) than 'freedom' if the regime that had been established in 1860–61 was to survive. 'The task is certainly difficult,' Salandra declared in the Chamber in 1913. 'We cannot offer paradise in heaven, like our Catholic colleagues, nor can we offer paradise on earth, like our socialist colleagues ... But we do have a flame, an ideal: the flame of idealism at the heart of Italian liberalism is patriotism – love of the fatherland.'[5]

The Nationalist movement emerged at the turn of the century as a reaction against socialism and the perceived weakness of Italy's ruling classes, and from the outset it had a strongly intellectual flavour. Its leading exponents – young men such as Giuseppe Prezzolini, Giovanni Papini and Enrico Corradini – were all highly educated and in many cases nurtured fierce literary ambitions: Corradini, who was to become spokesman for the movement's dominant imperialist wing, trained as a priest before turning his hand (unsuccessfully) in the 1890s to writing novels and plays with *fin de siècle* titles such as *Virginity* and *After Death*; and throughout his career he continued to produce fiction and drama alongside political works and a vast amount of journalism. Many of the Nationalists were inspired by a crusading idealism born of sublimated Catholicism ('I have always sensed in the depths of my soul a religious and priestly mission,' Giovanni Amendola confessed in 1904),[6] or else of a desire to reactivate the frustrated national hopes of Mazzini – whose reputation underwent a remarkable resurgence from the start of the century. As Giovanni Papini wrote in 1906:

I feel – like a Mazzinian of the old days – that I can have a mission in my country and that I must do everything to make Italy less deaf, less blind and less craven ... Rome has always had a universal, dominating mission ... [It] must become once again the centre of the world and a new form of universal power take its seat there ... The Third Rome, the Rome of the ideal, must be the fruit of our will and our work.[7]

From the outset the main vehicles for Nationalist ideas were journals, in the main based in Florence: *Il Marzocco*, which began in 1896, *Leonardo* and *Il Regno*, founded in 1903, *Hermes*, 1904, and, most influentially, *La Voce*, set up in 1908 and edited initially by Prezzolini and later, and until its demise in 1913, by Papini. They never had very large circulations – at its peak in 1911 *La Voce* sold around 5,000 copies – but their contributors included nearly all the most talented younger writers and thinkers in the country; and they came together on a common platform of dislike of the status quo and a belief that a 'party of intellectuals' should be established to save Italy from its current degenerate ruling class. They sought a spiritual revolution: there was a widespread recognition, as Prezzolini later recalled, that 'everything was mediocre and unworthy of the past and inferior to what was being done in the rest of Europe and America'.[8] But quite what the upshot of such a revolution would be was unclear.

The Nationalists had a much sharper sense of what they disliked than what they liked. They hated parliament: 'Montecitorio is the worst of Italy's burdens; and the governmental bourgeoisie is the most factitious aristocracy in existence because it is useless ...'[9] 'Those in power are the only people in the whole of Italy with no following outside parliament. They live solely for parliamentary life ... without roots in the nation.'[10] They loathed the corruption of the capital: 'Rome is the central leech of Italy ... the fundamental cause of all our economic, moral and intellectual backwardness ... Fish begin to stink from their heads: Italy, from Rome.'[11] They saw socialism as dangerous: they considered its doctrines materialistic, devoid of higher spiritual values and selfish; and contrary to what Giolitti thought, they believed Italy was economically and politically too fragile to benefit from the free interplay of class forces. And they were critical of the provincialism and complacency of much of Italian life, and of the deep flaws marring the national character: 'the absence of discipline, the weak conception of duty, the disregard for accuracy, the indifference to commitments, the limited or non-existent sense of initiative, the readiness to tolerate squalor'.[12]

The solution, in broad terms, was greater moral energy, an energy that would galvanize the middle classes around a programme of national renewal and allay the threat of socialism. Giolitti's materialism and piecemeal reforms were too tepid; more passion was needed to counter the scepticism and lethargy that had dogged the Italian bourgeoisie for so long and left the country prey to those, whether within or without, who possessed conviction and will. Indeed an important strand running through Nationalism was a celebration of aggression and a scorn of humanitarian and pacific values (Corradini claimed that it was Italy's spineless response to Adua in 1896 that had converted him to Nationalism). For, in a world of Darwinian struggle, how could any class or nation hope to survive without a preparedness to fight? Giolitti's policy of trying to buy off the socialists with concessions was wholly misguided: 'The [bourgeoisie] must make the class struggle . . . into a reality,' wrote Prezzolini in 1904, 'but with the intention specifically of bringing it to an end. When an enemy provokes you and, after provoking, attacks, the best way to secure peace is to strike back and win.'[13]

The supreme embodiment of aggression was war, and though Nationalism was initially divided over whether the principal focus of its energies should be domestic or foreign policy, it was foreign policy, and in particular colonial conquest in Africa, that emerged as the victorious line in the years immediately before the First World War. This was largely because war was seen as salutary. 'War, and war alone,' wrote the prominent Nationalist (and distinguished Dante scholar) Luigi Valli in 1911, echoing Turiello, 'arouses and rekindles the highest moral virtues and the purest ideal forces, and in many cases can scorch in a purifying flame a people that grows corrupt in peacetime and gets dragged into petty, narrow-minded interests and wastes itself in wretched local or party disputes – as is happening now with the Italian people.'[14] And that same year, in an article in *La Voce*, the young democrat Giovanni Amendola dismissed the claim made by the British intellectual Norman Angell that conflicts had primarily economic causes, saying that wars were attractive for moral reasons as, despite their horrors, they produced 'an infinitely superior being to the cautious sybarite who finds the best expression for his voluptuary view of life in the cradle of peace'.[15]

War had another crucial function: to redirect the class struggle outwards (Italy as a whole, according to the Nationalists, was a 'proletarian nation' competing for its rightful place in the world) and heal the country's internal fractures. 'The ideal of Nationalism is to create a collective national soul in place of the collective regional souls we have today,' declared the distinguished sociologist Scipio Sighele.[16] And what better mechanism could there be for generating 'the awareness of belonging to a great collective organism', as the future fascist minister Luigi Federzoni put it, and teaching individuals that their lives were as nothing compared to the superior interests of the nation, than war? 'From a national perspective,' said Corradini, 'the individual has no more importance than a single drop in the sea, than a falling leaf in a forest as vast as the surface of the earth ... The disregard for death is the supreme factor in life.'[17]

The Nationalists were a curious mixture of radical and conservative. While they loathed many aspects of Italian political life, parliament especially, and hankered after a great spiritual revolution, their opposition to socialism, their concern with discipline and order, and their belief in the need to subordinate the individual to the interests of the nation drew them towards the right – towards the monarchy, the army, the Church, big business and landowners. Indeed by the time the first Nationalist Congress convened in Florence in December 1910 to bring together the various currents of the movement, launch the Italian Nationalist Association and agree a common programme, sympathy for Nationalism had spread far beyond the ranks of middle-class intellectuals who had made up most of the early support. A major downturn in the economy from 1908 had caused large sections of the propertied classes, already sceptical about Giolitti's policies, to grow increasingly angry at the government's failure to deal with socialism: profit margins were now being rapidly eroded as strikes pushed up the costs of labour. A mood of desperation was beginning to overtake the country. 'Italy is now becoming *Nationalist*,' Vilfredo Pareto told Sorel early in 1911. 'The only talk is of a future war ... I am afraid it will all end badly.'[18]

LIBYA

Italy's sudden invasion of Libya in the autumn of 1911 was greeted with an enormous outpouring of excitement. The Nationalists were exultant: for months they had been calling for a war in north Africa from the columns of their newspaper, *L'Idea Nazionale* – launched on 1 March, the anniversary of the defeat at Adua and the date when the ancient Romans had traditionally mustered their armies. Their fear, and the fear of many, the prime minister, Giolitti, included, was that France might have stepped in first; and Italy could not afford a repeat of the Tunisian fiasco of 1881, particularly as its claim to Libya had long been recognized as strategically paramount – and historically: had it not been an important province of the Roman Empire? The Catholic press was enthusiastic: the Church had large financial holdings in Libya, and the invasion was soon being heralded as a new crusade against the infidel. Even some right-wing socialists backed the initiative on the grounds that it might assuage the land hunger of the peasants. D'Annunzio dashed off a series of celebratory odes in the *Corriere della Sera*, while a few weeks after the start of the campaign another leading poet, Giovanni Pascoli, delivered a speech that quickly became a classic text of Italian patriotism:

The great proletarian nation has stirred . . . Just fifty years after its return to life, Italy, the great martyr among nations, has done its duty and contributed to the advancement and civilization of the peoples, and asserted its right not to be penned in and suffocated in its own waters . . . Oh fifty years of miracle! What a transformation there has been! . . . Whoever wishes to know what [Italy] is now, behold its army and its navy . . . Land, sea and sky, mountains and plains, peninsula and islands are perfectly fused. The fair-skinned solemn Alpine soldier fights beside the slim dark Sicilian, the tall Lombard grenadier rubs shoulders with the short lean Sardinian fusilier . . . Run your eye over the lists of the glorious dead, and wounded – who rejoice in their radiant wounds: you will find yourself remembering and revising the geography of what was, but a short time ago, just a geographical expression . . . Oh, you blessed men who have died for the fatherland! . . . Fifty years ago Italy was made. On the sacred fiftieth anniversary . . . you have proved that Italians too have been made.[19]

Even liberals who had been strongly opposed to the Nationalist calls for war, such as the distinguished expert on the problems of the south

Giustino Fortunato, were carried along on the tide of patriotism. For many years Fortunato had argued that Italy should use its limited resources to improve the social and economic conditions of the peasants and not waste them on extravagant foreign-policy gestures; but once the invasion had been launched he started to change his tune. As he told Pasquale Villari in December 1911:

I was fearful for the Tripoli expedition and continue to be fearful. But I have one great, one immeasurable, consolation. For the first time since Italy was created amid the sea and beneath the sky, the southern peasants (and I know them well and they are not easily aroused to enthusiasm) are finally conscious of a duty to fight for a fatherland, their fatherland, and that this has a name: Italy. Yes, indeed, half a century of unity has not been wasted![20]

What a transformation from the late 1880s, he felt, when Crispi had brought the country to the brink of war and the peasant reservists he had talked to had been totally indifferent: 'Italy is Piedmont, we are Naples,' they had told him, 'and if the French come down here, it will be much the same. At most . . . you and other landowners will change.'[21]

The rhetoric and euphoria at home were in stark contrast to the reality on the ground in Libya. The initial expeditionary force of some 34,000 men succeeded in taking the main towns of Tripoli, Benghazi, Homs and Tobruk in the first two weeks of October without encountering much resistance from the Turkish garrisons. But the assumption that the Arab population would welcome the Italians as liberators proved a serious miscalculation. At dawn on 23 October some 10,000 well-armed Arabs and Turks launched a savage attack on the Italian lines in the oasis of Sciara Sciat near Tripoli, killing over 500. Corpses were nailed to palm trees, eyes sewn up and genitals cut off – apparently in retaliation for sexual offences committed against local women.[22] The Italian response was extreme: several thousand Arabs were massacred indiscriminately and thousands more sent off to penal islands. Gallows were set up in the main squares, and public hangings conducted as a warning to the 'rebels'.

It was an inauspicious start; and the situation scarcely improved. The Italian army found it hard to advance inland beyond the coast, and by the time a peace treaty with Turkey was signed in October 1912, only about 10 per cent of the country had been secured – and this despite the expeditionary force being increased to 100,000 men. It was to be another twenty years before the colony was finally brought under control, at the cost of around 100,000 Libyan lives – about an eighth of the entire population. The tactics employed against the resistance, particularly in the eastern territory of Cyrenaica, were extreme, and in December 1913 Filippo Turati felt obliged to ask in the Chamber whether the claims of 'a great civilizing mission' in Libya were justified given the frequent recourse to exemplary executions (with Italian soldiers being paid to act as hangmen when locals refused): 'I ask myself . . . if the Government is aware that a certain Cesare Beccaria was born in Italy?' However, there were many who were prepared to argue that Italy's problems in Libya were on the contrary due to insufficient ruthlessness – to what a leading Nationalist volunteer who had taken part in the battle at Sciara Sciat and the ensuing bloody reprisals condemned as liberal 'sentimentalism', that 'characteristic enervating illness of our race'.[23]

One particularly strong critic of the government's handling of the war was the well-known writer Filippo Tommaso Marinetti, who travelled to Libya as a newspaper correspondent and denounced what he called the 'stupid colonial humanitarianism' that was hampering the military operations.[24] Marinetti was the leading figure of the movement known as Futurism, which had been launched in 1909 with a manifesto calling for a new artistic and cultural value system based on the celebration of energy, danger, courage, aggression, speed, subversion and modernity ('a roaring car that seems as if it is mounted on a machine gun is more beautiful than the Victory of Samothrace'). Among its members were some of the most talented artists of the day, including Umberto Boccioni, Mario Sironi, Giacomo Balla and Carlo Carrà. Article nine of the manifesto had hailed the cathartic power of violence: 'We want to glorify war – the only source of hygiene in the world – militarism, patriotism, the destructive act.'[25]

Such views were unlikely to resonate with the rank and file peasant conscripts who were sent to Libya – except to fuel their ignorance and their fear and encourage them to treat the local inhabitants brutally ('the Arabs are like animals – killing one of them is just like killing a snake').[26] Some at least of the soldiers appear to have set off for Africa with optimism, believing that they would be welcomed as liberators and discover a 'second America' to which they might subsequently emigrate.[27] Instead they found a barren land and an indigenous population that was united against them:

[E]ighteen months in tents in the desert . . . We thought: 'Why should so many people be killed to come and get some sand, four palms and a few lemons?' . . . There was nothing, nothing, only sand blowing around and filling in the holes, and so many dying from illness or the fighting . . . and forty-five or fifty degrees of burning heat from the *ghibli*. We were always thirsty, and all we ever wanted was to drink. And the Moors hated us . . .[28]

But the idea that a successful war would be the answer to Italy's problems and purge centuries of weakness and division continued to haunt even sober-minded intellectuals like Giustino Fortunato. In November 1912 Fortunato wrote to his friend Gaetano Salvemini of how the campaign in Libya had laid bare Italy's continuing moral shortcomings and the need still for Italians to demonstrate they were worthy of nationhood:

I have come to the firm conclusion that only when Italy has secured a virile victory of its people over an enemy – no matter who . . . only then will it be able to say that it has avenged a millennium and a half of shameful history and be able to face the future with confidence. For the first time in my life I have a vision of the sanctity of war . . . Ever since the fall of the Roman Empire we have never displayed any courage as a people, have never been able to repel a single one of the hundred invaders, have never shown a willingness to die rather than flee. Between the Five Days of Milan [in 1848] and Porta Pia [in 1870] no more than 6,000 soldiers and volunteers gave their lives . . . And do not imagine for a moment that if France had not helped us in 1859 we would one day have managed to find 'ourselves'. God! Even Greece was able to act on its own in 1823. We, never. This, for Christ's sake, is what the history teachers ought to be explaining in our schools . . .[29]

THE FAILURE OF
GIOLITTI'S PROGRAMME

The invasion of Libya provided a dramatic coda to the celebrations that had taken place in the spring and summer of 1911 to mark the fiftieth anniversary of Italian unity. In Turin a huge International Industrial Fair had been staged to underscore the bonds of brotherhood and peace that work and economic progress could bring, with thirty participating countries and a string of grandiose pavilions along the banks of the Po, opened by the king in April in a newly constructed stadium with 70,000 spectators and a lavish display by 6,000 children. In Rome the highpoint of the festivities had been the inauguration of the monument to Victor Emmanuel II, the Vittoriano, at the beginning of June, with the liberal press heralding the enormous influx of crowds as evidence of the solidarity of the people with both the nation and the dynasty. Other events in the capital had included an exhibition showcasing the country's regional artistic traditions, the opening of a huge archaeological park and the staging of Italy's first beauty contest, with 302 girls wearing modern 'Italian' clothes ('not Parisian or London fashions, but our own costumes . . .') competing for the title 'Queen of Rome'.[30]

But behind the patriotic rhetoric and the spectacle it was difficult in 1911 for most observers to ignore the fractured reality. The Church formally boycotted the celebrations while the socialists dismissed the idea of political unity as meaningless ('North and south are two nations; and one, the most wretched, is fleeing across the seas. City and countryside are two nations . . . A single fatherland does not exist').[31] Moreover the celebrations themselves highlighted the depth of regional tensions and divisions and, as in the case of the 'national' art show in Rome, struggled to see 'Italy' other than in terms of an aggregate of the discrete achievements of its parts; and while some argued that diversity was positive and to be acclaimed, and that any attempt to force everyone 'into a bed of Procrustes' would be counterproductive,[32] many continued to feel that such laissez-faire empiricism was dangerous and that a far more ethical approach was needed. The eminent philosopher Benedetto Croce was deeply troubled by what he saw as the declining spirit of 'social unity' in Italy and the increase in corrosive, self-interested impulses ('bad individualism'), and he longed for terms like 'king', 'fatherland' and 'nation' to be injected with emotional, unifying power.[33]

Giolitti hoped that success in Libya would bolster his position in the country: win over the Nationalists, draw the moderate Catholics into the institutional fold, and reinforce his alliance with the reformist socialists, leaving the revolutionaries isolated. This was especially important as he was planning a major extension of the suffrage: like his old adversary Crispi more than twenty years before, he wanted to broaden the foundations of the state while simultaneously trusting to a vigorous foreign policy to minimize the danger from the subversives by 'nationalizing' the electorate. But it all went badly wrong. The Nationalists claimed credit for having pushed the government into invading Libya, increased their popularity and standing, and launched their own political party; and far from siding with Giolitti they denounced him for his lax prosecution of the war and became more dismissive than ever of liberal parliamentary democracy and its failure to impart energy and idealism (except under Crispi), oppose socialism robustly and elevate collective over individual rights. And many Catholics agreed: liberalism was certainly better than socialism, but Nationalism seemed better still.

But the biggest disappointment came with the socialists. Giolitti had offered Turati and his parliamentary colleagues a place in his new administration in March 1911 – they had refused, but they had been sorely tempted. Libya dashed hopes of any further progress, inflaming rank and file socialist feeling against the government's 'militarism' and precipitating a general strike. The reformist leadership was isolated. At the party congress in Reggio Emilia in July 1912 the revolutionaries won control, and Bonomi, Bissolati and a number of other deputies were expelled for supporting the war (or more precisely for having gone to the Quirinal in March to congratulate the king on surviving an assassination attempt). They set up the Italian Reformist Socialist Party, but it had no significant support. Turati and a number of other moderates remained in the old party, but they were at the mercy of the extremists, who occupied the key posts. Among the revolutionaries who were now catapulted to prominence was Mussolini, from December the editor of the main party newspaper, *Avanti!*

Italy was profoundly split. In the elections of 1913 – the first to be held under a new law that granted the vote to nearly every adult male (increasing the electorate from 3 million to 8.5 million) – the 'constitutional' parties secured just 56.7 per cent of the poll, with the socialists, radicals, Catholics and Nationalists all gaining significantly. To make matters worse, it was claimed after the elections by the head of Catholic Action's Electoral Union that 228 liberal deputies had owed their seats to support from the Church in return for signing up to a seven-point agreement on such issues as religious education and divorce. Giolitti strenuously denied that any agreement had existed, but the firm suspicion remained, and in the spring of 1914 his government fell after the anti-clerical radicals withdrew their support. Antonio Salandra took over at the head of a conservative administration, hoping to revive the fortunes of liberalism through 'exaltation of the fatherland' and a celebration of those feelings of 'national solidarity' that had recently been demonstrated by the 'officers and soldiers – members of the aristocracy and middle classes, workers and peasants' – who, 'had spilled their blood together on the fields of Libya'.[34] (Understandably he did not say 'deserts'.)

How little sense of 'national solidarity' there was became terrifyingly apparent early in June, when three young demonstrators were shot dead by the police in Ancona and the Socialist Party proclaimed a general strike. Anarchists, republicans and syndicalists joined in, and for a week much of northern and central Italy was in a state of turmoil. Public buildings were burned, barricades erected, tax registers destroyed, telegraph wires cut, trees of liberty planted, railway stations seized and churches ransacked. Hundreds of workers were killed and wounded in pitched battles, and in many places vigilante gangs were set up to protect property and save the country from what seemed an imminent revolution. In Milan Mussolini harangued vast crowds, urging them to take to the streets, and in an incident in Piazza Duomo he was struck to the ground and nearly trampled to death. The trade unions eventually called off the strike – much to the irritation of the revolutionaries – and order was restored. But 'Red Week' had underlined clearly just how far removed Italy was from Salandra's dream of national cohesion. And the solution seemed no less elusive than it had been to the patriots of the Risorgimento nearly a century before. 'The remedy,' Salandra confessed gloomily, 'will be slow; it will be the work of many governments and perhaps of many generations . . . It is a question of political education, of substituting a new moral order for the old one, whose sanctions are in many places crumbling.'[35]

INTERVENTION

Italy did not need to enter the First World War. Though it was still formally allied to Austria and Germany under the Triple Alliance, first signed in 1882, the fact that Austria failed to consult Italy before declaring war on Serbia at the end of July meant that Italy's treaty obligations technically did not apply. Thus, as Europe mobilized its armies and slipped towards Armageddon in August, Italy announced its neutrality. And many thought that it should remain neutral, including Giolitti and a majority of deputies in the Chamber. They believed that Italy was economically too fragile to sustain a major conflict, particularly so soon after the invasion of Libya; and Giolitti suggested that the country could in fact gain 'a great deal' by bargaining with both sides to stay out of the war. But Salandra and the Foreign Minister, Sidney Sonnino, negotiated in total secrecy with the British and French governments on the one hand and Austria and Germany on the other, in the spirit of what Salandra referred to as 'sacred egoism', to see what price Italy could secure for intervention. Britain and France made the most attractive offer, and on 26 April 1915 the Treaty of London was signed, pledging the South Tyrol, Trentino, Istria, Trieste and much of Dalmatia to Italy.

When rumours of what had been agreed began to leak out at the beginning of May pandemonium erupted. Parliament was closed, but more than 300 deputies went to the hotel where Giolitti was staying and left their visiting cards to signal their support for neutrality. Realizing he lacked a majority, Salandra resigned. But Giolitti found it impossible to form a new government: to reject the Treaty of London and betray the British and French after having repudiated the Triple Alliance and angered the Austrians and Germans would have been too humiliating and might have cost the king his throne. Meanwhile supporters of war took to the streets in their tens of thousands, led by Nationalists, Futurists, syndicalists and dissident socialists. Among the latter was Mussolini, who the previous autumn had decided that the best way of bringing about a revolution would be to plunge the country into the maelstrom of a great conflict: he had been dramatically expelled from the party for his renegade views.

The crowds calling for intervention were fired as much by anger towards Giolitti and the neutralists as by enthusiasm for war. Indeed, in a speech in Rome on 14 May, D'Annunzio denounced them as traitors and incited his audience to kill them ('should blood flow, that blood would be as blessed as any shed in the trenches').[36] And the anger of the demonstrators was also directed generally towards parliament and an entire political system that was felt to have betrayed the hopes of the Risorgimento. As an article in the leading Nationalist newspaper explained on 15 May:

Parliament is Giolitti; Giolitti is parliament: the binomial of our shame. This is the old Italy. The old Italy that is unaware of the new, the true, the holy Italy that is rising again in history – and the future . . . The struggle is mortal. Either parliament will destroy the nation and over her trembling sacred body resume its profession of procurer, and prostitute her once again to the foreigner, or the nation will overturn parliament, destroy the barrators' benches and purify with iron and fire the boudoirs of the pimps . . .[37]

Against this menacing and unruly backdrop the king reinstated Salandra as prime minister. Giolitti admitted defeat and left Rome. His former allies quickly trimmed their sails to the prevailing wind, and on 20 May the Chamber granted full emergency powers to the government by a majority of 407 to 74. The Socialist Party voted against, and became the only European party of the far left, outside Russia, not to lend its support to the conflict. On 24 May, Italy declared war on Austria; and a week later, from the heights of the Capitol, where the Romans had once celebrated their military triumphs, Salandra set out the country's goals, reminding Italians that only by 'dissolving [their] internal discords' in 'marvellous moral unity' would the nation find the strength to secure victory and complete the work of the Risorgimento:

Since the Fates have assigned to our generation the tremendous and sublime task of realizing the ideal of a great Italy that the heroes of the Risorgimento were not able to see finished, we accept this task with undaunted spirit, ready to give ourselves totally to the Fatherland, with all that we are and all that we have.[38]

With the fractures in the moral fabric of the nation for the moment concealed beneath a torrent of patriotic enthusiasm, Italy's forces advanced into the Alpine valleys along the borders with Austria in the vague expectation of some regenerative 'baptism of blood'.

20

The Great War, 1915–18

Remember the school, the church tower, the town hall
Every corner that contains a living memory
Of gentle joy, of grief and honest toil.
Fair Italy, from her mountains to the sea,
Can bring all this to your mind.
(Mothers, children, smiles, every memory:
This is what the Fatherland is, this is what it means.)

Oh, said the [soldier], now I understand:
Fatherland and Home are the same thing . . .
                'Geografia', poem in the trench newspaper
                        San Marco, 24 May 1918

> *On the road to Monte Pasubio*
> *Bom borombom*
> *A long column climbs slowly*
> *Bom borombom*
> *Those who won't return are marching*
> *Those who will stay up there to die . . .*
>
> *On the road to Monte Pasubio*
> *Bom borombom*
> *There's nothing left but a cross*
> *Bom borombom*
> *No voice can be heard any more*
> *Except the wind that kisses the flowers*
>   'Monte Pasubio',
>   song of the First World War

DEFEAT AT CAPORETTO

The first signs of an imminent attack came at two in the morning of 24 October 1917, when the Austrian artillery opened fire along a fifteen-mile stretch of the Isonzo front, in the mountains above the small town of Caporetto (present-day Kobarid, in Slovenia). Ever since Italy entered the war the Chief of General Staff, Luigi Cadorna, had concentrated his operations along the valley of the Isonzo, a river that wound its way through gorges and thickly wooded valleys southwards from the Julian Alps to the Gulf of Trieste. Italy's western front, in the Trentino, was too inhospitable and too well defended to allow for any serious offensives. Cadorna was an old-fashioned Piedmontese general of forbidding and authoritarian character and limited imagination who regarded courage and infantry assaults as the key to success, and between June 1915 and September 1917 he had launched eleven battles across the Isonzo, taking the town of Gorizia and a few kilometres of Austrian territory, but not achieving the breakthrough that would have allowed him to push towards Vienna and Budapest. The cost of these battles had been enormous: around a million killed and wounded.[1]

There had been plenty of warnings that something major was afoot. Reports from aerial reconnaissance and deserters had indicated the arrival of German troops in the Isonzo sector, but the precise scale of the build-up had apparently not been clear. Furthermore the general in command of Italy's eastern front, Luigi Capello, was a man of very different character and background to Cadorna – a genial middle-class Freemason, where the other was a reserved Catholic aristocrat – and though the two men had a reasonable working relationship, Capello's ambition to succeed Cadorna as Chief of General Staff had led him almost instinctively to think primarily in terms of attack and a spectacular success (such as he had achieved the previous summer in capturing Gorizia). As a result Italy's defences on the Isonzo, especially behind Caporetto, were inadequate. And to compound the problems, Cadorna had come to the conclusion at the beginning of October that the campaigning season was over and had gone on leave for three weeks, while Capello was seriously ill and unable to issue orders.[2]

The artillery bombardment was interspersed with gas attacks and culminated in thirty minutes of heavy-mortar fire; and by dawn on

24 October, when the Austrian and German troops started pouring forward through the rain and fog, the Italians had suffered serious casualties and their communications were badly disrupted. The Austrians and Germans met with little resistance and quickly broke through the lines of the 4th and 27th Army Corps, wheeling right into the valley towards Caporetto, and encircling several divisions. By evening of the first day some 15,000 prisoners had been taken and a huge breach opened in the Italian front, with additional breaches appearing to the north and south. Bemused and war-weary soldiers everywhere gave themselves up with little or no fight. One young German officer with a distinguished career ahead of him, Erwin Rommel, recalled coming across 1,500 men of the Salerno Brigade who, when challenged to surrender, threw down their weapons and rushed towards him: 'In an instant I was surrounded and hoisted on Italian soldiers. "*Evviva Germania!*" sounded from a thousand throats. An Italian officer who hesitated to surrender was shot down by his own troops.'[3] The failure of the 27th Army to put up effective resistance was particularly noteworthy, and its commander, Pietro Badoglio, later faced strong criticism from the commission looking into the disaster. But Badoglio was well connected, and the thirteen pages dealing with his part in the rout were omitted from the final published report. He went on to become Chief of General Staff.[4]

Cadorna initially thought that his forces could fall back onto the line of the Tagliamento river, but the speed with which the Austrians and Germans pushed westward and the near total breakdown of the Italian command structures made this look increasingly unlikely. By the beginning of November many divisions were in a state of complete disintegration: according to official figures, of the million or so men that had comprised the Isonzo army, 10,000 were killed during the Caporetto disaster, 30,000 wounded and 300,000 taken prisoner, while a further 400,000 simply vanished – in most cases, it would seem, back to their homes in the countryside (a majority of the front-line troops were peasants). It was clear that the only possible line of defence was along the Piave, the broad river that ran from the Dolomites, above Belluno, to the east end of the Venetian lagoon, and on 9 November, the same day as General Armando Diaz replaced Cadorna as Chief of General Staff, the last remaining bridges were blown up and the Austrian and German advance brought to a halt. Stiffened by the arrival of French and British divisions and a new draft of seventeen-year-olds, the Italian army was able to regroup and make a successful stand. But for a year a large swathe of territory in the north-east of Italy remained under the occupation of the Austrians.

The dissolving army presented a harrowing spectacle. Everywhere muddy roads were choked with dishevelled, sometimes barefooted, soldiers who had thrown away their rifles as if the war were finished, moving in a slow stream together with the hordes of refugees – men, women and children, an estimated 600,000 – who had decided to flee their homes ahead of the advancing enemy, taking with them what possessions they could in carts and carriages. Broken vehicles, discarded matériel of every description, and dead horses, their flanks routinely darkened with blood where the flesh had been cut away with a knife or bayonet for food, littered the waysides. Men too exhausted, too sick, or too drunk to move lay on the ground. Rivers and streams, swollen with the autumn rains, were clogged with corpses and debris. And most disturbing, perhaps, was the sight of thousands of wounded and shell-shocked troops who had escaped terror-stricken from the military hospitals, 'wrapped in sheets, blankets and bandages, many half naked, screaming, gesturing in agony . . . unleashed furies, wild beasts'.[5]

There was disorder and in places an almost bacchanalian spirit. Indeed one observer, the writer Curzio Malaparte, felt that the events of these days constituted, in retrospect at least, an Italian version of the Russian revolution (which took place at almost exactly the same time), with the masses rebelling anarchically (and in his view justly) against the 'political Italy' of bourgeois armchair patriots who had sent them to suffer and die for the fatherland; and he depicted the soldiers sweeping across the plains of the Veneto, like apocalyptic figures out of a painting by Hieronymus Bosch, looting, burning, drinking and raping, and bearing aloft in triumph prostitutes from the army brothels, 'naked and indecent': 'And often they hoisted on their shoulders, cheering, along with the prostitutes, some fat, pot-bellied senior officer – Bacchus and Ariadne – while the orgy of the "sans-fusils" dissolved into brawls and riots, cries of lust and lewd songs.'[6] But in reality such episodes were rare. The prevailing mood among the retreating soldiers was much more sober, a feeling of resignation in the face of a terrible disaster that lay beyond their control – as if it had been an earthquake or a landslide –

and a sense of relief at leaving behind an alien and senseless world, where men died in their tens of thousands for a few hectares of stony ground.

Another radical writer (who, like Malaparte, was to become an enthusiastic supporter of fascism) was a Futurist, Ardengo Soffici. He too served on the Isonzo front and witnessed at first hand the dissolution of the army, but rather than attribute it to a revolt of the unruly peasant masses, thirsting for justice and revenge, he saw it as a consequence of the natural fatalism of a people that had been let down by the state – a state that had failed to make them comprehend why they should be taken away from their tranquil, familiar rural lives, and made to endure such inhuman conditions:

What most struck me . . . was the calm of many of the soldiers . . . Some lay stretched out in the sun, on their backs, their arms folded beneath their heads, their mouths open, or else on their fronts, face down in the grass, enjoying the deep sleep of adolescents . . . Others were in their shirtsleeves, hanging jackets out on the trees to dry . . . or wandering here and there examining carefully the nature of the crops and the soil . . . Are these beaten men, deserters, rebels, traitors? Are they – let us not mince words – cowards? No . . . They are victims. They are uncomprehending. They are deceived. And the evil does not lie in them. We are the flower, now wilting, of a plant whose roots are in miserable soil. The evil is in the roots. The evil is down there beneath us: in the ignominy of those [in Rome] who divide, sow discord, lie and haggle. Of those who abandon. The evil is everywhere; but not here. Here there is only suffering. This is not the way of shame. This is the way of the cross.[7]

There had been clear signs in the months before Caporetto that the morale of the 2.5 million men at the front and of the civilian population as a whole was declining. In the early stages of the war Giustino Fortunato had been deeply impressed by the stoicism and commitment displayed by the peasants in his town of Rionero in Basilicata ('The calm, the good will, the dignity of all classes, and the peasantry especially, in this, the first great unitary war that Italy has fought, is astonishing, truly astonishing. Yes, Italy is made!'),[8] but from the end of 1916 he had grown increasingly alarmed at the number of deserters and at the mounting anger of the local people. By the summer of 1917 the situation seemed desperate. The women were incandescent with fury (like 'harpies') at the fate of their husbands and sons; deserters were roaming everywhere in the countryside; and woodland and forests were being set on fire. Much of the anger was directed towards landowners like himself (and it pained him deeply: 'until last year I was much loved'), who were accused of conspiring with the government to prolong the conflict and deliberately massacre the peasants; and he himself was the victim of a violent assault in August. He warned his friend Salandra that an insurrection, or worse, brigandage, was about to erupt.[9]

A number of factors contributed to the declining morale, but the abnormally harsh treatment of the conscripts was certainly one of the most important. The bitterly low temperatures on the Alpine front made nutrition of paramount importance; but rations, already far from generous in the first year of the war, were cut sharply at the end of 1916, and average consumption in the winter of 1916–17 was less than 3,000 calories a day compared to nearly 4,000 the previous winter. Pay was derisory – half a lira a day for an infantryman and a similar sum for his family (scant compensation for the loss in many cases of the principal breadwinner) – and leave was restricted to a single period of fifteen days in the year, a source of particular resentment to the peasants as it gave them insufficient time to attend to sowing and harvesting.[10] Very little consideration was given to entertainment (apart from improvised army brothels). There were no war newspapers and troops were banned from entering cinemas or bars in the so-called war zones, even when on leave. The only leisure initiative of note was that of a Catholic priest, Giovanni Minozzi, who founded the 'Soldiers' Homes' – usually a rather spartan building behind the lines, with a piano, some books and possibly a film projector. About 250 had been set up by October 1917. However, the military authorities regarded them with considerable indifference and even with suspicion.[11]

Behind the callous attitude of the military authorities towards the rank and file lay a good deal of mistrust, a belief that most of the conscripts (and only 8,000 of the 5.5 million Italians who were mobilized down to 1918 were volunteers) lacked the requisite patriotism and discipline to be treated other than with an iron rod. Punishments were accordingly severe, even by contemporary standards. Around 400,000 officers and men were arraigned before military tribunals in the course of the war, and over a quarter of these were convicted and punished; 4,028 received death sentences (mostly *in absentia*), of which 750 were carried out.[12] There was also regular use of random summary executions and decimations (permitted under the military penal code), though exactly how many is unclear. The documentary evidence suggests between 100 and 200 instances, though the real figure was certainly much higher as officers were understandably reluctant to report them. With frustration growing in the trenches in 1916–17 and the number of desertions mounting, the signs are that nervous commanders became increasingly dependent on terror to maintain order.[13]

Indicative of the brutal atmosphere in the trenches was an episode recalled by a peasant from the province of Cuneo, Alessandro Scotti, which took place on Monte Pasubio, a key strategic point high on the Trentino front to the south-east of Rovereto, on 9 October 1916. The commanding general had been informed that a company of *alpini* (Alpine troops) in the 'Monte Berico' battalion had shouted 'Long live the fog!' before they were due to go into action, hoping that bad weather would force a delay in the attack. The general immediately came down to the trenches and ordered the ninety *alpini* to be bound and shot. While the firing squad was being assembled military chaplains intervened (the 2,400 Catholic priests who served as chaplains in the war earned much gratitude from the troops for their humanity), and after fifteen minutes of parleying the order was changed to decimation, and every tenth man told to step forward. The chaplains intervened again; and once more the general was induced to back down: 'Take Pasubio for me and you will all be deemed absolved,' he declared. 'Otherwise I will proceed with the executions after the assault.' Virtually the entire company was wiped out in the ensuing battle. Scotti managed to reach the top of the Groviglio peak where he lay down under a rhododendron bush and slept, concealing his head beneath a corpse; and when darkness came, he and four other surviving *alpini* returned to the Italian lines. He was awarded a bronze medal ('because I had done my duty in full') and went on to survive the war and become a teacher.[14]

The lack of faith in the motivation of the troops was one important reason why the authorities refused, in contrast to other countries, to provide aid to those who had been captured. There was a fear that if the soldiers heard that conditions in prisoner-of-war camps were tolerable, they would surrender too easily. The government thus did all it could to foster the idea that imprisonment was shameful and hampered relief efforts, and as a result the 600,000 Italians who ended up interned in Austria and Germany were forced to make do with rations that frequently fell below 1,000 calories a day. Many died of hunger and hunger-related illnesses – around 100,000 (five times the figure for French prisoners, who, like the British, were in regular receipt of food parcels).[15] Those who survived were understandably resentful. One, Angelo Bronzini, wrote with bitter sarcasm after the war of how the 'government of our fatherland' had 'completely abandoned' him and the other Italians in the camp, forbidding access to essential supplies and hampering communication with families (only postcards were permitted).[16] Another, a peasant from Treviso, recalled how he used to look enviously at the French prisoners, 'whose government passed them bread and tins of meat every week, while we went around begging with our bowls in our hands'.[17]

In these circumstances it is not surprising that most rank and file soldiers seem to have remained largely untouched by the patriotic language and sentiment that continued to punctuate the rhetoric of pro-war intellectuals and politicians. Surviving letters of conscripts from the front, some of them probably written with the help of junior officers or chaplains, periodically contain phrases such as 'barbarian enemy', 'beautiful Italy', 'defence of the fatherland' and 'unredeemed lands' (*terre irredente* – rarely spelled correctly), suggesting that official propaganda had, if nothing else, supplied the conceptual tools with which to make a degree of sense of the suffering and carnage. But such formulae usually sound a discordant note in correspondence whose dominant themes are not surprisingly fear of death, horror at the killing, pain at separation from loved ones, anguish at having lost all that is familiar and comforting ('There are not even the chimes of bells here, just the continual roar of cannons that do not give us a minute of peace'),[18] and a longing to return home at the earliest possible opportunity.

There is little evidence that the peasant troops were ideologically motivated. The attitude of many is probably well summed up by a Piedmontese soldier who recalled: 'We understood nothing. We only tried not to die. We did not care about killing Austrians, but we had to kill them because if they came forward they killed you.'[19] Nor was there much identification with the state and its institutions: the king, parliament, the army. Such concepts, indeed, are almost entirely absent from letters. As for *Italia* and *la patria*, these seemed to be lacking in 'national' content and certainly had none of the literary and historical baggage with which the educated middle classes had often invested them. The writer Mario Mariani spoke of how there were two kinds of soldiers in his platoon, 'those for whom the fatherland was their town or at most their province – the consequence of ten centuries of enslavement – and those for whom the fatherland was the world – the consequence of fifty years of evangelical internationalist preaching'.[20] And for the majority the experience of the trenches may well have reinforced the feeling that abstractions in the end did not count for much and that only one *patria* really mattered. When an elderly *alpino* who had taken part in the bloody campaigns on Monte Ortigara on the Trentino front was asked many years after the war what *patria* he had been fighting for, he banged his fist angrily on the table and said: 'Christ! My fatherland was leave, family, home.'[21]

For many intellectuals abstractions did matter, and the sight of the army along the Isonzo dissolving at Caporetto was profoundly distressing. The distinguished senator Leopoldo Franchetti was so overwhelmed with grief that he shot himself. It had been widely hoped that the war would serve to bind the masses to the state and give the country the moral unity that it had hitherto lacked. Benedetto Croce wrote in 1916 of how great nations were characterized by a willingness of their citizens to die 'for an ideal'; and he quoted with approval the lines of the French poet Lamartine: 'A large people without a soul is just a vast crowd . . . / Sparta lived for three hundred years on one day of heroism.'[22] And only a month before Caporetto, Croce spoke enthusiastically of how Cadorna's army was eradicating 'a stain fifteen centuries old' by demonstrating that Italians had finally achieved 'national and political cohesion'.[23] Men and women, even 'street gossips and urchins', from every corner of the land, now felt 'truly one', he said; and what particularly gratified him was a sense that the growing unity was part of an upward curve of constant moral progress: 'Every step has been a step forward, every mistake a lesson. 1848 was better than 1821, 1859 than 1848, 1915 than 1866; and accordingly this war will not only be an improvement on the past, but will also be an experiment that will provide us with a clearer picture of ourselves . . .'[24]

Caporetto shattered these illusions, and in the atmosphere of fear and bitter recrimination that followed the disaster the reality of the deep fractures in the country became abundantly clear. Italy had entered the conflict split, profoundly split – between interventionists and neutralists, piazza and parliament – and it was these divisions that were now widely seen as responsible for the collapse of morale on the Isonzo front. According to *Unità*, the newspaper of Gaetano Salvemini (himself a passionate supporter of the war on the grounds that it would help the masses to secure a greater political, economic and social stake in the nation), Caporetto was 'a moral reverse' brought about by the failure of the government to stop the propaganda of 'the forces hostile to the conflict' – socialists, Catholics and Giolittian liberals – seeping perniciously 'from the interior of the country – from the factories and the homes of the peasants – to the trenches'. And in line with virtually all interventionist opinion, the newspaper called for a strong prime minister who would crack down on the 'defeatists' and prosecute the war with far greater energy than had hitherto been shown.[25]

The inevitable result was to deepen still further the rifts in the nation. The anger and violence that had been such disturbing features of the so-called 'radiant days of May' in 1915 resurfaced. There was inflammatory talk of revolution, military coups, republican plots and putting the 'neutralist' politicians on trial for treason – a majority of the Chamber had remained loyal to Giolitti and were known to be at best lukewarm towards the war. Police reports referred to secret societies with Carbonaro-style rites and oaths committed to the assassination of leading socialists such as Turati ('We are now surrounded and followed night and day by an escort of plainclothes policemen,' he told Anna Kuliscioff in December)[26] or to blowing up the Vatican with dynamite: a great many Catholics and Catholic associations had given their backing to the war, but the Pope, Benedict XV, had refused to declare the conflict 'just', and in August 1917 he had issued a Note describing it as a 'useless slaughter' and urging disarmament and arbitration. This had probably done serious damage to troop morale, and there were calls in the top echelons of the army for Benedict to be arrested and hanged.

One interventionist with particularly strident views following Caporetto was Benito Mussolini. Mussolini had been called up in September 1915 and had served in a *bersagliere* unit on the Isonzo front and risen (like Hitler) to the rank of corporal, before being wounded by an exploding grenade thrower in a training exercise and invalided out in June 1917. He had resumed the editorship of *Il Popolo d'Italia*, the newspaper he had founded in Milan towards the end of 1914, and had used its columns to denounce the attempts of 'His Holiness Pope

Pilate XV' at peacemaking and demand a more resolute government, 'total war' and improved propaganda to strengthen the 'moral health' of the army.[27] News of Caporetto left him distraught (according to his sister he was so depressed he talked of dying), but he quickly rallied, and called for the Italian socialists to be treated without mercy as 'a more dangerous enemy' than the Austrians and for the nation to be fused in spirit with the army. He wanted peasant troops to be promised land, so as to raise their morale, and he urged a more disciplined attitude on the home front and the closure of theatres, concert halls, race courses and cafés.[28] Above all, he said, Italy needed a forceful leader to turn the 'lacerated organism' of the nation into something beautiful, noble and strong:

In this moment the Italian people is a mass of precious minerals. It needs to be forged, cleaned, worked. A work of art is still possible. But a government is needed. A man. A man who, when the situation demands it, has the delicate touch of an artist and the heavy fist of a warrior. Sensitive and determined. A man who knows the people, loves the people, and can direct and bend it – with violence if necessary.[29]

VICTORY AT VITTORIO VENETO

The man chosen by the king to take over the reins of government after Caporetto was Vittorio Emanuele Orlando, a stocky white-haired professor of constitutional law of Sicilian origin (he had been born in Palermo a few days before Garibaldi's Thousand entered the city: hence his name), with great intelligence and considerable energy – he was proud of having produced three children in thirty-one months.[30] And the new prime minister responded to the catastrophe by urging 'national unity' – though in reality 'unity' now meant one nation pitted against another. In the Chamber, Giolitti and more than a hundred of his supporters closed ranks in a 'Parliamentary Union', while interventionist groups of all shades – Nationalists, conservatives, democrats – retaliated in December 1917 by setting up a Parliamentary Union (*Fascio*) for National Defence, with over 150 deputies and ninety senators, which pressed Orlando's government into introducing harsher censorship and tougher measures against the 'neutralists'. Across the country 'Resistance Committees' and 'Fasci of National Defence' sprang up (the term *fascio* – ironically of socialist provenance – was fast embedding itself in the patriotic lexicon) to help root out 'defeatists': such as the worker from Modena who was sentenced to forty days in prison and a fine of 100 lire for refusing to subscribe to a national loan on the grounds that 'he had not wanted the war'.[31]

In this heavily polarized atmosphere the interventionists clung to their belief that war would be salutary and curative, and in contrast to many other European countries Italy witnessed very little intellectual backlash against the carnage. Filippo Tommaso Marinetti, who volunteered and served on the Isonzo and Piave fronts, remained true to his Futurist principles and recounted his experiences during the conflict in a tone of exultant enthusiasm, glorying in the sensory cocktail of exploding shells, machine-gun fire and human cries, and relishing the strong emotions (not least erotic) that accompanied the violence and danger.[32] D'Annunzio adopted a similarly celebratory and aesthetic approach, engaging in a series of carefully choreographed and highly publicized raids by air and sea that earned him one gold, three silver and two bronze medals for valour, recording his exploits in exuberant prose and poetry full of mystical, classical and religious allusions. He also coined a number of rallying cries that became much celebrated nationally. Among them were *Memento audere semper* ('Remember always to dare'), *Iterum rugit leo* ('The lion roars again': the slogan given to his bomber squadron based near Venice; an inversion of Venice's more pacific motto, 'Peace be unto thee, Mark, my evangelist'), and *Eia, eia, eia, alalà*, a war-cry (later taken up by Mussolini's fascists), apparently of classical Greek origin, that D'Annunzio made his aviators use in place of the more conventional *Ip, ip, urrah!*[33]

Other interventionists viewed the war in less flamboyant terms, but almost all the memoirs produced during and after the conflict were written in terms of a patriotic officer sharing the harsh life of the trenches with stoical, long-suffering, rank and file soldiers, who were learning through war to subordinate local and familial ties to the needs of the nation. Some of the most successful of these accounts adopted the keynote that De Amicis had struck in his earlier portrayals of military life: hardship made bearable, often joyous, through the bonds of frater-nal camaraderie and the 'lofty principles that we accept with our eyes closed as if they were a faith: fatherland, necessity, discipline'[34] – as in

Paolo Monelli's highly popular *Shoes in the Sun* (1921), with its subtitle: *Chronicle of Joyful and Sad Adventures of Alpini, Mules and Wine*. And even the least belligerent of intellectuals felt drawn to the myth of national solidarity, a myth that seemed to gain in emotional and ideological allure when it was juxtaposed with the reality of pain and slaughter; for as the young writer Renato Serra explained poignantly in 1915, shortly before being killed in action on a mountainside near Gorizia, fusion with the collectivity, whether in death or life, seemed almost a moral imperative to those, like himself, who identified passionately with the nation and yet inhabited an elite world, estranged from the 'real Italy' of the masses. To have had the opportunity to leap, and to have faltered, would have been shaming:

We had been on the brink, on the very edge. The wind had been buffeting us, throwing back our hair; and we had stood, the vertigo welling up inside us, trembling – and had not jumped. With this memory we would have grown old . . . I have been living in another place. In that Italy that seemed to me, when I was merely looking at it, deaf and empty. But now I feel that it can be filled with men like myself, gripped with the same anxiety and marching along the same route, able to support each other, and live and die together – should the moment come – even without knowing why.[35]

National solidarity seemed all the more imperative in the wake of Caporetto given that a large section of north-eastern Italy was once again, as before 1866, under direct Austrian rule. Many inhabitants of the Veneto and Friuli had fled in advance of the enemy – chiefly land-owners and local government officials, mayors especially it seems (the sense of having been abandoned by 'the *signori*' – the wealthy – rankled subsequently in popular memory) – but the majority of the population had stayed behind and now had to endure considerable hardship. Looting and lawlessness were widespread, and it took several months for order to be imposed. And there was extensive raping by Austrian and German soldiers (a fact emotively exploited by Italian propaganda to support the new image of a 'violated nation'). Requisitioning resulted in serious food shortages, and mortality rates rose sharply: according to a later commission of enquiry some 30,000 deaths were attributable, either directly or indirectly, to the occupation. Yet despite the often brutal conditions prevailing in the north-east, there is very little to suggest that the local peasantry felt hostile to the invaders. Indeed there were reports of the enemy being enthusiastically welcomed in places.[36]

The sense that the nation needed to pull together in order to avenge the shame of Caporetto resulted in an escalation of propaganda. State employees, professionals, businessmen, traders and other middle-class groups were subjected to intense patriotic mobilization, with bodies such as the 'Union of Italian Doctors for National Resistance' and the 'General Union of Teachers for Spiritual Assistance to the People' being formed to stiffen resolve and stifle defeatism.[37] There was a major morale-boosting campaign for the army, with a newly formed Propaganda Office organizing programmes of lectures (or 'conversations' as they were more democratically styled) by well-known figures such as Salvemini and commissioning leading writers and artists to help produce lively and illustrated 'trench newspapers'.[38] Rations were raised, annual leave increased by ten days, and free life insurance provided (psychologically not very sensitive, perhaps). There were frequent promises of land for the peasants after the war was finished, and a servicemen's association, the Opera Nazionale Combattenti, was established in December 1917 to look after the welfare of the soldiers and their families.

These initiatives were accompanied by a shift in military tactics. General Diaz was a more cautious commander than his predecessor, concerned above all to hold the line on the Piave and not deplete his army with unnecessary offensives. And with the focus more firmly on defence, casualty rates fell (143,000 killed and wounded in 1918 compared to 520,000 the previous year) and the obsession with discipline declined: there were no more decimations. By the late summer of 1918 it was becoming clear that the Austro-Hungarian empire was crumbling and that with German troops pinned down on the western front there was no prospect of reinforcements coming to help the Austrians and stiffen their flagging resolve. But still Diaz hesitated to attack. Orlando urged him on: he badly needed a victory to strengthen his negotiating hand at any future peace conference. So, too, did the British and French commanders, who sensed that a major breakthrough was possible. Early in October, Diaz finally gave his consent and three weeks later an offensive was launched on Monte Grappa, followed by an advance across the Piave. There was some initial resistance, but it was not great, and on 30 October, Italian forces were able to enter the town of Vittorio Veneto, so splitting the Austrian army in two, and proclaim victory.

Trento was taken on 3 November and troops disembarked at Trieste. The Austrians signed an armistice and on 4 November the war in Italy formally came to an end. With its principal ally defeated, Germany had little choice but to surrender too.

In a ceremony held in Rome a fortnight later, Antonio Salandra, the man who had led Italy into the war, hailed the victory as the summation of the patriotic spirit of those many generations of men (women still did not get a mention) who had striven for the well-being and glory of their fatherland; and if Italians could maintain the discipline and self-sacrifice that they had displayed during the previous three and a half years of fighting, he predicted that the nation would become 'greater and more honoured still':

[We are] the spokesmen and delegates of the martyrs, the poets, the statesmen, the soldiers, the princes and the common people, of the great and the humble, of all those who loved this Italy, who willed this Italy, and who celebrated this Italy; of all those who worked for her, of all those who suffered for her, and of all those who died for her. Their spirit resonates in our spirits. It is immortal Italy that has awoken, wreathed in her glories and her sorrows, wishing to reconquer her throne . . . To Her, who is immanent, eternal, timeless; to Her, who has been received into the heavens of history amid the purest emanations of blood of her best sons, to Her we swear to consecrate all that remains to us of strength and life. Long live Italy! For ever, and above all else, Long live Italy![39]

PART SIX

Fascism
1919–43

21

Civil War and the Advent of Fascism, 1919–22

*When I returned from the war, like so many, I hated politics and politicians . . .
To come home, after struggling and fighting, to the country of Giolitti, who
offered every ideal as an object for sale? No. Better to deny everything, to destroy
everything, so as to rebuild everything from scratch . . . It is certain, in my view,
that without Mussolini, three-quarters of Italian youths who had returned from
the trenches would have become Bolsheviks.*

Italo Balbo, *Diario 1922*

Rise . . .
Oppressed of all the world
At the victorious eruption
Of the forces of the proletariat.
Remember
The horrendous carnage
The massive destruction.
The ancient anger of slaves
Rises ineluctably.
Spartacus prevails.

Socialist war memorial, Montella

THE WAR ECONOMY

Despite Caporetto, and despite all the charges of weakness, incompetence and even treachery that had been hurled at parliament by the
interventionists, Italy's victory in the First World War constituted in
many respects a remarkable achievement on the part of the liberal
state. It had been widely feared in 1915 that the country would prove

economically too fragile to sustain a prolonged conflict. And there had certainly been severe strains and major episodes of social unrest – most notably in Turin in August 1917, when riots triggered by food shortages had swept through the city, killing some fifty people. But overall the country's performance had been impressive. FIAT had emerged as Europe's leading manufacturer of trucks and lorries, turning out 25,000 vehicles in 1918, six times as many as in 1914. An aeronautical industry had been created almost from nothing, with 6,500 planes being produced in 1918. And while the army had begun the war with just 613 machine guns, by the time of the armistice it had nearly 20,000 and over 7,000 pieces of heavy artillery in the field – more than the British. All this had been achieved in the teeth of persistent shortages of essential raw materials, especially coal, and with only a fledgling domestic steel industry.[1]

The key to this success had lain in a ruthless programme of economic planning. A new under-secretariat (later ministry) of Arms and Munitions had been created, headed by an energetic and pragmatic general, Alfredo Dallolio, to ensure production at all costs and oversee the allocation of government contracts, cheap loans and raw materials. Firms regarded as 'auxiliary' to the war effort – and there were nearly 2,000 of them by November 1918 – were subjected to 'industrial mobilization', under which wages and hours of labour were strictly regulated, strikes banned and employees bound by tight military discipline, with armed guards patrolling the factories.[2] More than a third of the 900,000 workers in these plants were men who had been exempted from military service or else released from the army on secondment; many of the remainder were recruited from among the peasantry. Women also featured prominently, and nearly a quarter of the employees in munitions factories were female.[3] Although the lifestyle of these auxiliary workers was far from easy – a seventy-five-hour week was quite normal at FIAT in 1916, and in real terms wages for most industrial labourers declined in the course of the war – the general perception of soldiers fighting at the front was that they were little more than cosseted *imboscati* (shirkers) – another source of division and bitter vituperation in Italy after 1918.

Some sectors of society profited – and profited enormously – from the war. The main firms involved in the industrial mobilization programme grew rapidly, and in the process swallowed up many of their competitors. FIAT's capital increased from 25 million to 125 million lire, and its workforce from 6,000 to 30,000; and companies such as Breda (engineering), Ansaldo and Ilva (steel), and Montecatini (chemicals) witnessed a similar expansion. But this huge growth had been the result almost entirely of massive state spending on matériel and other war-related items (around 41 billion lire at pre-war prices, according to one estimate), most of it paid for by raising foreign loans and printing money (with inevitable inflationary consequences); and as a result the major firms were acutely vulnerable to the return of peacetime conditions and the end of government orders.[4] Already in 1918 Ansaldo, Ilva and other industrial giants were engaged in a scramble to buy leading banks and so guarantee themselves credit and deny it to their competitors – a rather unseemly spectacle. And the anger of workers and veterans towards war profiteers or 'sharks' was to be a further rift in the nation.

So, too, was the increased gap between the north and south of the country. The emergence of the 'southern question' in the 1870s, and the campaigns of politicians, economists and historians such as Fortunato, Salvemini and Nitti to highlight the gulf between the two halves of the peninsula and suggest possible remedies, had done little to assuage the feelings of many southerners that they were victims of northern arrogance and exploitation or of many northerners that they were being dragged down by a corrupt and barbarous society. Ironically, indeed, the torrent of literature from the 1880s on the problems of the *latifondi*, the mafia, the camorra, general crime and poverty in the south may well have hardened old stereotypes, as a letter sent from the Veneto and published by the Sicilian radical Napoleone Colajanni in 1906 suggested:

Dear Professor, if only you could hear the ideas that most people up here have about the poor south! How many prejudices they instil into us from our earliest years! We northerners, they say, belong to a superior race, are honest and hard-working. In short we have every good quality. The southerners, by contrast, belong to an inferior race and have none. They add that it was a grave mistake for Garibaldi to have gone and conquered the Kingdom of the Two Sicilies, as we northerners now have to pay taxes as well for those wretches in the south who do not want to work. Everything down there is mafia and camorra . . . And believe me, Professor, these are not just the views of the poor and ignorant, but also of virtually all the leading members of the educated classes.[5]

The industrial surge between 1915 and 1918 was concentrated in the north-west of the country, with the population of the main cities of

Piedmont and Lombardy growing by at least 20 per cent between 1911 and 1921, and this reinforced the sense of there being 'two Italies': a modern and increasingly prosperous urban north and a backward rural south. And the fact that agricultural production in the southern half of the peninsula had scarcely fallen during the war, despite 2.5 million peasants being drafted into the army, underlined dramatically the huge surfeit of manpower. The demobilized soldiers who returned to their impoverished villages in Campania or Calabria vented much of their anger on the *galantuomini*, forcibly occupying hundreds of thousands of hectares of land in a bid to realize their dreams of becoming smallholders. But there was also bitterness towards the government and resentment at continuing northern disparagement, and this led in places to intensified regionalism. One manifestation of such sentiments was a revival of the traditional idea that 'the mafia' had been a northern invention to discredit Sicily, and that in reality 'mafia' was a form of noble behaviour characteristic of the island. The former prime minister Orlando won rapturous applause at an electoral rally in Palermo in 1925 when he announced: 'I declare myself to be *mafioso*, and I am proud to be such.'[6]

THE MUTILATED VICTORY

The liberal regime deserved much credit for its handling of the war, but it was to receive little. The Socialist Party had been driven further than ever into the political wilderness, and after 1918 it retaliated by adopting a vehement revolutionary stance, inspired by the success of the Bolshevik coup in Russia. Church and state were still a long way from any formal conciliation, despite their increased cooperation in 1915–18; and the various interventionist groups – the Nationalists, the Futurists, the syndicalists and the dissident socialists – were still deeply hostile to parliament: wedded to the myth that Italy had only entered the conflict in May 1915 through their will and determination, and strongly convinced that the victory at Vittorio Veneto had been theirs and theirs alone. And the peace was now to be theirs, too; and woe betide any liberal politician – Orlando, or the Foreign Minister, Sonnino – who failed to secure Italy its just deserts after the sacrifice of 600,000 men. As D'Annunzio wrote in a celebrated poem published a few days before the armistice, questioning the right of the United States' President, Woodrow Wilson, and the other allied leaders to speak for those who had 'exceeded in their suffering the limits set by the pity of the Lord':

> Who is it today that arises as arbiter of all future life, over the wailing and smoking land?
>
> Where has he come from? From the depths of suffering or the summits of light, as the exile Dante?
>
> Or is he just a sage sitting in his unmoved chair, ignorant of the trenches and circles [of Hell]? . . .
>
> Who would transform the greatness and beauty of this violence into a long debate between old men, in a senile council of trickery?
>
> The ink of scribes for the blood of martyrs? . . .
>
> Oh victory of ours: you will not be mutilated. Nobody will break your knees or clip your wings.[7]

From the outset the position of the Italian delegation at the peace conference that convened in Paris in January 1919 was extremely difficult. Whipped up by D'Annunzio and the interventionists, public opinion back home was expecting the maximum possible territorial gains: not just Trentino, the South Tyrol, Trieste, Istria and northern Dalmatia – which had been promised under the Treaty of London of 1915 – but also the port of Fiume (Rijeka) on the Croatian coast, a town with long-standing economic and political ties to Hungary, but which from the middle of the nineteenth century had developed a large community of middle-class Italians, welcomed in by the authorities in Budapest in an attempt to create a counterweight in this strategically important centre to the potentially hostile local Slav population. But in asking for 'the Treaty of London plus Fiume' Italy risked muddying the ideological waters and creating an impression of cynical opportunism, for the Treaty of London had been premised on old-fashioned considerations of *Realpolitik* (to ensure Italy's security in the Adriatic), while Fiume was being claimed on the basis of the 'principle of nationality' – though it was in fact questionable whether a majority of the town's population was Italian, as the adjacent working-class suburbs were almost entirely Croat.

To make matters worse for the Italian delegation at Paris, stereotypes and prejudices abounded in the deliberations of the three most senior figures at the peace conference – Woodrow Wilson, the British prime minister, Lloyd George, and the French prime minister, Clemenceau – who clearly regarded Italy as something of a parvenu and undeserving of full membership of the great powers' club. And such condescension served further to inflame nationalist feelings in Italy, forcing Orlando and Sonnino to be yet more insistent in their demands in order to avoid being vilified back home as authors of what was already being widely spoken of as 'the mutilated victory'. Orlando was generally well received in Paris – Lloyd George warmed to his expansive Mediterranean manner (though Harold Nicolson probably reflected more mainstream English opinion in describing him, waspishly, as 'a white, weak, flabby man');[8] but Sonnino was the very antithesis of a conventional Italian with his rigid and austere character, severe demeanour and intellectual outlook; and he created a bad impression. Moreover he was forced to do much of the talking as the British and Americans found Orlando very hard to understand, despite his frequent expressive gestures.

The problem with Fiume was that the French were eager to support a strong Yugoslavia as part of a chain of new states in central Europe penning Germany in on its eastern flank. But there was another, less easily voiced, consideration. Franco-Italian relations had been deeply strained ever since 1860; and though Italy had abandoned the Triple Alliance in 1915, it had done so primarily on the basis of short-term expediency. In the long term, as Crispi and others had argued, it was more logical for Italy to aspire to an alliance with Germany against France – its rival for supremacy in the Mediterranean. The elderly Clemenceau knew this, and harboured few illusions, and while the Italian government did all it could to weaken Yugoslavia, sanctioning plans to foment civil war there by sending in agents provocateurs and even encouraging Italian soldiers to heighten tensions by seducing local women, the French worked to keep the new state united as a means of holding an unpredictable Italy in check. Orlando lamented that it was galling to have defeated Austria only to have another major power replace it in the Adriatic. But he attracted little sympathy in Paris.[9]

A further difficulty facing the Italian delegation was that neither France nor Britain believed that the contribution of Italy to the war effort had been sufficient to merit the extensive territorial claims it was now making: in addition to Trentino, the South Tyrol and Istria, the Treaty of London had promised the Dodecanese islands and major footholds in the Balkans, including the port of Vlorë on the far side of the Strait of Otranto and a protectorate over central Albania. It was pointed out that Italy had sustained far fewer casualties than France and

Britain, and there was much anger that Diaz had apparently only been willing to launch an offensive when victory had looked certain ('They all say that the signal for an armistice was the signal for Italy to begin to fight,' noted the British ambassador).[10] There was irritation that the Italian navy had hardly ventured from port, despite promises to patrol the Mediterranean and the Adriatic, and considerable resentment at the huge sums that the hard-pressed allies had been forced to lend to Italy (15 billion lire in the case of Britain), not all of which had then been spent on the war. The old idea that Italians were charming but utterly unscrupulous played through the minds of many of the delegates in Paris. As Clemenceau put it: '[T]he Italians met [me] with a magnificent *coup de chapeau* of the seventeenth-century type, and then held out the hat for alms at the end of the bow.'[11]

And what of the 'principle of nationality' that the high-minded Wilson had proclaimed to be the touchstone of the new European order? Was not Italy the home of this sacred ideal? In January 1919, shortly before the peace conference began, Wilson travelled to Genoa to pay homage at the tomb of Mazzini and, on being presented with a bound edition of the great patriot's writings by the mayor of the city, he revealed that he had studied Mazzini closely during his time as a professor at Princeton and that he was now aiming to implement the vision of this solitary thinker who had 'by some gift of God been lifted above the common level'. In private he added that perhaps only Lincoln or Gladstone had seen so clearly into the essence of liberalism.[12] How, then, could Italy insist on annexing territories that were clearly not 'Italian' (only Trentino and Trieste had a majority of Italophones)? Wilson was bemused, and as Orlando and Sonnino clung doggedly to the formula 'the Treaty of London plus Fiume', bringing the conference to an impasse, he grew increasingly frustrated: 'It is curious how utterly incapable these Italians are of taking any position on principle and sticking to it,' he announced, with unconcealed contempt and anger.[13]

But as the distinguished philosopher Giovanni Gentile (soon to be appointed Mussolini's first education minister) explained in a book published in 1919, Mazzini had never been in favour of the kind of democratic nationalism, based simply on self-determination, that Wilson was advocating in Paris. That was to miss the essence of Mazzini's thought, which was hostile to liberalism and rooted in a deeply religious vision of life. For Mazzini, rights derived from duties, and a nation could only claim rights when its citizens had demonstrated a capacity to struggle in pursuit of a shared ethical goal. Nations were spiritual entities, and freedom consisted of the individual immersing his moral being in that of the whole. Language, geography and race were mere epiphenomena, 'indications' of nationality, not their essence. And since the health of a nation was gauged by its success in mobilizing people to action, there was no automatic veto, according to Gentile, within the Mazzinian schema on expansion or conquest. Hence, Mazzini's claim in 1871 that the Roman Empire had been 'the most powerful nationality of the ancient world', despite being composed of many different peoples: 'In questions of nationality, as in everything else, the end alone is sovereign.'[14]

With demonstrations and violent clashes escalating in Italy in the spring of 1919, particularly along the interventionist–neutralist fault-line, Orlando and Sonnino felt in no position to compromise. Orlando claimed that a secret society had sworn to assassinate him if he returned home without having secured Dalmatia, while Sonnino spoke portentously of how a 'mutilated victory' would tip the country into anarchy. Orlando was desperate, and on Easter Sunday, during a particularly difficult meeting with the British, French and Americans, he was forced to leave the table in tears, while Clemenceau looked on impassively and the British incredulously (Sir Maurice Hankey, the conference secretary, said he would have spanked his son for such a disgraceful show of emotion).[15] Four days later, with the talks deadlocked, Orlando left Paris in disgust. Crowds cheered his train as he travelled down through Italy, and when he reached Rome he was greeted with pealing church bells, aeroplanes circling overhead dropping patriotic leaflets, and enthusiastic cries of '*Viva Orlando! Viva Fiume! Viva l'Italia!*' Everywhere walls were covered in slogans demanding the annexation of Fiume, and in Turin students went along the Corso Wilson, so named in honour of the president's recent visit to the city, changing all the signs into 'Corso Fiume'.[16]

Orlando received a ringing endorsement from the Chamber, by 382 votes to 40, for his firm stand in Paris, declaring that Italy's claims were based on 'such high and solemn reasons of right and justice' that they needed to be recognized by the allies in full. But he was painting himself into a corner, perhaps deliberately so ('I am . . . a new Christ, and must suffer my passion for the salvation of my country,' he had declared a few days before),[17] and when he returned to the conference table early in May, having aged, according to one observer, ten years, his negotiating hand was weaker than ever. Britain and France had proceeded in his absence to carve up Germany's African colonies among themselves, while the last vestiges of Wilson's thin veneer of patience had finally cracked, leaving the Italian delegates exposed to the full force of his cold Protestant censoriousness. Orlando pleaded for his political life. 'I must have a solution. Otherwise I will have a crisis in parliament or in the streets in Italy', he told Lloyd George. 'And if not,' the British prime minister asked, 'who do you see taking your place?' 'Perhaps D'Annunzio.'[18] But Orlando's entreaties were to no avail, and on 19 June he lost a vote of confidence in the Chamber and resigned, leaving his successor, Francesco Saverio Nitti, a radical economics professor from Basilicata, to concede Dalmatia to Yugoslavia and agree to Fiume becoming a neutral city under the protection of the newly formed League of Nations.

THE OCCUPATION OF FIUME

Against a backdrop of spiralling inflation and mounting unemployment, as millions of demobilized troops exchanged the horrors of the trenches for the bleak economic realities of civilian life, and with labour relations deteriorating as militant socialists, many of them newly released from prison, prepared for a revolution, 'as in Russia', staging strikes, protests, factory occupations and riots, D'Annunzio stoked the fires of nationalism with his intemperate rhetoric. In two major speeches in May, buoyed by the recent academic accolade of an honorary doctorate from the university of Rome, he railed against the treachery of the allies, claiming that Italy, the poorest of the belligerent powers, had 'saved the world' through its heroism and copious sacrifice of blood during the war, and he accused the 'triumvirs' of the three richest nations of conspiring to keep Italy impoverished and isolated, using the League of Nations as their tool. He talked of France's historic perfidy (had they not been responsible for Mentana, Tunisia and even the catastrophe of Adua?), and caricatured Wilson, the 'Croatified Quaker', as a grotesque hollow figurine with a 'long equine face' and false teeth.[19]

D'Annunzio was a major threat to the authority (such of it that remained) of the government in Rome. He had a cult following in the army, particularly among the *arditi* or shock troops that had been formed after Caporetto to help raise morale at the front and whose celebration of ruthlessness and daring, bravura exploits and violent language mirrored well the poet's own feverish *Weltanschauung* (their motto, *Me ne frego* – soon to be taken up by the fascists – was a slang expression meaning 'I don't give a damn'). In the course of the spring and summer of 1919 he was heavily involved in negotiations with disaffected generals and officers, Nationalists, Futurists and other patriotic groups to seize Fiume by force; while in Fiume itself the groundwork for a possible coup was being laid by a society of Mazzinian inspiration called Young Fiume, whose activities helped to feed a mood of ugly chauvinism in the city: in one incident Italian police opened fire on a party of children returning from a picnic who had failed to shout 'Viva Italia', killing nine and wounding twenty.[20] The new prime minister looked to avert the gathering storm by buying off D'Annunzio with a government post. D'Annunzio declined it, and turned his withering rhetoric on Nitti, dubbing him, in one of his most celebrated neologisms, *Cagoia* – 'shit-itis'.

D'Annunzio had a competitor in the war of words (and deeds; there was to be no disjuncture between thought and action) in Mussolini, who back in March 1919 had founded a new movement, the *Fasci di combattimento* ('fighting units'), in a rented hall overlooking Piazza San Sepolcro in the heart of Milan. This was one of a number of initiatives launched at that time in the no-man's land between liberalism and socialism, and the event had gone almost unnoticed in the press. A hundred or so people had turned up for the inaugural meeting, for the most part ex-combatants and interventionists of very differing backgrounds and inclinations – Futurists (including Marinetti), anarchists, syndicalists, republicans, Nationalists, Catholics and *arditi* (among them the patriotically named Ferruccio Vecchi, the group's main national spokesman) – and this heterogeneity had been one important reason why Mussolini had not wanted to adopt a precise political programme. The *Fasci* were to be a spiritual force, embracing all those who had believed in the war (an eclecticism underlined when ten people had been chosen at random from the front row to sit on the executive committee). And the most powerful bond uniting them was not what they hoped to build but what they hated. In April Marinetti and Vecchi had organized the ransacking of the headquarters of the Socialist Party newspaper, *Avanti!*, with the captured sign-board being taken in triumph to the offices of Mussolini's *Il Popolo d'Italia*.[21]

Sitting at his editor's desk, sipping a glass of milk and surrounded by pistols, daggers, grenades and cartridges, Mussolini poured out a steady stream of journalism intended to outdo D'Annunzio in vehemence if not literary inventiveness. He attacked the government for its flaccid handling of the peace negotiations: 'The Italy that deals and barters in Paris . . . is not the Italy of the Grappa and the Isonzo. It is the Italy of foreigners and storytellers, of beggars and lawyers, the Italy which sadly still survives on high, but which lower down among the people, who have a sense of her pride and her glory, is dead and buried.' He called Orlando a 'lachrymogen', an 'invertebrate who gets by propped up on strong zabagliones', and urged him to have the courage to break with Wilson and the other 'bandits of international plutocracy'.[22] He denounced Britain as 'the fattest and most bourgeois nation in the world',[23] and railed against the Bolsheviks, 80 per cent of whose leaders, he alleged, were Jews operating in the service of Jewish bankers in London and New York: 'Race does not betray race.'[24] And following D'Annunzio's lead he mocked Nitti as 'Franz Joseph Cagoia', 'Saverio Cagoia' and 'His excrescency Cagoia'.[25] Nothing, according to Mussolini, was sacrosanct, other than the nation: 'We are loyal to Italy and to the fatherland alone.'[26]

During the summer of 1919 Mussolini and his fascist supporters were in close touch with D'Annunzio and the other senior figures in the army (the king's cousin, the Duke of Aosta, included) who were toying with the idea of taking Fiume by force. D'Annunzio himself was growing distracted by plans for a long-distance flight to the Far East (and by a new love affair), and when in August the Italian troops that had been stationed in the city since the end of the previous year were ordered out by allied commissioners eager to enforce Fiume's neutrality, it was to Mussolini and General Peppino Garibaldi (grandson of the great patriot) and to the Nationalist leaders Enrico Corradini and Luigi Federzoni that they initially turned for help with a coup. When they did approach D'Annunzio, they couched their appeal in language redolent of the Risorgimento:

The Great Mother does not know Fiume; she is not permitted to know the finest of her daughters, the purest and most holy of Italian women . . . We have sworn upon the memory of all who died for the unity of Italy: *Fiume or death!* . . . And you do nothing for Fiume? You who have all Italy in your hands – great, noble, generous Italy – will you not shake her out of the lethargy into which she has so long fallen?[27]

D'Annunzio was persuaded, and on 12 September he set out from the small town of Ronchi to the south of Gorizia with around 200 Italian troops and twenty-six armoured trucks purloined from a local depot. As he advanced along the road to Fiume, he was joined by patriotic veterans, mutineers (including many *arditi*), Futurists, students, adventurers and even schoolchildren, and by the time the column reached the outskirts of the city it had swollen to more than 2,000. The commander in Fiume, General Vittorio Emanuele Pittaluga, had been given strict orders to halt the march. He parleyed with D'Annunzio at a roadblock, telling him that Italy would be ruined by his actions and face 'incalculable consequences'. 'It is you who will ruin Italy if you prevent her destiny being fulfilled,' retorted the poet. And in a scene reminiscent of Napoleon's famous gesture at Lake Laffrey in 1815, when the former emperor had bared his chest to the French troops sent to arrest him, D'Annunzio pulled back his coat and invited Pittaluga's men to aim at the medals pinned over his heart (D'Annunzio had always craved a beautiful death in a noble cause: throughout his life he had been haunted by the martyrdom of Saint Sebastian). Pittaluga hesitated, and then stepped forward and shook D'Annunzio's hand. 'I will not shed Italian blood nor be the cause of a fratricidal war . . . Long live Italian Fiume!'[28] D'Annunzio carried on into the city, with flags waving, bells tolling, laurel leaves tumbling from the balconies and the *arditi* singing their marching song, 'Giovinezza' ('Youth-time'):

> Youth-time, youth-time
> Beauty's springtime
> In the bitterness of life
> Your song rings far and wide

In keeping with the spirit of this anarchic anthem (soon to be appropriated by the fascists as their official hymn), the occupation of Fiume provided an extraordinary spectacle of theatricality, political innovation and licentiousness, with carefully choreographed parades, marches, histrionic speeches and mock battles, public dances, riotous drinking, drug-taking and sexual promiscuity, and outlandish experimentation with fashion and appearance. A young English writer, Osbert Sitwell, described the febrile and almost operatic character of the city after visiting it in the autumn of 1920:

The general animation and noisy vitality seemed to herald a new land, a new system. We gazed and listened in amazement. Every man here seemed to wear a uniform designed by himself: some had beards, and had shaved their heads completely so as to resemble the Commander himself . . . others had cultivated huge tufts of hair, half a foot long, waving out from their foreheads, and wore, balanced on the very back of the skull, a black fez. Cloaks, feathers and flowing black ties were universal, and every man – and few women were to be seen – carried the 'Roman dagger'.[29]

A striking aspect of the occupation of Fiume – which was to last for over fifteen months as the government in Rome sought for a solution, fearful of sending in the army in case it mutinied – was the constant interplay between the sacred and the profane. D'Annunzio's speeches, often delivered impromptu to crowds that gathered beneath the balcony of his residence, were full of religious imagery and language, oaths and liturgical exchanges ('A noi!', 'Eia, eia, alalà!') intended to create a close emotional dialogue with the audience ('the first example of such interplay since Greek times,' D'Annunzio claimed).[30] There was much talk of martyrdom, blood and faith, and the entire experience of Fiume was presented in terms of a redemptive sacrifice – a 'calvary', a 'passion' – that was being made by the city (the 'Holocaust City' as D'Annunzio called it) so Italy might rise again. Civic ceremonies were often linked to religious occasions – such as the feast day of St Sebastian on 20 January, when the city's women solemnly presented D'Annunzio with a dagger ('To you . . . chosen by God to radiate the light of renewed liberty through the world . . . [we] offer this holy dagger . . . so you may carve the word "victory" in the living flesh of our enemies') and the poet thanked them with an impassioned sermon on the meaning of the saint's death:

> The Archer of Life cried out in his death agony: 'I die in order not to die.'
> He cried, bleeding: 'Not enough! Not enough! Again!'
> He cried: 'I will live again. But in order to live again, I must die.'
> Immortality of love! Eternity of sacrifice!
> The paths of immolation are the surest; and the blood of the hero and the heroine is inexhaustible.
> You know this, sisters in Christ, brothers in the living God. This is the sense of the mystery.[31]

THE ELECTIONS OF 1919

Mussolini was eager to capitalize on D'Annunzio's success in seizing Fiume and humiliating the government in Rome, and from the columns of his newspaper, *Il Popolo d'Italia*, he pledged his full moral support to 'the Hero' and launched a subscription. But D'Annunzio was annoyed that the fascist leader had not participated directly in what he called 'the most beautiful exploit since the departure of Garibaldi's Thousand',[32] and he wrote him a stinging letter (which not surprisingly remained unpublished until after Mussolini's death) accusing him of cowardice and of making empty promises. Determined to show that he was as much a man of action as the poet, Mussolini responded by proposing a full-scale *coup d'état*, including a march on Trieste, the deposition of the king, Victor Emmanuel, a constituent assembly and the landing of troops in the Romagna and the Marche in support of a republican insurrection. But in reality Mussolini was not keen to get embroiled too heavily with D'Annunzio. He wanted his own political space, and his overriding concern was to build up his fledgling movement, which by the early autumn of 1919 numbered around 150 autonomous local sections and 40,000 members.[33] And when on 7 October he flew to Fiume for talks with the poet, his principal aim was to secure good publicity ahead of the first national congress of the *Fasci*, which was due to be held in Florence two days later.

It was no coincidence that the Socialist Party had just staged its own national congress: Mussolini wanted his movement to appear as a credible alternative for interventionists to the far left (though Marinetti's appeals in Florence for the Senate to be replaced by a 'dynamo' chamber of young men under thirty, the 'devaticanization' of Italy and the forcible enrolment of artists in government probably did not help his cause).[34] The socialists had certainly raised the political temperature at their congress, proclaiming the Russian revolution 'the most auspicious event' in the history of the working classes, and voting overwhelmingly for a new constitution that called for 'the violent conquest of political power', the dictatorship of the proletariat, and the destruction of every instrument of bourgeois domination and oppression. And on occasions the militant rhetoric of the delegates was matched by equally aggressive gestures. A former Party Secretary, the aptly named Nicola Bombacci, a hirsute man of ferocious appearance, responded to a taunt from a colleague during the 1921 congress that he was no more than a 'penknife revolutionary' by pulling out a pistol.[35] Bombacci was to be one of the founders of the Italian Communist Party, but during the 1930s he gravitated towards fascism and ended his days a passionate supporter of Mussolini's puppet government, the Republic of Salò. In April 1945 he was shot by partisans.

The combination of ideological extremism, economic chaos, unbridled anger and the erosion of central authority helped generate a dangerously volatile situation. Across huge areas of southern Italy millions of peasants demanded compensation for their suffering in the trenches, and with banners waving and drums beating, and led by representatives of veterans' associations or Catholic cooperatives, they marched onto uncultivated land, staked out plots and began digging. With the government unwilling to intervene, many owners were forced to sell. In northern and central Italy it was the left-wing unions – the socialist General Confederation of Labour (whose membership rose from 250,000 in 1918 to 2 million in 1920), the anarchist Italian Syndical Union and the recently formed Catholic confederation – that took the lead in mobilizing angry workers, and during 1919 more than a million people went on strike in protest at soaring prices and unemployment. In the rural communities of the Po valley the Chambers of Labour provided the focal point for militancy, with local bosses known as *capilega* – often ardent socialists convinced that a revolution was imminent and defiant of all bourgeois (indeed any) authority – controlling the peasantry, imposing strict labour quotas on the landowners, and dictating wages and general conditions of work.

In this atmosphere violence was rampant. Socialist leaders encouraged their followers to clash with the police, desecrate the tricolour, intimidate blacklegs and taunt soldiers. There were countless instances of arson, sabotage, theft, assault and murder, in many cases the result of crowds getting out of control as tempers flared and insults were exchanged. Everywhere graffiti appeared calling for revolution and applauding Lenin and the Bolsheviks, socialism and communism, daubed in red paint on even the most celebrated national buildings and monuments. The most publicized instances of disorder took place in regions such as Piedmont, Lombardy, Emilia Romagna and Tuscany, where the presence of socialism was strongest and the influence and ambition of its grass roots leaders greatest ('I do not recognize your authority – in fact I am here to strip you of your authority,' the head of the Bologna Chamber of Labour told the local prefect defiantly at the end of 1919),[36] but in parts of the south, too, less well reported, there was a terrifying escalation of lawlessness as old patterns of feuding and banditry broke to the surface. In western Sicily rival factions and gangs (schematically referred to as 'old' and 'new' mafias) vied with one another for supremacy, leaving thousands dead. In the province of Trapani alone there were some 700 killings in the space of just one year, with 216 in the small town of Marsala.[37]

It was against this backdrop that Italy's first post-war elections were held in November 1919. The government had hoped to draw some of the sting of subversion by passing a new suffrage law giving the vote to all who had served at the front, irrespective of their age, and to every other male over twenty-one. This increased the electorate by more than a quarter, to 11 million. But an even more decisive change was the introduction of proportional representation and provincial electoral colleges, which at one blow severed the link between deputies and local clienteles on which liberal politicians had traditionally based their power, handing the initiative instead to parties with the machinery to mobilize a mass turn-out.[38] The principal beneficiaries were the socialists, who secured 32 per cent of the vote and 156 deputies, three times as many as in the previous legislature, and a newly formed Catholic (though strictly speaking non-confessional) party, the Italian Popular Party, which got 100 deputies. The result was that more than half of the new Chamber was made up of politicians who were either deeply sceptical of the liberal regime (the Catholics) or who were overtly hostile to it and who now aimed to use their platform in parliament to vilify the state (the socialists). The remaining deputies consisted of assorted liberals, radicals and social democrats, who found cooperation hard. The fascists won fewer than 5,000 votes and none of their seventeen candidates, including the conductor Arturo Toscanini, was returned.[39] Mussolini thought of emigrating, while the socialists gleefully paraded a coffin through the streets of Milan to symbolize his political demise.

THE RISE OF THE FASCIST SQUADS

With parliament deeply split, effective government became almost impossible. Nitti limped on as prime minister until June 1920, unable to resolve the problem of Fiume, sort out the public finances or tackle the growing militancy of the socialists. And with central government perilously weak, the extremists became increasingly aggressive, encouraging property-owners (and not a few workers) in many parts of northern and central Italy to set up resistance associations and leagues in conjunction with local fascists and other patriotic groups in a bid to stem the tide of lawlessness. Italy was fast slipping towards anarchy, and as the chaos intensified, old anxieties about the lack of moral cohesion resurfaced. Giovanni Amendola lamented how the moment Italians no longer had an external enemy to fight they reverted to traditional partisan habits and set upon each other in 'the factional spirit that in former centuries had kept [them] divided',[40] and early in 1920 a group of leading intellectuals – among them Giuseppe Prezzolini, Giovanni Gentile and the brilliant young radical liberal Piero Gobetti – launched a passionate appeal for a '*Fascio* of National Education' to improve the quality of schools and teachers, lay the foundations for 'the granitic national unity and greatness of the fatherland', and bring an end to the country's long-standing internal divisions.[41]

The socialist leadership had little faith that a revolution could succeed in Italy – apart from anything else, they knew that the French and British would not tolerate a socialist state in the heart of western Europe – but in the polarized climate of 1919–20 they dared not use the language of moderation and so did nothing to rein in grass roots activists or disabuse the rank and file. Equally they failed to make plans for a national takeover, leaving the socialist movement uncoordinated, heavily dependent on local initiatives and vulnerable to counter-insurgency. Strikes continued unabated; and in September 1920, amid fears that a number of employers were about to impose a lock-out as part of a pay dispute, more than 400,000 workers occupied factories and shipyards, running up red or black (anarchist) flags and expelling the management. Giolitti, who had recently returned as prime minister (he was widely considered the only man with sufficient authority and guile to restore order, despite being seventy-eight) feared a full-scale insurrection (he pointed subsequently to the huge quantities of arms and explosives that were found in the factories to prove his point)[42] and pressurized the industrialists into making major concessions, including the principle that trade union representatives could sit on management boards. Giolitti wanted to buy time, convinced the current political turmoil was little more than a 'neurasthenic' post-war hangover which could, with appropriate inducements, be tamed and steered into constitutional channels. But few shared his optimism; indeed many felt angered by his leniency towards the far left and thought the time had come for a more robust response.

The local government elections early in November 1920 were for many the last straw. The far left made sweeping gains across northern and central Italy, and in the socialist heartlands of the lower Po valley, in old provincial centres such as Bologna and Ferrara (where a red flag now flew triumphantly above the Renaissance town hall), there was a new mood of defiance. On 21 November some 300 armed fascists marched through the streets of central Bologna to Palazzo d'Accursio, where the socialist administration was being sworn in. The attack had been announced in advance, and the councillors had taken the precaution of barricading themselves inside the building. 'Red guards' threw five grenades, causing panic in the crowds that were gathered outside, and in the ensuing confusion ten socialists or socialist sympathizers were killed, seven of them by fascists. Inside the city hall an opposition councillor was shot (by a policeman), providing the fascists with their first important 'martyr'.[43]

In the weeks that followed, similar punitive attacks were launched against socialists in other parts of the Po valley, and to the intense surprise of most observers, Mussolini included, the fascist movement suddenly began to escalate. There were 1,065 new subscriptions in October–November 1920: the following month the figure leapt to nearly 11,000; and total membership rose from 20,165 with just eighty-eight sections at the end of December to 187,588 and over a thousand sections five months later.[44] This remarkable growth was fuelled by an unwillingness on the part of the police and army to step in and prevent or even punish the fascist assaults, despite repeated government orders to prefects for the law to be upheld impartially, and also by a realization that the socialist movement was far more fragile than its confident rhetoric had suggested, a point underlined at the party's national congress in January 1921 when a number of important delegates walked out to found the Italian Communist Party. There was also a new air of militant patriotism circulating in the towns and villages of northern Italy, as one authoritative observer, the social democrat Ivanoe Bonomi, later recalled:

After the tragedy in Bologna, the rural propertied classes were stirred to action and began to meet and organize themselves. In the towns of the Po valley young officers who had served at the front summoned their landowning friends and relatives and told them that they needed to defend themselves against those who had been opposed to the war and now repudiated the victory, against those who were inciting violence and disorder, against those forces that wanted to establish the dictatorship of the proletariat and repeat the Russian experiment. A spirit of battle hovered over the countryside. During patriotic ceremonies the men of order no longer remained firmly indoors, frightened of violence, but displayed the national flag and went out into the piazza to cheer. The slogans on walls – so much a part of Italian political culture – were now not just communist ones. Alongside the numerous 'Viva Lenins!' and 'Long live the dictatorship of the proletariat!' were others celebrating the fatherland and the victory.[45]

The fascist assaults were carried out by 'action squads'. These were composed typically of a dozen or so men, for the most part war veterans or students, and often extremely young: under twenty years of age. They travelled to the scene of the attack by bicycle or train, or in cars and lorries provided by relatives, friends or sympathetic landowners and businessmen, and used an array of weapons: clubs (the notorious *manganello*, sometimes weighted with lead or thick leather), revolvers, daggers, grenades, rifles and even machine guns. These arms were sometimes supplied by local police stations or army barracks. On occasions more bizarre weapons were used: one Mantua squad became well known for beating opponents around the head with dried cod-fish. Each squad had a sobriquet – 'Satan', 'Desperado', 'Dauntless', 'Lightning', *Me ne frego*, or the name of some patriotic hero or event – and carried a banner with a skull and cross-bones or similarly macabre motif. The leader emerged spontaneously, through seniority or charisma, and was known as a *ras*, from the Ethiopian word for a local chief.

The exotic and sometimes ludic overtones to the activities of the fascist squads owed a good deal to the aestheticization of violence that the Futurists, the *arditi* and D'Annunzio had made fashionable. Indeed quite a few leading *squadristi* had spent time at Fiume prior to joining

Mussolini's movement, and often sought to mimic the decadent and flamboyant lifestyle of the poet-commander. Alcohol and cocaine were freely consumed before raids, while in Ferrara the 'Celibano' squad made a practice of pouring libations of cherry-brandy ahead of their attacks (the name 'Celibano' was a drunken version of 'cherry-brandy').[46] But behind the histrionic facade was a core of well-targeted brutality designed to break the working-class movement. Party and trade union buildings were ransacked and the offices of left-wing newspapers devastated, while key figures in the Socialist Party such as deputies, mayors, councillors and *capilega* were singled out for intimidation, beatings, torture and on occasions murder. According to official figures more than 200 people were killed and about a thousand wounded in clashes between *squadristi* and socialists in the first five months of 1921.

But the fascist violence was far more than just a tool of war. It was also an instrument of propaganda, a means of disseminating the 'myth' of the fatherland and generating a spirit of crusading idealism and fervour. As Mussolini declared in Naples on the eve of the March on Rome: 'We have created our myth. A myth is a faith, a passion . . . Our myth is the nation, our myth is the greatness of the nation.'[47] The *squadristi* accompanied their raids with songs proclaiming the holiness of their cause, with the *manganello* – 'Saint Manganello' as it was often known – singled out for particular veneration (the fascists of Monteleone Calabro had a statue of Our Lady wearing a starred halo and holding the infant Christ and a fascist club – the 'Madonna of the Manganello' – as their tutelary saint).[48] The punishments inflicted on enemies were frequently couched in terms of Catholic penitence, as in the case of the forced ingestion of castor oil, which, as one fascist newspaper explained, was intended 'to purge [a man] . . . of his faults, of the old sins of Bolshevism'.[49] (The powerful laxative qualities of castor oil appealed to the scatological humour of the squads.) And the general emphasis in the movement on faith, duty and enthusiasm linked fascism in the minds of many *squadristi* with what they saw as a distinctively Italian tradition of militant idealism going back to the time of Mazzini, with the 'religion of the nation' at its heart.[50]

With fascism growing exponentially, Mussolini found himself in the role of the sorcerer's apprentice, struggling to contain a movement that risked breaking away from its radical roots and becoming a crude anti-socialist strike force in the pay of the conservative middle classes.

A further threat was posed by the prime minister, Giolitti, who having failed to lure the more moderate socialists into his orbit following the occupation of the factories, now set his sights on the fascists, looking to use them as a tool with which to curb the far left and the Catholic Popular Party (*popolari*). He accordingly invited Mussolini to participate in his 'national' bloc in the elections that were due to be held in the late spring of 1921. The risk for Mussolini was that his movement might become further detached from its political origins (which were fiercely anti-parliamentary), but equally a foothold in the Chamber would provide him with an authoritative platform from which to try to control the unruly local *ras*. It would also furnish the fascists with official endorsement (extraordinary given the extent to which they had been openly flouting the law). Giolitti's hope was that fascism could be tamed and brought into the constitutional fold, and thus provide the anaemic body politic of Italian liberalism with a much-needed injection of fresh blood.

The 1921 elections were a great personal triumph for Mussolini. He secured an overwhelming victory in both Milan and Bologna, gaining nearly 400,000 votes, and was returned to parliament along with thirty-six other fascists. All but two of these new deputies came from colleges in the north and centre of Italy. The socialists lost ground, though not disastrously, and remained the largest party in the Chamber with 123 seats, while the Popular Party increased its tally to 107. Buoyed by this success Mussolini began to walk the tightrope between the competing expectations of his radical and conservative supporters, reaffirming the republican tendency of fascism, its commitment to major social and economic reforms, and even his willingness to enter a coalition with the socialists, while simultaneously stressing the need for order and discipline in his movement. In his first speech to parliament he mingled threats to the socialists ('on the plain of violence the working masses will be defeated') with offers of conciliation, albeit heavily qualified: 'For us violence is not a system, nor an aestheticism, far less a sport: it is a brutal necessity to which we have been driven. And I add: we are prepared to disarm if you, too, will disarm – your spirits, especially . . . for if we continue like this, the nation runs a serious risk of plunging into the abyss.'[51]

In the weeks that followed Mussolini repeatedly urged a cessation of violence ('the civil war is coming to an end . . . Bolshevism is beaten'):[52] he feared political isolation if the lawlessness persisted. But it was hard to curb the anarchic impulses of the squads, who continued their attacks almost unabated. In July, Mussolini proposed a 'pact of pacification' between the fascists and the socialist unions – and even went as far as to sign one early in August – but there was little chance of it being accepted by grass roots members, particularly after eighteen *squadristi* were killed in a pitched battle with police and the local peasantry at a town in Liguria. A crisis of authority now gripped fascism, with many of the squad leaders in open revolt against Mussolini; and two of the most influential *ras*, Dino Grandi of Bologna and Italo Balbo of Ferrara, even went to see D'Annunzio in his villa on Lake Garda and ask him to take over the movement. But D'Annunzio was not interested, and with the *ras* aware that there was nobody else of sufficient stature to dominate fascism, a compromise was eventually reached: in the autumn Mussolini agreed to abandon the pact in return for the movement becoming a party – the National Fascist Party – with a centralized command structure and local branches to help offset the power of the squads.[53]

But the tension between centre and periphery, order and violence, persisted – indeed it was to continue for many years to come as fascism struggled to decide how to balance the competing claims of spontaneity and discipline in a 'moral revolution'. Moreover, as Mussolini came to recognize by the autumn of 1921, fascism stood to gain most from perpetuating the violence and using it to blackmail the government, as neither of Giolitti's successors as prime minister in 1921–2, Ivanoe Bonomi and Luigi Facta (Giolitti had been compelled to resign after the spring elections, unable to hold together his increasingly fractured and vituperative parliamentary coalition) showed any sign of being able to bring the squads to heel. The police were openly fraternizing with the fascists ('The *carabinieri* travel around with [them] in their lorries . . . sing their hymns and eat and drink with [them],' reported a priest from the Veneto in July 1922),[54] and the prefects almost invariably took their side against the socialists (one, Cesare Mori, who famously endeavoured to make a firm stand against fascist aggression in Bologna, was transferred to a less sensitive post in southern Italy). Even the judiciary made little attempt to uphold the law impartially: seven fascists were brought before the Mantua courts charged with six counts of murder during the spring of 1921, and all were acquitted; in the same period sixteen socialists were found guilty of the murder of two fascists and sentenced to a total of 100 years in prison.[55]

From the end of 1921 the activity of the fascist squads continued relentlessly, with Mussolini now giving the *ras* his wholehearted backing. The party expanded rapidly, developing an extensive network of female and youth sections and claiming over 320,000 members by the late spring of 1922. There was also a growing network of fascist trade unions, with nearly half a million workers enrolled by the early summer of 1922 (for the most part agricultural labourers), built up over the ruins of the socialist organizations and led by a former revolutionary syndicalist from Ferrara, Edmondo Rossoni. In addition there were five national newspapers, two journals and some eighty local newspapers, all closely tied to the party's central machinery in Rome.[56] Although fascism was still very much a movement of the north and centre, with only two areas of strength in the south – the city of Naples and Puglia – it could plausibly claim to be the first genuinely national party in Italy appealing to men and women of all classes and regions. As such it felt increasingly entitled to demand power.

The cause of fascism was greatly assisted by the ineptitude of its enemies. At the end of July 1922 the elderly leader of the reformist socialists, Filippo Turati, desperate for a government that would make a stand against the *squadristi*, went to the Quirinal Palace for the first time in his life to discuss the political situation with the king and offer his support for an anti-fascist coalition. But the liberals could not agree on what to do. Orlando talked of a government of national unity, but Giolitti found the idea of sharing power with the Catholic *popolari* repellent, and claimed that a policy of resistance to the fascists would only plunge the country into a full-blown civil war. The trade unions then made matters worse by declaring a general strike. It was poorly supported – fewer than a thousand of FIAT's 10,000 workers downed tools – but it played straight into the hands of the fascists, who declared themselves defenders of the nation against a weak state and a still dangerous Bolshevik menace, kept the public services running with volunteers, and launched a fresh wave of attacks. In Genoa, Milan, Livorno, Ancona, Bari and elsewhere armies of fascists, several thousand strong, rampaged through the streets in the first days of August, destroying socialist buildings, occupying town halls, forcing the resignation of left-wing councils, and leaving a trail of dead and wounded in their wake. The only serious resistance took place in Parma, where the *squadristi*, led by the Ferrara *ras* Italo Balbo, were halted by troops and units of armed civilians led by a local socialist deputy.[57]

It was now a question not of if but when Mussolini's party would come to power. The organizers of the general strike had hoped to provide an overwhelming demonstration of support in the country for 'the defence of political and trade union liberties' and the 'conquests of democracy'. But liberty and democracy had for long been synonymous with governmental impotence, subversion, and economic and social chaos, and these words did not have the emotional force to stir Italians to action. The will to oppose fascism was lacking. On 10 August the Chamber gave its endorsement to a compromise coalition government led by a colourless Piedmontese lawyer, Luigi Facta, by 247 votes to 122, with the fascists, socialists and communists voting against. Explaining why his party was opposing the new administration one fascist deputy declared: 'Either the State will absorb fascism, injecting fresh life-blood into its vital organs, or fascism will replace the State . . . Any solution imposed by parliament against us would be an act of concrete violence at the expense of the wishes of the country.'[58] With this threat ringing in its ears, the Chamber adjourned for the summer recess.

THE MARCH ON ROME

Facta was contemplating using the anniversary of Italy's victory on 4 November 1922 to launch a programme of national reconciliation; and there was talk that Mussolini's rival D'Annunzio might be lured from his retreat on Lake Garda to deliver a speech calling on all patriotic Italians to bury their differences and unite behind the flag. This was a serious threat to Mussolini, though the threat was somewhat attenuated when D'Annunzio fell from a window of his villa on the evening of 13 August and was seriously hurt: he appears to have lost his balance while high on cocaine and fondling the sister of his mistress.[59] Mussolini accordingly needed to act quickly, and during the early autumn preparations began to be made for a march on Rome. In mid-October plans were firmed up. They envisaged the occupation of public buildings such as post offices in the principal cities (to hamper communications from the centre), the concentration of *squadristi* at muster points in central Italy, an ultimatum to the government to hand over power, and a descent on the capital and the capture of ministries.[60]

A key issue was the monarchy. Mussolini had always maintained that fascism was 'republican in tendency', but faced with the prospect of the king ordering the army to open fire on the rebels, he quickly modified his position, declaring in a major speech in late September that the Crown had nothing to fear from his party and urging Victor Emmanuel not to oppose the 'fascist revolution'. In the same speech he stressed how his intention was to bring about the spiritual regeneration of Italy in keeping with the unique traditions of Rome and the glorious, unfulfilled hopes of the Risorgimento:

But if Mazzini and Garibaldi tried three times to reach Rome, and if Garibaldi had presented his redshirts with the tragic and inexorable dilemma of 'Rome or death', this signifies that for the men of the Italian Risorgimento Rome had an essential role, of paramount importance, to play in the new history of the Italian nation. Let us therefore turn our thoughts to Rome, which is one of the few cities of the spirit in the world, with hearts pure and free of rancour . . . And it is our intention to make Rome the city of our spirit, a city that is purged and disinfected of all the elements that have corrupted it and dragged it into the mire. We aim to make Rome the beating heart, the galvanizing spirit of the imperial Italy that we dream of.[61]

On 27 October fascist squads began converging on major towns and cities throughout the country, occupying telephone exchanges, telegraph offices, town halls and prefectures, in most cases peacefully. The autumn rain and cold, as well as uncertainty over how the government would respond to the crisis, discouraged many from turning out, and the mobilization went less well than expected. Only about 16,000 *squadristi*, mostly from Tuscany, reached the main assembly points around Rome, from where they were due to descend on the capital. The majority had no weapons or food, and it was clear that minimal army pressure would have been needed to disperse them. The prime minister met in emergency session with senior generals and ministers in the early hours of 28 October, and later with his full cabinet, and it was unanimously agreed that a state of siege should be introduced across the whole country, beginning at midday. A telegram to this effect was dispatched to all prefects at 7.50. But when Facta went to see the king at nine o'clock and asked him to sign the decree, Victor Emmanuel refused. Why, remains a mystery: the previous evening he had apparently been determined not to give in to fascist pressure.[62] He may have come to doubt the loyalty of his troops or feared that his cousin had struck a deal with the fascists and was planning to depose him. Or he may simply have wanted to avoid bloodshed. Whatever the reason, his decision ensured that the 'march on Rome', which was an exercise in political blackmail rather than a serious revolutionary or military operation, a *coup de théâtre* more than a *coup d'état*, brought the fascists to power.[63]

Facta resigned at 11.30. Half an hour later a telegram was sent to all prefects announcing that the state of siege had been revoked: jubilant fascists took to the streets. The king initially asked Salandra to form a new administration, and Mussolini came under huge pressure, particularly from the Nationalists, to accept this solution. But he knew that he was in a position now to dictate terms. 'Much of northern Italy is under total fascist control,' he wrote in *Il Popolo d'Italia* on 29 October. 'Central Italy is completely occupied by blackshirts . . . The victory must not be mutilated . . . The government must be unequivocally fascist.'[64] Salandra declined the mandate, and Victor Emmanuel turned instead to Mussolini, who arrived in Rome from Milan on an overnight train on the morning of 30 October. He drove to the Quirinal, dressed in a black shirt. 'Sire, I bring you the Italy of Vittorio Veneto,' he (allegedly) told the king.[65] Victor Emmanuel invited him to form a government. He also asked him to disband the squads, but Mussolini considered this impossible, and it was agreed that the *squadristi* should be allowed a victory parade in the capital before being sent home. The next day some 50,000 fascists marched, or more precisely roamed, through the streets of the Eternal City, singing 'Giovinezza' and other songs and brandishing clubs, knives and guns, many of them purloined from army barracks. A group of around sixty broke into the house of the former prime minister, Nitti, and ransacked it. The local people watched the 'black devils', as they called them, with a good deal of unease.[66]

15. The warlord Ras Makonnen pursuing Italian troops at the Battle of Adua in 1896 in a contemporary Ethiopian painting. At the top, the patron saint of Ethiopia, St George, lends his support.

16. An emigrant family from southern Italy searching for lost luggage at Ellis Island, New York, 1905. A photograph by the celebrated American documentarist Lewis W. Hine. Around 6 million Italians emigrated in the first decade of the twentieth century, many of them to the United States.

17. Giovanni Giolitti – the man who dominated Italian political life in the first years of the twentieth century – in a photograph of 1908. Giolitti was vilified by idealists on both left and right for what was seen as his uninspiring bourgeois pragmatism.

18. Nietzschean superman. The poet Gabriele D'Annunzio on board an Ansaldo biplane on the occasion of a celebrated flight to drop 400,000 propaganda leaflets on Vienna, 9 August 1918.

19. The fascist squad of Fermo (Ascoli Piceno) posing in dandyish fashion for the camera, 1922. The aestheticization of violence owed much to the influence of D'Annunzio and the Futurists.

20. Holy violence. The *Madonna del manganello* ('Madonna of the bludgeon'), the patron saint of the fascists of Monteleone Calabro (Vibo Valentia) in Calabria. The statue was destroyed after the fall of fascism.

21. Living dangerously. A young fascist leaping over bayonets in a gymnastics display in the Foro Mussolini (now known as the Foro Italico) in Rome during the 1930s.

22. The entrance to the exhibition in Rome marking the bimillennium of the birth of the emperor Augustus in 1937. In contrast to Nazism, fascism favoured modernism in both art and architecture.

23. Fascism's place in the sun. Camel troops from Africa parading before the monument to Victor Emmanuel II (Vittoriano) in Rome during the first annual review of the foundation of the Empire, 1937.

24. Hitler, with Mussolini on his left, being given a Renaissance-style reception at Florence railway station on the occasion of his visit to Italy in 1938. Hitler was enchanted by the magic of Florence and its Renaissance art.

25. The front cover of the first number of *La difesa della razza* (*The Defence of the Race*), the best known of the many party publications issued in the wake of the racial laws of 1938. A Roman sword protects the Aryan from contamination by Semitic and Negroid types.

26. Piazzale Loreto, Milan, 29 April 1945. The bodies of Mussolini, his mistress, Claretta Petacci, and several prominent fascists strung up by their feet from a petrol station.

27. 'Mother! Save your children from Bolshevism! Vote Christian Democracy'. A poster from the bitterly fought general election of April 1948. The far-left used the face of Garibaldi (with shades of Saint Joseph and Karl Marx) as a campaign symbol.

28. The advent of television. The screening of a film in the small town of Carpi, near Modena, in 1956 is halted to allow the cinema audience to watch the hugely popular quiz programme *Lascia o raddoppia?* (*Quit or Double?*).

29. The launch of the new FIAT 500 at the Mirafiori factory, Turin, July 1957. This car replaced the equally diminutive 'Topolino' (1937–55) and became an icon of Italy's 'economic miracle'. Nearly 4 million models were built between 1957 and 1975.

30. In the shadow of Mussolini and consumerism: Ravenna, May Day, 1961. An Italian communist reading the party newspaper against a backdrop of a poster commemorating the sixteenth anniversary of Mussolini's death.

31. The weight of modernity. A newly arrived immigrant from the south of Italy in front of the Pirelli tower, Milan, 1969. Around 1.5 million southerners moved to the far north in search of work in the 1960s.

32. The triumph of image. Silvio Berlusconi addressing a meeting of leading Italian business figures in Milan in April 2004. Berlusconi promised 'a new economic miracle', but he turned out not to have heavenly powers when it came to dealing with the country's disastrous public finances.

33. Mafia violence. The wife and daughters of Benedetto Grado at the scene of his murder in Palermo, 15 November 1983. Grado was one of several hundred victims of a war between rival factions of the organization known as Cosa Nostra in the early 1980s.

22

The Establishment of a Dictatorship,
1922–5

Mankind is perhaps tired of liberty. It has had an orgy of it. Liberty is no longer the austere chaste virgin for whom the generations of the first half of the last century fought and died. For the brave, energetic, robust youths who face the glimmering dawn of the new history other words exercise a much bigger fascination, namely order, hierarchy, discipline.

Benito Mussolini, in *Gerarchia*, March 1923

Fascism has simply destroyed with its violence what we had destroyed in thought with twenty years of criticism: Italian democracy.

Giuseppe Prezzolini, in *La Rivoluzione liberale*, 1, 36 (1922)

Excellency, I feel this is the moment to declare a faith that has been nurtured and adhered to in silence.

If Your Excellency deems me worthy of entering the National Fascist Party, I will consider it the greatest honour to occupy the post of your most humble and obedient follower. Luigi Pirandello, telegram to Mussolini, 17 September 1924

THE NEW PRIME MINISTER

At thirty-nine, Mussolini was Italy's youngest ever prime minister. By temperament imaginative, impulsive and emotional, with a deep-seated strain of cynicism and a conviction that force ultimately determined the course of all human affairs, and a nervous energy that spilled over readily into cruelty (not for nothing was he a great admirer of Machiavelli), he nevertheless possessed a remarkable political intelligence. He had an extraordinary capacity to feel his way around obstacles, wrong-footing his opponents by spinning a web of ambiguity that left them uncertain as to exactly what he was thinking or planning to do, and alternating threats with blandishments. Often he himself had no clear idea where he was going: chance and intuition might easily determine his next step. And the fact that he was young, and even more that he came from a humble background and lacked the sophisticated veneer of the liberal elites – his plebeian table manners and uncouth language were a source of much anxiety to the Foreign Ministry – inclined his enemies to underestimate him. They mistook his gaucheness and insecurity for weakness, and imagined they could manipulate and use him and in due course push him aside when he tripped up and no longer suited their purposes.

Mussolini was appointed prime minister in a constitutional manner and he was to remain prime minister until July 1943. The *Statuto* continued in force throughout this time, and Victor Emmanuel III was head of state and commander-in-chief of the armed forces, with responsibility for signing all decrees and laws. That so little is known the crucial role played by the king during the interwar years – a consequence of the Savoy archives remaining firmly closed – is deeply frustrating, especially as the monarchy had traditionally viewed foreign policy and the conduct of war as its privileged domains.[1] However, from the beginning of his administration Mussolini combined obeisances to order and respectability with threats of subversion, claiming in his first speech to parliament that it was his intention to make 'the revolution of the blackshirts' a 'force for development, progress and stability in the history of the nation', and that while he could have turned 'this grim grey chamber into a bivouac for soldiers', he had instead decided to work towards 'the unification of spirits'.[2]

Most observers believed that the advent to power of Mussolini marked the beginning not of a new era but of 'normalization', a return to order after the chaos of the preceding years; and the fact that the cabinet included four liberals, two *popolari*, Nationalist Luigi Federzoni, the eminent philosopher Giovanni Gentile, and two distinguished military figures – Marshal Diaz and Admiral Thaon di Revel – seemed a guarantee that stability would indeed be the order of the day. Mussolini retained the key Foreign and Interior ministries for himself, and there was a heavy sprinkling of fascist under-secretaries; but the overall balance of this so-called National Government was reassuringly conservative. The business community (a large part of which had been extremely nervous at the prospect of the unpredictable Mussolini at the helm) was reassured by the appointment of the orthodox financier Alberto De' Stefani as Minister of Finance, while the country's most prestigious intellectual, Benedetto Croce, who on the eve of the March on Rome had attended a huge rally of blackshirts in Naples and applauded Mussolini 'fervently', was full of praise for the new prime minister.[3]

Crucial to the support given to Mussolini by the old ruling classes during his first two years in office (and to a large extent thereafter also) was his ability to look and sound conservative. After his first meeting with the king dressed in a black shirt, he took to wearing a morning suit and top hat for royal audiences, and spats, butterfly collar and bowler hat for most other public occasions (although bowler hats were discarded after it became clear to him that these were only worn by Laurel and Hardy in the Hollywood comedies he so much enjoyed watching).[4] In speeches he referred constantly to the importance of 'discipline', 'order' and 'hard work', and he repeatedly touched on many of the traditional leitmotifs of Italian patriotism: the need for Italy to be 'reborn', shake off its old vices, and become strong, feared and respected, and not just a land of 'museums and libraries';[5] the search for 'moral unity' as an antidote to the divisions caused by factions, parties and localism ('[fascism] will abolish parish pumps so that Italians see nothing except the august image of the fatherland');[6] and the necessity of 'making Italians' in accordance with d'Azeglio's celebrated injunction ('Italians are being fashioned through the rigours of the war, the harsh post-war conflicts and the fascist revolution').[7] He also made highly respectful comments about the Catholic Church, describing religion as a 'sacred patrimony of peoples',[8] and reinforcing his words with a number of high-profile gestures such as increasing clerical stipends and reinstating the crucifix in schools, courtrooms and the Colosseum.

But alongside the conservative gestures and statements were more subversive comments, in the main delivered to cheering *squadristi* at party rallies – though the fact that these comments had been part of mainstream criticism of the Italian state for over half a century blunted their capacity to shock conservatives. Indeed many liberals would very happily have endorsed them. One particular target of attack was parliament, an institution that Mussolini repeatedly disparaged as weak and corrupt, and whose activities in recent years had, he claimed, caused general revulsion in the country and evoked ideas of 'Byzantium'.[9] In a speech to party members in October 1923, explaining why the March on Rome a year before had been necessary, he said:

For twenty, perhaps thirty, years the Italian political class had been growing steadily more corrupt and degenerate. Parliamentarism – with all the stupid and demoralizing associations that go with this word – had become the symbol of our life and the hallmark of our shame. There was no government: there were just men continually under the thumb of the so-called ministerial majority . . . When people could read what were referred to as parliamentary proceedings and see what might be described as an exchange of the most banal insults between the so-called representatives of the nation, they felt disgusted, and a sense of nausea welled up inside them.[10]

Another object of attack was liberty, though here, too, Mussolini's insistence that freedom should not be confused with licence, and that the state should take adequate measures to defend itself against subversion, struck a powerful chord with those who had been horrified by the behaviour of the socialists in 1919-22 (that of the *squadristi* was evidently a different matter). As Mussolini put it in October 1923, 'If by liberty is meant the right to spit on the symbols of religion, the fatherland and the state, then I – head of the government and Duce of fascism – declare this liberty will never be allowed!'[11] As a corollary to this, he rejected the idea that freedom was a right, endorsing instead Mazzini's belief that it was a duty, a means to an end rather than an end in itself, and as such subject to modification according to circumstances. And he pointed out to those who claimed that liberalism was at the very root of united Italy that many of the most important patriots of the Risorgimento had in fact not been liberals:

Careful, let us not exaggerate. To start with I dispute the claim that there was a liberal party during the Risorgimento, a party, that is, in the modern sense of the word. There were liberal currents and groups. But alongside the liberals, splendidly represented by Camillo Cavour, there were men who were not liberals, such as Mazzini, Garibaldi, the Bandiera brothers and Carlo Pisacane, who, together with his companions, set off to be massacred for a dream of freedom and resurrection.[12]

What was deeply unclear in 1923 and 1924 was just how far Mussolini was prepared to travel along the road to subversion. That he wanted the March on Rome to be considered as the start of a revolution of some sort is evident from the frequent comparisons that he drew when addressing party members between fascism and Bolshevism (to the inevitable detriment of the latter: 'Moscow gives the impression of a terrible leap forwards and a resulting broken neck. Rome gives the impression of a march of compact legions').[13] But since he had often spoken of fascism inaugurating a 'moral' or 'spiritual' revolution, it was legitimate for liberal observers to assume this was what he was aiming to achieve. (He himself maintained that his attacks on parliament were only meant to goad this decadent institution into working more effectively.)[14] Furthermore – and this was critical to the political situation in Italy during his first two years in power – he could argue that the *squadristi* needed to be brought under control as part of the 'normalization' process, and that the best way of achieving this was to assuage their radical expectations with intransigent rhetoric while all the time working to contain them within the institutional framework of the state.

And from the outset of his administration there was every sign that Mussolini was indeed trying to bring the unruly squads to heel – though he carefully cloaked each move he made in political ambiguity. In January 1923 the Fascist Militia was set up – a party-based paramilitary organization that absorbed the *squadristi* and whose declared purpose was to provide the army and the police with support in 'defending the fascist revolution'. Such a body was potentially unconstitutional, not least because Mussolini and not the king was its commander; but the fact that it was centrally controlled meant it could be justified as an instrument for disciplining the rank and file and weakening the provincial *ras*. A similar line of defence could be applied to another important innovation at this time, the Grand Council of Fascism. This was a high-profile consultative body that appeared to elevate the fascist leadership to a similar plane as the cabinet, but once again Mussolini could argue that it was a way of tightening his grip on the party while simply compensating the *squadristi* for lost autonomy.[15] Moreover the party changed dramatically in character in the months after the March on Rome, more than doubling in size to 783,000 members by the end of 1923, as 'respectable', mainly middle-class, converts moved in and swamped the old guard.

A further sign that Mussolini was serious about curbing the revolutionary tendencies of fascism was the absorption of the Nationalist Association in February 1923. The Nationalists were a small but influential party, monarchist, authoritarian and pro-Catholic in orientation, with strong support in the upper reaches of the army, the diplomatic service, big business and academia. They had much in common with the fascists and even possessed their own paramilitary force, the blue-shirted *Sempre Pronti!* ('Ever Ready!'). But relations with the *squadristi* had not always been smooth, and many radical fascists were strongly opposed to the merger, fearing that it would pull the party in a sharply conservative direction. But from Mussolini's point of view the fusion offered considerable attractions: it served to underline the growing respectability of his party, while providing him with (much needed) cadres of able administrators and links to important sections of high society. The Nationalists were to exert a huge influence on the future development of the regime, far more than their modest numbers might have allowed them to expect, and figures such as Luigi Federzoni and Alfredo Rocco were to be pivotal in shaping the architecture of the new state.[16]

But it was not so much the Nationalists as the mood of frustrated nationalism that Mussolini appeared most in thrall to during his first months in office, and his repeated calls for Italy to assert itself on the world stage probably did more than anything else to endear him to conservative opinion. He spoke scathingly of the League of Nations (a 'Franco-British duet'; an 'insurance scheme for the established nations against the proletarian nations'),[17] and declared that it was imperative for the prolific 'Italian race' to find outlets for its fast-growing population of more than 40 million.[18] He celebrated Francesco Crispi, unveiling a plaque to him in the Foreign Ministry and declaring that he should be set permanently beside Mazzini, Garibaldi, Victor Emmanuel and Cavour as one of the country's founding fathers (there was to be a day of national commemoration for the Sicilian statesman in 1927).[19] And on the rare occasions that he ventured abroad he made it clear that he was determined to uphold Italy's right to be considered a great power. At a congress at Lausanne in November 1922 to discuss the Turkish peace treaty he demanded that the British and French representatives publicly declare in advance that Italy would be treated on an equal footing, while at a conference in London a few weeks later to discuss German war reparations he attempted to have the French delegates ejected from their rooms in Claridge's on the grounds that they had been allocated a more luxurious suite than the Italians.[20]

The most dramatic instance of Mussolini's attempts to conduct an assertive foreign policy occurred in the summer of 1923. On 27 August four Italian members of an international boundary commission working in northern Greece were murdered in mysterious circumstances. Relations between Rome and Athens had been strained for some time on account of the disputed ownership of the Dodecanese islands, which Italy had seized in 1912 at the time of the Libyan war, and although the killers (who were never caught) had almost certainly come from Albania, Mussolini immediately delivered an ultimatum to the Greek government demanding a formal apology, a large indemnity and a solemn funeral for the victims in the Roman Catholic cathedral in Athens attended by the entire Greek cabinet. When the Greek government objected, Mussolini ordered the occupation of the island of Corfu. Unfortunately the naval squadron arrived several hours behind schedule, leaving insufficient time for the formalities of a peaceful surrender, and the Italian commander proceeded to bombard the island's fortress even though he was aware that it was packed with Armenian refugees, including hundreds of children. Sixteen people were killed and dozens wounded.[21]

The Corfu episode was a blatant challenge to the authority of the League of Nations and to its central principle of collective security, and attracted worldwide condemnation. The British press was particularly critical of Italy's action, much to Mussolini's indignation, and relations between London and Rome grew dangerously strained. Mussolini hoped to annex the island, but after a month of intense diplomatic activity he was forced to withdraw the Italian troops in return for the Greek government agreeing to pay compensation of 50 million lire. Postage stamps bearing the overstamp 'Corfu' had to be quickly removed from circulation.[22] Despite this disappointing outcome Mussolini was determined to present the Corfu incident as a major success, claiming that it had raised the prestige of the nation greatly. At a blackshirt rally in October he described it as the 'most important and interesting experience' since 1860, in that Italy had 'carried out a gesture of absolute autonomy for the first time and had the courage to deny the competence of the Genevan Areopagus'.[23]

Some senior officials in the Foreign Ministry were shocked by Mussolini's behaviour over Corfu, most notably the Secretary General, Salvatore Contarini: he had been on leave at the time of the crisis and had refused to return to Rome to participate in what he called 'such statesmanship'.[24] But in general the Italian public appears to have been highly enthusiastic about the *coup de main*, seeing it as going some way to restoring national pride after the 'mutilated victory' and the rebuffs at Versailles. The distinguished liberal editor of the *Corriere della Sera*, Luigi Albertini, backed the government wholeheartedly throughout the crisis, criticizing the British for their reaction and claiming that Italy was displaying moderation and restraint towards the 'brutally offensive' Greeks.[25] Most other Italian newspapers took a similar line. Italy's representative at the League of Nations, Antonio Salandra, pledged his full support to Mussolini and had no qualms about defending his country's position vigorously in Geneva, maintaining that 'no Italian government could have acted otherwise'.[26] In his memoirs Salandra wrote that the Corfu affair 'increased the prestige of Italy's name – as always happens in such instances – through an act of force, albeit one carried out in contravention of the new rules . . . of international law'.[27]

As Mussolini sensed, the painful legacy of military defeats and set-backs in foreign policy, and the deep hurt at having for so long been dismissed by foreigners as too undisciplined, enervated and lacking in cohesion to be other than 'the least of the great powers', could be drawn on to attract widespread support for his government. The imagery of decadence and regeneration that had been at the heart of the national movement in the nineteenth century had left the prestige of Italy closely bound up in the minds of many patriots with the pursuit of international 'glory and power', as Mussolini put it.[28] Tellingly it was not so much Mussolini as the conservative Piedmontese aristocrat and former *aide de camp* to King Umberto, Admiral Thaon di Revel, who was the main instigator of the attack on Corfu, seeing a strike against Greece as indispensable for restoring the country's battered prestige.[29] And the greatness of the fatherland was a goal of such pre-eminent moral stature, even for convinced liberals, as to justify the most painful moral sacrifices. When in the spring of 1924 Vittorio Emanuele Orlando, the former prime minister, had to decide whether to back Mussolini in the forth-coming elections, he was torn between his love of liberty and devotion to *la patria*:

[T]here are two ideals to which I have dedicated my life: the fatherland and liberty . . . In giving my support [to fascism] I am aware that I would be obeying the passion and ideal of the fatherland . . . At the same time I do not feel inclined to sacrifice my other ideal, liberty. I am thus in a terrible dilemma . . . But knowing I have to sacrifice one ideal I cannot possibly sacrifice the fatherland, so I sacrifice liberty.[30]

THE MATTEOTTI CRISIS

The elections of 1924 were held under yet another voting arrangement. Proportional representation was widely considered to have been a disaster, except by the socialists and the *popolari*, who had been its main beneficiaries, and in the spring of 1923 the Grand Council of Fascism proposed a 'corrected' proportional system under which the group of parties with the largest number of votes would automatically receive two-thirds of the seats, provided it had secured more than a quarter of all votes cast. This was a radical break with past practice and called into question the very principles of representative government, but after years of weak majorities and an intimidating socialist presence in the Chamber, there was a widespread willingness to swallow such a reform. The main threat to the proposal came from the Popular Party; but the *popolari* had become deeply divided over whether or not to support fascism, with many senior Church figures, above all Pope Pius XI, unhappy at the increasing opposition shown by members of the party, including its Secretary, Don Luigi Sturzo, to Mussolini. Early in July, under pressure from the Vatican, Sturzo resigned, and the Popular Party began to disintegrate. A few days later the Acerbo Law, as the reform was known, passed by 223 votes to 123. Giolitti, Salandra and Orlando all voted in favour.[31]

The elections held on 6 April 1924 were bitterly contested. Mussolini had hoped that violence could be kept to a minimum, but this was wishful thinking. There were numerous killings and assaults by fascists, strings of attacks on opposition headquarters and other buildings, and frequent disruptions of rallies. There were also countless instances of intimidation and fraud. The government slate of approved candidates (the so-called *listone*) included former Nationalists, right-wing liberals and *popolari*, as well as fascists. The opposition groups were heavily divided: there were two socialist parties, a communist party, a republican party, social democrats, *popolari* and various liberals (among them Giolitti). They found it extremely hard to cooperate and failed to form a united bloc, making it easier for fascism to claim that it was the only 'national' force capable of providing a government.[32] The turn-out at the polls was high at nearly 64 per cent. The *listone* secured two-thirds of the votes (making the Acerbo Law in effect redundant) and 374 of the 535 deputies in parliament. Support for the government and its allies was particularly strong in the south, where the old liberal clienteles had been jostling since the March on Rome to jump on the fascist bandwagon.[33]

When parliament reopened on 30 May the man who had replaced Turati as the leader of the reformist socialists, Giacomo Matteotti, a young, fearless and highly educated lawyer from the province of Rovigo, stood up and delivered a damning indictment of the elections. He described in graphic detail the systematic violence and corruption perpetrated by the fascists that had prevented the 'expression of popular sovereignty'. 'Perhaps in Mexico they are used to conducting elections not with ballot papers but with courage in the face of revolvers. And I apologize to Mexico if this is not true!' Throughout the speech he was subjected to repeated barracking and abuse from the government benches. The prominent socialist and editor of *Avanti!*, Pietro Nenni, who back in 1911 had shared a prison cell with Mussolini, described the scene:

MATTEOTTI: We have a proposal from the Committee for Elections to confirm numerous colleges. We are opposed to this proposal . . .

(A voice: This is provocation)

MATTEOTTI: . . . because if the government majority has obtained 4 million votes, we know that this result is the consequence of obscene violence.

(From their benches, the fascists brandish their fists at the speaker. In the centre of the Chamber the most violent try to throw themselves on Matteotti. Mussolini watches impassively from his bench, frowning, silent, making no gesture.)

MATTEOTTI: The leader of fascism has himself explicitly declared that the government did not consider its fate as tied to the outcome of the elections. Even if it had been in a minority, it would have remained in power . . .

[ACHILLE] STARACE: That is true: we have power and we will keep it.

(The whole Chamber descends into uproar. A voice shouts: We will teach you to respect us by kicking you or shooting you in the back! Another exclaims: You are a bunch of cowards! Matteotti remains calm and allows the tumult to die down, ignoring the interruptions.)

MATTEOTTI: To support these government proposals, there is an armed militia
... *(Voice on the right: Long live the Militia!)* ... which is not at the service
of the state, nor at the service of the country, but at the service of a party ...
(Shouts on the right: Enough! Enough! Throw him out of the hall!) ...

MATTEOTTI: You want to hurl the country backwards, towards absolutism. We
defend the free sovereignty of the Italian people, to whom we offer our salute
and whose dignity we will defend by demanding that light be shed on the
elections.

*(The left rises to acclaim Matteotti. On the right there are cries of: Villain!
Traitor! Provoker!)*

MATTEOTTI (smiling to his friends): And now you can prepare my funeral
oration ...

*The 'duce' no longer hides his irritation ... The previous day he had interrupted
a speaker, saying: Twelve bullets in the back are the best remedy for enemies
who are in bad faith.*[34]

The speech was embarrassing to Mussolini and potentially highly
damaging, not least because Matteotti was a very well-regarded and
well-connected figure in international socialist circles. But far more
alarming for the government were rumours that Matteotti had built up a
substantial dossier on corruption in the Fascist Party and was about to
divulge its contents. One potential scandal related to the sale of huge
quantities of surplus war matériel at knock-down prices to fascist loyal-
ists, who then sold it on at an enormous profit. Among the beneficiaries
of this scam was a Tuscan *squadrista* of particularly violent character,
Amerigo Dumini, who had moved to Milan in the early 1920s pursued
by charges of arson and murder and become a protégé of one of Mussolini's most powerful and trusted lieutenants, Cesare Rossi. Thanks to
his political contacts Dumini was able to acquire thousands of rifles and
other weapons from the army, which he then passed to a bank in Trieste,
which in turn exported them to Yugoslavia. He netted the massive sum
of 1.5 million lire. Whether he was acting as a front man is not known,
but it was clear that leading fascists were able to abuse their positions
to transfer state resources to private pockets or party coffers.[35]

Potentially far more serious were allegations that massive bribes had
been paid to high-placed fascists by an American firm, Sinclair Oil, in
its endeavour to secure the exclusive rights to petroleum distribution in
Italy. The American bid certainly seemed to be working: in the summer

of 1923 one of the leading advocates of an alternative proposal for a national distribution company, the powerful Milanese businessman and Minister of Agriculture Giuseppe De' Capitani, was removed from the cabinet.[36] One of those rumoured to be heavily involved in the party's underhand financial transactions was Mussolini's brother and close confidant Arnaldo, who had taken over the editorship of *Il Popolo d'Italia* after the March on Rome. Another was the influential Under-Secretary at the Ministry of the Interior, Aldo Finzi, who was also very close to Mussolini (he acted on occasions as his second in duels), and who, like Matteotti, came from a wealthy family in the Polesine district of northeast Italy.[37] Mussolini's cynical view of human nature inclined him to be indulgent towards financial (and other) irregularities in his colleagues, and the fascist regime was to have remarkable levels of corruption. What Mussolini did not want was public scandal. The prospect of Matteotti delivering another exposé of fascist crimes was intolerable.

On the afternoon of 10 June five men led by Amerigo Dumini, who for a while had constituted a semi-official terror squad nicknamed the *Ceka* (after the Soviet secret police), controlled by the fascist party Treasurer, Giovanni Marinelli, whose function it was to intimidate government opponents, seized Matteotti as he walked along the Tiber towards parliament, pushed him into a car and after a violent struggle stabbed him to death. The killers drove around Rome for a few hours, apparently trying to decide what to do, before disposing of the body in a shallow grave fifteen miles outside the city. The corpse was not discovered for more than two months, but it was immediately clear to all that a serious crime had been committed. A bystander noted down the numberplate of the vehicle, and it was quickly traced. It belonged to the editor of the fascist newspaper *Il Corriere Italiano*, formerly the mouthpiece of Aldo Finzi, but now controlled by Mussolini's press secretary, Cesare Rossi. The night before the murder the car had been parked in the courtyard of the Ministry of the Interior. Late on 10 June, Dumini came to Mussolini's office, apparently quite calm and collected, and showed the prime minister a small piece of blood-stained upholstery.[38]

The attack had been ordered by Marinelli and perhaps by Rossi, too, and both men were in daily contact with Mussolini and would not have acted without his knowledge. Whether the intention had been to kill Matteotti, or to administer instead a brutal drubbing of a kind that had become commonplace in recent years and which might have been passed off as a regrettable 'spontaneous' gesture by undisciplined *squadristi*, is not clear. But Mussolini knew immediately that his government was in serious danger. He told his staff to create 'as much confusion as possible' about the incident, adding, 'If I get away with this we will all survive, otherwise we shall all sink together'.[39] And when the killers were traced and arrested, following the discovery of the car, Mussolini ordered the initial investigations be taken out of the hands of the magistrates and given (illegally) to the fascist chief of police, who promptly interviewed Dumini accompanied by two senior members of the Militia.[40] Dumini was eventually to serve two years in prison for the crime, but for a long time after that he was able to extract enormous sums of money – well over 2 million lire by 1939 – from Mussolini, a man whom he clearly saw as his patron, for all he had done, as he put it in one of his supplicatory letters, 'in the years of danger . . . for the Idea'.[41]

Mussolini vehemently denied any responsibility for the murder, and the country seemed willing to give him the benefit of the doubt. There were almost no protests or strikes, even in the big cities, where until recently the trade unions had been so militant (a sign of just how rapidly the working-class movement had been broken). The Vatican's *Osservatore Romano* preached forgiveness: 'Let him who is without sin cast the first stone.'[42] And the king did nothing. The principal threats to the government came from the press – particularly the *Corriere della Sera*, which now established itself, belatedly, as a beacon of opposition – and the cabinet. Several ministers threatened to resign unless the administration was broadened so as to hasten the process of 'national reconciliation'.[43] Mussolini complied, handing the Interior Ministry to the respectable Nationalist Luigi Federzoni and the Justice Ministry to another Nationalist, Alfredo Rocco. The opposition parties had decided to boycott parliament in protest at the murder in what became known as the 'Aventine secession', but this gesture only served to ensure that the government did not get defeated in a confidence vote. Mainstream conservative opinion was still behind the government (the playwright Luigi Pirandello pointedly joined the Fascist Party at this time) and on 26 June the Senate gave Mussolini its backing by 225 votes to 21. Explaining why he had voted with the majority, Benedetto Croce said that fascism had 'done much good' and ought to be given time 'to complete its process of transformation'.[44]

But the prime minister's concessions to respectability aroused fears in the radical fascists that their 'revolution' was in danger, and during the summer of 1924 Mussolini went out of his way to reassure them, mobilizing the Militia, staging mass rallies, and openly declaring his support for the party's 'intransigent' rural wing led by such extremists as Roberto Farinacci, the violent ex-*ras* of Cremona. He called on the members of the Militia to remain vigilant: to lay to one side the *manganello*, yes, but not to put on 'slippers and a skull cap', for while they were advancing with 'every possible olive branch, even a whole forest', their enemies might be preparing to crush them.[45] Such talk inevitably did little to allay conservative doubts, particularly when combined with a new decree law restricting freedom of the press. During the late summer Mussolini toured the country energetically, proclaiming his solidarity with the working classes ('I too have had calluses on my hands')[46] and declaring his commitment to solving the country's economic and social problems. But by the time parliament reopened in November it was clear that his support at the centre was waning.

Giolitti was the first major liberal to come out openly against the government, on 15 November. But Mussolini's biggest concern was Salandra, who was wavering: if he defected, the king might finally be driven to act. The main opposition groups were still boycotting the Chamber, which ruled out the possibility of defeat in a parliamentary vote, but Mussolini nonetheless felt he had to take further steps towards normalization, and he ordered the Fascist Party to cease all violence and purge the ranks of unruly and discreditable elements. This did not go down well with the *squadristi*, who showed signs of mounting impatience with their leader. And the fact that senior army generals (who were close to the king) were putting heavy pressure on Mussolini to curtail the autonomy of the Militia added to the tension. On 27 December the opposition parties played what they hoped would be their winning card, publishing a memorandum issued by Cesare Rossi to the police in which he stated explicitly that Mussolini had been responsible for setting up the *Ceka* and ordering attacks on opponents (though he claimed not to know if Matteotti was one of them).

Mussolini had no further room for manoeuvre. On 29 December, Salandra went into opposition. The next day Mussolini narrowly averted the resignation of his cabinet, but on 31 December he was told by a delegation of commanders of the Militia that unless he acted immediately to defend the fascist revolution against the opposition, the party would seize the initiative. And already in Tuscany and the Romagna tens of thousands of armed *squadristi* were descending on the cities, attacking the properties of anti-fascists and in places trying to break into prisons to free fellow blackshirts. Rumours began to abound of Mussolini's imminent dismissal and the declaration of martial law. But the king failed to make a move. Perhaps he feared civil war; or maybe he thought that as a constitutional monarch he had to wait for parliament to provide him with a lead. Whatever the reason, Mussolini was given a final chance to salvage his political career when the Chamber reopened on 3 January. The intervention he made that afternoon was not, as he admitted, a conventional parliamentary speech but a direct challenge to his opponents to invoke article 47 of the *Statuto* and impeach him:

It has been said that I set up a *Ceka*. Where? When? How? Nobody can tell us!

There has indeed been a *Ceka* in Russia ... But the Italian *Ceka* has never existed ...

It has been said that fascism is a horde of barbarians encamped in the nation, a movement of bandits and marauders! Attempts have been made to turn the issue into a moral question, and we know the sad history of moral questions in Italy. (*Strong signs of approval.*)

But there is no point in wasting time, gentlemen. I come to the point. Here, in front of this Assembly and in front of the entire Italian nation, I declare that I, and I alone, assume political, moral and historical responsibility for all that has happened. (*Prolonged and very loud applause. Many shouts of 'We are all with you! We are all with you!'*)

If some more or less garbled comments are enough to hang a man, then bring out the gibbet and the rope! If fascism has been simply castor oil and *manganello*, and not the magnificent passion of the very flower of Italian youth, the fault is mine! (*Applause.*) If fascism has been a criminal association, I am the head of that criminal association! (*Very loud applause. Many cries of: 'We are all with you!'*) ...

Gentlemen! You have deluded yourselves! You thought that fascism was finished because I was disciplining it ... But if I employed one-hundredth of the energy that I have used in disciplining it in unleashing it, you would see something indeed. (*Very loud applause.*)

But there will be no need for this, because the government is strong enough to stamp out fully and for good the sedition of the Aventine. (*Very loud and prolonged applause.*)

Italy wants peace, tranquillity and calm industriousness, gentlemen. We will give her this tranquillity and calm industriousness with love, if possible, and with force, if necessary. (*Loud applause.*)

You can be certain that in the forty-eight hours following my speech, the situation on every front will be clarified. (*Very loud and prolonged applause. Comments.*)

We all know that I am driven neither by personal caprice, nor by love of power, nor by ignoble passion, but solely by strong and boundless love for the fatherland. (*Very loud, long and repeated applause. Repeated cries of 'Viva Mussolini!' . . .*)[47]

Nobody picked up the gauntlet thrown down by Mussolini, and as darkness fell on 3 January liberal Italy quietly and ingloriously came to an end. The Minister of the Interior instructed the prefects to enforce law and order rigorously, monitor subversives and close down any organizations that tended to 'undermine the powers of the state' – a reference, naturally, to the far left, not to fascism.[48] The opposition groups lingered on for some months, hoping that there might be some reaction in the country and debating whether or not to return to the Chamber. But they were little more than voices crying in the wilderness, and it was only a matter of time before they were finally silenced. In November 1925, following an assassination attempt on Mussolini, the reformist socialists became the first party to be proscribed. The *popolari* deputies tried to return to Montecitorio in January 1926 but were driven away by fascist guards. In October another attempt on Mussolini's life led to the remaining opposition parties being banned. Italy was now a one-party state and a *de facto* dictatorship, committed to realizing the dreams of national regeneration that had so long been a central component of patriotism and which liberalism had failed to fulfil.

23

The Fascist Ethical State

It is the State that educates citizens to civil virtue; makes them aware of their mission; encourages them to be united ... When the sense of the State declines and the disaggregating and centrifugal tendencies of individuals and groups prevail, national societies come to an end.   Benito Mussolini, 10 March 1929

Fascism is a spiritual movement ... For centuries there has been a remarkable imbalance between the nobility, quality and energy of our cultural life in Italy and the inadequacy of our civil education. This problem ... has for centuries tormented the noblest Italian thinkers. It was the last thought of the dying Cavour. Massimo d'Azeglio summed it up after unification had been achieved in a phrase that has become famous with us: 'Italy has been made; now we must make Italians.' Fascism is the greatest experiment in our history in making Italians.

Benito Mussolini, interview with the *Chicago Daily News*, 24 May 1924

The relative ease with which Mussolini established a dictatorship in 1925 was in large part the result of the complex array of hopes and anxieties that since the Risorgimento had crystallized around the idea of *la patria*, investing it with a transcendent force against which the shibboleths of liberalism ultimately proved impotent. As dreamed of by a succession of nineteenth-century writers, nurtured on the glories of ancient Rome and the nostalgic laments of Dante, Petrarch and Machiavelli, the Italian nation was to be a resurrection of past greatness, an awakening after centuries of decadence and sleep. It was to be a fully united community, an extended family of brothers and sisters who had agreed to renounce their evil legacy of fratricide and division in order to work selflessly for the good of the whole. The liberal state had failed to live up to these expectations. Italy – or 'Italietta' as it was so often slightingly referred to – had since 1860 been morally fractured, militarily weak, corrupt, economically backward and culturally undistinguished. Freedom had not released the pent up virtues of an enslaved people, as some had fondly hoped. Instead, it appeared to have let loose on an unprecedented scale, as if from Pandora's box, all the old vices of indiscipline, materialism and factiousness that had long been considered the bane of the country's history.

Fascism offered for many a new hope and a new dawn. 'We wait nervously . . . straining our eyes to the horizon whence a star might arise to bring us again the longed-for day,' Giovanni Gentile had written in 1919 in an essay entitled *The Moral Crisis*.[1] And in keeping with such heartfelt yearnings Mussolini embarked from 1925 on a series of initiatives designed to galvanize almost every aspect of Italy's moral, economic and cultural life, using the machinery of the state and the rhetoric of war to mobilize the population and forge a united, disciplined, industrious and aggressive community whose entire spiritual being would be bound up with that of the nation. It was a Herculean task, as he told a gathering of party leaders in October 1930, since the damage that had been inflicted on the Italian psyche in recent centuries had been immense:

We need time, a great deal of time, to complete our work. And I am not speaking here of the material but of the moral work. We have to scrape off and crush the sediments that have been deposited in the character and mentality of Italians by those terrible centuries of political, military and moral decadence between 1600 and the rise of Napoleon. It is a prodigious undertaking. The Risorgimento was just the beginning, as it was the enterprise of just tiny minorities. The world war was profoundly educative. It is now a question of continuing on a daily basis this task of remaking the Italian character. For example, we owe it to the culture of those three centuries that the legend grew up that Italians cannot fight. It required the sacrifice and heroism of Italians during the Napoleonic wars to demonstrate the opposite. The Italians of the early Renaissance, of the eleventh, twelfth and thirteenth centuries to be precise, had temperaments of steel, and brought all their courage, their hatred and their passion to bear in war. But the eclipse we suffered in those centuries of decadence weighs still upon our destiny, as yesterday, as today, the prestige of nations is determined almost exclusively by their military glories, their armed might . . . This enterprise is my cross and my mission . . .[2]

In order to achieve its moral revolution, fascism set out greatly to strengthen the powers of the state, taking as its fundamental premise that the nation had claims prior to those of the individual, and that the government was accordingly entitled to use whatever measures were needed to protect society, irrespective of any liberal notions of 'rights'. Censorship was tightened up, and all newspapers were brought under *de facto* government control. Local government lost much of its autonomy, and from 1926 elected mayors were abolished and replaced by *podestà* appointed by the prefects. A new Public Safety Law of 1926 gave the police increased powers of arrest and made them, in effect, unaccountable, while a 'Special Tribunal', applying military law (including the death penalty – though it was rarely applied), was instituted to deal with terrorists and other dangerous political opponents. A new punishment of *confino* was introduced under which a person could be sent into exile in a remote community (usually in the deep south) for five years simply for being suspected of the intention of engaging in subversive activity. By the end of 1926 fascism was to all intents and purposes a police state, intolerant of any opposition and bent on forging a homogeneous national community. And one of the first and most widely publicized demonstrations of its new resolve came in the campaign it waged in Sicily against the mafia.

'EVERYTHING IN THE STATE, NOTHING OUTSIDE THE STATE, NOTHING AGAINST THE STATE'

When Mussolini visited Sicily in May 1924 his itinerary included a trip to the small Albanian settlement of Piana dei Greci, a few miles to the south of Palermo. The road up into the mountains was tortuous and dusty, and care had been taken in advance to clear it of traffic so as to ensure that the prime minister did not arrive too dirty. Mussolini drove one of the cars himself, fast, dispensing with the normal comfort of goggles. On arrival he and his entourage of ministers and dignitaries were welcomed on the steps of the cathedral by the mayor, Francesco Cuccia, and a Greek Orthodox priest, who offered Mussolini a piece of bread as a traditional token of hospitality. A group of women dressed in ethnic costume sang songs of greeting. The church was packed, and noticing a child waving a small flag insistently and straining to see him, Mussolini went over, took him by the hand, and escorted him up the aisle – an act of 'exquisite gentility', as one local newspaper admiringly put it. After the service there was a reception in the town hall, with a speech by Cuccia and numerous photographs, choreographed by the mayor, who was determined to milk the occasion for all it was worth. Whether at this point or earlier, Cuccia expressed surprise at Mussolini's police escort: Piana was his town, and he could vouch for the prime minister's total safety.[3]

Cuccia was a man with a reputation, a *mafioso* in local parlance, and his high-handed manner and clear belief that he and not the state should hold sway in Piana dei Greci deeply angered the prime minister. Three years later, when reporting on the progress of the recent drive against organized crime in Sicily to the Chamber of Deputies, Mussolini referred specifically to 'that unspeakable mayor who found ways of getting himself photographed at every solemn occasion' who was now safely behind bars.[4] But in the early summer of 1924 it was still not politically expedient for Mussolini to launch an offensive against the mafia. He needed the support of senior Sicilian liberals such as Orlando; and given that *mafiosi* invariably had connections (whether solicited or not) with leading politicians, any operation against the mafia might lead to the government falling foul of important conservative interests. But after the speech of 3 January 1925 and the defeat of the opposition parties Mussolini had much more freedom of manoeuvre. And when in October of that year he proclaimed that the twentieth century would be the century of Italy's 'power' and that in order to achieve this the Italian state needed to be strong as never before – 'Everything in the State, nothing outside the State, nothing against the State'[5] – the way was open for an offensive against organized crime. After all, there had been no more flagrant symptom of the liberal state's impotence than the persistence of the mafia.

The man appointed to conduct the operations in Sicily was Cesare Mori. Mori came from Lombardy, and had been educated at the Turin Military Academy, but he knew the island extremely well, having served there as a policeman for many years prior to 1917, gaining a formidable reputation for courage in fighting banditry. On the face of it, therefore, his appointment as prefect of Palermo in October 1925 appeared logical. But Mori was a Nationalist, not a fascist, and as prefect of Bologna in 1921–2 he had earned the bitter enmity of the *squadristi* for his attempts to uphold the law impartially: after the March on Rome he had been summarily dismissed from service. But by the autumn of 1925 Mussolini was looking to rein in the party once again. A wave of brutal killings in Florence (under the eyes of tourists) early in October had infuriated him, and the party Secretary, Roberto Farinacci (who had been appointed following the 3 January speech as a sop to the radicals), had been soundly rebuked at a meeting of the Grand Council for failing to control his followers. There followed a fresh offensive to subordinate the party to the state, culminating early in 1927 with the Circular to the Prefects, which denounced *squadrismo* as 'utterly anachronistic' and declared that in 'a totalitarian and authoritarian regime such as the fascist' the prefect alone was to act as the guardian of both 'public order' and the 'moral order' in the provinces.[6]

It was these political parameters that determined not just the choice of Mori for the campaign against the mafia but also the character of the police operations. Like all those who knew Sicily intimately at this time, Mori was well aware that the mafia was not a secret criminal organization of the kind that sensationalist writers liked to describe. It was, as Franchetti had observed half a century before, a much more diffuse phenomenon arising from a culturally sanctioned use of private violence by ambitious individuals pursuing economic, social and political power in regions where the state had historically been very weak. As such the mafia was not a clearly circumscribed entity (though from time to time real secret societies with hierarchies and initiation ceremonies did emerge) but rather a complex set of networks of patron–client relationships generated by *mafiosi* using whatever means they could (and getting yourself photographed standing by the prime minister, like Francesco Cuccia, was the pinnacle of achievement). And given that the boundaries of the mafia were ill-defined, any decision by the police about where to draw the line was ultimately political.

Under Mori's direction the police rounded up dozens of members of so-called 'criminal associations' (*associazioni a delinquere*) in the course of 1926 and 1927 in the rural settlements of western and central Sicily, arresting more than 11,000 men (and not a few women). For the most part the targets were upwardly mobile peasants, artisans and small landowners who had taken advantage of the turbulent situation in the island during and immediately after the war to advance themselves. How many had actually committed crimes is difficult to say, as the charge of criminal association did not require the police to prove direct involvement in a specific offence. Often the basis for an arrest was hearsay – if someone was known locally as *mafioso*: a dangerous premise, as many witnesses pointed out, as this adjective was bandied about quite loosely at the time and with a variety of meanings – or else membership of some notorious individual's family, political faction or clientele. Given that men such as Francesco Cuccia were pivotal to the life of their communities, it was frequently hard for the police to decide whether to arrest a few dozen or a few hundred people in a town.[7]

Framing the arrests, though, were political considerations. Mussolini wanted to draw the powerful landowning elites in Sicily firmly inside the regime in 1926–7: many of the island's most prominent conservatives were uncomfortable with the radical character of the Fascist Party in cities such as Palermo, and had stood aloof. Since Mori knew that the wealthy had colluded with, indeed very often protected, *mafiosi* and were thus themselves open to the charge of 'criminal association', he had a powerful weapon for gaining their cooperation: either they support the government or they risk prosecution. To facilitate their compliance Mori launched an offensive early in 1927 against the island's most important fascist, Alfredo Cucco, accusing him and his followers of corruption and involvement with the mafia. Cucco was expelled from the party, leaving the way open for fascism in Sicily to be rebuilt on a conservative footing, with members of the aristocracy occupying many of the key positions. This move was in keeping with a national trend. In the course of 1926–7 thousands of former *squadristi*, among them several deputies, were purged from the ranks of the party and replaced with an influx of respectable middle- and upper-class members.[8]

Mori never envisaged destroying the mafia through police action alone: he was well aware that simply removing a few hundred networks of *mafiosi* would not produce a permanent solution. Since, according to his analysis, the mafia was not an organization in any strict sense of the term, but rather 'a morbid form of behaviour' stemming from centuries of weakness on the part of the authorities, the only way to deal with the problem effectively was to dissuade the landowners and the peasantry from colluding with *mafiosi* by demonstrating to them unequivocally that the state now had the power to dominate all aspects of Sicilian life.[9] It was a question (in nineteenth-century parlance) of bridging the deep gulf between 'legal Italy' and 'real Italy' or, as the government put it in April 1927 in a document setting out the fundamental principles that were to underpin the economic life of the country under fascism, of fusing nation and state together in one seamless whole: 'The nation is . . . a moral, political and economic unit that finds expression integrally in the fascist state.'[10]

Force was thus intrinsic to Mori's operation, not just to crush the mafia, but more importantly to impress upon the population as a whole that it was to the state alone that they now owed total obedience and respect. The days of supine collusion between *mafiosi* and a weak liberal regime, incapable out of respect for antiquated notions of freedom of imposing itself on Sicilian society, were over. It was a question, as the journal of the distinguished young radical writer Piero Gobetti declared in October 1925, of conducting 'an enlightened and clear-sighted process of political education', teaching Sicilians 'the necessity of the state', and making 'Italy' for the first time into 'a living experience'.[11] Hence, in the wake of the mass arrests, the symbolic importance of the trials that were staged in the island amid much publicity from 1927. In each case dozens, sometimes hundreds, of alleged *mafiosi* were packed into improvised court-rooms – a converted church or similar building – and subjected to a swift judicial process. The ritualistic nature of the proceedings was accentuated by the fact that the accused were locked into huge iron cages – as if they were wild animals. Almost all were found guilty of the crime of 'criminal association' and sentenced to long terms in prison. In such circumstances justice was inevitably rather rough; but that was hardly the point. The aim, as Mori said, was to show that 'fascism and mafia are irredeemably antithetical': 'Fascism is the state in all its force and prestige.'[12]

But alongside force there had to be a measure of propaganda and indoctrination, for the fascist state aimed to be ethical in character and rectify through education many of the nation's historic vices. Mori told a regional Congress of Fascist Teachers in June 1926 of how he had once met a shepherd boy 'isolated in the murky solitude of a *latifondo* [large estate] of ill repute'. 'His father? Wanted, and in America. His mother, sick and alone in the village with two babies. The village? Far away. How far? He did not know; he never went there. God, prayer, school? Nothing. The king, Italy, the nation? Nothing. Rights, duties, the law, good and bad? Nothing.' He urged the island's educators to do all in their power to eliminate such appalling ignorance and fashion a 'new soul composed of love and inspired by one faith: God, king and fatherland'.[13] Many teachers no doubt did what they could. A school-mistress from the small town of Prizzi sent Mori a number of tributes written by her pupils: 'Miss has told us,' ran one, 'that in Sicily there were lots of robbers, brigands and men who always stole and killed other men, and that you have been right to put them in prison.'[14] And in Milocca the schoolmaster dutifully informed the children that they were all Italians (not Sicilians) and that Italy was one of the greatest nations in the world, with a glorious past and a brilliant future. But the fact remained that most schools were too poorly attended and too ill-resourced to have much impact on their communities.

Mori himself toured the countryside of western and central Sicily rallying the peasantry to the cause of the state. He handed out subsidies to the wives and children of arrested men, distributed food parcels to the poor, and delivered stirring speeches to large crowds in piazzas decked out with tricolours and banners and festooned with swags and triumphal arches. Like Mussolini's, his rhetoric was punctuated with words such as 'discipline', 'faith', 'courage', 'work', 'sacrifice' and 'sobriety', and he urged his audiences to remember that the new, resurgent Italy was 'the Italy of Vittorio Veneto [which] advances irresistibly towards that future greatness . . . which was the radiant vision of 600,000 men, nobly slain' (a precept given tangible expression with the inauguration of numerous war memorials at this time).[15] And, again like Mussolini, he celebrated rural life, seeing in the stoical and resilient peasants those virtues that would guarantee the nation a destiny worthy of its glorious imperial past:

In the figure of the Sicilian peasant . . . silent, industrious and riveted to his place of work on the sun-baked *latifondo*, I see not only the worker of today . . . but also the bold pioneer who affirms the primacy of Italy beyond its shores. I also see the heroic infantryman through whose valour the warrior tradition of Italy was yesterday born again, and which will re-emerge tomorrow and shine forth for ever amid the flash and lightning of legends and epics.[16]

How much impact Mori's propaganda had on the Sicilian peasants (if indeed it was comprehensible: most would have found his Italian, with its strong northern accent, almost impossible to follow) remains unclear. In all probability, though, very little. Appeals to self-abnegation and hard work were unlikely to fall on receptive soil in a society where the epitome of success was the corpulent and wealthy *mafioso* with a leisured lifestyle, who held court in the central piazza of his home town every day, like a Spanish grandee, with supplicants begging him for favours and kissing his hand in gratitude. Nor is there anything to indicate that the recent war resonated with the local population. An American sociologist who lived in the village of Milocca in the province of Caltanissetta in 1928–9 noted an attitude of almost total indifference to it:

No criticism was heard of the two men who had permanently blinded themselves with the medicine they put in their eyes to make themselves unfit for military service. Another man told at length the devices he used, first to avoid being taken for the army, and later to keep from being put in active service . . . No one was pointed out as a hero of the war. Disabled veterans were preferred for employment in minor positions connected with local government, but their war records were never cited in their praise.[17]

Another problem with Mori's attempts to draw the Sicilian peasantry closer to the state, in accordance with the regime's objectives, was the absence of any serious economic inducements. In the years immediately following the First World War there had been a rapid rise in the number of smallholdings in the island as hard-pressed landowners sold off parts of their estates; but this trend began to be reversed in the later 1920s as many of the new peasant proprietors found themselves unable to meet their mortgage repayments following a revaluation of the lire in 1926, and had to sell up. Furthermore a campaign to increase national wheat production – the 'battle for grain', launched in 1925 – bolstered the profits of even the most inefficient large landowners and tightened the grip of the old elites on the island's economy. The Great Depression of the early 1930s further damaged the position of the poor, and rural workers began pouring in tens of thousands into the cities in an attempt to find jobs. Reports began to speak of near starvation conditions in many towns in the interior of Sicily.[18]

The campaign against the mafia formally came to an end in 1929 when Mori was removed from Palermo. His attack on the island's leading fascist, Alfredo Cucco, had angered many of the party's old guard; but the last straw was almost certainly a bitter clash with the distinguished Sicilian general Antonino Di Giorgio, a former Minister of War whom Mori had accused of protecting *mafiosi*. The government now declared that the mafia was defeated and newspapers and other public documents were instructed not to mention it any more. However, during the 1930s the signs are that violence, corruption and lawlessness remained a serious problem in the island. Indeed, they may even have got worse, as crimes went unreported in the press and officials were inclined to turn a blind eye to anything that might jeopardize the official view that Sicily had become a haven of tranquillity under fascism. Leading *mafiosi* – especially those with influential contacts – quickly emerged from prison; and according to many well-placed observers the situation in the island was soon little different to before. As a leading lawyer lamented to Mori in a letter of December 1931, describing the growing chaos around Termini Imerese, to the east of Palermo:

As for public security, strong orders are issued but people go ahead regardless and murder and rob at will . . . I realize that hunger, after two bad harvests, has not improved things; but it is above all the general lack of faith in the authorities that is to blame. In almost every town the leading *mafiosi* have had their sentences reduced and are back . . . leaving the small fry behind. In Caccamo, a dangerous place, the Azzarello brothers, among the worst mafia bosses in Sicily . . . were proposed by the local authorities for deportation, but were then let off by the Palermo Commission. Scandals such as this make honest people sick and do nothing but encourage the dishonest to commit crimes.[19]

In these circumstances was it any surprise if the peasantry in western and central Sicily continued to place more trust in *mafiosi* than in the representatives of the Italian state?

MOULDING FASCIST MINDS

As the campaign in Sicily showed, the attempts of the fascist government to extend the authority of the state and generate an integrated national community faced huge obstacles. Old loyalties, identities and patterns of thought and behaviour were hard to eradicate – much harder than the heirs of the Enlightenment, with their deep-seated faith in the power of education to shape a better world, often liked to imagine.

Coercion could produce alienation as much as obedience; and while propaganda might have a positive impact on those disposed to believe, the value system of fascism, with its stress on discipline and self-sacrifice for the greater glory of the fatherland, was unlikely, at least without the prospect of tangible rewards, to appeal much to those whose lives were taken up with the struggle for economic survival. Furthermore the fascist state could never hope to be truly monolithic, despite talk from 1925 of the regime being 'totalitarian' in aspiration. Mussolini was only ever prime minister, not head of state, and his capacity to control those sections of society such as the army, big business, the aristocracy and the major landowners who looked to the monarchy as the ultimate guarantor of their interests was limited. Nor, of course, could he dominate the Church, the most powerful source of moral authority in Italy.

Despite these limitations, fascism followed Catholicism and other leading religions in regarding education as critical to the attainment of a morally unified community. For many years prior to 1922 there had been a strong feeling that the Italian academic system, especially at the level of secondary schools and universities, had become little more than a factory, churning out diplomas and degrees with scant regard for how the students would eventually be absorbed into the workplace. Many conservative commentators had been inclined to attribute Italy's political problems before the First World War to the fact that the country had a massive 'intellectual proletariat' of teachers, lawyers, doctors, engineers and other graduates who, it was believed, were turning to the Socialist Party to find solace for their frustrated hopes and ambitions. And the problem had been getting worse. In 1919–20 there were twice as many university graduates as in 1913–14, while the numbers emerging from teacher-training schools (*scuole normali*) and technical institutes trebled in the same period.[20]

In 1923 Mussolini's first Minister of Public Instruction, Giovanni Gentile, introduced a series of major reforms that radically restructured Italy's educational system. The underlying principle was to promote quality over quantity ('few schools, but good ones') and the ultimate goal, as Mussolini declared, was to ensure that the universities produced a ruling class 'properly prepared for the great and difficult duties' of regenerating the Italian nation.[21] For the vast majority of the population schooling was to end at the age of fourteen, with the last three years being spent in a new tier of 'complementary schools' that offered no access to higher education and whose curriculum was built around the provision of basic vocational skills. One of the consequences (and aims) of this innovation was to debar working- and lower-middle-class children from proceeding up the academic ladder and thus (it was suspected) acquiring ambitions above their station. The elites, who had passed the necessary exams, went on to secondary schools (*licei, ginnasi* and *istituti magistrali*) and from there were entitled to progress to university. As a result of these reforms the numbers in secondary schools dropped from 337,000 in 1922-3 to 237,000 in 1926-7, while university enrolments fell from 53,000 just after the war to around 42,000 a decade later.[22]

What Gentile was hoping – and many patriotic intellectuals, Croce included, concurred – was not only that the number of over-qualified graduates in Italy would decline, but more importantly that those who emerged from the secondary schools and universities would feel organically bound to the national community as never before. After all, in Gentile's opinion (and Mussolini happily endorsed his view), true freedom consisted in the spontaneous fusion of the individual with the collectivity. This was largely why there was such a heavy emphasis in the new secondary school curricula on subjects such as classical studies (Latin especially), literature, history and philosophy that were believed to transmit most effectively the spiritual essence of Italy. Religion, too, was accorded a prominent place, above all in elementary schools, with the local clergy being allowed to oversee how it was taught; for though Gentile was himself a non-believer he saw Catholicism as 'a peculiarly Italian institution' and 'store-house of national tradition' that could serve to reinforce respect for hierarchy and authority.[23] Science was not favoured: it was seen as intrinsically cosmopolitan and materialistic. Nor did women gain much from the reforms. Gentile considered their natural place to be in the home, and while he accepted they might make good primary school teachers on account of their 'obvious maternal qualities', he attempted to steer them away from the workplace by creating a new set of 'female *licei*' in which classics and philosophy were replaced by singing, dancing and domestic skills.[24]

The problem with the Gentile reforms lay in the relationship between ends and means. According to a distinguished educationalist, Ernesto Codignola, fascist pedagogy should cast aside the 'agnosticism and indifference to supreme national goals' that had characterized the liberal period and instead aim to create a 'strong spiritual unity without which a nation cannot pursue common aims, manifest any harmony of will, or aspire to greatness'.[25] But in trying to inject the academic system with a markedly 'national' character – and among the innovations in 1923 were the introduction of a uniform 'state exam', for private as well as public schools, a daily 'salute to the flag', and a general tightening of ministerial control over both teachers and the curricula – the government risked imposing a bureaucratic straitjacket that would almost inevitably stifle the 'moral' renaissance that the reformers were looking to achieve. Gentile saw education as a process of spiritual interaction between master and pupil – a relationship that required spontaneity and autonomy if it was to work – and he hoped that fewer schools, better-qualified students and higher-calibre teachers would allow this. But in practice centralized prescriptiveness became the order of the day.

From 1925 teachers were subjected to increasing 'fascistization'. In December of that year Mussolini declared that schools 'at all levels and in all their teaching should educate Italian youth to understand fascism, to renew itself in fascism and to live in the historical climate created by the fascist revolution'.[26] The same month a law was passed allowing for the forcible retirement of any public employee who had displayed views 'incompatible with the general political aims of the government', and the ensuing purge carried out by the Ministry of Public Instruction seems to have been more thorough than for other government departments.[27] From 1929 every primary and secondary school teacher was obliged to take an oath of loyalty to the regime, while four years later membership of the Fascist Party became compulsory (as for all civil servants). In 1934 primary school teachers were instructed that during working hours they should wear the uniform of either the party or the Militia so as to impress upon their pupils that both 'in and out of school' they were 'officers, educators and commandants' who were preparing the younger generation 'for service to the fascist fatherland'.[28]

School curricula were subjected to a similar process of fascistization, with a growing emphasis from the late 1920s on the celebration of Mussolini, militarism and empire. To ensure the maximum degree of uniformity a single state textbook for use in all primary schools was introduced in 1929, with material selected and approved by a special ministerial commission. Italian language instruction started in the first grade with the learning of key words such as 'Benito', *fascismo, Duce* and *re* ('king'), and progressed in later years with compositions on aspects of the regime and its achievements and commentaries on speeches by Mussolini. Maths-teaching was framed to highlight the recent material progress of the country, while physics was supposed to 'illustrate the theories of Galileo and Marconi with remarks designed to emphasize the primacy and excellence of the Italian genius'. History had as its central focus Italy as the cradle of European civilization, with a particularly strong emphasis placed on imperial Rome and the Risorgimento (both seen as foreshadowing fascism; the Renaissance was frowned on as overly individualistic), and teachers were expected to impart to students a deep sense of pride at being 'born . . . on this soil bathed by so much blood, sanctified by so many martyrs, [and] made powerful by [the Duce's] great genius'. In addition to their state textbook all students received a 'national notebook' for their homework (with a photograph of a smiling Mussolini on the front cover) and a free copy of a hagiographic biography of the Duce by Giorgio Pini.[29]

Given their status and their traditional concern with freedom of enquiry, university academics were not as susceptible to state control as schoolteachers. Gentile endeavoured to rally the intellectual community to fascism, and in 1925 he published a manifesto, signed among others by Pirandello, Corradini, Marinetti, Soffici and Malaparte, which called for the cultural life of the nation to be placed at the service of the new regime in order that the dreams of Mazzini might be realized and the work of the Risorgimento finally be completed; but Croce replied with a counter-manifesto, bearing a more distinguished list of signatories, asserting the necessary autonomy of the arts and the sciences from politics.[30] Only at the end of the 1920s, after the conciliation with the Vatican (1929) had given Mussolini a major fillip to his authority, did the government feel confident enough to start putting serious pressure on universities. In 1930 the Grand Council required faculty deans and rectors to have been party members for at least five years, and in 1931 an oath of loyalty to the regime was instituted for all university professors. The Pope gave his assent (provided Catholics made a mental reservation that it would not conflict with their duties to God and the Church), and only a dozen out of some 1,250 academics failed to comply. This was a huge propaganda coup for Mussolini, even though many of the jurors probably heeded Croce's advice to swear in order to prevent the universities being taken over by party placemen. One of the non-jurors, the Bologna surgeon Bartolo Nigrisoli, was assaulted and badly injured by a gang of young fascists.[31]

The tightening of the government's grip on the educational system enabled syllabuses to be adjusted to fit in with the regime's shifting priorities. After the conciliation with the Vatican religious instruction (delivered by priests) was made compulsory in all secondary schools and writers such as Bruno, Rousseau, Kant, Hegel and Schopenhauer were dropped from philosophy courses. The invasion of Ethiopia in 1935 led to an upsurge in anti-French and anti-British propaganda (Italy's ungrateful former allies, who had forgotten 'that the World War had been won, above all, by Italy'),[32] and writers such as Tolstoy, Ibsen and Hugo were removed from the curriculum and replaced with bellicose and nationalistic authors such as Oriani and D'Annunzio. (After his exploits at Fiume – which Italy finally annexed in 1924 – D'Annunzio lived quietly in his villa on Lake Garda until his death in 1938, his vanity appeased by official honours and titles, and a luxurious national edition of his works.) The regime's increasingly racist stance in the late 1930s was reflected in the appearance in primary school textbooks of stories such as 'The White Soul of Black John', in which a missionary returns from Africa with a native boy who, he tells a group of children, had been 'little more than a beast' when found ('he went about nude and ate raw meat') but who, under the benevolent influence of Italy and the Church, had become civilized and Christian. The priest announces that the boy is now 'black outside and white inside', but the children remain unconvinced and one of them asks if it would not be best to put him through the laundry to make him clean again.[33]

To what extent all this centrally directed education succeeded in influencing the minds of the young is very hard to say. Despite the purges of the later 1920s many teachers inevitably continued to harbour beliefs derived from older value systems such as Catholicism and socialism, and their support for the regime and its directives was no doubt often superficial and based on pragmatism more than real faith (a common joke in the 1930s was that the initials of the Fascist Party, PNF – Partito Nazionale Fascista – stood for *Per Necessità Familiare*: 'For the sake of the family'). The constant stream of ministerial directives generated a great deal of frustration and resentment, especially it seems in secondary schools and universities, where traditional humanistic culture remained strongly entrenched. One of the more doggedly centralizing education ministers, the authoritarian Count Cesare Maria De Vecchi di Val Cismon (1935-6) ('an ass and a fanatic', in Gentile's opinion), was regularly referred to by teachers as unintelligent and overbearing, according to police reports, or more graphically as 'a pig', 'Tsar of all Russia' and 'Caligula'.[34] In these circumstances it is reasonable to suppose that the spirit if not the letter of fascism was frequently absent from classrooms. 'After twenty years of fascism,' wrote a commentator in the early 1940s, 'everyone agrees that we still lack the fascist educator – I mean the educator who is physically, morally, politically and militarily a fascist.'[35]

Another problem with schools as an instrument for making new Italians was the persistent high level of absenteeism, particularly in rural communities. While the numbers of those going to *licei*, *ginnasi*, and *istituti magistrali* and university (women especially) rose sharply in the 1930s, generating a huge surplus once again of middle-class graduates (according to a government survey there were 100,000 unemployed teachers in 1938),[36] the peasantry still saw primary education as having limited practical value and regularly kept their children at home in bad weather or when they were required for work in the fields. Most local councils remained dominated by conservative landowners and continued to allocate insufficient resources for teachers and classrooms. And sometimes bureaucratic regulations worked to discourage attendance. In the town of Milocca in central Sicily girls were not allowed to join the second grade unless they had underwear: most peasant women did not possess such garments.[37] Illiteracy levels nationwide continued to fall slowly during the interwar years, but 21 per cent of brides in the south were still unable to sign the marriage register in 1936.[38]

MOULDING FASCIST BODIES

Mussolini harboured considerable ambivalence towards academic learning. The decadence of Italy had set in during the Renaissance, when speculative thought and the obsession with material comfort and culture had distracted the ruling elites from active pursuits, generating the 'Guicciardini man' that De Sanctis had so lamented: highly educated and eloquent, but sceptical, critical, individualistic, passive, and lacking in conviction and assertiveness. The new Italy needed to shed this essentially bourgeois mindset ('a mindset that is totally antithetical to the fascist mentality')[39] and become harder and more aggressive. Foreigners considered Italians to be not 'a race, but a cowardly mishmash of men and women best known for serving and entertaining people abroad', a collection of mandolin and violin players, singers and dancers, not a disciplined and serious nation.[40] This had to change. As he declared in a speech in June 1925:

Only by creating a way of life, or rather a way of living, will we be able to leave our mark on the pages of history and not just chronicles. And what is this way of life? First and foremost, courage. Fearlessness, love of risk, and loathing of comfort and easy living. Being always prepared to dare in personal as in public life and to abhor all that is sedentary . . . Being proud every hour of the day to feel Italian. Discipline in the workplace. Respect for authority.[41]

The fascist regime accordingly aimed to mould the entire personality and not just the intellect – a point underlined in 1929 when the Ministry of Public Instruction was restyled the Ministry of National Education and given a new under-secretariat with specific responsibility for physical training. From the outset the party had been eager to induct children and adolescents into the spirit and practice of fascism through paramilitary organizations, and in 1926 these bodies were brought together in a single association, the Opera Nazionale Balilla (ONB), headed by the tall, athletic and good-looking (if uncouth) former *ras* of Carrara, Renato Ricci. There were four sections: the *Balilla*, for boys aged eight to thirteen (named after the child who according to tradition sparked a popular revolt in Genoa in 1746 by flinging a stone at an Austrian officer), the *Piccole italiane*, for girls aged eight to thirteen, the *Avan-guardisti* and the *Giovani italiane*, for boys and girls respectively aged between fourteen and eighteen. To these were later added the *Figli della lupa* ('Children of the She-Wolf') for children aged between six and eight.

The principal purpose of these organizations was to prepare the young for their future roles in society: boys to be soldiers and girls to be the mothers of warriors. After all, as Mussolini declared in characteristically aphoristic fashion in 1934, 'War is to man as maternity is to woman.'[42] Boys dressed in uniforms, paraded, sang marching songs and engaged in competitive sports, while girls practised first-aid, danced around poles, went to concerts, and attended courses on topics such as flower arrang-ing, embroidery, knitting and typing. Part of the training for future maternity consisted of a military-style drill, in which girls were passed in review carrying dolls 'in the correct manner of a mother holding a baby'.[43] Guns were central to ONB culture, and in 1930 Ricci called publicly for every Balilla gym to be furnished with them, on the grounds that practising with real weapons was indispensable to the formation of true men. One much-favoured ceremony, repeated in piazzas up and down the country, consisted of a member of the *Giovani italiane* handing a rifle to an *Avanguardista*, then to a *Balilla* and finally to a *Figlio della lupa*, as if it were the torch of fascist life.[44]

Camping was among the principal activities of the ONB, and by 1942 the government claimed there were 5,805 fascist campsites visited each year by almost a million children. The camp programmes were tightly scheduled and included games, gymnastics, lectures, prayers for the 'fascist martyrs', and a twice-daily salute to the king and the Duce. All members of the ONB were eligible to participate, but preference was given to certain categories, including children from poor families and the sons and daughters of war veterans. The ONB's main showpiece event was the annual *Campo Dux*, a week-long training exercise for *Avanguardisti* held from 1929 in a wooded district on the outskirts of Rome. Mussolini and other leading party figures regularly attended, as did delegations from overseas: the grand parade of the 1937 camp included 450 members of the Hitler Youth. Celebratory documentary films were made of each year's *Campo Dux* and screened in cinemas throughout the country.[45]

Membership of the ONB was not compulsory until 1939, but parents who did not want their children to join had to provide schools with a written explanation of why, and non-participants faced discrimination when it came to state scholarships and jobs. The ONB expanded its sphere of control fast as the government came to see the party youth programme as necessary for supplementing the deficiencies of traditional education and imparting the true spirit of the fascist revolution ('*libro e moschetto, fascista perfetto*' – 'book and musket, perfect fascist'). In 1928 a decree ordered the disbanding of all rival organizations – a measure that brought the government into conflict with the Church, whose own totalitarian aspirations had in recent decades led to the creation of a network of Catholic associations for the young. Mussolini came to a compromise as part of his bid for a conciliation with the Vatican and agreed to allow the youth circles of Catholic Action 'with prevalently religious ends' to continue in being, but the Catholic Boy Scouts were banned on the grounds that they were a 'semi-military organization'.[46] In 1929 the ONB was absorbed into the Ministry of National Education.

Sport was regarded as a 'national necessity for the prestige and progress of the race', as an editorial in *Il Popolo d'Italia* said in 1924, and an excellent way of forging the new fascist man. For women the situation was more ambiguous: they needed to be fit so as to fulfil their roles as healthy mothers, but, as the head of the association for fascist university students said in 1937, they should avoid 'useless and dangerous over-competitiveness' and engage instead in 'graceful' pursuits such as archery.[47] Little had been done in liberal Italy since De Sanctis's reform of 1878 to encourage sport among the masses, and neither the Catholics nor the socialists had looked to fill the vacuum. Activities such as football had been regarded by the Church as overly self-expressive, and encouragement had been reserved primarily for gymnastics, whose repetitive exercises mirrored well traditional Catholic ideas of spiritual self-discipline.[48] The Socialist Party had tended to dismiss sport as inherently bourgeois and a potential distraction for workers from the class struggle. As a result the main developments had been in elite pursuits such as mountaineering, fencing, cycling and motor racing, particularly in the wealthy parts of the north. Football, too, had initially been for the upper classes, and in the case of some of the best-known teams, for the English upper classes: Milan had begun in 1899 as the Milan Cricket and Football Club.[49]

The fascist regime gave enormous encouragement to a wide range of sports, celebrating individual courage as a cardinal fascist virtue and hailing team victories as evidence of the new spirit of national solidarity in the country. The Italian Olympic Committee was brought under party control in 1926, and the following year all local sporting federations were required to include representatives of the PNF on their boards. In the Los Angeles Olympics in 1932 a great deal of political capital was made out of the success of the Italian competitors, who finished second in the medal table. Four years later, in Berlin, they came fourth. The exploits of aviators such as Francesco De Pinedo – whom Mussolini hailed in a major speech in 1925 as an early example of the 'new Italian' (and who was made a marquis after a 34,000-mile round trip to the Far East) – received huge coverage, as did the achievements in the 1930s of

Italy's 6' 7'' world heavyweight boxing champion, Primo Carnera (the 'Ambling Alp'). Newspapers were forbidden to show photographs of him knocked down.

Despite a claim by a leading party journal in 1933 that rugby was the most fascist of games, having been introduced to the Welsh by Julius Caesar's legions,[50] football was in fact the team sport that the regime promoted with greatest vigour. By the end of the 1920s almost every provincial capital had a major football squad, and in 1929 a single national league was instituted with the top teams competing in Serie A. In Bologna a magnificent new stadium was built under the direction of the city's former *ras*, Leandro Arpinati, and opened in 1926 – the most modern sports stadium in Europe, with two international swimming pools, four tennis courts, a gymnasium, an Institute for Physical Education and stands for 50,000 spectators graced by a giant bronze equestrian statue of the Duce as a latter-day *condottiero* (melted down after the war and turned into figures of a male and female partisan).[51] In Florence another ex-*squadrista*, Alessandro Pavolini, was the driving force behind the building of an equally impressive stadium for the newly founded Fiorentina team. Completed in 1932, the Giovanni Berta stadium, as it was called (named after a local 'fascist martyr'), was the work of the brilliant engineer Pier Luigi Nervi and included a daring cantilevered roof and a dramatic 55-metre high modernist Marathon Tower, decorated with a giant *fasces*, with a huge jutting platform at its base from which to address public rallies.

These and other new and refurbished stadiums in Rome, Turin and elsewhere contributed to Italy's successful bid to stage the World Cup in 1934. The tournament provided an ideal opportunity for showcasing the regime and mobilizing the country around what in a relatively short space of time had become a genuinely national sport. There were commemorative stamps featuring the different venues, and an avant-garde promotional poster designed by Marinetti showing a goal, a black ball and the *fasces*, which was widely distributed throughout the country. Cigarette packets were used to carry publicity, and a special *Coppa del Duce* was commissioned, cast in bronze and 'unique in moral value' according to an official press release, to be presented by Mussolini alongside the main trophy. Mussolini himself attended many of the matches together with other senior party and government officials, and the national team dutifully saluted to the strains of 'Giovinezza' and the

'Marcia reale' ('Royal March'). The final in Rome, between Italy and Czechoslovakia, was turned into a political as much as a sporting occasion, with the crowd raucously chanting 'Duce, Duce' and the band of the Militia playing a succession of fascist hymns. Fortunately the game went to script and Italy won with a goal in extra time. In addition to the two trophies the victorious players were presented with gold medals (for military valour) and a signed photograph of Mussolini.[52]

Fascist propaganda frequently gave a strong martial gloss to the achievements of the national team, seeing success on the football pitch as evidence of the new spirit of discipline and aggression that would guarantee the nation victory on the battlefield. Italy retained the World Cup in France in 1938, but in a charged political atmosphere; and the link that fascism had always sought to make between sport and preparation for war became more apparent than four years earlier. The team coach, Vittorio Pozzo, recalled the moment in the opening match against Norway when the Italian players were greeted with a cacophony of whistles as they gave the fascist salute:

How long exactly that din lasted, I cannot say. I was standing rigid, with one hand stretched out horizontally in front of me, and naturally I could not gauge the time. The German referee and the Norwegian players, who were with us on the pitch, stood looking at us anxiously. At a certain point the uproar showed signs of dying down and then stopped. I gave the order to stand to attention. But no sooner had we put our arms down than the protests started up again violently. Immediately I said: 'Squad, attention. Salute.' And we raised our hands, as if to show that we were not afraid . . .[53]

If sport was to counter Italian decadence, and help resurrect the Italian nation, so too was greater fecundity. As a socialist Mussolini had favoured birth control, but by the mid-1920s he had become smitten by the arguments of Nationalist demographers such as Corrado Gini who had been alleging for a number of years that the economic and cultural vitality of a people was closely related to its birth-rate. The gloomy forecasts of the German philosopher Oswald Spengler, whose best-selling work *The Decline of the West* (1918–22) had raised the spectre of European civilization being undermined by democracy and materialism and overtaken by the more prolific Asian and African races, had helped to give pro-natalist ideas popular currency. Mussolini launched the so-called 'battle for births' in a major speech to parliament in May 1927, claiming that 'all nations and empires felt the pangs of decadence' when their birth-rates began to fall, and that if Italy wanted to 'count for something' in the world it would have to raise its population by 50 per cent over the next twenty years to at least 60 million.[54]

The following year, in a preface to the Italian edition of a work by a German sociologist (and future SS officer), Richard Korherr, entitled *Reduction in Births: Death of Peoples*, Mussolini spelled out more fully the demographic threats that were facing the nation. The 'black and yellow races', not to mention the Slavs, were proliferating at an alarming rate, and 'the entire white race' was in grave danger of being swamped. Much of the problem, he said, lay in the growth of cities in Europe and the systematic emptying of the countryside, for as all demographic studies showed, urban populations were much less fertile than rural ones. And this phenomenon was due not simply to economic factors: city life was inherently materialistic and lacking in spirituality, and created individuals who focused selfishly on their personal well-being and comfort:

The alarm bells are ringing . . . The challenge is to see if the soul of fascist Italy is or is not irreparably infected by hedonism, philistinism and bourgeois values. The birth-rate is not simply an index of the progressive power of the fatherland . . . but is also what will distinguish the fascist people from the other peoples of Europe, in as much as it will be a measure of its vitality and of its determination to pass on this vitality over the centuries. If we do not reverse the trend, everything that the fascist revolution has hitherto achieved and will achieve in the future will be completely useless . . .[55]

This, as much as a concern to celebrate what a number of influential fascist intellectuals (following in the footsteps of Vittorio Alfieri) maintained was the true essence of the Italian nation, was why so much emphasis was placed on 'rurality' by the regime. Mussolini regularly toured the countryside, meeting farmers and peasants, praising their vital contribution to the economic life of the fatherland, lauding their sobriety and industriousness and having himself photographed, sometimes stripped to the waist, working alongside them in the fields. A special radio service, the *Ente radio rurale*, was set up in 1933 to broadcast to farmers – though much of the air time was given over to political propaganda, choral singing and religion, and was unlikely to have made most peasants feel much better about their lot (even if they had access to a radio).[56] And measures were taken to make it as hard as possible for rural workers to migrate to the cities, culminating in two laws in 1938–9 that made it illegal for anyone to transfer their residency to a major centre unless they already had a job there.

The problem with much of the cult of rurality was that it drew heavily on conventional urban myths about the joys of the countryside and was likely to seem irrelevant (if not grotesque) to those whose main concern was simply to find enough work to live. Official encouragement was given to films and songs celebrating the life of the peasantry, especially in the later 1930s, but the results were almost inevitably sentimental and trite. A good example was the popular 1940 film *Mamma*, in which the well-known tenor Beniamino Gigli played a singer returning after a world tour to his farm in the country, which had been looked after in his absence by his mother. He is greeted by crowds of smiling peasants dressed in picturesque costumes, who join him in a song: 'A little house in the country / a little garden, a vine / whoever is born here despises / – and never seeks or dreams of – / the big city . . .'[57] In reality, though, Italian peasants did dream of the big cities, and despite government prohibitions millions abandoned the land in the 1920s and 1930s and moved to places such as Rome, Milan and Genoa – three of the fastest-growing centres in Europe in the interwar years.

The regime's other attempts to make Italy less bourgeois and thus more fecund proved similarly disappointing. But there was no want of trying. In 1926 a centralized statistics institute (ISTAT), headed by the demographer Corrado Gini, was created to calibrate the material health of the nation, and newspapers were instructed to print the latest population figures regularly. Mussolini (who quickly added two more children to his family in the late 1920s after a gap of nearly ten years, bringing his total to five) invited prefects to keep him informed of interesting demographic developments and personally intervened when he felt the situation demanded it ('I note that between the last census and today the population of Como has declined by 27 stop if all the provinces of Italy were to follow this brilliant example the Italian race would have its days numbered stop tell the mayor to do something for large families stop Como needs it').[58] A tax was placed on unmarried men, and the new fascist penal code of 1930 had a category of 'crimes against the race' with stiff penalties for anyone involved in carrying out abortions or promoting contraception. In 1933 an annual Day of the Mother and Child was instituted, held on Christmas Eve, during which bronze, silver and gold medals were solemnly awarded to those with six, eight or ten children.

Fascist propaganda worked hard to promote the ideal of the 'authentic woman' – fertile, rosy-cheeked, stocky, broad-hipped and ample-bosomed – and to counter what it saw as decadent foreign models of femininity: the so-called 'crisis woman' who was neurotically obsessed with her appearance, hedonistic, wasp-waisted and in all likelihood barren. Mussolini – whose own wife, the sturdily built Donna Rachele, conformed to the party stereotype (though his mistresses often did not) – made no secret of his dislike of feminism, declaring publicly that women had a duty to obey their husbands and should focus on 'their natural and fundamental mission in life' of child-rearing and not be distracted by thoughts of emancipation.[59] The party made repeated attempts to regulate female sexuality, issuing guidelines about the length of skirts and the shape of bathing suits, and ordering newspapers not to publish pictures of unusually thin women (dieting promoted infertility) or women with dogs (child substitutes).[60] Such puritanical strictures were not surprisingly welcomed by the Church, though the Vatican did object to some measures, such as the encouragement given to partici-pation by women in suitably decorous and healthy sports: 'If woman's hand must be lifted, we hope and pray that it may be lifted only in prayer or for acts of beneficence.'[61]

The regime also provided considerable institutional and financial sup-port for its population goals. A government agency, the National Service for the Protection of Maternity and Infancy (ONMI), was established in December 1925 to assist needy mothers and provide care for unwanted children and thereby, it was hoped, reduce Italy's very high infant mor-tality rates. Its funding rose from 8 million lire initially to over 100 million in the later 1930s, helped from 1927 by the proceeds of the tax on bachelors; but the persistent poverty of so much of the peasantry and the squalor in which the underclasses in the fast-growing cities lived ensured that its results were disappointing. Infant mortality (0–12 months) dropped in the late 1920s and early 1930s to around 100 per 1,000 births (nearly twice the level of England and Wales), but in the next few years it remained almost unchanged and even began to rise again towards the end of the decade. The situation was especially bleak in the south, where in several regions the rate of mortality continued to be in excess of 140 throughout the 1930s.[62]

Another important organization that sought to promote the fascist ideal of the 'authentic woman' was the Federation of Rural Housewives (*massaie rurali*), founded in 1933 by Regina Terruzzi, an energetic former socialist schoolteacher who had once lost her job for mothering an illegitimate child.[63] The federation aimed to mobilize peasant women up and down the country with a mixture of propaganda, education and pleasure, and had a membership card featuring a housewife balancing a tray of loaves on her head, and the motto *Alma Parens* ('life-giving mother'), and a uniform (for official occasions) of an ivory-coloured neckerchief sprinkled with the word 'DUCE' and decorated with ears of wheat, the *fasces* and flowers. There were training programmes, lectures, film-shows and prize competitions, and trips to Mussolini's home-town of Predappio, Rome or the monumental war cemetery of Redipuglia near Gorizia; and the monthly newspaper carried photographs of prolific mothers and farm life, and extensive information about childcare, domestic hygiene, animal husbandry and cooking (including how to make a patriotic green, white and red omelette). By the end of the 1930s the association had nearly 1.5 million members nationwide, though, as with most party organizations, the great majority were concentrated in the north.[64]

The regime's attempts to raise the birth-rate were thwarted in the end by a combination of mundane economic and cultural factors. The lack of jobs for the middle classes and the unremitting poverty of many urban and rural workers made later marriages more common and large families unrealistic. And rising expectations, and a desire for the comfortable lifestyle that the regime officially disparaged, no doubt played a part, at least in the larger towns and cities. A huge programme of land reclamation was embarked on from the late 1920s, with areas such as the Pontine marshes outside Rome being drained in order to make way for new settlements; and in the 1930s the Libyan interior was subjugated and Ethiopia invaded, it was claimed, partly to provide necessary living room for the nation. But such initiatives were hardly justifiable on demographic grounds. The birth-rate continued to drop steadily at least until 1936, falling below replacement levels in some parts of the north and centre, and only picked up slightly at the very end of the decade. And not even the top echelons of the party managed to set a good example: the average number of children per member of the Grand Council in 1937 was less than two.[65] Once again the gap between ideal and reality, expectation and reality, was proving frustratingly hard to bridge.

24
Community of Believers

Hail, O people of heroes,
Hail, immortal fatherland!
Your sons are reborn
With faith in the ideal.
The courage of your warriors
The valour of your pioneers
The vision of Dante Alighieri
Shines today in every heart . . .

The poets and the artisans,
The landlords and the peasants,
With pride at being Italian
Swear faith to Mussolini.
There is no poor quarter
That does not send its men
Does not unfurl the flags
Of fascism the redeemer.
The fascist anthem, 'Giovinezza'

The fascist state can only be conceived, believed in, served and glorified
religiously.   Paolo Orano, *Il fascismo* (1939)

THE PARADIGM OF CATHOLICISM

Mussolini was very conscious of his body. As part of the 'cult of the Duce', which became a key mechanism for generating popular support for the regime after 1925, he developed a set of mannerisms intended to convey the impression of an exceptional being. He would throw his chest forward, tilt his head back and push out his large jaw aggressively, or stand with his legs apart and hands on hips, scowling slightly (like Napoleon). For public speaking he developed an arsenal of flamboyant gestures, but in private he was restrained, even terse, often confining himself simply to rolling his large protuberant eyes in a manner that suggested (to some at least) great volition. He had a horror of being overweight (a sign of bourgeois self-indulgence) and ate very frugally: he used to say that meals should take no more than ten minutes a day. He also took regular exercise – horse-riding and fencing were his preferred sports – to keep his muscular frame in shape. Consequently he had few qualms about displaying his torso in public, and during family holidays taken at the seaside resort of Riccione on the Adriatic coast he regularly swam or jogged on the beach with crowds looking on.[1]

During one short family holiday at Riccione in August 1926 he took time off to visit a number of towns in the Marche. Among them was Pesaro, where from the balcony of the town hall he delivered a speech whose main purpose was to announce the government's campaign to support the flagging lira on the international exchanges ('from this piazza I declare to all the civilized world that I will defend the lira to the last breath in my body and my last drop of blood'). But he also took the opportunity to underline the degree to which fascism was far more than just a political movement:

Fascism is not only a party: it is a regime. It is not only a regime: it is a faith. It is not only a faith, it is a religion, which is conquering the working masses of the Italian people . . . [A]nd nobody will deflect us from the path that we must resolutely follow. Are you ready to follow it? (*Unanimous cry: 'Yes.'*) Follow it to the point of sacrifice? (*'Yes! Yes!'*) I will take your cries, then, as an oath . . . Long live fascism! Long live Italy![2]

In constructing itself as a religion, fascism turned to the Church as a model, partly out of instinct and partly out of deliberate calculation. As all the leading popular political movements in Italy since the Risorgimento had recognized, Catholicism was by far the strongest cultural template in the minds of the masses; and to win their emotional support it was felt necessary to draw on the language, iconography and practices of the Church. The liberal regime had been repeatedly denounced for its 'agnosticism', for failing to enthuse the population with strong ideals and arresting images. Fascism aimed to rectify this. Like Catholicism, it saw itself as a community of the faithful in which non-believers had no place (and should be persecuted) and dissent had to be stifled (through censorship); and it looked to employ art, music, architecture, colour, ritual, liturgy and ceremony to stimulate fervour and devotion among its followers. It created its own extensive pantheon of saints and martyrs, arranged mass pilgrimages to the new 'shrines' of the regime, and elevated 'the Duce' into an almost godlike figure.

The cult of the Duce owed much of its early momentum to Arnaldo Mussolini, who used his position as editor of *Il Popolo d'Italia* to portray his elder brother as a man of incomparable ability. From the mid-1920s the cult accelerated rapidly, fed by cohorts of obliging ministers and lesser party officials, and also by Mussolini's mistress, the talented Milanese intellectual and patroness of the arts Margherita Sarfatti, whose biography, *Dux* (1925–6), depicted her lover as a quintessential Italian genius, the embodiment of all that had been great in the peninsula since the time of the Romans. It went through seventeen editions, sold 200,000 copies in Italy, and was translated into eighteen languages.[3] In the years that followed, an army of journalists and writers turned out a ceaseless flow of pamphlets and books extolling the prime minister and vying with one another in the extravagance of their hyperboles. Mussolini was compared to almost every illustrious figure in history, and was deemed superior to, among others, Socrates, Caesar, Washington, Napoleon and Lincoln. To what extent the authors of these works were driven by genuine belief in their leader's gifts, political zeal, or hope that adulation might lead to a good job, is difficult to know.

Mussolini himself took a very close interest in the cult, monitoring carefully what was written about him and scrutinizing reports from the police, party officials and prefects for indications of his standing in the country. He always maintained that the masses were deeply impressionable, citing fashionable crowd theorists such as Gustave Le Bon in support, and he repeatedly compared Italians to children who could be manipulated quite easily through rewards and punishments ('two things are utterly indispensable for ruling the Italians: policemen and music in the piazzas').[4] His speeches, a crucial ingredient in his charismatic appeal, were intended as theatrical performances, to generate enthusiasm and unthinking faith ('the crowd does not have to know; it must believe'),[5] and in keeping with his assessment of his fellow countrymen

477

as infantile and credulous he developed a histrionic style of oratory that was at once pantomimic and liturgical, with wildly exaggerated poses, melodramatic hand movements, striking modulations in the tone and pitch of his voice, and exchanges between speaker and audience of the kind that D'Annunzio had made fashionable.[6]

An enormous variety of media were used to propagate the cult of the Duce. Newspapers were obliged to give extensive coverage to his daily activities and report his speeches in glowing terms (the applause he received was invariably described as 'delirious', 'formidable', 'unstoppable', 'prolonged', 'frenetic', 'vibrant', 'deafening' and 'enthusiastic'). It became mandatory to print the words 'Duce' and 'he' (when referring to the prime minister) in capital letters, and among the epithets that journalists attached to his name were 'sublime', 'magnificent', 'divine' and 'tireless' (the myth that he worked long hours was fostered by leaving a light visibly burning in his office overlooking Piazza Venezia after he had left). Mussolini's (imputed) aphorisms – 'Believe, obey, fight', 'Live dangerously', 'Better one day as a lion than a hundred years as a sheep' – were reproduced in inscriptions and painted on walls all over the country, while his facial features and profile, often reworked in a modernist idiom, were made the subject of innumerable paintings, posters, sculptures, statues and medals. Radio and film became increasingly important vehicles for the cult during the 1930s.

Allusions to the Duce's 'messianic' status were frequent. Much was made of his 'miraculous' survival of four assassination attacks in 1925–6 ('Insane attempt on the life of Mussolini. God has saved Italy,' ran one headline)[7] and Pope Pius XI's description of him in 1929 as 'a man of providence' lent pontifical backing to the cause of sanctification. Manuals in elementary schools frequently injected a religious note into their descriptions of the Duce – as with the second-grade text called 'The "Yes" of the Deaf-Mute', in which a little boy is suddenly cured of his affliction while listening in a crowd to a speech by Mussolini, and is able to shout out enthusiastically: 'Yes! Du-ce! Du-ce!' in answer to his leader's questions. The story concluded: 'A star is watching from the heavens. It is the eye of God.'[8] Countless allusions were made to the parallels between Mussolini's character – his selflessness, his scorn of worldly goods, his stoicism in the face of the hardships of exile or the pain of his war wounds (so many, according to Sarfatti in her biography, that he seemed like 'Saint Sebastian, his flesh pierced as if with arrows')[9] – and the qualities shown by Christ and the great saints.

Mussolini's simple origins were also an important element in the cult, and their emotional resonance was again reinforced by explicit parallels with the life of Jesus. The Duce's blacksmith father became the carpenter Joseph, while his patient and long-suffering mother, the schoolteacher Rosa, took the part of Mary ('They are but Mary and Joseph in relation to Christ,' wrote Edgardo Sulis in his 1932 *Imitation of Mussolini*: 'instruments of God and history ordained to look after one of the greatest of national messiahs – indeed the greatest of them all').[10] The Duce's home-town of Predappio was extensively redeveloped from the mid-1920s as a centre for mass tourism, with the house where Mussolini had been born and a newly constructed family crypt containing the sarcophagi of his parents acting as the focal points. Visitors were invited to see themselves as pilgrims and behave with reverence; and most, it seems, did, quite spontaneously, as a report on a typical trip made in 1937 by 820 members of the national association of *massaie rurali* from Pesaro suggests:

> The previous evening, the *massaie rurali* decorated coaches and lorries with wild flowers from their fields and they also brought enormous bunches of them to lay on the tombs [of the Duce's parents]. The endless queue of *massaie*, in their characteristic costumes and their arms filled with flowers, was a splendid, lovely sight … Then the *massaie* heard a mass for Mussolini's parents, celebrated in the Predappio church … Then, with religious emotion they visited the Duce's house, poor, rustic like their own, where a mother has worked, loved, suffered, living a life like theirs, simple and loving, a life of sacrifice and happiness, teaching Her Great Son goodness, discipline and self-sacrifice.

One *massaia* was said to have 'religiously kissed' everything she could touch in the house.[11]

The cult of the Duce was in many respects the principal unifying force in the fascist regime, holding together men and women of different backgrounds and acting as a common denominator for the various ideological currents that continued to run through the Fascist Party – and indeed Italian society as a whole – after 1925. It functioned on a number of intellectual and emotional levels, not least the erotic: Mussolini was officially a respectable married man, but little was done to counter the idea that he had a fatal allure to women and was sexually voracious (according to his private secretary he made love, briskly, with a different partner almost every day in his office in Palazzo Venezia).[12] But the intensity and pervasiveness of the cult derived ultimately (as it had done with Crispi) from the plethora of hopes surrounding the idea of Italy, which the monarchy and parliament had repeatedly failed to satisfy. It was these hopes – political, moral, economic, cultural, military – that the regime was able to manipulate into a form of salvationism, with the aid of familiar religious iconography.

Ceremonies and symbols were extensively employed by fascism to highlight the religious character of fascism. As one of the party's leading intellectual figures, Giuseppe Bottai, explained in 1923, 'Religions often conquer souls and spirits through the solemnity of their rituals more than through the sermons of their priests.'[13] From the outset fascism developed an array of distinguishing attributes, sites of memory, and dates around which it could build a framework of liturgy and commemoration and thereby preserve, as Mussolini said, 'the pathos' of the movement[14] – the salute, the black shirt, the *fasces*, 'Giovinezza', 28 October (the March on Rome), 21 April (the foundation of ancient Rome: to replace the socialist May Day), 24 May (the entry into the war), 4 November (victory in 1918), the tomb of the unknown warrior (in the Vittoriano), the battlefields and cemeteries of 1915–18. In 1927 a new calendar was introduced alongside the Christian one, with the year beginning on 29 October and dates, written with a Roman numeral, starting from 1922–3 ('year one of the fascist era').

Like Catholicism, fascism made a cult of the dead. The '3,000 fascist martyrs' who had lost their lives in the struggle against socialism between 1919 and 1922 were a major focus of veneration throughout the regime – commemorated in speeches and monuments and in the names of public buildings, party sections and streets – while 'the fallen of the Militia' were frequently celebrated in both prayer and print. An anthology published by the party in 1935 with photographs and biographies of 370 blackshirts killed defending the revolution between 1923 and 1931 contained a characteristic mixture of religious and military imagery, with a frontispiece of a flaming crucifix flanked by *fasces* and erect bayonets, and an invocation to the fascist dead:

> GOD, you who light every fire and strengthen every heart, renew each daymy passion for Italy.

Make me ever more worthy of our dead, so that they – the strongest –
may reply to the living: PRESENT!
You nourish my book with Your wisdom and my musket with Your
will . . .
When the future soldier marches beside me in the ranks, may I hear his
faithful heart beating . . .
Lord! Make Your cross the insignia that goes before the banner of my
legion.
And save Italy, in the DUCE, always and at the hour of our beautiful
death.
Amen.[15]

The Catholic paradigm of the communion of the living and the dead
offered scope for bringing large swathes of Italy's past inside the emotional parameters of fascism, so enabling the regime to pose as the
embodiment of the historically (and providentially) ordained nation.
And likewise those elements that were considered foreign or unworthy
could be excised from the record or held up for execration – as with
much of the period between 1860 and 1922. A good example of how
fascism used the cult of death to link past and present was the reburial
on the twelfth anniversary of the March on Rome of thirty-seven 'fascist
martyrs' in the crypt of Santa Croce in Florence in a ceremony that
established a continuum between the regime, the Risorgimento (via
Foscolo and his great patriotic poem *On Tombs*) and the 'Italian glories'
already interred in the church, such as Machiavelli, Michelangelo and
Galileo. The lavish ceremony, in which each coffin was carried through
the streets of the city preceded by a banner with the martyr's name and
the word '*Presente!*', was attended by Mussolini and all the top party
figures. And the press underlined how the event bore witness to fascism's
success in unifying the nation through religious zeal:

[A] few hours separate us from a rite which the entire Italian soul is preparing
itself for and towards which it stretches as to a supreme and intimate source of
religious energy without which life would be a colourless succession of meaningless days . . . The civil liturgy of fascism testifies to the discipline of the masses
and their great faith in the Duce.[16]

Among the most important expressions of fascism's attempts to see
itself as a spiritual community of the dead and living were the celebrations

in 1932 to mark the tenth anniversary of the March on Rome. In the summer a major exhibition of the life and legacy of Garibaldi was held in the Palazzo delle Esposizioni in Rome, and its underlying political purpose was to highlight the affinity between the 'redshirts' and the 'blackshirts'. In the final room visitors walked down a long gallery of uniforms worn by three generations of Garibaldian heroes from the mid nineteenth century to the First World War, with the clear implication that the events of 1848–9, 1860, 1862, 1867 and 1915–18 were manifestations of the same faith (and all similarly sanctified by blood) that culminated in the fascist seizure of power in 1922. The curator of the exhibition, the distinguished Risorgimento historian Antonio Monti, was especially pleased with the uniform of Giuseppe Sirtori, one of Garibaldi's leading generals, in which the red shirt was hidden beneath a black frock-coat. It evoked, to his mind, the bloodstained shirt of a *squadrista* who had been killed at Mentana in October 1922, 'a magnificent signification of the spiritual relationship that links the two marches on Rome'.[17]

No sooner had the Garibaldi exhibition closed than the beaux-arts facade of the Palazzo delle Esposizioni was dramatically transformed for the opening on 28 October 1932 of the Exhibition of the Fascist Revolution: four towering black fasces, modernist in design and nearly eighty feet high, were set imperiously against a backdrop of red over the entrance staircase – as if to highlight the nation's recent metamorphosis from liberal effeminacy to fascist virility, discipline and strength. The exhibition, which was designed by some of the most talented architects and artists of the period, including Mario Sironi and Giuseppe Terragni, set out to chronicle the turbulent years in Italy from 1914 to 1922 using thousands of original documents and photographs displayed in rooms of often remarkable aesthetic originality. On the surface the political narrative was paramount, with Mussolini and other leading party figures playing key roles, but the underlying message was that the fascist revolution had been a supremely spiritual movement whose purpose had been to reconnect the people with the nation and so enable Italy to fulfil its rightful destiny as a force in the world.

This message was already implicit in the early rooms of the exhibition, where the narrative thread of events following the outbreak of the war was provided by *Il Popolo d'Italia*, with texts and quotations displayed prominently on the walls and the pilasters – as if the real protagonist of the revolution was 'the people of Italy' speaking through Mussolini.

But it was in the final rooms that the idea of fascism as author and agent of a new spiritual community was most powerfully expressed. In the Gallery of Fasces visitors passed through a church-like hall with giant cantilevered pilasters rising upwards on either side in the shape of a fascist salute towards a ceiling inscribed with 'DUCE'; while in the next room, the Hall of Mussolini, there was a reconstruction of the fascist leader's last office in Milan, with the phone receiver lying on the desk as if he had just been called away hurriedly, and cases of documents, framed to resemble death notices, detailing the assassination attempts on his life. The stress on Mussolini's mortality served (with a note of admonition) to emphasize that fascism's message was eternal, a point that was dramatically underlined in the final room, the Shrine of the Martyrs, a darkened hemispherical space dominated by a huge metallic cross bearing the inscription 'For the immortal fatherland' and surrounded by the word *'Presente!'* written up around the walls a thousand times on small metallic plates.[18]

FASCISM AND THE VATICAN

As a young man Mussolini had been fiercely anti-clerical, attacking the Church for its obscurantism and immorality, denouncing priests as 'black microbes', and publishing a scurrilous novel in 1910 about a cardinal who murders his young mistress;[19] and though he softened his tone markedly from the early 1920s as he looked to win the support of the Vatican against his liberal and socialist opponents, he remained at heart deeply hostile to Catholicism. Many fascists, especially those of radical left-wing backgrounds, were similarly opposed to an institution whose moral power threatened the party's monopoly of the hearts and minds of the masses; and the attempts to turn the regime into a secular religion often strayed quite deliberately – as had happened in the mid nineteenth century with the cult of Garibaldi – into the realms of blasphemy. Pupils in Italian schools in Tunisia in the mid-1920s were subjected to a version of the Creed which must have caused considerable offence to many Catholics as well as the clergy:

I believe in the high Duce – maker of the blackshirts. – And in Jesus Christ his only protector – Our Saviour was conceived by a good teacher and an industrious blacksmith – He was a valiant soldier, he had some enemies – He came down to Rome; on the third day – he re-established the state. He ascended into the high office – He is seated at the right hand of our sovereign – From there he has to come and judge Bolshevism – I believe in the wise laws – The communion of citizens – The forgiveness of sins – The resurrection of Italy – The eternal force. Amen.[20]

That the Church did not raise its voice in condemnation of such travesties reflected its ambivalence towards fascism. It was heartened from the outset by the government's support for Catholicism and its opposition to liberalism and socialism, and it welcomed the party's commitment to hierarchy and order, its preference for rural over urban life, its encouragement of cooperation between classes, and its conservative views on the role of women. But it had serious difficulties when it came to the goals of fascism. The battle for births, for example, accorded well with the Church's horror of contraception and its belief in the sancity of family life and procreation; but the purpose of sexual activity should be to help the dissemination of Christian values, not make Italy economically stronger and better able to fight a war, as Mussolini maintained. And in general the Church was highly uncomfortable with the regime's aggressive and militaristic culture and its insistence that the material and moral energies of the country should be directed wholly towards achieving worldly glory for Italy ('the pagan worship of the state', as the Pope put it in a moment of anger).[21]

But the biggest problem for the Church was the threat that fascism's totalitarian ambitions posed to organizations such as Catholic Action; and it was largely fear of being squeezed out of civil society that impelled Pope Pius XI into serious secret negotiations from 1926 for a concordat and settlement of the Roman Question. On 11 February 1929, in a magnificent ceremony at the Lateran Palace, the Vatican's Secretary of State and Mussolini signed the Lateran Pacts, which brought to an end nearly seventy years of formal dissension between Church and state. 'Italy has been given back to God and God to Italy,' announced the *Osservatore Romano*.[22] In return for recognizing the territorial settlement of 1870 as final, the Vatican City was made a fully independent state with forty-four hectares of land, and the Pope received an indemnity of 750 million lire plus a further 1,000 million in bonds as compensation for the loss of Church property since 1860. An accompanying concordat declared Catholicism to be the official religion of the state, and gave the Church a number of important privileges, such as the exemption of trainee priests from military service. Most significant of all for Pius, the concordat guaranteed the position in Italy of Catholic Action and its organizations, 'in so far as they carry out their activities independently of all political parties . . . for the diffusion and realization of Catholic principles'.

The pacts were of enormous political benefit to Mussolini as well as the Church. They were hailed internationally as a great diplomatic triumph and they consolidated the strong support for fascism that already existed in nearly every sector of Italian society. The level of consensus was indicated by the plebiscitary election held in March 1929 for 400 new parliamentary deputies, in which the government secured over 8.5 million 'yes' votes (98.33 per cent of those cast) in a turn-out of more than 90 per cent. Inevitably there was coercion, especially in the smaller centres, where the mayor and local party officials could easily control the result ('We will vote as they tell us, but God knows what is in our hearts,' a peasant in the Sicilian village of Milocca told an American observer as he was marched off to the polls accompanied, in time-honoured fashion, by the local band);[23] and the absence of any alternative to the list of government candidates inevitably meant the poll had limited significance. But there can be little doubt that the conciliation with the Vatican healed one of the most damaging moral fissures running through Italian society and permitted millions of Catholics to identify with the state to a degree that had not been possible since 1860.

However, in guaranteeing the independence of Catholic Action, Mussolini was imperilling his totalitarian dream of a fascist community of believers. He knew this, and in 1931 he launched a violent attack on the Vatican, and closed down all Catholic youth organizations, claiming that they were pursuing political goals (in contravention of the concordat). The Pope retaliated with an encyclical recommending that anyone who took an oath of loyalty to the regime should do so with 'mental reservations'.[24] A compromise peace was reached in due course whereby the youth organizations were allowed to continue, as long as they kept to purely religious activities (and did not engage in sport). But it was the Church, rather than fascism, that emerged as the real victor. Having succeeded in securing niches in civil society, the Vatican set out to capitalize on them. Membership of the Catholic youth groups increased swiftly in the 1930s to nearly 400,000, while the Church's student movement, FUCI, which aimed to train a Catholic lay elite, also flourished, nurturing in its ranks many of those who were to lead the Christian Democrat party after 1945. And private Catholic secondary schools prospered, with pupil numbers rising from 31,000 in 1927 to 104,000 in 1940.[25]

The idea of a community of believers bound together by faith in the fatherland, working to shed the vices of past centuries and restore the nation to a position of moral, cultural and political pre-eminence in the world, enjoyed the powerful sanction of some of the most important currents of the Risorgimento. And the fact that so many Italian intellectuals – artists, architects, novelists, playwrights, poets, musicians, journalists, teachers, academics and film-makers – felt able to collaborate with the regime and contribute, often passionately, to discussions about the nature and direction of fascism was testimony as much to the allure of the myths of regeneration and greatness as to the capacity of the state to co-opt through patronage. As Davide Lajolo, later to be a leading figure in the Italian Communist Party, recalled of his time as a young man in Piedmont in the late 1920s and early 1930s:

I never came across an anti-fascist who could make me understand that the ardour and eagerness with which I was burning for fascism was totally misplaced. Fascism was the only thing you heard at school, in cafés, among friends. 'Only with war will the world be healthy,' said fascism; only by 'conquering a place in the sun' will the majority of poor Italians become better off . . . Only by 'daring the undareable' – as D'Annunzio put it in his poetry (and it was deeply seductive) – could you make yourself worthy of life. Rhetoric? Certainly . . . But that rhetoric excited me. I believed so sincerely in going to the people that I was willing to seize a rifle and stand shoulder to shoulder in the front line with the infantry, in any war, facing bullets. Yes, yes: 'book and musket, perfect fascist'. And with all that this entailed: companions dead at my side, hopes consecrated with blood. A terrible legacy.[26]

But not everyone absorbed the messages of fascism as earnestly as Lajolo, and the reception of the fascist message was inevitably contingent on factors such as literacy, access to the media, and the rootedness or otherwise of rival value systems. In much of the countryside, and especially in the south, the party and its teachings made little headway, it seems, and the old rhythms of life, dominated by issues of family and the local community, and above all by the need to survive in the face of unremitting poverty, continued unaltered. 'Fascism? I don't remember anything of fascism,' said an elderly peasant in the 1970s. 'We only thought about our work. I never saw a newspaper . . .'[27] And even where the regime's propaganda operated most insistently, as in the large urban centres, traditional frameworks of thought and feeling – Catholic, liberal humanist, socialist – proved hard to eradicate, ensuring that some of the party's more extreme ideas were greeted with scepticism, sarcasm or hostility. As the limits of the regime's attempts to penetrate hearts and minds and create new fascist men and women became ever more apparent in the late 1930s, Mussolini grew increasingly desperate, and frequently railed to his colleagues about the seeming impossibility of transforming what he called a 'race of sheep' into one of wolves:

It is the material that I lack. Even Michelangelo needed marble to make his statues. If he had had nothing else except clay, he would simply have been a potter. A people that for sixteen centuries has been the anvil cannot in a few years become the hammer.[28]

And in his frustration, he turned, like many frustrated patriots before him, to war:

[Italians] have to be kept drawn up in uniform from dawn till dusk. What they need is stick, stick, stick . . . To make a people great you have to take them off to fight, even if it means kicking them up the backside. That is what I will do.[29]

25

A Place in the Sun, 1929–36

If, little black girl, slave among the slaves
You look down from the plateau to the sea
You will see, as in a dream, many ships
And a tricolour waving for you.

Chorus

Little black face
Pretty Abyssinian
Waiting and hoping
The moment is drawing close.
When we are with you
You'll have new laws and another king.
                    'Faccetta nera', popular song, 1935

Italy and Ethiopia are two entirely distinct entities. The former is a great nation,
the cradle of three civilizations. The latter is a conglomerate of barbarian tribes.
Ethiopia is a negative factor for Europe, a source of dangers. Italy, on the other
hand, is a linchpin of European collaboration . . .
                    Benito Mussolini, 9 October 1935

BREAD . . .

Fascism was concerned above all with the life of the spirit, but it could
not ignore financial matters. Beyond restoring a measure of stability,
Mussolini had no clearly defined economic policies when he came to
power. Moreover his hands were firmly tied by political considerations:

he needed to win over conservative business interests. He accordingly reduced government spending (axing nearly 100,000 public sector jobs), rescued the Banco di Roma, ended the compulsory registration of shares, lowered tariffs and abolished several taxes. These measures contributed to the boom in manufacturing that occurred (as elsewhere in Europe) between 1923 and 1925. In agriculture he curtailed the post-war trend towards the division of major estates, and in 1925, following a poor harvest, he launched a campaign to make Italy self-sufficient in food. The 'battle for grain' was of benefit mainly to large arable farmers. So, too, was the 'integral land reclamation' programme, which was designed to raise production levels through extensive investment in irrigation works, road building and reafforestation. Private landowners were supposed to contribute to the costs of the schemes, but in the absence of serious penalties for non-compliance many failed to do so.[1]

Once Mussolini had consolidated his grip on power in 1925, he set out to establish greater central direction over the economy. For some years the Nationalists had been talking of the need to 'discipline' labour through state-controlled syndicates, and in 1926 the government introduced a major new law confirming the fascist trade unions' monopoly over the representation of workers, banning strikes and making arbitration compulsory in collective disputes. In theory this was intended as a staging post towards a fully fledged 'corporativist state' of a kind aspired to by many left-wing fascists, who had been influenced by the pre-war ideas of the revolutionary syndicalists, with every economic category in the country – employers as well as employees – being represented on an equal footing in corporations so that the nation's resources could be harnessed rationally to the needs of the collectivity: a so-called 'third way' between capitalism and socialism. But in practice fascism was never in a position to control the industrialists to the same degree as the workers, and though some government measures – such as the revaluation of the lira in 1926–7 – were taken in opposition to the wishes of parts of the business community, the fascist economy in general tended to favour the middle classes more than peasants and urban labourers.

Italy felt the impact of the Great Depression from 1929 less severely than many other European countries (as a consequence principally of its still very restricted industrial base) but there was still considerable hardship. Wages were cut by 25 per cent between 1928 and 1934; and although the cost of living also fell sharply during the same period, the fact that the average working week was reduced by around 10 per cent meant that many industrial workers were on balance probably worse off than before. (Some fascist leaders welcomed this economic asperity: according to Bottai it would 'have valuable psychological and moral consequences by enforcing a more rigorous way of living'.)[2] The most damaging consequences of the depression were in the countryside, where the shift towards wheat production that the 'battle for grain' had encouraged was accelerated by the collapse of the export market for goods such as citrus fruit, olives, nuts and wine. Smallholders now faced serious difficulties. Unemployment rose sharply and consumption declined, especially in the south, where the traditional safety valve of overseas emigration and remittances had been shut off as a result of the United States and other countries introducing strict quotas after the war.

The government responded to the country's economic difficulties with a huge increase in public spending. The number of civil servants doubled during the 1930s to around one million, while the outlay on welfare schemes, including maternity benefits and family allowances, went up from 1.5 billion lire to 6.7 billion lire – over 20 per cent of the country's total receipts from taxation – thereby creating a prototype for a modern welfare state.[3] Expenditure on public works also soared. Italy had fewer than 200,000 private cars on the roads in 1930, compared to over a million in both Britain and France, but this did not prevent the state embarking on an ambitious programme of motorway construction – partly to provide jobs, and partly for prestige purposes. The *Italian Encyclopaedia* claimed that motorways were 'an entirely Italian creation': they were not, but they accorded well with the image that fascism liked to project of itself as the epitome of dynamism and modernity.[4] Car ownership in Italy rose to more than 300,000 in the 1930s, helped by the introduction of FIAT's cheap 500cc model known affectionately as the 'Topolino' ('Mickey Mouse') – a modern, but hardly dynamic, vehicle.

The state also responded to the depression with the creation of two important new agencies – the Istituto Mobiliare Italiano (IMI, 1931) and the Istituto per la Ricostruzione Industriale (IRI, 1933) – to rescue ailing banks and businesses. IRI in particular proved immensely important for the development of the Italian economy, intervening to save enterprises ranging from steelworks, shipyards and shipping lines to electrical and machine-tool industries and the telephone system. The aim initially was to provide capital and managerial advice that would enable companies to be restored to financial health and then sold back to the private sector, but in practice many of the firms remained fully or partially under the control of the state, run with considerable flare by a generation of progressive entrepreneurs, a number of whom were later to spearhead Italy's 'economic miracle' during the 1950s and 1960s. On the eve of the Second World War it was estimated that the Italian state owned a larger proportion of the industrial sector than any other European country outside the Soviet Union.[5]

The regime liked to present IRI as an aspect of the 'corporativist state', which was inaugurated in 1934 with the establishment of twenty-two vertically structured corporations of employers and workers, each (supposedly) articulating the needs of a different sector of the economy. But in reality IRI remained largely independent of these new institutions. Indeed the corporations turned out to be considerably less important than government propaganda initially made them out to be. They were supposed in theory to regulate wages, levels of production and conditions of work in accordance with the general needs of the community, but in practice their powers remained limited, with most of the key decisions on the economy continuing to be made by the party-controlled workers' syndicates, the autonomous employers' organization, Confindustria, and Mussolini. But this did not stop an enormous amount being written in Italy and abroad about the corporativist state. The historian Gaetano Salvemini, one of a small group of Italian intellectuals who emigrated, noted from his base at Harvard in 1935 how 'Italy ha[d] become the Mecca of political scientists, economists and sociologists' eager to examine a system that appeared to offer a revolutionary solution to the evils of both capitalist individualism and communist collectivism.[6]

. . . AND CIRCUSES

Objectively a majority of Italians may have witnessed a fall in their living standards in the late 1920s and early 1930s, but subjectively many probably felt better off. The Duce often spoke scathingly of his desire to 'Prussianize' his fellow countrymen and rid them of their image as sensual, fun-loving idlers, but the need to ensure mass support for the regime led, paradoxically, to extensive government promotion of leisure activities. In 1925 a national federation was established of recreational institutes and clubs, many of them formerly run by the socialists, and two years later it passed under the control of the party. The Opera Nazionale Dopolavoro ('National After-Work Agency'), as it was known, proved extremely popular, going from 280,000 members in 1926 (mostly railwaymen and postal workers) to 1.4 million in 1930 and nearly 4 million in 1939. It organized concerts, plays and dances, screened films, ran bars and billiard halls, promoted local carnivals and festivals, and arranged sports events, day trips and seaside holidays. As with so much of fascism its impact was far greater in the towns than the countryside, the north than the south, but it was certainly one of the most successful initiatives in generating consent during the interwar years.[7]

But circuses as compensation for shortages of bread (particularly white bread) carried political risks. While the government did its best to use entertainment to foster 'national' sentiment – for example by organizing festivals of song and dance, staging parades of traditional peasant costumes, and reviving (or in some cases effectively inventing) ancient sports such as 27-a-side football (*calcio in costume*) in Florence (1930) or the 'Saracen Joust' in Arezzo (1931) – some of the most popular leisure activities became powerful vehicles for foreign cultural influences. This was the case with cinema, which despite heavy encouragement from the government for films of a patriotic character remained dominated in the 1930s by escapist comedies featuring 'white telephones' and other symbols of bourgeois affluence. Some films purveying 'fascist' values were successful at the box office, including *Luciano Serra, pilota*, which Mussolini's son, Vittorio, helped to make; and the regime used import controls and censorship to try to restrict the distribution of foreign productions. But with limited success: almost three-quarters of ticket sales in 1938 were for American films.[8]

Nor was the promotion of popular festivals and folklore without its problems. Displays of provincial art, music and dress, re-enactments of traditional ceremonies and commemorations of local historical episodes were intended, as one party publication explained, 'to stop Italians blindly loving and imitating what is foreign, encouraging them instead to make use of what is theirs and arouse "that national spirit without which nothing great has ever been achieved in this world"'.[9] But celebrating the glories of 'little fatherlands' risked reinforcing those fierce municipal attachments that had long been regarded as a particularly Italian vice and which the regime was ostensibly committed to curbing – as its campaign to stigmatize local dialect and promote the use of Italian suggested. And certainly passions often did run high. Siena grew increasingly angered in the 1930s by other cities imitating its *palio*, and Mussolini had to intervene to ban other cities from using the word.[10] And in Puglia attempts by the town of Trani to have a monument to the 'duel of Barletta' erected in its territory, where it claimed the famous encounter between Italian and Spanish knights in 1503 had really occurred (and not in Barletta), led to pitched battles in 1932 in which two people died and sixteen were injured. Relating the unfortunate events to the Chamber, the Under-Secretary of the Interior said that the causes of the violence lay in 'an accursed survival of the spirit of *campanilismo*'.[11]

EMPIRE

Fascism liked to make out that colonies were an economic necessity for Italy. 'Our peninsula is too small, too rocky, too mountainous to be able to feed its 40 million inhabitants,' Mussolini told parliament in 1924.[12] But in reality such talk was no more than window-dressing for the regime's conviction that conquest and expansion were necessary tools for proving (and improving) the moral health of the nation. After all, if the country was so overcrowded, there was little conceivable logic in the 'battle for births'. Great claims were made for the potentially huge economic benefits to be had from Libya and the other colonies in east Africa (Eritrea and Somalia, which Italy had clung on to after the defeat at Adua), and there was talk of settling 300,000 or even half a million peasants along the north African littoral, amid the oases and fertile palm groves, and giving them access to levels of prosperity they could not have dreamed of back home. But by the outbreak of the Second World War only 39,000 Italian farmers had been lured to Libya.[13] Nor did the colonies do anything for the public finances: between a half and three-quarters of each colony's budget in 1941 had to be paid by Rome.

Almost from the outset of his government, Mussolini spoke of Italy's right to an expanded empire. The humiliation of Versailles, when the country had received 'just a few crumbs of the rich colonial booty' from its perfidious allies in return for its 'supreme contribution of 670,000 dead, 400,000 mutilated and a million wounded', rankled;[14] and behind much of the regime's obsession with creating a morally integrated, demographically strong and economically self-sufficient nation, peopled by a new race of bellicose Italians, lay a determination to make amends for the disappointments of the past – 1866, 1896 and 1917, as well as 1919 – and secure for Italy its due place in the world as a major imperial power. And Mussolini had a fairly clear idea of when this would be. As he said to the Chamber of Deputies in 1927:

We need to be able, at any moment, to mobilize 5 million men; and we need to be able to arm them. We must strengthen our navy and make the air force – in which I believe increasingly – numerically so strong and powerful that the roar of its motors will drown out every other sound in the peninsula and the surface of its wings will blot out the sun across our land. In this way we will be able, tomorrow – between 1935 and 1940, when we will once again be at a crucial juncture in European history, I believe – to make our voice heard and finally see our rights recognized. (*Very loud and repeated applause.*)[15]

And in the same speech he reminded deputies that he had always been an apologist for violence and the 'bath of blood' as necessary instruments of political and moral progress.[16]

Fascism was determined to bring an end to what it saw as the weak and tentative policies of its liberal predecessors in Africa. Much of Somalia was still not under full Italian control in 1922, and the new governor, Cesare Maria De Vecchi, one of the leaders of the March on Rome and a future Minister of National Education, set about subduing it with methods that earned him the nickname of 'butcher of the Somalis'. Even Mussolini claimed to be shocked by his cruelty and violence.[17] In one episode De Vecchi invited a group of *squadristi* that he had brought with him from Turin to punish a religious leader suspected of stirring up resistance among the thousands of natives who had been forced to work on Italian-owned banana plantations to the south of Mogadishu. 'Do not forget that you have been victorious soldiers of the Great War,' he told them. The *squadristi* duly obliged, opening fire randomly on local people and forcing the sheik and his terrified followers to take refuge inside a mosque. When the rebels refused to surrender, the mosque was shelled with artillery. Some managed to escape, but were later hunted down. On the governor's orders no prisoners were to be taken, and more than 200 Somalis died during the operation.[18]

In Libya the situation at the time of the March on Rome was similar to that of Somalia, with Italian jurisdiction confined to a narrow fringe along the Mediterranean coast. Under the energetic governorship of Giuseppe Volpi much of the northern part of Tripolitania was subjugated, in keeping with fascism's belief, as Volpi explained, that Italy possessed 'not only military superiority, but also, and above all, a *moral* superiority, deriving from the quality and strength of our historical traditions and the greatness of the civilizing mission that Italy has for centuries carried out'.[19] After 1925 the pace of military operations was intensified as the government made the development of its colonies and the strengthening of Italy's position in the Mediterranean key goals of fascist foreign policy. As Giuseppe Bottai explained in a pamphlet published shortly after Mussolini had paid a high-profile visit to Tripoli in 1926:

The imperial future of the Italian nation hinges in large part on the Libyan coast and on the political efficiency of its hinterland. It should not be forgotten that *mare nostrum* is not ours. The Mediterranean is everything to us, and yet we count for nothing in it. We are penned in this sea thanks to the criminal inertia of past governments and the power of other countries.[20]

The key military figure in the operations in Libya was Rodolfo Graziani, a soldier of enormous ambition whose exploits soon led to his being hailed as a fascist 'new man' and compared to the great Roman general Scipio Africanus. Graziani, who became a marshal and a marquis, enjoyed an extraordinary cult status in the 1930s, in part as a result of his own assiduous self-projection as a romantic intellectual who in moments of uncertainty turned to Caesar, Livy, Tacitus and Sallust ('my lords and masters') for inspiration. He frequently faced criticisms that he acted with excessive cruelty; but again he found comfort in literature. As he explained at a conference in 1931:

If sometimes I begin to have qualms and feel unsettled by the atrocities attributed to my actions, I love to reassure myself by reading what the great Machiavelli says: 'A prince must not worry about acquiring a bad reputation for cruelty when keeping his subjects united and loyal, as it is more merciful to make a few examples than to allow disorders, which can give rise to robberies and killings, to persist out of an excessive sense of pity' . . . I know from the history of every epoch that nothing new can be built if a past, no longer acceptable in the present, is not partly or entirely destroyed.[21]

By the spring of 1930 Graziani and the new governor of Libya, Marshal Pietro Badoglio, had succeeded in bringing the western half of the colony under control, but Cyrenaica, to the east, was proving much harder to subdue. Part of the problem lay in the almost complete lack of understanding on the part of the Italian authorities of the culture, at once fiercely proud and religious, of the nomadic tribesmen who inhabited the region. As far as Graziani was concerned the Senussi were scarcely more than barbarians, led by an elderly warlord, Omar el Mukhtar ('a Beduin . . . with no culture or idea of civilized life . . . an ignorant fanatic'),[22] who were misguidedly opposing the forces of civilization. In fact el Mukhtar was a man of considerable learning and almost saintly austerity, who had taught in a Koranic school for many years before becoming leader of the resistance in Cyrenaica. He enjoyed immense standing with his fellow countrymen and possessed quite exceptional military skills; and there were never any problems finding new recruits for his mobile army of around a thousand *mujahedin*.

In a desperate bid to crush the Senussi resistance Graziani and Badoglio drew up a plan in June 1930 to sever the supply lines to el Mukhtar's forces by interning the entire nomadic and semi-nomadic population of Cyrenaica in concentration camps. In the course of the next few months at least 100,000 people, for the most part women, children and elderly men, were marched across the desert, in some cases more than 1,000 kilometres, to a series of barbed-wire compounds erected around Benghazi. Any stragglers were summarily shot. According to fascist propaganda the camps were oases of modern civilization – hygienic, clean and efficiently run – but in reality the sanitary conditions were poor, with upwards of 20,000 Beduin crowded into an area about one kilometre square, together with their camels and other animals, and with only rudimentary medical services: the two camps of Soluch and Sisi Ahmed el Magrun, with 33,000 internees, had access to just one doctor between them. Typhus and other diseases rapidly took their toll on constitutions severely weakened by meagre food rations and enforced manual labour, and by the time the last camps were closed in September 1933, more than 40,000 of the inmates had perished.[23]

With the population of Cyrenaica interned, the prospects for el Mukhtar and his followers were bleak. To isolate them still further and prevent supplies coming in from Egypt, Graziani ordered the construction of a 275-kilometre barbed-wire barrier, four metres deep, running from the port of Bardia southwards across the desert to the oasis of Giarabub. The final operations against the rebel forces and their families were carried out with clinical efficiency, with bombers supporting the ground troops and dropping high explosives and (illegal) mustard gas shells on enemy placements and machine-gunning their lines. No prisoners were taken in engagements: even women and children were executed. One senior Italian official who tried to restrain Graziani was recommended for transfer back to Italy. 'The *forma mentis* of Dr Daodiace,' Graziani explained to the ministry, 'had become stuck in the old ways and I was constantly having to try to bully him into accepting the new.'[24] The capture of the Senussi holy site of Cufra and the massacre of many of its inhabitants provoked particular condemnation in the Islamic world. What possible connection was there between fascism's 'medieval methods' and 'civilization', asked one leading Arabic newspaper?[25]

In September 1931 the 73-year-old el Mukhtar was captured by Italian troops, summarily tried for what amounted to treason ('having taken up arms to detach this colony from the mother homeland'), and sentenced to death.[26] The army captain who defended him received ten days' solitary confinement for showing too much sympathy. El Mukhtar was hanged in the concentration camp of Soluch in front of 20,000 of his Beduin followers, and was immediately hailed as a martyr throughout the Arab world. In Palestine there were calls for his body to be buried in the holy city of Jerusalem. Italy's military hold over Libya was now almost complete, but the damage done to relations with the local population was beyond repair. In October 1933 the Cairo newspaper *Al-Jihad* published an open letter to Mussolini from a prominent Libyan exile pointing out the shortcomings of fascism's approach in Africa:

Thanks to your military equipment you have succeeded in conquering a country after a war waged in our midst for twenty-two years. But I can tell you that you have not conquered a single heart among the people of Tripoli. For hearts are not like forts: they are not captured with bombs, but are won over with justice and good deeds . . . You are seeking with your methods to eliminate the population in order to replace it with those who cannot find bread in your own country. This is a sterile policy . . .[27]

A major, and largely accurate, historical film, *The Lion of the Desert*, released in 1981, about Omar el Mukhtar and the suppression of the Senussi resistance in Libya, remains banned in Italy on the grounds that it is 'damaging to the honour of the Italian army'.

THE CULT OF ANCIENT ROME

As the pursuit of empire became more central to fascism, so the iconography of the regime grew increasingly imperial. In 1929 Mussolini transferred his governmental headquarters to Palazzo Venezia, the former residence in Rome of the ambassadors of Venice, the city-state whose mission it had been to dominate the Mediterranean (as D'Annunzio had reminded the audiences of his play *La nave*). The Duce's personal office in the Sala del Mappamondo – a sumptuous Renaissance room eighteen metres long, fifteen metres wide and twelve metres high, in the corner of which Mussolini sat at his desk, in imperious isolation ('You virtually need a pair of binoculars to see him,' one journalist commented)[28] – had a newly installed mosaic floor with a series of mythological and naval motifs around a large rectangular panel depicting the Rape of Europa by Jupiter. The subject, according to the designer, was supposed to symbolize the conquest of the world by Italian art, but it also lent itself readily to a much more bellicose interpretation, especially as the image was flanked by a pair of imposing *fasces*.[29]

As the quest for colonies moved up the political agenda, imperial Rome became the overwhelming point of cultural reference for the regime. Like Mazzini and Garibaldi before him, Mussolini claimed to have been intoxicated since childhood by the mystique of Rome ('For love of Rome I dreamed and suffered . . . Rome! The word itself was like a boom of thunder in my soul');[30] and fascism, with its rejection of democracy and celebration of authority, discipline, patriotism and war, made it possible for the state to embrace the history and symbols of ancient Rome in a way that liberalism never could. The disjuncture between past and present that had tormented so many patriots in the Risorgimento and deprived Italy after 1860 of powerful referents with which to sanction the new order appeared ended. Fascism was imperial Rome reborn. As a teaching manual for members of the Balilla explained:

If you listen carefully . . . you may still hear the terrible tread of the Roman legions . . . Caesar has come to life again in the Duce; he rides at the head of numberless cohorts, treading down all cowardice and all impurities to re-establish the culture and the new might of Rome. Step into the ranks of his army . . .[31]

The most potent expression of fascism's ambitions in the world was to be Rome itself. Mussolini called for a building programme that would make the city as 'vast, well-ordered and powerful' as in the era of the emperor Augustus. The principal Roman monuments – the Pantheon, the theatre of Marcellus, the tomb of Augustus, the Capitol – should be cleared, he said, of all the ramshackle housing that had grown up around them 'during the centuries of decadence' and turned into mighty beacons in the urban landscape. Magnificent buildings, befitting a great imperial power, were to replace the 'filthy picturesque' structures that everywhere abounded; and he proposed creating the longest and widest rectilinear motorway in the world to bring 'the imports of *mare nostrum*' from the rejuvenated port of Ostia to the heart of the city. Despite his campaign against urbanization he wanted Rome to expand massively – more than doubling its population and spreading twenty kilometres west down to the sea. Italy would finally have a capital that was both 'morally and politically' worthy of the nation.[32]

Inevitably such grandiose plans stood little chance of being realized, but one important project that Mussolini did see completed was the creation of a major new road running through the heart of the old Roman forums between the Colosseum and the Capitol. Built as the subjugation of Libya was nearing completion and inaugurated on the tenth anniversary of the March on Rome, the Avenue of the Empire involved the destruction of eleven streets and the levelling of some 40,000 square metres (causing in the process extensive archaeological damage). It was intended primarily as a route for military parades, and it drew a symbolic as well as physical line between the Rome of the Caesars and the Third Rome of modern Italy – symbolized by the huge marble monument to Victor Emmanuel II (the Vittoriano) and embodied in the jubilant crowds that thronged Piazza Venezia to listen to the Duce's speeches from the balcony of his palace. Along the west side of the new avenue were placed a series of giant marble and bronze maps illustrating the phases of growth of the Roman Empire.

Romanità pervaded the cultural life of Italy during the 1930s. Painters and sculptors drew heavily on classical forms in an attempt to create distinctive 'national' idioms of art, while architects used Roman motifs to produce an 'imperial' style of building that was at once both monumental and modernist. Triumphal arches became a feature of fascist ceremonies and festivals, and in places such as Bolzano they were used to underscore the recent successes of Italian arms. In Libya a huge arch was built in the Sirte desert between Benghazi and Tripoli, on the ancient border of Carthage, inscribed with an imperialistic quotation from Horace: 'O life-giving sun, may there be nothing more in your sight than the city of Rome.'[33] A number of high-profile bimillenary anniversaries – for Virgil in 1930, Horace in 1935 and Augustus in 1937 – allowed the regime to draw parallels between fascism and the golden age of Rome. Virgil and Horace were celebrated as poets of rural life and of concord after bitter civil war, who had placed their talents at the service of the state, while Augustus was presented as a glorious precursor of the Duce. A major exhibition in Rome in 1937, the 'Augustan Show of *Romanità*', aimed to illustrate how the ancient imperial values had been reborn in fascist Italy. Over the entrance were Mussolini's words: 'Italians, you must ensure that the glories of the past are surpassed by the glories of the future.'[34]

ETHIOPIA

The catastrophic defeat that Italy had suffered at the Battle of Adua in 1896 was often referred to by fascism as a stain on the national character that needed to be purged, and after the subjugation of Libya it was little surprise that Ethiopia should become the next target of Italy's imperial ambitions. There had been periodic talk in the 1920s of an invasion of the ancient east African kingdom, not least because its conquest would link the two colonies of Eritrea and Somalia, but Mussolini had more pressing concerns at the time and had been content to build up influence in the region through economic penetration alone. However, in the autumn of 1932, flushed with the success of the celebrations for the tenth anniversary of the March on Rome, he asked the Minister of the Colonies to draw up plans for a possible attack. These sparked off a long debate among the leading military authorities – the Chiefs of Staff of the army, the navy and the air force and the Chief of General Staff, Marshal Badoglio – about how the operations should best be conducted, a debate that exposed how little coordination there was at the top of the armed forces. Though nominally the most senior general, the Chief of General Staff had no powers of effective command over the three services. The only person who could impose centralized control was Mussolini, who from the end of 1933 held the War, Marine and Air Force portfolios (as well as those of the Foreign Ministry, Interior Ministry and Ministry of Corporations).[35]

The decision to invade Ethiopia was taken against the backdrop of the new international situation created by the advent to power of Hitler in 1933. Mussolini calculated that with Britain and France distracted by developments in Germany, there would be little international opposition to Italian aggression in Africa, provided it were swift. There was also the question of Austria. When Mussolini met Hitler for the first time in Venice in June 1934, the German Chancellor talked at length of his plans for a European war and indicated that he would like to install a pro-Nazi government in Vienna. Mussolini apparently did not demur – perhaps because he had failed to understand fully what Hitler was saying (no interpreter was present) – and he may thus have given the misleading impression that he was not too worried about Austrian independence. The following month the Austrian chancellor, Dollfuss, Mussolini's protégé, was murdered by Nazis, and it now seemed only a matter of time before Austria was annexed. The invasion of Ethiopia thus needed to be carried out before Hitler (who at this point was far from being considered by Mussolini as an obvious ally) could complete German rearmament and pose a threat to Italy along its northern border.

At the end of 1934 Mussolini issued a secret memorandum to the country's senior political figures to prepare for the 'total conquest of Ethiopia', and nine months later, on 2 October 1935, Italians gathered in piazzas up and down the country to hear the declaration of war transmitted over loudspeakers from the balcony of Palazzo Venezia. 'Fascist and proletarian Italy,' said Mussolini in a speech that contained echoes of Cavour and Manzoni (as well as Pascoli), was moving in unison to secure its rightful living space and avenge the injustices of which it had long been a victim:

Blackshirts of the revolution! Men and women of all Italy! . . . Listen. A solemn hour is about to strike in the history of the fatherland. Twenty million men are at this moment occupying the piazzas in every corner of Italy . . . Twenty million men: one single heart, one single will, one decision . . . It is not just an army that is moving towards its objectives, but an entire people of 44 million souls; a people against whom attempts have been made to commit the blackest injustice: that of depriving us of a little place in the sun . . . We have been patient for thirteen years, during which time the noose of selfishness that has stifled our natural energy has been pulled ever tighter! With Ethiopia we have been patient for forty years. Enough![36]

As soon as news of the first victories came through, including the capture of Adua, support for the war began to escalate; and when in the second week of October the League of Nations condemned Italy for violating the Covenant and fifty-two of its fifty-five member states voted to apply economic sanctions, a mood of extraordinary defiance swept the country. Distinguished liberal critics of the regime, among them Vittorio Emanuele Orlando, Luigi Albertini and Benedetto Croce, pledged their support to the government. So, too, did the eminent socialist Arturo Labriola, who now apologized for his opposition to fascism and returned to Italy from exile. Among those who volunteered to fight in Africa was the 61-year-old physicist and Nobel laureate Guglielmo Marconi. Popular songs circulated acclaiming the latest military triumphs, and in particular the victory at Adua ('Adua is conquered / The heroes rise again'),[37] while the widow of General Baratieri wrote to Mussolini to express her gratitude that her husband's honour had finally been avenged. Even the peasantry, usually almost impervious to the regime's rhetoric, got caught up in the excitement, attracted by the wild talk of land, work and wealth that the empire would bring.[38]

After years spent lauding the virtues of war, and denouncing liberalism for the weak humanitarianism that had shattered the dreams of the Risorgimento at Custoza, Lissa, Adua and Caporetto, fascism could not afford anything short of a crushing victory. On the face of it, this should not have been difficult to achieve. The army of the emperor Haile Selassie numbered no more than 300,000 men, and was feudal in both spirit and organization, with loyalty owed on a personal basis to individual warlords or *ras*. Most of the Ethiopian troops had access to modern rifles, but there were no military planes, very few machine guns and virtually no artillery. Against these ramshackle forces Mussolini mobilized the largest army ever seen for a colonial war. Initial plans for the campaign had suggested that three divisions would suffice, but Mussolini wanted to be safe and decided to send ten divisions (and eventually twenty-five). In all around 650,000 men were dispatched to east Africa, together with 2 million tons of supplies. They were supported by 450 aircraft, including over 200 bombers.[39]

Despite this massive superiority, the lack of passable roads in Ethiopia made it difficult to keep such large forces adequately supplied, and the campaign stalled badly after the initial successes. Mussolini promptly sacked the elderly commander, General De Bono, and replaced him with Marshal Badoglio; and, as in Libya, Badoglio was fully prepared to breach international law in pursuit of the rapid victory that the Duce needed. At the end of December, Mussolini sent Badoglio a telegram authorizing him to 'employ any kind of gas . . . even on a massive scale'. In fact Badoglio was already using mustard gas, and over the next three months around 1,000 heavy bombs filled with the chemical were dropped on enemy positions or, more lethally, sprayed as a vapour from aircraft, killing combatants and non-combatants alike and poisoning rivers and lakes.[40] Shells filled with arsine (a compound of arsenic) were also fired. In February, with heavy fighting still continuing, Mussolini urged Badoglio to use bacteriological weapons. But Badoglio felt this was unnecessary given that the enemy was already sufficiently weakened.[41]

Mussolini endeavoured to keep the truth about what was happening in Ethiopia hidden from the outside world. When photographs of mustard gas victims reached London, the Italian embassy succeeded in passing them off as cases of leprosy; and in general the line taken by the regime was that the allegations of atrocities were simply calumnies intended to discredit fascism. It was even suggested that the British – against whom a barrage of propaganda was launched following the imposition of sanctions – were themselves supplying mustard gas to the Ethiopians.[42] In Italy the press was heavily censored and the campaign portrayed as an unequivocal triumph, both moral and military, for the regime. None of the many accounts of the war published subsequently by those who had taken part referred to the use of illegal weapons – whether from genuine ignorance or a desire to protect the honour of the army is hard to know. And even after 1945 there remained a heavy blanket of public silence, even in the face of incontrovertible documentary evidence.

Only in 1996 did the Ministry of Defence finally concede that mustard gas and arsine had been used in Africa.[43]

The ruthless methods employed in Ethiopia were driven by Mussolini's need to secure a speedy victory and fostered by a widely held view in elite fascist circles that Italians had to acquire a sense of racial superiority as part of their re-education ('Racism is a catechism which, if we do not know it already, we must quickly learn and adopt,' wrote the young journalist Indro Montanelli in January 1936. 'We will never be dominators without a strong sense of our predestined superiority').[44] But the violence also drew on the powerful currents of thought that from the early years of the century, under the influence of the Nationalists and Futurists, had viewed war as an aesthethic and sensual experience that taught superior, anti-humanitarian values. Among the numerous memoirs of the fighting was one by Mussolini's eldest son, Vittorio, who served as a pilot in Ethiopia together with his brother, Bruno (both were awarded silver medals for their bravery). Vittorio told his readers that war was above all 'a sport, the most beautiful and the most complete', that conferred on those who took part 'the diploma of manhood'; and his favourite adjective for describing the military action was 'entertaining'. It was sad but 'extremely entertaining' to see a group of Ethiopians 'blooming open like a rose' after being hit by one of his bombs, and it was 'extremely entertaining' to set fire to the straw roofs of houses and watch those inside leap out and run for their lives 'like men possessed' (though he also admitted that it was disappointing that the flimsy Ethiopian huts simply collapsed when hit rather than produce the dramatic explosions that he had seen in American films).[45]

On 5 May 1936 Badoglio entered the Ethiopian capital of Addis Ababa, three days after Haile Selassie had fled, and when the news reached Italy the sirens sounded and more than 30 million people emerged into the piazzas to hear the news of victory. In Rome 400,000 people packed Piazza Venezia and the surrounding streets to listen to the Duce declare that the war was over and that Ethiopia was '*de iure* and *de facto*' Italian; and such was the acclaim that Mussolini was compelled to come out onto the balcony ten times to acknowledge the cheering. Meanwhile a choir of 10,000 children sang a newly composed 'imperial hymn' on the steps of the adjacent Vittoriano. Four days later, under arc lights, an even more ecstatic crowd applauded as the Duce hailed the 'reappearance of the empire after fifteen centuries on the fatal hills of Rome' and announced that the king had assumed the title of Emperor 'for himself and his successors'. He asked the crowd if they would be 'worthy' of this empire that he had given them. And when the cry came back resoundingly 'yes', he declared: 'This cry is like a sacred oath that binds you before God and man, in life and death.'[46]

In reality Ethiopia had not been secured '*de facto*'. Large parts of the country were still outside Italian control, and because Mussolini insisted against all advice on ruling the colony directly without the mediation of the local *ras*, the new viceroys – Badoglio first and later Graziani – were forced into a war of attrition against an extensive resistance movement, with mustard gas and arsine again being used on a large scale.[47] Insecurity led easily to over-reaction. When in February 1937 two young Eritreans threw grenades at Italian officials during a ceremony in Addis Ababa, killing seven and wounding some fifty others (including Graziani), between 3,000 and 6,000 Ethiopians were killed randomly in reprisals in the space of just forty-eight hours; and in the weeks that followed thousands more were executed, deported or sent to concentration camps. Graziani proposed razing the old city to the ground. Mussolini thought this was excessive, but did agree that any Ethiopian leaders 'even vaguely suspected' of opposition should be shot.[48] When evidence came to light of possible links between rebels and the most important Coptic Christian centre in Ethiopia, the ancient monastery complex of Debrà Libanòs, Graziani ordered its 'complete liquidation'. According to official figures more than 400 monks were shot, though the total number of victims, including sympathetic local laity, teachers and students, may well have been closer to 2,000.[49] Graziani also had itinerant singers, fortune-tellers and witches executed, on the grounds that they served as possible conduits of information about the resistance. In these circumstances it is little surprise that relations between the local population and the Italian occupying forces remained tense, and by the outbreak of the Second World War Ethiopia was far from being subdued.

26
Into the Abyss, 1936–43

My wife was down in the vineyard with my father-in-law . . . I shouted out to [them]: 'Armistice, the war is over!' . . . The three of us climbed back up the slope in silence.

The end of Badoglio's message had been obscure – but at the same time all too clear: 'Any attempt at aggression, whatever side it comes from, will be repelled with arms.' Who could this aggression come from, except from the Germans?

The farm workers are celebrating. As I write I can hear the faint sound of songs issuing from the town: everyone is in the tavern. The common people are happy. We are not. Why should that be? Did we not want peace as well? But this evening the common people have no idea of the abyss into which we have fallen. Or perhaps they realize all too well, and do not care. Peace, everyone home, drunk on Sunday, and to hell with the government . . .

A peaceful night. A short while ago I went out into the yard and looked up at the sky, empty except for the stars. No more roaring of enemy bombers. A great silence reigns around the corpse of the fatherland.

Andrea Damiano, *Rosso e grigio* (1947)

THE BRUTAL FRIENDSHIP

With the conquest of Ethiopia, Mussolini reached the pinnacle of his popularity in Italy. The king, who had wept with joy on hearing of the fall of Addis Ababa and then spent a sleepless night staring proudly at a map of Africa, awarded him the country's highest military honour for having won 'the greatest colonial war in history, a war that he . . . conceived and willed for the prestige, the life, the greatness of the fascist fatherland'.[1] From his villa on the shores of Lake Garda the elderly D'Annunzio wrote to congratulate Mussolini on his magnificent achievement, saluting the Duce 'in immortality' and describing the victory as an 'incomparable and courageous gesture' that had left his soul stirred 'by a kind of spiritual revelation': 'You have subjugated all the uncertainties of fate and defeated every human hesitation . . . You have nothing more to fear, you have nothing more to fear.'[2] Other tributes poured in from every quarter, and propagandists hurried to proclaim the Duce an instrument of God, a 'genius', a 'Caesar', a 'Titan', 'divine', 'infallible', 'ineluctable', the 'founder of a religion' ('the name of this religion is Italy').[3] Giovanni Gentile declared that the Empire had finally dissipated 'every doubt and uncertainty' and ushered in 'a new Italy'.[4]

In fact the war in Ethiopia had in many respects been disastrous for Italy. The costs in human terms had been quite light (something in the order of 4,500 Italians killed, against anything between 70,000 and 275,000 on the Ethiopian side), but the financial burden of transporting and supplying an army that most experts reckoned to be many times larger than was really needed was huge: probably well in excess of 40 billion lire or the equivalent of virtually the entire national income for a year.[5] One result of this was that Italy was in no position to invest in developing its armed forces either numerically or qualitatively at a time when other countries were engaging in massive rearmament programmes in preparation for the impending European war. Equally devastating were the political consequences of the invasion. By defying the League of Nations and acting in Ethiopia in ways that shocked the civilized world, Italy was pushed away from Britain and France and drawn inexorably closer to Nazi Germany.

For Mussolini personally, the adulation that surrounded him in Italy after the declaration of empire encouraged a growing detachment from reality and a tendency, as many of his closest collaborators noticed, to believe in his own myth. He seemed possessed by a sense of infallibility, and became increasingly impervious to rational discussion, trusting instead to what he called his 'good star' and instinct ('I have never made a mistake following my instinct, but always have when I obeyed reason').[6] Moreover the relative ease with which Ethiopia had been conquered inclined him to imagine that a decade of fascist education had begun to pay off and that Italians were finally acquiring the 'unity of faith and action' that would enable them to achieve a position of dominance in the new world order that was fast unfolding: a world order in which the decadent democracies of the West – France and

Britain especially, with their falling birth-rates, materialism, effete ruling classes and aversion to war – would be supplanted by the virile peoples of Italy and Germany. To those who dared to suggest that Italy might be too financially exhausted to sustain the burden of further wars he brusquely retorted that economic issues had never halted 'the march of history'.[7]

The outbreak of the Spanish Civil War seemed to lend credence to the idea that fascism was an ideology of potentially universal application, and though Mussolini had a low regard for Spaniards on account of what he took to be an Arab element in their racial make-up, he agreed to send 50,000 troops to support the rebel forces of General Franco. He presumed that the war would be over quickly, but in March 1937 three Italian divisions under the command of General Mario Roatta were routed at Guadalajara while attempting an ill-judged push on Madrid. The defeat received huge international coverage and revived old taunts about the incapacity of Italians to fight (Lloyd George spoke mockingly of the 'Italian skedaddle'),[8] and it was made all the more galling in that the victorious Republican units had included members of an Italian anti-fascist 'Garibaldi brigade'. Mussolini was now obliged to try to salvage the honour of his fascist 'new men', and got sucked deeper into the war, sending huge quantities of aircraft, artillery, machine guns and armoured vehicles to Spain at a cost of at least 8.5 billion lire by the spring of 1939. Much of this matériel never returned to Italy.

The drain on the country's economic resources was made all the worse by the sanctions imposed by the League of Nations in the wake of the invasion of Ethiopia. Though these remained in force only until July 1936, and did not include oil, they hit imports severely and compelled the government to shift much of its trade towards Germany. A campaign of self-sufficiency or 'autarky' was launched and efforts were made to produce a range of *ersatz* goods – such as rayon for cotton and 'lanital' (from milk) for wool – but they could not compensate for Italy's chronic shortage of raw materials, and by 1939 only about a fifth of the nation's needs in primary goods was met from domestic production.[9] New taxes and capital levies were introduced, and in December 1935 Italians were asked to pledge their wedding rings and any other gold items 'to the fatherland'; but such initiatives did not stop the budget deficit soaring. In October 1936 the gold standard had to be abandoned and the lira was devalued by 41 per cent. Inflation rose, and the quality of living began to drop alarmingly. By the eve of the Second World War the economy was bordering on collapse and reports spoke of widespread popular disillusionment and discontent.[10] When in May 1939 the Duce came to Turin to inaugurate the FIAT Mirafiori factory, only a few hundred of the 50,000 assembled workers applauded him. The rest stood silently with their arms folded.[11]

The intervention in the Spanish Civil War fostered the seemingly inexorable rapprochement of Italy and Germany. In the autumn of 1936 Mussolini's new Foreign Minister, his 33-year-old son-in-law, Count Galeazzo Ciano, visited Hitler and came away enthused by the prospect that had been held out to him of Germany expanding eastwards and into the Baltic and Italy being left free to dominate the Mediterranean – the division of power in Europe that Crispi had once dreamed of and worked to achieve. Mussolini, too, was excited, and on Ciano's return he delivered a major speech in which he reminded the world that 'the life of the Italian people' could never be separated from 'the sea that was the sea of Rome', and warned that any attempts to 'suffocate' Italy within the confines of the Mediterranean would only result in conflict. He also announced that an 'understanding' had been reached between Germany and Italy, and that Berlin and Rome now formed 'an axis around which all the European states motivated by a desire for cooperation and peace can collaborate'.[12]

By September of the following year relations between the two countries had grown sufficiently close for Mussolini to pay an official visit to Germany. The Nazis did everything they could to impress him, laying on huge military parades and staging the most spectacular army manoeuvres ever seen in the country (though Badoglio reassured the Duce that the Italian forces were superior).[13] He was taken to visit arms factories, blast furnaces and the tomb of Frederick the Great, and on the evening of 28 September, amid torrential rain and thunder, he addressed an estimated crowd of nearly a million people at an outdoor rally in Berlin. Speaking in German, he talked of how fascism and Nazism were indicative of the close historical parallels between two nations that had achieved unity at a similar time and in a similar fashion, and he stressed just how much their world views had in common: hostility to communism and materialism, an acceptance of will as the principal motor of history, an exaltation of work and of youth, a belief in the virtues of discipline, courage and patriotism, and a scorn of comfort and easy living. He said that the Rome–Berlin Axis existed to promote peace in the face of the 'dark forces' that were operating to foment war, and he concluded by insisting that the two peoples, who together constituted 'an imposing and ever-increasing mass of 115 million spirits', should be united 'in one unshakeable will'.[14]

Mussolini came back from Berlin confident that the Axis powers would prevail in any future war (indeed Ciano wondered if it might not be best to start 'the supreme game' right away),[15] and by the time Hitler paid a return visit to Italy in May 1938, Mussolini had withdrawn from the League of Nations, signed an anti-Soviet pact with Germany and Japan, and acquiesced (albeit uncomfortably) in Germany's annexation of Austria. However, he was reluctant to commit to a formal alliance, as it made little sense to break irrevocably with France and Britain until he had seen just how far these countries were prepared to go to maintain his friendship. And although he took great trouble to ensure that Hitler derived from his six-day tour of Italy an impression of discipline, wealth and military strength – every part of the itinerary was carefully scrutinized, and shabby buildings pulled down or encased in artificial facades, trees planted and appropriate works of art installed (a copy of Donatello's statue of *Saint George*, a suitable prototype of the fascist 'new man', was erected along the route of the motorcade in Florence)[16] – he refused to accede to the Führer's wish for a military convention.

But war was clearly approaching; and to prepare Italians for the rigours ahead and further accentuate the anti-bourgeois and military culture of the regime, Mussolini and his dull-witted but zealous party Secretary, Achille Starace, introduced a series of measures to 'reform the customs' of the people. Handshaking was suddenly declared unhygienic and banned: the more martial 'Roman salute' was to be used instead. The polite form of address, *lei*, was condemned as a foreign import with connotations of 'servility' and a fierce campaign was waged to replace it with the more fraternal and manly *voi*. Civil servants were obliged to wear uniforms to work, and coffee-drinking was discouraged as decadent. And in order to underline the vital importance of physical fitness party leaders were required to take part in gymnastic displays and jog in public (an unedifying sight in many cases). One reform that Mussolini set particular store by was the introduction in the course of 1938 of a more aggressive marching step, the *passo romano*. To most observers this seemed an imitation of the German goose-step, but Mussolini claimed that it was in fact Piedmontese in origin and that it was important to adopt it in order to dispel the myth that Italians were physically inferior (the king could not do it – he had abnormally short legs – and was mortified). The new march was intended as a manifestation of 'will' and 'moral force'.[17]

The most brutal of the 'anti-bourgeois' measures was the introduction of racial legislation. References to an Italian *razza* or *stirpe* had punctuated the speeches and writings of Mussolini and other senior party figures from the outset of the regime, but such language derived more from a Nationalist preoccupation with generating a spirit of national cohesion and identity in Italy than from any obvious biological platform. However, the work of Cesare Lombroso and his followers had penetrated lay culture, and especially socialism, deeply, and many fascists (including Mussolini) had grown up in an environment in which 'race' was regarded as a modern and progressive intellectual category. Enrico Ferri, one of the most authoritative figures within the school of criminal anthropology and a key exponent of theories of racial degeneracy, was a strong supporter of fascism until his death in 1929. In most Italian universities in the interwar years anthropology departments were located in faculties of science and were dominated by biological approaches to the subject. Assumptions about the inferiority of the coloured races were widespread. As the distinguished ethnologist Lidio Cipriani (who had recently volunteered to fight in Ethiopia) said in 1938:

We Italians have already irrevocably fixed our attitudes towards the coloured races in Africa. We are convinced that a fundamental inferiority, linked to biological causes and therefore transmittable from generation to generation, distinguishes these races from whites.[18]

Such views underpinned the government's attempts to prevent miscegenation in the colonies. A decree of April 1937 made it a crime, punishable with up to five years in prison, for an Italian citizen to have a 'conjugal relationship' with an African subject, and other measures in the course of the next few years endeavoured to keep blacks and whites as segregated as possible so as to 'defend the prestige of the race'.[19] The drift towards Nazi Germany inevitably favoured the introduction of racial laws in Italy, but there was never any direct pressure from Berlin; and the emphasis under fascism remained as much on the psychological and moral advantages to be had from fostering a sense of racial superiority as on the biological benefits. As Mussolini explained in October 1938, Italians had long suffered from 'an inferiority complex' in so far as they saw themselves as a 'mixture of races' rather than 'one people' – with a particularly dangerous cleavage between north and south – and convincing them that they were 'pure Aryans of a Mediterranean type' would generate the mind-set needed to ensure that they acted as 'standard-bearers of civilization' in the eyes of conquered peoples.[20]

The legislation against the Jews that was introduced from the autumn of 1938 was similarly intended to give the 'bourgeoisie a heavy punch in the stomach', as Mussolini put it, and create a more pitiless and aggressive cultural environment in Italy. (Had not the belligerence of the ancient Romans derived in large part from their being 'racists to a quite extraordinary degree'?)[21] For many years Mussolini and other leading fascists had denied that the country's 48,000 Jews constituted a problem; and Jews had in fact been disproportionately well represented in the party from the outset, even at the highest levels. Aldo Finzi, Under-Secretary of the Interior at the time of the murder of Matteotti, was Jewish, as was Margherita Sarfatti, Mussolini's mistress for much of the 1920s and a pivotal cultural figure of the regime. Guido Jung, Minister of Finance from 1932 to 1935, was also Jewish. It was only when race became a central concern of the regime following the conquest of Ethiopia that anti-semitism suddenly emerged as a serious political issue. Symptomatic was the publication in 1937 of a book by one of the most authoritative spokesmen for fascist culture, Paolo Orano, rector of the University for Foreigners in Perugia, which argued that there was a fundamental incompatibility between Jewish identity and Italy's need to defend its 'national patrimony in every field and manifestation, at the centre of which stands the immense work of the Church, which is entirely Roman and entirely Italian'.[22]

The fact that Catholicism had for centuries nurtured a deep vein of hostility towards the Jews undoubtedly helped the reception of the anti-semitic laws in Italy; and though the Pope protested at the more extreme aspects of the new racism, issuing the encyclical *Mit brennender Sorge* in 1937 and telling a group of Belgian pilgrims in September 1938 that anti-semitism was 'unacceptable', centuries of persecution, discrimination and enclosure of the Jews in ghettos had left the Church morally compromised and in no position to take a strong stand. Among the most outspoken supporters of the racial legislation were a number of Catholic intellectuals, and in 1938 Pius XI was obliged to refrain from condemning the laws – which debarred Jews from marrying 'Aryans', teaching in schools and universities, owning more than fifty hectares of land, being members of the Fascist Party, and serving in the armed forces – as much from fear of splitting the Church as from concern with possible retaliation by the government. The Vatican confined itself simply to endeavouring to secure more favourable treatment for Jews who had married Catholics or who had converted to Christianity.[23]

Most of the fascist leadership gave their backing to the anti-Jewish laws (as did the king, who signed them), whether from a desire to ingratiate themselves with Mussolini, moral conviction, or a belief that such measures would serve to strengthen the fabric of the nation and the revolutionary profile of the regime. Giorgio Almirante, who for many years after 1945 was to be the outspoken Secretary of Italy's neo-fascist party, wrote in the newly established periodical *La Difesa della razza* (*The Defence of the Race*) of how the campaign against the Jews constituted 'the biggest and most courageous recognition of itself that Italy has ever attempted',[24] while the Minister of National Education, Giuseppe Bottai, used his journal *Critica fascista* as a platform for proclaiming the 'eminently spiritual' character of fascist anti-semitism, which, he said, summed up 3,000 years of Italian 'history, thought and art'.[25] At a more popular level, an enormous number of magazines and newspapers spread the racist message through the medium of satirical articles and cartoons that lampooned the somatic features of blacks and Jews and caricatured their supposed defining traits: infantility in the case of Africans, mercenariness and moral deviancy in the case of Jews.[26]

There was some resistance to the new laws, but it was very limited. A number of senior fascists made it a token of their personal authority to protect Jewish friends or clients – as the otherwise vehemently anti-semitic Farinacci did in the case of his private secretary – but in general the legislation was complied with fully, and between 1938 and 1943 Italy's Jews were subjected to increasing levels of persecution. Some 6,000 emigrated, but those who were left behind faced expulsion from professional positions, ejection from societies and clubs, the exclusion of their children from schools, and ostracism and humiliation in numerous, often petty, ways. Bottai was especially punctilious as Minister of National Education, stipulating that universities apply strict racial segregation during oral exams and even banning Jews from public libraries.

To some contemporaries the level of compliance was frightening. As a high-minded anti-fascist observer from Trento recorded in her diary in the autumn of 1938:

The law is a reagent that brings out the worst instincts in Aryans, exposes stupidity and ignorance, and revives superstitious hatreds . . .

The reaction of Aryan Italians:

One: in public, no protest.

Two: in private, rumours of petitions presented by one or two senior figures . . .

Three: Supine obedience to the orders to remove the names of even distinguished Jews from cultural, intellectual and business associations . . . One professor who had come out of a meeting of an elite cultural institute, which had that day struck off the names of eminent Jews, said to me: 'And yet we had all been opposed.' When I asked him why then they had acted as they did, he replied: 'We are all sheep' (this is what they are reduced to after sixteen years of an absolutist regime).[27]

With Italy's entry into the war in the summer of 1940 all the country's foreign Jews were interned along with other groups considered to be dangerous: gypsies, ethnic minorities (such as Slavs) and anti-fascists. Several thousand Jews were sent to a concentration camp at Ferramonti in Calabria, from where they had the good fortune to be liberated by Allied soldiers in September 1943. Jews of Italian nationality faced mounting restrictions on their liberty, culminating in May 1942 in a government order requiring their conscription for heavy manual labour (an appropriate punishment, according to the press, given that 'the tribe of Israel' had always been parasitic and work-shy).[28] By this date information was coming through to the Italian government that the Nazis were exterminating the Jews systematically, and in the months that followed the evidence available mounted; and though it is true that the Italian authorities resisted pressure from the Nazis to hand over Jews in occupied territories – in France, Greece and Yugoslavia – it is also the case that Italy made no attempt to curb the actions of its ally. In the autumn of 1943, the Minister of the Interior in the newly founded Republic of Salò, Guido Buffarini Guidi, ordered the internment in concentration camps of all Jews in northern and central Italy and the confiscation of their goods. Around 7,000 were later deported to Auschwitz and other camps.[29]

NON-BELLIGERENCE

Mussolini spoke wildly from 1936 of having '8 million bayonets' at his disposal; and the phrase was often repeated in the Italian press. But in reality the armed forces were much weaker than the regime's bombast suggested. The infantry had access to good rifles, machine guns and artillery, but in many cases the weapons were in short supply, and the firepower of Italian divisions was thus considerably less than that of many other armies. Even more problematic was the lack of tanks. The General Staff had failed to appreciate the importance of armoured vehicles (partly because they were still thinking of a static war in the Alps – 'men, mules, rifles and cannons' were the keys to an effective fighting unit, according to Badoglio),[30] and this error, together with the country's growing insolvency, meant that in 1939 the only tank available was a small three-ton machine. Similar deficiencies dogged the air force and the navy. The relative weakness of the industrial base meant that it took nearly five times as long to build an aeroplane in Italy as in Germany, and the main fighters produced by FIAT were far slower and more lightly armed than the new generation of Spitfires and Messerschmitt 109s. The fleet was impressive in size, but it had major problems with its guns (not one shot fired by an Italian battleship hit its target in the war), and largely because of the admiralty's refusal to cooperate with the other services it had no aircraft carriers or air cover of its own, which made it hard for Italian ships to leave port.[31]

If the Duce's martial posturing helped to conceal the truth about the country's military strength from the Italian public (and many foreign observers, too), it also had the effect of encouraging Hitler in his aggression. After acquiescing in the annexation of Austria, Mussolini made it clear to Berlin that he would not stand in the way of a German invasion of Czechoslovakia, and that if it came to a general war Italy was ready to fight (and would use poison gas to ensure a quick victory, if need be).[32] In September the British Prime Minister, Neville Chamberlain, urged Mussolini to use his influence to restrain Hitler, indicating that London might accept a partial annexation of Czechoslovakia, and Mussolini took the opportunity to gain international credit by brokering a much-acclaimed deal in Munich, relishing the fact, as he said afterwards, that Chamberlain had 'licked his boots' and declaring to loud applause in Rome that for the first time since 1861 Italy had played a 'preponderant and decisive role' in Europe.[33] Mussolini was becoming increasingly confident that Britain and France did not have the stomach for a conflict, and when Chamberlain paid him a visit in January in a last attempt to prise Italy away from the Axis, he was scornful of the British Prime Minister's bourgeois demeanour and claimed that 'people who carry an umbrella' could 'never understand the moral significance of war'.[34] Two months later Hitler completed the annexation of Czechoslovakia and Mussolini responded by launching an invasion of Albania, a country that for some time had been a *de facto* Italian protectorate.

Germany and Italy were now dancing to the same tune, and there was no realistic prospect of a return to cordial relations with the Western democracies. Hitler was speaking of Poland as his next target; Mussolini was talking of pushing on from Albania further into the Balkans: to Greece, Turkey or Romania. And despite growing signs of public disquiet at the enormous risks that the country was facing Mussolini believed that the moment had come to conclude a formal alliance with Germany. He announced it in May, without any consultation of colleagues; and the terms of the Pact of Steel (the Duce's initial preference had been for 'Pact of Blood') were drawn up almost entirely in Berlin, with little being done by Rome to place restraints on its partner. Italy committed itself to supporting Germany in any defensive or aggressive war in which it became involved; and although there had been much talk of the need for Italy to buy time for rearmament, no temporal clauses were inserted into the treaty. The Germans repeatedly told Ciano that they did not have plans to attack Poland at the moment. And Ciano was apparently reassured. But as soon as the pact was signed Hitler issued secret orders to his generals to make preparations for the invasion of Poland.[35]

In the weeks that followed Mussolini repeatedly ignored requests from Hitler for a meeting, but continued to indicate to Berlin that Italy would be fully behind Germany in the event of war. His hope was probably that he could continue to exploit German aggression – as he had in the previous four years – to secure further territorial gains. When it became clear early in August that an attack on Poland was impending, Ciano (who was fast becoming conscious of his own naivety with regard to Hitler) was sent to Germany to explain that Italy was not ready to fight in what would almost certainly become a generalized European conflict and to request a delay of two or three years. But Hitler had no intention of stopping at this juncture. He was confident, he said, that France, Britain and Russia would not enter the fray; and he told Ciano (to his great relief) that he was not expecting any direct Italian help with the invasion of Poland. He also invited Italy to consider taking Yugoslavia or Greece as its part of the deal. Mussolini was initially hesitant, but when towards the end of August it was announced that Hitler had signed a pact with the Soviet Union (to Mussolini's astonishment: Italy had not been consulted or informed in advance), he became much more confident and issued fresh orders to the army to prepare for a limited war in the Balkans.[36]

But Britain's announcement in the wake of the Nazi–Soviet pact that it would guarantee Poland's independence made it clear that the war would not be localized. Hitler pressed Mussolini to say whether or not he would support Germany. Fear of repeating the abhorrent behaviour of the liberal neutralists in 1914–15 inclined him to say yes; but faced with overwhelming evidence that the army was desperately short of basic equipment and in no position to sustain a prolonged conflict, he told Hitler that he would intervene 'immediately', but only if Germany supplied, among other things, 6 million tons of coal, 7 million tons of petrol and 2 million tons of steel – impossible quantities, as he well knew. Hitler scathingly remarked that Italy was acting towards Germany just as it had done at the outbreak of the First World War.[37] In order to deflect accusations of cowardice and disloyalty, Mussolini informed the Italian public, with an air of statesmanship, that despite having 100 divisions and 12 million troops at his disposal he had decided to remain 'non-belligerent' in keeping with his long-standing desire to achieve 'peace based on justice' in Europe.[38] In reality, as he confessed ruefully to Ciano, the army had only ten divisions ready to fight.[39]

APPOINTMENT WITH HISTORY

As Hitler's armies swept almost effortlessly through eastern Europe, the Baltic and Scandinavia between the autumn of 1939 and the spring of 1940, Mussolini became increasingly uncomfortable at watching from the sidelines. He described himself as a cat eying up its prey and waiting for the right moment to jump;[40] but without any clear idea about where exactly he intended to strike – whether in north Africa, the Balkans, Corsica or Malta – it was not possible to undertake any serious military planning. Nor were appropriate command structures created, as Mussolini refused to appoint his own general staff or do anything that might remedy the congenital lack of cooperation between the army, the navy and the air force. But when in the early summer it looked as if France was on the verge of defeat Mussolini decided that the time had come to keep his 'appointment with history'. On 10 June, from the balcony of Palazzo Venezia, he announced to a country that by all accounts was more perplexed than enthusiastic (and not a little ashamed by the opportunistic timing),[41] that the moment had finally arrived to 'break the chains' that were shackling Italy in the Mediterranean and embrace the struggle of the 'young and fecund peoples' against those who were trying to monopolize the world's wealth but who were 'impotent and nearing their sunset'.[42]

Mussolini was certain that the fighting was nearly over, and that all he needed were 'a few thousand dead' to guarantee Italy a seat at the peace table. Accordingly (and to Hitler's astonishment) the army of 300,000 men, massed in the north-west of the peninsula, was ordered to remain on the defensive for ten days after hostilities had formally begun. Only when Paris had fallen and the French requested an armistice was the decision made to attack. But without any serious planning (once again), the results were disastrous. The artillery were positioned too far to the rear, and the air force had not received any training in bombing enemy positions in the Alps; and as a result the infantry were thrown against well-defended forts with very little chance of success. All along the line the Italian advance ground to a near standstill, and by the time the armistice was signed on 25 June virtually no French territory had been taken. In the meantime Italy had sustained nearly 4,000 casualties (compared to just 104 on the French side), while inadequate clothing and footwear (rubber-soled boots made of the milk-derived cloth lanital) had resulted in more than 2,000 instances of frostbite.[43]

Despite this chaotic failure, Ciano was despatched to Berlin to press Italy's claims to large swathes of territory, including Nice, Corsica and Malta, and huge parts of northern and central Africa. But Hitler now had the full measure of his ally's worth and suggested instead that they wait until Britain had been defeated before making any decisions. Meanwhile the fascist press discussed Italy's impending dominance of the Mediterranean, and there was talk of creating an Italian sphere of influence that stretched from north-west Africa and Spain across Europe to the Balkans, Turkey and even the Middle East. It was generally agreed that Palestine should be acquired by Italy, because of the Church's moral claims to the Holy Land and the fact that one of Victor Emmanuel's ancestral titles was 'King of Jerusalem'.[44] In order to improve his future bargaining position at the peace table, Mussolini pressed Hitler to be allowed to take part in the invasion of Britain, and even sent 300 aircraft to Belgium to help with the bombing of London (the Germans soon sent them back when they discovered how out of date they were). But Hitler urged Mussolini to concentrate his limited resources instead on north Africa, which he correctly foresaw would be a critical sector of the war.

Hitler's advice went unheeded, and on 15 October Mussolini announced to a meeting of ministers and army generals (for some reason representatives of the navy and air force had not been invited) that Italy would invade Greece in two weeks' time. The strength and morale of the Greek forces were greatly underestimated and it was widely assumed that the campaign would be swift and easy. The heavy autumn rains were not seen as a problem, nor was the fact that Albania had no ports large enough to keep a major army adequately supplied. As soon as the attack began on 28 October it became clear that the Italian forces would be in trouble. They quickly got bogged down in the mud and snow of almost impassable roads, so allowing the Greeks time to mobilize and launch concentrated counterattacks. Reinforcements poured in, and by the early spring there were half a million Italian soldiers stretched along a 250-kilometre front. But they failed to break through the Greek defences. Only when Hitler decided that control of the Balkans was a necessary prerequisite for his forthcoming attack on the Soviet Union was the stalemate ended and, on 6 April, German troops crossed into Yugoslavia and Greece, overrunning both countries with ease. The Greeks initially refused to surrender to the Italians, on the grounds that they had not been defeated by them (28 October is still celebrated as a national holiday in Greece in honour of the successful resistance to the Italian invasion), but Mussolini begged Hitler to be allowed a share of the victory: Italian losses had after all amounted to nearly 100,000 men. Hitler agreed, and an armistice was signed with both Italy and Germany on 23 April.

By now the regime was facing disasters on all fronts. Three heavy battleships were sunk by British torpedoes while lying unprotected in the harbour of Taranto in November 1940, and the following March the fleet paid the price for having no aircraft carriers (or radar) in an engagement with the British at Cape Matapan off the coast of Greece in which a further five Italian warships were lost. Thereafter the navy hardly ventured out to sea again. In Libya, Rodolfo Graziani's serious shortcomings as a general were underlined when his huge but under-equipped army of nearly 250,000 men was routed early in 1941 by 30,000 British troops supported by a few hundred tanks. More than 130,000 prisoners were taken, and film footage of interminable columns of demoralized and poorly clothed soldiers quickly made its way into cinemas around the world, exposing the hollowness of fascist claims to have forged 'new men' and reactivating the old stereotype of Italians who cannot fight.[45] At the same time Somalia and Ethiopia were attacked by British forces from Kenya and were quickly overrun. In May 1941 Haile Selassie entered Addis Ababa exactly five years after he had been forced to flee, and Italy's new Roman empire came to an end.

With the regime showing signs of crumbling, Mussolini found scape-goats wherever he could. He pinned the blame for the fiasco in Greece on Badoglio and forced him to resign as Chief of General Staff along with the under-secretaries in the ministries of War and the Navy (but resisted calls for the dismissal of Ciano, even though his son-in-law had been perhaps the strongest advocate of the Balkans campaign).[46] After the Libyan disaster he sacked Graziani as the army's Chief of Staff, and in moments of anger he even talked of having him shot – though Graziani was too much a man after the Duce's own heart to remain in disgrace for very long, and he went on to become Minister for the Armed Forces in the Republic of Salò in 1943. But Mussolini's most vehement invective was reserved for the Italian people in general and their failure, after nearly twenty years, to absorb the central tenets of fascist education. He denounced their levity, their egoism, their cowardice, their corruption, their disobedience, their indiscipline, their disorganization, their lack of faith and their materialism. They were not a serious nation, he claimed, but rather a collection of individuals; and he feared that Italy would only ever be a country for tourists – a large Switzerland. And to support his case he maintained a dossier in his private archives which he labelled 'immaturity and blameworthiness of the Italian people'.[47]

On the home front, the situation was growing increasingly grim. In the north aerial bombardments disrupted production and shattered morale. By the end of 1942, 25,000 dwellings had been destroyed in Turin and around 500,000 people had moved out of Milan. Shortages of food and fuel for heating caused severe hardship, especially in the cities, and essential items such as shoes, soap and medicines all but disappeared. Rationing – which was introduced relatively late (only in October 1941 in the case of bread), partly in the hope of sustaining the illusion that the war would be short – allowed adults little more than 1,000 calories a day; and widespread corruption and administrative inefficiency meant that even with heavily restricted quantities staple items were often unavailable. Those with money were forced to turn to the black market, which flourished: by the spring of 1943 eggs were selling at fifteen times the official price in Rome (whose cats had long since vanished from the streets and forums).[48] Petrol supplies dwindled, and in 1942 private cars were requisitioned, leaving many towns eerily silent and empty except for pedestrians and bicycles.

Defeatism and political opposition grew. Years of patriotic rhetoric and calls to 'believe, obey and fight' seemed to have had little impact as young men hurriedly enrolled in universities to avoid conscription: student numbers doubled between 1940 and 1942, and in all nearly a million Italians found ways of securing exemption from military service during the war.[49] Clandestine newspapers, often linked to embryonic communist, socialist or Christian democrat anti-fascist groups, began to circulate, and strikes broke out, culminating in March 1943 in more than 100,000 workers downing tools in Turin for a week. Even more subversive, perhaps, was the escalation of sardonic humour ridiculing the regime, and the police struggled hard to contain those who peddled it – like the Milanese hairdresser Leonardo Patanè, who was arrested in February 1942 for distributing a list of alternative titles to current films: *A Hopeless Affair* was 'The War', *It's a Joke*, 'Fascism', *The Eternal Illusion*, 'Victory', *One Hour with You is Enough*, 'Mussolini', and *The Miserable Ones*, 'The Italians'.[50]

By the spring of 1943 the last hopes of salvaging something from the war had gone. Hitler's invasion of the Soviet Union, launched in the summer of 1941, had ground to a catastrophic halt in the snows around Stalingrad, and of the 200,000 soldiers that Mussolini had insisted on contributing to the campaign half never returned. In Slovenia, Dalmatia and Croatia the Italian occupying forces had been confronted with a ferocious resistance movement, and General Roatta had responded with a brutal reign of terror and mass deportations of local civilians in which thousands, probably tens of thousands, ended up dying in concentration camps.[51] In north Africa the German forces under the command of Field Marshal Rommel, which had been sent in to help the Italians prosecute the campaign against the British after Graziani's army had collapsed, had been driven back towards Tunisia following the Battle of El Alamein. Mussolini had wanted Libya held to the last man. But this was clearly futile, and in May 1943 General Messe, one of the few Italian commanders to emerge with some credit from the war, surrendered after a brave final resistance. British and American troops now controlled the entire north African seaboard and were poised to invade Italy.

For some time Mussolini had been losing touch with reality more and more, seeking distraction from his stomach pains, insomnia and other nervous conditions in the arms of his young mistress, Claretta Petacci, or in administrative minutiae – such as deciding whether *Parsifal* or *Tannhaüser* was a more appropriate opera for the Rome season – or in intellectual diversions such as translating Manzoni's *The Betrothed* into German. He was no longer capable of making rational decisions, and to some observers he resembled a sleepwalker who was oblivious to all that was going on around him. And without any obvious successor who could replace him, the Germans made preparations for a possible occupation of the peninsula in the event of the regime collapsing. At the same time a number of senior fascists, including some of the Duce's closest associates such as Ciano and Grandi, desperately began searching for ways to mitigate the imminent débâcle. At the centre of the web of conspiracy was the king, who as head of state still had the constitutional right to dismiss his prime minister.

On 10 July, British and American forces landed in Sicily, with little resistance, and two weeks later at a specially convened meeting of the Grand Council in Rome a motion calling on the king to resume the full military powers accorded him under the *Statuto* was passed by nineteen votes to seven. Among those who supported the measure were such leading fascists as Bottai, Grandi, Federzoni, De Bono, De Vecchi and Ciano. Mussolini had five of the 'traitors' executed a few months later. The precise implications of the vote were not clear at the time, but when the Duce went to see the king on the afternoon of 25 July, Victor

Emmanuel told him that the army's morale had utterly collapsed and that he had decided to appoint Marshal Badoglio as prime minister. Mussolini left the audience in a daze, and was promptly arrested. Later that evening a radio broadcast announced that the Duce had 'resigned' and called on the Italian people to rally round their sovereign. There were some celebrations, but popular excitement was muted by Badoglio's ominous statement that the war would continue. Nowhere in the country did any serious gesture of protest occur at the overthrow of the man whom millions had supported passionately for two decades.[52]

In the next few weeks the king, Badoglio and other senior generals secretly negotiated the terms of Italy's surrender to the British and the Americans. Despite the relative ease with which Sicily had fallen (most of the 300,000 Italian troops stationed in the island having simply melted away leaving the German divisions to fight a fierce rearguard action near Messina), the Allies were in no position to conduct a full-scale invasion of the mainland given that they needed to conserve the bulk of their forces for the anticipated landings in France. Consequently any further swift and significant gains in Italy required the support of the Italian army; and when Badoglio agreed to the armistice on 3 September at Fairfield Camp in Sicily he pledged to secure all airfields and ports against the Germans and hand over the entire fleet and air force. The Allies were particularly intent on capturing Rome, so cutting the peninsula in half, and this necessitated the aid of the 60,000 Italian troops – far more than the Germans had in the area – that were based in and around the capital under the command of General Roatta.

The tragic events of the next few days revealed just how fragile was the sense of the state – and perhaps of the nation, too – in the minds of more than 40 million Italians. When news of Italy's surrender was made public on 8 September, neither Badoglio, nor Victor Emmanuel, nor any of his senior generals showed a willingness to take responsibility for the fate of the country at this critical juncture. Lack of confidence in the armed forces – not unfounded, but probably excessive – and fear of the Germans almost certainly contributed to their inertia. No orders were issued to the army – apart from a near meaningless statement by the prime minister that troops should retaliate if attacked – and nothing was done to secure the airfields and ports as the armistice had required. The only action taken by General Roatta before he fled Rome was to instruct an armoured corps to withdraw to Tivoli so as to avoid 'grave and sterile losses' in the city. The minister in charge of the navy, Admiral De Courten, was supposed to send his battleships to north African waters under cover of darkness and surrender to the British. Instead he ordered them to proceed to Sardinia, where they were intercepted by German planes. One, the *Roma*, was sunk with heavy loss of life.[53]

At dawn on 9 September, as German forces were pouring into Italy, the king, Badoglio and more than 200 generals and senior officers left Rome for the safety of Allied protection in the extreme south of the peninsula. All across the country – and beyond, too, in the occupied territories of Greece, the Balkans and southern France – chaos and confusion spread. In the absence of orders from the top, panic-stricken Italian soldiers everywhere flung away their rifles and their uniforms. Many surrendered to the Germans, who ended up taking nearly a million prisoners. Feelings of terror mingled with resentment and anger: anger above all towards the country's leaders, who had added to the humiliation of defeat with what seemed like a double act of betrayal – of both the Germans and the Italian people (not to mention the British and the Americans).[54] And in the maelstrom of emotions that followed in the wake of the armistice, some who had believed blindly in fascism found solace in the prospect of a new redemptive faith: like Nuto Revelli, who went home, threw his weapons into a rucksack, and set off to find a communist or socialist partisan unit, convinced that the only 'fatherland' in which it was worth believing was 'that of the poor devils who ha[d] paid for the sins of others with their lives'.[55] Others chose to cling to the idea that the fatherland was best represented by fascism – particularly after the behaviour of Badoglio and the king – and pledged their support to the Republic of Salò, the puppet state that was set up in northern and central Italy after the Germans had freed Mussolini from imprisonment on the Gran Sasso mountain in a commando raid on 12 September.

But for many, perhaps the vast majority, the events of these days provided no discernible way forward. Instead they seemed to offer a terrible summation of decades of hopes that, however noble in their origins, had led ultimately to a terrifying abyss – an abyss into which the ideas of 'Italy', 'nation' and 'state' now risked being hurled and shattered. The elderly Benedetto Croce lay awake at night racked by the thought that 'everything that generations of Italians had for a century constructed, politically, economically and morally' had been 'irremediably destroyed',[56] while his fellow philosopher Giovanni Gentile saw in the turmoil and lacerations that followed 8 September the tragic end of all his dreams of building 'the Italy of the Italians':

Suddenly the Italy in which we had believed, the Italy of the Italians, where we had lived and wanted to live united in both feeling and thought, seemed to have vanished. What Italy should we now live for, think, make poetry, teach and write? For it will always be hard, if not impossible, to open one's spirit and be creative, even in abstract thought, without having the fatherland to lean on – in other words that spiritual patrimony by which everyone exists – without being able to participate in that eternal dialogue of the living with the dead through which Italians can feel themselves Italian. And when the fatherland vanishes, air and breath vanish too . . . Today's incalculable disaster is not the foreign invasion and the devastation of our cities . . . It lies in our spirit, in the discord that rends us . . . in the dissolution of what had been our common faith, through which we had looked with the same eyes at our past and with the same passion at our future: the sense of no longer recognizing or understanding one another, and thus of no longer feeling at ease with ourselves.[57]

A few months after writing these words, Gentile was shot by a band of communist youths as he sat in his car in front of his house in Florence. His assassin allegedly cried as he fired at point blank range that it was not the man he wanted to kill, but his ideas.[58]

But most Italians could not articulate the catastrophe in such intellectual and rarefied terms. For millions of ordinary people it was simply a matter of survival at any cost. 'Like ants when their nest is being destroyed, the Italians race hither and thither, on foot, horse, train and ship,' recalled the journalist Leo Longanesi. 'They must now save their skins and their homes: they must save that little Italy that we all carry around with us.'[59] And for the great majority of the population that 'little Italy' meant those elements that had shaped the moral and material horizons of humble men and women for centuries: family, friends and native village, with its familiar peal of bells and parish priest, its patron saint and festivals, its dialect, folklore and ancestral memories. For decades idealists had sought to expand these contours into the greater unit of the nation; but amid the wreckage of defeat appeals to anything as remote and abstract as the 'state', the 'nation' or 'Italy' seemed to have little meaning. A young Milanese bank clerk, Luigi Berlusconi, was typical of many of those serving in the Italian army on 8 September who were faced with a moral choice. As his son, Silvio, explained years later, Luigi decided to put his own and his family's interests first:

Then 1943 arrived: the great crisis, the fall of fascism, 8 September, the Germans, the fear, the bombardments. My father was serving in the army at the time of the defeat. The Germans had started hunting down Italian soldiers, and he was persuaded by a group of his friends to go with them to the safety of Switzerland. He made the right choice. He saved his life and saved the future of all the members of our family.[60]

After so many years of trying to create a sense of the nation, what nation could Italy now be?

PART SEVEN

Parties

27

The Foundations of the Republic,
1943–57

*I feel entitled to speak . . . as a democratic antifascist, as a representative of the
new republic, which, combining in itself the humanitarian aspirations of Giuseppe
Mazzini, the universal ideas of Christianity, and the international hopes of workers,
is set now on achieving that lasting and reconstructive peace that you seek . . .*
Alcide De Gasperi to the Peace Conference, Paris, 10 August 1946

*The reorganization, under any form whatsoever, of the dissolved fascist party, is
forbidden.*
Article of the Constitution of the Italian Republic, 27 December 1947

*We must present ourselves for what we truly are, and that is as fascists of the
Italian Social Republic . . . We alone are extremists . . . And our courage, or
rather our audacity, consisted in 1946 of inserting ourselves into this democracy
as the MSI, in other words as an active party.*
Giorgio Almirante, Fifth Congress of the Movimento Sociale Italiano,
Milan, November 1956

'WHAT ITALY?'

On the morning of 27 April 1945, the war in Europe almost at an end,
a column of cars, trucks and armoured vehicles, filled with German
soldiers and Italian fascists, was halted by communist partisans of the
52nd Garibaldi Brigade at a road block just south of the small town of
Dongo on the western shore of Lake Como. Exactly where the column
was heading is unclear: the countryside was swarming with members of
the resistance and the chances of crossing the border into Switzerland
or travelling east into the Valtellina and thence into Austria were slight.

After several hours of parleying it was agreed that the Germans would be allowed to proceed but that any Italians should be handed over. The vehicles began to be searched, and a man with a German helmet and greatcoat, the collar turned up over his face, was spotted under a blanket in the corner of one of the lorries, apparently asleep. 'Drunk, wine,' the Germans said. But the partisans became suspicious, and pulled off his helmet. The man stood up, his eyes glazed with exhaustion rather than fear, surrendered his sub-machine gun and pistol without a struggle, and was escorted to the nearby town hall of Dongo. Excited onlookers shouted: 'It's him, it's him, Mussolini.' Other prominent fascists in the column, many of whom had tried to find sanctuary in local houses or hidden in the water among the rocks beside the lake, were also rounded up and brought to the town hall. Among them were Marcello Petacci and his sister, Claretta, Mussolini's long-standing mistress. They had been travelling disguised as the Spanish consul and his wife.[1]

That night there was discussion among the partisan leaders in Milan as to what to do with Mussolini. Some favoured handing him over to the British and Americans, but the majority wanted him to be dealt with immediately by a popular tribunal. Fascism may have been destroyed primarily by the Allied armies, who had spent much of the preceding eighteen months fighting their way up the peninsula, but at least the representatives of the Italian 'people' would claim credit for having killed the Duce.[2]* The decision was accordingly taken to send Walter Audisio, whose battle name was Colonel 'Valerio', a communist who had spent five years in *confino* for anti-fascism in the 1930s, at the head of an armed unit to administer justice. He arrived in Dongo in the early afternoon of 28 April and learned that Mussolini and his mistress had spent the night under guard in a farmhouse in the nearby hamlet of Bonzanigo.

When they reached Bonzanigo, Valerio and his men found the Duce dressed in a grey overcoat standing listlessly in a bedroom with Petacci. The contrast between the heroic public image of the dictator and the mundane private reality was striking. 'His appearance [was] very differ-

---

* The allegation advanced by some historians that Winston Churchill had dispatched Intelligence Service officers to infiltrate the partisans and ensure that Mussolini was shot (perhaps to prevent damaging evidence of the British Prime Minister's personal correspondence with the Italian leader coming to light) and not put on public trial, as the Americans wanted, has never been substantiated.

ent from that of the strong and energetic man built up by fascist propaganda,' one of the partisans recalled. 'He had his forearms slightly raised and was holding a spectacle case in each hand.'[3] Valerio announced that he had come to rescue Mussolini. Mussolini was initially incredulous, but as they left the house his confidence seemed to grow and he turned to Valerio and said: 'I will offer you an empire.'[4] The small party walked down a slope (Petacci stumbling on the wet surface in her black high-heeled suede shoes) to the small piazza, where a waiting car was parked. Three local women were scrubbing clothes in the village fountain. Mussolini and Petacci were driven a short distance to the gates of the Villa Belmonte in Giulino di Mezzegra, where Valerio ordered them to get out. He pushed them against a wall. Whether he read out the death sentence ('By order of the general command of the Army of volunteers of liberty, I am charged with rendering justice to the Italian people') is unclear. Possibly not. Petacci threw her arms around Mussolini. Valerio shouted to her to let go. He pulled the trigger of his sub-machine gun, but it jammed, and he had to borrow another weapon: a French sub-machine gun taken from one of the fascists arrested the previous day, with a tricolour ribbon tied round the end of the barrel. Before being shot, the Duce apparently opened his coat and cried: 'Aim at my heart!'[5] 'Official' communist accounts of his death contained no suggestion of heroism.

It was shortly after four in the afternoon, and Valerio immediately set off back for Dongo. Two hours before, he had been shown a list of the fascist prisoners being held in the town, and despite vigorous protests from members of the 52nd Garibaldi Brigade, who were unsure exactly what authority the Milan emissary had to dispense summary justice to 'their' captives, Valerio had placed a cross against the names of those who were to be shot. They included the former revolutionary socialist and founder member of the Italian Communist Party, Nicola Bombacci, who had gravitated to fascism in the later 1930s and become a close supporter and friend of Mussolini in the Republic of Salò, and Alessandro Pavolini, the one-time Florentine PNF leader, who had been made Secretary of the reconstituted Fascist Party in northern and central Italy in September 1943. After their death sentences had been read out, fifteen men were escorted into the central piazza in Dongo, in front of crowds of onlookers, and lined up against the parapet wall looking out over Lake Como, their backs to the firing squad. Francesco Barracu, a former under-Secretary in the republic of Salò, turned and demanded to be shot in the chest: he had a gold medal for valour. Valerio refused. Before the final order to fire was given, the condemned raised their arms in fascist salutes and shouts were heard of '*Viva l'Italia!*' Valerio apparently retorted angrily: 'What Italy?' To which the reply came back: 'Our Italy, not yours, you traitors!' Bombacci was reported to have cried: '*Viva Mussolini!* Long live socialism!' Pavolini's last words were: '*Viva l'Italia!* Long live fascism.'[6]

The corpses were gathered up and thrown into the back of a lorry, which set off for Milan. The intended destination was Piazzale Loreto, where on 10 August the previous year fifteen political prisoners had been shot by Italian fascists (on German orders) as a reprisal for a partisan raid, and the bodies left gruesomely piled up in the baking sun for a day as a warning to the public. After stopping at Giulino di Mezzegra to collect the remains of Mussolini and Petacci, the lorry arrived in Piazzale Loreto in the early hours of 29 April, and deposited its load haphazardly on the ground. Huge crowds quickly gathered, and the bodies became the object of every possible form of desecration – spat on, shot at, urinated over, kicked, beaten and taunted ('Make a speech now! Make a speech now!').[7] Mussolini, Petacci and several other of the better-known figures were strung up by their feet from the gantry of a petrol station. They were soon joined by the former Secretary of the PNF, Achille Starace, whose lifelong obsession with physical fitness had proved his undoing. Spotted on 27 April jogging near Porta Ticinese by a passer-by, who had tipped off some partisans, he had been taken to a People's Tribunal and summarily tried and sentenced to death (his curious offer to help educate the younger generation of communists had not surprisingly elicited only mirth). He was brought to Piazzale Loreto on the morning of 29 April, his hands tied behind his back. When asked who the man hanging upside down beside the woman was, he answered, with some defiance it seems: 'My Duce!' Just before he was shot he turned towards the suspended bodies and raised his hand in a Roman salute.[8]

Italy emerged from the Second World War, as it had done from the unification process in 1860 and the Great War in 1918, deeply split and profoundly uncertain as to its identity. For over twenty years fascism had striven to appropriate state and nation, embracing the monarchy, the constitution, the administrative system and (from 1929) the Church, seeing itself as the rightful heir of the Risorgimento with all its aspirations to unity, spiritual revival and political greatness, and proclaiming itself the embodiment of more than 2,000 years of history in the peninsula. Now, amid the wreckage of the regime and the visceral anger – summed up in the macabre scenes in Piazzale Loreto – being directed at those deemed most responsible for the country's débâcle, where could Italy turn to find building blocks for its future? At the heart of fascism had been obsessive and paroxysmal nationalism: could anything with truly 'national' resonance ever be used again with conviction? Socialism and communism had of course both been anathematized in the interwar years, and thus had powerful moral claims to a place in the new order; and Catholicism, despite the settlement of 1929, could legitimately maintain that it had endeavoured to preserve a certain degree of independence from the regime. But all three of these ideologies were markedly universal in outlook and had enjoyed a highly problematic relationship with 'Italy'. To what extent could they be expected to provide solid bases for a reconstituted nation?

The need for new shared ideals seemed especially pressing given that the war had resulted in major regional as well as political cleavages in the country, with the north–south divide in particular having widened as a consequence of the very different experiences of the two halves of the peninsula since September 1943. After fleeing Rome ahead of the advancing Germans, Victor Emmanuel and Badoglio had set up a Kingdom of the South in the territories liberated by the Allies (and by the autumn the British and Americans had reached Naples, with the Germans dug in a little to the north in a series of heavily fortified defensive lines running across the Apennines); but in practice this reincarnation of the Italian state enjoyed very little autonomy, and most of the south was ruled directly by the Allied Military Government. The king desperately tried to enhance his standing by entering the conflict as a fully fledged 'ally'. But Churchill was firmly opposed; and though Victor Emmanuel did declare war on Germany on 13 October (with what little remained of his army: at best some twenty poorly equipped divisions), he did so only with the ill-defined status of 'co-belligerent'.

The consequence of this situation was that the south of Italy (in contrast to the north) had almost no experience of active anti-fascism in 1943–5, and the appalling hardship and suffering of the last phase of the war, with rampant inflation, food shortages, disease, broken infrastructures and widespread homelessness, failed to generate political currents or ethical positions that could feed constructively into post-war national politics. Instead southerners fell back on time-honoured methods of survival, living from hand to mouth through black-marketeering, petty crime, corruption, clientelism and banditry in ways that further eroded the already fragile sense of the state. And in Sicily, mafia activity flourished once again on a huge scale (the idea that the mafia was deliberately reintroduced into the island by the Americans has no basis: *mafiosi* simply resurfaced, as they had done at every moment of major political crisis, taking advantage of the new opportunities opened up in the semi-anarchy that followed the Allied invasion). It was a sordid and unedifying spectacle, that horrified high-minded observers like the writer Curzio Malaparte, who felt that the country had been struck by an extraordinary medieval plague that somehow left the flesh intact but gnawed away at the soul, leaving everyone 'defiled, vitiated and debased'.[9]

What was particularly disconcerting in this moral decay, at least to those with patriotic leanings, was the sensation that more than eighty years of unity had barely touched the surface of society. There was little apparent remorse or shame at the disaster that had befallen the country, and the occupying forces were everywhere greeted with wild enthusiasm, the poor clamouring for chocolates and cigarettes, the wealthy hurrying to throw open their doors and lay on receptions for the victors. As the Calabrian writer Corrado Alvaro noted with a mixture of horror and amazement, public opinion seemed to think that 'national dignity' and 'national honour' involved no more than trying to curb the swarms of shoe-shiners and prostitutes that were thronging the streets.[10] It was almost as if people were happy to be liberated not just from fascism but from 'Italy' ('I hope the Anglo-Americans will never go away . . . [T]hey have a vision of life that is different from the wretched one that we have known up to now,' wrote a Neapolitan in a letter in January 1944).[11] To those conscious of history, there was a horrible sense of *déjà vu* – the same vices ('the eternal Italian psychology of looking to foreigners for salvation', as the Florentine academic and anti-fascist Piero Calamandrei lamented) requiring, it seemed, the same remedies: 'Once again [we need] to make Italians . . . We have to turn them from subjects into citizens.'[12]

In contrast to the south, the north and centre of Italy had experienced a bitter civil war in the eighteen months following the armistice. The Republic of Salò – or the Italian Social Republic as it was officially called – was a puppet regime with a string of ministries dotted around the main northern cities and its capital in the small resort of Salò on the western shore of Lake Garda, near to where Mussolini had his personal residence in the Villa Feltrinelli at Gargnano. The Duce tried to preserve what autonomy he could, but real power lay with the Germans. It was they who controlled much of the machinery of government and issued orders to the Republic's ill-equipped and relatively small conscript army headed by Marshal Graziani (around 600,000 former Italian soldiers were kept in prison camps in Germany and deployed as slave labour). They ran (or attempted to run) sections of the Republic's ramshackle and factious police forces, composed largely of former members of the Militia and ex-*carabinieri*; and it was they who were chiefly responsible for rounding up and deporting some 7,000 Italian Jews, nearly all of whom subsequently died in the gas chambers.

But German dominance of the Republic of Salò did not preclude support for the new state among significant sections of the Italian population. The reconstituted party – the Fascist Republican Party – set out to recapture the anti-bourgeois spirit of the early fascist movement, and a number of radical measures were introduced, including the 'socialization' of large firms and the election of workers onto boards of management. But what backing the Republic secured did not derive so much from any of its policies as from Mussolini's residual appeal and from the capacity of the government to employ the language of patriotism and denounce as enemies of 'the fatherland' those who had overthrown fascism and surrendered to the Allies (five of the conspirators of 25 July 1943, including Galeazzo Ciano, the Duce's son-in-law, were shot in Verona, on Mussolini's orders, in January 1944). The Republic's propaganda agencies worked tirelessly to link the defence of the Republic to the honour of *la patria*, and the names of Mazzini, Garibaldi and the other heroes of the Risorgimento were invoked constantly. Letters from those who volunteered to fight for Salò, many of whom had been born after Mussolini came to power and had grown up immersed in the nationalistic language and culture of fascism, indicate that this patriotic rhetoric fell on highly receptive soil. As one seventeen-year-old wrote:

Italy, resurrected, once more marches towards its predestined goal, with an iron will. The sacrifice of so many years could never have been wrecked in dishonour in so unseemly a fashion ... Out of the abyss into which we have fallen, overwhelmed by lightning events and betrayed by the traitors, we – we volunteers in particular – have raised ourselves up with all our strength to redeem the path of honour. And we sing new songs of war, with the same immutable faith in our hearts, and with one great name on our lips: ITALY![13]

But the Republic did not enjoy a monopoly of the language of patriotism in northern and central Italy, for the resistance movement that began to emerge in the autumn of 1943 among ex-soldiers fleeing the German and Italian authorities after the armistice likewise appealed to the 'honour of Italy', 'the ideal of the fatherland' and the 'independence of the nation'.[14] Estimates as to how many Italian partisans there were in 1943–5 have varied considerably. There was never a 'mass' popular rising against fascism, as communist mythology subsequently tried to claim; but equally the resistance was far from being a wholly negligible entity. According to the Salò government there were over 80,000 'rebels' at large by the early summer of 1944, most of them young men who had taken to the hills to avoid being drafted into the Republican army; and by the spring of the following year this figure had more than doubled. But not all of those who deserted became active partisans. Many were simply in hiding, indifferent to the competing claims of nation and fatherland, and waiting for peace to return so that they could go home and resume their normal lives.[15]

Those who did fight were impelled by a complex array of motives. Some saw the resistance as primarily a war of liberation, to drive the German occupying forces out of the country. Others were inspired by socialist ideals, and viewed the struggle as primarily one for the emancipation of the poor and greater social justice. Still others regarded the destruction of 'fascism' as the overriding goal. These varied objectives were soon to crystallize into distinct political positions as representatives of the communists, the Christian Democrats, the socialists and the other anti-fascist parties that were fast emerging in the major cities in 1943–4 began to infiltrate the partisan formations and draw them into their orbit. But as the distinguished socialist Vittorio Foa later recalled, at the heart of the resistance lay a common desire to try to find some positive new meaning for Italy after the catastrophic experience of fascism:

Fascism had driven nationalist propaganda to excess. It had raised the nation up on an altar, like a god, and had destroyed it. It had obliterated the nation in the eyes of Italians with the collapse of 8 September; and it had obliterated the nation in the eyes of the world in the way it had entered the war – cravenly, and at the last moment – in the way it had fought it, and in the way it had lost it. Fascism had deprived the nation of all value. This was the fundamental feeling . . . that lay at the root of the resistance: . . . the need to reconstruct an identity for ourselves in the face of fascism . . .[16]

But whatever the inspiration to take up arms, and however noble the aims, the resistance involved Italians fighting against Italians in a civil war of great viciousness. According to official figures 44,720 partisans were killed between September 1943 and April 1945 and a further 10,000 civilians died in reprisal raids; and most of these deaths came at the hands of the various police and militia units that made up the sprawling, semi-anarchic, public security machinery of the Republic of Salò. Exactly how many fascists were killed in the same period remains unknown.[17] The celebration of violence and the rejection of humanitarian values that had been central to interwar culture ensured that the Republican forces had few qualms about acting with brutality towards their enemies; and a desire to assuage some of the humiliation of defeat by showing that they could behave as ruthlessly as their Nazi allies also encouraged atrocities. Torture, rape, public executions, the display of corpses (often with crude inscriptions pinned to the bodies to indicate the crimes) and the annihilation of entire communities for having given support to partisans were all features of this grim struggle.[18]

Both sides saw the violence as necessary; and for many partisans, certainly those in communist or socialist units, the armed struggle and the terrible punishments frequently meted out to innocent civilians following attacks on fascists or Nazis could be justified by the thought that the resistance was on behalf of 'the people'; and if, as a consequence of the reprisals, the masses were goaded into hating the enemy more and giving active support to the partisans, so much the better.[19] Like the Risorgimento democrats a century earlier, the resistance fighters hoped that out of sacrifice and bloodshed would emerge an engaged people and a regenerate nation; and it pained many of them to see just how much Italian society was still afflicted by its 'secular inertia', 'like a giant rusty wheel' that was almost impossible to turn, as the communist

Franco Calamandrei noted in his diary.[20] Alfredo Pizzoni, President in
1943–5 of the National Committee for the Liberation of Upper Italy,
the supreme organ of the resistance, recalled 'the huge, abject category
of so-called *benpensanti* . . . who at that time had only one preoccupation: to come back home each evening with their bags full of the meat,
rice, butter and flour they needed to support their families':

That Italy was disarmed, rent to pieces, and torn in every possible way, and
appallingly so, mattered less to them. They thought about it, perhaps, yes; but
only on the fringes of their material concerns. They cared solely about their own
private affairs, and got ready to criticize what had taken place once the war was
over, . . . unaware that they ought themselves to have done something, oblivious
to the heroic efforts that had been made and the great results achieved.[21]

Here was yet another formulation of the old problem that had taxed
Francesco De Sanctis in the years after unification: that of the insouciant
'Guicciardini man' and the divorce between thought and action. But
given what 'Italy' had signified for most inhabitants of the peninsula in
the preceding decades – the persistent poverty, the false hopes, the social
conflicts and the ruinous wars – it was perhaps not altogether surprising
that the standard-bearers of the new gospels of national redemption
should have been greeted with considerable scepticism. According to
Nuto Revelli virtually all the peasants in the Piedmontese province of
Cuneo regarded the events of 1943–5 as a largely meaningless 'fratricidal war', from which it was best to stand aside and not get involved.[22]
And for many of them the resistance fighters appeared no more than
dangerous trouble-makers who requisitioned scarce food and other supplies and risked precipitating reprisals – of the kind that occurred in and
around the small town of Marzabotto in the countryside to the south of
Bologna in late September and early October 1944, when German troops
punished the peasants for giving assistance to local partisans by mass-
acring nearly 1,000 people, including over 200 children.

THE 'VALUES OF THE RESISTANCE'

Though popular support for the partisans was in reality far less than
was subsequently maintained by governments eager to assert to the
outside world that post-war Italy was built on the 'values of the resist-

ance', politically it was hard in 1944–5 to ignore the claims of the anti-fascist forces to a monopoly of power. Following the capture of Rome by the Allies in June 1944, the leaders of the communists, the socialists, the Christian Democrats and the 'Actionists' (a liberal democratic formation, heavily involved in the resistance, but whose elitist character led to its rapid disappearance after 1945) emerged from hiding and succeeded in wresting control of the government from Badoglio (with the backing of the Americans – President Roosevelt had the wishes of 600,000 Italo-American voters back home to consider – but to Churchill's annoyance: 'I am not aware ... that we have conceded to the Italians, who have cost us so dear in life and materials, the power to form any Government they choose without reference to the victorious Powers and without the slightest pretence of a popular mandate').[23] And once the war in Europe was over in May 1945, these same anti-fascist parties continued in power – in coalition – and, with the exception of the Actionists, were to dominate the Italian political landscape for the next forty-five years.

The ethical foundations of post-war Italy were provided by the 'values of the resistance', celebrated annually in a new national holiday on 25 April and endorsed solemnly by all the leading parties. But the events of July–September 1943 and the ensuing civil war in the north and centre – which continued long after May 1945, with at least 20,000 fascists being hunted down and killed by vigilantes in the next two years – left a legacy of anger and bitterness that was to fester beneath the surface of society for decades to come. As a result millions of Italians openly refused after 1945 to identify with the official political orientation of the state, with on average around 7 per cent of the electorate regularly voting for neo-fascist parties. And well into the 1950s clandestine formations such as the Mussolini Action Squads, the Italian Army of Liberation, the Fasci of Revolutionary Action and the Italian Anti-Bolshevik Front carried out terrorist operations in the name of fascism. One of these formations, the Fascist Democratic Party, attracted international publicity in April 1946 by stealing the body of Mussolini at night from its unmarked grave in a cemetery in Milan. (The remains were found a few months later hidden in a cupboard in the Charterhouse of Pavia).[24]

A further problem with the 'values of the resistance' was that they belonged almost exclusively to the north. Many southerners, especially among the propertied classes, had experienced 1943–5 as a period of lawlessness and social upheaval, with peasants occupying estates in time-honoured fashion and demanding a share of the land. In these circumstances fascism could easily be viewed with nostalgia as a time of 'order' and the new democratic parties – the communists and socialists in particular – as a threat. In Sicily the landowners responded by organizing a movement in 1944–6 to make the island independent, even financing a sizeable private army, with bandits and *mafiosi* in its ranks, to fight the 'Italian' security forces. In the mainland south the Fronte dell'Uomo Qualunque ('Average Man Front'), created shortly after the end of the war by a flamboyant Neapolitan playwright called Guglielmo Giannini, showed its disdain for the 'values of the resistance' by championing the cause of those who simply wanted to be left in peace to enjoy their lives without meddling 'professional politicians' imposing taxes, passing laws and talking loftily about the 'nation' and the 'fatherland' ('If anything is mortal on earth, the most mortal thing of all is the idea of the fatherland').[25] The Front gained well over a million votes in the elections held in 1946.

Perhaps the most dramatic indication of the limited resonance of the 'values of the resistance' (and also of the political fracture between north and south) came over the question of the monarchy. Victor Emmanuel's close involvement with Mussolini and his unheroic flight from Rome after the armistice had compromised his political credibility heavily (and seemingly beyond repair), and on 2 June 1946, the same day as elections were held for a Constituent Assembly, Italians went to the polls to decide the fate of the Savoys in a referendum. A month earlier Victor Emmanuel had abdicated in favour of his son, Umberto II. But it was not enough to save the dynasty, and on 13 June, after several days of mounting tension as the king tried to insist that the Court of Cassation ratify the vote (in the end the government took it upon itself to proclaim the Republic, allowing the king to talk of a 'coup'), Umberto left the Quirinal Palace for exile in Portugal. Yet the vote had been close – 12.7 million to 10.7 million. And while almost every province in the north and centre had followed the lead of the communists, socialists and Christian Democrats in favouring a republic, in Rome and the south the monarchists had secured a clear majority (nearly 80 per cent in Naples).

The Constituent Assembly that was returned on 2 June by universal male and (for the first time in Italy's history) female suffrage was dominated by the three main anti-fascist parties: the Christian Democrats, who secured 207 of the 556 seats, the communists, who had 104, and the socialists, who had 114; and the constitution that emerged from the Assembly's rapid deliberations in 1946–7 was a forceful affirmation of the 'values of the resistance'. The Republic was to be democratic, liberal and decentralized – the antithesis of fascism – with an elected president, an executive answerable to parliament, a powerful Chamber of Deputies, proportional representation, regional government, an independent judiciary, a Constitutional Court, and mechanisms for allowing the general public to propose or repeal legislation. Numerous civil and political liberties and social rights were guaranteed. Potentially the most divisive question related to the Church, with the Christian Democrats eager to maintain Catholicism as the state religion and the lay parties opposed. But with the Cold War setting in, the Communist Party leader, Palmiro Togliatti, did not want to inflame popular opinion unduly, and with his support the 1929 Lateran Pacts were embedded in the new constitution. The socialists were furious. 'When Togliatti announced the vote in favour, anger erupted on the socialist benches . . . [with] cries of treachery,' recalled a young Christian Democrat deputy, Giulio Andreotti. 'Many of us had tears in our eyes.'[26] Here was yet another deep emotional fault-line running through Italian society that was to add to the fractured political landscape in the years ahead.

As in so many other moments of Italian history, the principles embodied in the constitution (which came into force in January 1948) underlined the gap between the mass of the population and the elites and thereby the limits of the latter's moral authority in the country. Nor was the cause of the anti-fascist leadership assisted by the British and Americans, who, in drawing up the peace treaty in 1945–6, refused to recognize that Italy's contribution to the defeat of Germany had been significant, and certainly not enough to atone for the sins of fascism. Benedetto Croce and a number of other prominent Italian intellectuals had been endeavouring since 1943 to argue that the interwar years had been no more than a mysterious parenthesis in the country's history, an aberration from the true path of liberalism and peace laid down during the Risorgimento. But such attempts to minimize the significance of fascism, and effectively to absolve the nation of responsibility for it, were not met with much sympathy by the victorious powers, and Italy was obliged in the peace treaty that was signed in Paris in February 1947 to accept a large measure of blame for the outbreak of the Second World War. As punishment it was stripped of its colonies, forced to hand over Dalmatia, Istria and Fiume to Yugoslavia, and saddled with a heavy bill for reparations.

But the biggest blow to hopes that the 'values of the resistance' might provide the basis for a cohesive sense of nationhood lay in the splintering of the anti-fascist coalition with the onset of the Cold War. From the moment he returned from exile in Moscow in March 1944, the bespectacled, cautious and austerely intellectual Palmiro Togliatti had tried to give his party a reassuring face, stressing its commitment to democracy and national unity, and using the writings of his old friend Antonio Gramsci (who, like Togliatti, had been a founder of the Italian Communist Party (PCI) in 1921) to argue that the road to socialism in Italy lay not through a violent seizure of power but through the peaceful and gradual establishment of moral, cultural and political 'hegemony' over society. But there was no escaping the fact that the PCI was a communist party with close links to the Soviet Union – Togliatti had been Vice-Secretary of the Comintern (Third International) and was a loyal supporter of Stalin. And as the world began to polarize sharply between Eastern and Western blocs in 1946–7, so pressure grew, both within and outside Italy, for the PCI and its socialist allies (early in 1947 the Italian Socialist Party split between its pro- and anti-Moscow wings) to be excluded from power. In May 1947 Alcide De Gasperi, the Christian Democrat prime minister, announced the formation of a new government without the far left. The anti-fascist front was broken and the pattern was set for Italian politics over the next forty-five years, with the Christian Democrats dominating a succession of centrist coalitions and the PCI permanently consigned to opposition.

What made the split particularly acrimonious was the position of the Church. The collapse of fascism and the humiliation of surrender in 1943 presented Pope Pius XII with a golden opportunity, it seemed, to 'reconquer' Italy for Catholicism. And the fact that millions of Italians looked spontaneously towards the Papacy for solace and leadership amid the wreckage of defeat appeared to justify the hope that Italy could be turned into a flagship of 'Christian civilization'. But 'Christian civilization' did not embrace the communists and socialists, and after 1945 the Vatican used every available tool, traditional and modern, to mobilize the faithful against the enemies of the Church: radio broadcasts, newspapers, sermons, Catholic Action, pilgrimages, reports of miracles, cults of saints (above all the Virgin Mary – appealing to women was seen as especially important now that they had the vote) and films – a documentary about Pius XII, *Pastor Angelicus*, portraying him as a charismatic leader *super partes*, toured the country to large audiences. And with the Italian 'nation', such as it had been conceived in the course of the preceding century or so, now stripped of much of its ethical credibility, the Church hurried in to pick up the mantle, with one authoritative Catholic newspaper describing the pontiff as 'the supreme pinnacle of our fatherland' to whom Italy owed 'its independence, liberty, glory, life, beauty – everything!'[27]

With Italy ideologically polarized between the Christian Democrats and the Catholic Church on the one hand and the communists and the socialists on the other, and with the United States raising the political temperature further by making it clear to De Gasperi that American aid for economic reconstruction was contingent upon the far left being kept at bay, the 'values of the resistance' lost any residual capacity to provide a clear ethical platform for the new Republic. And with neither camp able to appeal with conviction to 'the nation' as an overarching pole of reference (what, after all, was the 'fatherland' of Catholics if not the international communion of believers, and of communists, the Soviet Union?), the essence of Italian political life became, as it had been for so much of its history, more a struggle against an internal enemy than a pursuit of collective goals. For those whose faith in the ideal of an Italian nation had not been shattered by fascism, the spectacle of so much mutual vituperation was dispiriting. As the non-conformist anti-fascist priest Primo Mazzolari wrote in 1949:

Everything is being rebuilt: roads, bridges, factories. But we are not. Even though we continue to grow in number and speak the same language as the men of our Risorgimento, it is hard to say that we have returned to being Italians . . . The communist proletariat calls Russia its fatherland, while the rest look to America . . . Italians are still in the position they were on 8 September, when, from love of liberty, some rebelled. The resistance is still going on, but in the name of a party pitted against the fatherland, perpetuating and aggravating the divide . . . How can we move towards peace when we lack a shared political consciousness, shared sentiments and a shared altar on which to lay our fratricidal arms? I see collective suffering and collective poverty that could soon become collective ruin.

But I do not see a collective fatherland. I see fascists and partisans, not brothers and Italians.[28]

With Italy caught up in what amounted to a war of religion, with each side fighting for what it felt to be an entire cultural universe rather than just a programme of government, the principles underlying the 'values of the resistance' were widely dismissed as too idealistic to be practicable – with enormous damage, as a result, to the credibility of the state. Large swathes of the constitution were glossed by the conservative Court of Cassation as merely aspirational or 'programmatic' and not implemented.[29] Thus, apart from in Sicily, Sardinia and the Alpine fringes, there were no regional governments until the 1970s: the Christian Democrat-led administrations found the prospect of the communists holding power in areas such as Emilia Romagna, Tuscany and Umbria, where their support was concentrated, unacceptable. A Constitutional Court was not created until towards the end of the 1950s, and in the meantime many laws and legal codes that had been introduced by the fascists were left in force despite being in flagrant contradiction of the democratic precepts of the Republic. Tools of control and repression were after all useful for containing left-wing militancy, whether in the south, where the communists were active in organizing land occupations by the peasantry in the late 1940s (three demonstrators were killed and fifteen wounded in a clash with the police in a village in Calabria in October 1949), or in the more industrialized north. In the province of Bologna between 1948 and 1954 there were nearly 14,000 trials for offences against public order, including such 'crimes' as putting up posters and selling the Communist Party newspaper, *L'Unità*.[30]

Even more telling of the gulf between the 'values of the resistance' and the reality of the post-war Republic was the failure to rid the state of former fascists. A number of decrees were issued in 1944 calling for the bureaucracy to be purged, but they were not implemented with any rigour. This was partly because of the practical difficulties of trying to prove who had been 'fascist' (or at least sincerely 'fascist') in a regime where party membership had been compulsory for all civil servants, but more fundamentally because the Christian Democrats, and behind them the British and the Americans, had no wish to see the administrative machinery decimated and replenished with communists and socialists. As a result the courts, run still by judges appointed under Mussolini, gave credence to lines of defence of great suppleness – as in the case of Guido Leto, head of the Duce's secret police, OVRA, and later Deputy Chief of Police in the Republic of Salò, who was acquitted in April 1946 of the charge of having helped to maintain the regime in being, on the grounds that he had simply been carrying out his duties as a public official and so had not been in a position to decide on the constitutionality or otherwise of the laws and institutions of the state.[31] An alternative defence, widely used and with equal success, was to claim to have been in reality a secret anti-fascist: many of those accused of collaborating with the Republic of Salò found friends (and often fabricated documents) to attest their links to partisans.[32]

A particularly perverse aspect of the failure of the courts to uphold the 'values of the resistance' related to the prosecution of war crimes. An amnesty for political and military prisoners, issued in June 1946 as part of an attempt to inject a note of reconciliation into the newly proclaimed Republic, excluded those who had been responsible for 'especially heinous tortures'. But the judiciary often decided that the atrocities perpetrated by fascists against members of the resistance had been neither 'tortures' nor 'especially' brutal. Thus the captain of a unit who had allowed a female partisan prisoner to be tied up, blindfolded and repeatedly raped by his troops was deemed not to have committed 'torture' but 'only the maximum offence to the honour and modesty' of the woman.[33] By contrast partisans frequently found themselves branded by the police and judges as common criminals rather than resistance fighters, and thus excluded from the amnesty. In 1954 the Supreme Military Court went so far as to rule that the Republic of Salò had been a legitimate government, 'albeit through error', and that those who had fought for it had thus not committed a crime, whereas partisans had been irregular troops and so could not claim the protection of military law.[34]

The consequences of the failure to prosecute war crimes adequately were far-reaching. Many of the most senior figures of the fascist regime who had not been captured and shot in 1945 escaped serious punishment; and without a set of high-profile trials, comparable to those at Nuremberg, in which the regime's responsibility for the Second World War, the atrocities committed in Libya, Ethiopia, the Balkans and elsewhere, and such domestic policies as the racial laws and the persecution of the Jews could be publicly aired and condemned, the Republic failed to define itself clearly in relation to fascism (and indeed to the rest of recent Italian history). And a succession of former supporters of the regime profited from the climate of political ambivalence to produce a number of best-selling works that sought to soften and humanize fascism, and above all Mussolini. (What had the Duce done that was 'terrible', asked Indro Montanelli in his 1947 book, *Il buonuomo Mussolini* (*The Good Soul Mussolini*), except 'grimace'? And aside from sending a few hundred people to *confino*, had the fascist government not been characterized by 'mildness'?)[35] Such views derived powerful support from the heavily Catholic culture suffusing Italy (and especially the middle classes) in these years, with its injunctions to forgiveness and mercy.[36]

Despite the Republic's claims to be built on 'the values of the resistance', anti-fascism was in fact a hard article of faith only for the communists and the socialists, who were confined to a ghetto of political opposition during the height of the Cold War (albeit a substantial one: 31 per cent of the votes in the 1948 elections; 35 per cent in 1953). And in the absence of a significant purge, the state showed a remarkable degree of continuity from fascism. It was calculated in 1960 that sixty-two of the country's sixty-four prefects had been functionaries under Mussolini; and the same applied to every one of the 135 police chiefs and their 139 deputies.[37] Many senior figures in the army and the judiciary had likewise established their careers in the fascist period: Gaetano Azzariti, who became President of the Constitutional Court in 1957, had been the President of the Race Tribunal in 1939–43. Of course not all of these officials had shared the illiberal and virulently anti-socialist values of fascism. But many had; and as a result large parts of the bureaucracy had concentrations of civil servants who were profoundly unsympathetic to the principles expressed in the constitution and willing to hamper the operation of democracy in Italy or even actively to conspire against it.

On 31 August 1957, a little over twelve years after huge crowds had desecrated and taunted the corpse of Mussolini in Piazzale Loreto, two Capuchin friars dragged a large wooden box from the back seat of a car outside the gates of the cemetery of San Cassiano, near Predappio. Ever since being recovered from the Charterhouse of Pavia, the remains of the Duce had been secretly stored in a monastery near Milan, and requests by the family to have them handed over for burial in Predappio had gone unheeded. Now, with the recently installed Christian Democrat prime minister Adone Zoli (whose family also came from Predappio) dependent for survival in parliament on the votes of neo-fascist deputies (among them, Domenico Leccisi, the man who had stolen Mussolini's body in 1946: opposite him, on the far left of the Chamber, sat Walter Audisio, Mussolini's executioner), the government decided the time had come to relent. On 1 September, with a throng of faithful supporters looking on, their right arms raised in salute, the box with Mussolini's body was laid in the mausoleum in San Cassiano, where it remains to this day, a site of pilgrimage for a steady stream of visitors.[38]

28

The Economic Miracle, 1958–75

Come, come to the city
Why hang around in the country
If you want a good life
You've got to come to the city

The city is beautiful
The city is big
The city is lively
The city is fun

It's full of streets and shops
And shop windows brightly lit
With lots of people working
And lots of people producing

With bigger and bigger advertisements
With stores and escalators
With taller and taller skyscrapers
And so many, so many cars
  Giorgio Gaber, 'Com'è bella la città'
            (popular song, 1969)

At the beginning of the 1960s, due to the pollution of the air and, particularly in
the countryside, of the water ... the fireflies began to disappear ... After
[they] had gone, the 'values' ... of the old rural and paleo-capitalist universe
suddenly did not count any more. Church, fatherland, obedience, order, thrift
and morality lost their significance ... They were replaced by the 'values' of a

new type of civilization, one that was totally alien to the civilization of the peasantry . . .

Pier Paolo Pasolini, 'Il vuoto del potere in Italia', in *Corriere della Sera*,
1 February 1975

CHRISTIAN DEMOCRATS
AND COMMUNISTS

The Republic had a low-key birth. Two decades of nationalist rhetoric had culminated in military defeat, economic destitution and civil war, and few were inclined to consider this latest incarnation of Italian unity as an occasion for patriotic celebration. And given the widespread feeling that it was not just fascism but the country's entire recent past that had been shattered in 1943–5 ('To see the destruction of the Italy that had been created by the men of the Risorgimento . . . is something that I cannot reconcile myself to,' wrote Croce disconsolately in September 1946),[1] it was very difficult to know what symbols might be deployed to celebrate the new regime. The commemorative stamps that were issued in October 1946 lacked any obvious 'national' allusions. There were references to the maritime republics of the Middle Ages and to the Florentine republic, but not to anything in the modern era (including the resistance). And there was no tricolour: not until 1952 did the national flag feature on a stamp, and then only discreetly in an image of the cathedral of Trieste (Trieste had been claimed by Yugoslavia at the end of the war, and remained a 'Free Territory' under British and American occupation until 1954, when it was handed to Italy).[2]

The weak identity of the Republic was evident in other areas of symbolism. The Royal March was no longer serviceable as a national anthem, but there was little consensus as to what might take its place. Many Italian soldiers had spontaneously sung Verdi's 'Va pensiero' as they were taken off to prison camps by the Germans in September 1943; and for many years after the war there were to be intermittent calls for this or for 'O Signore, dal tetto natio' from *I Lombardi* to be made Italy's official anthem. But the sentiment expressed in both choruses – yearning for an absent or lost fatherland – was hardly very apt for a collective affirmation of nationhood. The 'Hymn of Mameli' ('Brothers

549

of Italy') was provisionally indicated as the Republic's anthem in the autumn of 1946, and largely by default (no formal decision was taken on the matter) the choice was allowed to stand. But there was much disquiet about the hymn's bellicose wording, and the Republic never identified with it very strongly (the British authorities were evidently unsure what to play when Italy faced England in a football match at Wembley in May 1959 and performed the Royal March by mistake).[3]

In other areas, too, it was apparent that the Republic was short of cohesive national symbols. Streets with names or dates of obviously fascist origin – such as 21 April, 9 May (the proclamation of Empire) and 28 October – had to be changed, but it was hard to get agreement on what should replace them. The constitution declared 25 April, 1 May, 2 June and 4 November to be public holidays, but each of these dates, with the possible exception of 4 November (Italy's victory in the First World War), had resonances more of division than of unity. Nor was it possible to devise an emblem for the new Republic that could command a strong emotional (and aesthetic) response. A competition for the design was launched in January 1948 with several permitted themes: bees, a toothed wheel (both symbols of industry: the first clause of the constitution had declared Italy to be a democracy 'founded on work' – a compromise formula that had been agreeable to all parties), a star, a shield with a turreted crown, an eagle (probably a little too Roman for comfort), and a beacon.[4] The winning entry consisted of a five-point star set against a toothed wheel and flanked by laurel and oaks leaves – symbolizing peace and the strength and dignity of the Italian people.

In the absence of a solid base, rooted in national history, on which to found their legitimacy, the political parties that dominated the Republic from 1946 until the early 1990s relied for much of their authority on sources that were largely extraneous to 'Italy'. The Christian Democrats were heavily dependent on the Church. They were not a confessional party, and some of the political choices they made – the fostering of close ties with the USA and the sanctioning of American-style consumerism, for example – did not meet with the full approval of the Vatican, certainly in the 1950s. But the Christian Democrats were committed to upholding Catholic values and fighting the far left, and the Church accordingly threw its moral and organizational weight behind them, using the pulpit, the confessional, the press and the powerful machinery of Catholic Action to mobilize voters (especially women, who made up 60 per cent of Christian Democrat supporters). The drift of peasants from the countryside to the cities and the growth of secularization after the 1950s undoubtedly reduced the power of organized Catholicism to influence elections, but the continued support of the Church was an important factor in the Christian Democrats being able to secure around 40 per cent of the vote consistently down to the early 1980s (with a high of 48.4 per cent in 1948).[5]

The Socialist and Communist parties derived much of their cachet from the near mythic status of the Soviet Union among left-wing voters in Italy during the later 1940s and 1950s. The extraordinary achievements of the Red Army against the Nazis – the siege of Leningrad, the Battle of Stalingrad, the victories of 1943-5, the capture of Berlin and the Red Flag hoisted over the ruins of the Reichstag – became the stuff of legend to those whose own forces had performed so miserably during the war; and to these military achievements was added the image of a country that in the space of a little over two decades had transformed itself from a backward agricultural power into an industrial colossus. Stalin was an object of veneration to millions of Italians, the personification of superhuman strength and paternal kindness, his moustached features held aloft on placards at countless communist and socialist rallies. And when he died in 1953 there were extraordinary scenes of collective grief: one party activist recalled standing outside the gates of FIAT at dawn on 6 March distributing copies of *L'Unità*, with its large headline – 'The man who has done most for the liberation of the human race is dead' – and watching workers dissolve into tears as they took in the news.[6]

In order to consolidate their followings, the two main blocs into which the country was divided (the only other grouping of significance, aside from the neo-fascists, was that of the centrist lay parties – the Social Democrats, the Republicans and the Liberals – who had about 10 per cent of the vote between them) set about colonizing civil society, using as their model many of the techniques of the fascist regime. The communists built up a powerful network of institutions alongside those of the party and its affiliated trade union, the Italian General Confederation of Work (CGIL), and together these enabled millions of their supporters to move in what amounted to a parallel universe to that of their opponents. There were organizations for ex-partisans and women (the Union of Italian Women, with 3,500 local circles and over a million members by 1954); there were the *Case del Popolo* ('Houses of the People'), the focal points (together with the church) of community life in many smaller towns, which arranged debates and meetings, screened films, laid on children's activities and sports events, and in some cases even ran their own pharmacies and medical services; and there were the popular *feste dell'Unità*, designed as fund-raising events for the party newspaper, with barbecues, singing, dancing and other entertainments for the whole family.[7]

Although the Christian Democrats relied heavily on the organizations of the Church to mobilize their supporters, especially in the north, where Catholic Action (which had more than 2.5 million members in the mid-1950s) was strongest, they also built up their own extensive network of flanking structures. The most important of these were ACLI (the Association of Italian Christian Workers), CISL (the Italian Confederation of Free Syndicates) – a trade union rival to the communist and socialist CGIL – and the association for peasant farmers known as Coldiretti. The latter was particularly important in the post-war years, when Italy was still predominantly an agricultural country, and it was conceived from the outset as a militant anti-communist movement ('We will not defeat communism or build a dyke against it . . . [unless we] galvanize the masses on the basis of precise beliefs . . . and call on them to fight,' its founder declared).[8] It had its own newsletters and magazines, special divisions for women and the young ('Youth of the Fields'), and training schools, whose motto was *Provare, Produrre, Progredire* ('Strive, Produce, Progress'). By 1956 it had more than 13,000 local sections and 1,600,000 families as members.[9]

Whereas the fascists had endeavoured to mobilize Italians on behalf of the 'fatherland', the two blocs into which the country was now split made little attempt to encourage their supporters to see the state or the nation as overarching objects of loyalty. Instead each regarded itself as the standard-bearer of a set of supreme and embattled values (symbolized in the case of the Christian Democrats by their badge of a crusader shield emblazoned with the word *libertas*), whose defence against the benighted forces of the opposition – demonized by both sides in a manner often reminiscent of the crude propaganda techniques used by fascism – might necessitate even severe moral compromises: the appropriation, perhaps, of public resources for party or personal ends, connivance at support from known criminal elements, or the suppression of potentially damaging truths – such as the fact of the Stalinist purges of the 1930s, which many well-placed Italian communists (including Togliatti) would have known about, in some measure at least, well before the revelations made by Nikita Khrushchev at the twentieth congress of the Russian Communist Party early in 1956.[10]

If both sides inherited the view, deeply ingrained since the Risorgimento, of seeing politics largely as a pedagogic struggle to indoctrinate the masses, it was the communists who set the greatest store by education, ideas and culture. This was partly because the PCI attracted into its upper ranks a disproportionately large number of intellectuals – including many of the best-known writers, artists and film-makers of the period – but also because the dominance of idealism in Italian thought, amplified by twenty years of fascism, had dulled the left to the political power and importance of the economy. Thus, at a moment when the Western world was about to undergo one of the most dramatic material transformations in its history, the communists failed to offer a clear vision of how greater well-being might be secured through the promotion of the public sphere and its partnership with the private sector. Instead they devoted much of their energy to securing the citadels of high culture, disseminating Marxist history and critical theory, using newspapers and journals to attack bourgeois individualism and argue the merits of socialist values, encouraging the production of didactic social-realist films, and promoting texts by Antonio Gramsci and other approved communist writers.

If the communists succeeded in building up their own powerful subculture – a subculture in which party activists addressed one another as 'comrade', gave their children names such as Ivan, Vladimiro, Uliano and Illich, wore leather 'commissar' jerkins, celebrated the resistance, sang partisan songs, idolized the Soviet Union and sported works by Steinbeck and Dos Passos alongside those of Stalin and Gramsci on their shelves[11] – the capacity of the left to proselytize beyond its established heartlands in the centre and north of the country was severely limited by the growing challenge of consumerism. Faced with a barrage of images in the 1950s and 1960s of an opulent modern urban lifestyle, with luxurious apartments, domestic appliances, expensive clothes and Cadillacs, transmitted through Hollywood films, glossy magazines and television programmes, it was hard for the left's austere emphasis on work and self-denial in the name of social justice and the greater good of the collectivity to compete with much hope of success. The dreams of most Italians resided in New York, not Moscow; and increasingly from the late 1950s they had the wherewithal to realize them.

THE 'ECONOMIC MIRACLE'

The immediate post-war years were a time of severe hardship for most Italians. Real wages in 1945 were half what they had been in 1938–9, and it was estimated that a typical factory worker spent around 95 per cent of his income on food. Average daily calorie consumption in 1941–50 stood at 2,171 (compared to 2,834 in the 1920s), and a national survey in 1951–2 found that 869,000 families – 744,000 of them in the south – never ate meat or sugar. It also discovered that 48 per cent of households had no kitchen and 73 per cent no bathroom, and that only 7.4 per cent of homes were fitted with the basic necessities of running water, electricity and an indoor toilet.[12] The most common form of transport in the countryside was still the mule and cart, and in the city, the tram and bicycle – as in Vittorio De Sica's classic neo-realist film *Bicycle Thieves*, shot in the near noiseless streets of Rome in 1948. The cheapest car, the FIAT 500 'Topolino', cost about twice the annual income of industrial and white collar workers in 1950, and was thus unaffordable, and it was only with the appearance of the Vespa scooter (powered with a war-time aeroplane starter engine that had never gone into production) and shortly afterwards of its rival the Lambretta, towards the end of the 1940s, that most Italians began to experience their first taste of private mechanized travel.[13]

But in the space of a decade, between the mid-1950s and the mid-1960s, there was an extraordinary surge in manufacturing that in effect transformed Italy from a relatively backward agricultural country into one of the world's most powerful modern economies. The gross domestic product grew at an average rate of over 6 per cent per annum and industrial production doubled – faster than in any country in the world apart from Japan (and possibly West Germany). Most of this growth occurred in the 'industrial triangle' of the north-west (Turin–Milan–Genoa) and was led by FIAT – which by 1967 was selling more cars in Europe than any other company, Volkswagen included – and by a string of engineering firms specializing in electrical appliances such as refrigerators, washing machines, sewing machines and televisions. In 1951 Italy produced just 18,500 fridges annually; by 1957 the figure had gone up to 370,000; and by 1967 it stood at 3,200,000, making it the third-biggest producer after the USA and Japan. Italy had also become Europe's leading manufacturer of washing machines, with firms such as Candy, Zanussi and Ignis (quite literally) household names.[14]

Several factors lay behind this extraordinary development – which radically transformed the way Italy saw itself and was seen by outsiders: the land of *Bicycle Thieves* suddenly became the country of Federico Fellini's *La Dolce Vita* (1960), of Gina Lollobrigida and Sophia Loren, of Martinis, Cinzanos and Ferraris. In the first place Italian industry and infrastructure had been spared some of the worst ravages of war-time bombing and were able to recover relatively quickly; and the reconstruction process was greatly assisted by the influx of goods and cheap loans (worth more than $1,400 million between 1948 and 1952) under America's Marshall Aid programme, designed to restore European markets (and stop impoverishment fuelling support for the far left).[15] Italy's economy benefited, too, from the flair of a generation of highly talented business leaders, many of whom had honed their management skills in the progressive surroundings of fascism's Institute for Industrial Reconstruction. Fuel was also an important ingredient in the economic miracle: large supplies of natural gas were discovered in the Po valley towards the end of the war, and these, together with the massive oil imports that Enrico Mattei, the unscrupulous but dynamic head of Italy's state petroleum company, negotiated with overseas suppliers on extremely advantageous terms, ensured that Italian industry had the cheapest energy in western Europe.

Another major element in Italy's industrial growth was the European Economic Community. The combination of shattered national self-confidence, the Catholic universalism of the Christian Democrat leadership, and the urgent need for export markets for Italian goods and labour (to relieve the demographic pressures in the south) made De Gasperi and most of his successors as prime minister enthusiastic supporters of European cooperation. In 1952 Italy followed up its membership of NATO, which it had joined in 1949, by signing the European Defence Community plan; and in 1957 it became a founder signatory of the European Economic Community with the Treaty of Rome. The benefits of the new market opportunities that this agreement afforded became immediately apparent as the country's burgeoning manufacturing sector began shipping fridges, cars and washing machines in huge quantities over the Alps to meet the consumerist demands of the renascent west European economies. In 1955, 23 per cent of Italian products were exported to EEC countries. By 1960 the figure had gone up to 29.8 per cent; and by 1965 it stood at over 40 per cent.[16]

But probably the most important factor behind the 'economic miracle' was Italy's reservoir of cheap labour. Nearly 50 per cent of the country's population of over 45 million people at the end of the war was still dependent on agriculture, but, in the southern countryside especially, living standards were lower than almost anywhere else in Europe, with labourers earning just a few hundred lire a day (if they could find work) – about half what their counterparts in industry could make.[17] The Christian Democrats looked to assuage the land hunger of the peasants – or at least defuse the tensions caused by the forcible occupation of estates across the south after 1943 – by passing a series of reforms in 1950 that allowed for the expropriation of large properties and their distribution in lots to the poor. This was a radical initiative that finally broke the power of the centuries-old southern elites; but only a small proportion of peasant families ended up as beneficiaries, and those that did become smallholders were rarely able to make a decent living from the few hectares of poor quality soil that they acquired. As a result millions of rural workers began to abandon the land in the 1950s in search of employment in the cities, willing to take on almost any job.

For the industrialists this was an ideal situation; and the government assisted them by pursuing orthodox liberal policies (in reaction, largely, to fascist 'planning') that left unemployment high and the trade unions weak and unable to counter the often fiercely punitive measures taken by factory owners against organized labour. The peasants who arrived in the towns and cities of the north-west in search of work, many of them from the most impoverished regions of the south (around 200,000 southerners settled each year in the industrial triangle in the late 1950s and early 1960s), clutching battered suitcases and jars of olive oil, were forced to take jobs in factories where safety regulations and insurance payments were non-existent and the hours inhumanly long. Accidents and fatalities were common – eight people died in the space of just one month on building sites in Turin in the summer of 1961 – and average wages were among the lowest anywhere in Europe.[18] But at least the hours were regular and the pay considerably better than the migrants received back home. And despite the harsh and squalid conditions, the allure of the big cities remained almost unassailable: 'In Sardinia they talk of Turin as if it were a God,' remarked one contemporary.[19]

The 'economic miracle' radically transformed the lifestyle and expectations of countless Italians. Men and women whose families had for centuries lived in small towns and villages, and whose lives were attuned to the rhythms of the agricultural calendar and the seasons, who spoke dialect chiefly and perhaps only rudimentary Italian, suddenly found themselves in a new and often bewildering world. 'I felt alone, like in a forest without a single living soul,' recalled Antonio Antonuzzo, a Sicilian peasant who had come to Milan in 1962, after an unsuccessful period as a charcoal burner and miner in Tuscany.[20] And if in the past those who had migrated – whether to other parts of Italy or abroad – had done so in the hope of returning to their native community after they had saved enough money to buy a few hectares of land there, most of the estimated 9,140,000 Italians who moved away from their home regions between 1955 and 1971 were conscious that there was now nothing for which to go back.

But it was not just the need to make a living that uprooted so many Italians from the land. The 'economic miracle' spread a constellation of powerful new ideas and images that challenged many of the traditional values of rural society – built as they had been around the precepts of the Church and an embedded sense of moral and material immobility – and threatened to destroy a culture 'that had certainly remained unchanged for a span of time far greater than the two thousand years of Catholicism', as the writer and film-maker Pier Paolo Pasolini lamented.[21] Migration was a measure of the extraordinary appeal of consumerism, which permeated Italian society rapidly after the war through such media as American films (some 5,000 were being screened in cinemas across the country in 1953 to huge audiences), weekly magazines and (from 1954) television. The most popular television programme by the early 1960s, watched by more than 8 million viewers each day, was *Carosello*, a ten-minute compilation of comedy sketches, cartoons, stories, songs and music framing a series of advertisements for the latest products now on offer thanks to the 'economic miracle'.[22]

The Church observed the spread of the new consumerist values with horror, aware that the migration to the cities would erode its cultural

grip on Italians, and conscious, too, that the central message of consumerism – that happiness was to be found in the pursuit of material
well-being – was antithetical to its own teaching. Pius XII tried to find
crumbs of comfort in modern life where he could (he welcomed the
advent of television in so far as it offered 'the entire family the possibility
of honest pleasure together, away from the perils of unhealthy company
and unhealthy places'; though the prospect of programmes transmitting
the 'poisoned atmosphere of materialism, fatuity and hedonism', which
was so often found in cinemas, made him 'shudder'),[23] but he thought
American culture in general repugnant and during his last years (he died
in 1958) he spent much time denouncing its evils: its lax sexual mores,
its individualism, its utilitarianism, its weak sense of family, its obsession
with health and bodily functions, and its mistaken notions about the
place and role of women in society.

For much of the 1950s the Christian Democrats supported the
Church's battle to uphold strict Catholic morality. As head of the Central
Office for Cinematography from June 1947, the future prime minister
Giulio Andreotti ensured that films were subject to strict censorship,
with anything that might offend public decency carefully excised
(moments of sexual intimacy and bad language in particular). Journalists
and radio broadcasters were obliged to transfer the linguistic gymnastics
that they had developed in extolling the Duce and fascism to finding
ingenious circumlocutions and synonyms for sensitive terms. Thus
'abortion' became 'interruption of maternity'; 'pregnancy', 'interesting
condition'; 'suicide', 'insane gesture'; 'breast', 'chest'; and 'member',
'component' (even the phrase 'member of parliament' was banned). A
particular challenge was offered by the second Kinsey Report on the
sexual behaviour of Americans, which the weekly magazine *Oggi* ventured to publish in 1954 as a supplement. The word 'sexual' had to be
replaced with 'amorous' throughout, while the noun 'coitus' was
stripped of any suggestion of physicality by use of the bizarrely poetic
phrase 'sentimental expansiveness'.[24] Television was tightly controlled
from the outset, with the chief executive of the newly created state
broadcasting company, RAI (1954), Filiberto Guala, prohibiting any
material that might incite 'class hatred' or undermine the 'institution of
the family' or 'the sanctity of the matrimonial bond'.[25]

But the Christian Democrats knew that they were fighting a losing
battle, and that doggedly to uphold the moral injunctions of the Vatican

in the face of the rising tide of consumerism and growing secularization risked exposing them to unpopularity and, increasingly, to ridicule. In 1956 Guala was forced to resign after RAI tried to make amends for a live broadcast in which ballerinas had danced in almost transparent tights – allegedly causing the Pope to turn off his television in shock and retreat hurriedly to prayer – by instructing the dancers to wear what looked like long johns in subsequent transmissions: large sections of the press fulminated against RAI's apparent subservience to the Vatican. Guala shortly afterwards retreated to a Trappist monastery and was replaced at RAI by a tough-minded managerial party figure who was willing to be more attuned to the fast-shifting values of Italian society – and prepared to deliver the diet of quiz shows and light entertainment that the public relished.

The Church had little answer in the end to consumerism and its attendant values. During the pontificate of John XXIII (1958–63) the Vatican sought to steer Catholicism in fresh directions, opening up a dialogue with the left and trying, with the Second Vatican Council, to adapt to the changing world rather than campaigning against it. But attempts to reach out to the new Italy of the 'economic miracle', however imaginative, could not avoid a strong savour of incongruity and, increasingly, of anachronism – as when in October 1964 the prime minister, the directors of IRI and the archbishop of Florence gathered in a small church built in front of the Florence North service station to sing a *Te Deum* of thanksgiving to God for having allowed the completion of the latest section of the *Autostrada del sole* motorway from Naples to Milan.[26] For most Italians in the 1960s miracles (including the economic miracle) were made on earth, not in heaven. In 1956, 69 per cent of Italians attended mass regularly on Sunday. Twelve years later the figure had fallen to 40 per cent, and of these just 6 per cent could be classified as 'devout'. The situation was especially alarming among the immigrant workers in the sprawling suburbs of the northern cities, where in 1968 only 11 per cent of men were found to be going to mass regularly.[27] With the Church's authority dwindling, Italy's Christian Democrat rulers were forced to look elsewhere for a source of legitimacy to sustain them in power. But their moral choices were limited, and in the absence of God they had little else to call on but Mammon.

THE COLONIZATION OF THE STATE

The celebrations in 1961 to mark the centenary of the unification of Italy were deeply uncertain and strained in tone. Behind the speeches, the conferences and the laying of wreaths on the tombs of Garibaldi, Mazzini and Victor Emmanuel II ('The Italian Republic to Victor Emmanuel II, the father of the Fatherland'); behind the television documentaries and the films – including a specially commissioned work by the leading director Roberto Rossellini, *Viva l'Italia!*, re-enacting for modern cinema-goers the events of 1860; behind the major exhibitions dedicated to the Risorgimento, the regions and 'work' ('to illustrate . . . the most distinctive feature of this age, namely the staggering technical and social progress'), all held in Turin – selected primarily because it was the symbol of the resurgent Italy of the 'economic miracle' – the Italy of the gleaming production lines of FIAT;[28] behind all these official initiatives lay, for many observers, a sense of malaise, an awareness that the country's political unity had still not been matched by the moral unity that the patriots of the nineteenth century had so desperately hoped to achieve. As Italy's most authoritative newspaper, the *Corriere della Sera*, said in an article in April 1961:

Material progress, increased prosperity and economic dynamism are important . . . But what are also needed are a common basis, a foundation that will unite, and above all a moral centre – a state that invites loyalty and instinctive obedience. These are things that are hard to improvise once they have been destroyed, whatever the regime. But an attempt should at least be made to reconstruct them little by little, with patience, good will, sacrifice and faith in the principles underpinning public life . . . We have failed to do this in the fifteen years that have elapsed since the war and the resistance.[29]

The absence of a 'common basis' was evident in the polemics that took place in 1961 over Italian history. The Christian Democrats argued that the true Italy was the community of the Catholic faithful, who, thanks to the Lateran Pacts of 1929 and the establishment of the post-war Republic, had at last been brought into the fold of the state by the guiding hand of Providence, so giving the 'nation' its proper contours and character. The entire liberal period was written off largely as an aberration, a period of 'difficulties and shortcomings', as the Catholic press put it, caused by 'the Gordian knots that the hasty and almost improvised diplomatic-military solution of the Italian problem' had failed to cut.[30] The communists and socialists contested this reading of Italian history vigorously – and at the same time denounced the commemorations of 1961 as a vainglorious display of self-congratulation by the representatives of 'monopoly capitalism' who had plunged the country into 'a series of bloody wars and twenty years of dictatorship'.[31] The rightful protagonist of Italian history, they maintained, was the working class, which had been kept in ignorance by the Church and denied social justice by the liberals, the fascists and now the Christian Democrats, too. Only the small centrist lay parties were willing to defend the achievements of the Risorgimento, pointing to the extreme irony of celebrating the centenary of unification while depicting Cavour and the liberal state 'in roughly the same terms . . . as Radetzky and the Habsburg empire had been presented to our forebears: as little more than monumental obstacles blocking the path of the Italian people to the glorious achievements and progress that would otherwise have been secured without them'.[32]

The contested memories and fierce ideological divisions were especially striking given that the economic advances of the 1950s and 1960s were dissolving many of the traditional material impediments to unity: television, mass migration, education, cars, urbanization, improved infrastructures and rising levels of prosperity served to make Italians culturally more uniform than at any time in their history. They ate much the same food, wore similar clothes, had convergent patterns of work and leisure, and in most cases could communicate with one another in standard Italian (even if dialect remained the first language for over half the population in the 1970s).[33] But as a number of acute observers pointed out, Italy's rapid emergence as a modern industrial democracy made the need for shared national values and a strong sense of the state more important than ever. For how could the growing economy be properly planned and regulated, and social tensions be mediated, if there was not a willingness on the part of individuals and interest groups to make sacrifices on behalf of the community as a whole? As the political commentator Domenico Bartoli observed in 1959 (echoing similar reflections by Mazzini, De Sanctis and others a century before):

A democracy without patriotism will struggle to exist. It is easier in such circumstances for a society that is ruled by an authoritarian government to survive, where the cracks can be covered up and the sores contained. But patriotism cannot be imposed from above ... It has to be found within each person. And to find it, people need to suppress their feelings of egoism and become conscious of their duties as citizens ... Now that our dangerous nationalistic illusions have been destroyed for good, the only appropriate patriotism (and it is, in fact, the only genuine form of patriotism) is something resembling the proud national sentiment of the Scandinavians, the Swiss or the English today. Pride in reforms accomplished or intended; pride in a well-ordered society; pride in progress made. Patriotism does not exist without good governance. But equally there can be no good governance without patriotism.[34]

Such warnings owed much to a realization that the pedagogic impulses that had operated since the Risorgimento to counter the country's historic divisions had all but evaporated, and that with the 'economic miracle' Italy seemed in danger of falling back once again into the exaggerated individualism and materialism that the high-minded patriots of the nineteenth century had sought to correct. The problem lay partly in the fact that the spheres in which 'national' sentiment could legitimately be expressed had become so constricted after fascism and were now confined primarily to sport (and particularly to the achievements of the *azzurri* in football);[35] and it was also the case that many politicians and intellectuals (like their counterparts elsewhere in Europe) were inclined to see the nation-state as essentially an anachronism and were looking instead to the supra-nationalism of European integration as the best long-term guarantee of peace, prosperity and political stability. But the situation in Italy was made worse by the inability of the Christian Democrats to provide an ethical vision of citizenship or the state that would serve to offset the centrifugal tendencies of party politics.

Much of the reason for this failing lay in the preoccupation of the Christian Democrats with dominating government at all costs and excluding the communists from power. Hence, from the early 1950s, their adoption of a strategy designed to reduce their dependence on the Church and build up an autonomous party machine, using the state's resources to create huge networks or clienteles of support, especially in the economically dependent south. The result was an accentuation of the tendency, already heavily pronounced under both liberalism and fascism, for the public sector to be regarded as a tool of partisan political ambitions rather than as a neutral instrument for the implementation of law and policy. But the inability of the Christian Democrats to put forward an ethical model of citizenship also derived from the feeling that it was ultimately the Catholic Church and not the state that should be the principal source of moral instruction in Italy. After all, as De Gasperi said in 1946, it was God who was the supreme arbiter of human affairs: 'To rule a state is to generate an intimate link with the Almighty, our Father, and . . . to create an immediate responsibility towards the people, but only in so far as the state is the mediator of the divine will that governs us.'[36]

The colonization of the state by the Christian Democrats – and in due course by their coalition partners, too – was far from being systematic. Much of the impetus came from the largely haphazard competition for power between the various factions into which the party was divided. The leaders of these rival currents – men such as the right-wing Mario Scelba, the centrists Mariano Rumor and Giulio Andreotti, and the left-leaning pragmatist (and former fascist) Amintore Fanfani – endeavoured to build up networks of political support by ensuring that their friends and allies were placed in key positions within the public administration and the state-controlled industries. These appointees in turn bolstered their own positions by recruiting allies, and so on down the bureaucratic chain, thereby creating vast capillary networks that penetrated into almost every corner of Italian society. The result was a diffuse and fragmented state with archipelagos of competing power in which the dominant ethos was not so much public service as the provision of jobs for the party faithful – irrespective, very often, of whether those who were employed were in possession of the appropriate qualifications.

The consequences of this system were most conspicuous in the south, where the relationship between politicians and the electorate had traditionally hinged on the exchange of favours – jobs, pensions, contracts – for votes: in the north ideology had tended to figure more prominently. The agencies set up to implement the land reforms of 1950 quickly became dominated by Christian Democrats, who made sure that peasants bearing suitable letters of attestation from their parish priest were given preferential treatment and that communist supporters were rejected.[37] The proliferation of public agencies controlled by the local authorities provided especially fertile terrain for the exercise of state clientelism. In the Sicilian city of Catania by the mid-1970s there were eighteen agencies dealing with health, pensions, sickness benefit and social security, eleven operating public services (such as water and gas) and five running public housing. In 1950 the Christian Democrats had just seventeen directors and eight presidents on their boards; in 1955 the figures had gone up to thirty-three and thirteen respectively; and by the mid-1960s they stood at seventy-nine and twenty-two.[38]

From a political point of view, state clientelism was a remarkably powerful tool. The huge sums of public money that flowed into local government coffers could be channelled towards the friends and allies of Christian Democrat politicians who tendered for the massive development contracts on offer in the 1950s and 1960s. The *Cassa per il Mezzogiorno* ('Fund for the South'), set up in 1950 to assist the economic regeneration of the poorest regions of the country, spent more than 1,000 billion lire during the first years of its existence on roads, electricity, housing, water supplies and other infrastructure works in the south, and over 8,000 billion lire between 1957 and 1975 on (for the most part failed) schemes to promote industrialization. The chief beneficiaries were often unscrupulous entrepreneurs like Francesco Vassallo, the man who dominated the Palermo construction sector during the 1950s and 1960s thanks to his close association with Giovanni Gioia and Salvo Lima, two of Sicily's most powerful Christian Democrat politicians (both of whom were widely regarded as having extensive mafia connections: Lima was murdered in 1992).[39]

With party interests taking precedence over financial prudence or considerations of the common good, the public sector in Italy became increasingly bloated, corrupt and inefficient. State industries, which had remained largely competitive in the course of the 1950s, went into the red in the 1960s as managers were appointed according to political criteria and clientelism undermined efficiency. Local government pay rolls lengthened as the drive to build up Christian Democrat support intensified. In Naples the number of municipal employees quadrupled between the early 1950s and 1968, and in Palermo, according to one estimate, over 35 per cent of the entire labour force consisted of public sector workers in 1976.[40] Services such as street cleaning and refuse collection had veritable armies of staff on their books (though southern cities remained notoriously among the most squalid in Europe). And even the health service got sucked into the vortex of clientelism. The Vittorio Emanuele Hospital in Catania was the city's third-largest employer, with every post from consultant to cleaner filled (or not filled: keeping aspirants dangling was an excellent way for local politicians to expand their client base) according to party considerations. In 1963 the president of the hospital, a Christian Democrat senator who was desperate to get re-elected, had patients specially transferred to the hospital so that they could vote for him from their beds.[41]

The colonization of the state by the Christian Democrats and their allies was to have disastrous long-term effects on the economy. As the appeal of the government came to lie almost exclusively in its capacity to deliver prosperity to its clients and keep the communists out (and from the 1960s the threat posed by the PCI in the eyes of many voters was not so much its commitment to socialism as its stronger sense of the law and public morality), so successive administrations had to resort to borrowing heavily to stay afloat (enforcing higher taxation would have been counter-productive). There were also deleterious consequences throughout the public sector, as local and central bureaucracies became unaccountable and increasingly sclerotic, and services such as postal and telephone communications, health care and education grew ever more inefficient. Planning, too, went out of the window. Emblematic was the situation in the Sicilian town of Agrigento, where in July 1966 a hillside development of new high-rise flats, built illegally and in contravention of engineering reports, began slipping down the valley towards the ancient Greek temples below. Party political concerns and private speculative interests had prevailed over considerations of public welfare.

Behind state clientelism, with all its corruption and inefficiency, lay an insidious circularity. The more pathological the public sector became, the more necessary it was for private individuals to have patrons ('saints in Heaven') who could intercede on their behalf. In a world where jobs, contracts, licences and so much else depended on having access to the appropriate contacts, it was hard for even the most high-minded to avoid succumbing to the system and fostering the cycle of dysfunctionality. And with the state weak and the judiciary unwilling to take a stand (judges who tried to uphold the law and oppose corruption could find themselves accused of behaving 'politically' and have their careers ruined), it was logical for people to take refuge in what one American anthropologist described as 'amoral familism'[42] (encouraged by the Church's celebration of the family as the inviolable cell of society) – or even, in more extreme cases, in subterranean bodies such as the mafia networks of the south or 'P2', an apparently subversive secret Masonic organization that came to light in 1981 and whose membership included hundreds of prominent politicians, civil servants and journalists.

The mass migrations from the countryside to the cities, the decline of traditional practices and values, the onslaught of consumerism, the rise in material expectations, the strengthening power of the trade unions as Italy approached full employment, and a growing sense that the Christian Democrat state was too impotent and backward-looking to deal with the demands posed by the 'economic miracle' led at the end of the 1960s to an explosion of discontent. As in other Western countries where the extraordinary pace of recent economic change had given rise to huge social and cultural tensions, students took to the streets in protest at the overcrowded and ramshackle universities; and their anger soon fanned out into a broad denunciation of many of the key features of post-war Christian Democrat Italy: capitalism, pro-Americanism, sexual repression, conformism, individualism and authority. Millions of industrial workers voiced their dissatisfaction at low pay and poor working conditions and at the failure of the state to provide the housing, transport, education and welfare to match the country's self-image as a modern industrial democracy. The Communist Party was widely attacked for having been unable to orchestrate effective opposition.

The Christian Democrats and their coalition allies – including the socialists, who since 1956 had distanced themselves from the communists and moved towards the centre ground of politics – responded to the unrest with a string of piecemeal reforms. In a bid to make the state more responsive to the country's socio-economic needs regional government was finally introduced in the spring of 1970, twenty-two years after it had been enshrined in the constitution, with elected councils being given the power to legislate in areas such as health, social welfare, town planning and public works. The upshot, as the Christian Democrats had always feared, was the creation of a 'Red Belt' of communist-led regions in Emilia Romagna, Tuscany and Umbria. New laws were also passed on pensions, public housing and index-linked pay; spending on the south was greatly increased; and from 1975 workers who were made redundant were entitled to receive at least 80 per cent of their pay for up to a year from a state insurance fund. There were also important social reforms, most notably, in 1970, the introduction of divorce – despite strong opposition from the Christian Democrats, the neo-fascists and the Church. In 1978 (the same year as the first non-Italian for more than 450 years was elevated to the throne of St Peter) a further milestone on the march of secularism was reached with the legalization of abortion.

But these changes did little to alter the fundamental weaknesses of the state; and the fact that the government had responded to the demands of the trade unions and other pressure groups with such extraordinary largesse (Italy had the most generous welfare provisions in Europe by the mid-1970s, and Italian workers were among the best paid, best treated and most protected) underlined the extent to which the authority of the Christian Democrats depended on their capacity to guarantee material well-being – and little else. Despite a succession of high-profile financial scandals and indications that corruption was rife in government circles, voters continued to back the Christian Democrats: in the elections of 1976 the party secured nearly 39 per cent of the vote. But the dangers inherent in supporting a government that had failed to maintain a clear commitment to the national good were evident in the massive budget deficits, unrestrained borrowing and spiralling public debt of the 1970s and 1980s. The fear of many nineteenth-century patriots that 'parties' would prove ruinous in Italy, given the absence of any strong tempering sense of the collectivity, seemed in danger of being realized.

29

Towards the 'Second Republic'

Padania is our pride, our great source of wealth, our only means of expressing
ourselves freely in the fullness of our individual being and our collective identity.
*   The history of the Italian state, by contrast, has become a history of colonial*
oppression, of economic exploitation and moral violence . . . The Italian state has
deviously compelled the Peoples of Padania to endure the systematic exploitation
of the economic resources created by their hard work, and see them squandered in
the thousand streams of support for the mafia clienteles of the south . . .
*   WE, PEOPLES OF PADANIA,*
*   solemnly proclaim,*
*   PADANIA IS A FEDERAL, INDEPENDENT AND SOVEREIGN*
REPUBLIC

Declaration of the independence of Padania by the Northern League,
15 September 1996

At school, almost all the teachers say that Berlusconi is a fascist, that he'll sell
the school to whoever can afford to buy it . . . But if Berlusconi is a fascist, why
is he always laughing and happy? I learned that the fascists wore black shirts,
were always in uniform, wanted the war and used their clubs on people . . . And
so they certainly had no reason to laugh . . . But if Berlusconi put on a uniform,
started clubbing people and wanted to go to war, then his televisions wouldn't
be watched by anybody.

Thirteen-year-old child writing about Silvio Berlusconi, Rome, 1994

COSA NOSTRA

During the 1950s and 1960s the problem of organized crime in the
south of Italy had been seen largely in terms of economic backwardness.

The mafia was felt to belong primarily to the semi-feudal world of the great estates of western and central Sicily, a world of orange and lemon groves and cattle rustling, of bandits, archaic codes of honour, arcane rituals and symbols and exotic legends peddled by travelling bards. It was widely believed that this rural sub-culture would quickly disappear once the island became fully absorbed into a modern capitalist society. There was certainly consternation in the immediate post-war years at the high murder-rate (particularly of left-wing activists); and in the 1950s, the appearance of gangster-style violence on the streets of Palermo, linked, it seemed, to the new opportunities for enrichment afforded by the massive influx of public money into the island, led to increasingly insistent demands for a formal government enquiry – especially from the communists, who correctly surmised that it would be the Christian Democrats who would emerge most embarrassed by any findings. But even after a parliamentary commission had been instituted in 1962 to investigate 'the phenomenon of the mafia', it was still believed by many that the problems of Sicily would best be resolved through economic investment.[1]

During the 1970s, however, faith in the salutary effects of 'modernization' began to diminish. Far from changing old patterns of behaviour it was becoming clear that mafia methods were flourishing in a society where Mercedes cars, Rolex watches and an urban jet-set life-style were the hallmarks of success (as opposed to land and leisure, as formerly). The massive investments by the government in infrastructure and industry had not produced a self-sustaining economy: instead vast sums had been squandered on initiatives that, as a result of clientelism, corruption and poor planning, had never stood a serious chance of success. Entire factories (nicknamed 'cathedrals in the desert'), built at great public cost and often in entirely unsuitable locations, stood idle as they were found to be uncompetitive to run. The onset from 1973 of a major international recession, sparked by the huge rise in world oil prices, further highlighted the futility of trying to solve the island's problems through industrial investment. Pessimism spread, and a century of discussions linking the regeneration of the island (and indeed the south in general) to economic, social and political reforms came quietly to an end, leaving the spotlight to be trained instead on law and order. The mafia was no longer seen as a symptom; it was the cause of Sicily's problems.

For a time in the 1970s the principal focus of the government's concerns lay more in the north of the country than the south. The explosion of left-wing militancy in 1968–9 produced a right-wing backlash, with support for the neo-fascists at the polls rising to nearly 9 per cent in 1972 and extremist paramilitary groups assaulting student leaders, trade unionists and communists and promoting a 'strategy of tension' – using random bombings to create an atmosphere of panic and uncertainty and (it was hoped) trigger an authoritarian military crack-down of the kind that had occurred in Greece in 1967. The first major act of terrorism took place in Milan in December 1969, when a bomb placed in a bank in Piazza Fontana near the centre of the city killed sixteen bystanders and wounded more than eighty others. The police hurried to pin the blame on anarchists, but it soon transpired that the most likely perpetrators were in fact a neo-fascist group from the Veneto with links to the Italian secret services. Calls for an investigation into the activities of Italy's secret services went unheeded on the grounds of national security.[2] Other neo-fascist attacks followed in the next few years, including a bomb on an express train north of Florence in August 1974, which killed twelve people. A device left on Bologna railway station in August 1980 killed eighty-four.

Alongside right-wing terrorism went an escalation from the mid-1970s of left-wing terrorism, as groups of revolutionary intellectuals, disenchanted with the lack of militancy shown by the Communist Party in recent years, endeavoured to bring about the collapse of capitalism by striking at the heart of what they called the 'Imperialist State of the Multinationals'. The leaders of these groups were often the sons and daughters of partisan fighters from the Second World War, who felt that the struggle for social justice had been betrayed since 1945; and some, like Renato Curcio and Margherita Cagol, the founders of the most famous terrorist organization, the Red Brigades, came from strongly Catholic families.[3] In contrast to the neo-fascists, they selected their targets carefully: prominent magistrates, businessmen, journalists and politicians. And their most spectacular success occurred in the spring of 1978 when a Red Brigade unit kidnapped the most senior figure in the Christian Democrat party, Aldo Moro, subjected him to a public 'trial' and then shot him, after more than seven weeks of captivity. His body was left in the back of a car in via Caetani, in the centre of Rome, halfway between the headquarters of the communists and the Christian Democrats.

The kidnapping of Aldo Moro precipitated a crisis over the state and its values. Contrary to the hopes of the terrorists (whose highly abstract readings of Italian society, influenced by fashionable Marxist sociology, had blinded them to the reality of the conservative aspirations of most ordinary Italians), the country was not plunged into incipient civil war. Instead, as one of the kidnappers, the young feminist Anna Laura Braghetti, recalled despondently, a wave of indignation and solidarity swept the country, 'with piazzas full of red flags and students and workers calling us fascists'.[4] But if public condemnation of the Red Brigades was strong, there was far less clear-cut support for the line of no negotiation with the terrorists taken, rather reluctantly, by the Christian Democrats and, more insistently, by the communists. The socialists claimed that a humanitarian gesture to save the life of Moro would in fact strengthen Italian democracy, while others found the spectacle of Christian Democrats invoking a 'sense of the state' to justify their intransigence immensely hypocritical. What 'sense of the state' had the Christian Democrats ever displayed during thirty years in power, asked the well-known writer Leonardo Sciascia. Had they not consistently subordinated the interests of Italy to those of their party?[5]

The murder of Moro forced the state onto the offensive. The incompetence of the intelligence services had been exposed by their failure over a period of fifty-five days to locate the hideout of the Red Brigades in a suburb of Rome (leading to much speculation about conspiracies),[6] and in the summer of 1978 it was decided to give the fight against terrorism much greater cohesion. The man appointed to head the new operations was a highly efficient *carabiniere* general, Carlo Alberto Dalla Chiesa, whose family embodied a Piedmontese belief in service to the state and the need to impart a sense of the law to traditionally recalcitrant regions of the country: his father had participated in the campaign waged by Cesare Mori against the mafia in Sicily in the 1920s and he himself had been stationed in the island after the war and again from 1966 to 1973. Though left-wing violence increased in 1979–80, this was indicative of growing desperation on the part of the terrorists as Dalla Chiesa's security forces tightened the net around them and cells splintered and competed with one another for publicity. Public opinion, too, had lost all residual sympathy for the armed struggle. By 1981, aided by a new law that offered reduced prison terms to those who agreed to collaborate with the authorities and 'repent' (*pentiti*), terrorism was fast waning and the state was free to turn its new-found sense of determination towards organized crime.

Criminal gangs specializing in drug trafficking, arms smuggling, prostitution rackets and other criminal activities had become extremely powerful in the southern cities by the start of the 1980s, their ranks swollen by growing armies of unemployed, as the economic recession of the 1970s closed off the safety valve of emigration. Violence, too, escalated – especially in Naples, where the network of families known as the *camorra* had become well organized – and in Palermo. In the spring of 1981 a brutal war broke out between mafia factions in the Sicilian capital, leading to hundreds of killings in and around the city over the next few years. What made the situation particularly alarming to the authorities was the willingness of the criminals to target senior public officials, including magistrates and politicians. In January 1980 the Christian Democrat President of the Region was assassinated after attempting to liberate himself from his old mafia connections. He was followed by Palermo's chief prosecutor and in the spring of 1982 by the highly respected leader of the Sicilian Communist Party and energetic member of the Anti-Mafia Commission, Pio La Torre. It was immediately after La Torre's murder that Carlo Alberto Dalla Chiesa arrived in Palermo as the 58th prefect of the city since the island's incorporation into united Italy.

From the start Dalla Chiesa had the sensation that the supporters of Giulio Andreotti – the dominant Christian Democrat group in Sicily – were against him. In contrast to when he was fighting terrorism, he felt isolated; and, as he told a journalist on 7 August, when a man was simultaneously isolated and dangerous the mafia moved in to eliminate him.[7] Since arriving in Palermo he had faced the dilemma of many previous prefects: whether to surround himself with high security and risk becoming cut off from the general public, or to attempt to win local sympathy and support at the cost of personal safety. He had chosen the latter course. On the evening of 3 September 1982 he left his office in the centre of Palermo together with his young wife and got into a small beige-coloured car to return home to his official residence. He had only one guard following as an escort. As the vehicles entered via Isidoro Carini, two men on a large BMW motorbike pulled up and opened fire with an AK-47 sub-machine gun, killing Dalla Chiesa and his wife instantly. The guard was also assassinated. The funeral was held hastily the following day and was televised live nationally. Crowds threw coins at the government ministers who had come to pay their respects. Dalla Chiesa's brother-in-law shouted: 'You have murdered them, in parliament!'[8]

Dalla Chiesa's assassination resulted in the next few years in a relentless offensive against organized crime. A special 'pool' of investigating magistrates was created in Palermo headed by a group of Sicilians with an unusually strong sense of civic duty – men such as Giovanni Falcone and Paolo Borsellino.[9] And the press ensured that the government remained committed to the campaign through persistent coverage of their initiatives and graphic reporting of the innumerable atrocities for which the mafia had been responsible over the years: any residual 'romantic' ideas about the mafia (on which *mafiosi* had often traded in Sicily) were to be firmly scotched. A major breakthrough occurred in 1984, when a senior boss, Tommaso Buscetta, agreed to collaborate with the authorities and gave detailed information about a structured organization known as Cosa Nostra, with initiation ceremonies and 'statutes', that specialized in drugs and arms trafficking and was based in and around Palermo. On the basis of his testimony – and soon that of other 'repentant' *mafiosi* (*pentiti*), too – more than 450 members of this extensive criminal association went on trial in 1986 in a specially built underground 'bunker' courtroom in Palermo, and 344 were found guilty.

At the time there was widespread optimism that a decisive turning-point had been reached in Sicily's fortunes. Buoyed by the determination of the state and the successes of the police and judiciary, anti-mafia movements began to spring up across the island, and students and workers took to the streets to show their solidarity with the fight against Cosa Nostra. The Church, for the first time in its history, was taking a public stand (in 1976 the Archbishop of Palermo, Salvatore Pappalardo, had become the first prelate to denounce the mafia openly), while the Sicilian Christian Democrats had dispensed with their old corrupt leadership and were being guided by a charismatic young mayor of Palermo, Leoluca Orlando (a descendant of the prime minister of 1917–19), who had pledged to make the fight against the mafia his principal objective. Academics, too, lent their support. Older interpretations that had suggested the mafia was not a unitary organization but more a form of behaviour, rooted in popular culture, were replaced by a new orthodoxy declaring it always to have been a highly structured criminal association, like Cosa Nostra, based in Palermo.[10] Though such a view was not well supported by the historical evidence, it had the political advantage of drawing a clear distinction between the mafia and its social milieu and endorsing the idea that firm state action was the most appropriate solution.

But at the end of the 1980s the fight against organized crime ran into the same sort of difficulties that many earlier operations had faced. Buscetta and the other *pentiti* had refused to be drawn on the links between Cosa Nostra and politicians, and ugly disputes broke out within the judiciary about how much further to press the enquiries. In 1988 the most high-profile of the judges, Giovanni Falcone, was passed over for promotion to leadership of the Palermo 'pool' and left for a post in Rome, and the momentum of the investigations rapidly slowed. It was only after Falcone was murdered in 1992, blown up along with his escort by nearly 400 kilos of high explosives placed under a motorway near Palermo, that the campaign resumed some of its former intensity. Meanwhile the relentless media focus on the mafia provoked in some quarters an uneasy feeling that old stereotypes of the island as a land of crime and barbarism were being reactivated, and that the crusading zeal displayed by the authorities might lead to the perpetration of serious injustices and a strengthening of traditional Sicilian animosity towards the state. When Leonardo Sciascia voiced such concerns in two newspaper articles in 1987, he provoked a storm of fury and accusations that he had in effect become a mafia fellow-traveller.[11]

THE *SORPASSO*

The focus on organized crime during the 1980s deflected attention from the growing disparity between the north and south of Italy. The development programmes of the 1950s and 1960s, based on the idea that targeted intervention could kick-start the southern economy and lead to a sustainable industrial base, were discredited for good by the recession of the 1970s. There were some parts of the south – in the Abruzzi, Molise and Puglia, for instance – where local manufacturing had succeeded in putting down some roots, but elsewhere the general picture was bleak. By 1990 the gross domestic product (GDP) of the south, in proportional terms, was 59 per cent that of the rest of the country (lower than it had been in 1980 and in 1970) and unemployment, especially among the young, had climbed to perilously high levels: over 44 per cent of those aged 14–29 were classified as having no occupation, compared to 14.6 per cent in the centre and north.[12] Admittedly the living standards of most southerners had changed almost beyond recognition since the 1940s, and the trappings of modern consumerism had become nearly as conspicuous in the south as in the north. But much of this lifestyle was the result of cash transfers through the social security system (subsidies, pensions and invalidity benefits, often fraudulently assigned) and superfluous public sector jobs.

In northern and central Italy the recession of the 1970s gave way in the 1980s to a period of what some commentators called Italy's 'second economic miracle'. As in other Western countries, the manufacturing sector was dramatically restructured, with employers defying the trade unions (seemingly all powerful in the 1970s) and laying off hundreds of thousands of workers in a bid to reduce labour costs and shed the less profitable parts of their operations. Companies such as Pirelli were able to return a profit for the first time in a decade. Simultaneously a huge growth took place in the service industries – for example, leisure, entertainment, advertising, banking and insurance – so that by 1995 more than three-fifths of all jobs were in this sphere of the economy compared to less than half fifteen years earlier.[13] Television experienced a particularly spectacular boom after a ruling in 1976 that ended RAI's monopoly of broadcasting. In the space of a few years an ambitious Milanese property tycoon, Silvio Berlusconi, managed, with powerful political protection and in defiance of court rulings, to secure a near monopoly of all commercial stations in the country. By the middle of the 1980s 44 per cent of prime-time viewers were watching channels that he owned.[14]

But the thrust of Italy's economic dynamism in the 1980s was provided by small and medium-sized manufacturing firms, many of them family owned, clustered in specialized industrial districts of the north and centre – shoes in Vigevano, ceramics in Sassuolo, cutlery in Lumezzane, spectacles in Belluno, furniture in Poggibonsi, jewellery in Arezzo, clothes in Treviso (Benetton). They drew on traditional artisan, design and engineering skills, and through a combination of hard work, flexibility, paternalistic management, and strong support and cooperation at a local level, they were able to beat off stiff competition, especially from the Far East, and maintain a strong position in the European export market. They also benefited from contracts from larger manufacturers who had sought to reduce their costs by outsourcing.[15] At the beginning of the 1980s nearly 60 per cent of Italy's industrial workforce was employed in firms with fewer than a hundred people – a figure comparable to that for Japan, but far higher than that for the USA (23 per cent), the UK (25 per cent), France (29 per cent) and Germany (30 per cent).[16]

However, the success of these smaller businesses was also heavily dependent on the willingness of the state to turn a blind eye to numerous fiscal and other abuses. Tax evasion was rife throughout the sector, and when in 1983 a law was passed to try to rectify the situation, workers in a million private firms took action in protest (public sector employees simultaneously went on strike in favour of the law: they were paying an increasingly disproportionate share of the country's revenue from taxation).[17] The government was disinclined to force the issue, and only when Italy was facing exclusion from the mainstream of European economies in the early 1990s on account of its dire public finances did it begin to tackle the matter. Firms also kept their costs down by ignoring the health and safety directives emanating from Brussels (and successive governments again showed little willingness to address the problem), employing staff on short-term contracts without social security payments, and drawing on the huge pool of hidden or 'black' labour – those with undeclared second jobs, pensioners operating from home, immigrants from the Balkans or (increasingly) north Africa. In the early 1990s it was estimated that the black economy accounted for some 2 million people, many of them working in appalling conditions.[18]

The serious structural weaknesses behind the economic boom of the 1980s – above all the fact that the state was having recourse to massive borrowing to cover the low fiscal take and the persistent high levels of public expenditure – were largely ignored amid a widespread sense of euphoria at what seemed the country's definitive arrival in the ranks of the great industrial democracies. In 1976 Italy had been admitted (despite protestations from the French) to membership of the elite club of leading capitalist nations (the G7), and just over a decade later the government was able to notch up a further success when it announced with considerable satisfaction that Italy had overtaken Britain to become the fifth largest economy in the world. The British Chancellor of the

Exchequer contested the claim vehemently – a sign of the United Kingdom's own deep insecurity over its status after years of industrial decline
– but official figures for the GDP of both countries confirmed that the
sorpasso had indeed taken place. In the course of the next few years per
capita income and overall volume of GDP remained more or less the
same for the two economies, before the United Kingdom began to pull
ahead again quite sharply around the turn of the millennium.[19]

The economic optimism was matched by hopes that the political
stalemate that had marred the first decades of the Republic might be
coming to an end, as the grip of the Christian Democrats on government
loosened and the socialists under a dynamic leader, Bettino Craxi, set
out to supplant the communists as Italy's main party of the left. Craxi
came from Milan, and during the 1980s he and his followers embodied
much of the ethos of the 'second economic miracle' (to which Lombardy
had so greatly contributed). The new socialists were bullish and techno-
cratic, with sharp suits and mobile phones, and while they paid lip
service to old left-wing ideals of social justice and inclusiveness, their
prevalent values seemed to be more those of personal success – whatever
the means. Craxi was a close friend of Berlusconi: the two men went on
holiday together to Saint-Moritz and Portofino; and in 1984, a year
after Craxi had become prime minister, the socialist leader agreed to act
as godfather to Berlusconi's illegitimate daughter – a gesture redolent of
the transition from Catholic to post-Catholic clientelism. Over the next
few years Craxi helped Berlusconi to consolidate his media empire, and
in return Berlusconi's television stations flooded Italian households with
the modern consumerist values that Craxi and his party so admired.[20]

Craxi's accession to power was made possible by the declining appeal
of the communists and the waning authority of the Christian Democrats.
In 1973 the newly elected leader of the Communist Party, Enrico
Berlinguer, a shy but charismatic Sardinian of aristocratic background,
had proposed a 'historic compromise' between the three principal parties
as a way of defending Italian democracy in the face of terrorism; and
the Christian Democrats, worried by the spread of secularism and the
continued socio-economic unrest in the country, had edged towards an
alliance with the communists as a possible means of safeguarding their
electoral fortunes. But a sharp drop in the vote for the Communist Party
in 1979 coupled with an escalation of the Cold War after the invasion
of Afghanistan brought the 'historic compromise' to a sudden end,

leaving the Communist Party to return once again to sterile opposition. Meanwhile the Christian Democrats were rocked by a string of corruption scandals; and in 1981 the Italian President, Sandro Pertini, an elderly, austere, high-minded and combative former partisan leader, appointed the respected university professor and leader of the diminutive Republican Party, Giovanni Spadolini, as the first non-Christian Democrat prime minister since 1945. Two years later, in the wake of a disastrous electoral showing by the Christian Democrats, Craxi became prime minister.

Craxi's aggressive and flamboyant style of leadership (cartoonists delighted in showing him wearing Mussolini's riding boots and black shirt) was a marked contrast to the colourless Christian Democrat administrations of previous decades, but his four years in office did nothing to change the pathological imbalance between state and party, public and private, that had dogged the Republic from the outset. Corruption flourished during the 1980s on an unprecedented scale as ambitious members of the Socialist Party took their cue from the top and clawed out enclaves of patronage and power at the expense of their rivals using kickbacks and other illicit means; and their opponents, desperate not to lose ground, responded in kind. Local politicians took advantage of the eagerness of private companies to gain lucrative municipal contracts by insisting on huge clandestine payments as the price for a successful bid: typically about 10 per cent of the value of the contract. The money was transferred through a maze of foreign banks or handed over more prosaically (and commonly) in a briefcase stuffed full of old banknotes and then transferred to the party coffers or straight to private pockets.[21]

A good example of how the system worked was provided by a minor Milanese socialist politician, Mario Chiesa, whose arrest in February 1992 as he frantically tried to flush 30 million lire down a toilet after being caught *in flagrante* accepting a kickback, opened the door to the so-called *Tangentopoli* ('Bribesville') scandal that rocked Italy to its political foundations. Chiesa ran a council-subsidized old people's home in Milan and was a supporter of the local Socialist Party Secretary, Craxi's son, Bobo (the mayor of Milan was Craxi's brother-in-law, Paolo Pillitteri, a man who openly dismissed opponents of corruption as 'cretins who . . . do not understand how the world operates').[22] Chiesa also controlled sporting and recreational facilities and estimated that his little empire was worth 7,000 votes. The old people's home was especially useful: not only were its inmates easy fodder when it came to elections but the allocation of commissions gave Chiesa an important instrument of patronage. It was the owner of a small cleaning company, who had become fed up with being regularly bullied by Chiesa into paying a 10 per cent kickback in return for being given the contract to clean the old people's home, who eventually shopped him to the police.[23]

THE END OF THE 'FIRST REPUBLIC'

The boom of the 1980s left the north one of the most affluent regions of Europe, but the huge tide of money washing through the towns and countryside of Piedmont, Liguria, Lombardy, the Veneto, Emilia Romagna and Tuscany had almost drowned out any serious talk of Italy as a moral point of reference. There were shades of the Renaissance in the combination of opulence and cynicism, with family, clientele and party taking decisive precedence over the broader framework of national claims that the patriots of the nineteenth century had sought to construct. The fact that the prosperity of these years was overwhelmingly at the expense of the public finances went largely unheeded, and little effort was made by Craxi or the weak and short-lived Christian Democrat governments that succeeded him at the end of the decade to rein in public spending. Borrowing soared to levels unequalled in Europe, with the Treasury issuing huge quantities of high-yield bonds to savers (who often bought them with the surplus income that they should have handed over to the state in taxes). Between 1982 and 1990 the annual budget deficit doubled, and by 1992 the accumulated public debt had reached well over 100 per cent of GDP. And simply servicing the debt had become a major problem – it was costing some 10 per cent of GDP in 1990.[24]

With governments lacking the authority and the will to sort out this parlous situation, they turned to Europe for possible salvation. In 1990 Giulio Andreotti, prime minister again for the sixth time, took the lira into the band of currencies that comprised the European Monetary System, trusting the markets would not worry unduly about Italy's precarious public finances; and over the next two years he pressed the case for greater political and economic integration, shepherding

Europe's ministers towards the Maastricht Treaty, which laid down the criteria for monetary convergence. The treaty, signed in 1992, in effect put a gun to Italy's head: but at least it was a gun held by Europe, for which Italians had traditionally shown considerable enthusiasm. To qualify for entry into the single currency Italy would have to reduce its budget deficit to 3 per cent of GDP (down from 9.9 per cent) and bring the public debt to below 60 per cent of GDP. On the face of it this was an almost impossible task, but some leeway was provided with the final wording of the convergence criteria when it was stated that a public debt of more than 60 per cent might not be seen as an impediment provided there had been sufficient evidence of movement in the right direction.[25]

If Italy was now to avoid relegation from the top flight of European states – and the frequency with which this concern was aired in the press in the next few years indicated just how much the old anxieties about the country's standing in the world still reverberated two centuries after Napoleon's armies had swept through the peninsula and triggered the national soul-searching of the Risorgimento – there would have to be drastic reforms. And the seriousness of the situation was underlined in September 1992, when the lira was forced out of the European Monetary System and heavily devalued. Successive governments embarked on desperate programmes to try to deal with the public debt, selling off state companies, freezing wages, raising taxes, and reducing spending on pensions and the bureaucracy. But such measures were inevitably highly unpopular after years of affluence, and mass demonstrations were staged in protest at the cuts and the job losses. At the same time there were loud calls for institutional changes, with the focus as so often in the past on altering the voting system in the hope of creating stronger governments. A new electoral law of 1993 introduced single-member constituencies for three-quarters of the deputies, but it could not solve the fundamental problem: that Italy's parties lacked the authority and credibility needed to maintain internal cohesion and command widespread popular support.

As resentment spread and uncertainty grew, the fragile edifice of the Republic began to disintegrate. The conclusion of the Cold War at the end of the 1980s, and the collapse of the Soviet Union that followed, removed one of the principal pillars upon which the post-war order in Italy had been built. In January 1991, exactly seventy years after its foundation, the Italian Communist Party held its last Congress and voted to dissolve itself and become the Democratic Party of the Left (PDS) – though a sizeable minority found the breach with the past too hard to bear and separated off to form a group called Communist Refoundation. And with the red flag and hammer and sickle now replaced as the symbol of the PDS by a benign spreading oak tree, what justification was there for the crusader shield of the Christian Democrats? In the elections of 1992 the Christian Democrats secured less than 30 per cent of the poll for the first time in their history (the ex-communists managed just 16 per cent); and with public money no longer freely available to prop up their clienteles, and with judicial investigations into corruption gathering pace, recriminations and in-fighting escalated. In 1994 the Christian Democrats broke in two, with the centre and the left resuming the old name of the Popular Party and the right styling itself the Christian Democratic Centre.

A major catalyst for the disintegration of the old political system came with the eruption of the 'Bribesville' scandal following the arrest of Mario Chiesa in February 1992. The enquiry into the illegal funding of parties through kickbacks was led by the chief prosecutor of Milan, Francesco Saverio Borrelli, and a team of magistrates, of whom one, Antonio Di Pietro, rapidly acquired cult status as a result of his formid-able interrogatory skills and dramatic courtroom style (and probably humble southern origins as well) – graffiti such as 'Thank you Di Pietro' and 'Di Pietro, you are better than Pelé' became common on the walls of buildings in Milan.[26] The ease with which the investigators were able to extract confessions from a string of politicians and businessmen was due in large measure to the severely weakened state of the principal parties (attempts to probe the world of corruption had in the past been quickly snuffed out) and to the almost feverish desire of the general public to find scapegoats for the mess into which the country had descended. The enquiries spread rapidly upwards through the ranks of the socialists and the Christian Democrats (and some of the smaller parties, too – the ex-communists, whether rightly or not, were left largely untouched), and, by the summer of 1993, 130 members of parliament were facing investigation.

Craxi – who first received notice that he was under enquiry for corrup-tion at the end of 1992 – attempted, like others caught up in the scandal, to claim that he was the victim of a political witch-hunt.[27] But it was difficult to discern any obvious party bias among the Milan magistrates. Some undoubtedly had left-wing sympathies, but others, including Di Pietro (a former policeman), leaned towards the right. This said, the febrile atmosphere that surrounded the investigations, heightened by massive international media attention and an Italian press that was ready to report news of the latest issue of a 'Notice of Guarantee' to a suspect as if it were a clear indication of guilt, pushed the protagonists into seeing themselves as more than simple enforcers of the law. There was a sense in the country that a sea-change – indeed a revolution of some kind – was required; and the magistrates responded accordingly: 'Ours is a legal and wise revolution,' Borrelli announced proudly in May 1993, 'which has lasted a little more than a year. Remember that the French Revolution began in 1789 and was completed only in 1794.'[28] In such a climate of heightened expectations, it was almost inevitable (as in the fight against Cosa Nostra) that miscarriages of justice would occur.

As the constituent political elements of the Republic dissolved amid ignominy or a sense of redundancy, the old struggle to determine the identity of Italy resumed, and as it did so, the history of the preceding two centuries emerged as an ideological battlefield to be fought over by competing groups vying for popular legitimacy. In northern Italy a combination of the affluence of the 1980s, the spectacle (inflamed by the media) of a south seemingly dominated by organized crime, and the imposition of fiscal stringency in the early 1990s led to the rapid emergence of a major party of protest known as the Northern League. Led by Umberto Bossi, a rough-speaking Lombard senator with dishevelled hair and ill-fitting suits, his tie half undone as if he had just come out of a long and acrimonious board-meeting, the League celebrated the industry and entrepreneurial spirit of northerners, denounced the government in Rome for having squandered the hard-earned taxes of northern businessmen on the mafia-ridden clienteles of the south, and proclaimed unification in 1860 to have been a catastrophic error: north and south were two separate nations, and the country should at the most have been no more than a federation, as the Milanese writer Carlo Cattaneo had argued.[29]

The League appealed especially to small businessmen, shopkeepers and other self-employed groups in the small towns and cities of the north of Italy – groups that had developed increased feelings of xenophobia and particularism in recent years thanks to a heavy influx of immigrants from eastern Europe and Africa (though racist attitudes towards southern Italians had a long history, and may well have been more exacerbated than reduced by the migratory flows of the 1950s and 1960s).[30] Under Bossi's charismatic leadership, the League promoted a strong pseudo-ethnic culture, postulating the existence of a north Italian nation called Padania, celebrating Lombard and other local dialects, and drawing selectively on history to support its claim to the essential unity of the north. Much was made (ironically, given how it had been used by the 'Italian' patriots in the Risorgimento) of the twelfth-century Lombard League, and the party's badge showed the hero of the Battle of Legnano in 1176, Alberto da Giussano, raising his sword to rally the city-states of the Po valley against Frederick Barbarossa.

The growth of the Northern League – in the elections of 1992 it came from almost nowhere to win 8.7 per cent of the national vote (with 20 per cent in Lombardy, Piedmont, Liguria and the Veneto) – triggered a series of intellectual and political initiatives to counter what appeared to be a serious threat to the integrity of the state. If in the past the 'southern question' had been viewed as a way of acknowledging (and addressing) the problems of the most disadvantaged half of the country, it could now seem a liability in as much as it gave the League ammunition for its blanket dismissal of the south as a separate (and inferior) nation. An important new historical school emerged committed to demonstrating the artificiality of the concept of 'the south' and showing that southerners had often been just as entrepreneurial and modern-minded as their northern counterparts. (It also promoted vigorously the idea of 'the mafia' as a structured criminal organization like Cosa Nostra with no roots in popular culture – in part as an antidote to the League's crude claims that all southerners were to a degree *mafiosi*.)[31]

While some southerners responded to the League's claims that unification had been a disaster for the north by asserting that it had been a catastrophe for the south, too (books, pamphlets and websites proliferated in the 1990s dedicated to showing how the south had been the victim of brutal northern colonialism – even genocide – after 1860), the prevalent feeling among southerners was that the unity of the state had to be defended at all costs. After all, what future could the south look forward to if it was cut adrift from the rest of the peninsula? One symptom of the growing concern for the integrity of the state was a surge of support for the far right. In the autumn of 1993 the suave and demure leader of the neo-fascist party, the MSI, Gianfranco Fini, stood for mayor of Rome and was only narrowly defeated. And the same happened in Naples, where Alessandra Mussolini, the Duce's grand-daughter, a model and film actress (and niece of Sophia Loren), was a candidate. The following year, the far right – which had recently repositioned itself as a 'post-fascist' force and adopted the name National Alliance – won 13.5 per cent of the vote in the general elections. Ninety-four of its 109 deputies represented constituencies in Rome and the south.[32]

With the peninsula fracturing into discordant political pieces, and with the very idea of unity being called into question, many commentators began to ask – in a manner reminiscent of the agonized discussions that had taken place in the nineteenth century among patriots about the country's failure to achieve 'moral unification' – why Italy still displayed so little sense of nationhood. A string of books appeared by well-known intellectuals with alarmist titles such as *If We Cease to be a Nation*, *The End of Italy: The Decline and Death of Risorgimento Ideology* and *The Death of the Fatherland*, analysing who or what might be to blame for the current insalubrious situation.[33] History, geography, the Church and the national character were all indicted in varying measures (as they had been in many previous discussions); and so, too, were the parties that had dominated Italy since 1945 and failed to inculcate a strong sense of the law and the state or provide a clear framework of common memories and values.

With debates centring once more on the inveterate problem of the nation, the balance of moral power shifted sharply to the right, with the former communists (and communists) being subjected to increasingly vituperative attacks from broad sections of conservative opinion and above all from the resurgent forces of neo-fascism for their lack of commitment to 'Italy'. Among other things the far left were accused of having driven a wedge through the nation after 1945 thanks to their celebration of the 'values of the resistance' and their wilful distortion of the historical reality of fascism. Had not Mussolini's regime in fact been far more benign and moderate than that of Nazism, with which the communists had unjustly sought to confound it? And had not those who had supported the Republic of Salò been motivated by ideals of patriotism that made them fully as worthy of honourable commemoration as the partisans? And though the Duce had undoubtedly made mistakes, had he not at least tried to promote a sense of the 'fatherland' and heal the country's internal fractures? And, anyway, who were the communists to take the moral high ground against the far right given the atrocities that had been committed by the Soviet Union or, indeed, by the resistance itself?

On 26 January 1994, with the First Republic, as commentators were now calling it, lying largely in ruins, Silvio Berlusconi sent a short videocassette to RAI, Reuters and his own commercial television channels, in which he announced his intention to enter the political arena in the forthcoming general elections to be held in March:

Italy is the country I love. Here are my roots, my hopes, my horizons. Here I have learned, from my father and from life, how to be an entrepreneur. Here I have acquired my passion for life ... Never as in this moment does Italy ... need people of a certain experience, with their heads firmly on their shoulders, able to give the country a helping hand and to make the state function ... If the political system is to work, it is essential that there emerges a 'pole of liberty' in opposition to the left-wing cartel, a pole which is capable of attracting to it the best of an Italy which is honest, reasonable, modern. Around this pole there must gather all those forces which make reference to the fundamental principles of Western democracies; in the first place the Catholic world which has contributed generously to the last fifty years of our history as a united nation ... I tell you that we can, I tell you that we must, create for ourselves and for our children a new Italian miracle.[34]

With his principal political patron, Bettino Craxi, disgraced, and many of his business friends and associates caught up in the Bribesville scandal, Berlusconi knew that the best way to safeguard his massive media empire was in power. His companies were heavily in debt; and if a left-wing coalition won, there was a strong chance that it would legislate to end his near-monopoly of commercial broadcasting. Using the most advanced marketing, polling and advertising techniques, Berlusconi had recently created a new political party designed to have the maximum possible resonance with an electorate with few certainties about its past or its future, and little faith in the ideologies that had guided the thoughts and actions of Italians for so much of the nineteenth and twentieth centuries. Its name, Forza Italia, was taken from a football chant

('Go, Italy!') (part of Berlusconi's popular appeal lay in his ownership of the country's most successful team, AC Milan); and the values that it trumpeted were those of financial success, family, consumerism, Catholicism (of a non-committal kind) and freedom – understood mainly as freedom from the irksome shackles of the state.[35]

It was a winning formula, and in the spring of 1994 Berlusconi swept to power with his rather unlikely allies of the Northern League and the National Alliance. Forza Italia emerged as the biggest party in Italy with 21 per cent of the vote: much of its support had come from housewives, the young and the self-employed. But the victory was short-lived, and there was to be no 'new Italian miracle'. The coalition partners soon began to fall out, and when, in November, Berlusconi was served with a Notice of Guarantee (embarrassingly while presiding over a meeting of the G7 in Naples), informing him that he was under investigation for a number of counts of corruption, including bribing the finance police to ignore false tax returns, the Northern League took the opportunity to withdraw its support from the government. In the months that followed, fresh charges were lodged against Berlusconi and many of his closest business and political associates by the Milan magistrates. Berlusconi's future looked bleak.

But he survived: the judiciary succumbed to internal feuding (even Di Pietro found himself under investigation for a time) and the drive against corruption slowed. And when fresh elections were held in the spring of 1996, Forza Italia again managed to secure more than 20 per cent of the vote. But it was the centre-left that won, and for the next five years Italy was ruled by a succession of left-wing coalitions that struggled to deal with the country's financial problems and the parlous state of the public services. They offered no coherent vision or systematic programme for implementing reforms – perhaps inevitably given the strange mixture of communists, former communists, Catholics, Republicans, Greens and other groups in the government – and they accordingly failed to inspire much enthusiasm in the country. Their one significant achievement was to gain acceptance into the single European currency in 1998 – despite the public debt still being almost twice the level permitted by Maastricht. When fresh elections were held in May 2001 Berlusconi was returned to power with a considerable majority. He remained prime minister for the next five years (despite facing a string of corruption charges), but was unable to find a magic formula to sort out Italy's problems. In the elections of 2006 he was narrowly defeated by the centre-left.

At the beginning of the twenty-first century Italy had been transformed beyond all recognition from the impoverished country into which Mazzini, Garibaldi and Cavour had been born 200 years earlier. Most of its inhabitants were far better fed, much better educated, and considerably richer and healthier (and possibly happier) than at any other time in history. They were also undoubtedly more 'Italian'. But the concerns that had haunted the patriots of the Risorgimento – how to construct a nation with a shared past and a strong sense of collective destiny and purpose – remained almost as pressing in the age of Forza Italia as in the era of the Carbonari and Young Italy. The Italian nation had from the outset been difficult to define and even more difficult to build; and despite the endeavours of poets, writers, artists, publicists, revolutionaries, soldiers and politicians of varying hues and persuasions, it was clear that old patterns of thought and behaviour had remained deeply entrenched, and that faith in the ideal of 'Italy' had not been engendered in the way that so many patriots had hoped. Perhaps, though, the very insistence with which the project of 'making Italians' had been pursued down to the Second World War had contributed to the scant belief in collective national values. But if states are to function well they need an overarching sense of a greater whole to which the interests of the individual, the group or the party are ultimately subordinate; and at the start of the new millennium 'Italy' appeared still too uncertain and contested an idea to provide the emotional core of a nation – one at least that was at peace with itself and able to face the future with confidence.

References

Preface

1. J. Budden, *The Operas of Verdi. Vol. 2: From Il Trovatore to La Forza del Destino* (London, 1978), p. 435.
2. G. Verdi, *Letters of Giuseppe Verdi. Selected and Translated by Charles Osborne* (London, 1971), pp. 124, 129.

1: Deliverance, 1796–9

1. F. Venturi, 'L'Italia fuori d'Italia', in *Storia d'Italia. Vol. 3: Dal primo Settecento all'Unità* (Turin, 1973), p. 1131.
2. E. Passerin d'Entrèves and V. E. Giuntella (eds.), *Storia d'Italia. Vol. 3: Dalla pace di Aquisana all'avvento di Camillo Cavour* (Turin, 1959), p. 230.
3. Ibid., pp. 237–8.
4. R. Sòriga, *L'idea nazionale italiana dal secolo XVIII all'unificazione. Scritti raccolti e ordinati da Silio Manfredi* (Modena, 1941), pp. 35–7.
5. Venturi, 'L'Italia fuori d'Italia', p. 1036.
6. G. Angiolini, *Lettera di Gasparo Angiolini a Monsieur Noverra sopra i balli pantomimi* (Milan, 1773), pp. 11, 110.
7. Sòriga, *L'idea nazionale*, p. 39.
8. Stendhal, *La Chartreuse de Parme. Préface, commentaires et notes de Victor del Litto* (Paris, 1983), p. 21 (Ch. 1, 'Milan en 1796').
9. Sòriga, *L'idea nazionale*, p. 41.
10. G. R. Carli, 'Della patria degli italiani', in S. Romagnoli (ed.), *'Il Caffe' ossia brevi e vari discorsi distribuiti in fogli periodici* (Milan, 1960), pp. 297–302.
11. A. Saitta, *Filippo Buonarroti. Contributi alla storia della sua vita e del suo pensiero*, Vol. 2 (Rome, 1950–51), pp. 1–2.
12. G. Pécout, *Il lungo Risorgimento. La nascita dell'Italia contemporanea (1770–1922)* (Milan, 1999), p. 67.
13. Venturi, 'L'Italia fuori d'Italia', p. 1131.
14. A. Saitta, *Alle origini del Risorgimento. I testi di un 'celebre' concorso (1796)*, Vol. 1 (Rome, 1964), pp. x–xi.
15. Ibid., Vol. 2, pp. 51–2, 66, 73.
16. Ibid., Vol. 3, pp. 268–71.
17. Ibid., Vol. 2, pp. 191–6.
18. Ibid., Vol. 3, pp. 233–4.
19. Ibid., Vol. 2, pp. 337–40.
20. Ibid., Vol. 3, pp. 382–6.
21. Passerin d'Entrèves and Giuntella (eds.), *Storia d'Italia*, Vol. 3, p. 233.

22. A. De Fournoux, *Napoléon et Venise 1796–1814* (Paris, 2002), p. 210.
23. C. Cantù, *Della indipendenza italiana. Cronistoria*, Vol. 1 (Turin, 1872), p. 99.
24. Fournoux, *Napoléon et Venise*, pp. 213–14.
25. *Edizione nazionale delle opere di Ugo Foscolo. Vol. 2: Tragedie e poesie minori*, ed. G. Bezzola (Florence, 1961), pp. 331–41 ('Bonaparte liberatore (1797–99)').
26. Ibid. *Vol. 6: Scritti letterari e politici dal 1796 al 1808*, ed. G. Gambarin (Florence, 1972), p. xxv.
27. A. Lyttelton, 'The national question in Italy', in M. Teisch and R. Porter (eds.), *The National Question in Europe in Historical Context* (Cambridge, 1993), p. 75.
28. U. Dotti, *Storia degli intellettuali in Italia. Vol. 3: Temi e ideologie dagli illuminati a Gramsci* (Rome, 1999), p. 180.
29. V. Alfieri, *Il Misogallo*, in *Opere di Vittorio Alfieri. Scritti politici e morali*, Vol. 3, ed. C. Mazzotta (Asti, 1984), p. 200.
30. Ibid., pp. 199, 201.
31. Dotti, *Storia degli intellettuali*, Vol. 3, p. 177.
32. Alfieri, *Il Misogallo*, p. 411 ('Conclusione').
33. A. Pillepich, *Milan capitale napoléonienne 1800–1814* (Paris, 2001), p. 139 (to Eugène de Beauharnais, 18 May 1808).
34. S. Woolf, *A History of Italy 1700–1860. The Social Constraints of Political Change* (London, 1979), p. 175.
35. G. Candeloro, *Storia dell'Italia moderna. Vol. 1: Le origini del Risorgimento* (Milan, 1956), p. 174.
36. Stendhal, *La Chartreuse de Parme*, p. 24.
37. C. Capra, *L'età rivoluzionaria e napoleonica in Italia 1796–1815* (Turin, 1978), pp. 108–9.
38. Ibid., pp. 113–17.
39. R. Salvadori, 'Moti antigiacobini e insorgenze antinapoleoniche in Val padano', in *Storia della società italiana. L'Italia giacobina e napoleonica*, eds. G. Cherubini et al. (Milan, 1985), p. 192.
40. Ibid., pp. 120–21.
41. T. Coleman, *Nelson. The Man and the Legend* (London, 2002), pp. 177–8.
42. J. A. Davis, *Naples and Napoleon. Southern Italy and the European Revolutions 1780–1860* (Oxford, 2006), p. 44.
43. N. Moe, *The View from Vesuvius. Italian Culture and the Southern Question* (Berkeley, 2002), pp. 61, 67.
44. B. Croce, *La rivoluzione napoletana del 1799* (Bari, 1948), pp. 39–40.
45. Candeloro, *Storia dell'Italia moderna*, Vol. 1, p. 260.
46. R. De Felice (ed.), *I giornali giacobini italiani* (Milan, 1962), p. 455 ('Educazione della plebe', in *Monitore napolitano*, February 1799). Cf. Davis, *Naples and Napoleon*, pp. 99–100.
47. Capra, *L'età rivoluzionaria e napoleonica*, p. 138.
48. C. Albanese, *Cronache di una rivoluzione. Napoli 1799* (Milan, 1998), p. 111.
49. P. Colletta, *Storia del reame di Napoli*, Vol. 2, ed. N. Cortese (Naples, 1969), pp. 46–7.
50. Albanese, *Cronache di una rivoluzione*, p. 112.
51. Ibid., p. 120.
52. C. De Nicola, *Diario napoletano, dicembre 1798–dicembre 1800*, ed. P. Ricci (Milan, 1963), p. 277.
53. Albanese, *Cronache di una rivoluzione*, p. 135.

2: Searching for the Nation's Soul

1. A. Ottolini, *La Carboneria dalle origini ai primi tentativi insurrezionali (1797–1817)* (Modena, 1936), pp. 14–16.
2. R. Sòriga, *L'idea nazionale italiana dal secolo XVIII all'unificazione. Scritti raccolti e ordinati da Silio Manfredi* (Modena, 1941), pp. 45–7.

3. V. Cuoco, *Saggio storico sulla rivoluzione napoletana del 1799*, ed. F. Nicolini (Bari, 1929), p. 28.

4. Ibid., p. 90.

5. Ibid., p. 21.

6. S. Patriarca, 'Patriottismo, nazione e italianità nella statistica del Risorgimento', in A. M. Banti and R. Bizzocchi (eds.), *Immagini della nazione nell'Italia del Risorgimento* (Rome, 2002), p. 125.

7. G. Calò, *Pedagogia del Risorgimento* (Florence, 1965), pp. 4–6.

8. Ibid., p. 4.

9. V. Cuoco, *Platone in Italia*, Vol. 2, ed. F. Nicolini (Bari, 1928), pp. 157–8.

10. Calò, *Pedagogia*, p. 8.

11. E. Noether, *Seeds of Italian Nationalism, 1700–1815* (New York, 1969), pp. 79–82.

12. S. Woolf, *A History of Italy 1700–1860. The Social Constraints of Political Change* (London, 1979), p. 197.

13. G. Candeloro, *Storia dell'Italia moderna. Vol. 1: Le origini del Risorgimento* (Milan, 1956), pp. 308–9.

14. C. Capra, *L'età rivoluzionaria e napoleonica in Italia 1796–1815* (Turin, 1978), p. 160.

15. C. Zaghi, *Napoleone e l'Italia. Studi e ricerche* (Naples, 1966), pp. 309–22.

16. Stendhal, *La Chartreuse de Parme. Préface, commentaires et notes de Victor del Litto* (Paris, 1983), p. 38.

17. L. Patetta, 'Il neoclassicismo', in *Storia della società italiana. L'Italia giacobina e napoleonica*, eds. G. Cherubini et al. (Milan, 1985), p. 421.

18. P. Colletta, *Storia del reame di Napoli*, Vol. 2, ed. N. Cortese (Naples, 1969), p. 266.

19. M. Meriggi, *Gli stati italiani prima dell'Unità. Una storia istituzionale* (Bologna, 2002), pp. 72–4.

20. U. Foscolo, 'Orazione a Bonaparte pel Congresso di Lione', in *Edizione nazionale delle opere di Ugo Foscolo. Vol. 6: Scritti letterari e politici dal 1796 al 1808*, ed. G. Gambarin (Florence, 1972), pp. 212, 231–2.

21. U. Foscolo, 'Dei sepolcri', in ibid. *Vol. 1: Poesie e carmi*, eds. F. Pagliai, G. Folena and M. Scotti (Florence, 1985), p. 130.

22. U. Foscolo, 'Ultime lettere di Jacopo Ortis', in ibid. *Vol. 4: Le ultime lettere di Jacopo Ortis*, ed. G. Gambarin (Florence, 1955), p. 260.

23. U. Foscolo, 'Dei sepolcri', in ibid. Vol. 1, p. 130.

24. U. Foscolo, 'Essay on the present literature of Italy', in ibid. *Vol. 11, part 2: Saggi di letteratura italiana* (ed. C. Foligno), p. 476.

25. U. Foscolo, 'Dell'origine e dell'officio della letteratura', in ibid. *Vol. 7: Lezioni, articoli di critica e di polemica (1809–1811)*, ed. E. Santini (Florence, 1933), p. 17.

26. Ibid., pp. 33–4.

27. Ibid., pp. 36–7.

28. E. Francia, *Delfina de Custine, Luisa Stolberg, Giulietta Récamier a Canova. Lettere inedite* (Rome, 1972), p. 73.

29. F. Mazzocca, 'L'iconografia della patria tra l'età delle riforme e l'Unità', in Banti and Bizzocchi (eds.), *Immagini della nazione*, pp. 100–101.

30. Ibid., pp. 94–7.

31. Ibid., pp. 97–8.

32. E. Irace, *Itale glorie* (Bologna, 2003), pp. 124–7.

33. M. Gutwirth, *Madame de Staël, Novelist. The Emergence of the Artist as Woman* (Urbana, 1978), p. 285.

34. Madame de Staël, *Corinne, or Italy*, trans. S. Raphael (Oxford, 1998), pp. 11, 89.

35. J. C. Herold, *Mistress to an Age. A Life of Madame de Staël* (London, 1959), pp. 301–3.

36. S. Balayé, *Madame de Staël. Écrire, lutter, vivre* (Geneva, 1994), p. 326.

37. De Staël, *Corinne, or Italy*, p. 27.

38. Madame de Staël, *Correspondance générale. Vol. 6: De Corinne vers De l'Allemagne. 9 novembre 1805–9 mai 1809* (Klincksieck, 1993), p. 245.

39. De Staël, *Corinne, or Italy*, pp. 261–2.

40. Ibid., p. 24.

41. C. Garry-Boussel, 'L'homme du Nord et l'homme du Midi dans *Corinne*', in *Mme de Staël. Actes du colloque de la Sorbonne du 20 novembre 1999* (Paris, 2000), p. 62.

42. De Staël, *Corinne, or Italy*, p. 99.

43. Ibid., p. 99.

44. Ibid., p. 304.

45. Ibid., pp. 110–11.

46. G. Montanelli, *Memorie sull'Italia e specialmente sulla Toscana dal 1814 al 1850* (Florence, 1963), p. 30.

47. A. Codignola (ed.), *Goffredo Mameli. La vita e gli scritti. Vol. 2: Gli scritti* (Venice, 1927), pp. 279–80.

3: Conspiracy and Resistance

1. Cf. J.-E. Driault, *Napoléon en Italie (1800–1812)* (Paris, 1906), pp. 477–8.

2. D. Gregory, *Napoleon's Italy* (Madison, 2001), p. 181.

3. F. C. Schneid, *Soldiers of Napoleon's Kingdom of Italy. Army, State, and Society 1800–1815* (Boulder, 1995), p. 76.

4. F. Della Peruta, 'Dai particolarismi all'idea di nazione. L'esperienza degli anni "giacobini" e "napoleonici" ', in F. Tarozzi and G. Vecchio (eds.), *Gli italiani e il tricolore. Patriottismo, identità nazionale e fratture sociali lungo due secoli di storia* (Bologna, 1999), p. 71.

5. Schneid, *Soldiers of Napoleon's Kingdom of Italy*, pp. 129–30.

6. F. Della Peruta, *Esercito e società nell'Italia napoleonica* (Milan, 1988), pp. 422–3.

7. R. Salvadori, 'Moti antigiacobini e insorgenze antinapoleoniche in Val padana', in *Storia della società italiana. L'Italia giacobina e napoleonica*, eds. G. Cherubini et al. (Milan 1985), p. 205.

8. Ibid., p. 206.

9. M. Broers, *Europe Under Napoleon* (London, 1996), p. 132.

10. J. A. Davis, *Naples and Napoleon. Southern Italy and the European Revolutions 1780–1860* (Oxford, 2006), pp. 209–31.

11. Gregory, *Napoleon's Italy*, p. 171.

12. G. Cingari, *Brigantaggio, proprietari e contadini nel sud (1799–1900)* (Rome, 1976), pp. 44–60.

13. Ibid., pp. 77–9.

14. Cf. B. Amante, *Fra Diavolo e il suo tempo (1796–1806)* (Florence, 1904), p. 458.

15. Gregory, *Napoleon's Italy*, p. 173.

16. A. Ottolini, *La Carboneria dalle origini ai primi tentativi insurrezionali (1797–1817)* (Modena, 1936), p. 54.

17. G. Candeloro, *Storia dell'Italia moderna. Vol. I: Le origini del Risorgimento* (Milan, 1956), p. 362.

18. Ottolini, *La Carboneria*, pp. 48–9.

19. R. John Rath, ' "The Carbonari": their origins, initiation rites, and aims', in *American Historical Review*, 69, 2 (1964), pp. 359–61.

20. R. Sòriga, *Le società segrete, l'emigrazione politica e i primi moti per l'indipendenza. Scritti raccolti e ordinati da Silio Manfredi* (Modena, 1942), p. 99.

21. Ottolini, *La Carboneria*, pp. 124–6.

22. J. Rosselli, *Lord William Bentinck. The Making of a Liberal Imperialist 1774–1839* (London, 1974), p. 155.

23. D. Mack Smith, *A History of Sicily. Modern Sicily after 1713* (London, 1968), p. 350.

24. Rosselli, *Lord William Bentinck*, pp. 151, 161–3.

25. R. Sòriga, *L'idea nazionale italiana dal secolo XVIII all'unificazione. Scritti raccolti e ordinati da Silio Manfredi* (Modena, 1941), pp. 184–202.

26. Rosselli, *Lord William Bentinck*, p. 168.

27. Ibid., p. 172.

28. Ibid., p. 176.

29. C. Mozzarelli, 'Sulle opinioni politiche di Federico Confalonieri, patrizio e gentiluomo', in G. Rumi (ed.), *Federico Confalonieri aristocratico progressista* (Bari, 1987), p. 56.

30. Candeloro, *Storia dell'Italia moderna*, Vol. 1, pp. 371–2.

31. D. Mack Smith, *The Making of Italy 1796–1870* (London, 1968), p. 18.

32. A. Manzoni, 'Il proclama di Rimini', in *Tutte le opere di Alessandro Manzoni. Vol. 1: Poesie e tragedie*, eds. A. Chiari and F. Ghisalberti (Milan, 1957), pp. 119–20.

33. J.-P. Garnier, *Gioacchino Murat re di Napoli*, trans. G. F. Malquori (Naples, 1959), p. 346.

4: Restoration, Romanticism and Revolt

1. Cf. *Pelagio Palagi: artista e collezionista. Mostra organizzata dal Museo civico con il contributo della Regione Emilia Romagna* (Bologna, 1976).

2. F. Hayez, *Le mie memorie dettate da Francesco Hayez* (Milan, 1890), p. 21.

3. M. C. Gozzoli and F. Mazzocca (eds.), *Hayez* (Milan, 1983), p. 86.

4. I. Marelli, *Brera mai vista. Il Romanticismo storico: Francesco Hayez e Pelagio Palagi* (Milan, 2001), p. 16.

5. F. Mazzocca, 'La pittura dell'Ottocento in Lombardia', in E. Castelnuovo (ed.), *La pittura in Italia: l'Ottocento*, Vol. 1 (Milan, 1991), p. 102.

6. Cf. F. Venturi, 'L'Italia fuori d'Italia', in *Storia d'Italia. Vol. 3: Dal primo Settecento all'Unità* (Turin, 1973), pp. 1217–18.

7. Cf. A. Scirocco, *L'Italia del Risorgimento 1800–1860* (Bologna, 1990), pp. 35–55.

8. A. Balletti, *Storia di Reggio nell'Emilia* (Rome, 1968), pp. 615–32.

9. Cf. L. C. Farini, *Lo Stato Romano dall'anno 1815 al 1850*, Vol. 1 (Florence, 1853), pp. 6–15.

10. G. Candeloro, *Storia dell'Italia moderna. Vol. 2: Dalla restaurazione alla rivoluzione nazionale 1815–1846* (Milan, 1974), p. 61.

11. D. Laven, *Venice and Venetia under the Habsburgs, 1815–1835* (Oxford, 2002), pp. 122, 140–42.

12. Scirocco, *L'Italia del Risorgimento*, p. 61.

13. Ibid., pp. 64–5.

14. M. Meriggi, 'Centralismo e federalismo in Italia. Le aspettative preunitarie', in O. Janz, P. Schiera and H. Siegrist (eds.), *Centralismo e federalismo tra Otto e Novecento. Italia e Germania a confronto* (Bologna, 1997), pp. 52–5.

15. Candeloro, *Storia dell'Italia moderna*, Vol. 2, pp. 28–9.

16. Laven, *Venice and Venetia*, pp. 79–80.

17. Venturi, 'L'Italia fuori d'Italia', pp. 1218–19.

18. Madame de Staël, 'Sulla maniera e le utilità delle traduzioni', in *Biblioteca italiana* (Milan), January 1816, pp. 16–18.

19. G. Berchet, *Lettera semiseria di Grisostomo*, introduction by A. Galletti (Lanciano, 1913), pp. 109–12, 118, 121, 146–7.

20. Cf. M. Thom, *Republics, Nations and Tribes* (London, 1995), pp. 289–305.

21. Candeloro, *Storia dell'Italia moderna*, Vol. 2, pp. 33–4.

22. Cf. *Scritti editi ed inediti di Giuseppe Mazzini*, Vol. 39 (Imola, 1924), p. 9 ('Parties and affairs in Italy').

23. Candeloro, *Storia dell'Italia moderna*, Vol. 2, p. 106.

24. Cf. R. Balzani, 'I nuovi simboli patriottici: la nascita del tricolore e la sua diffusione negli anni della restaurazione e del Risorgimento', in F. Tarozzi and G. Vecchio (eds.), *Gli italiani e il tricolore. Patriottismo, identità nazionale e fratture sociali lungo due secoli di storia* (Bologna, 1999), pp. 146–7.

25. Candeloro, *Storia dell'Italia moderna*, Vol. 2, p. 114.

26. P. Giudici, *Storia d'Italia narrata al popolo. Vol. 4: Il Risorgimento* (Florence, 1932), p. 335.

27. L. Gigli, *Santarosa* (Milan, 1946), pp. 221–323.
28. G. Mazzini, *Note autobiografiche*, ed. R. Pertici (Milan, 1986), pp. 52–3.
29. F. Lemmi, *Carlo Felice (1765–1831)* (Turin, 1931), p. 182 (9 May 1822).
30. Cf. S. Romagnoli, 'Narratori e prosatori del Romanticismo', in E. Cecchi and N. Sapegno (eds.), *Storia della letteratura italiana. Vol. 8: Dall'Ottocento al Novecento* (Milan, 1968), pp. 150–57.
31. R. J. M. Olson, *Ottocento. Romanticism and Revolution in 19th-Century Italian Painting* (New York, 1992), p. 152.

5: Fractured Past and Fractured Present

1. C. Petraccone, *Le due civiltà. Settentrionali e meridionali nella storia d'Italia* (Rome, 2000), p. 6.
2. G. Bollati, 'L'italiano', in *Storia d'Italia. Vol. 1: I caratteri originali* (Turin, 1972), p. 954.
3. Cf. I. De Feo, *Manzoni. L'uomo e l'opera* (Milan, 1971), pp. 131–2, 158, 596–8.
4. A. Manzoni, 'Marzo 1821', in *Tutte le opere di Alessandro Manzoni. Vol. 1: Poesie e tragedie*, eds. A. Chiari and F. Ghisalberti (Milan, 1957), pp. 115–18.
5. Ibid., pp. 854–5.
6. A. M. Banti, 'Le invasioni barbariche e le origini delle nazioni', in A. M. Banti and R. Bizzocchi (eds.), *Immagini della nazione nell'Italia del Risorgimento* (Rome, 2002), p. 22.
7. A. Manzoni, *Il Conte di Carmagnola*, Act 2, Chorus, in *Tutte le opere di Alessandro Manzoni*, Vol. 1, p. 337.
8. Manzoni, 'Discorso sur alcuni punti della storia longobardica in Italia', in *Tutte le opere di Alessandro Manzoni. Vol. 4: Saggi storici e politici*, ed. F. Ghisalberti, pp. 198, 206–11.
9. Manzoni, *Adelchi*, Act 3, Chorus, in *Tutte le opere di Alessandro Manzoni*, Vol. 1, pp. 613–15.
10. A. M. Banti, *La nazione del Risorgimento. Parentela, santità e onore alle origini dell'Italia unita* (Turin, 2000), p. 47.
11. G. Mazzini, 'De l'art en Italie, à propos de "Marco Visconti", roman de Thomas Grossi', in *Scritti editi ed inediti di Giuseppe Mazzini*, Vol. 8 (Imola, 1910), pp. 45–7.
12. L. Settembrini, *Lezioni di letteratura italiana*, Vol. 2 (Florence, 1964), pp. 1072–3 ('La rivoluzione interiore. Il Manzoni').
13. M. L. Astaldi, *Manzoni ieri e oggi* (Milan, 1971), p. 319.
14. J. C. L. Sismondi, *Histoire des républiques italiennes du moyen age*, Vol. 10 (Paris, 1840), pp. 364–401.
15. Ibid., Vol. 2, pp. 42–4.
16. F. Venturi, 'L'Italia fuori d'Italia', in *Storia d'Italia. Vol. 3: Dal primo Settecento all'Unità* (Turin, 1973), p. 1177 (Sismondi to Madame de Staël, 20 March 1804).
17. Ibid., p. 1178.
18. Cf. M. O'Connor, *The Romance of Italy and the English Political Imagination* (Basingstoke, 1998), pp. 40–55.
19. C. Botta, *Storia d'Italia continuata da quella del Guicciardini sino al 1789*, Vol. 1 (Capolago, 1832), p. 42.
20. C. Botta, *Storia dei popoli italiani*, Vol. 2 (Pisa, 1825), p. 16.
21. Ibid., p. 111.
22. Botta, *Storia d'Italia continuata da quella del Guicciardini*, Vol. 1, p. 44.
23. Botta, *Storia dei popoli italiani*, Vol. 5, pp. 164–5.
24. Bollati, 'L'italiano', p. 972.
25. *Goffredo Mameli. La vita e gli scritti. Vol. 2: Gli scritti*, ed. A. Codignola (Venice, 1927), pp. 76–7.
26. G. Mazzini, *Doveri dell'uomo*, in *Scritti editi ed inediti di Giuseppe Mazzini*, Vol. 69 (Imola, 1935), pp. 61–2.
27. G. Pescosolido, 'L'economia e la vita materiale', in G. Sabbatucci and V. Vidotto (eds.),

Storia d'Italia. Vol. 1: Le premesse dell'Unità. Dalla fine del Settecento al 1861 (Rome and Bari, 1994), pp. 107–9; G. Montroni, *La società italiana dall'unificazione alla Grande Guerra* (Rome, 2002), p. 7.

28. A. Scirocco, *L'Italia del Risorgimento 1800–1860* (Bologna, 1990), pp. 239–43.

29. A. M. Banti, *La nazione del Risorgimento. Parentela, santità e onore alle origini dell'Italia unita* (Turin, 2000), pp. 19–22.

30. D. Mack Smith, *The Making of Italy 1796–1870* (London, 1968), p. 85.

31. R. Romeo, *Cavour e il suo tempo. Vol. 2: 1842–1854* (Rome, 1977), pp. 214–20.

32. A. M. Banti, *Storia della borghesia italiana* (Rome, 1996), p. 81.

33. S. Woolf, *A History of Italy 1700–1860. The Social Constraints of Political Change* (London, 1986), p. 286.

34. V. Zamagni, *Dalla periferia al centro. La seconda rinascita economica dell'Italia: 1861–1981* (Bologna, 1990), pp. 37–9.

35. Woolf, *A History of Italy*, pp. 285–6.

36. Banti, *Storia della borghesia*, pp. 82–3.

37. M. Petrusewicz, *Latifondo. Economia morale e vita materiale in una periferia dell'Ottocento* (Venice, 1989), pp. 185–219. Cf. S. Lupo, 'I proprietari terrieri nel Mezzogiorno', in P. Bevilacqua (ed.), *Storia dell'agricoltura italiana in età contemporanea. Vol. 2: Uomini e classi* (Venice, 1990), pp. 112–18.

38. Romeo, *Cavour e il suo tempo*, Vol. 2, pp. xii–xiv.

39. Ibid., p. 142.

40. L. Serianni, *Storia della lingua italiana* (Bologna, 1990), pp. 17–18.

41. G. Visconti Venosta, *Ricordi di gioventù. Cose vedute o sapute 1847–60* (Milan, 1904), p. 277.

42. E. J. Hobsbawm, *Nations and Nationalism since 1780. Programme, Myth, Reality* (Cambridge, 1990), p. 94.

43. Cf. R. Price, *A Social History of Nineteenth-Century France* (London, 1987), pp. 349–52.

44. T. De Mauro, *Storia linguistica dell'Italia unita* (Rome, 1984), p. 44.

45. Ibid., p. 31.

46. Ibid., p. 32.

47. Banti, *La nazione del Risorgimento*, p. 25 (Olimpia Savio).

48. Stendhal, *Rome, Naples and Florence*, trans. R. Coe (London, 1959), p. 316.

49. Ibid., p. 220.

50. Ibid., pp. 36–7, 51, 56–8, 68, 105, 128.

51. Ibid., p. 93.

52. Ibid., p. 122.

53. Ibid., p. 220.

54. Ibid., p. 453–4.

55. Cf. R. Damiani, *Vita di Leopardi* (Milan, 1992), pp. 41–77.

56. G. Leopardi, *All'Italia, Sopra il monumento di Dante, Ad Angelo Mai, Nelle nozze della sorella Paolina*, in *Opere*, Vol. 1, ed. S. Solmi (Milan, 1956), pp. 3–28.

57. Leopardi, 'Discorso sopra lo stato presente dei costumi degl' italiani', in *Opere*, Vol. 1, pp. 853–4.

58. Leopardi, *Zibaldone*, Vol. 1, ed. R. Damiani (Milan, 1997), p. 1004 (27 July 1821).

6: Apostles and Martyrs

1. C. Dédéyan, *Lamartine et la Toscane* (Geneva, 1981), pp. 36–42.

2. B. Croce, *Pagine sulla guerra* (Bari, 1928), p. 219.

3. G. Garibaldi, *Le memorie di Garibaldi nella redazione definitiva del 1872* (Bologna, 1932), pp. 321–2, 365.

4. G. Pécout, 'Philhellenism in Italy: political friendship and the Italian volunteers in the Mediterranean in the nineteenth century', in *Journal of Modern Italian Studies*, 9, 3 (2004), p. 408.

5. Cf. M. Isabella, 'Italian exiles and British politics before and after 1848', in S. Freitag (ed.), *Exiles from European Revolutions. Refugees in mid-Victorian England* (Oxford, 2003), pp. 61–9.

6. F. Della Peruta, 'Le teorie militari della democrazia risorgimentale', in F. Mazzonis (ed.), *Garibaldi condottiero. Storia, teoria, prassi* (Milan, 1984), pp. 63–4.

7. Ibid., p. 64.

8. G. Montanelli, *Memorie sull'Italia e specialmente sulla Toscana dal 1814 al 1850* (Florence, 1963), p. 7.

9. F. Chabod, *Storia della politica estera italiana dal 1870 al 1896. Vol. 1: Le premesse* (Bari, 1951), p. 16.

10. *Carteggi di Michele Amari*, Vol. 1, ed. A. D'Ancona (Turin, 1896), p. 452 (Amari to Arrivabene, 24 November 1848).

11. Ibid., p. 91 (Amari to Panizzi, 10 March 1843).

12. G. Procacci, *La disfida di Barletta. Tra storia e romanzo* (Milan, 2001), p. 63.

13. Ibid., pp. 56–60.

14. G. Candeloro, *Storia dell'Italia moderna. Vol. 2: Dalla restaurazione alla rivoluzione nazionale 1815–1846* (Milan, 1974), pp. 182–5.

15. R. Sòriga, *Le società segrete, l'emigrazione politica e i primi moti per l'indipendenza. Scritti raccolti e ordinati da Silio Manfredi* (Modena, 1942), p. 261.

16. G. Mazzini, 'La peinture moderne en Italie', in *Scritti editi ed inediti di Giuseppe Mazzini*, Vol. 21 (Imola, 1915), pp. 292, 301.

17. M. C. Gozzoli and F. Mazzocca (eds.), *Hayez* (Milan, 1983), p. 114.

18. Mazzini, 'La peinture moderne en Italie', pp. 301–3.

19. A. Lyttelton, 'Creating a national past: history, myth and image in the Risorgimento', in A. Russell Ascoli and K. von Henneberg, *Making and Remaking Italy. The Cultivation of National Identity around the Risorgimento* (Oxford, 2001), p. 35.

20. P. Barocchi, F. Nicolodi and S. Pinto (eds.), *Romanticismo storico* (Florence, 1974), p. 30.

21. F. Mazzocca, *Hayez dal mito al bacio* (Venice, 1998), p. 108.

22. S. Mastellone, *Mazzini e la 'Giovine Italia' (1831–1834)*, Vol. 1 (Pisa, 1960), pp. 89, 117–18.

23. D. Mack Smith, *The Making of Italy, 1796–1870* (London, 1968), pp. 48–9.

24. E. E. Y. Hales, *Mazzini and the Secret Societies* (New York, 1956), p. 26.

25. Mastellone, *Mazzini e la 'Giovine Italia'*, Vol. 1, pp. 334–8.

26. D. Mack Smith, *Mazzini* (New Haven, 1994), p. 156.

27. Hales, *Mazzini and the Secret Societies*, p. 188.

28. Ibid., p. 192.

29. G. Mazzini, *Della Giovine Italia* (1832), in *Scritti editi ed inediti di Giuseppe Mazzini*, Vol. 20 (Imola, 1907), p. 99.

30. L. Salvatorelli, *Il pensiero politico italiano. Dal 1700 al 1870* (Turin, 1949), p. 261.

31. A. M. Banti, *Il Risorgimento italiano* (Rome, 2004), p. 66.

32. A. Giardina and A. Vauchez, *Il mito di Roma. Da Carlo Magno a Mussolini* (Rome, 2000), p. 169.

33. N. Costa, *Quel che vidi e quel che intesi*, ed. G. Costa (Milan, 1983), p. 121.

34. Mack Smith, *Mazzini*, p. 5.

35. A. Scirocco, *L'Italia del Risorgimento 1800–1860* (Bologna, 1990), pp. 184–6.

36. Mastellone, *Mazzini e la 'Giovine Italia'*, Vol. 2, pp. 73–4, 82–3.

37. Hales, *Mazzini and the Secret Societies*, pp. 163, 166, 173.

38. E. Morelli, *L'Inghilterra di Mazzini* (Rome, 1965), pp. 14–15.

39. Mack Smith, *Mazzini*, p. 24.

40. Gozzoli and Mazzocca (eds.), *Hayez*, p. 98.

41. G. Rumi, *Gioberti* (Bologna, 1999), pp. 37–8, 47, 50.

42. L. Settembrini, *Ricordanze della mia vita*, ed. M. Themelly (Milan, 1961), pp. 68–71.

43. P. Alatri, 'Benedetto Musolino, biografia di un rivoluzionario europeo', in *Benedetto*

Musolino. Il Mezzogiorno nel Risorgimento tra rivoluzione e utopia. Atti del convegno storico in Pizzo 15/16 novembre 1985 (Milan, 1988), p. 26; Mack Smith, *Mazzini*, p. 86.

44. C. M. Lovett, *The Democratic Movement in Italy, 1830–1876* (Cambridge, 1982), p. 126.
45. Montanelli, *Memorie sull'Italia*, p. 156.
46. Mack Smith, *Mazzini*, p. 41.
47. L. Carci, *La spedizione e il processo dei Fratelli Bandiera. Con una appendice di documenti* (Modena, 1939), pp. 12–13, 89–90, 100.
48. Ibid., pp. 130–33.
49. G. Mazzini, *Ricordi dei fratelli Bandiera* (1844), in *Scritti editi ed inediti di Giuseppe Mazzini*, Vol. 31 (Imola, 1921), pp. 69–70.
50. Carci, *La spedizione e il processo dei Fratelli Bandiera*, pp. 28–35, 158–66.
51. Ibid., pp. 157–8.
52. Ibid., pp. 49–59; G. Ricciardi, *Martirologio italiano dal 1792 al 1847* (Florence, 1860), pp. 231–3.
53. Ricciardi, ibid., p. 233.

7: Educators and Reformers

1. A. Tennyson, 'Locksley Hall', in *Alfred Tennyson: In Memoriam, Maud and Other Poems* (London, 1977), pp. 58–64.
2. R. Romanelli, *Italia liberale (1861–1900)* (Bologna, 1979), p. 119.
3. A. M. Banti, *Storia della borghesia italiana* (Rome, 1996), p. 181.
4. G. Montroni, *La società italiana dall'unificazione alla Grande Guerra* (Rome–Bari, 2002), pp. 135–40.
5. S. Woolf, *A History of Italy 1700–1860. The Social Constraints of Political Change* (London, 1986), p. 333.
6. A. Scirocco, *L'Italia del Risorgimento 1800–1860* (Bologna, 1990), pp. 213–15.
7. Ibid., pp. 216–17.
8. R. Romeo, *Cavour e il suo tempo. Vol. 2: 1842–1854* (Rome, 1977), pp. 219–20.
9. D. Bertoni Jovine, *I periodici popolari del Risorgimento. Vol. 1: Il periodo prerisorgimentale (1818–1847). Le rivoluzioni (1847–1849)* (Milan, 1959), pp. xi–xii, xv–xvi, lviii–lx, 233–56.
10. M. Isnenghi, 'Il ruralismo nella cultura italiana', in P. Bevilacqua (ed.), *Storia dell'agricoltura italiana in età contemporanea. Vol. 3: Mercati e istituzioni* (Venice, 1991), p. 878; M. Berengo, 'Appunti su Luigi Alessandro Parravicini. La metodica austriaca della Resaurazione', in A. Mastrocinque (ed.), *Omaggio a Piero Treves* (Padua, 1983), p. 1.
11. Isnenghi, 'Il ruralismo nella cultura italiana', p. 883.
12. *Monumenti di Giardino Puccini* (Pistoia, 1845), p. 16.
13. Ibid., p. 533.
14. C. Mazzi and C. Sisi, 'La collezione di Niccolò Puccini', in *Cultura dell'Ottocento a Pistoia. La collezione Puccini* (Florence, 1977), p. 16.
15. S. von Falkenhausen, 'L'immagine del "popolo": dal centralismo al totalitarismo in Italia e in Germania', in O. Janz, P. Schiera and H. Siegrist (eds.), *Centralismo e federalismo tra Otto e Novecento. Italia e Germania a confronto* (Bologna, 1997), p. 196.
16. P. Luciani, 'Le committenze di Niccolò Puccini', in *Cultura dell'Ottocento a Pistoia*, pp. 25–6.
17. Bertoni Jovine, *I periodici popolari del Risorgimento*, pp. 42–3.
18. A. Gamberai, *Memorie storiche della vita di Niccolò Puccini* (no place, no date), pp. 7–8.
19. C. M. Lovett, *The Democratic Movement in Italy, 1830–1876* (Cambridge, 1982), p. 51.
20. C. Sorba, *Teatri. L'Italia del melodramma nel età del Risorgimento* (Bologna, 2001), pp. 96–8, 118, 145–6.
21. Ibid., pp. 26, 33–4, 40, 45.
22. C. Sorba, 'Il Risorgimento in musica: l'opera lirica nei teatri del 1848', in A. M. Banti

and R. Bizzocchi (eds.), *Immagini della nazione nell'Italia del Risorgimento* (Rome, 2002), p. 141; C. Sorba, ' "Or sia patria il mio solo pensier". Opera lirica e nazionalismo nell'Italia risorgimentale', in F. Tarozzi and G. Vecchio (eds.), *Gli italiani e il tricolore. Patriottismo, identità nazionale e fratture sociali lungo due secoli di storia* (Bologna, 1999), p. 187.

23. C. Sorba, 'La patria nei libretti d'opera verdiani degli anni '40', in P. Ballini (ed.), *La rivoluzione liberale e le nazioni divise* (Venice, 2000), pp. 345–6.

24. Sorba, 'Il Risorgimento in musica', p. 136.

25. J. Rosselli, *The Life of Verdi* (Cambridge, 2000), p. 77.

26. G. Mazzini, *Filosofia della musica* (1836), in *Edizione nazionale degli scritti di Giuseppe Mazzini*, Vol. 8 (Imola, 1910), pp. 131, 141, 150.

27. Sorba, 'Il Risorgimento in musica', p. 139.

28. Ibid., p. 145.

29. L. Settembrini, *Ricordanze della mia vita*, ed. M. Themelly (Milan, 1961), p. 163.

30. Scirocco, *L'Italia del Risorgimento*, pp. 223–4.

31. V. Gioberti, *Il rinnovamento civile d'Italia*, Vol. 1 (Milan, 1915), pp. 65–6.

32. Ibid., p. 55.

33. Ibid., Vol. 4, pp. 164–6, 192.

34. R. Romanelli, 'Nazione e costituzione nell'opinione liberale avanti il '48', in Ballini (ed.), *La rivoluzione liberale e le nazioni divise*, p. 276.

35. C. Balbo, *Le speranze d'Italia* (Turin, 1948), pp. 62–95, 141–2, 264–8.

36. Scirocco, *L'Italia del Risorgimento*, p. 225.

37. Balbo, *Le speranze d'Italia*, p. 133.

38. Ibid., p. 200.

39. Ibid., pp. 145–50.

40. A. M. Banti and M. Mondini, 'Da Novara a Custoza: culture militari e discorso nazionale tra Risorgimento e Unità', in W. Barberis (ed.), *Storia d'Italia. Annali 18: Guerra e pace* (Turin, 2002), p. 432.

41. M. d'Azeglio, *Epistolario (1819–1866). Vol. 2: 1841–1845*, ed. G. Virlogeux (Turin, 1989), p. 149.

42. M. d'Azeglio, *I miei ricordi* (Turin, 1949), pp. 553–4.

43. M. d'Azeglio, *Raccolta degli scritti politici* (Turin, 1866), pp. 13, 72–5.

44. G. Pallavicino, *Memorie di Giorgio Pallavicino pubblicate per cura della moglie. Vol. 2: 1848–1852* (Turin, 1886) p. 435.

45. Romanelli, 'Nazione e costituzione nell'opinione liberale avanti il '48', p. 304.

46. Ibid., pp. 285–6.

47. Ibid., p. 282.

48. G. Durando, *Della nazionalità italiana. Saggio politico-militare* (Lausanne, 1846), pp. 87–91, 176–80.

8: Revolution, 1846–9

1. G. Montanelli, *Memorie sull'Italia e specialmente sulla Toscana dal 1814 al 1850* (Florence, 1963), p. 150.

2. Ibid., p. 154.

3. C. Sorba, 'Il Risorgimento in musica: l'opera lirica nei teatri del 1848', in A. M. Banti and R. Bizzocchi (eds.), *Immagini della nazione nell'Italia del Risorgimento* (Rome, 2002), p. 143.

4. G. Mazzini, 'A Pio IX, Pontefico Massimo' (8 September 1847), in *Scritti editi ed inediti di Giuseppe Mazzini*, Vol. 36 (Imola, 1922), p. 232.

5. A. Scirocco, *Garibaldi. Battaglie, amori, ideali di un cittadino del mondo* (Rome–Bari, 2001), p. 135.

6. Cf. L. Settembrini, *Ricordanze della mia vita*, ed. M. Themelly (Milan, 1961), p. 34.

7. M. d'Azeglio, *Raccolta degli scritti politici* (Turin, 1866), pp. 213, 216, 247–8 ('Proposta di un programma per l'opinione nazionale italiana', July 1847).

8. Sorba, 'Il Risorgimento in musica', p. 148.
9. Montanelli, *Memorie sull'Italia*, pp. 259–60.
10. Ibid., p. 261.
11. R. Romeo, *Cavour e il suo tempo. Vol. 2: 1842–1854* (Rome, 1977), p. 314.
12. R. Marshall, *Massimo d'Azeglio. An Artist in Politics 1798–1866* (Oxford, 1966), p. 118.
13. M. Minghetti, *Miei ricordi. Vol. 1: Dalla puerizia alle prime prove nella vita pubblica (1818–1848)* (Turin, 1889), pp. 365–7.
14. M. d'Azeglio, *Lettere di Massimo d'Azeglio a Giuseppe Torelli*, ed. C. Paoli (Milan, 1870), p. 327 (to wife, 16 April 1848).
15. A. Scirocco, *L'Italia del Risorgimento 1800–1860* (Bologna, 1990), p. 304.
16. D'Azeglio, *Raccolta degli scritti polittici*, p. 475 ('Timori e speranze').
17. Ibid., pp. 432 ('L'onore dell' Austria e l'onore dell'Italia', 16 August 1848), 468–73, 501–4 ('Timori e speranze').
18. Ibid., p. 540 ('Ai suoi elettori', 8 January 1849).
19. G. Asproni, *Diario politico 1855–1876. Vol. 1: 1855–1857*, eds. C. Sole and T. Orrù (Milan, 1974), p. 584.
20. A. Ricci, *La repubblica* (Bologna, 2001), p. 94 (Cernuschi to Cattaneo).
21. Scirocco, *Garibaldi*, p. 149.
22. G. Garibaldi, *Le memorie di Garibaldi nella redazione definitive del 1872* (Bologna, 1932), p. 502.
23. Ibid., p. 624.
24. C. Osborne, *The Complete Operas of Verdi* (London, 1973), p. 201.
25. C. M. Lovett, *The Democratic Movement in Italy, 1830–1876* (Cambridge, 1982), p. 138.
26. Ricci, *La repubblica*, pp. 88–91.
27. *Goffredo Mameli. La vita e gli scritti. Vol 2: Gli scritti*, ed. A. Codignola (Venice, 1927), p. 370 (Mameli to Girolamo Boccardo, 29 August 1848).
28. Montanelli, *Memorie sull'Italia*, pp. 459–60.

9: Piedmont and Cavour

1. B. Tobia, 'Riti e simboli di due capitali (1846–1921)', in V. Vidotto (ed.), *Storia di Roma dall'antichità a oggi. Roma capitale* (Rome and Bari, 2002), pp. 372–3.
2. F. Mazzonis, *La monarchia e il Risorgimento* (Bologna, 2003), p. 93.
3. L. Cafagna, *Cavour* (Bologna, 1999), p. 84.
4. V. Gioberti, *Del rinnovamento civile d'Italia*, Vol. 3 (Milan, 1915), pp. 151–2, 157–61, 212–14, 239–44.
5. E. Casanova, 'L'emigrazione siciliana dal 1849 al 1851', in *Rassegna storica del Risorgimento*, XI (1924), pp. 841–3.
6. C. M. Lovett, *The Democratic Movement in Italy, 1830–1876* (Cambridge, 1982), p. 176.
7. D. Mack Smith, *Mazzini* (New Haven and London, 1994), p. 83.
8. S. Woolf, *A History of Italy 1700–1860. The Social Constraints of Political Change* (London, 1979), p. 419.
9. H. Adams, *The Education of Henry Adams. An Autobiography* (London, 1918), pp. 92–3.
10. H. Rudman, *Italian Nationalism and English Letters* (London, 1940), pp. 97–8.
11. Mack Smith, *Mazzini*, pp. 95–6.
12. E. Morelli, *L'Inghilterra di Mazzini* (Rome, 1965), pp. 40–45, 79–82, 108–12, 187.
13. Ibid., pp. 8–9.
14. S. Patriarca, 'Patriottismo, nazione e italianità nella statistica del Risorgimento', in A. M. Banti and R. Bizzocchi (eds.), *Immagini della nazione nell'Italia del Risorgimento* (Rome, 2002), p. 127.

15. G. Aliberti, *La resa di Cavour: il carattere nazionale italiano tra mito e cronaca, 1820–1976* (Florence, 2000), p. xvii.

16. *Carteggi di Michele Amari,* Vol. 2, ed. A. D'Ancona, p. 23 (Amari to Giuseppe Ricciardi, 11 October 1853).

17. R. Romeo, *Cavour e il suo tempo. Vol. 1: 1810–1842* (Bari, 1969), p. 241.

18. Cafagna, *Cavour,* p. 41.

19. D. Mack Smith, *Cavour* (London, 1985), p. 65.

20. R. Romeo, *Cavour e il suo tempo. Vol. 2: 1842–1854* (Rome–Bari, 1977), pp. 617–23.

21. D. Mack Smith, *Vittorio Emanuele II* (Rome–Bari, 1975), p. 353.

22. Ibid., p. 356.

23. R. Grew, *A Sterner Plan for Italian Unity. The Italian National Society in the Risorgimento* (Princeton, 1963), pp. 153–6.

24. Ibid., pp. 140–41, 151.

25. Cafagna, *Cavour,* p. 194; N. Moe, *The View from Vesuvius. Italian Culture and the Southern Question* (Berkeley, 2002), pp. 87–120, 139–53, 158–64.

26. R. Romeo, *Cavour e il suo tempo. Vol. 3: 1854–1861* (Rome–Bari, 1984), pp. 333–6.

27. Cf. N. Rosselli, *Carlo Pisacane nel Risorgimento italiano* (Turin, 1932), pp. 315–41.

28. C. Pisacane, 'Seconda dichiarazione a bordo del "Cagliari" ' (28 June 1857), in *Opere complete di Carlo Pisacane,* Vol. 3, ed. A. Romano (Milan, 1964), p. 364.

29. C. Pisacane, 'Testamento politico' (24 June 1857), in ibid., pp. 353–9.

30. L. Mercantini, *La spigolatrice di Sapri,* in *Poeti minori dell'Ottocento,* Vol. 2, eds. L. Baldacci and G. Innamorati (Milan, 1963), pp. 1079–80.

10: Unity, 1858–60

1. F. Orsini, *The Austrian Dungeons in Italy. A Narrative of Fifteen Months' Imprisonment and Final Escape from the Fortress of S. Giorgio,* trans. J. M. White (London, 1856).

2. M. Packe, *The Bombs of Orsini* (London, 1957), pp. 250–61, 272–3.

3. R. Romeo, *Cavour e il suo tempo. Vol. 3: 1854–1861* (Rome–Bari, 1984), p. 340.

4. C. Cavour, *Epistolario. Vol. 15: 1858 (January–July),* ed. C. Pischedda (Florence, 1998), pp. 520–30 (Cavour to Victor Emmanuel II, 24 July 1858).

5. D. Mack Smith, *Cavour* (London, 1985), p. 143.

6. J. Rosselli, *The Life of Verdi* (Cambridge, 2000), p. 77.

7. F. Nicolodi, 'Il teatro lirico e il suo pubblico', in S. Soldani and G. Turi (eds.), *Fare gli italiani. Scuola e cultura nell'Italia contemporanea. Vol. 1: La nascita dello Stato nazionale* (Bologna, 1993), pp. 257–8.

8. R. Villari, *Cospirazione e rivolta* (Messina, 1881), pp. 303–6, 373–80.

9. Romeo, *Cavour e il suo tempo,* Vol. 3, p. 515.

10. Ibid., p. 527.

11. Ibid., p. 538.

12. Mack Smith, *Cavour,* p. 163.

13. R. Martucci, *L'invenzione dell'Italia unita 1855–1864* (Milan, 1999), pp. 54–61.

14. Romeo, *Cavour e il suo tempo,* Vol. 3, p. 576.

15. Martucci, *L'invenzione dell'Italia unita,* p. 94 (Cavour to Farini, 3 July 1859).

16. Ibid., p. 70.

17. Mack Smith, *Cavour,* pp. 169–70.

18. L. Firpo (ed.), *Henri Dunant e le origini della Croce Rossa* (Turin, 1979), pp. xvii–xxx, 27–31.

19. *Il carteggio Cavour–Nigra dal 1858 al 1861. Vol. 2: La campagna diplomatica e militare del 1859* (Bologna, 1961), pp. 291–2.

20. A. Saffi, *Ricordi e scritti di Aurelio Saffi. Vol. 6: 1860–1* (Florence, 1901), p. 33.

21. Cf. D. Mack Smith, *Victor Emanuel, Cavour and the Risorgimento* (Oxford, 1971), pp. 256–9, 264.

22. F. Guardione, 'La spedizione di Rosalino Pilo nei ricordi di Giovanni Corrao', in *Rassegna storica del Risorgimento*, IV (1917), p. 822, n. 6.

23. L. Riall, 'Storie d'amore, di libertà e d'avventura: la costruzione del mito garibaldino intorno al 1848–49', in A. M. Banti and R. Bizzocchi (eds.), *Immagini della nazione nell'Italia del Risorgimento* (Rome, 2002), pp. 161–71.

24. F. Crispi, *I Mille, da documenti dall'archivio Crispi* (Milan, 1911), pp. 93–5.

25. C. Duggan, *Francesco Crispi. From Nation to Nationalism* (Oxford, 2002), pp. 179–85.

26. L. Riall, *Sicily and the Unification of Italy. Liberal Policy and Local Power, 1859–1866* (Oxford, 1998), pp. 71–4.

27. Crispi, *I Mille*, p. 193.

28. A. Scirocco, *Garibaldi. Battaglie, amori, ideali di un cittadino del mondo* (Rome–Bari, 2001), p. 289.

29. Romeo, *Cavour e il suo tempo*, Vol. 3, p. 762.

30. A. Mario, *La camicia rossa* (Venice, 1977), pp. 209–10. Cf. G. C. Abba, *Da Quarto al Volturno. Noterelle d'uno dei Mille* (Bologna, 1956), pp. 257–8.

31. Mack Smith, *Victor Emanuel, Cavour and the Risorgimento*, p. 253.

32. Duggan, *Francesco Crispi*, p. 598 (Costantino Nigra, 7 August 1890).

33. C. Tivaroni, *L'Italia degli italiani*, Vol. 3 (Turin, 1897), pp. 136, 207.

11: The New State

1. M. G. De Lucia, *Brigandage and Political Unrest in the District of Cerreto: The Case of Pontelandolfo, August 1861*, unpublished MPhil, University of Kent at Canterbury, 2001, pp. 51–2, 61.

2. Ibid., p. 51; G. Pescosolido, 'L'economia e la vita materiale', in G. Sabbatucci and V. Vidotto (eds.), *Storia d'Italia. Vol. 1: Le premesse dell'Unità. Dalla fine del Settecento al 1861* (Rome–Bari, 1994), pp. 22–3.

3. V. Zamagni, *Dalla periferia al centro. La seconda rinascita economica dell'Italia: 1861–1981* (Bologna, 1990), p. 44.

4. De Lucia, *Brigandage and Political Unrest*, pp. 52–6.

5. Ibid., pp. 66–7.

6. Ibid., pp. 67, 70–71, 119.

7. R. Martucci, *L'invenzione dell'Italia unita 1855–1864* (Milan, 1999), pp. 208–20.

8. Cf. F. Molfese, *Storia del brigantaggio dopo l'Unità* (Milan, 1964), pp. 63–6, 99–100.

9. De Lucia, *Brigandage and Political Unrest*, pp. 129, 139–41, 168, 171–2.

10. Cf. G. Di Fiore, *I vinti del Risorgimento. Storia e storie di chi combatté per i Borbone di Napoli* (Turin, 2004), p. 256; A. De Jaco (ed.), *Il brigantaggio meridionale. Cronaca inedita dell'Unità d'Italia* (Rome, 1969), pp. 190–92.

11. De Lucia, *Brigandage and Political Unrest*, pp. 150–53, 162–6.

12. Cf. C. Melegari, *Cenni sul brigantaggio. Ricordi di un antico bersagliere* (Turin, 1897), pp. 12–13, 17–19.

13. S. Lupo, 'Il grande brigantaggio', in W. Barberis (ed.), *Storia d'Italia. Annali 18: Guerra e pace* (Turin, 2002), p. 468.

14. De Lucia, *Brigandage and Political Unrest*, p. 159.

15. Ibid., p. 161.

16. Di Fiore, *I vinti del Risorgimento*, p. 339.

17. Cf. C. Levi, *Christ Stopped at Eboli*, trans. F. Frenaye (London, 1982), pp. 135–7.

18. De Lucia, *Brigandage and Political Unrest*, p. 169 (*Gazzetta di Torino*, 15 August 1861). Cf. P. Calà Ulloa, *Lettres napolitaines* (Paris, 1864), pp. 84–93.

19. Martucci, *L'invenzione dell'Italia unita*, p. 323 (parliamentary session of 20 November 1861).

20. Lupo, 'Il grande brigantaggio', p. 489.

21. *Carteggi di Camillo Cavour. La liberazione del Mezzogiorno e la formazione del Regno*

d'Italia. Vol. 3 (October–November 1860) (Bologna, 1952), p. 208 (Farini to Cavour, 27 October 1860).

22. Mack Smith, *Cavour*, p. 412.

23. C. Petraccone, *Le due civiltà. Settentrionali e meridionali nella storia d'Italia* (Rome–Bari, 2000), pp. 45–6.

24. N. Moe, *The View from Vesuvius. Italian Culture and the Southern Question* (Berkeley, 2002), pp. 172–3. Cf. N. Moe, ' "Altro che Italia!" Il Sud dei piemontesi (1860–61)', in *Meridiana. Rivista di storia e scienze sociali,* 15 (September 1992), pp. 78–84.

25. Moe, *The View from Vesuvius*, pp. 175–6; Petraccone, *Le due civiltà*, p. 31.

26. Moe, *The View from Vesuvius*, p. 183.

27. Molfese, *Storia del brigantaggio dopo l'Unità*, pp. 75–80.

28. I. Nievo, *Lettere garibaldine*, ed. A. Ciceri (Turin, 1961), p. 89 (29 October 1860).

29. Lupo, 'Il grande brigantaggio', p. 494 (to De Sanctis, August 1861).

30. Cf. Martucci, *L'invenzione dell'Italia unita*, p. 313; Lupo, 'Il grande brigantaggio', p. 494; L. Del Boca, *Indietro Savoia. Storia controcorrente del Risorgimento* (Casale Monferrato, 2003), p. 222.

31. F. De Sanctis, *La giovinezza*, ed. G. Savarese (Turin, 1961), p. 10.

32. Ibid., pp. 432, 477, 537.

33. F. De Sanctis, *Il Mezzogiorno e lo Stato unitario*, ed. F. Ferri (Turin, 1960), pp. 80–81 (16 October 1860).

34. Cf. R. Romanelli, 'Centralismo e autonomie', in R. Romanelli (ed.), *Storia dello stato italiano dall'Unità a oggi* (Rome, 1995), pp. 131–7; R. Romeo, *Cavour e il suo tempo. Vol. 3: 1854–1861* (Rome–Bari, 1984), pp. 859–63.

35. A. Scirocco, *L'Italia del Risorgimento 1800–1860* (Bologna, 1990), pp. 448–9.

36. A. Bertani, *Discorsi parlamentari di Agostino Bertani pubblicati per deliberazione della Camera dei Deputati* (Rome, 1913), p. 70 (19 June 1863).

37. *Il Mondo illustrato* (Turin), 23 February 1861.

38. F. Crispi, *Discorsi parlamentari di Francesco Crispi*, Vol. 1 (Rome, 1915), p. 11 (17 April 1861).

39. G. Barbèra, *Memorie di un editore. Pubblicate dai figli* (Florence, 1883), pp. 342–3.

40. A. C. De Meis, *Il sovrano. Saggio di filosofia politica con riferenza all'Italia*, ed. B. Croce (Bari, 1927), p. 15.

41. A. M. Banti, *La nazione del Risorgimento. Parentela, santità e onore alle origini dell'Italia unita* (Turin, 2000), p. 173; R. Leydi, *Canti sociali italiani. Vol. 1: Canti giacobini, repubblicani, antirisorgimentali, di protesta postunitaria contro la guerra e il servizio militare* (Milan, 1963), p. 112.

42. D. Mack Smith, 'Britain and the Italian Risorgimento', in M. McLaughlin (ed.), *Britain and Italy from Romanticism to Modernism* (Oxford, 2000), pp. 24–6; H. Rudman, *Italian Nationalism and English Letters* (London, 1940), pp. 296–305.

43. F. Venturi, 'L'immagine di Garibaldi in Russia all'epoca della liberazione dei servi', in *Rassegna storica toscana,* 6 (4) (October–December 1960), p. 313.

44. D. Mack Smith, *Mazzini* (New Haven and London, 1994), p. 159.

45. George Eliot, *Romola*, ed. D. Barrett (London, 1996), pp. 581–3.

46. Rudman, *Italian Nationalism and English Letters*, pp. 138–41.

47. Romeo, *Cavour e il suo tempo*, Vol. 3, p. 801.

48. A. M. Banti and D. Mondini, 'Da Novara a Custoza: culture militari e discorso nazionale tra Risorgimento e Unità', in W. Barberis (ed.), *Storia d'Italia. Annali 18: Guerra e pace* (Turin, 2002), p. 436.

49. Romeo, *Cavour e il suo tempo*, Vol. 3, p. 917.

50. C. Duggan, *Francesco Crispi. From Nation to Nationalism* (Oxford, 2002), p. 223.

51. J. Rosselli, *The Life of Verdi* (Cambridge, 2000), p. 123.

52. G. Verdi, *Letters of Giuseppe Verdi. Selected, Translated and Edited by Charles Osborne* (London, 1971), p. 126 (Verdi to mayor of Borgo San Donnino, 6 January 1861).

53. F. Della Peruta, 'Verdi e il Risorgimento', in F. Della Peruta, *Uomini e idee dell'Ottocento italiano* (Milan, 2002), p. 232.
54. Cf. Rosselli, *Life of Verdi*, pp. 82–5, 93, 128–31.
55. F. Chabod, *Storia della politica estera italiana dal 1870 al 1896. Vol. 1: Le premesse* (Bari, 1951), pp. 512–28.
56. A. Mattone, 'I miti fondatori del parlamentarismo italiano', in L. Violante (ed.), *Storia d'Italia. Annali 17: Il parlamento* (Turin, 2001), pp. 18–20.
57. G. Carducci, 'Il parlamento', in *Edizione nazionale delle opere di Giosuè Carducci. Vol. 4: Odi barbare e rime e ritmi* (Bologna, 1944), pp. 259–65.
58. F. De Sanctis, *I partiti e l'educazione della nuova Italia*, ed. N. Cortese (Turin, 1970), p. 516.
59. F. Petruccelli della Gattina, *I moribondi del Palazzo Carignano* (Milan, 1862).
60. F. Cammarano, 'Nazionalizzazione della politica e politicizzazione della nazione. I dilemmi della classe dirigente nell'Italia liberale', in M. Meriggi and P. Schiera (eds.), *Dalla città alla nazione. Borghesie ottocentesche in Italia e in Germania* (Bologna, 1993), pp. 142–5.
61. De Sanctis, *Il Mezzogiorno e lo Stato unitario*, pp. 201, 215 (2 July 1864).

12: The Road to Rome, 1861–70

1. R. Romeo, *Cavour e il suo tempo. Vol. 3: 1854–1861* (Rome–Bari, 1984), pp. 908–9.
2. M. d'Azeglio, 'Questioni urgenti. Pensieri', in M. d'Azeglio, *Scritti e discorsi politici. Vol. 3: 1853–65* (ed. M. De Rubris) (Florence, 1938), p. 374.
3. F. Chabod, *Storia della politica estera italiana dal 1870 al 1896. Vol. 1: Le premesse* (Bari, 1951), p. 320.
4. F. Curato, 'Aspetti nazionalistici della politica estera italiana dal 1870 al 1914', in R. Lill and F. Valsecchi (eds.), *Il nazionalismo in Italia e Germania fino alla Prima guerra mondiale* (Bologna, 1983), p. 17.
5. Chabod, *Storia della politica estera italiana*, p. 318.
6. E. Gentile, *La grande Italia. Ascesa e declino del mito della nazione nel ventesimo secolo* (Milan, 1997), p. 48.
7. Chabod, *Storia della politica estera italiana*, p. 203.
8. A. Scirocco, *Garibaldi. Battaglie, amori, ideali di un cittadino del mondo* (Rome–Bari, 2001), p. 311.
9. D. Mack Smith, *Vittorio Emanuele II* (Rome–Bari, 1975), pp. 169–77.
10. Scirocco, *Garibaldi. Battaglie, amori, ideali*, pp. 322–3; G. Garibaldi, *Le memorie di Garibaldi nella redazione definitiva del 1872* (Bologna, 1932), pp. 496–9.
11. D. Pick, *Rome or Death. The Obsessions of General Garibaldi* (London, 2005), p. 101.
12. C. Duggan, *Fascism and the Mafia* (New Haven and London, 1989), pp. 24–7.
13. Cf. A. M. Banti, *La nazione del Risorgimento. Parentela, santità e onore alle origini dell'Italia unita* (Turin, 2000), pp. 141–2.
14. M. d'Azeglio, *Lettere di Massimo d'Azeglio a sua moglie Luisa Blondel*, ed. G. Carcano (Milan, 1870), p. 523 (25 October 1864).
15. S. Sepe, 'Amministrazione e "nazionalizzazione". Il ruolo della burocrazia statale nella costruzione dello Stato unitario (1861–1900)', in M. Meriggi and P. Schiera (eds.), *Dalla città alla nazione. Borghesie ottocentesche in Italia e in Germania* (Bologna, 1993), pp. 310–35.
16. M. d'Azeglio, *Lettere di Massimo d'Azeglio a Giuseppe Torelli*, ed. C. Paoli (Milan, 1870), p. 440 (3 December 1864).
17. M. d'Azeglio, *I miei ricordi* (Turin, 1949), p. 38.
18. D'Azeglio, *Lettere di Massimo d'Azeglio a Giuseppe Torelli*, p. 212 (8 February 1865).
19. F. D'Amoja, 'La sinistra e i problemi di politica estera', in *Rassegna storica toscana*, XI, 2 (1965), p. 61.
20. F. Crispi, *Discorsi parlamentari di Francesco Crispi*, Vol. 1 (Rome, 1915), pp. 716–17 (8 May 1866).

21. F. De Sanctis, *Un viaggio elettorale*, ed. N. Cortese (Turin, 1968), p. 391 (31 May 1866).
22. Ibid., p. 400 (23 June 1866).
23. E. De Amicis, *La vita militare* (Florence, 1869), p. 384.
24. S. Sonnino, *Diario 1866–1912*, Vol. 1, ed. B. Brown (Rome–Bari, 1972), p. 43 (20 June 1866).
25. Ibid., p. 9 (17 May 1866).
26. A. Pollio, *Custoza (1866)* (Rome, 1925), p. 32.
27. Ibid., pp. 138, 233, 257, 315, 319.
28. Mack Smith, *Vittorio Emanuele II*, pp. 212–13, 253–4.
29. I. Massabò Ricci, 'L'Alta Corte di giustizia e il processo Persano', in L. Violante (ed.), *Storia d'Italia. Annali 17: Il parlamento* (Turin, 2001), p. 1100.
30. Ibid., pp. 1117–22.
31. C. Duggan, *Francesco Crispi. From Nation to Nationalism* (Oxford, 2002), p. 283 (Crispi to Bertani, 12 August 1866).
32. G. Fortunato, *Carteggio. Vol: 1: 1865–1911*, ed. E. Gentile (Rome–Bari, 1978), pp. 234–5 (Fortunato to Abba, 6 August 1910).
33. P. Villari, 'Di chi è la colpa? O sia la pace e la guerra', in P. Villari, *Le lettere meridionali e altri scritti sulla questione sociale in Italia* (Naples, 1979), pp. 113, 138.
34. E. Pantano, *Memorie. Dai rintocchi della Gancia a quelli di S. Giusto. Vol. 1 (1860–70)* (Bologna, 1933), pp. 232–6; M. Da Passano (ed.), *I moti di Palermo del 1866. Verbali della Commissione parlamentare di inchiesta* (Rome, 1981), p. 103.
35. Duggan, *Fascism and the Mafia*, pp. 29–30.
36. F. Petruccelli della Gattina, *Storia d'Italia dal 1866 al 1880* (Naples, 1882), pp. 46, 55–6; G. Candeloro, *Storia dell'Italia moderna. Vol. 5: La costruzione dello Stato unitario (1860–1870)* (Milan, 1968), p. 346.
37. F. Crispi, *Carteggi politici inediti di Francesco Crispi (1860–1900), estratti dal suo archivio, ordinati e annotati da T. Palamenghi Crispi* (Rome, 1912), p. 248 (27 September 1867).
38. G. Finali, *Memorie* (Faenza, 1955), p. 346.
39. G. Carducci, *Canto dell'Italia che va in Campidoglio*, in *Edizione nazionale delle opere di Giosuè Carducci. Vol. 3: Giambi ed epodi e rime nuove* (Bologna, 1944), pp. 85–8.
40. G. Carducci, 'Per Vincenzo Caldesi otto mesi dopo la sua morte', in ibid., pp 76–7.

13: The Threat From the South, 1870–85

1. F. De Sanctis, *Storia della letteratura italiana*, Vol. 2, ed. N. Gallo (Turin, 1962), p. 612.
2. Ibid., pp. 606–7.
3. Ibid., pp. 974–5.
4. Cf. G. Farrell-Vinay, *Povertà e politica nell'Ottocento. Le opere pie nello Stato liberale* (Turin, 1997), pp. 32–60, 95–124.
5. E. Sereni, *Il capitalismo nelle campagne, 1860–1900* (Turin, 1968), pp. 142–5.
6. Cf. V. Zamagni, *Dalla periferia al centro. La seconda rinascita economica dell'Italia: 1861–1981* (Bologna, 1990), pp. 219–29.
7. G. Candeloro, *Storia dell'Italia moderna. Vol. 5: La costruzione dello Stato unitario (1860–1870)* (Milan, 1978), p. 253.
8. L. Franchetti and S. Sonnino, *Inchiesta in Sicilia. Vol. 2: I contadini* (Florence, 1974), p. 184.
9. C. Duggan, *Francesco Crispi. From Nation to Nationalism* (Oxford, 2002), pp. 344–5.
10. Cf. A. Capatti, A. De Bernardi and A. Varni (eds.), *Storia d'Italia. Annali 13: L'alimentazione*, pp. xlix–liv.
11. G. Montroni, *La società italiana dall'unificazione alla Grande Guerra* (Rome–Bari, 2002), pp. 21–2.

12. Cf. M. Petrusewicz, *Come il Meridione divenne una Questione. Rappresentazioni del Sud prima e dopo il Quarantotto* (Catanzaro, 1998), pp. 35–8, 135–6, 144–50.

13. C. Duggan, *Fascism and the Mafia* (New Haven and London, 1989), pp. 33–6.

14. L. Franchetti and S. Sonnino, *Inchiesta in Sicilia. Vol. 1: Condizioni politiche e amministrative* (Florence, 1974), pp. 5–7, 23–5, 31–3, 92, 101, 106–7.

15. Ibid., pp. 52, 101.

16. Ibid., pp. 132–4, 224.

17. Cf. D. Frigessi, *Cesare Lombroso* (Turin, 2003), pp. 97–101; R. Villa, *Il deviante e i suoi segni. Lombroso e la nascita dell'antropologia criminale* (Milan, 1985), pp. 147–56.

18. M. Gibson, *Born to Crime. Cesare Lombroso and the Origins of Biological Criminality* (Westport, 2002), p. 100.

19. Ibid., p. 106.

20. C. Lombroso, *L'uomo delinquente in rapporto all'antropologia, alla giurisprudenza ed alle discipline carcerarie*, Vol. 1 (Turin, 1889), p. 85.

21. Ibid., p. 577.

22. Gibson, *Born to Crime*, p. 127.

23. F. Turati, *Il delitto e la questione sociale: appunti sulla questione sociale* (Bologna, 1913), p. 14.

24. Gibson, *Born to Crime*, pp. 29–30.

25. *Atti della Giunta per la inchiesta agraria e sulle condizioni della classe agricola (Presidente della Giunta: Conte Stefano Jacini)* (Rome 1881–5).

26. R. Molinelli, *Pasquale Turiello precursore del nazionalismo italiano* (Urbino, 1968), pp. 12–14.

27. P. Turiello, *Governo e governati in Italia. Fatti* (Bologna, 1889), p. 106.

28. Ibid., pp. 109–11.

29. Ibid., p. 309.

30. P. Turiello, *Governo e governati in Italia. Proposte* (Bologna, 1890), p. 113.

31. Ibid., p. 238; Turiello, *Governo e governati in Italia. Fatti*, pp. 8, 53, 319.

14: National Education

1. S. Pivato, 'Tricolore e simboli patriottici nell'onomastica post-risorgimentale', in F. Tarozzi and G. Vecchio (eds.), *Gli italiani e il tricolore. Patriottismo, identità nazionale e fratture sociali lungo due secoli di storia* (Bologna, 1999), pp. 161–5. Cf. A. C. Jemolo, *Anni di prova* (Vicenza, 1969), p. 4.

2. G. Bini, 'Romanzi e realtà di maestri e maestre', in *Storia d'Italia. Annali 4: Intellettuali e potere*, ed. C. Vivanti (Turin, 1981), pp. 1201–2.

3. E. Catarsi, 'Il suicidio della maestra Italia Donati', in *Studi di storia dell'educazione*, 1, 3 (1981), pp. 35–6.

4. S. Pivato, *Pane e grammatica. L'istruzione elementare in Romagna alla fine dell'800* (Milan, 1983), pp. 45–6.

5. Ibid., p. 53.

6. T. De Mauro, *Storia linguistica dell'Italia unita* (Rome–Bari, 1984), p. 325.

7. Ibid., pp. 88–9; A. Asor Rosa, *La cultura*, in *Storia d'Italia. Vol. 4: Dall'Unità ad oggi* (Turin, 1975), pp. 903–9.

8. A. Bertani, *Discorsi parlamentari di Agostino Bertani pubblicati per deliberazione della Camera dei Deputati* (Rome, 1913), p. 564 (22 June 1884).

9. Pivato, *Pane e grammatica*, pp. 43–4.

10. Catarsi, 'Il suicidio della maestra Italia Donati', p. 36.

11. Ibid., pp. 36–7.

12. C. Paladini, 'Le sventure di Italia Donati', in *Corriere della Sera*, 10–11 June 1886.

13. Ibid.

14. Catarsi, 'Il suicidio della maestra Italia Donati', pp. 41–2, 44–6.

15. Bini, 'Romanzi e realtà di maestri e maestre', pp. 1204–5.

16. M. Lessona, *Volere è potere* (Sesto San Giovanni, 1915), p. 6.
17. S. Lanaro, *Nazione e lavoro. Saggio sulla cultura borghese in Italia 1870–1925* (Venice, 1979), p. 121.
18. P. Pancrazi, 'Vita del Collodi', in *Tutto Collodi. Per i piccoli e per i grandi*, ed. P. Pancrazi (Florence, 1948), p. xxix.
19. C. Collodi, *Le avventure di Pinocchio. Storia di un burattino*, ed. F. Tempesti (Milan, 1983), p. 154.
20. G. Carducci, *Eterno femminino regale. Dalle mie memorie* (Rome, 1982).
21. Lessona, *Volere è potere*, p. 31.
22. A. Capatti, A. De Bernardi and A. Varni (eds.), *Storia d'Italia. Annali 13: L'alimentazione* (Turin, 1998), p. xlviii.
23. L. Magliaretta, 'Alimentazione, casa, salute', in S. Lanaro (ed.), *Storia d'Italia. Le regioni dall'Unità a oggi. Il Veneto* (Turin, 1984), p. 681.
24. F. Mazzonis, 'L'esercito italiano al tempo di Garibaldi', in F. Mazzonis (ed.), *Garibaldi condottiero. Storia, teoria, prassi* (Milan, 1984), pp. 204–5.
25. F. De Sanctis, *I partiti e l'educazione della nuova Italia*, ed. N. Cortese (Turin, 1970), pp. 227–30, 255–6.
26. G. Bonetta, *Corpo e nazione. L'educazione ginnastica, igienica e sessuale nell'Italia liberale* (Milan, 1990), p. 83.
27. G. Montroni, *La società italiana dall'unificazione alla Grande Guerra* (Rome–Bari, 2002), pp. 163–4.
28. Ibid., p. 84.
29. G. Oliva, 'La naja', in M. Isnenghi (ed.), *I luoghi della memoria. Strutture ed eventi dell'Italia unita* (Rome–Bari, 1997), pp. 98–9.
30. E. De Amicis, *La vita militare* (Florence, 1869), p. 257.
31. E. De Amicis, *Cuore. Libro per i ragazzi*, ed. L. Tamburini (Turin, 2001), pp. 47–8.
32. Oliva, 'La naja', p. 98.
33. Ibid., pp. 97, 100; R. Leydi, *Canti sociali italiani. Vol. 1: Canti giacobini, repubblicani, antirisorgimentali, di protesta postunitaria contro la guerra e il servizio militare* (Milan, 1963), pp. 348, 366, 382–94; S. Lanaro, 'Da contadini a italiani', in P. Bevilacqua (ed.), *Storia dell'agricoltura italiana in età contemporanea. Vol. 3: Mercati e istituzioni* (Venice, 1991), p. 938.
34. Cf. N. Revelli, *Il mondo dei vinti. Testimonianze di vita contadina*, Vol. 1 (Turin 1977), p. 57; Oliva, 'La naja', p. 100.
35. Mazzonis, 'L'esercito italiano al tempo di Garibaldi', pp. 240–1.
36. Ibid., pp. 206–7; Leydi, *Canti sociali italiani*, pp. 401–3.
37. R. Romanelli, *L'Italia liberale (1861–1900)* (Bologna, 1979), p. 55.
38. G. Verga, 'Cavalleria rusticana', in *Tutte le novelle di Giovanni Verga*, Vol. 1 (Milan, 1959), p. 107.
39. N. Labanca, 'I programmi dell'educazione morale del soldato. Per uno studio sulla pedagogia militare nell'Italia liberale', in *Esercito e città dall'Unità agli anni Trenta. Atti del Convegno di studi, Spoleto 11–14 maggio 1988*, Vol. 1 (Rome, 1989), pp. 523–5; Mazzonis, 'L'esercito italiano al tempo di Garibaldi', pp. 237–8.
40. Mazzonis, 'L'esercito italiano al tempo di Garibaldi', p. 205.
41. P. Del Negro, 'L'esercito italiano da Napoleone a Vittorio Veneto: fattore di identità nazionale?', in S. Bertelli (ed.), *La chioma della vittoria. Scritti sull'identità degli italiani dall'Unità alla seconda Repubblica* (Florence, 1997), p. 73.
42. N. Marselli, *Gli avvenimenti del 1870–71. Studio politico e militare* (Turin, 1871), pp. 141–2.
43. Mazzonis, 'L'esercito italiano al tempo di Garibaldi', p. 202.
44. A. Guiccioli, *Diario di un conservatore* (Milan, 1973), p. 22 (2 June 1877).
45. Marselli, *Gli avvenimenti del 1870–71*, pp. 31, 139; N. Marselli, *La politica dello Stato italiano* (Naples, 1882), p. 402.
46. Marselli, *La politica dello Stato italiano*, p. 398.

47. Del Negro, 'L'esercito italiano da Napoleone a Vittorio Veneto', p. 78.
48. I. Porciani, 'Stato e nazione: l'immagine debole dell'Italia', in S. Soldani and G. Turi (eds.), *Fare gli italiani. Scuola e cultura nell'Italia contemporanea. Vol. 1: La nascita dello Stato nazionale* (Bologna, 1993), pp. 398–9.
49. I. Porciani, *La festa della nazione. Rappresentazione dello Stato e spazi sociali nell'Italia unita* (Bologna, 1997), pp. 22–3, 37.
50. Ibid., p. 207.
51. Ibid., pp. 105–7.
52. Ibid., pp. 123–33.
53. 'L'isola sacra', in *La Riforma*, 10 June 1882.
54. E. Irace, *Itale glorie* (Bologna, 2003), p. 176.
55. R. Certini, *Il mito di Garibaldi. La formazione dell'immaginario popolare nell'Italia unita* (Milan, 2000), pp. 99–102, 117–18.
56. F. Crispi, *Scritti e discorsi politici di Francesco Crispi (1849–1890)* (Rome, 1890), pp. 655–8 ('Giuseppe Garibaldi', 1 June 1884).
57. C. Brice, *Monumentalité publique et politique à Rome. Le Vittoriano* (Rome, 1998), pp. 43–4.
58. Irace, *Itale glorie*, p. 188.
59. S. Montaldo, *Patria e affari. Tommaso Villa e la costruzione del consenso tra Unità e Grande Guerra* (Turin, 1999), pp. 312–13.
60. S. Soldani, 'Il Risorgimento a scuola: incertezze dello Stato e lenta formazione di un pubblico di lettori', in E. Dirani (ed.), *Alfredo Oriani e la cultura del suo tempo* (Ravenna, 1985), pp. 154–6.
61. D. Mack Smith, 'Documentary falsification and Italian biography', in T. Blanning and D. Cannadine (eds.), *History and Biography. Essays in Honour of Derek Beales* (Cambridge, 1996), pp. 182–4.

15: Sources of Authority

1. Cf. A. C. Jemolo, *Chiesa e Stato in Italia negli ultimi cento anni* (Turin, 1963), pp. 175–6, 186–7.
2. Cf. P. Scoppola, *Dal neoguelfismo alla democrazia cristiana* (Rome, 1963), pp. 32–68.
3. A. Bertani, *Discorsi parlamentari di Agostino Bertani pubblicati per deliberazione della Camera dei Deputati* (Rome, 1913), pp. 372–3 (25 July 1877).
4. Ibid., p. 374.
5. G. Finali, *Memorie* (Faenza, 1955), p. 525.
6. U. Pesci, *I primi anni di Roma capitale (1870–1878)* (Florence, 1907), p. 68.
7. D. Pick, *Rome or Death. The Obsessions of General Garibaldi* (London, 2005), pp. 1–9, 183–200.
8. A. Caracciolo, *Roma capitale. Dal Risorgimento allo Stato liberale* (Rome, 1956), p. 121.
9. A. Riccardi, 'La vita religiosa', in V. Vidotto (ed.), *Storia di Roma dall'antichità a oggi. Roma capitale* (Rome–Bari, 2002), p. 278.
10. G. Pécout, *Il lungo Risorgimento. La nascita dell'Italia contemporanea (1770–1922)* (Milan, 1999), p. 286.
11. C. Hibbert, *Rome. The Biography of a City* (New York, 1985), p. 280.
12. P. Alatri, *Gabriele D'Annunzio* (Turin, 1983), p. 27.
13. Caracciolo, *Roma capitale*, pp. 190–92.
14. A. Asor Rosa, *La cultura*, in *Storia d'Italia. Vol. 4: Dall'Unità ad oggi* (Turin, 1975), p. 831.
15. G. Carducci, 'Roma', in *Edizione nazionale delle opere di Giosuè Carducci. Vol. 4: Odi barbare e rime e ritmi* (Bologna, 1944), pp. 30–31.
16. Carducci, in ibid., *Vol. 24: Confessioni e battaglie, serie prima* (Bologna, 1944) pp. 127–8 (preface to *Levia Gravia*, 1881).
17. C. Dossi, *Opere*, ed. D. Isella (Milan, 1995), p. 1324.

18. L. Pirandello, *I vecchi e i giovani*, in L. Pirandello, *Tutti i romanzi*, Vol. 2, ed. G. Macchia (Milan, 2003), p. 273.

19. D. Mack Smith, *Vittorio Emanuele II* (Rome–Bari, 1975), p. 334.

20. Cf. U. Pesci, *I primi anni di Roma capitale (1870–1878)* (Florence, 1907), pp. 589–91.

21. C. Duggan, *Francesco Crispi. From Nation to Nationalism* (Oxford, 2002), pp. 379–81.

22. Ibid.; U. Levra, *Fare gli italiani. Memoria e celebrazione del Risorgimento* (Turin, 1992), p. 18.

23. A. C. De Meis, *Il sovrano. Saggio di filosofia politica con riferenza all'Italia*, ed. B. Croce (Bari, 1927), pp. 20, 53, 67.

24. S. Romano, *Crispi. Progetto per una dittatura* (Milan, 1973), p. 121.

25. *Nuova antologia*, 1 December 1878 (23), p. 535.

26. Duggan, *Franceso Crispi*, p. 393 (7 December 1878).

27. M. Casciato, 'Lo sviluppo urbano e il disegno della città', in Vidotto (ed.), *Storia di Roma dall'antichità a oggi*, p. 152.

28. B. Tobia, *Una patria per gli italiani* (Rome–Bari, 1991), pp. 140–41.

29. Cf. H. Busch (ed. and trans.), *Verdi's Otello and Simon Boccanegra (Revised Edition) in Letters and Documents*, Vol. 1 (Oxford, 1988), pp. 29, 37–41.

30. A. M. Banti, *Storia della borghesia italiana* (Rome, 1996), p. 239.

31. A. Mazzoleni, *Il popolo italiano. Studi politici* (Milan, 1873), p. 322.

32. F. Martini, *Confessioni e ricordi (1859–1892)* (Milan, 1929), pp. 120–21.

33. G. Lanza, *Le carte di Giovanni Lanza. Vol. 9 (luglio 1873–1877)*, ed. C. M. De Vecchi di Val Cismon (Turin, 1940), p. 445 (Dina to Lanza, 20 November 1876).

34. F. De Sanctis, *I partiti e l'educazione della nuova Italia* (Turin, 1970), p. 380 (11 May 1880).

35. F. De Sanctis, *Il Mezzogiorno e lo stato unitario* (Turin, 1960), p. 358 (*L'Italia*, 16 February 1864).

36. Duggan, *Francesco Crispi*, p. 333.

37. F. De Sanctis, *Un viaggio elettorale*, ed. N. Cortese (Turin, 1968), p. 32.

38. R. Romanelli, 'Le regole del gioco. Note sull'impianto del sistema elettorale in Italia (1848–1895)', in *Quaderni storici*, 69 (3) (December 1988), p. 699.

39. Ibid., p. 700.

40. Cf. G. Mosca, *Teorica dei governi e governo parlamentare. Studii storici e sociali* (Palermo, 1884), pp. 295–302, 318–22; Banti, *Storia della borghesia italiana*, p. 243.

41. De Sanctis, *I partiti e l'educazione della nuova Italia*, p. 389.

42. R. Bonghi, *Discorsi parlamentari*, ed. G. Gentile (Florence, 1934), pp. 282, 291 (13 May 1881).

43. *Atti parlamentari, Camera dei Deputati, Discussioni*, 18 June 1881, pp. 8726–8.

44. *La Riforma*, 25 April 1891 ('Il ritorno al collegio uninominale').

45. F. Crispi, *Discorsi elettorali di Francesco Crispi 1865–1886*, p. 230 (19 May 1886).

46. F. Soddu, 'Il ruolo del Parlamento nella costruzione dell'unità politica e amministrativa', in L. Violante (ed.), *Storia d'Italia. Annali 18: Il parlamento* (Turin, 2001), pp. 102–4.

47. C. Fumian, 'Patroni e padroni. La grande possidenza tra declino e metamorfosi', in S. Lanaro (ed.), *Storia d'Italia. Le regioni dall'Unità a oggi. Il Veneto* (Turin, 1984), p. 113.

48. F. Cammarano, 'Nazionalizzazione della politica e politicizzazione della nazione. I dilemmi della classe dirigente nell'Italia liberale', in M. Meriggi and P. Schiera (eds.), *Dalla città alla nazione. Borghesie ottocentesche in Italia e in Germania* (Bologna, 1993), pp. 144–5.

49. F. Chabod, *Storia della politica estera italiana dal 1870 al 1896. Vol. 1: Le premesse* (Bari, 1951), p. 385 (Minghetti to Luzzatti, 29 August 1881).

50. G. Sabbatucci, *Il trasformismo come sistema* (Rome–Bari, 2003), pp. 18–27.

51. Ibid., p. 26.

52. Martini, *Confessioni e ricordi*, p. 148.

53. *La Riforma*, 28 July 1885.

16: Francesco Crispi and the 'New European Order', 1887–91

1. F. Martini, *Confessioni e ricordi (1859–1892)* (Milan, 1929), pp. 213–14.
2. C. W. Dilke, *The Present Position of European Politics or Europe in 1887* (London, 1887), p. 251.
3. G. Astuto (ed.), *Crispi e Damiani. Carteggio (1876–1899)* (Catania, 1984), p. 15 (Crispi to Damiani, 28 June 1878).
4. P. Turiello, *Governo e governati in Italia. Fatti* (Bologna, 1889), pp. 302–3.
5. M. Biancale, *Michele Cammarano* (Milan–Rome, 1936), pp. 84–92.
6. F. Chabod, *Storia della politica estera italiana dal 1870 al 1896. Vol. 1: Le premesse* (Bari, 1951), p. 14.
7. A. Guiccioli, 'Diario del 1882', in *Nuova antologia*, 16 August 1936, pp. 439–41 (22 April 1882, 16 May 1882).
8. R. Bonghi, *Discorsi parlamentari*, ed. G. Gentile (Florence, 1934), p. 313 (14–15 May 1883).
9. C. Duggan, *Francesco Crispi. From Nation to Nationalism* (Oxford, 2002), p. 413 (19 May 1883).
10. Martini, *Confessioni e ricordi*, p. 224.
11. *I documenti diplomatici italiani. Seconda serie: 1870–1896*, Vol. 21 (31 July 1887–31 March 1888), ed. R. Mori (Rome, 1968), pp. 450–54 (31 January 1888).
12. *Die grosse Politik der europäischen Kabinette 1871–1914*, Vol. 6 (Berlin, 1924–7), n. 1293 (Solms to Herbert von Bismarck, 20 October 1887).
13. Duggan, *Francesco Crispi*, pp. 515–18.
14. Ibid., p. 531 (Salisbury to Dufferin, 28 December 1888).
15. *I documenti diplomatici italiani. Seconda serie: 1870–1896*, Vol. 22 (1 April 1888–31 August 1889), ed. G. Carocci (Rome, 1994), pp. 21–2 (Goiran to Cosenz, 22 April 1888).
16. Ibid.
17. A. Guiccioli, *Diario di un conservatore* (Milan, 1973), p. 157 (13 November 1888).
18. *La Riforma*, 27 May 1889.
19. Duggan, *Francesco Crispi*, p. 565.
20. Ibid., pp. 567–8.
21. Ibid., p. 567.
22. Ibid., p. 543 (Baron Blanc to Crispi, 10 January 1888).
23. Ibid., pp. 542–3.
24. G. Ferrero, *La reazione* (Turin, 1895), p. 7.
25. Ibid., pp. 12–15, 18–20, 28, 31, 35–8, 44–5.
26. Duggan, *Francesco Crispi*, p. 550 (1 December 1888).
27. D. Mack Smith, *Italy and Its Monarchy* (New Haven and London, 1989), p. 95.
28. Cf. N. Labanca, *Oltremare. Storia dell'espansione coloniale italiana* (Bologna, 2002), pp. 57–8, 70–73, 217–34.
29. F. Crispi, *Scritti e discorsi politici di Francesco Crispi (1849–1890)* (Rome, 1890), pp. 736–8.
30. Duggan, *Francesco Crispi*, pp. 599–605.

17: The Fin de Siècle Crisis

1. Public Record Office, FO 45 700, Edwardes to Rosebery, 6 December 1893.
2. V. Zamagni, *Dalla periferia al centro. La seconda rinascita economica dell'Italia: 1861–1981* (Bologna, 1990), p. 159.
3. N. Colajanni, *Banche e parlamentari. Fatti, discussioni e commenti* (Milan, 1993), pp. 236–7; N. Quilici, *Banca Romana* (Milan, 1935), pp. 74, 458–9, 514–15.
4. G. Manacorda, *Dalla crisi alla crescita. Crisi economica e lotta politica in Italia 1892–1896* (Rome, 1993), pp. 70–73. Cf. D. Farini, *Diario di fine secolo*, ed. E. Morelli (Rome, 1961), pp. 320–22 (22–7 August 1893).

5. *Atti Parlamentari, Camera dei Deputati, Discussioni*, 20 December 1893.
6. Ibid., 28 February 1894.
7. Cf. F. Fonzi, *Crispi e lo 'Stato di Milano'* (Milan, 1965), pp. xvi–xxiii.
8. Manacorda, *Dalla crisi alla crescita*, pp. 97–8; C. Duggan, *Francesco Crispi. From Nation to Nationalism* (Oxford, 2002), pp. 640–41.
9. News International Archive, Stillman Papers, William J. Stillman to Wallace, 18 March 1894.
10. Manacorda, *Dalla crisi alla crescita*, pp. 113–14.
11. P. Ballini, *Le elezioni nella storia d'Italia dall'Unità al fascismo. Profilo storico-statistico* (Bologna, 1988), p. 124.
12. Duggan, *Francesco Crispi*, pp. 673–4.
13. A. Guiccioli, *Diario di un conservatore* (Milan, 1973), p. 172 (16 September 1892).
14. Duggan, *Francesco Crispi*, p. 677 (2 January 1897); L. Mangoni, *Una crisi fine secolo. La cultura italiana e la Francia fra Otto e Novecento* (Turin, 1985), p. 162.
15. Duggan, *Francesco Crispi*, pp. 679–80.
16. Ibid., p. 665 (speech in Naples, 10 September 1894).
17. U. Levra, *Fare gli italiani. Memoria e celebrazione del Risorgimento* (Turin, 1992), p. 340.
18. Duggan, *Francesco Crispi*, p. 698.
19. S. Sonnino, *Diario 1866–1912*, Vol. 1, ed. B. Brown (Rome–Bari, 1972), pp. 209 (10 January 1896), 213 (15 January 1896).
20. Guiccioli, *Diario di un conservatore*, p. 201 (15 January 1895).
21. Duggan, *Francesco Crispi*, pp. 700–701.
22. *La Riforma*, 17 January 1896 ('L'Italia nuova').
23. H. G. Marcus, *The Life and Times of Menelik II. Ethiopia 1844–1913* (Oxford, 1975), pp. 171–3; A. Del Boca, *Gli italiani in Africa orientale. Dall'Unità alla Marcia su Roma* (Rome–Bari, 1976), pp. 645–8, 652, 691–2; J. Gooch, *Army, State and Society in Italy 1870–1915* (Basingstoke, 1989), pp. 90–92.
24. G. Candeloro, *Storia dell'Italia moderna. Vol. 7: La crisi di fine secolo e l'età giolittiana* (Milan, 1974), p. 60. Cf. U. Levra, *Il colpo di stato della borghesia. La crisi politica della fine del secolo in Italia (1896–1900)* (Milan, 1975), pp. 115–20.
25. L. Ferraris, 'L'assassinio di Umberto I e gli anarchici di Paterson', in *Rassegna storica del Risorgimento*, 55 (January–March 1968), pp. 51–4.
26. B. Anatra, 'Gaetano Bresci', in *Dizionario biografico degli italiani*, Vol. 14 (Rome, 1972), p. 169.
27. S. Turone, *Politica ladra. Storia della corruzione 1861–1992* (Rome–Bari, 1992), p. 80.

18: Rival Religions

1. J. Woodhouse, *Gabriele D'Annunzio. Defiant Archangel* (Oxford, 2001), pp. 59–60.
2. Ibid., p. 167; P. Alatri, *Gabriele D'Annunzio* (Turin, 1983), pp. 189–90.
3. Woodhouse, *Gabriele D'Annunzio*, p. 168.
4. Alatri, *Gabriele D'Annunzio*, p. 196.
5. U. Levra, 'Il parlamento nella crisi di fine secolo', in L. Violante (ed.), *Storia d'Italia. Annali 17: Il parlamento* (Turin, 2001), p. 163.
6. G. Manacorda (ed.), *Il socialismo nella storia d'Italia. Storia documentaria dal Risorgimento alla Repubblica*, Vol. 1 (Rome–Bari, 1970), pp. 106–7, 112, 117 (Bakunin, *Circolare ai miei amici d'Italia*, 1871).
7. A. De Jaco (ed.), *Gli anarchici. Cronaca inedita dell'Unità d'Italia* (Rome, 1971), pp. 212–14.
8. P. C. Masini, *Gli Internazionalisti. La banda del Matese 1876–1878* (Milan, 1958), pp. 79–102.
9. Cf. G. Cerrito, *Andrea Costa nel socialismo italiano* (Rome, 1982), pp. 209–22.
10. G. Candeloro, *Storia dell'Italia moderna. Vol. 6: Lo sviluppo del capitalismo e del movimento operaio* (Milan, 1970), pp. 383–8.

11. Ibid., *Vol. 7: La crisi di fine secolo e l'età giolittiana* (Milan, 1974), pp. 158–64, 362–3.

12. V. Zamagni, *Dalla periferia al centro. La seconda rinascita economica dell'Italia: 1861–1981* (Bologna, 1990), pp. 116, 121.

13. Ibid., pp. 128–9.

14. B. Mussolini, *La mia vita* (Rome, 1947), p. 28.

15. A. Labriola, *Spiegazioni a me stesso* (Naples, 1945), p. 118.

16. Cf. D. Cinel, *The National Integration of Italian Return Migration 1870–1929* (Cambridge, 1991), pp. 172–6, 230–31.

17. T. De Mauro, *Storia linguistica dell'Italia unita* (Rome–Bari, 1984), pp. 62–3.

18. R. Michels, *Storia critica del movimento socialista italiano. Dagli inizi fino al 1911* (Florence, 1926), p. 191. Cf. L. Ellena, ' "Una donna nel quadro può venire in prima linea con essi": genealogia di un'immagine', in M. Nani, L. Ellena and M. Scavino, *Il Quarto Stato di Pellizza da Volpedo tra cultura e politica. Un'immagine e la sua fortuna* (Turin, 2002), pp. 65–7.

19. R. Monteleone, *Filippo Turati* (Turin, 1987), p. 16.

20. Ibid., pp. 15–30.

21. C. Petraccone, *Le due civiltà. Settentrionali e meridionali nella storia d'Italia* (Rome–Bari, 2000), p. 183.

22. Monteleone, *Filippo Turati*, pp. 146–7.

23. Ibid., p. 148.

24. C. G. Lacaita, 'Politica e istruzione popolare nel movimento socialista', in G. Genovesi and C. G. Lacaita (eds.), *Istruzione popolare nell'Italia liberale. Le alternative delle correnti di opposizione* (Milan, 1983), p. 25.

25. G. Turi, 'Intellettuali e propaganda nel movimento socialista', in S. Soldani and G. Turi (eds.), *Fare gli italiani. Scuola e cultura nell'Italia contemporanea. Vol. 1: La nascita dello Stato nazionale* (Bologna, 1993), p. 490.

26. R. Michels, *Storia critica del movimento socialista italiano. Dagli inizi fino al 1911* (Florence, 1926), pp. 356–7.

27. Ibid., p. 197.

28. Turi, 'Intellettuali e propaganda nel movimento socialista', p. 487.

29. Michels, *Storia critica del movimento socialista Italiano*, pp. 367–8.

30. Ibid., p. 197.

31. Manacorda (ed.), *Il socialismo nella storia d'Italia*, Vol. 1, p. 156.

32. Cf. S. F. Romano, *Storia dei Fasci siciliani* (Bari, 1959), pp. 230–37.

33. I. De Begnac, *Vita di Benito Mussolini. Vol. 1: Alla scuola della rivoluzione antica* (Verona, 1936), pp. 319–20.

34. Michels, *Storia critica del movimento socialista italiano*, p. 218.

35. Monteleone, *Filippo Turati*, p. 146.

36. D. Mack Smith, *Modern Italy. A Political History* (New Haven and London, 1997), p. 185.

37. C. Treves, 'Giolitti', in G. Pischel, *Antologia della Critica Sociale*, ed. G. Arfè (Manduria, 1992), p. 85 (1 August 1899).

38. *Discorsi parlamentari di Giovanni Giolitti pubblicati per deliberazione della Camera dei Deputati*, Vol. 2 (Rome, 1953), pp. 632–3 (4 February 1901).

39. G. Giolitti, *Memorie della mia vita*, Vol. 1 (Milan, 1922), p. 166.

40. A. M. Banti, *Storia della borghesia italiana* (Rome, 1996), p. 293.

41. A. Capatti, A. De Bernardi and A. Varni (eds.), *Storia d'Italia. Annali 13: L'alimentazione* (Turin, 1998), p. xxxv.

42. Michels, *Storia critica del movimento socialista italiano*, p. 374.

43. L. Allegra, 'Il parroco: un mediatore fra alta e bassa cultura', in *Storia d'Italia. Annali 4: Intellettuali e potere*, ed. C. Vivanti (Turin, 1981), p. 945.

44. D. I. Kertzer, 'Religion and society, 1789–1892', in J. A. Davis (ed.), *Italy in the Nineteenth Century 1796–1900* (Oxford, 2000), p. 198.

45. U. Pesci, *I primi anni di Roma capitale (1870–1878)* (Florence, 1907), p. 48.
46. G. Miccoli, 'Chiesa e società in Italia dal Concilio Vaticano I (1870) al pontificato di Giovanni XXIII', in *Storia d'Italia. Vol. 5: I documenti (2)* (Turin, 1973), pp. 1508–9.
47. I. Porciani, *La festa della nazione. Rappresentazione dello Stato e spazi sociali nell'Italia unita* (Bologna, 1997), pp. 189–90.
48. M. Isnenghi, 'I luoghi della cultura', in S. Lanaro (ed.), *Storia d'Italia. Le regioni dall'Unità a oggi. Il Veneto* (Turin, 1984), pp. 348–9.
49. S. Pivato, *Pane e grammatica. L'istruzione elementare in Romagna alla fine dell'800* (Milan, 1983), pp. 128–9.
50. Ibid., pp. 131–4.
51. Isnenghi, 'I luoghi della cultura', p. 357.
52. Ibid., pp. 137–8.
53. Pivato, *Pane e grammatica*, p. 135.
54. Michels, *Storia critica del movimento socialista italiano*, p. 373.
55. M. Clark, *Modern Italy 1871–1995* (London, 1996), p. 149.
56. Giolitti, *Memorie della mia vita*, Vol. 2, pp. 307–8.
57. G. Pini and D. Susmel, *Mussolini: l'uomo e l'opera*, Vol. 1 (Florence, 1953), pp. 111, 146–7.
58. G. Salvemini, 'Il ministro della malavita', in *Opere di Gaetano Salvemini. Vol. 4: Il Mezzogiorno e la democrazia italiana (1)* (Milan, 1962), pp. 73–141.
59. Michels, *Storia critica del movimento socialista italiano*, p. 255.
60. J. E. Miller, *From Elite to Mass Politics. Italian Socialism in the Giolittian Era, 1900–1914* (Kent, 1990), p. 8 (*Avanti!*, 12 May 1903).
61. Mussolini, *La mia vita*, pp. 60–61, 69–71.
62. Ibid., pp. 25–6; Pini and Susmel, *Mussolini: l'uomo e l'opera*, Vol. 1, p. 32.
63. Pini and Susmel, *Mussolini: l'uomo e l'opera*, Vol. 1, p. 42.
64. De Begnac, *Vita di Benito Mussolini*, Vol. 1, p. 321.
65. R. Bosworth, *Mussolini* (London, 2002), p. 53.
66. D. Mack Smith, *Mussolini* (London, 1983), p. 15.
67. Pini and Susmel, *Mussolini: l'uomo e l'opera*, Vol. 1, p. 147.
68. R. De Felice, *Mussolini il rivoluzionario 1883–1920* (Turin, 1965), p. 116.
69. De Begnac, *Vita di Benito Mussolini*, Vol. 1, p. 239.
70. Pini and Susmel, *Mussolini: l'uomo e l'opera*. Vol. 1, p. 56; De Felice, *Mussolini il rivoluzionario*, p. 14.
71. Ibid., p. 77.
72. G. Prezzolini, *La Voce 1908–1913. Cronaca, antologia e fortuna di una rivista* (Milan, 1974), p. 933 (*Vita trentina*, 3 April 1909).

19: Nationalism

1. G. D'Annunzio, 'Canto di festa per calendimaggio', in *Tutte le opere di Gabriele D'Annunzio. Versi d'amore e di gloria*, Vol. 2 (Milan, 1952), pp. 543–8.
2. G. D'Annunzio, *La Nave*, in *Tutte le opere di Gabriele D'Annunzio. Tragedie, sogni e misteri*, Vol. 2 (Milan, 1950), pp. 3–210.
3. P. Alatri, *Gabriele D'Annunzio* (Turin, 1983), pp. 343–4 (to Maurice Paléologue, 16 June 1914).
4. *Discorsi parlamentari di Antonio Salandra. Pubblicati per deliberazione della Camera dei Deputati*, Vol. 1 (Rome, 1959), p. 375 (9 December 1901).
5. Ibid., Vol. 2, p. 792 (17 December 1913).
6. G. Amendola, *Carteggio. Vol. 1: 1897–1909*, ed. E. d'Auria (Rome–Bari, 1986), p. 87 (to Eva Kühn, 6 June 1904).
7. 'Gian Falco' (G. Papini), 'Campagna per il forzato risveglio' (*Leonardo*, 1906), in D. Frigessi (ed.), *La cultura italiana del '900 attraverso le riviste. Vol. 1: 'Leonardo', 'Hermes', 'Il Regno'* (Turin, 1960), pp. 312, 314.

8. G. Prezzolini, *L'italiano inutile. Memorie letterarie di Francia, Italia e America* (Milan, 1953), p. 93.

9. G. Prezzolini, 'Le due Italie' (*Il Regno*, 1904), in Frigessi (ed.), *La cultura italiana del '900 attraverso le riviste*, Vol. 1, p. 502.

10. E. Corradini, 'Tornando sul nostro programma' (*Il Regno*, 1904), in Frigessi (ed.), *La cultura italiana del '900 attraverso le rivirte*, Vol. 1, p. 518.

11. G. Prezzolini, *La Voce 1908–1913. Cronaca, antologia e fortuna di una rivista* (Milan, 1974), pp. 758 (11 August 1910), 761 (28 August 1910).

12. Ibid., p. 327 (1 September 1910).

13. G. Prezzolini, 'A chi giova la lotta di classe?' (*Il Regno*, 1904), in Frigessi (ed.), *La cultura italiana del '900 attraverso le riviste*, Vol. 1, p. 490.

14. L. Valli, 'Che cosa è e che cosa vuole il nazionalismo', in F. Perfetti, *Il movimento nazionalista in Italia (1903–1914)* (Rome, 1984), pp. 185–6.

15. Prezzolini, *La Voce 1908–1913*, p. 701 (2 March 1911).

16. Perfetti, *Il movimento nazionalista*, p. 67.

17. A. Asor Rosa, 'La cultura', in *Storia d'Italia. Vol. 4: Dall'Unità ad oggi (2)* (Turin, 1975), p. 1254.

18. G. Busino, 'Il nazionalismo italiano e il nazionalismo europeo', in *La cultura italiana tra '800 e '900 e le origini del nazionalismo* (Florence, 1981), p. 67.

19. G. Pascoli, 'La grande proletaria si è mossa', in *Prose di Giovanni Pascoli. Vol. 1: Pensieri di varia umanità* (Milan, 1952), pp. 557–69.

20. G. Fortunato, *Carteggio 1865/1911*, ed. E. Gentile (Rome–Bari, 1978), pp. 397–8 (18 December 1911).

21. G. Fortunato, *Carteggio 1912/1922*, ed. E. Gentile (Rome–Bari, 1979), p. 89 (6 October 1912).

22. A. Del Boca, *Italiani, brava gente?* (Vicenza, 2005), pp. 110–12, 122.

23. Ibid., pp. 115–16.

24. Ibid., p. 116.

25. V. Zecchini (ed.), *Futurismo e fascismo: manifesti e programmi* (Bologna, 2000), p. 20.

26. S. Bono, *Morire per questi deserti. Lettere di soldati italiani dal fronte libico 1911–1912* (Catanzaro, 1992), p. 27.

27. Ibid., p. 20.

28. N. Revelli, *Il mondo dei vinti. Testimonianze di vita contadina*, Vol. 2 (Turin, 1977), pp. 124–5.

29. Fortunato, *Carteggio 1912/1922*, pp. 97–8 (8 November 1912, 10 November 1912).

30. M. De Giorgio, *Le italiane dall'Unità a oggi. Modelli culturali e comportamenti sociali* (Rome–Bari, 1992), pp. 160–62.

31. E. Gentile, *La grande Italia. Ascesa e declino del mito della nazione nel ventesimo secolo* (Milan, 1997), p. 63 (*Critica sociale*, 16 April 1911).

32. S. Sighele, *Il nazionalismo e i partiti politici* (Milan, 1911), p. 118.

33. B. Croce, *Cultura e vita morale. Intermezzi polemici* (Bari, 1955), p. 163 ('Fede e programmi', 1911).

34. *Discorsi parlamentari di Antonio Salandra*. Vol. 3, p. 1429 (19 October 1913).

35. Ibid., Vol. 2, p. 893 (2 June 1914).

36. A. M. Banti, *Storia della borghesia italiana* (Rome, 1996), p. 335.

37. Ibid., p. 335 ('Il Parlamento contro l'Italia', in *Idea Nazionale*, 15 May 1915).

38. *Discorsi parlamentari di Antonio Salandra*. Vol. 3, pp. 1444–5 (2 June 1915).

20: The Great War, 1915–18

1. Cf. P. Pieri, *L'Italia nella prima guerra mondiale* (Turin, 1965), pp. 77–90, 111–21, 128–36.

2. G. Rocca, *Cadorna* (Milan, 1985), pp. 255–60.

3. C. Falls, *Caporetto 1917* (London, 1965), p. 75.

10. Mussolini, *Opera omnia*, Vol. 23, p. 523 (Carta del Lavoro).
11. P. Mignosi, 'La mafia', in *La Rivoluzione liberale*, 4, 38 (25 October 1925).
12. Duggan, *Fascism and the Mafia*, p. 145.
13. Mori, *Con la mafia ai ferri corti*, pp. 46–7; Duggan, *Fascism and the Mafia*, p. 209.
14. Ibid., p. 210.
15. Ibid., pp. 215–16.
16. Ibid., p. 214.
17. C. G. Chapman, *Milocca. A Sicilian Village* (London, 1973), p. 155.
18. Duggan, *Fascism and the Mafia*, pp. 264–70.
19. Ibid., p. 263.
20. M. Barbagli, *Disoccupazione intellettuale e sistema scolastico in Italia* (Bologna, 1974), p. 169.
21. Mussolini, *Opera omnia*, Vol. 20, p. 130 (13 December 1923).
22. Barbagli, *Disoccupazione intellettuale*, pp. 203–4.
23. T. Koon, *Believe, Obey, Fight. Political Socialization in Fascist Italy, 1922–1943* (Chapel Hill, 1985), p. 55.
24. Ibid., p. 51.
25. E. Codignola, *Il problema dell'educazione nazionale in Italia* (Florence, 1925), pp. 149, 225–6.
26. Mussolini, *Opera omnia*, Vol. 23, p. 23 (5 December 1925).
27. A. Lyttelton, *The Seizure of Power. Fascism in Italy 1919–1929* (London, 1973), p. 408.
28. Koon, *Believe, Obey, Fight*, p. 65.
29. Ibid., pp. 71, 84.
30. Asor Rosa, 'La cultura', pp. 1465–9.
31. Cf. J. Charnitzky, *Die Schulpolitik des faschistischen Regimes in Italien (1922–1943)* (Tübingen, 1994), pp. 257–60.
32. Koon, *Believe, Obey, Fight*, p. 80.
33. Ibid., pp. 72, 79–80.
34. Ibid., p. 70.
35. Ibid., p. 86.
36. Barbagli, *Disoccupazione intellettuale*, pp. 213–15, 237, 245.
37. Chapman, *Milocca*, p. 148.
38. M. Clark, *Modern Italy 1871–1995* (London, 1996), p. 278.
39. G. Aliberti, *La resa di Cavour. Il carattere nazionale italiano tra mito e cronaca, 1820–1976* (Florence, 2000), p. 149.
40. Ibid., p. 145.
41. Mussolini, *Opera omnia*, Vol. 21, p. 362.
42. Ibid., Vol. 26, p. 259 (26 May 1934).
43. Koon, *Believe, Obey, Fight*, p. 97.
44. R. Bosworth, *Mussolini's Italy. Life under the Dictatorship 1915–1945* (London, 2005), p. 290.
45. Koon, *Believe, Obey, Fight*, pp. 101–3.
46. Lyttelton, *The Seizure of Power*, p. 409.
47. Bosworth, *Mussolini's Italy*, p. 290.
48. P. McCarthy, 'The beginnings of Italian sport', in *Journal of Modern Italian Studies*, 5, 3 (2000), p. 324.
49. Clark, *Modern Italy*, p. 168.
50. Bosworth, *Mussolini's Italy*, p. 410.
51. S. Martin, *Football and Fascism. The National Game under Mussolini* (Oxford, 2004), pp. 125, 137.
52. Ibid., pp. 185–9.
53. S. Jacomuzzi, 'Gli sport', in *Storia d'Italia. Vol. 5: I documenti* (Turin, 1973), p. 929.
54. Mussolini, *Opera omnia*, Vol. 20, pp. 364–5 (26 May 1927).
55. Ibid., Vol. 23, pp. 209–16.

56. S. Lanaro, 'Da contadini a italiani', in P. Bevilacqua (ed.), *Storia dell'agricoltura italiana in età contemporanea. Vol. 3: Mercati e istituzioni* (Venice, 1991), p. 965.

57. M. Isnenghi, 'Il ruralismo nella cultura italiana', in Bevilacqua (ed.), *Storia dell'agricoltura italiana*, pp. 903–5.

58. C. Ipsen, *Dictating Demography. The Problem of Population in Fascist Italy* (Cambridge, 2002), p. 85.

59. D. Mack Smith, *Mussolini* (London, 1983), p. 186. Cf. E. Ludwig, *Colloqui con Mussolini. Riproduzione delle bozze della prima edizione con le correzioni autografe del duce* (Verona, 1950), pp. 164–6.

60. Koon, *Believe, Obey, Fight*, p. 25.

61. Mack Smith, *Mussolini*, p. 186.

62. Ipsen, *Dictating Demography*, pp. 165–9.

63. P. Willson, *Peasant Women and Politics in Fascist Italy. The 'massaie rurali'* (London, 2002), pp. 58–61.

64. Ibid., pp. 64, 90–92, 178–9.

65. Ipsen, *Dictating Demography*, p. 179.

24: Community of Believers

1. Cf. R. Bosworth, *Mussolini* (London, 2002), pp. 207–8, 211–12.

2. B. Mussolini, *Opera omnia*, Vol. 22, eds. E. and D. Susmel (Florence, 1951–62), pp. 197–8 (18 August 1926).

3. L. Passerini, *Mussolini immaginario. Storia di una biografia 1915–1939* (Rome–Bari, 1991), p. 43.

4. R. De Felice, *Mussolini il duce. Vol. 1: Gli anni del consenso 1929–1936* (Turin, 1974), p. 50.

5. D. Mack Smith, *Mussolini* (London, 1983), p. 145.

6. L. Passerini, *Fascism in Popular Memory. The Cultural Experiences of the Turin Working Class* (Cambridge, 1987), p. 113.

7. T. Koon, *Believe, Obey, Fight. Political Socialization in Fascist Italy, 1922–1943* (Chapel Hill, 1985), p. 17.

8. Ibid., p. 79.

9. M. Sarfatti, *Dux* (Milan, 1926), p. 185.

10. Passerini, *Mussolini immaginario*, p. 90.

11. P. Willson, *Peasant Women and Politics in Fascist Italy. The 'massaie rurali'* (London, 2002), pp. 155–6.

12. Q. Navarra, *Memorie del cameriere di Mussolini* (Milan, 1972), pp. 208–11.

13. A. Giardina and A. Vauchez, *Il mito di Roma. Da Carlo Magno a Mussolini* (Rome–Bari, 2000), pp. 217–18.

14. E. Ludwig, *Colloqui con Mussolini. Riproduzione delle bozze della prima edizione con le correzioni autografe del duce* (Verona, 1950), p. 121.

15. M. Berezin, *Making the Fascist Self. The Political Culture of Interwar Italy* (Ithaca and London, 1997), pp. 202–3.

16. Ibid., p. 120 (*La Nazione*, 26 October 1934).

17. C. Lazzaro and R. J. Crum (eds.), *Donatello among the Blackshirts. History and Modernity in the Visual Culture of Fascist Italy* (Ithaca and London, 2005), pp. 36–7.

18. Ibid., pp. 46–8. Cf. J. T. Schnapp, *Anno X. La Mostra della rivoluzione fascista del 1932* (Pisa, 2003), pp. 45–6, 51–60.

19. B. Mussolini, *The Cardinal's Mistress*, trans. H. Motherwell (London, 1929). Cf. Mack Smith, *Mussolini*, p. 20.

20. S. Falasca-Zamponi, *Fascist Spectacle. The Aesthetics of Power in Mussolini's Italy* (Berkeley, 2000), pp. 64–5 (published in *La Tribuna*, 25 July 1927).

21. Cf. A. C. Jemolo, *Chiesa e stato in Italia negli ultimi cento anni* (Turin, 1963), pp. 437–40, 447–50, 486, 502–3.

22. J. F. Pollard, *The Vatican and Italian Fascism 1929–1932: A Study in Conflict* (Cambridge, 1985), pp. 49–50.
23. C. G. Chapman, *Milocca. A Sicilian Village* (London, 1973), pp. 155–6.
24. Jemolo, *Chiesa e stato in Italia*, p. 487.
25. M. Clark, *Modern Italy 1871–1995* (London, 1996), p. 256.
26. E. Albertoni, E. Antonini and R. Palmieri (eds.), *La generazione degli anni difficili* (Bari, 1962), p. 170.
27. N. Revelli, *Il mondo dei vinti. Testimonianze di vita contadina*, Vol. 1 (Turin, 1977), p. 60.
28. G. Ciano, *Diario 1937–1943*, ed. R. De Felice (Milan, 1980), pp. 444–5 (21 June 1940).
29. Ibid., pp. 394 (7 February 1940), 418 (11 April 1940).

25: A Place in the Sun, 1929–36

1. V. Zamagni, *Dalla periferia al centro. La seconda rinascita economica dell'Italia: 1861–1981* (Bologna, 1990), pp. 324–30.
2. C. T. Schmidt, *The Plough and the Sword. Labor, Land, and Property in Fascist Italy* (New York, 1938), p. 165.
3. M. Clark, *Modern Italy 1871–1995* (London, 1996), p. 267.
4. 'Autostrada', in *Enciclopedia italiana*, Vol. 5 (Rome, 1930), p. 589.
5. Zamagni, *Dalla periferia al centro*, pp. 337, 378–80; G. Toniolo, *L'economia dell'Italia fascista* (Rome–Bari, 1980), pp. 245–56, 337–42.
6. G. Salvemini, *Under the Axe of Fascism* (London, 1936), p. 10.
7. Cf. V. De Grazia, *The Culture of Consent. Mass Organization of Leisure in Fascist Italy* (Cambridge, 1981), pp. 100–126.
8. G. P. Brunetta, *Storia del cinema italiano, 1895–1945* (Rome, 1979), p. 285.
9. S. Cavazza, *Piccole patrie. Feste popolari tra regione e nazione durante il fascismo* (Bologna, 1997), p. 99.
10. Ibid., p. 206.
11. G. Procacci, *La disfida di Barletta. Tra storia e romanzo* (Milan, 2001), pp. 79–90.
12. B. Mussolini, *Opera omnia*, Vol. 20, eds. E. and D. Susmel (Florence, 1951–62), p. 289 (29 May 1924).
13. C. G. Segrè, *L'Italia in Libia. Dall'età giolittiana a Ghedafi* (Milan, 1978), p. 188.
14. Mussolini, *Opera omnia*, Vol. 27, p. 159 (2 October 1935).
15. Ibid., Vol. 22, p. 386 (26 May 1927).
16. Ibid., pp. 381–2.
17. D. Mack Smith, *Le guerre del Duce* (Rome–Bari, 1976), pp. 46–7.
18. A. Del Boca, *Italiani, brava gente?* (Vicenza, 2005), pp. 153–5.
19. A. Del Boca, *Gli italiani in Libia. Dal fascismo a Gheddafi* (Rome–Bari, 1988), p. 6.
20. Ibid., p. 84.
21. Ibid., p. 16.
22. Del Boca, *Italiani, brava gente?*, pp. 175–6.
23. Del Boca, *Gli italiani in Libia*, pp. 179–89.
24. Ibid., p. 183.
25. Ibid., pp. 196–7.
26. Ibid., p. 207.
27. Ibid., p. 230.
28. E. Ludwig, *Colloqui con Mussolini. Riproduzione delle bozze della prima edizione con le correzioni autografe del duce* (Verona, 1950), p. 17.
29. V. Vidotto, 'La capitale del fascismo', in V. Vidotto (ed.), *Storia di Roma dall'antichità a oggi. Roma capitale* (Rome–Bari, 2002), pp. 398–9.
30. Mussolini, *Opera omnia*, Vol. 20, p. 234 (21 April 1924).
31. T. Koon, *Believe, Obey, Fight. Political Socialization in Fascist Italy 1922–1943* (Chapel Hill, 1985), p. 21.

32. Mussolini, *Opera omnia*, Vol. 22, p. 48 (31 December 1925); ibid., Vol. 25, p. 86 (18 March 1932).
33. J. Welge, 'Fascism *Triumphans*. On the architectural translation of Rome', in C. Lazzaro and R. J. Crum (eds.), *Donatello among the Blackshirts. History and Modernity in the Visual Culture of Fascist Italy* (Ithaca and London, 2005), pp. 87–8.
34. P. Cannistraro, 'Mussolini's cultural revolution: Fascist or Nationalist?', in *Journal of Contemporary History*, 7 (1972), p. 127.
35. G. Rochat, *Le guerre italiane 1935–1943. Dall'impero d'Etiopia alla disfatta* (Turin, 2005), pp. 15–19.
36. Mussolini, *Opera omnia*, Vol. 27, pp. 158–9 (2 October 1935).
37. A. Del Boca, *Gli italiani in Africa orientale. La conquista dell'impero* (Rome–Bari, 1979), p. 423.
38. N. Revelli, *Il mondo dei vinti. Testimonianze di vita contadina*, Vol. 1 (Turin, 1977), pp. cxii, 130.
39. Rochat, *Le guerre italiane*, pp. 32–8.
40. Ibid., pp. 66–7; Del Boca, *Gli italiani in Africa orientale*, pp. 490–91.
41. Ibid., p. 489.
42. Mack Smith, *Le guerre del Duce*, p. 97.
43. Del Boca, *Italiani, brava gente?*, p. 198.
44. I. Montanelli, 'Dentro la guerra', *Civiltà fascista*, 3, 1 (January 1936), p. 40.
45. V. Mussolini, *Voli sulle ambe* (Florence, 1937), pp. 27–8, 48, 78–9, 141, 150.
46. Mussolini, *Opera omnia*, Vol. 27, pp. 268–9.
47. Rochat, *Le guerre italiane*, p. 96.
48. Ibid., p. 83.
49. Del Boca, *Italiani, brava gente?*, pp. 217–21.

26: Into the Abyss, 1936–43

1. A. Del Boca, *Gli italiani in Africa orientale. La conquista dell'impero* (Rome–Bari, 1979), p. 711.
2. *Carteggio D'Annunzio–Mussolini (1919–1938)*, eds. R. De Felice and E. Mariano (Milan, 1971), pp. 364, 376.
3. R. Bosworth, *Mussolini* (London, 2002), p. 310.
4. Del Boca, *Gli italiani in Africa orientale*, p. 713.
5. Ibid., pp. 717–20.
6. R. De Felice, *Mussolini il duce. Vol. 2: Lo stato totalitario 1936–1940* (Turin, 1981), pp. 265–6.
7. Ibid., p. 266.
8. M. Knox, *Mussolini Unleashed 1939–1941. Politics and Strategy in Fascist Italy's Last War* (Cambridge, 1982), p. 6.
9. V. Zamagni, *Dalla periferia al centro. La seconda rinascita economica dell'Italia: 1861–1981* (Bologna, 1990), p. 341.
10. De Felice, *Mussolini il duce*, Vol. 2, pp. 182–90.
11. L. Passerini, *Fascism in Popular Memory. The Cultural Experiences of the Turin Working Class* (Cambridge, 1987), pp. 189–90.
12. B. Mussolini, *Opera omnia*, Vol. 28, eds. E. and D. Susmel (Florence, 1951–62), pp. 69–71.
13. D. Mack Smith, *Mussolini* (London, 1983), p. 250.
14. Mussolini, *Opera omnia*, Vol. 28, pp. 248–53.
15. G. Ciano, *Diario 1937–1943*, ed. R. De Felice (Milan, 1980), p. 45 (14 October 1937). Cf. ibid., p. 70 (19 December 1937).
16. R. J. Crum, 'Shaping the fascist "new man": Donatello's *St. George* and Mussolini's appropriated Renaissance of the Italian nation', in C. Lazzaro and R. J. Crum (eds.), *Donatello among the Blackshirts. History and Modernity in the Visual Culture of Fascist Italy* (Ithaca and London, 2005), pp. 136–7.

17. Mussolini, *Opera omnia*, Vol. 29, pp. 188–9.
18. M. Gibson, *Born to Crime. Cesare Lombroso and the Origins of Biological Criminality* (Westport, 2002), p. 118.
19. E. Collotti, *Il fascismo e gli ebrei. Le leggi razziali in Italia* (Rome–Bari, 2003), pp. 37–8.
20. Mussolini, *Opera omnia*, Vol. 29, pp. 190–91.
21. Ibid., pp. 188–90.
22. Collotti, *Il fascismo e gli ebrei*, pp. 42–3.
23. S. Zuccotti, *Under His Very Windows. The Vatican and the Holocaust in Italy* (New Haven and London, 2000), pp. 44–51.
24. R. Bosworth, *Mussolini's Italy. Life under the Dictatorship 1915–1945* (London, 2005), p. 421.
25. Ibid., p. 419.
26. Cf. *La menzogna della razza. Documenti e immagini del razzismo e dell'antisemitismo fascista*, ed. Centro Furio Jesi (Bologna, 1994).
27. Collotti, *Il fascismo e gli ebrei*, p. 84 (Ernesta Bittanti-Battisti).
28. Ibid., p. 114.
29. Cf. R. De Felice, *The Jews in Fascist Italy* (trans. R. Miller) (New York, 2001), pp. 448–72.
30. G. Rochat, *Le guerre italiane 1935–1943. Dall'impero d'Etiopia alla disfatta* (Turin, 2005), p. 183.
31. Ibid., pp. 216, 233–4.
32. De Felice, *Mussolini il duce*, Vol. 2, pp. 508–10; Mack Smith, *Mussolini*, p. 259.
33. Mussolini, *Opera omnia*, Vol. 29, p. 192.
34. Mack Smith, *Mussolini*, p. 263
35. D. Mack Smith, *Le guerre del duce* (Rome–Bari, 1976), pp. 218–23.
36. Ciano, *Diario*, pp. 326–33.
37. Mack Smith, *Le guerre del duce*, p. 265.
38. De Felice, *Mussolini il duce*, Vol. 2, p. 670 (1 September 1939).
39. Ciano, *Diario*, p. 349 (18 September 1939).
40. Mack Smith, *Mussolini*, p. 289.
41. R. De Felice, *Mussolini l'alleato 1940–1945. Vol. 1: L'Italia in guerra 1940–1943* (Turin, 1990), pp. 683–4.
42. Mussolini, *Opera omnia*, Vol. 29, pp. 403–5.
43. Rochat, *Le guerre italiane*, pp. 249–51.
44. Mack Smith, *Le guerre del duce*, pp. 306–7.
45. Rochat, *Le guerre italiane*, pp. 296–7.
46. De Felice, *Mussolini l'alleato 1940–1945*, Vol. 1, pp. 298, 329–32.
47. Mack Smith, *Mussolini*, p. 329.
48. M. Clark, *Modern Italy 1871–1995* (London, 1996), p. 290.
49. Bosworth, *Mussolini's Italy*, p. 476.
50. Ibid., p. 477.
51. D. Rodogno, *Il nuovo ordine mediterraneo. Le politiche di occupazione dell'Italia fascista in Europa (1940–1943)* (Turin, 2003), pp. 400–410, 416–26.
52. De Felice, *Mussolini l'alleato 1940–1945*, Vol. 1, pp. 1383–1402.
53. Rochat, *Le guerre italiane*, pp. 427–30.
54. C. Pavone, *Una guerra civile. Saggio storico sulla moralità nella Resistenza* (Turin, 1991), pp. 43–8.
55. N. Revelli, 'La ritirata di Russia', in M. Isnenghi (ed.), *I luoghi della memoria. Strutture ed eventi dell'Italia unita* (Rome–Bari, 1997), p. 374.
56. B. Croce, *Scritti e discorsi politici (1943–1947)*, Vol. 1 (Bari, 1963), pp. 223–4.
57. E. Gentile, *La grande Italia. Ascesa e declino del mito della nazione nel ventesimo secolo* (Milan, 1997), p. 225 (*Nuova antologia*, 1 January 1944).
58. S. Romano, *Giovanni Gentile. La filosofia al potere* (Milan, 1984), p. 299.
59. Gentile, *La grande Italia*, p. 229.
60. S. Berlusconi, *Una storia italiana* (Milan, 2001), p. 6.

27: The Foundations of the Republic, 1943–57

1. G. Bianchi and F. Mezzetti, *Mussolini aprile '45: l'epilogo* (Milan, 1979), pp. 52–63.
2. Cf. P. Milza, *Mussolini* (Paris, 1999), pp. 879–81.
3. Bianchi and Mezzetti, *Mussolini aprile '45*, p. 95.
4. Ibid., p. 100.
5. S. Luzzatto, *Il corpo del duce. Un cadavere tra immaginazione, storia e memoria* (Turin, 1998), pp. 45–6. Cf. F. Bandini, *Le ultime 95 ore di Mussolini* (Milan, 1959), p. 329.
6. A. Zanella, *L'ora di Dongo* (Milan, 1993), pp. 502–3.
7. Luzzatto, *Il corpo del duce*, p. 64.
8. Cf. G. Pansa, *Il sangue dei vinti* (Milan, 2003), p. 39.
9. C. Malaparte, *La pelle. Storia e racconto* (Rome–Milan, 1949), pp. 40–42.
10. C. Alvaro, *Quasi una vita. Giornale di uno scrittore* (Milan, 1959), pp. 341–3, 354.
11. N. Gallerano, 'L 'arrivo degli Alleati', in M. Isnenghi (ed.), *I luoghi della memoria. Strutture ed eventi dell'Italia unita* (Rome–Bari, 1997), p. 460.
12. E. Gentile, *La grande Italia. Ascesa e declino del mito della nazione nel ventesimo secolo* (Milan, 1997), pp. 240, 307.
13. Ibid., p. 235.
14. Cf. C. Pavone, *Una guerra civile. Saggio storico sulla moralità nella Resistenza* (Turin, 1991), pp. 169–89.
15. Cf. S. Peli, *La Resistenza in Italia. Storia e critica* (Turin, 2004), pp. 224–8.
16. C. Dellavalle (ed.), *8 settembre 1943: storia e memoria* (Milan, 1989), p. 209.
17. R. Battaglia, *Storia della Resistenza italiana* (Turin, 1964), p. 662.
18. Cf. M. Franzinelli, *Le stragi nascoste. L'armadio delle vergogne: impunità e rimozione dei crimini di guerra nazifascisti 1943–2001* (Milan, 2002), pp. 17–60.
19. Pavone, *Una guerra civile*, pp. 479–92.
20. Gentile, *La grande Italia*, p. 239.
21. A. Pizzoni, *Alla guida del CLNAI. Memorie per i figli*, (Bologna, 1995), p. 297.
22. N. Revelli, *Il mondo dei vinti. Testimonianze di vita contadina*, Vol. 1 (Turin, 1977), p. cxiv.
23. M. Clark, *Modern Italy 1871–1995* (London, 1996), pp. 306–7.
24. Luzzatto, *Il corpo del duce*, pp. 98–112.
25. A. Lepre, *Storia della prima Repubblica. L'Italia dal 1943 al 1998* (Bologna, 1999), p. 64.
26. G. Andreotti, *1947. L'anno delle grandi svolte nel diario di un protagonista* (Milan, 2005), p. 57.
27. Gentile, *La grande Italia*, p. 344 (*La Civiltà cattolica*).
28. Ibid., pp. 350–51 ('Ritorniamo italiani', in *Adesso*, 15 March 1949).
29. C. Pavone, 'La continuità dello Stato. Istituzioni e uomini', in *Italia 1945–48. Le origini della Repubblica* (Turin, 1974), p. 221.
30. P. Ginsborg, *A History of Contemporary Italy. Society and Politics 1943–1988* (London, 1990), p. 187.
31. Pavone, 'La continuità dello Stato', p. 242.
32. S. Lanaro, *Storia dell'Italia repubblicana. Dalla fine della guerra agli anni novanta* (Venice, 1992), p. 33.
33. Pavone, 'La continuità dello Stato', p. 252.
34. Ibid., pp. 249, 253.
35. Luzzatto, *Il corpo del duce*, pp. 123–4.
36. Cf. P. Spriano, *Le passioni di un decennio 1946–1956* (Milan, 1986), pp. 78–9.
37. Ginsborg, *A History of Contemporary Italy*, p. 92.
38. Luzzatto, *Il corpo del duce*, pp. 208–12.

28: The Economic Miracle, 1958–75

1. P. Scoppola, *La repubblica dei partiti* (Bologna, 1991), p. 90.

2. G. Vecchio, 'Tricolore, feste e simboli dello Stato nel primo decennio repubblicano', in F. Tarozzi and G. Vecchio (eds.), *Gli italiani e il tricolore. Patriottismo, identità nazionale e fratture sociali lungo due secoli di storia* (Bologna, 1999), p. 353.

3. Ibid., pp. 344–8.

4. Ibid., pp. 342–3.

5. Cf. G. Miccoli, 'L Chiesa di Pio XII nella società italiana del dopoguerra', in *Storia dell'Italia repubblicana. Vol. 1: La costruzione della democrazia. Dalla caduta del fascismo agli anni cinquanta* (Turin, 1994), pp. 596–602.

6. P. Spriano, *Le passioni di un decennio 1946–1956* (Milan, 1986), p. 153.

7. S. Gundle, *Between Hollywood and Moscow. The Italian Communists and the Challenge of Mass Culture, 1943–1991* (Durham and London, 2000), pp. 31, 65–7.

8. P. Ginsborg, *A History of Contemporary Italy. Society and Politics 1943–1988* (London, 1990), p. 171 (Paolo Bonomi).

9. Ibid.

10. Cf. A. Lepre, *Storia della prima Repubblica. L'Italia dal 1943 al 1998* (Bologna, 1999), p. 98.

11. Cf. P. P. D'Attorre, 'Sogno americano e mito sovietico nell'Italia contemporanea', in P. P. D'Attorre (ed.), *Nemici per la pelle. Sogno americano e mito sovietico nell'Italia contemporanea* (Milan, 1991), pp. 45–6.

12. S. Lanaro, *Storia dell'Italia repubblicana. Dalla fine della guerra agli anni novanta* (Venice, 1992), pp. 165–6.

13. Ibid., p. 166.

14. Ginsborg, *A History of Contemporary Italy*, pp. 214–15.

15. J. E. Miller, *The United States and Italy. The Politics and Diplomacy of Stabilization* (Chapel Hill, 1986), pp. 250–55.

16. Ginsborg, *A History of Contemporary Italy*, p. 214.

17. V. Zamagni, *Dalla periferia al centro. La seconda rinascita economica dell'Italia: 1861–1981* (Bologna, 1990), p. 418.

18. Ginsborg, *A History of Contemporary Italy*, pp. 223–4.

19. Lepre, *Storia della prima Repubblica*, p. 175.

20. Ginsborg, *A History of Contemporary Italy*, pp. 217–18.

21. P. P. Pasolini, 'Le Madonne oggi non piangono più' (*Lettere luterane*, 5 June 1975), in P. P. Pasolini, *Saggi sulla politica e sulla società*, eds. W. Siti and S. De Laude (Milan, 1999), p. 593. Cf. ibid., pp. 578–9, 651–2, 696–7.

22. Gundle, *Between Hollywood and Moscow*, pp. 79–80.

23. A. Ventrone, 'L'avventura americana della classe dirigente cattolica', in P. P. D'Attorre (ed.), *Nemici per la pelle*, p. 150.

24. Lanaro, *Storia dell'Italia repubblicana*, p. 187.

25. Cf. M. Caroli, *Proibitissimo! Censori e censurati della radiotelevisione italiana* (Milan, 2003), pp. 31–8.

26. S. Gundle, 'L'americanizzazione del quotidiano. Televisione e consumismo nell'Italia degli anni Cinquanta', in *Quaderni storici*, Vol. 21, 62 (1986), p. 588.

27. S. Burgalassi, *Il comportamento religioso degli italiani* (Florence, 1968), pp. 19, 27.

28. E. Gentile, *La grande Italia. Ascesa e declino del mito della nazione nel ventesimo secolo* (Milan, 1997), pp. 355–6.

29. Ibid., p. 369 (D. Bartoli, 'Italia centenaria', in *Corriere della Sera*, 18 April 1961).

30. Ibid., p. 360.

31. Ibid., p. 363 (*L'Unità*, 9 May 1961).

32. Ibid., p. 364 (R. Romeo, 'Gli abusi feudali', in *Il Mondo*, 25 July 1961).

33. A. L. Lepschy, G. Lepschy and M. Voghera, 'Linguistic variety in Italy', in C. Levy (ed.), *Italian Regionalism. History, Identity and Politics* (Oxford, 1996), p. 74–5.

34. Gentile, *La grande Italia*, p. 373.

35. Cf. D. Marchesini, 'Nazionalismo, patriottismo e simboli nazionali nello sport: tricolore e maglia azzurra', in Tarozzi and Vecchio (eds.), *Gli italiani e il tricolore*, p. 313; Lepre, *Storia della prima Repubblica*, p. 146.

36. A. Schiavone, *Italiani senza Italia* (Turin, 1998), p. 40.

37. Cf. Ginsborg, *A History of Contemporary Italy*, pp. 132–40.

38. M. Caciagli, *Democrazia Cristiana e potere nel Mezzogiorno. Il sistema democristiano a Catania* (Florence, 1977), pp. 274–9.

39. Cf. J. Chubb, *Patronage, Power and Poverty in Southern Italy* (Cambridge, 1982), pp. 67–71, 135–8.

40. Ibid., p. 89; P. Allum, *Politics and Society in Post-War Naples* (Cambridge, 1973), p. 38.

41. Ginsborg, *A History of Contemporary Italy*, p. 179.

42. E. Banfield, *The Moral Basis of a Backward Society* (Glencoe, 1958).

29: Towards the 'Second Republic'

1. Cf. F. Ferrarotti, *Rapporto sulla mafia: da costume locale a problema dello sviluppo nazionale* (Naples, 1978), pp. 34–41, 62–3, 280–82.

2. P. Ginsborg, *A History of Contemporary Italy. Society and Politics 1943–1988* (London, 1990), pp. 333–4.

3. G. Galli, *Storia del partito armato* (Milan, 1986), pp. 13–15; G. Bocca, *Il terrorismo italiano 1970–1978* (Milan, 1979), pp. 7–8.

4. A. L. Braghetti and P. Tavella, *Il prigioniero* (Milan, 2003), p. 45.

5. L. Sciascia, *L'affaire Moro* (Palermo, 1978), pp. 31–7.

6. Cf. A. Giovagnoli, *Il caso Moro. Una tragedia repubblicana* (Bologna, 2005), pp. 75–80.

7. G. Bocca, 'I Dalla Chiesa', in *Morte di un generale. L'assassinio di Carlo Alberto Dalla Chiesa, la mafia, la droga, il potere politico* (Milan, 1982), pp. 15–16, 22.

8. N. Cattedra, 'Cronaca dall'interno di una città violenta', in ibid., p. 188.

9. Cf. A. Stille, *Excellent Cadavers. The Mafia and the Death of the First Italian Republic* (London, 1996), pp. 22–5.

10. Cf. S. Lupo, *Storia della mafia* (Rome, 1993); J. Dickie, *Cosa Nostra. A History of the Sicilian Mafia* (London, 2004).

11. L. Sciascia, 'I professionisti dell'antimafia', in *Corriere della Sera*, 10 January 1987, and 'Contro la mafia in nome della legge', in ibid., 26 January 1987.

12. P. Ginsborg, *Italy and Its Discontents 1980–2001* (London, 2001), p. 22.

13. Ibid., p. 340.

14. Cf. P. Ginsborg, *Silvio Berlusconi. Television, Power and Patrimony* (London, 2004), pp. 32–44.

15. Cf. C. Trigilia, 'Dinamismo privato e disordine pubblico. Politica, economia e società locali' in F. Barbagallo et al. (eds.), *Storia dell'Italia repubblicana. Vol. 2: La trasformazione dell'Italia: sviluppo e squilibri. 1: Politica, economia, società*, pp. 736–44.

16. V. Zamagni, *Dalla periferia al centro. La seconda rinascita economica dell'Italia: 1861–1981* (Bologna, 1990), p. 438.

17. A. Lepre, *Storia della prima Repubblica. L'Italia dal 1943 al 1998* (Bologna 1999), p. 305.

18. Ginsborg, *Italy and Its Discontents*, p. 58.

19. Ibid., p. 6.

20. Ibid., p. 155; D. Lane, *Berlusconi's Shadow. Crime, Justice and the Pursuit of Power* (London, 2004), pp. 57–8.

21. Cf. D. della Porta, *Lo scambio occulto. Casi di corruzione politica in Italia* (Bologna, 1992), pp. 125–42, 162, 184, 243–7.

22. M. Andreoli, *Andavamo in Piazza Duomo* (Milan, 1993), p. 166.

23. Ginsborg, *Italy and Its Discontents*, pp. 182, 254.

24. M. Clark, *Modern Italy 1871–1995* (London, 1996), pp. 396–7.

25. Cf. K. Dyson and K. Featherstone, *The Road to Maastricht. Negotiating Economic and Monetary Union* (Oxford, 1999), pp. 523–5.
26. Ginsborg, *Italy and Its Discontents*, p. 268.
27. G. Bocconi, 'Tangentopoli in Parlamento', in L. Violante (ed.), *Il Parlamento. Storia d'Italia. Annali 17* (Turin, 2001), pp. 1066–9.
28. S. H. Burnett and L. Mantovani, *The Italian Guillotine. Operation Clean Hands and the Overthrow of Italy's First Republic* (Lanham–Oxford, 1998), p. 122.
29. I. Diamanti, *La Lega. Geografia, storia e sociologia di un nuovo soggetto politico* (Rome, 1993), pp. 69–85.
30. Cf. S. Lanaro, *Storia dell'Italia repubblicana. Dalla fine della guerra agli anni novanta* (Venice, 1992), pp. 235–43.
31. Cf. J. Morris, 'Challenging *Meridionalismo*: constructing a new history for southern Italy', in R. Lumley and J. Morris (eds.), *The New History of the Italian South: the Mezzogiorno Revisited* (Exeter, 1997), pp. 1–19.
32. Clark, *Modern Italy*, pp. 422–3.
33. G. E. Rusconi, *Se cessiamo di essere una nazione. Tra etnodemocrazie regionali e cittadinanza europea* (Bologna, 1993); S. Romano, *Finis Italiae. Declino e morte dell' idiologia risorgimentale. Perchè gli italiani si disprezzano* (Milan, 1995); E. Galli Della Loggia, *La morte della patria. La crisi dell'idea di nazione tra resistenza, antifascismo e Repubblica* (Rome–Bari, 1996).
34. Ginsborg, *Italy and Its Discontents*, p. 290.
35. P. McCarthy, 'Forza Italia: the new politics and old values of a changing Italy', in S. Gundle and S. Parker (eds.), *The New Italian Republic: From the Fall of the Berlin Wall to Berlusconi* (London–New York, 1996), pp. 134–40.

Index

Froude, James 187
Fucini, Renato 279
Futurism, Futurists 374, 383, 388,
    394, 401, 410, 416, 418, 504

Gaber, Giorgio 548
Galileo Galilei 5, 34, 36, 37, 40, 150,
    261, 281, 283, 462, 481
Galluppi, Pasquale 139
Galvani, Luigi 96
Garibaldi, Giuseppe 197, 201, 212,
    221, 237, 239, 247, 301, 333,
    560
  and Aspromonte (1862) 244–6
  character and views of 117, 207,
    211, 227
  cult of after death 293–5, 296, 349
  in exile in South America 134, 167
  and fascism 431, 436, 438, 482,
    535
  and Mentana (1867) 256
  popular appeal of 207, 234, 275,
    483
  and relations with Cavour 207,
    236, 297
  in revolutions of 1848–9 173–4,
    177, 178–9
  and socialism 353, 359, 361, 372
  and support for Victor Emmanuel
    II 194, 208, 210
  and the Thousand (1860) 185,
    207–11, 229, 230, 420
  and war of 1859 204, 206
  and war of 1866 251
  and Young Italy 133
Garibaldi, Peppino (Giuseppe) 417
Garofalo, Raffaele 269
Genoa 7, 11, 65, 74, 171, 175–6,
    354, 358, 429, 471, 507
Gentile, Giovanni 369, 423, 450, 464
  assassination of 525
  and manifesto of fascist
    intellectuals 462
  as Minister of Education (1922–4)
    434, 459–60
  views on Mazzini 413–14, 462

Germany, the Germans 64, 129, 345,
    415, 541, 554
  and Anschluss (Austria) 501, 515
  economic relations with 343, 508
  and First World War 388, 391,
    392, 396, 402, 404
  and formation of Axis (1936) 507,
    509–10
  and Italian armistice (1943) 523–4,
    533
  military convention with (1888)
    327–8
  and outbreak of Second World War
    515–17
  and plans for war with France
    (1888–90) 329–33
  and Republic of Salò 535, 537, 538
  in Second World War (1940–43)
    519, 521–2
  and Triple Alliance 324, 387, 412
  and Zollverein (customs union)
    147, 167
Giannini, Guglielmo 540
Gigli, Beniamino 471
Gini, Corrado 469, 471
Ginori (family), 104
Gioberti, Vincenzo xix, 91, 144, 150,
    161, 166, 191, 242, 269, 296
  early links of with Mazzini 132,
    134, 137
  and On the Civil Renewal of Italy
    183–4
  and On the Moral and Civil
    Primacy of the Italians 29,
    155–7
  in revolutions of 1848–9 174–5
Gioia, Giovanni 564
Gioia, Melchiorre 9, 10, 17, 49, 281,
    283
Giolitti, Giovanni xx, 336, 378, 400,
    407
  and Banca Romana scandal 340,
    343–4
  and Catholics 365, 368, 386
  character and ideas of 362
  and fascism 427, 429, 441, 446

INFCW 945
.08
D866

DUGGAN, CHRISTOPHER.
    THE FORCE OF DESTINY

CENTRAL LIBRARY
03/09